NEOLITHIC BRITAIN

By the same author

The Wilmington Giant: the quest for a lost myth

The Stonehenge People: an exploration of life in neolithic Britain, 4700–2000 BC

The Knossos Labyrinth: a new view of the 'Palace of Minos' at Knossos

Minoans: life in bronze age Crete

Book of British Dates: a comprehensive chronological dictionary of British dates from prehistoric times to the present day

NEOLITHIC BRITAIN

New stone age sites of England, Scotland and Wales

Rodney Castleden

Illustrated by the author

London and New York

First published 1992
by Routledge
11 New Fetter Lane, London EC4P 4EE

Simultaneously published in the USA and Canada
by Routledge
a division of Routledge, Chapman and Hall, Inc.
29 West 35th Street, New York, NY 10001

Printed in Great Britain by Butler & Tanner Ltd, Frome and London

British Library Cataloguing in Publication Data
Castleden, Rodney
Neolithic Britain: new stone age sites of England, Scotland and Wales
1. Great Britain. Antiquities
I. Title
936.101

Library of Congress Cataloging in Publication Data
Castleden, Rodney
Neolithic Britain: new stone age sites of England, Scotland and Wales/Rodney Castleden.
p.   cm.
Includes bibliographical references (p.   ) and index.
1. Neolithic period – Great Britain. 2. Great Britain – Antiquities. I. Title
GN776.22.G7C36   1992
936.1 – dc 20   91-16745

ISBN 0-415-05845-7

To Aubrey Burl

A wander witt of Wiltshire, rambling to Rome to gaze at Antiquities, and there skrewing himself into the company of Antiquaries, they entreated him to illustrate unto them that famous Monument in his Country, called **Stonage**. His answer was that he had never seen, scarce ever heard of, it. Whereupon, they kicked him out of doors, and bade him goe home, and see **Stonage**.

Robert Gay: *A Fools Bolt Soon Shott*
at Stonage (about 1665)

I never saw the Country about Marlborough, till Christmas 1648. Mr Charles Seymour and Sir William Button of Tokenham (a most parkely ground, and a Romancy-place) Baronet, mett with their packs of Hounds at the Greyweathers. . . . One might fancy it to have been the Scene where the Giants fought with stones against the Gods. 'Twas here that our Game began: and the chase led us through the Village of Aubury, into the Closes there: where I was wonderfully surprised at the sight of those vast stones, of which I had not heard before; as also at the mighty Banke and Graffe about it. I observed in the Inclosures some segments of rude circles, made with these stones, whence I concluded, they had been in old time complete.

John Aubrey: *Topographical Collections*
(written in the 1660s)

CONTENTS

List of illustrations   ix
Acknowledgements   xiii

Introduction: 'Saying it with stone'   1

ENGLAND
   Avon   9
   Bedfordshire   12
   Berkshire   16
   Buckinghamshire   17
   Cambridgeshire   19
   Cheshire   28
   Cornwall (excluding Scilly)   29
   Cumbria   54
   Derbyshire   62
   Devon   77
   Dorset   81
   Essex   103
   Gloucestershire   105
   Greater London   115
   Hampshire   116
   Hereford and Worcester   121
   Hertfordshire   123
   Humberside   126
   Kent   131
   Lancashire   135
   Leicestershire   135
   Lincolnshire   137
   Merseyside   140
   Norfolk   141
   Northamptonshire   145
   Northumberland   148
   Nottinghamshire   151

Oxfordshire	152
Scilly Isles	161
Shropshire	163
Somerset	164
Staffordshire	170
Suffolk	173
Surrey	175
East Sussex	179
West Sussex	187
Tyne and Wear	194
Warwickshire	194
Wiltshire	196
North Yorkshire	248
West Yorkshire	257

SCOTLAND

Borders	261
Central	263
Dumfries and Galloway	264
Fife	271
Grampian	272
Highland	278
Caithness	278
Inverness	291
Nairn	292
Ross and Cromarty	292
Sutherland	293
Lothian	297
Orkney	298
Shetland	330
Strathclyde	339
Tayside	350
Western Isles	353

WALES

Anglesey (part of Gwynedd)	361
Clwyd	370
Dyfed	374
Glamorgan	381
Gwent	386
Gwynedd (excluding Anglesey)	387
Powys	395

Appendix: Radiocarbon dates	403
Bibliography	405
Index	410

ILLUSTRATIONS

FIGURES

1	The North Circle and Cove at Avebury, drawn by Stukeley	2
2	Farmer Robinson, the 'stone-killer'	8
3	Stanton Drew	10
4	Stoney Littleton, a Cotswold–Severn chambered long cairn	11
5	Waulud's Bank	15
6	A lost stone circle complex at St Just	18
7	Maxey ritual complex	25
8	Ballowall Barrow	30
9	Boscawen-un, as drawn by J. T. Blight in about 1860	31
10	Brane Entrance Grave	32
11	Carn Brea fortified hilltop enclosure	33
12	Carn Gluze Barrow	34
13	The Hurlers	38
14	King Arthur's Hall	39
15	Men-an-tol	42
16	Sites near the Merry Maidens	44
17	Pennance Entrance Grave	46
18	The Pipers, drawn by J. T. Blight in 1861	47
19	Trethevy Quoit	52
20	Long Meg and Her Daughters	57
21	The Langdale axe factories	60
22	Arbor Low	64
23	Fivewells: one of the megalithic tomb chambers	69
24	Willington, a neolithic settlement	77
25	Maiden Castle	83
26	Ceremonial monuments in the Mount Pleasant area	93
27	Mount Pleasant: a plan of the circular timber structure	95
28	Two Wessex superhenges	97
29	The north-east end of the Dorset Cursus	98
30	The Knowlton Circles	101
31	Orsett causewayed enclosure	104

32	Crickley Hill causewayed enclosure	107
33	Crickley Hill: the distribution of flint arrow-heads	107
34	Eastleach causewayed enclosure	109
35	Opening a barrow at Snodland, Kent, in August 1844	117
36	Two partly destroyed long barrows: Badshot and Jullieberrie's Grave	133
37	Giant's Hills Long Barrow	139
38	Broome Heath	142
39	Briar Hill causewayed enclosure	146
40	Rollright	157
41	The Rollright Stones as engraved by Kip for Camden's *Britannia*	158
42	Wayland's Smithy	160
43	The Whispering Knights at Rollright	161
44	Axe factories and flint mines	165
45	South Cadbury, drawn by William Stukeley	168
46	A Stonehenge trilithon drawn by William Stukeley	173
47	A neolithic landscape in West London	177
48	Church Hill flint mine	184
49	Harrow Hill flint mine	191
50	Wolstonbury Hill	194
51	Stonehenge in 1875	197
52	Map of the Avebury area	199
53	Avebury	200
54	The South Entrance Stones at Avebury	201
55	The Avebury Cove	202
56	Durrington Walls	211
57	Fussell's Lodge: reconstruction of the mortuary house, porch and façade	214
58	Normanton Down mortuary enclosure	222
59	Stukeley's drawing of the Sanctuary	226
60	The Shelving Stones burial chamber, drawn by Stukeley	227
61	South Street Long Barrow	230
62	Stonehenge I	232
63	West Kennet Long Barrow: reconstruction of chambers and façade	240
64	West Kennet Long Barrow: plan	241
65	Windmill Hill causewayed enclosure	245
66	Woodhenge	247
67	Mill Barrow, Avebury: an invaluable sketch by John Aubrey	250
68	The Devil's Arrows	256
69	Lochhill Long Cairn	267
70	Mid Gleniron II: two stages in the tomb's development	269
71	Torhousekie stone circle	269
72	Balfarg: plan of the controversial timber structure	272
73	Balfarg Henge	273

74	Balbridie: a neolithic longhouse or 'hall'	273
75	Loanhead of Daviot	277
76	Balnuaran of Clava North-East	281
77	Camster Long: plan	281
78	Camster Long: view of the restored cairn	282
79	Cairnpapple	298
80	Knap of Howar: a neolithic house doorway	305
81	Knap of Howar: a plan of the two neolithic houses	311
82	Knowe of Lairo	313
83	Maes Howe	317
84	Mid Howe	319
85	Ring of Brodgar	324
86	The interior of House 7 at Skara Brae, as seen from the doorway	326
87	House 7 at Skara Brae: plan	327
88	Three stone houses in the Shetlands	333
89	Scord of Brouster	336
90	Stanydale	338
91	Glenvoidean, a multi-phase tomb	345
92	Three phases in the development of Croft Moraig	351
93	Forteviot: a large timber enclosure	352
94	Callanish: Colonel Sir Henry James's drawing of 1866	355
95	Callanish: plan and oblique view	356
96	Barclodiad y Gawres	362
97	Bryn-Celli-Ddu	364
98	Bryn yr Hen Bobl	366
99	Lligwy chambered tomb	367
100	Carreg Coetan Arthur	376
101	Pentre Ifan	379
102	Samson's Quoit	381
103	Parc-le-Breos, a Cotswold–Severn chambered tomb	383
104	St Lythans tomb chamber	384
105	Tinkinswood chambered tomb	385
106	Gaerllwyd Cromlech	386
107	Dyffryn Ardudwy	391
108	Trelystan	399
109	Ty Isaf chambered tomb	400
110	Radiocarbon dates conversion graph	404

PLATES (between pages 260 and 261)

1	Arbor Low, Derbyshire
2	Setta Barrow, Devon
3	Wor Barrow, Dorset
4	The Rudston Monolith, Yorkshire Wolds

5 Willie Howe, Yorkshire Wolds
6 The Rollright Stones, Oxfordshire
7 Wayland's Smithy: the façade, entrance passage and chambers
8 The Whispering Knights tomb chamber, Oxfordshire
9 Windover Long Mound, East Sussex
10 The King Stone at Rollright, Warwickshire
11 Avebury: the East Entrance causeway
12 The West Kennet Avenue, Avebury
13 A Stonehenge trilithon
14 One of the Rollright circle stones
15 Deepdale standing stone, Mainland Orkney
16 The Dwarfie Stane, Hoy
17 The Hill of Cruaday flagstone quarry
18 Langstane standing stone, Rousay
19 Skara Brae: the southern end of House 8
20 Taversoe Tuick chambered cairn, Rousay
21 Wideford Hill chambered cairn, Mainland Orkney
22 Barclodiad y Gawres chambered cairn: the entrance passage
23 Bodowyr tomb chamber, Anglesey
24 Bryn-Celli-Ddu Henge and passage grave, Anglesey
25 Bryn-Celli-Ddu passage grave entrance
26 Bryn-Celli-Ddu tomb chamber and pillar: entrance passage to the right
27 Bryn Gwyn stone circle, Anglesey
28 Bryn yr Hen Bobl, Anglesey: 'the hill of the old people'. The small tomb chamber is protected by the fence visible on the left
29 Plas Newydd burial chamber
30 Dyffryn Ardudwy chambered cairn: the smaller, older tomb chamber

ACKNOWLEDGEMENTS

A book of this kind cannot be written without the help and support of others. Much of the information used has been drawn from accounts published in a wide range of archaeological journals, books and other publications, a selection of which is listed in the Bibliography at the end of the book. I thank Mr Brian McGregor, Librarian at the Ashmolean Library in Oxford, for allowing me to read these archaeological sources in his library, and John and Celia Clarke for their hospitality during my reading weeks in Oxford.

Some of the most recent finds were kindly communicated by local authority archaeologists, many of whom found the time to send me details of new sites; some even sent printouts of all the neolithic finds ever made in their counties. Any doubts that enough material for a book might exist were soon dispelled. I am very grateful indeed to all the people who sent me data. Without this input, it would have been difficult to produce a 'state of the art' picture of neolithic Britain. The following people were all kind enough to send me data; Peter Yeoman of the Department of Economic Development and Planning, Fife Regional Council; Trevor Sprott, Director of Physical Planning, Grampian Regional Council; Geoffrey Steeley, County Planning and Estates Officer, Hertfordshire County Council; David Thompson, Records Officer of the Gwynedd Archaeological Trust; Frances Griffith, Countryside Officer, Devon County Council; John Steane, County Archaeologist, Oxfordshire County Council; John Shryane, County Planning and Development Officer, Staffordshire County Council; Alison Taylor, County Archaeologist, Cambridgeshire County Council; Peter Liddle, Archaeological Survey Officer, Leicestershire County Council; Glen Foard of the Northampton Archaeological Unit; Fiona Gale, Archaeology Assistant, Clwyd County Council Tourism and Leisure Division; John Hodgson, Sites and Monuments Record Officer, Warwickshire County Council; John Pickin, Antiquities Officer, Bowes Museum, Durham County Council; Lorna Main, Archaeological Officer, Central Regional Council; J. D. Hedges, County Archaeologist, West Yorkshire Archaeology Service; Edward Martin, Suffolk County Council; Michael Gwilliam, County Planning Officer, Bedfordshire County Council; Angela Simco, also of Bedfordshire County Council; David Thompson, Records Officer, Gwynedd Archaeological Trust; Jill Collins, County Planning

Office, Cheshire County Council; V. Baddeley, Planning and Transportation Office, Nottinghamshire County Council; Alexander Macgregor, Department of Physical Planning, Strathclyde Regional Council; Claire Pinder, Assistant to Laurence Keen, County Archaeological Officer, Dorset County Council; R. A. Canham, Field Officer, Wiltshire County Council; Tom Clare, Archaeological Officer, Cumbria County Council; Steve Hartgroves, Sites and Monuments Officer, Cornwall Archaeological Unit; David Bird and Phil Jones, Principal Archaeologist and Field Officer respectively, Surrey County Council Planning Department, Countryside and Heritage Division; M. E. Farley, Buckinghamshire County Museum; Harry Cowley, County Planning Officer, Derbyshire County Council; Andrew Woodcock, Archaeological Adviser, East Sussex County Council.

Aubrey Burl, the Rock of Ages in British neolithic studies, is an inspiration to all prehistorians. In his steady output of publications he has supplied us with profound insights into the nature of life in neolithic Britain, with an unusual combination of patient research and vivid writing. I am particularly grateful to him for his kind words about my book *The Stonehenge People* when his own book, with the same title, had come out only a month or two before, and for his patience in answering my questions about stone circles. It seemed natural, from the planning stage onwards, that this book should be dedicated to him.

Finally, I thank my wife, Kit, for coming with me to see many of the sites and enduring the rigours of some extraordinary British summers, from the drenching rainstorms of Orkney in 1986 to the blistering heat of Dorset in 1990.

R.C.
Brighton, 1991

INTRODUCTION: 'SAYING IT WITH STONE'

The celebrated seventeenth-century diarist, courtier and antiquary, John Aubrey, stumbled on Avebury by chance while out hunting in 1648 and expressed surprise 'that so eminent an Antiquitie should lye so long unregarded by our Chorographers'. In about 1663, in Aubrey's own words,

> King Charles IId discoursing one morning with my Lord Brounker and Dr Charleton concerning Stoneheng, they told his Majestie, what they had heard me say concerning Aubury, sc. that it did as much excell of Stoneheng as a Cathedral does a Parish Church. His Majestie admired that none of our Chorographers had taken notice of it: and commanded Dr Charleton to bring me to him the next morning. I brought with me a draught of it donne by Memorie only: but well enough resembling it, with which his Majestie was pleased: gave me his hand to kisse, and commanded me to waite on him at Marleborough ... and the next day, his Majestie left the Queen and diverted to Aubury, where I shewed him that stupendious Antiquity.... As his Majestie departed from Aubury to overtake the Queen he cast his eie on Silbury-hill, about a mile off: which he had the curiosity to see.

This episode illustrates the importance of personal discovery and insight in our collective perception of landscape. The villagers who had lived for centuries at Avebury were all too familiar with the earthworks and large circle-stones obstructing their fields and cottage gardens, but Aubrey in a very real sense *discovered* the site by seeing the remains, not as an impediment, but as components of a prehistoric monument that had once been of great importance to the people of the area. Aubrey also implicitly communicated the idea that if a monument was once of great importance, albeit within a culture very different in its precepts from our own, then we should treat it with respect as well as curiosity (Figure 1).

The large henge at Avebury is now internationally recognized as one of the great monuments of the later part of the British neolithic, or new stone age. All over Britain, we can find traces of this ancient proto-civilization. Some of the remains are standing monuments in good condition, easy enough for the non-specialist to identify: some even have cast metal notices erected by bodies such

1

Figure 1 The North Circle and Cove at Avebury, drawn by Stukeley. Several of the stones in this picture – the ones to the right of the Cove and, coincidentally, the ones that Stukeley is looking at – have gone since he drew them in August 1722. A – Avebury parish church, B – The Cove, C – Windmill Hill.

as the National Trust or English Heritage telling us what they were and when they were built. But many are unmarked and lie neglected and anonymous in field corners or on hilltops. It is still possible even for well-informed travellers to stumble upon remains from Britain's ancient past that they will never have heard of. One purpose of this book is to assist and amplify that experience of personal discovery, by locating the sites, suggesting what their original function might have been, and indicating where other, related sites may be found. It is too easy to see neolithic monuments as isolated and freakish.

Substantial areas of the new stone age landscape are still, surprisingly, retrievable, even though the surviving sites may seem like a multitude of archaic islands scattered across a rising sea of later developments, drowning in progress. Most of the remains from this remote period have been weathered, modified and fragmented out of recognition; many that survive have been covered by soil and vegetation and subsumed within the texture of the modern landscape, so that they are very hard to detect. The far-off world of the henges, megaliths and long barrows is so reticent that it seems useful to provide a guide for the general reader.

Within the limitations of a single volume, this book aims to serve as a comprehensive guide or vade-mecum for anyone with an interest in Britain's ancient heritage. My earlier book, *The Stonehenge People* (Castleden 1987), seeks to give an overall synthesis of the cultural achievement of the period. This book has been written to complement it by showing the sort of site detail, from more than a thousand different places, that supplied the evidence for the synthesis. It also includes details of some newly discovered sites. I hope that this approach will make clear to the general reader the scale and variety of the neolithic achievement in Britain.

There are several existing books about prehistoric sites, all of them good in their different ways, but because they extend themselves across the entire prehistoric period they are necessarily short-winded when it comes to the new stone age, and they cover relatively few neolithic sites. It seemed desirable, natural and timely to focus this guide on sites belonging to one period and one culture: it seemed the best way to ensure adequate coverage and coherence. It also seemed desirable to make the book as comprehensive as the format will allow, on the assumption that the more sites that are covered, the more useful the reader will find it.

Of the 1,100 sites included, perhaps a handful are world-famous monuments, many more will be well known among archaeologists and others with an interest in prehistory, and some will seem very obscure. A wide variety of sites of many different types has been included, partly as a reminder that our knowledge of the neolithic period does not come entirely, as some general readers may have assumed, from a few spectacular ceremonial monuments. There is far more to the British neolithic than Stonehenge and Maes Howe, inexhaustibly fascinating as those monuments are; enormous quantities of valuable information about neolithic diet, technology and social structures have been collected from some very humble, superficially unexciting domestic sites. Archaeologists and professional prehistorians know this already, but this book has been compiled every bit as much for the use of the general reader who may be curious about a cromlech seen on holiday in Wales, or wish to widen his or her understanding of the evolution of the rural landscape of Britain, or feel a need to fill in some of that long, yawning gap in our heritage – the long millennia before documented history began.

One major problem in compiling any book about this remote period is that of dating, or the lack of it, and the difficulties that exist in defining the beginning and end of the neolithic. I have taken the British neolithic to span the period 4700 BC to 2000 BC, beginning, in other words, with the first signs of experimentation with agriculture and ending with the building of the last stone circles to use very large stones and the introduction of bronze tools on a large scale.

The preceding period, the mesolithic or middle stone age, came to an end around 4700 BC, as agriculture was adopted. There were, nevertheless, many communities where mesolithic lifestyles, depending primarily upon hunting, fishing and gathering, continued long into the neolithic period. On rocky Scottish islands, for example, where farming was difficult to introduce and unlikely to sustain a reliable food supply, the mesolithic way of life went on, probably right through the period that we are calling the neolithic. Even in southern England, where the adoption of agriculture was fairly rapid and successful, people who settled close to a river estuary, with all the varied micro-habitats it offered, opted for a mixed economy, farming but also drawing heavily on the old mesolithic practices. So the British neolithic does not have a sharply defined beginning. The period from 4700 to 4300 BC was a pioneering phase, leading to the early neolithic, 4300–3600 BC.

The middle neolithic period that followed, 3600–3200 BC, was a period which some prehistorians, such as Colin Burgess (1980) and Paul Ashbee (1978), treat as a major economic and social crisis; the true nature of that crisis is discussed in *The Stonehenge People* (1987). After it came a period of recovery, evolution and social stratification. It was during this late neolithic period, from 3200 BC until 2000 BC, that most of the great monuments of the new stone age, such as the henges and stone circles, were built. It was also during the second half of this very important culmination phase that the large earthen enclosures, or superhenges, were raised and the first high-status burials, presumably of chiefs, appeared. Clearly, by 2600 BC, things were on the change.

Defining the close of the neolithic is very difficult. The problem is that the end of the neolithic and the beginning of the bronze age does not appear to have been a sudden event: changes were under way, with the appearance of very small quantities of what are called 'Beaker' artefacts, from about 2600 BC onwards. Nevertheless, I was very struck by Colin Renfrew's perceptive observation in a television documentary about Stonehenge ('Who built Stonehenge?' 1986), to the effect that the people of the new stone age liked to 'say it with stone', which seems to express very well one of the leitmotivs of the culture. While Britain

4

remained in a stone-dominated culture, with the great majority of tools still being made of stone, and the stone monuments still being constructed out of ambitiously large stones, the new stone age lived on. At the same time, we must remember that neolithic people were saying it with earth and timber as well, and that many of their ceremonial enclosures used these materials instead of stone.

Yet even identifying what we might call 'lithocentricity' as the hallmark of the neolithic leaves us with problems, because the period when stone circles were built straddles our end-date of 2000 BC. Some stone circles have been radiocarbon dated to the neolithic, i.e. between 3000 BC and 2000 BC, others to the bronze age, i.e. between 2000 and 1500 BC, but the great majority remain undated by the radiocarbon or any other absolute dating method. There is therefore an area of uncertainty about which to include and which not. At one stage I considered leaving out all the stone circles, which would have meant leaving out some that I knew to be neolithic, but I also knew that including all the stone circles would involve some that I knew were bronze age. It seemed essential to find the boundary between the generally larger monuments of the neolithic, which usually utilized larger stones, and the generally smaller bronze age circles, which usually were made of smaller stones. I sought Aubrey Burl's advice on this 'Catch 23', and I am very grateful to him for his thoughts on the subject. The solution, an attempt to identify those stone circles that are likely to have been built before 2000 BC, has not been an easy one. The earlier recumbent stone circles of old Aberdeenshire, for example, are likely to belong to the late neolithic, and are therefore included, whereas the apparently degenerate type of stone-setting known as the four-poster, which is agreed to be late, i.e. bronze age, has been left out.

I have resolved the problem as best I can using the few available radiocarbon dates and the morphological evidence of the circles' architecture, but only absolute dating for a great many more stone circles will give us a final resolution. The situation is nevertheless improving all the time. Each new radiocarbon date adds a little more detail to the overall picture, and the recalibration of 'raw' radiocarbon dates gives that picture a sharper focus. In the next, I have followed the usual convention in presenting raw, uncalibrated or uncorrected radiocarbon dates in years bc, and the recalibrated or corrected dates in calendar years BC. The uncorrected date is usually quoted first, followed by the equivalent in calendar years BC in brackets. The conversion graph used is shown in Figure 110 and explained in the Appendix.

The guide attempts to be comprehensive, and it is to be hoped that all the sites that are of interest to the reader are included. Unfortunately it is inevitable that someone's favourite site will have been omitted; in spite of the large number of sites included, the book is still a personal selection. The book had to be kept short enough to be easily portable: a guide that can be carried without difficulty in the car or rucksack. Detailed directions for reaching the sites have been omitted for a number of reasons. They would, for instance, be very space-consuming and yet still not be definitive. I have found when using other, comparable guides that even after three or four lines of detailed directions I have had to consult a 1:50,000

Ordnance Survey map in order to work out where the monument was and the best way of approaching it; sometimes that varies significantly according to mode of transport. In nearly every case it has been possible to supply a six-figure grid reference, and this standard procedure seems easily the most economical and unambiguous way of locating the sites. In the background there was also a disquieting feeling that guiding readers along specific tracks and paths would be tantamount to encouraging them to visit, and this leads on into the very important issue of access.

The inclusion of a site in this book does not guarantee any right of access. Every monument in Britain stands on land that belongs to someone. In some cases, such as the National Trust or English Heritage, and a good proportion of private landowners, the owner is enlightened enough to care for the monument and still allow controlled public access. Nevertheless, there are some private landowners who are hostile, and they are within their rights if they refuse access to monuments standing on their land: it is as well to make sure before undertaking a long journey to see a site that your visit will be well received. It is the would-be visitor's responsibility to seek the owner's permission. However keenly you may wish to see any site, the law of trespass is clear. Trespass is

> the act of entering or remaining upon land of another without his permission. If the permission originally given is later withdrawn, a trespass will be committed. A landowner can take a person trespassing to court without proving loss or damage to his land. Any actual damage he can show will entitle him to increased compensation.

It may be that the Ordnance Survey map indicates a road with a Ministry of Transport classification, or a public footpath, passing right beside or even through the monument, in which case access is assured. In other words, the book really needs to be used in conjunction with an Ordnance Survey map of the area in question.

One further disclaimer needs to be made. The inclusion of a site in this guide does not necessarily mean that anything interesting remains to be seen there. Some sites have been discovered accidentally, for instance during gravel extraction: after a rescue dig, the site will have been destroyed utterly. Sites have been destroyed by urban or industrial development, road widening, by-pass building, and deep ploughing. In some rare cases, monuments have even been destroyed by archaeologists. Neolithic sites have been damaged and lost at an alarming rate. We can only guess at the numbers of sites that were destroyed before the modern period, but the known losses during the last 200 years alone have been catastrophic. The traditional sheep pasture of the downlands of southern England helped to conserve a great many sites until 1940, but the government-subsidized craze for ploughing from then onwards has annihilated many a long barrow and other neolithic sites as well. It is for this reason that entries on specific sites sometimes refer to or draw upon the notes, plans and sketches made by antiquaries of the seventeenth, eighteenth or nineteenth centuries, as well as the scientific investigations of twentieth-century archaeologists. The observations of antiquaries such as John Aubrey and William Stukeley are invaluable in helping us to reconstruct the appearance of monuments that have long since been damaged beyond recognition.

My hope is that this book will contribute in a small way to raising public awareness of the very real threat that exists to our neolithic heritage. Greater awareness of the whereabouts of the sites, and their significance can only help to conserve what is left.

In 1990, English Heritage drew attention to the implications of the Department of Transport's road-building schemes as outlined in the 1989 Government White Paper 'Roads for Prosperity' and the 1990 Government Report 'Trunk Roads: England into the 1990s'. The road works, if carried out, are likely to involve nearly 300 km of roads and the use of more than 14,800 hectares of land. They would cause the destruction of at least 840 known archaeological sites of various periods; a proportion of these will be new stone age sites. The figure of 840 is bound to be an underestimate. When large areas of topsoil are stripped off in preparation for extensive road works, new and previously unsuspected sites inevitably come to light, and it may be that as many as 5,000 sites will be imperilled.

It is difficult to be other than alarmist. We like to believe that we live in educated and enlightened times, and that our media-saturated society is so well-informed and well-equipped that it cannot help but devise successful strategies for managing the environment, managing the future and managing the past. And yet ours is a society that is prepared to allow its bureaucrats to contemplate adding a second carriageway to the A303, which would destroy six prehistoric barrows, as well as an unknown number of yet-undiscovered features, very close to the key neolithic ritual centre of Stonehenge. As I write, Dr Alastair Whittle is conducting one of the most exciting archaeological excavations of the decade, uncovering the remains of two large post circles close to Silbury Hill and the West Kennet Avenue. These monuments, which are as yet imperfectly understood, were clearly an important element in the ceremonial complex centring on Avebury, a ritual landscape that, as Professor Peter Ucko (Ucko *et al*. 1991) reminds us, we are only beginning to understand. And yet, as I write, plans to build a large hotel on the post circle site are being discussed.

Officially sanctioned vandalism may be large in scale, but an enormous amount of damage has been done piecemeal, by private individuals with varying motives (Figure 2). It is important to remember that many of the sites described are protected by their status as scheduled ancient monuments, and it is illegal to excavate, bury, or damage them in any way without formal permission from the Department of the Environment. The consequences of vandalism can be serious. In 1990, the company responsible for excavating part of Legbourne Priory in Lincolnshire and burying another part of the site was fined £15,000 for the offence. Unfortunately, many of the neolithic sites are remote and damage to them often goes unnoticed for a long time. Readers can help in reducing this

Figure 2   Farmer Robinson, the 'stone-killer' who used fire and water to smash many of the Avebury stones. William Stukeley drew this villainous portrait as a tailpiece for his 'Abury' in 1743. The background includes a stone being broken over a fire pit, a bat, a presiding hag, and further megaliths awaiting destruction.

kind of damage by reporting at once to the police any activity they see causing damage to a monument.

An improved understanding of the true nature of these monuments, and what they once meant to our ancestors, will also help us to see a new dimension in the British landscape. If we can see the ruined, degraded and overgrown remnants as fragments of a new stone age scene, then we are close to seeing the landscape not through our own eyes alone, but through those of our forefathers. As William Stukeley wrote in the eighteenth century, 'If we examine into the antiquities of nations that had no writing among them, here are their monuments. These we are to explore; and the more we reason upon them, the more reasons shall we find to admire the vast size of the minds of our predecessors.'

ENGLAND

AVON

CHEW PARK

c. ST: 5757

In the new stone age, an irregularly shaped house 3.5m by 3m supported by about six vertical posts, and with an entrance on the southern side, stood here. The remains were obscured by those of a Roman villa, but the neolithic house seems to have been roughly hexagonal or possibly D-shaped in plan.

DRUID STOKE   Bristol   ST: 561762

This possible chambered long barrow site consists of a rectangular area of displaced stones. One massive slab 3m long is still supported by a smaller stone upright. The site was excavated in 1913, but without any positive results or finds, so its status remains uncertain.

FAIRY TOOTE   Nempnett Thrubwell   *c*. ST: 5360

This destroyed Cotswold–Severn tomb was first opened in 1788. Although the monument was almost entirely destroyed by 1835, some of its details were recorded. The number of pairs of side chambers varies according to source – some say six, others eight – but it is a large number, whichever is correct. The chamber complex was larger than that at Stoney Littleton, about 26m long, compared with Stoney Littleton's 18m. Bones were found in the chambers in some numbers: 'in one of them 7 skulls were found, one quite perfect; in another a vast heap of small human bones and horses'. At Fairy Toote, it looks as if the human remains were disarticulated and sorted before they were buried in the tomb, suggesting a two-phase funerary ritual that seems to have prevailed throughout Britain.

STANTON DREW

ST: 601634

This group of three stone circles lying low on the Chew valley floor includes the second largest circle in Britain, and yet the monument is far from well known. The site's potential impressiveness is greatly reduced by its low-lying location, backing onto a farmyard, the low ridge separating the South-West Circle from the Great Circle, and the positioning of the parish church of St Mary's between

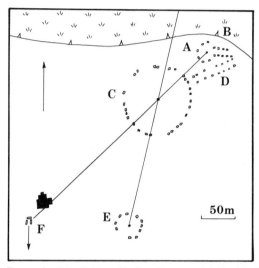

Figure 3 Stanton Drew. A – North-East Circle, B – stone avenue leading from North-East Circle to water meadows, C – Great Circle, D – stone avenue leading from Great Circle to water meadows, E – South-West Circle, F – Cove, facing south. The site's geometry has been drawn in, showing the alignment of the Cove, Great Circle and North-East Circle, and the alignment of the South-West Circle, Great Circle and Hautville's Quoit, which is off the map.

the Cove and the rest of the ritual complex. The monument as a whole is generally considered to consist of the three stone circles, the Cove, two short and badly damaged stone avenues, and an outlying stone known as Hautville's Quoit. Although at first sight the arrangement of these elements looks casual and informal, there are detectable alignments which are almost certainly part of the original design. The North-East Circle, the Great Circle and the Cove all lie on the same straight line (SW–NE). The South-West Circle, the Great Circle and Hautville's Quoit lie on a different line running SSW–NNE.

Of the 30 stones in the Great Circle, only 3 are still standing: the rest have fallen. They make a circle 113m in diameter. One or two of the stones are sarsens, the rest are the local dolomitic conglomerate. The Great Circle stands in a level meadow a little above the Chew floodplain, the edge of which lies only 40m away to the north; a short avenue of stones leads away to the north-east, as if to connect the Great Circle to the watermeadows. Near the north-east end of the avenue is the North-East Circle, a much smaller monument 30m across and consisting of only eight stones, four of which are still upright. The North-East Circle has its own avenue, also of eight stones, which leads eastwards and seems to get tangled up with the terminus of the Great Circle avenue. Their orientation towards the wet floodplain of the River Chew suggests that water may have played some part in the religious beliefs of the monument builders.

The South-West Circle, on the southern slope of a low ridge that separates it from the Great Circle, is a little larger than the North-East Circle, 40–43m across. It consisted of 11 or 12 stones, all of which have now fallen. Due west of the South-West Circle is the Cove, a box-like setting of three very large stones arranged along three sides of a square. The fourth side, to the south, is open, suggesting an orientation to the sun's zenith. The back or central stone has unfortunately fallen. The building of the parish church right next to the Cove is reminiscent of the juxtaposition of church and monolith at Rudston. Hautville's Quoit, now also fallen, lies some 360m NNE of the Great Circle; as an outlier, it may have served as an astronomical marker of some kind, but this has not been proved.

Rather surprisingly, Stanton Drew has been neglected by archaeologists. It has never been excavated, but it seems likely to belong to the late neolithic, possibly around 2600 BC (Figure 3).

STONEY LITTLETON   ST: 735572

This very fine chambered long barrow of Cotswold–Severn type was carefully and beautifully restored in 1858. The grass-covered mound is 30m long and 15m

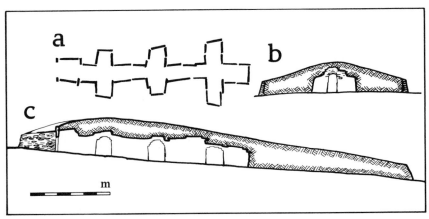

Figure 4   Stoney Littleton, a Cotswold–Severn chambered long cairn. a – plan of the transepted chambers,   b – cross section,   c – long profile.

wide, contained within a well-made drystone retaining wall, which gives it the appearance of a turf-roofed house. At the south-east end there is a horned entrance with a fossil ammonite cast on the western door jamb; whether the positioning of the decorative fossil at the tomb entrance was inadvertent is open to speculation, but the form is reminiscent of the neolithic spiral carvings deliberately placed at tomb entrances at Newgrange and Pierowall, so it may well have been selected for its symbolic value. The entrance leads into a low-ceilinged gallery with three pairs of side chambers and an end chamber. The gallery is 15m long but only a metre or so high: crawling is easier than walking here. In 1816, the Revd John Skinner broke in through the roof to explore the tomb chambers. He found many human bones and fragments of pottery (Figure 4).

BEDFORDSHIRE

BARTON HILL FARM   Streatley   TL: 094282

This middle neolithic henge barrow was discovered from air photographs in 1948. The foundation trench of a wooden mortuary enclosure and two crouched burials were enclosed inside a circular ditch 30m in diameter. The ditch and external bank were broken by an entrance causeway, and from this a row of posts led to a site consisting of a number of overlapping pits.

BISCOT MILL LONG   Luton   TL: 079232
BARROW

The exact location of this destroyed long barrow is not known for certain, although it seems likely that it was the mound on which Biscot Windmill was built. This stood behind what is now the Biscot Mill public house. Two polished greenstone axes have been found here, which suggests that it was a neolithic site of some kind.

CARDINGTON CAUSEWAYED ENCLOSURE   TL: 093484

A causewayed enclosure site in a field called Stonyland Furlong. The misshapen circular precinct is enclosed by three closely spaced interrupted ditches. The small straight-sided enclosures which lie within it, and also across the ditches and outside, probably relate to a later prehistoric occupation of the site. Close by, at TL: 092502, cropmarks indicate the existence of mortuary enclosures, an oval barrow and a cursus.

DUNSTABLE DOWN LONG BARROW TL: 012222

An earthen long barrow 30m long, forming part of the Five Knolls Barrow Cemetery on Dunstable Down.

FURZENHILL FARM CURSUS TL: 196466

A possible cursus showing as a cropmark.

GALLEY HILL LONG BARROW   Streatley   TL: 086268

This long barrow, destroyed in about 1900, lay to the west of Galley Hill. Air photographs show it to have been 90m long; this seems incredibly long for a Chiltern long barrow, but it may be that it was spread during destruction and was originally significantly shorter. Excavation produced Windmill Hill pottery and human bones.

GOLDINGTON HENGES TL: 078504

The earliest monument at this complex ritual site was a henge with a single entrance to the south-west. Its ditch, 2.5m wide and 2m deep, encircled a precinct 25m in diameter. The ditch was open for a time and full of water, forming a kind of moat, before it was deliberately filled in using material from its inner bank. There was apparently no external bank. The ditch was subsequently recut and once again backfilled, perhaps as part of some recurring ritual act. The refill contained pottery, flints and hazel nuts. Within the henge, and probably contemporary with the first cutting of the ditch, were seven pairs of post-pits, 0.6m deep and 0.6m in diameter, regularly spaced round the circumference. A single cremation was found near the centre. The henge was re-used for burial in the bronze age; there is a cremation pit of the later period dug through the windblown sands that seal in the neolithic levels.

A second site nearby (at TL: 078502) also seems to have begun as a single-entrance henge. Its irregular, sub-circular ditch 2.5m wide and 0.8m deep enclosed an area 34–40m in diameter. There was a single, narrow entrance on the north side. There were several small pits on the enclosure circumference; three contained cremated bone, while the others contained deposits of hazel nuts, potsherds and a broken flint axe. Two pits dug in the centre of the henge each contained the body of a child, one of them accompanied by a small pot, some flints and a stone ball. A post-pit near the child burials probably carried a marker or totem pole, and the burial area was defined by a circle of stake-holes. This encircling fence was quickly replaced by a low turf mound 0.4m high and 14m in diameter; the mound was later enlarged, and further burials followed. Whether the central child burials represent evidence of child sacrifice as a foundation offering for the monument is open to speculation, but parallels with Woodhenge and other sites inevitably spring to mind. The burial monument was re-used, still for burial, in the ensuing bronze age, and seems to have retained its original neolithic function until about 1200 BC.

HOUGHTON CONQUEST LONG BARROW   TL: 055405

Unusually located on sand hills, this long barrow runs from north-west to south-east up a hill slope. It is 50m long, 10m wide and 1.5m high, with traces of side ditches. About 90m away to the east there is a round barrow 18m in diameter.

KNOCKING KNOLL   Pegsdon   TL: 133311
LONG BARROW

This large long barrow straddles the county boundary; its Hertfordshire half has been destroyed by the plough, giving it the appearance of a large round barrow 30m in diameter. A chalk cist incorporating a crouched burial was set in the east end. The barrow was opened by William Ransom in about 1855, and William Stukeley mentioned it over a hundred years earlier, but the only other record of it seems to be a watercolour in Hitchin Museum.

LEAGRAVE LONG BARROW   TL: 057247

An earthen long barrow 30m long.

MAIDEN BOWER   Houghton Regis   SP: 997224

Beneath the small iron age plateau fort lie the remains of a neolithic causewayed enclosure. In the nineteenth century, several sections of flat-bottomed ditch were found, and some of these can still be seen in the side of the quarry that is eroding away both fort and neolithic enclosure on the north side. The ditches have yielded bones, Windmill Hill pottery and an antler comb. Bones found in the neolithic ditch in 1898 had been split 'for the extraction of marrow', or so it was believed. The iron age ditches, with their distinctive V-shape, are also plainly visible.

MAULDEN HENGE   Barton-in-the-Clay   TL: 095275

A large henge monument 150m in diameter, discovered by James Dyer in 1962. It shows up on air photographs, where it appears to have an entrance on the south side. A line of pits, possibly representing a post row, leads from the henge southwards for about 1km. A section through the pits produced fragments of neolithic pottery.

MILL HILL LONG BARROW   Dunstable   TL: 012222

This long barrow once stood in Union Street, Dunstable. It was mentioned by William Stukeley in 1724, but unfortunately it was never excavated. It seems to have been about 30m long and oriented W–E. It was destroyed in the twentieth century.

WAULUD'S BANK   Luton   TL: 061246

A D-shaped enclosure at the source of the River Lea. It is probably late neolithic, replacing the earlier and higher enclosure of Maiden Bower. The semi-circular bank defining this monument is now difficult to trace, although it is still 2.5m high in places. There is a silted-up outer ditch 6m wide. Ditch and bank sweep up in an arc from the source of the Lea, past blocks of flats, and round the crest of the hill to Youth House. Excavation has proved that the site is neolithic, and it exhibits some significant points of similarity with henge monuments. A comparison with the great henge at Marden suggests itself; like Marden, Waulud's Bank uses a stream as part of its perimeter, apparently for ritual rather than defensive reasons. No entrances or internal features have as yet been found at Waulud's Bank, although Grooved ware pottery and many arrow-heads have; the arrows may be interpreted as evidence of warfare or of hunting in marshes and woodland. A long barrow site was been tentatively identified nearby, at TL: 057247 (Figure 5).

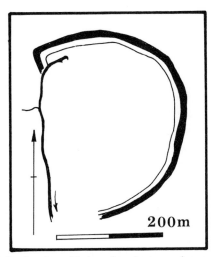

Figure 5 Waulud's Bank, a large D-shaped enclosure at the source of the River Lea, which is in the north-west corner of the enclosure. The thick black line shows the enclosure ditch.

BERKSHIRE

BEENHAM RING DITCH   Marley Tile Pit   SU: 604678

A chance find of a Great Langdale greenstone axe in the scoop of a mechanical grab led to the discovery of a ring ditch 55m in diameter. The axe probably came from the ditch fill. Other remains included fragments of pottery, including one piece that might have belonged to a Grooved ware vessel. The ring ditch has been quarried away.

CANNONS HILL   SU: 896792

One of the few earlier neolithic pottery assemblages of the region has been found here. The pottery was undecorated ware, including carinated, round-based bowls tempered with crushed flints.

ENGLEFIELD RING DITCHES   SU: 624702

These four conjoining ring ditches were discovered from the air in 1962; one of them was excavated by Paul Ashbee and J. J. Wymer in 1963. The excavated ring ditch was the easternmost and smallest of the four, about 15m in diameter. The other three were about twice this size. Their centres lay in an approximately straight line. Pottery fragments from the ditch represented remains of Windmill Hill, Grooved ware, Mortlake and Fengate styles. There were also flint flakes, two transverse arrow-heads and some scrapers.

LAMBOURN LONG BARROW   SU: 323834

At the southern end of the Westcot Wood lies this ruined long barrow. It is about 80m long and 20m wide, and still 1m high at its eastern end. Martin Atkins dug into it in the nineteenth century and found skeletons, but left no details. More recently, John Wymer found a crouched female skeleton, with an unusual necklace of whelk shells, in a sarsen stone cist at the barrow's eastern end. This did not form part of the primary deposit, but had been tucked into the core of sarsen stones some time after the barrow had been built. Charcoal from the barrow gave a radiocarbon date of 3415 bc (4250 BC).

This is the only long barrow in Berkshire to have been scientifically investigated, and it turns out to be very early. The use of turves in the construction speaks of an open, pastoral environment even at this early date, as at Wayland's Smithy. The chalk country of Berkshire has rather surprisingly yielded no major ceremonial enclosures – at least none have been discovered so far. The fact that the area lies on or close to the edge of the long barrow distribution (in the main confined to the chalk outcrops) may have meant that unusual conditions prevailed there.

SONNING   SU: 75 75

A sub-rectangular ritual enclosure 40m by 30m, surrounded by a ditch 2–3m wide. There was an apparently random scatter of eight storage or votive pits within the enclosure. No domestic debris was found at the site, which suggests strongly that it may have had a sacred or funerary use.

——————— BUCKINGHAMSHIRE ———————

PITSTONE HILL   SP: 949142

Two flint mines have been identified here, at the north-western end of the chalk escarpment. The surface hollows are still about 3m deep. Although such sites are common enough in the South Downs, they are surprisingly rare in the Chilterns, although some more have been identified in Whipsnade Zoo, not far away. Immediately to the east of the Pitstone Hill flint mines there are traces of a discontinuous (i.e. causewayed) ditch, which may well turn out to be the remains of a neolithic causewayed enclosure.

WHITELEAF BARROW   Princes Risborough   SP: 822040

False-crested and located just above the medieval Whiteleaf Cross are the damaged and overgrown remains of Whiteleaf Barrow. It was excavated in the 1930s. The barrow was kidney-shaped and 20m across, surrounded by a circular ditch 24m in diameter, with a concave 'forecourt' area on the eastern side. Its shape is unusual for a southern tomb. Under the mound was a wooden burial chamber or mortuary house 2.4m long and 1.7m wide. The left foot of a middle-aged man was found in the chamber, but the rest of his bones were scattered across the forecourt. Fragments of over 50 neolithic pots and hundreds of pieces of worked flint were found throughout the barrow mound; presumably this neolithic occupation debris was lying about on the ground when the mound material was scraped up. The pottery fragments found in the barrow carry impressions of two types of wheat grain, *Triticum dicoccum* and *Triticum compactum*. The grain must have been lying about on the surface on which the pottery was made: the neolithic British were not particularly clean or tidy. The Whiteleaf Barrow has the distinction of being the only known neolithic mound burial in Buckinghamshire.

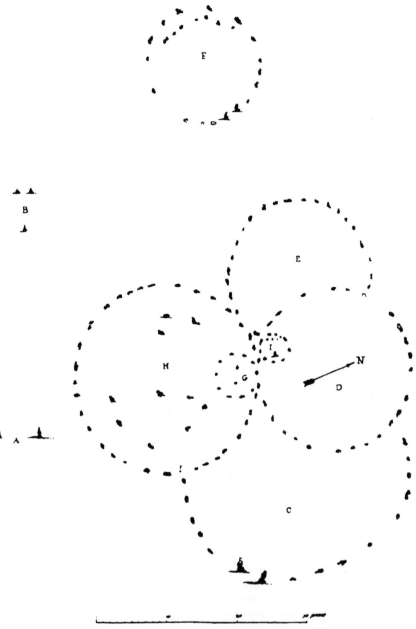

Figure 6 A lost stone circle complex at St Just, Cornwall. The stones were removed for building. The overlapping design is very unusual and one might suspect that it had been misinterpreted, but Dr William Borlase, who recorded it in 1754, was a careful and accurate observer. The largest of these circles had a diameter of more than 30 paces.

CAMBRIDGESHIRE

BARNACK CURSUS   TF: 082065

A cursus monument.

BUCKDEN GRAVEL PIT   TL: 202680

An occupation site on gravels of the River Cam's third terrace. Several pits were found, one containing a neolithic pot.

BUCKWORTH LONG BARROW   TL: 139768

A long barrow 100m long and 15m wide; it was ploughed down in 1945.

BURWELL   TL: 570675

A neolithic and early bronze age settlement about 3m above sea level in Hallard's Fen. Large numbers of flint implements have been found in the fenland of Burwell parish, and the concentration of flints in Hallard's Fen shows that there was a settlement site here. Finds include quantities of flint cores and a number of polished axes, leaf-shaped arrow-heads, scrapers and burins. There were also late neolithic ring ditches in the area, at TL: 601688, 596656, 596565, 587653, 593646 and 583646, but they have all been ploughed out.

CAMBRIDGE   TL: 475547

An occupation site. A pit containing late neolithic Grooved ware pottery was revealed when an anti-tank ditch was cut in the 1940s.

CHERRY HINTON   TL: 4857

An occupation site. Excavation revealed a pit containing three sherds of neolithic Grooved ware, flint flakes, a scraper and a core.

ELTON HENGE   TL: 082962

A henge about 100m in diameter was inferred from cropmarks visible from the air in 1960 and 1977. The entrance is slightly west of south and the ditch itself seems to be very broad. Other cropmarks nearby may not be contemporary with the henge. One ring ditch, to the north-west, straddles the henge ditch, indicating that the henge was already disused when the ring ditch was dug. Air photographs show a large sub-rectangular enclosure with internal divisions inside the henge, and circular, linear and rectangular features both inside and outside the circle. The henge ditch is 5.5m wide but only 1m deep, with steep sides and a floor that is nearly flat. A few small plain black sherds were found and a number of flint flakes. Thick lenses of burnt soil containing charcoal near the ditch bottom have given a radiocarbon date of 4070 bp (2600 BC). Just inside and parallel to the ditch was a narrow trench, which was evidently a bedding trench for a palisade. The site is likely to be destroyed by mineral extraction; at the time of writing, planning consent had already been given.

ELTON   TL: 085927

An early neolithic D-shaped enclosure, measuring 12m by 12m, with an entrance to the west. It was later remodelled with a new entrance to the east. Its ditches contained artefacts that show beyond much doubt that the enclosure was domestic. Probably contemporary with the D-shaped house-enclosure was an open pit grave, which contained the disarticulated remains of at least five people. Also contemporary was a straight-sided cairn made – unusually for lowland England – of river gravel pebbles. It had a semi-circular entrance façade made of ten posts at its southern end. The whole complex was replaced in the late neolithic by a rectilinear field system aligned at right angles to the stream channel. The late neolithic fields, nestling in the floor of the Nene valley, were in their turn buried beneath slopewash in the ensuing bronze age. Now, the site has been designated as part of the route of the A605 Elton–Chesterton bypass.

ETTON CAUSEWAYED   **Maxey**   TF: 138073
ENCLOSURE

A settlement and ceremonial site at the eastern end of the Maxey ritual complex. The causewayed enclosure consists of a single segmented ditch enclosing an oval area 180m (W–E) by 140m (N–S); the southern end of the Maxey Cursus runs close to it. The site was probably occupied for a hundred years around 2700 BC, although radiocarbon dates have yet to confirm this, and probably mainly in the summer months. Even so, the lower parts of the ditch must always have been wet; when digging it out, the neolithic workers must often have been standing up to their knees in water. The ditch was cleaned out several times. A low-lying turf-fronted platform was built and fires were lit on top of it.

The waterlogged layers in the enclosure ditch preserved the remains of twigs, leaves, seeds, wood chips and pointed sticks. An axe handle, probably made of ash, was apparently split during use across the axe-head socket; this must have been a common enough problem for neolithic wood-cutters. Also from the lower ditch came many large sherds of middle neolithic Mildenhall pottery, some with remnants of food still sticking to them. The pottery was all very similar, showing a narrow range of shapes and decorative motifs. The ditch yielded fragments of antler and 4,000 pieces of wood. There was evidence of coppicing: rather surprisingly, coppice stools were allowed to grow in the bottom of the ditch. It may be that the Etton people made something coarser in texture than basketwork, perhaps producing objects akin to the Sussex trug.

Cattle were reared and the bones even of relatively young cows show evidence of arthritis; the slopes here are very gentle, so they may have been used for drawing ards, sleds or carts. There were symbolic or dedicatory deposits near the ditch terminals, such as a small heap of butchered animal bones, a complete pot on a birch bark mat, a neat bundle of calf ribs beside a pile of hazel nuts, a length of vegetable fibre twine and a piece of squared-off birch bark. These were carefully placed deposits, and not merely tips of rubbish. The enclosure had two clearly differentiated halves, one funerary, the other non-funerary, and they were separated by a line of post-holes. The enormous quantity of detail from this site gives us an unusual insight into people's everyday lives, not least the curious dovetailing of secular and ritual elements.

ETTON WOODGATE   Maxey   TF: 138073

A settlement on what is now cultivated land, 80m WNW of the causewayed enclosure. A length of ditch followed the curve of a low, buried scarp, and was broken by a broad entrance, which was located opposite one of the entrances of the causewayed enclosure. Just inside the settlement entrance there were small pits, one of them containing a crouched burial, and post-holes containing blade-like flints of early neolithic form, as well as fired clay, burnt stone and some plain pottery. The settlement seems to have spread out across a hectare of land, on both sides of the ditch. Patterns of post-holes suggest that people were living in straight-sided wooden houses.

FENGATE SETTLEMENT AND FIELD SYSTEM   TL: 213989

The first forest clearings here were made and occupied by 3500 BC. Among the remains at Fengate are those of an early neolithic house to the west of Cat's Water; its four foundation trenches formed a rectangle 7m by 8.5m, and there were also a few associated pits and post-holes. The house dates from around 3500 BC. Pottery found in the trenches belongs to the Grimston/Lyles Hill tradition, which spanned a period of 1,000 years and so is not in any way definitive in dating the house. Pieces of 'burnt clay' may be the remains of wattle-and-daub walls, although no impressions of wattles survive. Four people, perhaps the occupants of this house, were buried in a pit beside it. One of them had an arrow-head between his ribs, implying a violent death.

A later building was raised inside a ring ditch and therefore may have been a shrine; this has been radiocarbon dated to 1860 or 1930 bc (2300–2400 BC). Four phases of activity can be detected at this site. In Phase 1, dated to 2030–2010 bc (2550–2500 BC), a straight-sided enclosure and a droveway for livestock were in use. In Phase 2, around 1860 bc (2300 BC), the drainage ditches were deepened and the ring ditch was made. After the abandonment of the ring ditch, at the beginning of Phase 3, 1460–1360 bc (1800–1700 BC), the field system continued in use, largely unchanged, but the people appear to have moved elsewhere; there is no sign of permanent settlement among these fields. The ring ditch was left to silt up, although it was still visible in the early bronze age, when it was cleaned out to supply material for a burial mound. In Phase 4, the field system still continued in use, though it is assumed that it finally went out of use when the well was abandoned in about 1050 bc (1300 BC). The Fengate field system shows us in unique detail a pattern of gradually changing land use and occupation right through the middle and late neolithic, and on into the bronze age; the site is nevertheless a very difficult one to interpret.

FOULMIRE FEN   TL: 420766

A middle and late neolithic settlement on the southern edge of the sand and gravel island in Foulmire, 100m to the south of the Haddenham Long Barrow. Finds here include large quantities of flintwork, including leaf-shaped and barbed-and-tanged arrow-heads, Fengate pottery, and a large spread of bark evidently cut by human hand. Possibly this was a centre for salt production: the sea is known to have encroached in the Fens in the late third millennium BC, and the site was eventually sealed in by the resulting deposits of Fen Clay.

GODMANCHESTER ENCLOSURE   TL: 255709

A large trapeze-shaped enclosure (7ha) on level terrace gravels at Rectory Farm, Godmanchester, which has been excavated in advance of gravel working. A ditch 4m wide and 1m deep ran round three sides of an almost rectangular enclosure 336m long, 180m wide at the narrower south-west end and 230m wide at the open north-east end. At the north-east end the ditch terminals turned inwards but left a broad entrance gap 176m wide. The upcast from the ditch formed an internal bank. Within that were 24 large post-holes, evidently sockets for substantial totem poles, arranged round the perimeter of the enclosure. The biggest posts stood at each end of the enclosure, on its axis. The spacing of the posts along the sides was fairly regular, mostly 36–38m, but not exactly uniform, which suggests that pacing was probably used to lay out the design. The more significant posts at the ends were unevenly spaced, which implies that they were laid out according to some other criterion.

A radiocarbon date of 2270 bc (2950 BC) from an antler at the bottom of one of the post-holes tells us when this remarkable, and undoubtedly important, monument was built.

The Godmanchester Enclosure has no known counterpart anywhere in the British Isles or Brittany, which makes its loss to gravel extraction all the sadder. Aubrey Burl and Jon Humble have established alignments among the post-holes to *all* the major risings and settings of the sun and moon. For example, a line from the axial post at the south-west end, post 13, to the northern gatepost, post 2, marked the midsummer sunrise; a diagonal line from the north-west corner, post 11, to the southern gatepost, post 24, marked the equinox sunrise and sunset.

It could be argued that 24 posts will offer a very large number of possible sightlines and that some of these are bound to hit significant astronomical events by chance. Nevertheless, the posts that define solar and lunar alignments in 2900 BC – and *only* those posts – were treated in a special way with ritual deposits of antlers, ox skulls or ox jawbones.

Though the shape and design of the Godmanchester Enclosure are different from those of Stonehenge I, the astronomical and ritual preoccupations seem to have been very similar. It was also, significantly, built only a century or so after Stonehenge I, at a time when the same ideas were in the air.

GREAT WILBRAHAM   TL: 539578

A causewayed enclosure site on low-lying ground at 15m OD, close to a stream. The site is a knoll or low spur made of gravels of the Cam's second terrace. It was, in other words, always above flood level. Surface finds of struck flakes, some with secondary working, appear to belong to the earlier neolithic. The land has only recently come under the plough, yet nothing is visible at ground level. The site was excavated in 1975–6. The two concentric ditches yielded a lot of pottery, as well as animal and plant remains. Excavations in the mere which surrounds the gravel knoll on three sides have turned up a great deal of organic material, pottery and flint, some of it contemporary with the causewayed enclosure.

HADDENHAM CAUSEWAYED ENCLOSURE   TL: 412736

A neolithic causewayed enclosure at the edge of the Fens. It has two encircling ditches; the inner one, 1.5–2.0m deep, is middle neolithic, the outer one, 0.8m deep, is late neolithic. Waterlogging at the bottom of the ditch allowed the preservation of some oak planks and other cultural material that does not normally survive in the archaeological record. It was excavated in 1981. Set back about 10m inside the ditch was a palisade trench for substantial posts, implying that the entrances must have been formal. There was also a placed deposit or offering of a polished axe and fragments of three or more human skulls in the primary fill of the ditch. The site was modified in the middle iron age, apparently for funerary purposes, indicating the continuity of the site's sanctity.

HADDENHAM LONG BARROW   TL: 420767

15km north of Cambridge, where the Great Ouse enters the Fens, the Haddenham Long Barrow forms the focal point for a major barrow cemetery. The barrow mound is 49m long and 18m wide, and was excavated by Ian Hodder in the 1980s. Under its broader north-eastern end, there was a rectangular wooden mortuary chamber: the 7m-long, box-like chamber was made of massive oak planks up to 25cm thick, 1.3m wide and 4m long. Axial posts at the ends may have supported the roof. There seems to have been an oaken floor too. Immediately in front of the mortuary chamber was a straight 12m-long façade, with limbs returning towards the west for 3 or 4m at each end. The façade was probably originally a free-standing structure, like the one at Giant's Hills, and probably made of oak trunks 60cm in diameter. There were 60–80cm gaps at the corners, implying entrances of some kind. Finally, a trapezoid barrow was raised over the façade and mortuary chamber, making a mound 50m long and 1.2m high. But first the wooden chamber was dismantled and set on fire; burnt and smashed pottery in front of the tomb shows that this was part of a funerary ritual, which has parallels at other tomb sites, such as Nutbane in Hampshire. The site is exceptional in that the carpentry of its oak burial chamber has been well preserved, and replicates megalithic masonry techniques. The monument must have been overwhelmed by peat and waterlogging shortly after its construction. Tree-ring analysis suggests that only one or two 1.5m diameter oaks were felled to construct the tomb chamber.

LITTLE PAXTON   TL: 183627

The site of a D-shaped wooden house, now destroyed. The straight side of the house, marked by a row of post-holes, was exposed during road works. The curved sides were bounded by an irregular trench with a vertical face which was supported inside by stakes. The southern half of the floor of the house had been cut away 0.3–0.4m below ground level, to leave a bench or bed running the length of the house from the entrance along the northern side. The lower half had been covered with straw. The house was strongly built with turf walls on three sides, 0.6m thick and supported by posts and stakes. The door was at the north-west corner and the rest of the west wall and the straight wall of the D were marked by two large post-holes. Between these two post-holes the floor finished in a straight line, showing that boards, skins or wattles must have formed a solid boundary there. It seems that there were rafters radiating from a large post in the north wall, possibly indicating a hut roof that was a half-cone. The interior dimensions were 3m by 2m. A sherd of Peterborough pottery was found in the trench bottom and many worked flints were found nearby. This important example of a D-shaped turf house illustrates that there may have been many variants in neolithic house design. It may also throw some light on the significance of the C-shaped and D-shaped ritual enclosures, which could have been derived from domestic architecture.

MAXEY CURSUS   TF: 127077

Part of an important neolithic and early bronze age ritual focus, the Maxey Cursus seems to have had its beginning – or ending – at the banks of the River Welland. It ran south-east for about 850m and then turned slightly to run on a new alignment a further 900m to the ESE. This reorientation took the cursus very close to the Etton causewayed enclosure. It may have run tangentially past the enclosure or stopped at its entrance: it is difficult to infer the exact relationship because the crucial section has been destroyed by the excavation of Maxey Cut. It is not known whether the cursus ended at the causewayed enclosure or continued even further to the south-east. About 50 circular structures of various kinds are clustered round and on the cursus, most of them significantly later in date.

Construction of the cursus was piecemeal, and it is thought that the north-west segment is much later then the south-east. The cursus ditches are about 2.5m wide, 58m apart, and seem to have misaligned sections: halfway between Maxey Great Henge and Etton causewayed enclosure, for example, there is a 'step', where the north ditch slips off course. There are also gaps. It seems that it was the general effect or the overall alignment that was important, rather then the finish of the monument.

The site has been scheduled for destruction by gravel extraction (Figure 7).

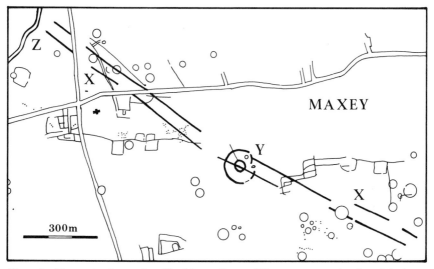

Figure 7   Maxey ritual complex. The Maxey Cursus (X) passes across the site of the later henge (Y) to the River Welland (Z).

MAXEY GREAT HENGE   TF: 127077

This large henge monument straddled the Maxey Cursus and had several unusual features, including a round mound at its centre and an oval barrow actually in its entrance causeway. The first stage in the development of the site was turf-stripping in the centre of the henge and the entrance area, where the oval barrow was later to be built. Then the main monument was constructed, starting with a ring ditch at the centre, spoil from the ditch being cast up inside to form a mound. The outer ditch was probably dug out at the same time and the spoil from this

25

thrown outwards to make the characteristic external henge bank; this was 125m in diameter, making it slightly larger than the earthwork at Stonehenge. After this, the site of the oval barrow was developed, initially as an imposing oval enclosure 15m by 10m, formed out of 156 massive squared oak beams set upright to make a continuous wooden wall. Substantial though this was, it was not allowed to stand for long. It was burnt down and, at the same time, the bounding outer bank of the henge was pushed back into its ditch and the central mound was similarly pushed back into the ring ditch. As a result, the monument was virtually destroyed.

The final phase of construction of the Maxey Great Henge followed quickly. A new mound was built at the centre, covering the entire area of the earlier ring ditch; as no burial was included in it, it cannot really be considered a barrow. At the same time, an oval turf barrow was built at the henge entrance, on the site of the burnt-out oval enclosure; first a crouched burial was deposited at the centre of the blackened enclosure, and then the barrow mound was piled on top. The soil below the barrow was found to be enriched in a way that implies that the earlier enclosure had been used as a mortuary enclosure.

Despite all this activity, none of the episodes seems to have lasted very long. The whole flurry of ritual was probably over in as little as a decade.

Within the outer ditch of the henge, but close to it on the north-west side, were two circles of pits, one 14m and the other 10m in diameter. Each circle consisted of ten pits, and one of them overrode the south-west ditch of the cursus, which runs right through the henge, proving that at least one post circle post-dated the cursus.

The Great Henge yielded some unique carved ritual objects. Two of them were antlers, a third was a red deer rib. The antlers were highly polished and ornamented with geometric chevrons cut into them, the designs being similar to those seen on Boyne megaliths and Grooved ware pottery. The incisions carry traces of red paint (ferric oxide). The deer rib also had carvings on it, but was painted all over, two-thirds black, one-third red.

The site of Maxey Great Henge is on the River Welland's first terrace and, despite its undoubted archaeological importance, is scheduled for destruction by gravel extraction.

ORTON LONGUEVILLE   TL: 160963

A settlement site, indicated by storage pits, a scatter of Peterborough ware, and a few sherds of Grooved ware pottery – all found during gravel working in the early 1930s. The site is now built over, so that it is a settlement once more.

SHIPPEA HILL

A settlement site which supplied Sir Harry Godwin with evidence of the problematic 'elm decline', believed to have occurred rather suddenly around 3400–3300 BC. It is thought now that the elm decline detected in the pollen record was not caused by climatic change but by elm disease or some kind of land management technique. The settlement itself has been radiocarbon dated to 3000–2920 bc (3700–3600 BC).

STONEA GRANGE   Wimblington   TL: 449936

Two parallel ditches, tentatively identified as a cursus, are aligned on the barrow excavated in 1961–2. No artefacts were found in the cursus ditches, which in itself suggests a prehistoric date and is consistent with the negative evidence found in cursus ditches generally: they tend to be 'clean' monuments. A second barrow and a circular cropmark have been located nearby, and two flint arrow-heads and some late neolithic sherds show that the area was occupied.

SWAFFHAM PRIOR   TL: 561650

An occupation site on Lower Chalk on the fen edge, which was first settled in the mesolithic period. Neolithic flint and stone axes, arrow-heads and awls prove that the site was occupied in the new stone age too. There were ring ditches in the area as well, at TL: 587615, 599630, 581645 (still visible), 580636, 579636, but they have mostly been ploughed out.

WIMBLINGTON   TL: 450931

A low ploughed round barrow of bronze age date was found to rest on top of a late neolithic occupation surface. The neolithic occupation comprised pits, stake-holes, worked flints, charcoal, bone, 600 sherds of coarse red pottery (many comparable with Ebbsfleet, Mildenhall, Whiteleaf and Grooved ware styles). A slightly later horizon yielded two beaker sherds.

CHESHIRE

THE BRIDESTONES   Congleton   SJ: 905621

One of only two known megalithic monuments in Cheshire, this stands 5 km E of Congleton at a height of 250m OD; it really belongs to the Pennines rather than to the Plain. The burial chamber now stands denuded of its covering mound, which was at one time, in the eighteenth century, 110m long and 11m wide. The chamber is 5.5m long and 1.5m wide, and lies W–E. Halfway along its length is a broken porthole stone: an upright slab with a hole in it just large enough to pass fragments of a corpse through. It is recorded that there were originally two additional chambers. A second chamber in the centre of the mound was 2m square and 0.7m high. Traces of the third chamber were noticed in 1766. These chambers and the covering mound were destroyed in the eighteenth century. In 1764, several cartloads of stone were taken from the monument to construct Dial Lane. Successive plans of the forecourt stone circle show how it too was progressively reduced. At the eastern end of the chamber, there are still visible traces of a semicircular forecourt, marked by large stones. The forecourt has been badly damaged and overgrown, but it seems that it was originally surrounded by at least a partial and probably a complete circle of standing stones, of which three survive. They enclosed a cobbled area covered by pyre ashes. The style of the monument suggests that it might be an outlier of the Scottish 'Clyde–Carlingford' type of tomb. It nevertheless has affinities with at least one other monument in the area – the forecourt tomb at Five Wells near Taddington, not far away in Derbyshire.

HENBURY HENGE   SJ: 887728

The site of an oval setting of ball-shaped boulders. Ploughing in 1971 at Brickbank Farm revealed two large erratic blocks 30–40cm in diameter. More boulders were found built into the field boundaries and into a nearby stile. The stones had passed unnoticed because the field had, as far as is known, only been ploughed once before 1971. Systematic excavation of the site revealed 11 stone sockets up to 0.5m deep, arranged in an oval surrounding a central pit. A thirteenth pit, which lay outside the oval setting to the east, showed signs of great heat: it was, moreover, associated with a large deposit of charcoal. It has been suggested that the setting may have been designed to mark the winter solstice but, given the compass bearing of the thirteenth pit, this seems unlikely. The monument has yet to be dated, but it is probably late neolithic.

LINDOW MOSS   **Mobberley**   SJ: 819807

Under the peat layer where Lindow Man was found, there is a layer of charcoal which represents the neolithic forest clearance episode. The charcoal has been radiocarbon dated to 4980 bp (3700 BC). On a sand island in the bog, a thin scatter of worked flints gives us further, if scanty, evidence of the presence of neolithic people in the area.

CORNWALL

BALLOWALL BARROW   **St Just**   SW: 356312

A large, complex and multi-phase chambered tomb. It consists of a large closed chamber sealed inside a central conical cairn, which in turn is surrounded by a later collar or cairn-ring. The central chamber contained a number of stone cists and a T-shaped ritual pit: this alone remains. Two further cists can be seen in the narrow corridor between the central cairn and the collar, which contains a smaller chamber, again with a pit dug into its floor. Set into the outer wall of the collar, on the south-west side, is an entrance grave with two capstones still in place.

Probably the monument began as a conventional neolithic Scillonian chambered tomb, and it was developed in the middle bronze age with the building of the conical cairn and cists, and finally with the addition of the collar. But the dating sequence is uncertain, and the monument as it stands is unique (Figure 8).

THE BLIND FIDDLER   **Sancreed**   SW: 425282

A standing stone 3.3m high, also known as the Trenuggo Stone. Fragments of bone were found buried at its foot in the nineteenth century, but it is not known whether these were contemporary with the raising of the stone: they may have been deposited much later.

BOSCAWEN-UN STONE CIRCLE   **St Buryan**   SW: 412274

Nineteen regularly spaced stones are enclosed within a modern field wall. This low-lying stone circle is 23m in diameter, with a leaning stone pillar 2.5m high at its centre. This central stone may have been the focus for foundation deposits and offerings; it does not appear to have any astronomical significance. The circle

Figure 8 Ballowall Barrow. A reconstruction, showing what the monument originally looked like.

was restored in 1862, when three fallen stones were re-erected and a hedge cutting the circle in two was removed. It is to be hoped that similar consideration will one day be given to the stone rings at Avebury. An experimental trench cut through the site revealed nothing. A west-facing gap in the circle may have been the monument's entrance. There are two outlying stones to the north-east, at SW: 415276 and 417277.

This circle is probably the 'Beisgawen yn Dumnonia' named in the old Welsh Triads as one of the Three Principal Gorsedds of the Island of Britain, which implies that it held some considerable importance in ancient times as a ceremonial centre. Appropriately, the modern Cornish Gorsedd was inaugurated here in 1928 (Figure 9).

BRANE ENTRANCE GRAVE Sancreed   SW: 401281

This is the best example in mainland Cornwall of a type of entrance grave more commonly found in the Isles of Scilly. The barrow is 6m in diameter and 2m high, and held in place by a remarkably heavy wall of large granite blocks. On the south-east is an entrance passage that leads directly into the chamber. The chamber is 2.2m long and 1m wide and roofed with two capstones: a third, the outermost, capstone has been removed. The tomb stands on private land; permission to visit it must first be sought at Brane Farm. It is situated, unusually, on good farmland near the valley floor, but it is difficult to find. It is one of the smallest but best-preserved chambered tombs in Britain. Only discovered as late as 1863, and first recorded in 1872, it has not been tampered with since then. For some reason, the ground level both outside and inside the mound seems to have been lowered by about 0.3m since the time when the tomb was built, which may

Figure 9 Boscawen-un, as drawn by J. T. Blight in about 1860.

explain why three or four of the big kerbstones are missing; they probably collapsed outwards when their foundations were undermined, and were carted away by farm labourers. The mound has been made only just big enough to contain the chamber, which is also unusual (Figure 10).

BRANE LONG BARROW   Sancreed   SW: 401279

The long barrow is located just downstream from the Brane Entrance Grave, beside the footpath from Brane to Crows an Wra. It is on a valley floor, oriented NE–SW, at right angles to the stream. Only recently identified as a long barrow, its status is still unclear. In form, it is a long mound about 40m long and 10m wide, with a height of 2.5m. Ploughing has reduced the height and also spread the mound laterally. The south-west end has been truncated by stream erosion and the resulting river cliff has become a rabbit warren. It is one of two suspected long barrows in western Cornwall: the other is the Lanyon Mound. The Brane Long Barrow remains unexcavated.

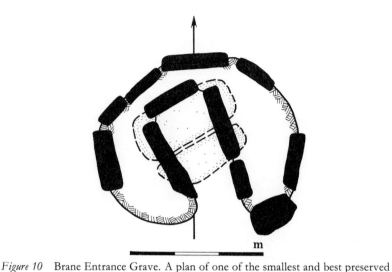

Figure 10   Brane Entrance Grave. A plan of one of the smallest and best preserved chambered tombs in Britain. The two capstones are shown with dashed lines.

CARN BREA   Redruth   SW: 686407

This large tor enclosure is capped by a medieval castle on a summit to the east and a monument to Sir Francis Basset on the west. Between the two, along the northern side of the hill, runs a single drystone wall, with two others looping round the south side. It seems likely that the iron age fort, to which *some* of the walls belong, was built in several stages, making interpretation of the site very difficult. A concentration of neolithic objects focused archaeological interest on the stone-walled enclosure surrounding the 0.7 hectares of the castle summit. Excavation indicated that the wall round the castle was of neolithic origin. Within it are irregular huts, including one leaning up against the wall, which are without doubt among the oldest in Britain. They have been dated to 3100–2700 BC. Large quantities of pottery have been found across the whole area, indicating that it is possible that all the fortifications were built in the neolithic.

This is the most important earlier neolithic settlement in Cornwall, and one of the oldest to have been discovered in Britain. It was permanently occupied by perhaps as many as 200 people, and areas that could have been used for crop production exist on the slopes below the defensive walls. The village was defended by a substantial wall, which is the only feature still to be visible. The neolithic villagers at Carn Brea enjoyed a peaceful existence for 300–400 years before their settlement was attacked and burnt down. The 700 arrow-heads found here have been seen as evidence of a fierce attack, one of the rare instances of warfare in the neolithic record (Figure 11).

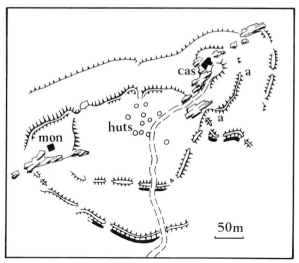

Figure 11   Carn Brea fortified hilltop enclosure. Neolithic walling at (a) has been positively identified; it may be that the other defences are neolithic in origin too.

CARN GLUZE BARROW   St Just   SW: 355312

This impressive site, one of the most dramatic in Britain, is easy to find on waste land beside the lane from St Just to Carn Gluze. It stands above the highest cliffs on this section of the coast, overlooking the sea. The barrow was excavated in 1878–9 by W. C. Borlase, who restored the site and, in doing so, radically changed its appearance.

The central feature was a high mound of rubble contained in two concentric walls of drystone about a metre apart. This made an oval, drum-shaped building 11m across from east to west and 9m across from north to south. It was 3.5m high when excavated and the top was evidently missing. The outer wall mainly consisted of a 1.5m high plinth of carefully selected square stones. The present inner wall is a modern rebuilding designed to keep the central area open so that visitors can see the interior structure: originally the mound was solid. Within the mound at ground level were three small cists; the cist at the centre was destroyed in 1881. Another cist was found 1.5m above ground level.

The central mound was surrounded by a layer of ashes and charred wood. Two large paved cists were built against the outer wall. Borlase built an additional wall so that these could remain visible, but it was not part of the original design. The outer mound, with a diameter of about 21m, was revetted by the kerb of large square blocks which supported a drystone wall, apparently only a metre or so high. An entrance grave was inserted on the south-west side; it still has two of its capstones in place. The building sequence is uncertain, but two phases seem likely: first, the central mound with its two outer cists, and then the outer mound with the entrance grave (Figure 12).

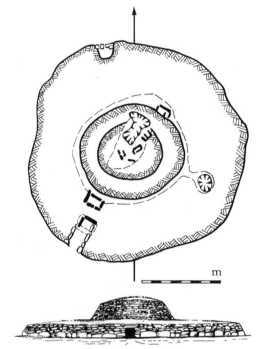

Figure 12   Carn Gluze Barrow: plan and reconstruction.

CARWYNNEN QUOIT   Troon   SW: 650373

A wrecked Penwith chambered tomb also known as the Giant's Quoit and the Giant's Frying Pan. The capstone, 3.3m by 2.5m by 0.3m, was once raised up on three supporters at a height of 1.5m, to make the tomb chamber, or quoit. The quoit collapsed in 1834 and was subsequently rebuilt. It collapsed again in 1967, since when it has been left in its present sorry state. The capstone rests on one of its supporters: the other two lie on top. Other stones lying around are field clearance boulders. The quoit in its present condition is a quite meaningless pile of boulders, and really should be restored without delay.

CASTILLY HENGE   Lanivet   SX: 031627

An oval henge with a maximum dimension of 66m, Castilly stands on a gentle northward slope beside the A391, 200m south of its junction with the A30. There is an oval bank nearly 2m high enclosing a ditch dug 2m deep into weathered slate. The ditch surrounds a flat oval precinct 49m long from north to south by 27m wide, with two diametrically opposed entrances consisting of gaps in the bank and causeways across the ditch. The north entrance seems to be the original one: the south entrance is a late addition. It was identified as a possible henge in 1953 and partially excavated by Thomas in 1962. Borlase in 1871 interpreted it as a 'Plain an Gwarry', a medieval open-air theatre, and it may well have been used as such in the thirteenth century, when the south entrance was made. Only medieval sherds have been found, so the site's status as a neolithic henge is still uncertain.

CASTLEWITCH HENGE   Callington   SX: 371685

On the summit of Balstone Down is an outcrop of Cornish greenstone, one of the sources of polished stone axes in the neolithic. Less than half a kilometre to the south is the Castlewitch Henge, a small monument, oval in shape, with the usual external bank and internal ditch. It lies 1km SE of Callington, on a gentle slope near the head of a stream and well below the crest of a NW–SE trending ridge: there are only restricted views towards the south-west. Castlewitch Henge was first identified by Lady Fox in 1952. It has a ditch 9–13m wide and about 1m deep. Outside this is a ploughed-down bank which must originally have been substantial: it is still 1m high and 12m wide. On the northern side, the bank has been badly damaged by ploughing. The bank is roughly circular with an external diameter of about 96m. The nearly circular central precinct is 49m by 45m. Contrary to Lady Fox's report, there seems to have been no entrance causeway; it is possible that a wooden bridge was used. There is no sign of a central mound either, and this suggests that the site was not a barrow – a possible alternative interpretation. It has been described as ideally situated for a trading centre. It is next to greenstone outcrops that were quarried for stone axes; it is midway between Dartmoor and Bodmin Moor, with unbroken ridges stretching away to north-west and south-west, and there is a route southwards leading to the Tamar estuary. The henge probably functioned as a ceremonial centre for the community of quarrymen and axe-makers living in the area.

CHAPEL CARN BREA   SW: 385280

On the summit of Carn Brea, at 200m OD, is the wreckage of a complex barrow. Borlase excavated the barrow in 1870, and found at its centre a chamber of rough drystone walling half sunk in a pit. It was 2.3m by 1.1m in plan and 1.2m high. Perhaps it was an unusual entrance grave or an eccentric type of cist: it can be viewed in either way. There were several other features which are difficult to interpret, including three internal vertical drystone walls, a strange drain-like feature, and a later enlargement of the mound with at least one cist above ground level, the last being the only surviving identifiable feature. In its final form, the mound was 21m by 18m and 4m high, and it was later used as a foundation for a medieval chapel. There are, altogether, eight barrows on Carn Brea, including at least one more entrance grave.

CHUN QUOIT   Morvah   SW: 402339

A large mushroom-shaped capstone 3.4m by 3.1m by 0.8m thick, supported by four wallstones, forms one of the finest surviving burial chambers in Cornwall. The chamber measures 1.8m long by 1.7m wide. A few scattered stones on the south may mark the position of the entrance passage. The remains of a circular enclosing mound about 12m in diameter can be seen, together with remnants of a retaining kerb on the north-east side.

THE DEVIL'S COYT   St Columb Major   SW: 923619

A destroyed chambered tomb site. The large chamber was probably a simple box type of portal dolmen. It collapsed in the mid-nineteenth century and its stones were carted away in 1871. Descriptions survive from that time, but no detailed plan. There were three tall supporters; the back slab, on the west side, had already gone. The capstone had a tilt to the west, probably because a supporter was missing on that side. The chamber was approximately cube-shaped and 2m across.

Fragments of this tomb were rediscovered in 1977 by the Cornwall Committee for Rescue Archaeology, while pipe-laying was under way. Dowsing has indicated the location of what may be the original capstone, measuring 3m by 2m; it corresponds to the dimensions given in the early descriptions.

DRY TREE MENHIR   Goonhilly   SW: 726212

A standing stone 3.2m high stands sentry near the Goonhilly Down dish aerials. It is made of Crousa Downs gabbro, and must therefore have been dragged at least 3km to this site. The place was notorious in the late eighteenth and early nineteenth centuries as the haunt of the Goonhilly highwaymen. The menhir may originally have been erected in the neolithic or bronze age. It was re-erected in 1927 in its original socket, after lying uprooted for many years.

EATHORNE MENHIR   SW: 746313

A fine standing stone 2.4m tall, and made of local granite. It is unusual in shape, tall and slender with a curious bend two-thirds of the way up, which makes it look like a pointing finger. Its age is unknown, but it is likely to be neolithic or bronze age.

FERNACRE STONE CIRCLE   SX: 144799

Fernacre, the largest circle on Bodmin Moor, measures 46m by 44m, with a slightly flattened circumference. Its 70 small stones are of local granite, and 39 are still standing. Two others lie near the centre of the circle. There are signs that the circle was retained by an earth bank, although it is odd that traces of this survive only on the south-east. The circle lies on a level site surrounded by four hills, Rough Tor to the north, Brown Willy and Garrow Tor to the east and south, Louden Hill to the WNW. Together with Louden Hill and Stripple Stones, Fernacre is one of the largest rings in Cornwall. It is as irregular as Stannon and likely to have been designed and built by eye. It probably originally consisted of 80–90 stones. The north-west quadrant has been damaged at some time during the twentieth century; two stones have been removed and a third has been broken. Not far away are the remains of three large prehistoric and undated settlements: they may prove to be contemporary with the circle.

GIANT'S QUOIT   Pawton   SW: 966696

An enormous rectangular capstone, originally measuring 4m by 2.1m and 0.8m thick, is supported by three out of its original seven wallstones. Two further stones would have supported the front of the stone, which has broken off. The chamber is in a ploughed field, and access is difficult except in winter. There are traces of an oval mound 21m by 15m.

HELMAN TOR   Lanlivery   SX: 061617

A tor enclosure on the rocky summit of Helman Tor. The battered remnants of this earth and stone wall enclose a long narrow area measuring 170m N–S and 60m E–W. It is similar in size and construction method to the enclosure on Carn Brea, and may be assumed provisionally to be neolithic.

HIGHER DRIFT   Sancreed   SW: 437283
STANDING STONES

Two standing stones, 2.7m and 2.3m high, stand 5.5m apart. They are also known as The Sisters or Triganeeris Stones. In 1871, excavation showed that a rectangular pit 1.8m long had been cut just north of a line between the two stones, but apparently it contained nothing.

THE HURLERS   Minions   SX: 258713

Three fine stone circles lie in an approximately straight line on the desolate, mine-ravaged east side of Bodmin Moor. They are very close together and run from SW–NE up the hillside. The smallest circle, which is now badly damaged, is on the south side. It contains nine stones still standing and is 35m in diameter. Next to it is the largest circle, 42m in diameter, egg-shaped and with a standing stone located just off-centre; it has 14 stones still standing out of an original 28. To the north is a circle 33m in diameter and consisting of 15 stones out of its original 28 or 30. Excavation has shown that the interior of this circle was roughly paved with granite blocks. The stones of the circles were originally shaped and then set up in sockets of varying depths, so that their tops would all be level (Figure 13).

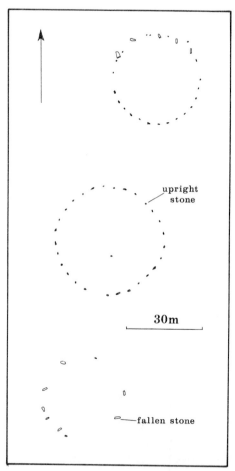

Figure 13 The Hurlers. The South Circle is so badly damaged that many people walk through it without noticing it. The Central and North Circles are in better condition, partly through restoration work.

Two standing stones, the Pipers, lie 120m WSW of the central circle. John Barnatt (1980) thinks these are not prehistoric, for several reasons: they are squarer stones than those in the circles, they stand on the parish boundary, which has some stone markers that are known to be modern, and they were not noted by Borlase.

In 1935–6, the two northern circles were partially restored by Raleigh Radford, who raised fallen stones and placed small marker stones on the sites of the missing stones. Astronomical alignments have been proposed but, on the whole, Thom's proposed star lines to first magnitude stars are not convincing because the circles' centres were unmarked. The Hurlers stone circles seem to have formed the centre of a major prehistoric ceremonial complex. To the south-east is the important barrow cemetery on Caradon Hill: to the north is the Rillaton Barrow and the Stowes Hill enclosure.

KING ARTHUR'S HALL   St Breward   SX: 130777

This substantial rectangular earthwork on an exposed moorland summit has been the subject of argument and debate for centuries. Its true origin, purpose and date are still a mystery. Today, 56 stones, varying in height from 0.3m to 1.8m, are arranged in an incomplete rectangle 48m by 21m. They were clearly intended to retain the inner side of a bank of earth and stone 6m wide and still rising to a height of 2m, and which is broken by a narrow entrance gap in the south-west. The interior is marshy in summer, a pond in winter, and devoid of any prehistoric features. Many of the stones lean inwards, but they were evidently all originally vertical. In other respects, the structure has not changed much. Guesses at its date vary from medieval to neolithic. It may be significant that very similar enclosures exist in south-west Wales and in Ireland, where they proved to be neolithic, which is why King Arthur's Hall is included here. The general form is that of an English mortuary enclosure, so we may tentatively identify it as an unusually substantial neolithic mortuary enclosure, a place where corpses were laid out to be stripped by carrion (Figure 14).

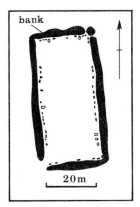

Figure 14   King Arthur's Hall. The bank is represented by the thick black line.

KING ARTHUR'S STONE CIRCLES   St Breward   SX: 135775

Midway between King Arthur's Hall and the Leaze stone circle are the remains of two stone circles very close together: their edges are only 2m apart. The western circle is the better preserved. It is 23m in diameter, with two upright stones, four stumps and two fallen stones; there are also two recumbent fragments at the centre. Only six stones remain of the eastern circle, which is more precisely ESE of the first: one stone is erect, two are stumps and three are fallen. The second circle seems to have had the same diameter as the first. Many stone circles – perhaps the majority – are bronze age. These two are included here because they are close to, and may therefore be associated with, King Arthur's Hall. Proximity is not proof of contemporaneity, but it is suggestive. It may well be that the stone circles and the mortuary enclosure were used together in late neolithic or early bronze age funeral rites.

LAND'S END

There was an axe factory, producing axe-heads of petrological type II, somewhere in the Land's End peninsula, but its exact location is unknown.

LANIVET QUOIT   Lanhydrock   SX: 072628

Three stones survive in the middle of a ploughed field. One of them is a huge capstone 4.5m long and 2.7m wide; the others are thought to be the uprights on which it once rested.

LANYON QUOIT   Madron   SW: 430337

Like an enormous table, a capstone 5.8m long is held up by three uprights, each 2.5m high. Once it was taller than it now is, but the monument fell down in 1815 and some of the stones were broken; as a result, its overall height was lower when it was set up again nine years later. Some stones lie beneath it, and a few metres further south are others that may belong to a burial cist. It was once thought that all were contained in a long N–S mound, which can still be made out in spite of being overgrown: it measures 27m by 12m. Large human bones (a giant's, of course) are reputed to have been found in the tomb, although cremation was more common in these south-western graves. It is now considered more likely that the site is the spread remnant of two round barrows that were built very close together. The southern barrow contains a jumble of stones which are probably the remains of two or three cists. The whole site has been very badly disturbed. Lanyon Quoit chamber was excavated in 1754, when a pit was dug into soil that had been previously disturbed; it was said that a rectangular pit 1.8m deep had been dug there a few years before.

Only two stones of the West Lanyon Quoit have survived (at SW: 432338). One stands about 1.5m square, and a capstone leans against it.

LEAZE STONE CIRCLE   St Breward   SX: 137773

This impressive stone circle 25m in diameter is 300m to the south-east of the King Arthur's Downs circles. There are 14 surviving stones – 10 of them still standing – out of an original 22. They are about 1m tall and spaced 3.7m apart. A hedge cuts the site, which may be neolithic or bronze age, in two.

LESQUITE QUOIT   Trebyan   SX: 070627

A chambered tomb on sloping ground on the south-east spur of a prominent ridge, 1.5km SW of Lanhydrock House. Like Carwynnen Quoit, it is on the edge of a granite outcrop. It stands above the marshy springs of two streams draining out of Red Moor, with Helman Tor and its possible neolithic enclosure beyond them to the south-west.

Now, the monument consists of a high supporter, nearly 2m high, with a massive capstone leaning against it. Another upright stands a short distance up the slope: this is 1.7m high and partly buried by a possibly modern mound. In 1973, the excavation of a pipe-laying trench running immediately south of the visible remains revealed several new features – a post-hole and three stone-holes, which could have been part of a low kerb for a mound or possibly a subsidiary stone setting of some kind. It is, in fact, generally the case that areas adjacent to neolithic monuments have been insufficiently explored; even the area surrounding the much-studied Stonehenge is turning out to have previously unsuspected outlying features – features that may prove to be integral to the original design and so shed light on the way in which the central area was used.

THE LONGSTONE   Prospidnick   SW: 659316

A standing stone 3m high, on gently sloping terrain at 165m OD, just below the summit of Prospidnick Hill. It may be neolithic or bronze age.

THE LONGSTONE   Roche   SW: 986601

This fine menhir was moved to its present position in the twentieth century, as its original site on Longstone Downs (at SW: 984561) was due to be destroyed by expanding china clay workings. Excavation at the time of its removal revealed that this broad-based, pointed slab, 3.2m high, had replaced an earlier stone and that this in turn had taken the place of a wooden post. This provides an interesting parallel to the larger ceremonial monuments, which were also repeatedly modified and replaced, and were in use for long periods. The Longstone's new home is on a green at Holmleigh Crescent, St Dennis Road, Roche.

MEN-AN-TOL   **Madron**   SW: 427349

Men-an-tol, literally 'the holed stone', is the central block of a line of three. It is a thin slab with a perfectly circular hole through its centre. On either side are upright pillars, one of which has been moved in historic times. It is possible that the whole monument once formed part of a burial chamber, but it is not certain. The perspective drawing and careful plan drawn by Dr Borlase in the eighteenth century show that the holed stone was then about 0.5m south of a line passing through the other two standing stones, and skewed at a 45° angle to that line. By 1856, when the monument was redrawn by J. T. Blight, the stones appear to have been moved in line with each other (Figure 15).

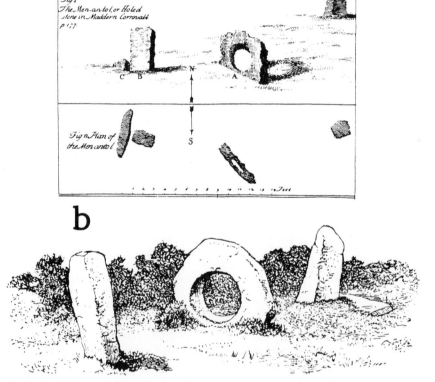

Figure 15 Men-an-tol. a – as recorded by Dr Borlase in the eighteenth century, with the holed stone out of line,   b – as drawn by J. T. Blight in 1856, by which time the holed stone had apparently been moved into line.

MEN GURTA   **Wadebridge**   SW: 969683

A standing stone 3m high on St Breock Downs. It fell in 1945 and was re-erected 11 years later. Its overall length is 4.6m and, at 16.5 tonnes, it is the heaviest megalithic stone in Cornwall. Excavation showed that a layer of white quartz stones, redolent of neolithic magic at other sacred sites too, had been laid round the menhir. Possibly the quartz was originally raised into a low cairn 4.5m in diameter, with the standing stone sticking up from the centre.

A second stone, 2.4m tall, stands 400m to the east at SW: 973683; it rises from the centre of a low mound 6m in diameter.

MERRY MAIDENS   **St Buryan**   SW: 432245

This is one of the most perfect and best preserved stone circles in Britain. It measures 24m in diameter, and is composed of 19 rectangular blocks, each 1m high and evenly spaced except on the north-east side, where there seems to be an entrance gap. Beside the B3315, about 0.5km away to the north-east, are two big standing stones known as the Pipers. They cannot be seen from the stone circle, although another, to the west, and known as the Fiddler, can be seen;

The circle was restored in 1862–9. Nineteenth-century drawings show stones 6 and 7, in the south-east, fallen and a space where stone 1 stands today. Stone 6 was reset correctly: stone 7 was reset at 90° to its original position, its long face now radial. The spacing is very regular and the ring is exactly circular; all the stones but one are within 9cm of the circumference of a true circle. The stones are also graded, with the tallest stones to the SSW, though it is not known why: there is no obvious orientation to any topographical feature or an astronomical event in that direction.

There was once a second stone circle (Boleigh) close by. It was recorded by Borlase in the eighteenth century. Two hundred metres away to the south-west, at SW: 431244, it was 30 paces in diameter, with four standing stones and three recumbent stones. It was described again in 1861, but probably destroyed soon after that date (Figure 16).

MOORGATE STANDING   **Camelford**   SX: 113819
STONE

A fine pointed standing stone 3m high, at 245m OD on a gentle north-eastward slope, 3.5 km WNW of Rough Tor. It is a thin slab of weathered granite and has the distinction of being the tallest stone on Bodmin Moor. It may be neolithic or bronze age in date.

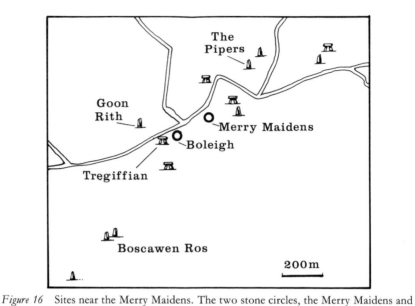

Figure 16 Sites near the Merry Maidens. The two stone circles, the Merry Maidens and the now-lost Boleigh Circle, formed the focus for an important linear ritual complex in the late neolithic and early bronze age. The table symbol represents a chambered tomb; the pillar represents a menhir or standing stone.

MOUNTS BAY   SW: 5230

An axe factory, producing axe-heads of petrological type I was located here, although it is not known exactly where; possibly it was on a site now covered by the sea. The bay itself was used as a trading harbour in the neolithic. Axe-heads and other commodities were exported from here along the south coast to Wessex, East Anglia and even as far afield as Yorkshire. The axe factory was probably in use from about 2300 BC.

MULFRA QUOIT   **Madron**   SW: 452353

Three upright stones form a rectangular cist and a large capstone has slipped off, leaning on the western side with one end firmly planted in the ground. There are traces of a small circular mound about 12m in diameter. Mulfra Quoit stands near the summit of Mulfra Hill and must once have looked like Chun Quoit. Dr Borlase dug within the chamber in 1749 and found a pit 0.5m deep: he found that it contained a 'black, greasy loam'.

NINE MAIDENS   **St Columb Major**   SX: 937676

The remains of a row of nine standing stones, of which six are still upright and three broken. The stones are each about 1.5m high and the line is about 110m long. Almost 1km further north of the stone alignment there is a single block, known as the Magi Stone. There is a round barrow a little to the south of it. The date of these monuments is unknown, and they may well prove to be bronze age rather than neolithic.

PAWTON QUOIT · Wadebridge · SW: 966696

A Penwith chambered tomb consisting of nine short uprights forming a chamber 2.3m by 1.1m. The massive capstone is 3.6m by 2.1m by 0.8m thick; it was originally 4.6m long, but a chunk has broken off and now lies in front of the façade formed by three of the support stones. There is no antechamber. The tomb stands just to the south of the centre of a mound 21m by 15m, which has been ploughed down but is still over a metre high. The capstone, with an estimated weight of 14.4 tonnes, is the heaviest in Cornwall.

PENNANCE ENTRANCE GRAVE · near Zennor · SW: 447375

This site is on private land and permission to visit it must first be sought at Pennance Farm. The chambered tomb is sited on gently northward-sloping land at the foot of a steep hillside; from it, there is a good view across agricultural land towards the sea, now only 1.5km away. The tomb consists of an irregular, disturbed mound 1.5m high and about 7–8m in diameter, surrounded by high kerbstones up to 1.2m tall. Near the entrance, the uprights are well preserved and large stones appear to have been alternated with small in a deliberate pattern. Some have collapsed, others have been taken away. Eleven of the stones are visible, but originally there must have been about 25.

The gallery-shaped chamber, about 3m long, is partly filled with earth and so is now only 0.5m high: probably originally it was about 0.8m high, although Blight, who first recorded it in 1865, reported that it was 1.3m high. Subsequent stone collapses explain how mound soil has found its way into the chamber. Five capstones are still in position. The outermost one is lower than the rest and this may have been part of a deliberate attempt to constrict the entrance – a feature of a great many chambered tombs. As at Treen, the grave is on relatively marginal land (Figure 17).

THE PIPERS · Lamorna · SW: 435248

These standing stones are about 100m above sea level, on gently sloping land above the Lamorna valley. The north-east Piper, the one nearer to Boleigh Farm, is 4.6m high, the tallest neolithic or bronze age standing stone in Cornwall. Its neighbour, 99m to the south-west, is the second tallest, at 4.1m. A line drawn from one to the other and continued towards the south-west touches the north-west quadrant of the Merry Maidens stone circle about 300m away. This may well be a coincidence, as the circle is not visible from either of the Pipers (Figure 18).

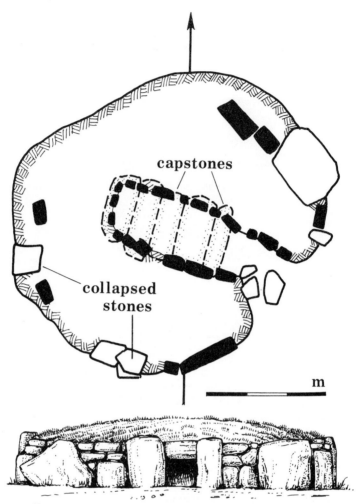

Figure 17 Pennance Entrance Grave: plan and reconstruction.

ROUGH TOR   **St Breward**   SX: 141815

A possible neolithic enclosure with two lines of stone walls, now much degraded, has been identified between the two rocky summits of the tor, Rough Tor and Little Rough Tor, at a height of 400m OD. Some of the walls are of piled stones, others of large slabs wedged upright. The piled stone walls have now spread laterally as much as 5m and stand no more than 1m high. The tor enclosure might be assumed to belong to the bronze age, but for the neolithic enclosure on Carn Brea, to which this bears similarities. About ten round houses have been traced in the south-western part of the interior. The extraordinary and very striking granite tor formations surmounting the main summit at the south-west must

Figure 18   The Pipers, drawn by J. T. Blight in 1861.

surely have provided a focus for cult activity for the people living in the enclosure. Indeed, comparison with nearby Showery Tor suggests that this is very likely. The enclosure is nevertheless of uncertain date. Some suggest that it belongs to the bronze age/iron age transition, around 1000 BC, while others think it may be neolithic; Barnatt (1980) points out, in support of a neolithic origin, that the general contraction in the agricultural use and occupation of Bodmin Moor during the iron age makes this an unlikely spot for iron age development.

Below the enclosure to the south are remains of circular stone huts, livestock pounds and the Fernacre stone circle. These are undated too, and may belong to the bronze age.

SHOWERY TOR   **Camelford**   SX: 149813

The tor itself is a naturally weathered outcrop of granite, standing up some 5m above the hill summit like a piece of primitive sculpture. It is surrounded by a massive ring cairn of piled stones, 30m in diameter and up to 1.2m high. The site is important in proving that the tors were being used as religious focal points, as one senses at Rough Tor, the next summit to the south-west. As far as is known, the site has not been excavated, so it is not known whether it was used for burials, nor is its date known for certain. It is probably neolithic or bronze age.

SPERRIS QUOIT   Zennor   SW: 470382

A chambered tomb site 300m NE of Zennor Quoit. Only one upright is visible. This ruined site was rediscovered in 1954 by Thomas and Waites; it was partially excavated. Five upright stones of a possible chamber were found, two standing, one reduced to a stump, and two fallen, all set in a 12m diameter low cairn. A small cremation pit was found just outside the chamber, perhaps in a south-facing antechamber, and probably dating to the period immediately before the tomb was built as a dedicatory deposit. The site was so wrecked as to be virtually impossible to reconstruct, and it has deteriorated further since the excavation. One upright and three fallen stones can be seen, and there are only indistinct traces of the mound, covered in thick vegetation.

STANNON STONE CIRCLE   St Breward   SX: 125801

A circle of 64 closely spaced stones, 42m in diameter; originally there were about 80 stones. The circle stands on a flat shelf with Rough Tor rearing above it to the north-east. Although on the ground it looks like a regular circle, it is really a polygon, consisting of a series of seven arcs. Many of the stones are only 0.3 to 0.7m high. About 84m to the north-west from the centre of the circle is a setting of four small stones arranged in a crude line; they have no apparent astronomical alignment and are well below the skyline when seen from the circle. Several astronomical orientations have been proposed which may be significant; Rough Tor may have acted as a horizon marker for the sunrise on May Day and Lammas, and the summit of Brown Willy as a marker for the equinox sunrise.

STOWE'S POUND   Minions   SX: 258725

A tor enclosure spared from quarrying, which has encroached towards the site from the south. There are two enclosures next to each other on the windswept summit of Stowe's Hill.

The southern enclosure, 130m by 80m, is adjacent to the Cheesewring, a strangely shaped and entirely natural landform, which may nevertheless have held some cult significance. The enclosure has a pear-shaped plan which tapers towards the south as if deliberately to exclude the Cheesewring. The single, unditched rampart that encloses it is still up to 5m high externally and 1.5m high internally. Before reduction by weathering it was probably a metre or so higher. Its single entrance is to the south-east, close to the edge of the quarry. No hut sites are known within this enclosure, which seems to have had no communication with the enclosure adjoining to the north.

The northern enclosure, 300m by 200m, is defined by an unditched and degraded wall up to 1.5m high externally. On the western side, where some coursing is evident in the masonry, there is a well-defined entrance, with a walled approach through a roughly rectangular annexe and a hollow way into the main enclosure. Within the enclosure there were no less than 39 round houses. The northern half of the enclosure is paralleled by further, lower walls which may be prehistoric field walls.

Neither of the enclosures has been firmly dated, but they are thought to be bronze age or neolithic.

STRIPPLE STONES   Blisland   SX: 144752

A henge 44.5m in diameter with the usual external bank and internal ditch. When excavated in 1905, the ditch was found to be very irregular, with an average width of 2.7m and an average depth of 1.2m. An entrance faces the Trippet Stones on the south-west. Inside the henge is an irregular circle of 15, out of an original 28, blocks of granite; 4 of the stones are still standing. A single stone lies near the circle's centre, and three other stones lie outside. The monument is undated but, since it combines a stone circle and a henge, it is probably late neolithic.

THE THREE BROTHERS   St Keverne   SW: 761198
OF GRUGWITH

A burial chamber or cist. A heavy capstone 2.4m by 1.5m balances on two supporting stones, which made up the parallel sides of a tomb chamber 2.4m long, 0.9m wide and 0.9m high. The slabs making up the other two sides are missing, and there is no trace of any supporting mound that may once have covered the tomb chamber. There are shallow depressions in the capstone, and these have been interpreted as deliberately made cupmarks, but it is equally likely that they are the result of weathering.

THE TOLVAN STONE   Gweek   SW: 706283

This monument is not open to public view; it stands on private land, in the back garden of Tolvan Cross Cottage. It consists of a large, triangular, upright slab, 2.3m high and 2.2m wide at the base. The centre of the slab has been laboriously drilled out to make a round hole 44cm in diameter. The purpose of the hole, and indeed of the stone itself, is unknown. It is possible that it was the entrance or septal slab of a large chambered tomb and that the 'port-hole' was designed for posting bundles of bones. It was one of the last places in Britain where a pre-Christian baptism rite took place. In this rite, babies were passed nine times through the hole and then laid to sleep on a grassy hillock.

TREEN ENTRANCE GRAVES   SW: 438371

Two small Scillonian chambered tombs on the hillside above the road from Treen to New Hill, on a gentle slope with a fine view towards the coast. In high summer they are hard to see because of dense bracken.

The southern entrance grave has a well-preserved mound just over a metre high and 7.6m in diameter, barely covering the coffin-shaped chamber 4m long and 0.9m high, made of large uprights and, probably, originally three capstones. A fragment of a kerb two courses high survives on the south-eastern side. Near it are two more badly damaged barrows and the remains of a settlement.

The northern entrance grave, 60m away to the north, is 6m in diameter, but only the inner end of its chamber and one capstone survive. The chamber of this tomb faces south-west; the chamber of the southern tomb faces north-west.

The small size of both tombs suggests a purely local significance. Standing at 145m and 155m OD, in other words at heights comparable with that of the Pennance Entrance Grave, the family graves at Treen were probably located at the upper margins of the agriculturally viable land, implying a link between grave ritual and declining land fertility.

TREGESEAL ENTRANCE   St Just   SW: 380321
GRAVE

Difficult to find, and in any case on private land, this grave is located on a gentle south-facing slope. The 16m oval mound is 0.5m high, and much of it has been removed. There are traces of a low kerb which seems to have become taller towards the entrance at the south-eastern, downslope, end. The chamber now consists of four pairs of uprights and two capstones: at least two more capstones have been removed. Photographs taken at the time of W. C. Borlase's excavations in 1879 show that the chamber was originally 0.8m high. The inner end of the chamber was blocked off with a vertical slab which has since disappeared. Immediately behind this, at the centre of the mound, was a secondary cist containing a large urn with a cremation: this cist has also disappeared. The chamber was paved and covered with ashes, burnt bones, broken pottery and a perforated whetstone: small stones were used to seal the south-east end.

The site has been claimed as an unusually large cist grave, on the grounds that the chamber does not reach the mound edge and that there is no drystone walling, only vertical slabs. In the light of the Tregiffian excavation, it seems more likely that Tregeseal is a two-period site, with a first period entrance grave walled up in the second period.

TREGIFFIAN ENTRANCE   Lamorna   SW: 430244
GRAVE

The B3315 cuts across and has destroyed half of this barrow. The tomb stands near the floor of a valley with only restricted views of the surrounding landscape, like the Brane Entrance Grave; it is just below the Merry Maidens circle. The 1m high mound is 15m in diameter, with a ring of kerbstones set 1.5m inside the edge. The kerbstones were originally set in a circle and then reset in a polygonal arrangement. The later ring consists of low stones increasing in height towards the entrance, which is marked by a large slab flanked by two slim pillar-like stones. Just inside the slab are two uprights flanking the chamber entrance; one of them is uniquely carved with cupmarks. The original has been removed for safety and replaced by a cast. There are 13 circular and 12 oval cups in an apparently random arrangement that covers the outer face of the stone. The chamber is 4.7m wide, 1.8m across, with walls of vertical slabs infilled with drystone. Near the entrance a collapsed capstone blocks the passage; at the inner end, three capstones have been re-erected. The large mound was badly damaged by roadmakers in 1846, and excavated by W. C. Borlase in 1868. Both above and below the large fallen capstone near the entrance he found a lot of bones and ashes; he also found a small pit lined with shell sand containing a cremation sealed underneath a small stone. The monument was partially restored in 1968, and has been radiocarbon dated to 1540 bc (1950 BC).

TREMENHEERE FARM MENHIR   St Keverne   SW: 778210

A finely shaped, tapering standing stone 2.9m tall, close to the road leading south-west from Trevallack. It stands on a level plateau about 100m above sea level.

TRENCROM CASTLE   Lelant   SW: 518362

A tor enclosure with iron age hut circles and enclosing walls. Finds of neolithic axes on the hillslopes surrounding it imply that the hill summit was occupied in the new stone age as well, and it may be that a neolithic enclosure was built here before the iron age enclosure.

TRENOW   SW: 530300

An axe factory site where stone axe-heads of petrological type III were produced.

TRETHEVY QUOIT   St Cleer   SX: 259688

'A little howse raysed of mightie stones, standing on a little hill within a feilde' wrote John Norden in 1584, and the description still fits the monument. Seven upright stones form a rectangular burial chamber 2m by 1.5m and more than 3m high on the southern side. Resting on top is a great sloping capstone 4m long with a small, unexplained hole piercing its highest corner. Although the capstone is still aloft, it slopes alarmingly owing to the collapse of the western supporting upright into the chamber, where it still lies: some restoration work is needed here. The chamber is divided into two parts by the great doorstone at the eastern end. The inside is almost completely sealed off, apart from a small rectangular hole made in the corner of the doorstone, just big enough to pass a bundle of bones through. Outside is an antechamber, created by the two side stones that jut forward towards the east. In the nineteenth century, Lukis reported an oval mound 7m by 6m, but virtually nothing of this survives today (Figure 19).

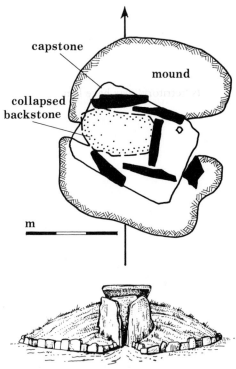

Figure 19 Trethevy Quoit: plan and reconstruction. When the back wallstone of the chamber fell inwards, some time before 1850, the back of the capstone dropped but did not slide off as at Zennor: it came to rest, somewhat skewed, on the two side-slabs. Although still in place, the capstone is more steeply tilted than the builders intended. The monument needs restoring, for its own safety.

TRIPPET STONES   Blisland   SX: 131750

There were originally about 26 stones forming a circle 33m in diameter, of which 12 remain – eight standing and four fallen. The stone in the centre is a modern boundary stone.

WOOLEY LONG BARROW

SS: 262166

The grass-covered mound, 2.5m high, is clearly visible in a field next to a crossroads. It is very close to the northernmost tip of Cornwall, only 0.5km from the Devon border, 5km from the sea, on the crest of a broad ridge. The mound is aligned ENE–WSW along the ridge crest. It tapers at both ends, but – as is usual – the eastern end is higher. Recent disturbances include trenches cut at both ends and across the summit of the mound, but large areas of it appear undisturbed and it is possible that an undetected chamber still remains. A small-scale excavation in 1976 on the north-west side revealed a quarry ditch 1.5m deep, diamond-shaped, 72m long and up to 20m wide. The odd form of the ditch seems to have been dictated by the presence of hard rock outcrops, which were avoided. Tests with augers suggest that there was no ditch on the south side. Close by, and now underneath the new A39 road, there was a large round barrow. The site of the long barrow may have been chosen for its commanding position at the head of the Tamar valley, where its 'territory' may have lain.

ZENNOR QUOIT

SW: 469380

This great neolithic tomb stands high up on a bleak, windswept ridge at 220m OD. Unlike the lower tombs at Pennance and Treen, it does not command a view over coastal lowlands, but squats on a high plateau. Its large capstone, 5.5m by 2.9m by 0.4m thick, has fallen to an angle of 45° so that one end rests on the ground and the rest of it completely covers the five wall stones of the burial chamber. On the east is a narrow antechamber in which a perforated whetstone was found, indicating that the tomb was still in use as late as 1900 BC. In front of that stand two large stones that give a straight façade to the barrow, the narrow gap between them forming the entrance to the antechamber. The chamber is 2.4m high and once stood within a stone mound 13m in diameter, little of which survives.

There was an unsuccessful attempt to break open the tomb with gunpowder in the nineteenth century; a farmer wanted to build a shed here. A sketch of the monument in 1762 by Dr William Borlase shows substantial remains of the stone barrow, as well as the capstone in its original position. R. J. Noall later excavated it and discovered cremated bones, flints and neolithic pottery.

Dr Borlase, along with many another eighteenth-century antiquary, believed that megalithic monuments like Zennor Quoit were the work of the Druids. He nevertheless made one very important, and undoubtedly correct, deduction about them. 'It is very unlikely', he wrote in 1763, 'that ever the Cromlech should have been an altar for sacrifice, for the top of it is not easily to be got upon, much less a fire to be kindled on it, sufficient to consume the victim, without scorching the Priest that officiated, not to mention the horrid Rites with which the Druid was attended, and which there is not proper room, nor footing, to perform in so perilous a station. It is a Sepulchral Monument.'

CUMBRIA

BLAKELEY RAISE   Ennerdale   NY: 068132

A circle of 12 stones, each about 0.5m high; it may originally have surrounded a barrow 10m in diameter.

BRATS HILL   Miterdale   NY: 173023

A group of stone circles at 260m OD on a subdued ridge separating Brat's Moss and White Moss. The largest of the stone circles is flattened on its northern side and measures 32m by 26m. Of its 42 stones only 8 are still standing, although the others can be seen. The circle is unusual in that there are five cairns, each 7m in diameter, standing inside it, clustered in its south-western half. The cairns, which are now very low, are surrounded by the remains of stone kerbs, and when two were excavated in 1827 they revealed mounds of stones covering cremations, animal bones and antlers.

At White Moss, 130m NW of Brats Hill, there are two circles 16m in diameter. Both of them appear to contain central cairns that have not been opened. On Low Longrigg, 450m to the north, are two more circles. One of them, which is 15m in diameter, contains a cairn. The second, to the north-east, is oval, 22m by 15m, and contains two cairns, one of them with a well-defined kerb.

CASTERTON   SD: 640799

A stone circle on a steep west-facing slope at 250m OD, perched high above the River Lune. The circle is 18m in diameter, and may originally have had an outer bank. Twenty stones, all under 0.5m tall, surround what may once have been a cairn circle.

CASTLEHOWE SCAR   Crosby Ravensworth   NY: 587155

A stone circle 6.4m in diameter on a knoll in undulating terrain at about 310m OD, about 1km E of the M6 motorway. Ten of its 11 stones are still standing.

CASTLERIGG   near Keswick   NY: 292236

There is no stone circle in England with a more beautiful site than Castlerigg, with its superb views of the north Lakeland mountains. Castlerigg stands on an inconspicuous spur, some 215m high, projecting into the Greta valley from the north side of Castlerigg Fell; the site nevertheless gives the sensation of being raised above the valleys (of the Derwent, Greta and Naddle Beck) which flank it on three sides, and allows spectacular views of the encircling mountains. It shows beyond any doubt that the people who chose sites for ceremonial monuments had an acute and sensitive awareness of landscape. The nodal situation of Castlerigg, at a fork in the trade routes used by the stone axe traders, made it an excellent meeting-place.

Nearly all of the 38 stones in the circle still stand in their original position, forming a slightly flattened circle 85m in diameter. A gap 3.5m wide on the north side indicates the entrance: it is emphasized by two massive flanking portal stones. Ten stones arranged in a rectangle touch the inside of the circle on the eastern side. The purpose of this unusual feature is not known. It has been suggested that they may have formed a burial chamber, but they are too low and too far apart to have held up a roof of any kind. It is more likely that this is a variant of the cove idea, a symbol of the tomb chamber rather than an actual tomb. About 3.5km away to the east stands Threlkeld Knott, the hill above which the sun rises on the equinoxes.

THE COCKPIT   Waverton   NY: 483222

This monument may have been either a stone circle or a ring cairn. Two concentric circles of stones 25–30cm in diameter form the outer faces of a wall. There are traces of a cairn on the wall on the south-east.

COLD FELL CAIRN   Midgeholme   NY: 606556

A heap of stones 15m in diameter and not much more than a metre high represents what seems to be an unopened cairn. There are traces of a ditch round the edge.

DRUIDS' TEMPLE   Birkrigg Common   SD: 292739

This stone circle may belong to the late neolithic or to the early bronze age: more likely the latter. It consists of two concentric rings of limestone blocks. The outer circle, which is 26m in diameter, consists of 14 stones standing low in the bracken. The inner circle is 8.4m in diameter with ten stones enclosing five cremation pits, one containing an inverted urn. The tallest stone is on the north side, while to the south-west two more high stones flank the lowest stones, as if to form ceremonial portals. Excavations in 1911 and 1921 revealed burnt patches where corpses may have been cremated, immediately outside the inner circle, along with a cobbled pavement which was probably used for processions or ritual dances. At 70m OD on the moderately steep eastern flank of Birkrigg Common, the Druids' Temple commands a fine view across Morecambe Bay; the coast lies only 0.5km away to the east. Even though the site may well eventually prove to belong to the early bronze age, the unusual evidence it offers us may well help us to understand the ritual practices performed at the truly neolithic sites, with which it shows many affinities.

EHENSIDE TARN   south of St Bees   *c.* NX: 990100

A settlement site, marked by a series of domestic hearths surrounded by occupation debris along a lake shore. The finds were made at the base of a bed of forest-peat, mainly oak and beech. Below the occupation layer was a 'leaf bed', which indicated the forest clearance phase immediately before the foundation of the settlement. The settlement was occupied in 3014 bc (3700 BC), according to radiocarbon-dated material, and it has yielded some very important finds of wooden artefacts, including a club, a throwing stick and an axe haft; such well-preserved wooden artefacts are rare in Britain.

Ehenside gives us evidence of a sequence of temporary forest clearance episodes, probably for very small-scale agriculture. Forest was cleared, the land was cultivated and exhausted, and then the forest was allowed to return; we can imagine this cycle being repeated several times over before the land was permanently cleared. There was no pronounced expansion of the areas under grass or cereals until the late neolithic, from about 2500 BC onwards.

ELVA PLAIN   Setmurthy   NY: 173317

The tallest of the 15 surviving stones in the circle is only a metre high. The stone ring is 34m in diameter, with an outlying stone standing to the south-west, pointing the way along the ridge that runs westwards to the coast. Originally the circle was formed of about 30 stones.

GAMELANDS CIRCLE   Orton   NY: 640082

This ruined stone circle, 42m in diameter, stands on a col with extensive views. Once it had 40 stones, but ploughing in the nineteenth century damaged many of them and reduced their number to 33. The rounded boulders are made of Shap granite. The circle has an external bank, and an entrance on the south-east side.

GRETIGATE STONE CIRCLES   Gosforth   NY: 058036

A segment of a large stone circle some 31m across has survived in a field wall to the north-west of Sides Farm. Further to the west are two more circles. One, which is about 21m in diameter, originally contained about 16 stones, of which 9 survive; the other, which touches it, is 7m in diameter. Probably both of these adjacent circles originally contained cairns. There are several cairns between the circles.

GREY CROFT   Seascale   NY: 034024

This stone ring is oval, measuring 27m by 24m. There were 12 stones at the time of its destruction in the nineteenth century. It was excavated and restored in 1949, when ten of the stones were re-erected. A low cairn at the centre was excavated and produced a cremation burial and a fragment of a ring made of jet. A partly polished stone axe head made at Langdale (Figure 21) was also found beside one of the stones. Alexander Thom suggested that an outlying stone was deliberately aligned on the setting of the star Daneb, but, since starset positions shift rapidly, it is difficult to know what value to put on this idea.

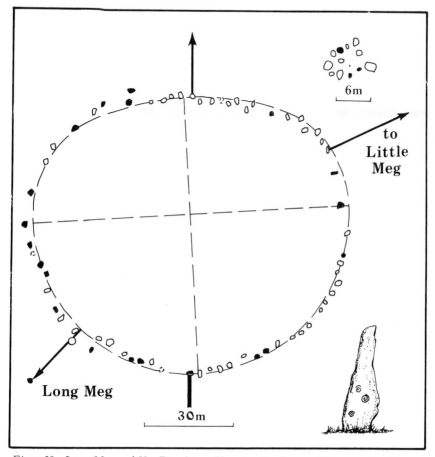

Figure 20 Long Meg and Her Daughters. Plan showing its possible geometry: the two principal axes are shown by dashed lines, and solid black indicates upright stones. The small ruined satellite circle, Little Meg, lies off the map to the ENE. The sketch in the bottom right-hand corner shows the elevation of Long Meg with its spiral carvings.

GUNNERKELD   Rosgill   NY: 568178

This stone circle stands in undulating hill country at 255m, right beside the south-bound carriageway of the M6 motorway. A good view of it can be had from the M6, although it would of course be unsafe to look down the embankment at it while driving along. Gunnerkeld is one of the Shap group of circles. Its ring of two concentric ovals encloses a low mound and a cist. The inner ring, 18m in diameter, is the more complete of the two. Of the outer ring of stones, which is 28m in diameter, only 3 of some 18 stones are still standing.

KING ARTHUR'S ROUND   Penrith   NY: 523284
TABLE

A badly damaged henge monument 90m in diameter, originally with two opposing entrances; only the south-east entrance now survives. The north entrance was once flanked by two portal stones. The bank still stands 1.5m high and is separated by a berm from a 9m wide ditch which is 1.5m deep. Bersu's excavations implied that there might once have been a stone circle on the berm. At the monument's centre there was a trench, 2.4m long, 0.8m wide and 0.25m deep, which had been used to cremate a corpse, using hazel wood as fuel; this established an important connection between the ceremonial circles and funerary ritual, a connection which has been confirmed at other sites as well.

KIRKBY MOOR   Kirkby Irelith   SD: 251827

A stone and earth bank 3m wide and 0.5m high marks out a circle 22m in diameter. This ring cairn is partly retained on the inner side, at least on the east, by a kerb of stones. There is no obvious entrance, but it looks as if it must have been on the north-east side; about 30m to the north-east three pairs of small stones form what appears to be part of an avenue. About 300m to the north-east, at SD: 251830, there is a stone cairn 24m across and 1m high. It has a burial cist on its south-west side: a cremation was found inside it.

LACRA CIRCLES   Millom   SD: 150814

The five small Lacra circles were excavated in 1947. Circle A is badly damaged; 15m in diameter, six of its stones are still standing. The second circle, Circle B, lies 360m to the east; six of its original 11 stones mark out a ring 16.2m in diameter. It had a low cairn in the centre: this covered a turf stack, which in turn covered a cremation burial with a good deal of charcoal, presumably from the funeral pyre; the cairn had a ring of stones placed upon it. Only four stones survive of Circle C, 100m east of Circle B: it too produced pyre-charcoal when it was excavated. Circle D, 150m to the ESE, produced the most interesting results. It is oval, 18m by 16m, with a central stone and an avenue of stones running WSW; there is also a single stone row on the opposite side, running ENE. Although obviously much smaller in scale than either Avebury or Callanish, the architectural vocabulary of Circle D at Lacra is similar. Oak and hazel charcoal was found, and a hazel nut indicating an autumn burial. Circle E, only 5m across, has only six stones in its ring, with another stone in the centre. It lies only 8m to the north-west of D and excavation yielded nothing. To the south-west of Circle E are the remnants of another stone avenue, 15m wide and running for about 70m. The small diameter of these as yet undated circles suggests that they may well belong to the bronze age rather than to the neolithic.

LONG MEG AND HER DAUGHTERS   Hunsonby   NY: 571373

This is one of the largest stone circles in Britain, where folklore has it that a witch and her coven were turned to stone. Long Meg is a slender column of red sandstone 3.7m tall, and decorated on its north-eastern face with a cup-and-ring mark, a spiral and an incomplete concentric circle. These undoubtedly significant but so far undeciphered carvings face the stone circle, which stands 18m away. Oval in plan, the ring (the Daughters) measures 109m by 93m and slopes downhill from west to east. Here the shape seems to have been deliberately designed to counteract foreshortening by perspective. At the long barrows, too, neolithic architects used false perspective to deceive the eye and create special visual effects. There were originally up to 66 stones, forming a magnificent ring with an entrance on the south-west side, close to Long Meg. Two of the largest stones stand to east and west on the circumference, perhaps as markers for the sunrise and sunset on the equinoxes. There are traces of an earth bank on the west side of the circle: presumably it originally ran all the way round. Two cairns may have stood inside the circle, but this is not certain (Figure 20).

MAYBURGH   Penrith   NY: 519285

A high and impressive tree-crowned bank of rounded river boulders, 6m high and 65m in diameter, forms a substantial circular amphitheatre. The bank rises in height as it approaches the precinct's single entrance on the east side, which faces King Arthur's Round Table. This belongs to the family of single-entrance henge monuments, although very unusually it has no quarry ditch: the boulders must have been carried to the site from elsewhere, for reasons that are not obvious. At the centre of Mayburgh stands just one of the original group of four stones recorded by William Stukeley. Other observers have mentioned four more stones, also gone, that once stood inside the entrance, forming a kind of ceremonial gateway. The two projections of the bank outwards from the entrance are probably part of the original design.

Mayburgh, King Arthur's Round Table and the Little Round Table should probably be considered together, as a triad of rings, like Thornborough, or

Stanton Drew, or indeed the original three-ring design for Avebury. As the largest and most impressive of the circles at Penrith, Mayburgh must surely have been the centrepiece of this major neolithic cult centre.

PIKE OF STICKLE   Langdale   NY: 272072

In 3000 BC, neolithic axe makers squatted on the south-west slopes of Langdale Pikes, roughing out thousands of stone axes, mainly from stones picked up among the scree. Their waste flakes and discarded broken implements can still be seen (but not picked up) today between the head of Pike of Stickle at 600m and the foot of the scree at about 150m. The site deserves better conservation, and it is worth emphasizing that the removal of archaeological material is illegal. The rock is an epidotized tuff of the Borrowdale Volcanic Series and can easily be ground

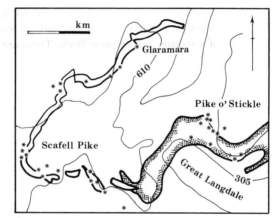

Figure 21   The Langdale axe factories. Each asterisk represents an axe factory. The hatched area represents the outcrop of bedded tuffs and Wrengill andesite. The unhatched band surrounding Scafell Pike represents the outcrop of hornstone. As the map shows, quite a large area was involved in the industry, and at quite high altitudes (contours in metres).

into a fine, sharp cutting edge. Many axes from this site have been found all over Britain, with large numbers finding their way to Wessex. Axes of this tuff are designated Group VI to distinguish them from axes made of other types of rock. The finished Langdale axes have a broad-butted, tapering form with a parallelogram or diamond-shaped cross section; they are commonly 25cm long. At first only one chipping site was identified, close to the Stake Pass, north of Langdale. By the 1940s, more sites were being recognized, from the evidence of chippings, waste flakes and rejected rough-outs. Quite a large area was involved in the industry, including a major working site below Scafell Pike itself; it formed an arc-shaped industrial zone which closely followed the rock outcrop, and shows us that the axe makers had a keen awareness of Lakeland geology (Figure 21).

RAISET PIKE   Crosby Garrett   NY: 683073

This long cairn is badly damaged, probably as a result of excavation by Canon Greenwell. The cairn is 55m long and 19m wide at the south-west end. It appears that there was a mortuary building running along the cairn's long axis from close to the south-west end to a standing stone 2m high. In the wreckage of this collapsed structure were the disarticulated bodies of three adults and three children, along with plenty of timber. A flue trench enabled both wood and human remains to be set on fire and to continue to burn within the cairn. To the north-west of the standing stone more disarticulated corpses were found, this time unburnt, and many of them children.

SAMSON'S BRATFUL   Stockdale Moor   NY: 098080

This long cairn is 28m long, with its long axis aligned roughly W–E. It stands on a moderately steep south-west facing slope on the flank of Stockdale Moor, very close to the source of a stream, Scalderskew Beck. There are also traces of ancient field systems within a few hundred metres of the cairn to north, south and east.

SHAP   NY: 567133

Shap South Stone Circle lies on a gentle westward-facing slope at 260m OD, about 0.5km from the River Lowther, and close to the A6 just south of Shap. The stone circle is badly damaged and only six of its huge Shap granite boulders now remain, each of them over 2m long. The circle was originally some 24m across.

Traces of at least eight stones of an important megalithic avenue 3,000m long can be found running NNW to the Skellaw Hill Barrow 2.4km away at NY: 556154, and then on towards the massive Thunder Stone, 600m further on at NY: 552157. Surviving avenue stones can be seen at NY: 562147, 559150, 558152 and 555152; all four of these are marked on the 1:25,000 OS map, three of them accessible beside public footpaths. The stone at 559150 is known as the Goggleby Stone. The fields to the south and west of Shap were evidently an important megalithic ceremonial centre, though little now remains of it.

SWINSIDE   Millom   SD: 172883

A fine stone circle 27m in diameter, consisting of 52 closely set stones. On the south-east side there is a clearly marked entrance: the portal stones are emphasized by doubling. Excavation has shown that the stones are seated on a layer of pebbles; fragments of burnt bones and charcoal were also found, reinforcing the association of the stone circle with burial rites. The circle is sometimes called

Sunken Kirke, because the Devil is supposed to have made the stones, used in building a church by day, sink into the ground by night.

THUNACAR KNOTT   Great Langdale   NY: 280080

A chipping floor or axe factory above Great Langdale. It was evidently associated with the much better known axe factory at Pike of Stickle, which faces it across the shallow valley of Dungeon Ghyll. The industry has been radiocarbon dated to 4680–4474 bp (3400–3150 BC), at a time when the area was being cleared of pine and birch woods for the second time. There had already been an earlier clearance episode here around 4600 BC, which must have been at the end of the mesolithic or at the very beginning of the neolithic period.

WILSON SCAR   Thrimby   NY: 550184

This small stone circle is really one of the Shap group. It contains 32 small stones and measures 15m in diameter.

DERBYSHIRE

ARBOR LOW   Middleton   SK: 160636

The grass-covered banks of this two-entrance henge monument enclose a circle of weathered white limestone blocks. The henge is oval, measuring 83m by 75m, with entrances at the north-west and south-east. The rather irregular internal ditch was dug out of solid limestone, purely to provide the 1,500 cubic metres of stone needed for the bank. The bank today is a little over 2m high and very irregular in appearance, especially on the eastern side, where its surface has been robbed to build the later round barrow that rests on top of it.

On the flat interior of Arbor Low lie some three dozen limestone blocks, that seem once to have stood upright in an egg-shaped ring 37m by 42m. There has always been controversy as to whether the stones were ever upright, but there is strong evidence that they were. There are seven stumps which mark the positions of uprights that have been broken off; and some of the recumbent stones are cracked in a way that could well have resulted from their falling over. Excavations have failed to produce any stone-holes, so we must assume that the stones were in many cases propped up by smaller packing stones (Plate 1).

At the centre of the precinct, three large stones formed a cove, whilst just to the east lay an extended male skeleton surrounded by stones.

The stones of Arbor Low are severely weathered, and it is clear that the weathering preceded their use in building the stone circle. Possibly to save the effort of quarrying new stone, possibly because the old stones were more interesting shapes, the neolithic builders of Arbor Low collected weathered boulders from areas of limestone pavement.

Leading west from the south-east entrance is a long, low, curving bank. It runs some 320m to the south-west, passing the large round cairn called Gib Hill. It may be that originally the 6m-wide ditch and bank feature continued to the SSW and curved round about 100m to the south of Gib Hill. It is not clear what this strange linear feature was, but it seems never to have had a pair, turning it into a true avenue.

Gib Hill was opened by Bateman in 1848, when a small limestone cist was found, containing a cremation burial and a food vessel. It has been suggested that Gib Hill is really a neolithic long cairn 35m long, 20m wide and 1m high, with a secondary, later, circular round barrow built on top of it. The long cairn is not a burial mound in the usual sense, but some sort of fertility monument. Its central core of red clay was formed into four small mounds. Covering this were layers of burnt material, including bones of oxen, hazel twigs and flints, which in turn were covered with stones and then a final thick layer of earth and stones. A second phase of building was the raising of a late neolithic or early bronze age burial mound nearly 30m in diameter and 3m high. Some aspects of the construction method, and indeed the ritual precepts that lie behind it, are reminiscent of Silbury Hill. Next to Gib Hill, J. Radley identified a proto-henge, which may be referred to as Arbor Low II, but it seems likely that Arbor Low II is nothing more than a string of quarry pits, supplying material for the various mound and bank structures close by.

Arbor Low stands close to the 'centre of gravity' of a scatter of five neolithic tombs, and at the geometric centre of a diamond-shaped area of light limestone soils some 20km by 7km. The site would have made a natural, communal focus for the neolithic farming groups of this area (Figure 22).

ASHOVER   SK: 340630

An occupation site, indicated by finds of flint scrapers, burins and arrow-heads.

ASH TREE CAVE   **Whitwell**   SK: 514761

A neolithic burial cave. Excavation has uncovered three separate deposits of disarticulated human bones. Each deposit represented the remains of two people. Two of the deposits were buried underneath heaps of stones, the third was in a cist; all of them were accompanied by minimal offerings or grave-goods of flint flakes.

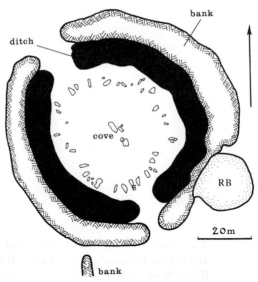

Figure 22 Arbor Low, a henge enclosing a collapsed stone circle. 'RB' indicates the position of the later round barrow, built out of material robbed from the henge bank.

ASTON BARROW   Aston-on-Trent   SK: 421292

A circular cropmark identified on an air photograph proved on excavation to be a round barrow. The barrow itself was early bronze age in date, but the old land surface underneath it carried neolithic pottery, suggesting that it had been a neolithic occupation site before it became a burial place.

ASTON CURSUS   Aston-on-Trent   SK: 4128

Cropmarks visible from the air show a cursus and other features. The parallel lines of the cursus are visible for 1800m from the south-west end, and about 110m apart. There is a side entrance into the cursus some 60m from the south-west end. Ring ditches lie within and outside the cursus: one actually crosses it, so it is possible that they may all be later additions to the monument. A large double ring ditch within the cursus has been excavated, and it showed two phases of Beaker burial and a pit containing early neolithic pottery. A small square enclosure was also excavated: this is thought to have been a square barrow. The cursus and related features may well be contemporary with the adjacent neolithic settlement, which has been radiocarbon dated to 2750 bc (3450 BC).

ASTONHILL — **Brassington** — SK: 203586

A settlement site, indicated by several types of neolithic pottery (Grimston, Mortlake, Fengate, and Windmill Hill with Ebbsfleet traits) and a variety of flint and chert tools.

AULT HUCKNALL — SK: 489644

An occupation site on a ridge. Finds here include flint tools, such as cores, scrapers, burins, a saw blade and waste flakes.

BARBROOK CIRCLES — **Ramsley Moor** — SK: 278755

There are three stone circles in this group. The southern circle consists of 13 stones on the inner edge of a rubble bank 13m in diameter. A circle of similar size, 275m to the north of the first, surrounded a burial mound. This contained two cremations in urns which were radiocarbon dated to 1500 bc (1900 BC). A further 450m to the NNE is a third circle with 22 stones set into the edge of a bank 30m in diameter. The radiocarbon date suggests that the circles were built right at the end of the neolithic or the beginning of the bronze age, in about 2100 BC.

BONSALL LANE — **Bonsall** — SK: 248599

The rock shelters overlooking Bonsall Lane seem to have been occupied by people in the neolithic period. Flint scrapers, a leaf-shaped arrow-head and waste flakes and cores were found here. Large stones have been arranged to form an enclosed platform in front of the rock shelters.

BRETTON RACECOURSE — SK: 203778

An occupation site, indicated by some 20 flint artefacts, including arrow-heads, a saw and waste flakes, and a polished Group VII (Graig Lwyd) stone axe.

BRIERLOW GRANGE — **Hartington** — SK: 096690

A flint-working site, discovered during ploughing at Brierlow Grange, close to a former swallow-hole. No implements were found – only waste flakes and a core. A Group XX (Charnwood Forest) stone axe also came from this area.

BROWN EDGE — **Holmesfield** — SK: 280790

An occupation site. Flint tools have been found here and at Flask Edge close by (SK: 280780).

BRUSHFIELD HOUGH BARROW   SK: 168708

This cairn stands on steeply sloping ground above the valley floor, and was opened in about 1925 by Major Harris after earlier robbing. It may be a horned long cairn, with four slabbed graves positioned along its main axis and one on each horn. No human bones were recovered from the graves – only a piece of bronze age pottery and some Roman pottery. One grave contained two flint scrapers. Two other circular drystone structures built into the mound may also have been graves. A piece of Peterborough pottery was found outside the mound edge.

The site is difficult to interpret. Today, it consists of a rather shapeless mound 12m by 6m, with pits along its south-west side. To the north-east, and beyond the mound, is a ruined stone setting at right angles to the mound's long axis. The mound's status as a neolithic barrow is not yet certain, and there have been suggestions that the so-called graves and other structures were the product of an over-active imagination; no neolithic burials were recovered from the site, and the drystone walling need not be prehistoric. The site really needs careful re-examination in order to establish its true status.

BULL RING   Dove Holes   SK: 078783

A two-entrance henge monument which has been badly damaged by quarrying. Today the outer bank made of limestone rubble stands 1.2m high and is 76m in diameter. Excavation in 1949 revealed that the ditch was 2m deep and 10m wide. Once there was a ring of stones inside the monument, but only one of the ring-stones remains. This would have made the site rather like Arbor Low; another similarity is a large barrow 2.4m high standing to the SSW, like Gib Hill at Arbor Low. The similarities suggest that Arbor Low and the Bull Ring may even have been designed by the same architect.

CALLING LOW DALE   Youlgreave   SK: 183654

A rock shelter that was used in the neolithic for burial. It was excavated by Colonel Harris in 1936–9, when it was found to have two cists built into it, one of them containing a bundle of human bones, some arrow-heads and a Peterborough ware bowl. Further burials were found outside the cists. A double-edged polished stone axe was found here in about 1830.

CALTON HILL   SK: 118714

A settlement. Many neolithic artefacts were discovered over an area 900m by 200m, but they were particularly dense in an area of 100 square metres. Tools found here include 29 polished stone axes, at least one of which came from the Langdale area of Cumbria, 43 scrapers, 7 knives, and some fragments of Peterborough-type pottery.

CHATSWORTH PARK FARM SHOP   SK: 242707

A neolithic industrial site, where narrow blades were manufactured from flint and chert. Many blades were found here, as well as some waste, cores and a scraper.

CRESWELL CRAGS   Whitwell   SK: 536745

An occupation site indicated by flint flakes, blades, points, scrapers and cores.

CURZON LODGE   Aldwark   SK: 233561

An occupation site, where seven polished stone axe heads were found. They belonged to Groups vi (Langdale), vii (Graig Lwyd), xv (Southern Lake District) and xviii (Whin Sill). A mace belonging to Group i (Land's End) was also found here. These finds show that trading links were widespread and complex in the neolithic period.

DERWENT RESERVOIR   SK: 170919

An occupation site located south of the point where Abbey Brook enters the reservoir. Finds here include a hollow-based arrow-head made of black chert, a flint scraper and a well-fired piece of pottery.

DOWEL CAVE   Hollinsclough   SK: 075676

A burial cave. Ten people were buried here, some extended, and at least one crouched, together with late neolithic and Beaker pottery. Seven of the bodies were near the cave entrance, two in a sealed-off area and another in a second blocked-off area. The one crouched skeleton was accompanied by two flints, one on each side of the pelvis; another was placed close to the headless skeleton of a dog.

EDENSOR   SK: 238693

An occupation site indicated by three distinct concentrations of flints at SK: 240694, 237692 and 238693. The finds include large quantities of arrow-heads, scrapers, burins, cores and blades, made of chert and flint. The separate patches of debris suggest that tool-making was focused on three dwellings or three open-air working floors.

ELTON COMMON   SK: 215598

A settlement site, indicated by large quantities of flint and stone artefacts. The flint material includes arrow-heads, scrapers and axes. Fragments of stone axes were found as well as a piece of neolithic pottery, a rim of coarse black ware with finger-nail decoration along the top of the flanged rim: the complete vessel would have been about 20cm in diameter. More neolithic tools were found on another part of the Common, at SK: 207593 – half of a fine-grained greenstone axe, a flake of stone from a Langdale axe, and a flint knife.

FINDERN CURSUS   SK: 320389

Cropmarks show two parallel lines spaced about 100m apart and 500m long. Neither end of the Findern Cursus has been seen. There are also two ring ditches, one inside and one outside the cursus.

FISSURE CAVE   **Hartle Dale**   SK: 164803

This cave in a narrow fissure was excavated in 1961–5 by A. L. Pill, and produced a polished stone axe of unknown origin, sherds of Peterborough ware and a flint scraper. To judge from the occupation debris and pottery, the cave may have been used for habitation. Whether these 'cave dwellings' were in any sense permanent dwellings, or just used as seasonal hunting lodges, is open to speculation.

FIVEWELLS   **Taddington**   SK: 124710

A circular cairn with two back-to-back burial chambers approached by separate passages to east and west. Both chambers are now roofless, with two portal stones at their entrances. Thomas Bateman found a dozen skeletons in 1846; five more were discovered later. Neolithic pottery, arrow-heads and a flint knife have also been found. The cairn is made of thin limestone slabs (Figure 23).

FOX HOLE CAVE   **Hartington**   SK: 099661

This cave seems to have been used as some sort of dwelling in the new stone age. Pieces of Peterborough ware and Grooved ware pottery were discovered in the first chamber in the 1960s and 1970s, together with a small polished greenstone axe. Neolithic sherds were also recovered from outside the cave entrance in 1928–9.

GRANGE FARM   **Taddington**   SK: 130705

A settlement site. A large quantity of neolithic stone material was found here by

Figure 23 Fivewells: one of the megalithic tomb chambers. The two portal stones can be seen to the right.

Mr Bagshaw, the farmer, including 9 stone axes, 2 perforated tools, 14 scrapers and 4 knives.

GREEN LOW   Aldwark   SK: 233580

This circular cairn, 18m in diameter, was excavated in 1964. A straight façade was revealed on the south side of the barrow and, from the centre of this, a narrow passage (constricted as always) led into a chamber about 2m square. Bateman found pieces of a human skeleton in the chamber in 1843; in 1964 the disarticulated remains of another skeleton were found in the cairn material. Neolithic pottery was also found.

Roman coins and pottery dating from the third century AD were found in the tomb's passage and chamber. What these finds mean, exactly, is hard to tell, but they prove at least interest in the monument during the Romano-British period; whether that interest was religious, or motivated by greed or curiosity, is impossible to say.

GREEN SITCHES   SK: 180907

An occupation site indicated by a scatter of flint, chert and stone tools. Originally, the site was bare of vegetation, with implements coming out of the layer of grey sand; now it is covered with grass. Finds include leaf-shaped arrow-heads and petit tranchet derivative arrow-heads, scrapers, cores, a knife, an awl, and waste flakes. More of this occupation debris was found close by, at SK: 182910.

HADDON GROVE   **Over Haddon**   SK: 177658

An occupation site, indicated by several flint tools, such as scrapers, knives and a leaf-shaped arrow-head. The neolithic debris was found on the old land surface, buried and preserved under a bronze age barrow.

HARBOROUGH CAVE   SK: 242552

This cave may have been used as a dwelling during the neolithic. Occupation debris and some pieces of Peterborough ware pottery were found here; a polished neolithic stone axe was found in a spoil heap on the slope immediately outside the cave.

A chambered round cairn 14m in diameter and 1m high is situated on the summit of Harborough Rocks, just east of the Ordnance Survey triangulation pillar. The site was excavated in 1889 and appears to have been a fairly small chambered tomb. The single chamber contained the remains of at least 16 people, together with three leaf-shaped arrow-heads. Six of the skeletons were buried in the crouched position. There appears to have been a passage to the north-west. There is another artificial mound, 15m long, 2m wide and 0.5m high, leading from the Rocks to the brow of the hill, but it is not known whether this was in any way connected, in time and function, with the neolithic round cairn.

HARROD LOW   **Peak Forest**   SK: 098805

A robbed and mutilated long barrow 42m long, 16–22m wide and 1m high, standing on a rock outcrop. It is aligned W–E and there are traces of a ditch on the south side. It was reported in 1775 that bones had been found at Harrod Low.

HAWKSLOW FARM   **Parwich**   SK: 172562

An occupation site or flint working floor. A large collection of flint tools came from this site, including over 60 flakes, blades, scrapers and saws: they are now in Derby City Museum.

HICKEN'S BRIDGE — Shardlow — SK: 429299

Cropmarks indicate the presence here of a triple ring ditch with an adjacent circle and enclosure.

LATHKILL DALE — Monyash — SK: 167659

The remains of three neolithic fissure burials – the disarticulated remains of an adult and two children – were found here in 1961.

LIFFS LOW — SK: 153576

A badly mutilated round cairn 17m across and 2m high on the Liffs near Biggin. It was opened by Thomas Bateman in July 1843. In an octagonal cist he found a skeleton accompanied by an unusual pot with both neolithic and Beaker affinities. There were also two flint axes and two knives, all with polished edges, a perforated antler mace-head, two flint spear-heads, two flint arrow-heads and two boar's tusks. The recurrence of the number 2 suggests some sort of religious or magical purpose, and the presence of pieces of red ochre in the burial reinforces this interpretation: from very early times the bones of the dead have been painted with red ochre. This was nevertheless a very late neolithic or Beaker burial ritual, performed at a time when some people in the community, chiefs perhaps, were attaining high social status.

LISMORE FIELDS — Buxton — c. SK: 0573

When this meadow on the outskirts of Buxton was excavated in 1985 in advance of housing development, the remains of a substantial neolithic house were uncovered. A well-defined group of post-holes formed a rectangular structure, 15m long and 5m wide, which was divided into four compartments or rooms, with hearths set in the partitions between the first and second compartments, and between the third and fourth. The compartments were marked by lines of internal post-holes, in some cases accompanied by shallow slots, showing that they were originally joined by horizontal planks to make solid wooden walls. It looks as if the initial structure was later doubled in size by extension to the east or west; the design is nevertheless unusually orderly for a neolithic house. The compartments suggest that it may have functioned as four terraced dwellings, each pair sharing a hearth, or perhaps two semi-detached houses, each with two rooms. There is as yet no radiocarbon date for the Lismore Fields house, but it seems from the finds to have been early–middle neolithic in date.

LONG LOW — Wetton — SK: 112547

A cairn 30m in diameter, with a stone cist and the bones of 13 people. A drystone structure was added to the cairn in antiquity; it consisted of a narrow ridge of masonry extending 200m to the south-west, where it ended in a smaller cairn which was an integral part of the ridge's structure. Cremation burials were found both in the stone ridge and in the second cairn. Although this extension is unusual, it is by no means unique in neolithic architecture. It may be seen as a variant of the 'phallus' at Bryn yr Hen Bobl, if indeed that interpretation is valid, and the 'tail' at Broome Heath.

LONGSTONE MOOR LONG BARROW — Longstone Moor — SK: 197747

This monument close to a summit at over 335m OD was previously thought to be a round barrow. Now, because of the 'tail' that exists on its east side, it is thought likely to be a neolithic long barrow instead. It is 44m long, 16m wide and 2m high, with its long axis aligned W–E. It may have a similar history to Gib Hill, where a round barrow was apparently built on top of an earlier long barrow.

MELBOURNE — SK: 389252

An occupation site. A pit, which was possibly a domestic storage pit, was found to contain neolithic pottery.

MIDDLE HILL — Wormhill — SK: 106771

An occupation site, indicated by a large number of flint tools (mainly scrapers and arrow-heads), stone axe fragments, large quantities of waste chippings and some sherds of plain and decorated pottery.

MILL FARM — Scarcliffe — SK: 517711

An occupation site, indicated by a large number of neolithic flint tools.

MINNING LOW — near Ballidon — SK: 209573

This, the largest chambered barrow in the Peak District, is one of two mounds in a plantation. Originally, the monument must have been very impressive, at least 35m in diameter and enclosed by a circular wall. It is now ruined, but contains at least four burial chambers. The first, at the centre, was built into a small cairn and approached by a drystone-walled passage. This initial mound was later enlarged when the second chamber on the south side was added. Both of these chambers have their capstones still in place. Later chambers were added to the west and south-west. Most of the chambers were emptied of their contents by Thomas Bateman in 1851, although some robbing had probably gone on in earlier centuries. One chamber contained bronzes and pottery from the Romano-British period, which suggests a late re-use of the tomb. There may have been a neolithic settlement 100m to the south, at SK: 209570; hut sites have been identified and a flint saw and a scraper have been found there.

NEWBRIDGE FARM   **Baslow and Bubnell**   SK: 289723

A settlement site, where over 500 neolithic flint artefacts were found, including 76 scrapers, 13 leaf-shaped arrow-heads and 5 petit tranchet derivative arrow-heads.

NEWHAVEN HOUSE   **Hartington**   SK: 160600

An occupation site or forest clearance site. Five stone axes were found close to the house, when the fairground was being planted up in 1826. Another three axes were found in neighbouring fields during the next 30 years. Two of the axes have been identified as Group VI.

NEWHAVEN LODGE   **Hartington**   SK: 152626

An occupation or forest clearance site, where five neolithic stone axes were found between 1843 and 1860. Those that have been petrologically identified belong to Groups I, VII and XX.

NINE LADIES STONE CIRCLE   **Stanton Moor**   SK: 247634

Ringed by a low modern stone wall is a circle of at least nine stones, all under 1m tall. They stand on the inner edge of a degraded bank, which is broken by entrance gaps on the north-east and south-west sides. There was at one time a small mound at the centre of the stone circle, but this has gone. The stone circle is 10m in diameter. The tenth stone lay unnoticed until the 1976 drought, combined with accelerating tourist erosion, uncovered one edge of it. Some unknown person, probably with the aid of a Swiss Army knife, uncovered the whole stone in August 1977. There may well have been an eleventh in the gap between stones 5 and 6; probably the site will go on being called 'Nine Ladies' no matter what the final count is. This site suffered appreciable damage in the 1970s from witchcraft drinking ceremonies and fires.

NINE STONES CLOSE — Harthill — SK: 225626

Only four large stones remain from this 13m circle, although a block in the field wall to the south may represent a fifth. An excavation by Thomas Bateman in 1847 yielded a few pieces of pottery and flint.

ONE ASHE CAVE — Monyash — SK: 172655

Excavation here in 1927 yielded flint tools, including a disc-shaped knife and a leaf-shaped arrow-head. The cave may have been used as a seasonal hunting lodge in the neolithic.

PERRYFOOT LONG BARROW — Peak Forest — SK: 109811

A large mutilated long barrow 55m long, 27m wide and 0.6m high, which has been severely robbed for its stone. In the eighteenth century, large quantities of (allegedly) human bones were found here, although more recent finds imply that many of them may have been animal bones. The long axis follows the contour, on the edge of a low, flat-topped ridge at the head of the Peak Forest basin. Two crouched inhumation burials were accompanied by a piece of pottery and large numbers of animal bones, including those of ox, red deer, roe deer, horse, pig, goat and dog.

RAINS'S CAVE — Longcliffe — SK: 225553

This small cave in the limestone ridge near Longcliffe was excavated in 1890–2 by J. Ward. Seven skeletons were found together with Peterborough, Mortlake and Grimston ware pottery. The burials were thought by the excavator to be bronze age, but it now seems clear that they were neolithic.

RAVENCLIFFE CAVE — Great Longstone — SK: 174735

A neolithic burial cave, where the remains of at least 20 people were buried. The cave was excavated in 1902–8, and the cleared stone is stacked neatly outside the cave entrance. Two neolithic stone axes and several flint scrapers were found in the cave.

REYNARD'S CAVE — Tissington — SK: 145525

This cave, about 35m above the road, has a 5m wide entrance and extends horizontally into the hillside for some 7m. Excavation in 1959 showed that it had been occupied in the neolithic; finds included two flint scrapers and two sherds of pottery that was reminiscent of Ebbsfleet ware.

RINGHAM LOW   **Over Haddon**   SK: 169664

An oval-chambered barrow, now badly·damaged, stands mainly in a plantation with a fieldwall cutting off its northern end. An early engraving implies that it once had a horned forecourt. It had four or five burial chambers which, between them, housed some 20 human burials as well as flint tools, arrow-heads and animal bones. Some of the chambers were paved. Originally, the barrow was a long cairn, 48m long.

Ringham Low stands on private land and may not be visited.

ROSELAND WOOD   **Scarcliffe**   SK: 491677

An occupation site indicated by a scatter of flint artefacts.

ROUND HILL HENGE   **Twyford**   SK: 334284

This seems to be a single-entrance henge with a large round barrow placed centrally within it. It has been identified from air photographs, but not yet excavated.

SMERRILL MOOR   SK: 184608

A round cairn 10m in diameter and 1m high. The slab-built stone chamber within the cairn contained the disarticulated bones of 12 people (adults and children), some fragments of plain pottery, a flint knife and some animal bones.

STADEN LOW   **Buxton**   SK: 069721

A doubtful henge – and even its exact plan is unclear. It was first recorded by William Stukeley and later by Jewett, as an oval bank 61m by 43m, with an internal ditch and a single entrance to the south-east. Later plans show an additional entrance to the NNW, but this could have resulted from robbing; an enclosure, also with an internal ditch, was shown abutting the henge on its west side. A destroyed mound was reported to have existed 40m to the north-east of the henge – if indeed it is really a henge.

STONEY LOW   **Aldwark**   SK: 218578

A round chambered tomb that was destroyed early in the nineteenth century for road building. A contemporary sketch shows an exposed chamber in the body of the barrow mound. When it was levelled, a large 'cist' or chamber was discovered, containing three skeletons and a secondary urn cremation.

Close by, at SK: 417367, there was a settlement. The neolithic occupation debris consisted of flint tools, a stone axe fragment, and the bones of pigs and oxen. Interestingly, it rested on top of mesolithic occupation debris, implying that perhaps the site was in use for a long time, surviving large-scale cultural changes. In the vicinity, fragments of 4 greenstone axes, 22 flint scrapers and 3 arrow heads (petit tranchet derivative type) were also found.

TIDESLOW ROUND BARROW
Tideswell　　　　　　　SK: 149779

A neolithic round barrow 34–38m across and 2m high. A series of cists containing human bones was discovered in 1818; in 1946–7, the disarticulated skeletons of at least three people were found in a cist. Excavation in 1968–9 revealed two cists edged by paving with scattered human bones; it is thought that the cists were originally free-standing structures with paved surrounds. There were stretches of internal kerbs, which suggests that perhaps the monument was multi-phase, and also a stone-lined pit containing the bones of both animals and people. The animal remains include those of deer, ox, sheep, pig and wolf; whether these represent the remains of sacrificial offerings, or of totem animals, or simply food for the journey to the other world is open to speculation.

TORSIDE RESERVOIR
SK: 065982

An occupation site on the south side of the reservoir, indicated by a scatter of neolithic flint artefacts and a fragment of a (possibly Langdale) stone axe.

TREAK CLIFF CAVERN
Castleton　　　　　　　SK: 137828

A burial cave where at least three people were interred, together with a small polished stone axe and red deer antler pick. The remains were found in a limestone fissure above the cave mouth in 1921 by workmen mining fluorspar; the site is now blocked up with quarry spoil.

TWYFORD CURSUS
Twyford　　　　　　　SK: 317289

Cropmarks showing on air photographs indicate the existence of a cursus here.

WHALEY ROCK SHELTER
Elmton　　　　　　　SK: 511721

This cave was apparently used as a dwelling. Neolithic material found in it includes scrapers, arrow-heads and Peterborough ware pottery.

WIGBER LOW
Kniveton　　　　　　　SK: 204514

An occupation site, indicated by leaf-shaped arrow-heads, neolithic pottery and fragments of Langdale stone axes. The occupation debris was preserved on the old land surface, underneath a bronze age round barrow.

WILLINGTON

SK: 288278

The site of a third millenium BC settlement. The remains of both circular and rectangular wooden houses from the late neolithic were discovered here, partly by the study of air photographs, partly by excavation in 1970–2. The settlement was enclosed, perhaps for defence, at the end of the neolithic. A cursus, at SK: 316288, may have been contemporary with the Willington settlement (Figure 24).

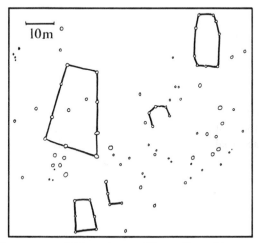

Figure 24 Willington, a neolithic settlement. The outlines of houses, shown by solid lines, are only tentatively reconstructed; other shapes could be created by joining the post-holes in different ways.

DEVON

BEER HEAD

Seaton

SY: 230885

An axe factory on the South Devon coast. Flints worked here were traded in the West Country, although exclusively to the north and west (to such places as Hembury, High Peak, Haldon, Hazard Hill and Carn Brea), and not, it seems, to the east. The people of the Maiden Castle enclosure were presumably supplied by Dorset rather than Devon miners. The flaking floors at Beer Head have been identified, and it seems that flints were quartered on the spot. The flint was then probably traded in this semi-manufactured state, but at least some finished axes were produced at Beer Head; some creamy white flint axes were exported in a finished state to the people of the Hembury enclosure, where no trace has yet been found of any of the waste flakes that would have been created during axe manufacture.

BLACK HILL   Manaton   SX: 766792

North of the road from Haytor to Manaton are the remains of a ring cairn 14m in diameter. Leading northwards from it down the slope is a row of 16 stones, 9 of which have fallen. This was probably a double row originally. The row, which may well date from the bronze age rather than from the late neolithic, stretches over a distance of about 120m and ends at a larger stone set at right angles to the axis of the row.

BROADSANDS PASSAGE GRAVE   Paignton   SX: 892573

A wrecked passage grave on a south-facing slope. Originally, it had a polygonal stone chamber made of 11 small orthostats about 1m high: the gaps were filled with drystone walling. The chamber was roofed by a single capstone. The entrance was by way of a very narrow passage built of small stones. The cairn was probably circular and 10m across. It seems likely that the tomb is early; comparison with passage graves in Brittany suggests that Broadsands belongs to the fourth millennium BC. Its wrecked state is regrettable, and all the more so since it seems to be the only tomb of its type in the West Country. Obscured by a thick hedgerow, the site was only discovered by Guy Belleville in the 1950s.

CHAPMAN BARROWS   Challacombe   SS: 695435

A linear cemetery of about nine round barrows: the easternmost barrow was opened by J. F. Chanter in 1905. In it he found burnt bones covered by a layer of turves; the barrow was enclosed by a stone kerb, although the weathered mound had spread across and covered it. 450m SE of this barrow is the tallest and most imposing standing stone on Exmoor, the Long Stone, a slab of Morte slate 2.7m high poised, false-crested, above a moorland valley-head. These monuments may be late neolithic or bronze age in date.

CORRINGDON BALL GATE   South Brent   SX: 670614

A long barrow 40m long and 20m wide, with its long axis oriented NW–SE. At the higher, south-east end are the remains of a collapsed burial chamber. One supporting stone of the chamber still stands upright 1.3m high, and beside it lie two others measuring 4m by 2m.

DRIZZLECOMBE   Sheepstor   SX: 592670

The main feature in a cluster of monuments is a large bracken-covered barrow 3m high and 21m in diameter, with a hollow in the top called the Giant's Basin. North-east of the large barrow are three smaller barrows in a row. From the central barrow of these a single line of stones runs south-west for 150m, ending at a larger stone 2.4m high. To the south a second line of stones 84m long ends at another standing stone 4.2m high. These monuments may be late neolithic or bronze age in date.

FERNWORTHY STONE CIRCLE SX: 655841

This stone circle is 18m in diameter and composed of about 30 granite blocks, which are graded in size with the largest, 1.2m high, on the south side. A damaged double stone row approaches the stone circle from the south, emphasizing the circle's orientation. The floor of the circle was covered with charcoal, so it may have been used for cremations, but nothing else was found when the circle was excavated in 1897.

GREY WETHERS Lydford SX: 638832

Two stone circles that were restored in the late nineteenth century are situated on a saddle east of Sittaford Tor. The northern circle is 31m in diameter and the southern 36m. In the mid-nineteenth century only nine stones were standing in the northern circle, and seven in the southern, but today almost all the stones are standing again, spaced about 3m apart and each about 1m high.

HALDON SX: 874862

A large rectangular house high on the 250m ridge which forms the Teign–Exe watershed. The house was 7.5m by 4.7m in plan and had a gabled ridge roof carried on a ridge pole, with a timber frame and daub walls resting on a rough foundation of gravel set in clay. There was a doorway in the north-east corner, significantly and very sensibly facing away from the prevailing wind, and a hearth in the south-east corner. The clay floor was trodden hard, and raised and renewed during the two phases of occupation. A thick layer of hearth-ash swept up against the north wall of the cottage also implies a long period of occupation. The Haldon house is archaeologically important in representing in some detail a type of rectangular timber dwelling that seems to have been very common right through the neolithic.

HAZARD HILL SX:755593

An early neolithic settlement that has produced radiocarbon dates of 2970 and 2750 bc (3650 and 3450 BC).

HEMBURY CAUSEWAYED ENCLOSURE ST: 113031

A hillfort with a long history beginning in the neolithic period, when a causewayed enclosure was built on the hill on the site of the southern half of the fort. Eight sections of neolithic ditch, each about 1.8m deep and between 8 and 17m long lay in an arc from west to east, with traces of a bank on their southern side. At the western end, under the iron age entrance another segment of neolithic ditch was uncovered with a line of palisade holes outside it. Finds at Hembury, clearly an important settlement site, include over 1,600 flints, 15 greenstone axes, pottery and a substantial amount of charred wheat. Charcoal from the neolithic ditch has given us radiocarbon dates of 4000–3750 BC.

HIGH PEAK near Exeter SY: 103859

An eroded causewayed enclosure on a cliff top site, which was inhabited in about 3000 BC. Its boundary ditch has the typical neolithic flat bottom. There were many hearths and shallow pits. Like Hembury, this neolithic enclosure was only discovered by chance during the excavation of later earthworks.

MERRIVALE STONE CIRCLE Walkhampton SX: 553746

A stone ring, three stone rows and several cairns. The ring is oval, 18m by 20m, with a single standing stone outside to the south. About 180m NE is a large stone cist, which may have contained a single burial long since destroyed in the acidic soil. North of the cist are two almost parallel double stone rows running W–E. The southern row, 238m long, has a round barrow at its centre; the northern is 78m long. Both are terminated by triangular stones at the eastern end. These monuments may be late neolithic or bronze age.

SCORHILL STONE CIRCLE Gidleigh SK: 655874

One of the finest Dartmoor stone circles, a jagged circle 27m in diameter, with 23 of its original 70 stones still standing. Most of the stones are pointed in shape and the tallest is over 2m high.

SETTA BARROW High Bray SS: 726381

Setta Barrow is conspicuous for its kerb of retaining stones. It has been used as a field boundary and also as a county boundary marker, measuring 30m in diameter by 2m in height (Plate 2).

SPINSTERS' ROCK   **Drewsteignton**   SX: 700908

Three upright stones over 2m high support a large capstone. The tomb chamber collapsed in 1862 and was re-erected slightly inaccurately. Camera lucida drawings made in 1858 suggest that the entrance to the burial chamber faced north-east. No traces remain of the retaining mound that presumably once surrounded the chamber.

YELLOWMEAD DOWN   **Sheepstor**   SX: 575678

This was once a burial cairn, traces of which can still be made out. It was defined by four roughly concentric circles of kerbstones with diameters of 6m, 12m, 15m and 20m. These were restored in 1921. There are 21 stones still standing and almost touching each other in the central circle. The stones in the surrounding circles are graded in size, with the largest in the outer ring. There may also have been an avenue of stones leading up to the cairn.

───── DORSET ─────

ALINGTON AVENUE LONG   Dorchester   SY: 702898
BARROW

A long barrow site on the south-eastern edge of Dorchester. Its ditches were discovered together with a double-lobed bronze age barrow that had been built onto the long barrow. The long barrow's long axis, oriented WSW–ENE, became the axis of a linear barrow cemetery. Peter Woodward suggests that this axis was later projected further to the east and west to fix locations for the major monuments of Maumbury Rings (to the west) and Mount Pleasant (to the east): the barrow cemetery lies about halfway between them. The infill from the long barrow ditches was dated to 4450 bp (3150 BC).

BERE DOWN LONG   **Bere Regis**   SY: 829972
BARROWS

The Bere Down North Long Barrow, at SY: 829972, is 58m long, 12m wide and 3m high. It is parallel-sided and oriented SW–NE. Sarsen stones protrude from the centre of the mound. Bere Down South, at 826966, is very fat, making it appear more like a round barrow than a long barrow; it is 32m long, 32m wide and 1m high. Its orientation seems to be WSW–ENE.

BIG WOOD LONG BARROW   Winterbourne Abbas   SY: 614896

An almost completely destroyed long barrow in an unusual valley-floor location, near Loscombe Farm. Two large stones mark its eastern end.

BINCOMBE HILL LONG BARROW   Bincombe   SY: 688851

A long barrow 82m long, 14m wide and 1m high, on grassland surrounded by cultivated land.

BOKERLEY LONG BARROWS   SU: 041187

The Bokerley I Long Barrow, at SU: 041187, is 102m long, 18m wide and 2m high. Bokerley IIa, at SU: 041190, is 92m long, 22m wide and 1m high. Bokerley IIb, at SU: 040191, is 53m long, 21m wide and 1m high. The Bokerley III Long Barrow, at SU: 039195, is 29m long, 21m wide and 1m high.

BRADFORD PEVERELL   SY: 669919

There are four long barrows in this area. One, at SY: 669919, is 46m long and was partly excavated in 1954. Another, at SY: 648924, is 64m long. A third, in a coniferous plantation at SY: 637923, is 37m long and grass-covered. A fourth, in mixed woodland at SY: 647924, is 27m long and in rather poor condition.

BROADMAYNE LONG BARROW   SY: 702853

This is of the Royal Commission on Historical Monuments' three 'official' bank barrows of Dorset. Two of them, the Broadmayne Long Barrow and the Martins Down Long Barrow, bracket the Dorset Ridgeway cemetery, apparently placed as deliberate end markers at its eastern and western extremities. The third is the very long bank barrow at Maiden Castle (Figure 25). Like many other long barrows, the Broadmayne Long Barrow became the focus of a small bronze age cemetery; it has a round barrow at each end. The bank barrow itself is 183m long, 16m wide and 1.5m high, with its long axis oriented WNW–ESE, on cultivated land. It is in a rapidly deteriorating condition, described as being in 'good condition' in 1983, with 80–99 per cent of the barrow surviving, and in 'bad condition' in 1988, with only 1–19 per cent surviving.

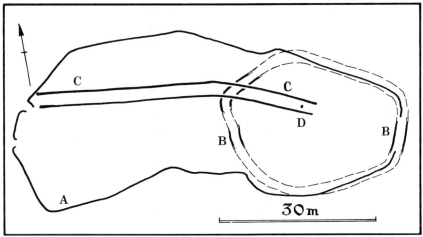

Figure 25　Maiden Castle. A – inner rampart of the iron age fort,　B – ditches of the neolithic causewayed enclosure,　C – ditches of the Long Mound,　D – ritual burials.

CAME DOWN　　　　　　**Bincombe**　　　　SY: 675858

A settlement site that was fully excavated in 1963. Like the settlement at Sutton Poyntz, 3km away to the south-east, the Came Down settlement was located close to, but may well have preceded, a linear barrow cemetery built along the crest of a ridge.

CAME WOOD BARROW　　**Broadmayne**　　　SY: 699855
CEMETERY

The key to this barrow group seems to be the Broadmayne Long Barrow, running WNW–ESE. Most of the other barrows seem to be aligned on it. These include bowl barrows, pond barrows and bell barrows, and extend in a long scatter from Came Wood for a thousand metres eastwards along the Ridgeway. The Culliford Tree Barrow, at SY: 698855, is the only one to have been excavated. From the Ridgeway, there are fine views across to other barrow groups to the south and south-west.

CHETTLE LONG BARROW ST: 937135

A long barrow 58m long, 20m wide and 3m high. In the eighteenth century it was reported that 'many human bones' had been found there. The barrow's long axis is aligned NNW–SSE. A second long barrow, 100m long, lies south of the village, at ST: 950127, with a long axis oriented almost exactly W–E.

CLANDON LONG BARROWS Winterbourne Monkton SY: 665887

A long barrow in a poor state of preservation on cultivated land, immediately outside the north-west ramparts of Maiden Castle. It may have served as a burial place for the people of the Maiden Castle causewayed enclosure. A second long barrow, also in a poor state and also on cultivated land, is at SY: 665893.

CONQUER BARROW Mount Pleasant SY: 707898

A large late neolithic round barrow, built on the western edge of the site of the later Mount Pleasant superhenge. The infill of the ditch that surrounds it has been radiocarbon dated to 2600 BC. It is contemporary with the unenclosed late neolithic settlement which occupied the Mount Pleasant site immediately before the superhenge was laid out.

COWLEAZE LONG BARROW Black Down SY: 604883

A poorly preserved long barrow 55m long, 23m wide and 0.3m high.

CULLIFORD TREE LONG BARROW Came Wood, Broadmayne SY: 699856

An earthen long barrow 52m long, 15m wide and 3.5m high on the eastern edge of Came Wood. 300m to the south-east is the Came Wood linear barrow cemetery, commanded by its huge bank barrow, but the Culliford Tree Long Barrow seems to stand aloof from this alignment. When it was excavated in 1858, it was found to contain four secondary burials, one accompanied by an amber necklace and two gold-plated beads, and a cremation in an urn.

CURSUS LONG BARROW Dorset Cursus SU: 025169

A long barrow 43m long, 18m wide and 1.5m high. Its long axis is oriented SW–NE and seems to have guided the positioning and orientation of the Dorset Cursus. The long barrow has itself actually been incorporated into the western bank of the cursus. It is believed that the purpose of the cursus was specifically to link together several long barrows and form a processional way for funerary rites.

DOGHOUSE HILL   Chideock   SY: 428913

A settlement site on the cliff overlooking East Ebb Cove.

DORSET CURSUS   SU: 040193 to ST: 970124

Stretching almost 10km from Bokerley Down at Pentridge to Thickthorn Down, this is one of the longest, but also one of the least impressive prehistoric monuments in Britain. Two parallel banks with outer ditches lie an almost constant 90m apart, and the ends are carefully closed off by transverse banks and ditches. The Dorset Cursus encloses an area of 90 hectares, compared with the Stonehenge Greater Cursus's 28 hectares. The earthwork, slight though it now appears, involved moving some 184,000 cubic metres of soil and stone, almost twice the amount of earth-moving necessitated by the creation of the Avebury henge.

At the south-west end are the two Thickthorn long barrows, and similar long mounds lie clustered near the north-east end; others are incorporated in it along its course. The Dorset Cursus was built in at least two sections, the section from Thickthorn to Bottlebush Down being earlier than that from Bottlebush to Bokerley. Today, much of the cursus has been ploughed out, but it must have been an awe-inspiring landmark when it was first created. Its precise purpose is unknown, but it has been suggested that its various sections contain astronomical alignments. Whether that was the original intention is by no means clear, but it seems certain that the monument was connected with the cult of the dead, in that its course was evidently determined by the locations of the long barrows; even so, it is unlikely that the cursus's precise function will ever be known. William Stukeley's proposal, that the cursus monuments were used as race-tracks, has no academic support today. It is much more probable that they were used for some sort of processional rite connected with a funerary cult.

A small amount of material from the ditch has been radiocarbon dated to 4490 bp (3250 BC). This overturns a long-cherished assumption that the larger and more ambitious monuments belong to a time when social and political units were aggregating and enlarging in the late neolithic; it is clear from the evidence of the Dorset Cursus that some large-scale projects were launched in the middle neolithic too.

DOWN FARM   Gussage St Michael   SU: 999146

140m to the north of the Dorset Cursus, and 130m NE of a ring ditch, is a middle bronze age farmstead site. Underneath its remains were traces of a comparatively prosperous late neolithic Grooved ware occupation site; 16 pits and a number of stake-holes were found.

The ring ditch, at SU: 999145, was first cut in the neolithic, almost certainly as a cemetery for the Grooved ware settlement, but continued in use into the bronze age. Nine Deverel-Rimbury cremations (bronze age) were found there. It is a site which shows that some settlements, together with their burial places, continued in use across what is usually regarded as a major cultural divide.

DRIVE PLANTATION LONG BARROW
Monkton Up Wimborne   SU: 014147

A long barrow that was possibly originally 36m long, 27m wide and 1m high. It stands on arable land and one end has been ploughed down. The barrow's long axis is oriented N–S.

EGGARDON BARROW
SY: 551944

An uncertain site, which may be a mutilated long barrow, on the floor of a steep-sided and enclosed valley. When examined in 1936, it was 45m long, 18m wide and 1.8m high. It was aligned E–W.

FLAGSTONES
Max Gate, Dorchester   SY: 703899

The Flagstones ritual enclosure on the south-east edge of Dorchester was half-excavated as a rescue operation in the 1980s, in advance of the building of the Dorchester by-pass. The remaining, unexcavated half survives, protected in the grounds of Thomas Hardy's house, Max Gate. The monument is carefully sited on a ridge crest, on the rough alignment that connects Maumbury Rings, the Alington Avenue Long Barrow and Mount Pleasant.

Several infant burials were found in the enclosure's ditch. A radiocarbon date from an early pit containing Hembury pottery, 4080 bp (2600 BC), agrees closely with dates from the pre-superhenge settlement at Mount Pleasant, 4070 bp (2600 BC), and the infill of the Conquer Barrow ditch, 4077 bp (2600 BC). The ring ditch, the central pit-burial of a crouched adult sealed by a large sarsen stone and covered by a round barrow, and the outer ditch were probably all contemporary, belonging to the very end of the neolithic.

The most striking thing about Flagstones has been the discovery of neolithic chalk engravings, carved in the near-vertical walls of the ditch. The site was eroded, so there may have originally been more carvings round the ditch rims. This is a rare survival of British neolithic two-dimensional art, and one that illustrates well the neolithic fusion of art, monument-building and burial ritual.

FORTY ACRE PLANTATION

Bradford Peverell   SY: 668920

A long barrow 46m long, 21m wide and 1m high on the crest of a spur overlooking the floodplain of the River Frome.

GREYHOUND YARD

Dorchester   SY: 697904
(centre)

A very large circular, or possibly D-shaped, enclosure discovered in Dorchester during the excavation of the Greyhound Yard car park in 1984. An arc of post-pits was found 5m inside a curving ditch. The regularly spaced post-pits, which were 1m in diameter and 1m apart, had vertical walls on the east side and entry ramps for the erection of the posts on the west side. There was no sign that the posts had been removed at the close of the period of use, and it can be assumed that they were left to rot in position. The curvature of the arc excavated implies that it was part of a circle 240–290m in diameter. It was radiocarbon dated to 2140 bc (2750 BC). Another segment of the same perimeter setting was found on the east side of Church Street, and the curvature of this second arc implies an even larger diameter, perhaps as large as 380m. The monument was abandoned in the early bronze age, when the site was turned over to the plough.

This extraordinary enclosure may have been part of a major ceremonial complex which included Mount Pleasant, just over 1km ESE, and Maumbury Rings 750m to the south-west. Alternatively, it may have been a palisaded proto-urban settlement similar to Durrington Walls. If so, there has been a remarkable recurrence of interest in the site, now occupied by the modern town of Dorchester, once occupied by the Roman town of Durnovaria, and more than 2,500 years before that occupied by the nameless new stone age settlement. Unfortunately, subsequent and continual urban redevelopment on the site has removed the neolithic land surface, so it may not be possible to learn anything about what went on inside this very large, intriguing and undoubtedly very important monument.

THE GREY MARE AND HER COLTS

Long Bredy   SY: 584871

An untidy pile of stones representing the remains of a rectangular burial chamber with three wallstones and a slipped capstone. At the south-east end of the barrow it is possible to make out a crescent-shaped forecourt. The mound is approximately 24m long, 14m wide and 1m high, with traces of a retaining wall round it. Excavations in the early nineteenth century revealed human bones and some pottery. It is the southernmost and most isolated tomb of its type in Britain.

GUSSAGE DOWN LONG BARROWS

Gussage St Michael ST: 994136

An important cluster of three long barrows which were possibly the 'destination' of the first, south-western, segment of the Dorset Cursus. Gussage Down North (or Gussage St Michael I), at ST: 993138, is 50m long, 21m wide and 3m high. Gussage Down Centre (or Gussage St Michael II), at ST: 994136, is 52m long, 30m wide and 3m high. Gussage Down South (or Gussage St Michael III), at ST: 992131, is 64m long, 26m wide and only 0.6m high.

The North and Centre Barrows are built on the same axis, pointing to the midwinter sunrise in 3000 BC. In the nineteenth century, the Centre Barrow was excavated to reveal two post-holes, which were big enough to support large posts. One post was set on the axis, the other was offset from it by 3m. Viewed from the rear end of the North Barrow, the slot between the two posts would have been about the same as the diameter of the sun disc as it appeared on the horizon. Many of the other Cranborne Chase long barrows are oriented to the south-east, suggesting that the people of this area were consciously making a regular ritual gesture towards the midwinter sunrise.

There are more long barrows at ST: 970123 and 971122. Both are in good condition, and the second of the two was partly excavated in 1933.

HAMBLEDON HILL ENCLOSURES

ST: 852123

The southern summit of Hambledon Hill, outside the great iron age hillfort, is ringed by a neolithic causewayed enclosure of about 8 hectares. Along the three spurs leading away from the enclosure are substantial outworks. Excavation of the inner enclosure has shown that the ditches were recut many times and frequently filled with deposits of human skeletal remains, including crouched infant burials, that were repeatedly dug into. Pieces of neolithic pottery, leaf-shaped arrow-heads, stone axes and animal bones were associated with these human remains. The outer earthworks were constructed on a large scale, with timber revetting, which suggests that defence may have been a motive. There is a small long barrow 26m long just outside the southern outer defence work. Both barrow and enclosure probably date from 3500 BC.

The main causewayed enclosure and a recently discovered smaller enclosure nearby, called Stepleton, were both set within a large-scale system of earthworks enclosing some 60 hectares. In 1981, the small Stepleton enclosure with its timber reinforced outwork was totally excavated. It was apparently rebuilt several times. The sequence culminated in the destruction of the site in a single catastrophic event, apparently an armed attack of some kind; there were several intact skeletons, one with a leaf-shaped arrow-head in the rib-cage. Evidently Stepleton was a settlement site, even if of a specialized nature. It had two gateways: one was 4m wide, possibly for people, the other 12m wide with incurving ditch terminals, which was probably used as a livestock entrance. Adjoining the enclosure to the north-west were some massive timber structures, as yet uninterpreted. The ditches of the Stepleton causewayed enclosure yielded radiocarbon dates of 4850, 4700 and 4570 bp (3550, 3400 and 3300 BC). A pit close to the enclosure yielded a single grape pip, which gives us the rather surprising evidence that grapes were part of the British neolithic diet.

HAMBLEDON HILL LONG BARROWS ST: 845126

Two long barrows closely associated with the causewayed enclosures on the hill. Hambledon Hill North Long Barrow, at ST: 845126, is 69m long, 15m wide, 2m high and well preserved. Hambledon Hill South Long Barrow, at ST: 849120, is 26m long, 12m wide and 1.5m high.

HAMPTON BARN LONG BARROW Portesham Hill SY: 595868

A robbed and degraded chambered long barrow which stands on the northern crest of Portesham Hill, overlooking the Valley of Stones. It seems to have been 16m or more long, 16m wide and at least 2m high. There are also two large stones, which may represent the eastern end of a tomb chamber.

HAMPTON STONE CIRCLE Portesham SY: 596865

This sarsen circle was excavated in 1964–5, when it was shown that the visible stone circle was a relatively recent reconstruction of an ancient circle that still lay buried, out of sight, to the west. The true circle is 6m in diameter and consists of nine stones set in two arcs on the north and south sides. An old track led to the north-east entrance and was marked out by stakes and two sections of ditch. After the 1964–5 excavation, the stones were replaced in the original sockets.

HAND-IN-HAND FLINT CAIRN Farnham ST: 948157

A poorly preserved neolithic cairn standing on cultivated land. It was partly excavated in 1984. It may have been the burial place and territorial marker of the flint-knappers who worked the Rookery Farm flint factory about 1km to the north, although no bones were found in it.

HELL STONE Portesham SY: 606867

A poorly preserved barrow mound 27m long and about 12m wide. At the eastern end is a stone chamber with nine wallstones wrongly restored by Martin Tupper in 1866. There are traces of a retaining wall close to the chamber; it probably did not mark the edge of the barrow but served as an internal support, stabilizing the mound material. Early drawings show the burial chamber with only three uprights and a sloping capstone; as such, it was a useful shelter for shepherds in wet weather.

HOLDENHURST LONG BARROW

Bournemouth   *c.* SZ: 120950

The site of an earthen long barrow oriented NNW–SSE, with burials secreted under the slightly broader SSE end. The rectangular mound 75m long and 12m wide was kept in shape by a turf revetment wall. Its side ditches continued right round the south end of the barrow, making a rather unusual horseshoe shape; two other long barrows in the same area, both at Whitsbury, have similar ditches. The elongated rectangular shape is thought to be a symbolic reference to the rectangular longhouses of the North European Plain although, curiously, such houses seem never to have been built in England for the living.

KINGSTON RUSSELL LONG BARROWS

Long Bredy   SY: 580905

Two unusually long barrows, at SY: 580905 (90m long) and SY: 580904 (75m long), which stand on the crest of a high, steep hill, Whatcombe Down. Their great length means that they can be treated as bank barrows, and they are marked as such on Ordnance Survey maps. The crest of this ridge is thick with neolithic barrows, the Martin's Down bank barrow standing 1,100m away to the west.

KINGSTON RUSSELL STONE CIRCLE

SY: 577878

A stone circle on the narrow crest of the Tenant's Hill ridge. The 18 stones which compose this ring all lie flat in the grass, which makes the monument rather difficult to see. The stones are arranged in an oval setting 27m by 20m with the longest stones on the north side.

KNIGHTON

Poole   SZ: 046974

A neolithic settlement site, found on the north-west of the built-up area of Poole. It was partly excavated in 1985, in advance of mineral extraction. The settlement was sited on a low terrace beside the River Stour's floodplain.

KNOWLTON CIRCLES

Knowlton   SU: 025100

Three circular earthworks form a line of henge monuments on a rough SSE–NNW axis. The largest, the South Circle, is 244m in diameter, and is rather inaccessible and damaged since it straddles the B3078 and contains farm buildings. The Central Circle is the only part of the ritual complex to be in the care of

English Heritage; it is beautifully presented and maintained and survives in an excellent state of preservation. The Central Circle, although by no means the largest, is certainly one of the finest henges in Britain. It occupies a rather unusual position on a hilltop, commanding extensive views. The henge is about 96m in diameter, with entrances to south-west and north-east, and what seems to be an additional modern entrance to the east, opening in the direction of the Great Barrow. A ruined twelfth-century church stands at the centre of the Central Circle and two of its churchyard yews survive on the eastern edge of the henge, adding a uniquely picturesque touch.

This is a site that is bound to appeal to those who like to argue for the long-continuing sanctity of sacred sites from age to age, although there are in reality very few sites which can be claimed in support of this view. Neolithic monuments at Rudston, Stanton Drew and Avebury admittedly have churches built next to them, but few others can be proved. This means that, as far as the archaeological evidence goes, 99.9 per cent of British churches are not built on or adjacent to neolithic monuments, and equally that 99.9 per cent of neolithic monuments were not later on to become sites for churches, so the argument for enduring sanctity is not as strong as is popularly supposed.

The North Circle is really D-shaped in plan and 84m across. It stands on privately owned farmland and is not accessible to the public. Due east of the Central Circle, and plainly visible from it, is the Great Barrow, a round barrow densely covered with trees; it has a buried surrounding ditch and bank making it about 150m in diameter overall. It may well be that the Great Barrow Circle was originally a fourth henge, and there are other barrows in the neighbourhood, implying that this shallow dome was a ritual focus of great importance in the late neolithic and early bronze age.

The Knowlton Circles are situated at the southern end of a major cluster of round barrows, and just south of the centre of a major concentration of older long barrows. Together with the Dorset Cursus, which passes not far away to the north-west, the Knowlton Circles seem to have formed a major ceremonial focus for the people who lived in that part of Dorset between the valleys of the Nadder and the Stour, including Cranbourne Chase. Knowlton appears to have had a status rivalling that of the late neolithic superhenges of Mount Pleasant, Stonehenge-Durrington, Marden and Avebury (Figure 30).

LITTON CHENEY   SY: 556917

A settlement site with an earthwork that was fully excavated in 1974. The site is now occupied by a widened A35 (T), which at this point follows the crest of the South Dorset Downs; it is probable that the ridge was a neolithic line of communication too, to judge from the dense scatter of barrows along it.

In the 1930s it was suggested that the circular bank was the site of a stone circle, but this is now considered unlikely. In the first phase at Litton Cheney a bank was raised with an external, V-shaped ditch. The interior of the site was levelled and the fill was deliberately thrown back into the ditch. There was a circular timber structure, almost certainly a house, that may have been contemporary with this activity: it was set back against the bank in the south-west quadrant of the enclosure. The house remains consisted of a shallow foundation trench filled with flints. There were some post-holes and also some gaps among the flint nodules, every 2m. The diameter of the house was about 7m. It had its entrance to the east, facing the enclosure entrance, which was on the south-east side. Inside the house was a small pit containing a cremation, but there is no reason to suppose that the burial and the house were contemporary with each other. The site may have been a small farmstead, perhaps used only during the summer months when livestock were brought up onto the hilltops to graze. The exposed site suggests that it may not have been inhabited in the winter. Later, in other words after the late neolithic occupation phase, the site was used for cremation burials. If the building is indeed a house, the site will be a rarity – one of the few sites in England and Wales to have yielded a definite house plan. The possibility also remains that the site had a ritual function in the late neolithic as well as in the early bronze age, in which case the 'house' may need to be reinterpreted as a cult-house of some kind.

LONGLANDS LONG BARROW Winterbourne Abbas SY: 604900

A long barrow 30m long, and possibly once longer, 11m wide and only 0.3m high; it is now ploughed down and in a poor state.

LUTON DOWN LONG BARROW Tarrant Rawston ST: 915066

A long barrow 38m long, 24m wide and 2m high. Its long axis is oriented NW–SE. It yielded two pieces of pottery and two pieces of bone when it was excavated.

MAIDEN CASTLE near Dorchester SY: 669885

The hill which carries the magnificent iron age hillfort takes the form of an E–W ridge with prominent knolls at each end. It was the eastern knoll that was occupied first, in about 3500 BC, when two concentric rings of ditches were dug to create a causewayed enclosure. The ditches were steep-sided and flat-bottomed, and the sections that have been excavated were 1.5m deep. The neolithic banks have vanished, presumably because they have been pushed back into the ditches.

When the neolithic ditches were three-quarters full of chalk rubble and soil, and the site had – apparently – passed out of use, in about 3200 BC, an unusual bank barrow was constructed. It runs along the crest of the ridge and rides right over the degraded remains of the enclosure's western perimeter. The barrow is a remarkable 546m long, which makes it far and away the longest long barrow in the country. It is 18m wide and 1m high. Because of the high relief of the iron age earthworks, the neolithic barrow is nevertheless scarcely noticed by most visitors to the site.

The child burial in the causewayed enclosure ditch has been dated to 4810 bp (3500 BC), and this is the earliest radiocarbon date to have come from Maiden Castle, although it may at first sight appear that this burial could represent some kind of foundation offering – and possibly a sacrifice – parts of the ditch were being dug out as early as 3100 bc (3900 BC), with the final fill dating to between 3450 and 3050 BC. The Maiden Castle enclosure was the principal ceremonial focus in the area in the middle neolithic; in the late neolithic it was given up in favour of a ritual complex on lower ground, stretching from Dorchester to Mount Pleasant (Figures 25 and 26).

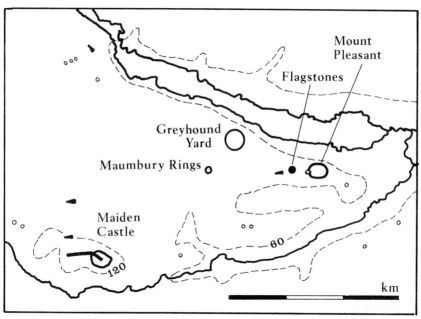

Figure 26 Ceremonial monuments in the Mount Pleasant area, near Dorchester (contours in metres).

MARTIN'S DOWN BANK BARROW   **Long Bredy**   SY: 571911

This extraordinarily long and well-preserved bank barrow, also known as Martin's Down West, is 197m long, 12m wide and about 2m high. Along each side there are quarry ditches. It is broken at one point by a gap, which gives it the appearance of being two unequal long barrows.

93

Apart from being in itself an extraordinary and imposing monument, with its dramatic hilltop location and command of distant views, it marks the western end of the South Dorset Downs Ridgeway cemetery. There is a very marked falling off in barrow density to the west of the bank barrow, which suggests that it was intended as an end marker and may have held some regional significance as a landmark.

Martin's Down East, at SY: 573909, 180m to the east, is a more modest long barrow, 33m long, 27m wide and 1.5m high. It seems not to have been excavated, Martin's Down North, at SY: 580905, is 91m long, 12m wide and 1.5m high. Martin's Down South, at SY: 580904, is 26m long, 14m wide and 1.5m high.

MARTIN'S DOWN CURSUS   Long Bredy   SY: 573192

A cursus monument immediately south of the A35 between Dorchester and Bridport. Today, nothing can be seen on the ploughed land surface at all. The western end of the cursus is located close to the bank barrow on the summit of Martin's Down. The eastern end has not been found.

MAUMBURY RINGS   Dorchester   SY: 690899

A Roman amphitheatre and Civil War gun emplacement make this an impressive site, but excavation by H. St George Gray in 1908–13 showed that there were much more ancient elements in it, although his findings were not to be published until 1975. In the late neolithic period, it was a henge monument with a bank about 100m in diameter and an internal ditch. There was a single entrance on the north-east side, beneath the modern entrance. In the bottom of the ditch about 45 shafts were cut into the chalk, some over 10m deep and 2–4m in diameter. Into these, caches of bones and tools were carefully and deliberately placed and buried, and then the shafts themselves were deliberately refilled. The only datable find was a piece of neolithic Grooved ware, the pottery type usually associated with henge monuments, but chalk balls and a chalk phallus were found on the western perimeter, and these were probably neolithic cult objects too. Antler picks found in the shafts have been radiocarbon dated to 1690 and 1700 bc (2150 bc), showing that the shafts filled up rapidly. The dates are also earlier than had been expected; the monument is not intermediate in time between Maiden Castle and Mount Pleasant, as once thought, but belongs to the same period as the cove and palisade at Mount Pleasant. Maumbury probably evolved over a long period, in just the same way as many of the other great ceremonial monuments, and further work may show that it developed as a satellite to the huge late neolithic enclosure at Greyhound Yard in Dorchester (Figure 26).

94

MOUNT PLEASANT   **Dorchester**   SY: 710898

A superhenge monument 300m by 270m, situated on a low ridge near Dorchester. It is the the smallest of the four giant Wessex henges, and has been virtually destroyed by ploughing. Like Avebury, it has four entrances: unlike Avebury,

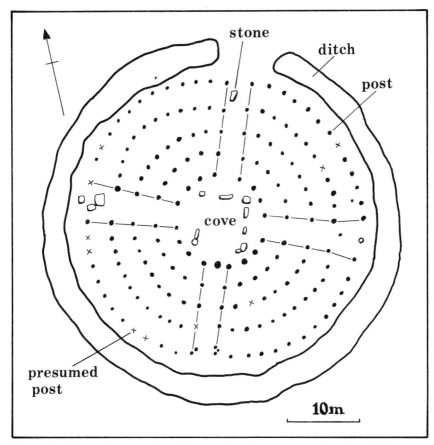

Figure 27 Mount Pleasant: plan of the circular timber structure, showing a high degree of order and symmetry. The north and south 'corridors' are parallel-sided, whilst the west and east corridors are flared. The numbers of posts in each quadrant appear to have been the same. In the outermost circle, for instance, there were 13 posts in each quadrant: in the innermost circle 4. It is not known whether these numbers (13, 12, 9, 6 and 4) or their totals (52, 48, 36, 24 and 16) held some significance for the builders.

its entrances are irregularly spaced. Mount Pleasant seems to have formed part of an extensive late neolithic ceremonial complex which included Maumbury Rings and the newly discovered Greyhound Yard enclosure, and which replaced the older, higher ceremonial centre at Maiden Castle. A similar process of ritual migration from high to low ground can be seen at other sites too, such as Avebury, which supplanted the older centre on Windmill Hill.

Excavation in 1970–1 revealed a circular timber structure with its own ditch and bank 60m in diameter and with a single entrance; this was, in effect, a substantial henge erected within the precinct of the superhenge, but actually built before the outer works were begun: as at Durrington Walls, the roundhouse came first, the ditch and bank later. The timber building itself was similar in concept to Woodhenge, which also has its own surrounding ditch and concentric post-rings. The building was different from Woodhenge in being divided carefully into quarters by four axial corridors. Later, it was replaced by a rectangular stone cove 6m square and open to the south: this was raised at the centre of the enclosure. To the north, west and east there were outlying marker stones, which lay on the axes of the earlier corridors. The transformation or symbolic reduction of a wooden monument into a stone acronym recalls the sequence of events at the Sanctuary in Wiltshire (Figure 27).

A substantial timber stockade surrounded the flat hilltop, about 3m inside the 3m deep ditch. The depth of the bedding trench implies a palisade as much as 5m high, composed of timbers 40cm in diameter, standing against one another side by side in the trench. If it followed the whole perimeter, as it may well have done, it would have been 850m long and consisted of some 2,500 separate timbers. On the western side, the palisade crossed one of the entrances, showing that it was not part of the original henge design but added afterwards. The ditch was dug in 1780 bc (2200 BC) and the palisade was raised about 30 years later. There were two narrow entrances through the palisade opposite the north and east entrance causeways across the ditch: these were marked by pairs of huge posts, 1.5m in diameter and set 1.5m apart. Their enormous girth implies that they may have risen to a great height, perhaps as ceremonial dipylon gates, and may therefore have been major landmarks in their own right.

The monument as a whole represents an enormous collective endeavour, comparable to Avebury, but executed in timber rather than stone. Whether the enclosure was designed as a purely secular defensive settlement or as a religious sanctuary is not known. Nevertheless, at the end of the neolithic, Mount Pleasant had emerged as the most important 'central place' in south Dorset, and was probably a tribal centre rivalling Knowlton, Stonehenge, Marden and Avebury (see Figures 26 and 28).

NEW LITTLEWOOD FARM   **Muckleford**   SY: 627925
LONG BARROW

An earthen long barrow 40m long.

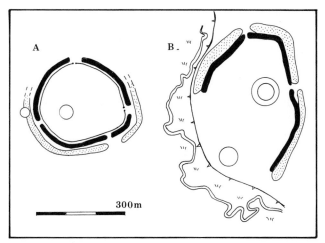

Figure 28   Two Wessex superhenges. A – Mount Pleasant, Dorset,   B – Marden, Wiltshire.

NINE BARROW DOWN LONG BARROW

Corfe Castle   SY: 995815

A well-preserved earthen long barrow 34m long, 14m wide and 2m high, oriented roughly W–E on the summit of the Purbeck Hills. It forms the focus of a linear barrow cemetery consisting of some 17 round barrows which vary considerably in size. The second barrow from the western end is conspicuous, with four causeways across its circular ditch suggesting an inheritance from the causewayed enclosure tradition of the middle neolithic.

NINE STONES

Winterbourne Abbas   SY: 610904

Carefully protected inside an enclosure of iron railings, this beautiful little circle 8.5m in diameter contains nine stones of very unequal sizes. Two are large, approaching 2m in height, while the rest stand no higher than stools. Two of them have been engulfed by the roots of a beech tree and the monument as a whole has been enveloped in woodland. The circle may be complete, although a gap on the side nearest the road implies that there may once have been a tenth stone. The Nine Stones stand right in the bottom of a narrow valley, an unusual site for a stone circle.

PARSONAGE HILL

Gussage St Michael   ST: 981113

An oval barrow 26m long, 20m wide and 0.6m high.

PENTRIDGE BANK BARROW

Pentridge

SU: 040190

Richard Bradley (1983) has suggested that the two substantial long barrows 91m and 54m long at the northern end of the Dorset Cursus should be treated as a single bank barrow. Bradley follows Richard Atkinson in thinking that there is a close relationship between bank barrows and cursus monuments. The cursus is often much longer than the bank barrow, and the bank barrow has only a single ditched bank, but the main difference should be seen as one of scale. The 'tail' at Pentridge seems to be an extension of the original long barrow, to turn it into a longer feature in much the same way that the Dorset Cursus was itself lengthened, at least once and perhaps twice. On the other hand, there is a distinct, well-marked gap between the two long barrows, just as there is between the 'tail' barrow and the round barrow beyond, so the issue must remain open.

Other long barrows at Pentridge, the destination of the Dorset Cursus, include one at SU: 041187 (100m long and in poor condition), one at 039195 (30m long) and another at SU: 025169 (40m long). It is regrettable that the terminus of the Dorset Cursus itself has been obliterated by ploughing, and that so little survives here of what must have been an important ceremonial focus. Interestingly, the linear zone marked by the Dorset Cursus terminus and its row of accompanying barrows was to become an important boundary in the Romano-British period, when it was marked by the Bokerley Dyke (Figure 29).

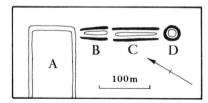

Figure 29   The north-east end of the Dorset Cursus (A). It may be that long barrow C was added to long barrow B to make a bank barrow. Barrow D is a round barrow built on the same axis. Neolithic and bronze age barrow builders were fond of developing linear cemeteries of this kind.

PENTRIDGE HILL

Cranborne

SU: 041169

A settlement site in the hollow of a south-east-oriented valley on the flank of Pentridge Hill, about 200m SE of the hilltop. The site was found as a result of surface finds of flint implements.

PIGEON HOUSE LONG BARROW
Winterbourne Abbas   SY: 627925

A poorly preserved long barrow 43m long, 18m wide and 1m high. Its long axis runs NW–SE. Another long barrow stands on the next spur to the east, at the same altitude and with the same orientation.

PIMPERNE LONG BARROW   **Tarrant Hinton**   ST: 917105

This was the medieval meeting place of Longbarrow Hundred. The hundred takes its name from this very fine and well-preserved chambered barrow 107m long, 27m wide and 2.4m high. It has well-marked side ditches, which are separated from the mound by a level berm. Its long axis is oriented NNW–SSE.

PISTLE DOWN LONG BARROW
Verwood   SU: 097105

The site of a small long barrow, once 20m long, 16m wide and 1.5m high, but now gone. Its exact location on Boveridge Heath is not known.

PORTESHAM HILL LONG BARROW
SY: 605867

A chambered long barrow site. Its long axis was oriented NW–SE and it stood on the summit of the steep hill overlooking Portesham.

RACE DOWN LONG BARROW
Blandford Camp   ST: 929088

A long barrow 35m long, 15m wide and 1.5m high. The site is hemmed in by buildings on three sides, but is nevertheless in fairly good condition.

RED BARN LONG BARROW   **Winterbourne Abbas**   SY: 637923

A long barrow 37m long, 18m wide and 1m high, with no visible ditches. Its long axis is oriented NNW–SSE.

ROOKERY FARM   **Farnham**   ST: 942168

A flintworking site indicated by surface finds or large quantities of worked flint debris. The site is on a gently sloping spur, just south of Tollard Royal.

SEVEN BARROW PLANTATION SY: 647923

A short long barrow 27m long, 13m wide and 1m high; there is a longer long barrow close by at SY: 648924, which is 64m long and 11m wide.

SLAUGHTER BARROW Gillingham ST: 787272

A long barrow 40m long, 12m wide and 2m high on undisturbed grassland. Its N–S long axis lies along the contour. It was partly excavated in 1951 and is now in a poor condition. Unlike most of the Dorset long barrows, this one is on limestone, not chalk.

SMACAM DOWN LONG BARROW Cerne Abbas SY: 657993

This well-preserved earthen long barrow 30m long, 12m wide and 1.5m high has its long axis oriented N–S and its larger end towards the south. An oddity of the barrow is that its ditch departs from usual neolithic practice by having a U-shaped ditch rather than one with a flat bottom. The barrow stands on undisturbed grassland, and a bronze age settlement was built beside it.

SUTTON POYNTZ Bincombe SY: 703847

A settlement site on the crest of a ridge which carried a distinct linear barrow cemetery. The settlement may well have existed before the barrow cemetery was established.

TELEGRAPH CLUMP LONG BARROW Blandford Camp ST: 922093

A long barrow 96m long, 24m wide and 3m high. Its long axis is oriented NW–SE.

THICKTHORN LONG BARROWS Gussage St Michael ST: 970124 and 971122

Two long barrows lying parallel to the road, at the south-west end of the Dorset Cursus, for which they may well have been the starting point. The northern barrow, Thickthorn Long, is 46m long, 20m wide and 2m high, and is enclosed by a U-shaped ditch. It appears not to have been opened. The southern barrow, Thickthorn Short, was totally excavated in 1933. Before excavation it was 30m long, 18m wide and 2m high; it too had a U-shaped ditch. No primary burials were discovered, but traces of a turf structure within the barrow suggest that there may have been some kind of mortuary building or mortuary enclosure at

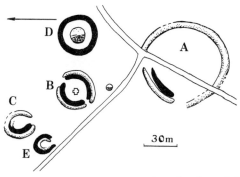

Figure 30 The Knowlton Circles. A – South Circle, B – Central Circle, C – North Circle, D – Great Barrow, E – 'Old Churchyard'. The ditch surrounding the Great Barrow has been filled in.

the east end. Outside it was a large post-hole, with two others close by. Windmill Hill pottery was found in the barrow. Three secondary burials were later added to the mound, two of them with beakers. Two chalk phalli were found in the ditch. A red deer antler from the buried soil under the barrow has been radiocarbon dated to 3210 bc (3840 BC). It has been suggested that the dated antler was contaminated in some way to give a false date; but, even if the barrow seems unexpectedly old, we should take the early date at its face value. The history of British neolithic studies over the last 50 years has been one of repeated revision in favour of older dates; time and again we have been surprised to find that a particular monument or type of monument is earlier than we thought.

TOLLARD FARNHAM LONG BARROW   Farnham   ST: 947157

A long barrow 44m long, 15m wide and 0.6m high. It was discovered in 1981 on arable land.

VALLEY OF STONES   Littlebredy   SY: 597877

This is the likely source of stone for most of the megalithic monuments in southern Dorset. The blocks seem to have been weathered, transported and deposited as a result of periglacial action during cold stages of the ice age.

WOR BARROW   Sixpenny Handley   SU: 012172

A long barrow 46m long, imposingly sited on gently sloping land near the broad convex summit of a ridge; it is false-crested, implying that it was meant to be seen from the valley slopes to the east. It is also within a few hundred metres of the Dorset Cursus, a funerary processional way which passes to the south. Wor Barrow is still clearly visible as a skyline feature from the road, although it only becomes apparent on close inspection that it is not the original barrow that we see but the spoil-heaps of Pitt-Rivers' classic 1893–4 excavation. Visible at the site is the only permanently exposed long barrow ditch in southern England, since the excavation was deliberately not back-filled. Pitt-Rivers had the ditch fill and the mound material carefully shaped into a surrounding rampart to make an amphitheatre in which his private band could give alfresco performances.

The barrow was apparently built in two stages. First, a rectangular wooden mortuary enclosure 27m by 11m was built, with a narrow entrance at the south-east. Outside this, a shallow ditch was dug as a series of connected pits. A large totem pole was erected inside the enclosure, and beside it were deposited the bodies of six people. Turves were placed over the bodies to make a kind of hut. Then a larger ditch was excavated, destroying most of the earlier ditch. The material quarried out of the ditch was piled up over the mortuary enclosure to make a long barrow 46m long, 22m wide and about 6m high. It looks as if the walls of the mortuary enclosure may have formed the original outer retaining wall of the barrow, producing the chalk longhouse form familiar from other sites, such as Fussell's Lodge. At the south-east end, two projections of the palisade bedding trench imply that there may have been a 'blind' porch, also reminiscent of the design of Fussell's Lodge.

All the mound material was cleared away by Pitt-Rivers, and it now stands in heaps forming an enclosing rampart. It would be a relatively simple matter to rebuild this once-fine long barrow, and restore it to its neolithic splendour. It is a great pity that no long barrow in southern England has been fully restored to its original state, and Wor Barrow would seem the obvious candidate for a restoration of this kind (Plate 3).

WYKE DOWN HENGE   Woodcutts   SU: 006153

A single-entrance henge marked by a ring of pits. The ditch fill has been radiocarbon dated to 4040–4150 bp (2600–2750 BC). This is therefore one of the earlier henges, some 500 years older than Maumbury Rings. The comparable dates for the Down Farm neolithic pits suggest that this settlement site was in use at the same time as the henge. Both are associated with Grooved ware pottery and may have been used by the same people.

ESSEX

CHELMSFORD CURSUS

This cursus monument is clearly visible on air photographs as a cropmark. It has the usual straight parallel sides and a squared-off end. There are also probable examples of cursus monuments at Lawford, Great Hollow, Wormingford, Little Horkesley and Dedham.

GRANGE FARM LONG BARROW   Lawford

The status of this monument is uncertain, but it is of particular interest in that it may prove to be the only long barrow in Essex. In 1970 it survived to a height of 1m and was 50m long. There are several rectangular and oval enclosures 75–100m long in Essex which may turn out to be the ploughed-down remains of long barrows; alternatively, they may prove to be the remains of mortuary enclosures in which case they will still date from the neolithic period.

LITTLE BROMLEY HENGE   TM: 274089

A circular enclosure with two entrances, diametrically opposed. The enclosing ditch, which is 3.5m wide, forms a circle 20m in diamater. It is visible on air photographs, but has not been excavated. There are other likely Essex henges at Tendring, Great Wigborough (45m in diameter), Boxted, Lawford and Romford.

ORSETT CAUSEWAYED ENCLOSURE   TQ: 653806

A causewayed enclosure discovered as a result of aerial survey in 1973. It occupied a prominent position on sloping ground on a remnant of the Boyn Hill Terrace, overlooking the Thames valley, with what seems to have been its main entrance to the north-west. It was surrounded by three concentric circuits of interrupted ditches. The inner circuit was about 80–95m in diameter; a gap of 30–40m separated the inner circuit from the next. The third, outer, circuit lay some 10m beyond this. The circuits of ditches are incomplete on the south side; they may have been eroded away there, or perhaps the monument was C-shaped from the beginning, like the enclosure at Broome Heath. The 2m-high bank between the outer and middle ditches was made of gravel and probably revetted with turf to hold it in place. Three metres inside the middle ditch was a palisade trench which was dated to 3500 BC. Controversy over the enclosure's function continues, but at the time of writing a ritual, and particularly a funerary, use seems the most likely (Figure 31).

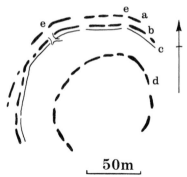

Figure 31 Orsett causewayed enclosure. a – outer ditch, b – middle ditch (bank between a and b not shown), c – timber palisade, d – inner ditch, e – entrances, one at least with a complicated gateway.

SPRINGFIELD CURSUS
TL: 726066

This cursus monument was discovered as a cropmark near the River Chelmer, east of Chelmsford. The ditches were 3.5m wide, 1m deep, 40m apart, and ran SW–NE for about 670m. The ends were neatly squared off. Within the cursus was a C-shaped setting of post-holes; it may well originally have been a complete circle 25m in diameter. Although the cursus ditches were composed of regular, straight segments, they show slight variations in direction, just like the ditches of the causewayed enclosures; probably the different segments were made at different times.

STONE POINT
Walton-on-the-Naze TM: 248257

A settlement site. The settlement consisted of circular pit dwellings 4.5m in diameter and made of interlaced branches.

TYE FIELD
Lawford TM: 088308

An enclosure which is sometimes referred to as a henge, but is more probably a settlement site. When excavated in 1962–3, the site still survived as a low mound: by 1971, it had been almost completely flattened by ploughing. The enclosure was defined by an irregular segmented ditch, with entrance causeways on opposite sides. The outer face of the internal bank was held up by a post and wattle fence. Within the bank was an area 12m by 11m, with a small centrally placed dwelling. No trace of the post-holes of the dwelling survived, but there was a thick layer

104

of black ash which had been trampled down to make its floor. Most of the finds from the site – Grooved ware pottery, flints, bone pins, pig and cattle bones, and four arrow-heads – were discovered on this dwelling-floor.

GLOUCESTERSHIRE

AVENING BURIAL CHAMBERS   ST: 879983

In 1806 the Revd Nathaniel Thornbury excavated a long barrow that lay to the south-east of the hamlet of Nag's Head: this was probably the long barrow 61m long and 23m wide at ST: 895978. Inside it he found three stone chambers, one containing eight skeletons and another containing three. After his excavation, Thornbury had the chambers taken out of the barrow and reconstructed in a field next to the rectory gardens, which is where they still stand today.

The westernmost chamber is rectangular in plan and measures 1.5m long by 0.9m wide. There is no capstone. The central chamber is also rectangular, 1.7m long and 0.9m wide, walled with five uprights and roofed by a single capstone. A notched stone at the front is probably one half of a porthole entrance to the chamber. The eastern chamber is also rectangular, measuring 1.8m by 2m, with six wallstones and a large roofstone. It has a porthole entrance, a hole created by making semicircular cuts into the adjoining faces of two upright stones, just large enough to pass a bundle of human bones through.

BELAS KNAP   **Charlton Abbots**   SP: 021254

By the beginning of the twentieth century, this fine Cotswold-Severn chambered tomb had already been reduced to a ruin by many digs; it consisted then of little more than a pile of stones with a deep trench running through it from north to south.

Careful restoration in 1928 has produced the tomb as we now see it. The barrow is 52m long, 18m wide at the northern end, 3.7m high, and enclosed by its original revetment wall, a conspicuous feature of this type of tomb. The most attractive feature of the barrow is the false entrance between the bulging, convex horns at the north end. The door lintel and much of the walling of the horns belongs to the twentieth-century reconstruction. The skull of a man and the bones of five children were discovered in the rubble blocking behind the false door during the 1928–31 excavations; this area was already badly disturbed, so the original position of these remains is not certain. There are two burial chambers halfway along the barrow, a third chamber on the south-east side and a cist, which has been restored, at the south end. The 'side chambers' may originally have been free-standing tombs, later incorporated in the long cairn, as at Dyffryn Ardudwy in Gwynedd. All the entrance passages to these chambers were sealed off in the neolithic, but since restoration they have been left open so that their interiors can be seen. It is not certain what the original form of the chamber roofs may have taken, but corbelling seems likely. The remains of about 30 people have been found in the barrow during the excavations, together with a few pieces of neolithic pottery and flint.

CONDICOTE HENGE   SP: 153284

North of Bourton-on-the-Water lies the only known example of a henge in Gloucestershire. It has a single entrance and is 100m across. Charcoal from the secondary fill of the ditch has been radiocarbon dated to 3700 bp (about 2150 BC).

COW COMMON LONG   Swell   SP: 135264
BARROW AND CEMETERY

The overgrown and badly damaged long barrow is of the false entrance type, 45m long, 23m wide and 1.5m high. Two stone-built chambers contained the remains of ten adults and an infant, as well as pieces of neolithic pottery and clay 'spoons'.

The round barrows in the cemetery have also suffered from the plough. On the edge of the field to the west of the long barrow are the remains of five round barrows in a row: some of them overlap. Canon Greenwell opened them and found both crouched and cremated burials inside them. The second barrow from the south covered a circular, beehive-shaped chamber which was entered by a 6m long passage from the west. It had been robbed of its contents, but its architectural type has been seen elsewhere in Gloucestershire.

CRICKLEY HILL   Coberley   SO: 928161

The iron age promontory fort represents only the last stage in the development of a site which had a long, complex and turbulent history (Figure 32). In about 3500 BC two arcs of causewayed ditches with internal stone banks were constructed across the neck of the spur. During succeeding years the ditches were filled and recut several times, a procedure followed at other causewayed enclosures, and one which seems to have had some ritual significance. The whole site was then remodelled, with new, deeper quarry ditches and a rampart faced with drystone walling on its outer side and a timber stockade on the back, the whole structure topped with a wooden fence. Inside this substantial fortification, there were houses and roadways, the site as a whole then constituting nothing less than a fortified village. This feature alone makes Crickley Hill a fascinating site, because there are very few neolithic sites in Britain that show an undisputable interest in defence – and defence, in its turn, implies aggression from another quarter. Two gateways pierced the defensive wall, 3m and 5m wide, with post-holes showing that they were closed by substantial gates. Clear evidence of burning and a scatter

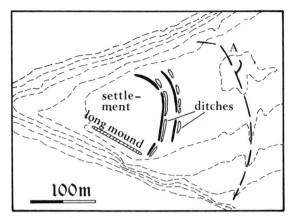

Figure 32 Crickley Hill causewayed enclosure. A – line of iron age fortification.

of over 200 arrow-heads imply that Crickley Hill was attacked and burnt down in about 2500 BC, giving us a rare glimpse of warfare in the late neolithic period (Figure 33).

There were other late neolithic settlement sites in the area (such as Carn, Gloucester, Barnwood, Tewkesbury, Salmonsbury and Bourton-on-the-Water), but they all had Peterborough ware. Crickley Hill alone (so far) has yielded Grooved ware pottery, which suggests that it was a special site of some kind.

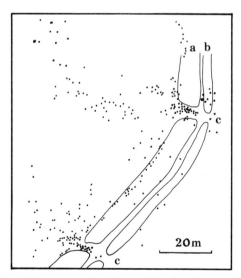

Figure 33 Crickley Hill causewayed enclosure. The distribution of flint arrow-heads vididly shows the pattern of an attack on the neolithic defences. a – bank with palisade along the top, b – ditch, c – entrances.

The western tip of the spur was developed as a shrine area early on. In 2700 BC the sacred area was marked out with a cobbled stone platform surrounded by low fences and approached by a narrow fenced path. A stone barred direct access to the platform from the path, and wear marks on the land surface show that people went round it to the left and passed through some sort of gate onto the platform. This was kept scrupulously clean, and yet piles of bone, antlers, flint and pottery were gradually built outwards from its edges: these may have been heaps of votive offerings. A small, three-sided wooden and stone building was raised at the west end of the platform, with its open side facing the path, and fires were lit outside this cult house. The ritual platform was later destroyed.

Much later on, towards 2300 BC, the west end of the processional way was covered with a cairn and a stone circle raised there. The interior of the stone circle was cobbled and at its centre a large stone was placed; burnt offerings were made at this slab. The cairn was later extended, to make a long mound, 100m long and 4m wide, out of topsoil that seems to have been brought into the site from elsewhere. At the east end of the long mound was a semi-circular paved area, in effect a forecourt, and a large post-hole, which may have been a socket for a marker post or a totem pole: this could have its shadow the length of the mound, perhaps at the midwinter sunrise. At the west end another paved area served as some sort of ritual focus. The long mound was built right across the razed site of the neolithic settlement.

Wear by trampling suggests that many people processed along the side of the long mound, and then moved (walking or dancing?) clockwise round inside the stone circle. This is one of the first, exciting, detailed glimpses of neolithic ritual activity, and it implies that a whole world once thought to be unknowable and lost beyond recall may one day be accessible to us.

The long mound can still be seen on Crickley Hill, but not the stone ring at its west end, which has been reburied for its own safety. There is no surface trace of the destroyed neolithic settlement, and, in fact, little to suggest that this is a key site in British archaeology (see Figure 32).

EASTLEACH CAUSEWAYED ENCLOSURE   SP: 215048

This causewayed enclosure was discovered from air photographs in the 1970s; a peculiarity of the site is that it seems to become more distinct on successive air photographs. Photographs taken in 1986 show as many as four circuits of interrupted ditches, arranged in two pairs. The inner pair, set close together, are narrow. The outer pair, 40m further out, are much broader. The enclosure belongs to a small elite – just out of about 50 known sites – of causewayed enclosures with four rings: the other two are the Trundle and Whitehawk in Sussex. The difference in style between the inner and outer rings suggests two separate phases of building, but the sequence of events at Eastleach has yet to be unravelled (Figure 34).

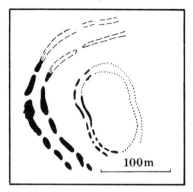

Figure 34 Eastleach causewayed enclosure. The ditches are shown in black.

GATCOMBE LODGE BARROW

Minchinhampton   ST: 884997

At the beginning of the nineteenth century, a poor woman known as Molly Dreamer dug into this long barrow in search of treasure of which she had had a prophetic dream. Whether she found any is not recorded; it seems very unlikely, in that neolithic people had no 'treasure', in the modern sense, to bury in their barrows. In 1870 Samuel Lysons opened the mound. At its east end was a false doorway set between stone horns, with a low wall made of thin drystone surrounding the rest of the mound. It is a typical Cotswold-Severn chambered tomb. In front of the false entrance Lysons found a human skull and some prehistoric pottery. He did not find a burial chamber, but one was discovered the following year on the north side; this is overgrown but still visible. An entrance 1m high leads into a chamber 2.4m long, 1.2m wide and 1.7m high. Five stones form the chamber walls, and its roof is an enormous block of stone 3m by 1.5m. A crouched skeleton was found at the inner end of the chamber. A large slab 10m from the western end of the barrow may be a capstone for another chamber.

HAZLETON NORTH LONG BARROW

SP: 073189

A totally excavated Cotswold–Severn chambered long cairn with an unusual orientation towards the WSW, where it had a forecourt. The 54m long, roughly trapeze-shaped mound had a straight external stone revetment wall. There were entrance passages opening off the sides of the mound and leading to small burial chambers. The radiocarbon dates fell in the period 4950–4800 bp (3650–3500 BC). The cairn's 19 internal cells were defined by stone walls, presumably to allow phased building, perhaps at a rate of one compartment per year. The dense flint scatter beneath the forecourt contained some mesolithic microliths.

    The Hazleton barrow contained its burial deposit intact, a deposit which included two complete skeletons placed there at the end of the tomb's life. The skeleton of a man of 45 or so, a left-handed flint-knapper, was the last; he was buried with a hammer stone, a quartzite pebble, close to his left hand. The site was cleared of its forest, probably by burning, to judge from the charcoal, and then cultivated for at least 30 years before the barrow was built.

Of about 70 surviving Cotswold–Severn tombs, half are currently suffering damage resulting from ploughing; this one was utterly destroyed by archaeologists.

HETTY PEGLER'S TUMP   Uley   SO: 789000

A Cotswold–Severn chambered tomb that has been badly vandalized. When it was first opened in 1821, workmen smashed the stones of the north-eastern burial chamber, and the excavation that followed was little better. Another dig in 1854 revealed the plan of the barrow and gave a fair idea of its original design.

The mound is 36m long, 25m wide and surrounded by a drystone revetment wall, double at the east end; the revetment is now covered by the barrow turf. The entrance with its massive lintel stone is a modern construction, and the genuine, neolithic, tomb begins at the second stone inside the doorway. On the left are two chambers or transepts, and the end of the passage forms a third. Two more chambers on the right have been sealed off as they are unsafe. The gaps between the wall-slabs are filled in with drystone walling, a characteristic neolithic architectural technique. The various excavations have uncovered at least two dozen skeletons in the tomb and the remains of two more people in the forecourt fronting the entrance. Hidden walls cross the barrow at its west end and must have been connected in some way with the building ritual.

The key to the tomb can be obtained from the house 800m along the road to the south, towards Uley. Visitors are advised to take a torch.

LAMBOROUGH BANKS   Bibury   SP: 107094

Overgrown and badly damaged, this long barrow is 85m long, 30m wide and 4m high. It is surrounded by two drystone walls, which curve inwards to create horns at the south end. Between the horns is a slab of stone 1.5m wide and 1.4m high, which forms a simple, symbolic false entrance to the tomb. In 1854, Thurnam found a long, narrow burial chamber containing a single skeleton.

LECHLADE CURSUS   SP: 212004

This fragmentary cursus was identified from cropmarks immediately north of Lechlade, to the west of the River Leach. The cursus was aligned NW–SE, and ran for about 160m, its ditches 50m apart. Only the squared-off north-west end was seen. It was excavated in 1965, in advance of gravel working; nothing was found except a post-hole near the terminus. There was nothing unusual in this: cursus monuments were, for possibly ritual reasons, deliberately kept free of debris of any kind by the neolithic people. One result of this cleanliness, of course, is that it is difficult to learn much about them: they remain the most enigmatic neolithic monuments.

LEIGHTERTON BARROW   ST: 819913

This is one of the highest long barrows in Britain, standing almost 6m high, the same height as Wor Barrow before Pitt-Rivers demolished it. It is covered with trees and is enclosed by a modern stone wall. About 66m long, it was opened in about 1700 by Matthew Huntley, who found three corbelled chambers; at the mouth of each one there were urns containing cremations, although the skulls and thigh bones were unburnt, implying that these bones had been kept apart from the others during a scorching ritual. Huntley did not fill in his excavations, which were mainly at the east end, and the barrow has decayed. It is impossible to identify any of the original walling with any confidence, although Crawford thought he could trace some on the south side in 1920. John Aubrey recorded a stone at the east end which may have been a false portal.

LODGE PARK   Farmington   SP: 143125

A fine long barrow which appears not to have been excavated. It is 46m long, 23m wide and 2.4m high. At the south-east end two parallel stones and a collapsed roofstone can be seen. There has been discussion as to whether they represent a false entrance or a burial chamber. Other large stones protrude from the surface of the mound.

THE LONGSTONE   Minchinhampton   ST: 886999

This standing stone, 2.5m high, is pierced by two large holes and several smaller ones, which are almost certainly the result of natural weathering. A second stone, less than 1m high, forms a stile in the wall 10m away. Both may once have formed part of a burial chamber. Early documentation suggests that they once stood on a barrow, but there are no traces of this today. Superstitious mothers used to pass their babies through the holes in the larger stone in the hope of preventing rickets, but it is not recorded whether it worked.

LOWER SWELL   SP: 170258

A barrow 46m long, 15m wide and 3m high and planted with trees. At the east end is a trench, which suggests either a collapsed side chamber or unrecorded early excavation.

NOTGROVE LONG BARROW   SP: 096212

After lying open to the sky for nearly 40 years, this tomb has now been grassed over. About 49m long and 24m wide, it is trapezoid in plan. It was excavated in 1881 and again in 1934–5, revealing a central gallery with an antechamber and two pairs of side chambers. In the chambers were found the remains of at least six adults, three children and a new-born baby. There were also many animal bones, including those of a young calf. Sealed in the centre of the barrow was a circular domed cairn covering a polygonal stone burial chamber which held the crouched skeleton of an elderly man. This may suggest that the barrow had its origins as a monument built for a specific dead headman or bigman, later becoming a collective tomb associated with long-enduring ancestor-worship. There are other neolithic tombs, like Quanterness, which seem to share a similar history. Above the cairn were the bones of a young woman 17–19 years old at the time of her death. At the east end of the barrow, between two horns made of drystone masonry, there had been a forecourt – a focus for ceremonies. Here considerable evidence had survived of fires, scattered animal bones and the skeletons of two more young people.

NYMPSFIELD LONG   **Frocester**   SO: 794013
BARROW

Nympsfield has been excavated at least three times, in 1862, 1937 and 1974. It has been consolidated and now lies open to the sky for all those who come to the picnic area to see. The barrow's plan is rectangular, 27m by 18m, with drystone walls curving round the east end to form horns on each side of the central entrance. From here a short antechamber leads into a small gallery with chambers on the north and south sides and an end chamber. In 1937, evidence of burning and a small pit were found in the forecourt at the east end of the barrow, where, it seems, elaborate funeral rituals were carried out. The remains of 20–30 people were found in the tomb, as well as neolithic pottery and a leaf-shaped arrow-head.

PEAK CAMP   SO: 924150

A neolithic causewayed enclosure on a steep-sided spur, almost exactly like Crickley Hill – in site, shape and size – but with a single ditch and bank. Peak Camp is about 2km to the south-west of Crickley Hill.

For many years it was assumed that Peak Camp was an iron age hillfort, but finds of neolithic flint arrow-heads altered the picture. An exploratory dig by Timothy Darvill in 1980 produced exclusively neolithic material: arrow-heads, scrapers, cores, a fragment of an axe head, and a fine serrated blade. The site has also yielded Abingdon-style pottery.

POLES WOOD EAST LONG BARROW   Swell   SP: 172265

The barrow is about 37m long, 12m wide and 1.5m high, and trapezoid in shape. It has a horned forecourt without a false entrance at the north end. Across the centre a trench-like burial chamber, entered by a narrow passage from each side of the barrow, seems to have been cut into the subsoil. Finds from the barrow include the bones of 19 people, animal bones, neolithic pottery and worked flints. It was excavated in the nineteenth century, and the chamber can no longer be seen.

POLES WOOD SOUTH LONG BARROW   Swell   SP: 167264

This tree-covered barrow, excavated in 1874, is still about 55m long, 21m wide and 3m high. Its east end was horned, with a forecourt, but there is no sign now of either a chamber or a false entrance at its centre. On the north side near the west end a rectangular burial chamber can be seen. An overgrown passage 1.8m long leads into the chamber, which is another 2m long. The remains of six people, some animal bones and two pieces of neolithic pottery were found in it. In the entrance passage were the bones of two more people.

RANDWICK BARROW   SO: 825069

A long barrow 35m long, although before quarrying it was significantly longer. G. B. Witts excavated the Randwick Barrow in 1883 and found that it was trapezoid in plan, and surrounded by a drystone wall. At the larger north-east end there were two horns; between the horns was a small rectangular burial chamber only 1.5m across. This chamber had evidently been opened in the Romano-British period and on the floor was 'a confused mass of human bones, broken up into very small pieces'. It is not clear whether this damage and confusion relate to the Romano-British break-in or to the original neolithic burial practice. Witts noted a complete lack of thigh-bones and few pieces of skull among the debris. The implication is that either these bones were treated as special and so were not included in the burial deposit or they were removed subsequently for some magical purpose; either of these possibilities would be consistent with what we know of neolithic magico-religious practices.

Witts also found some 'very old British' pottery and a few flint flakes. Outside the barrow but very close to it on the south side were several crouched skeletons, which seem to have been deposited there during the new stone age. When the excavation was over, the owner, the aptly named Mrs Barrow, instructed that the site be covered over again in order to ensure its preservation.

RENDCOMB CAUSEWAYED ENCLOSURE   Southmore Grove   SP: 003099

This causewayed enclosure stands at 220m OD on the gently sloping eastern shoulder of a south-pointing spur. It was discovered from air photographs in 1983, and consists of two concentric interrupted ditch circuits with a diameter of about 125m. It was probably open on the south side, where a steep slope supplied a natural boundary, as at Combe Hill in Sussex.

TINGLESTONE BARROW   Avening   ST: 882990

In spite of being planted with beech trees, whose roots must be disturbing the barrow's interior, and in spite of being encroached upon by ploughing, this long barrow is remarkably well preserved. It is still about 40m long. It gets its name from a slab of oolitic limestone 1.8m high which stands on the higher, northern end. According to folklore, this stone, the Tinglestone, runs across the field when it hears the church clock strike twelve. Megaliths are often alleged to be freed, on special occasions, to roam, run, turn or dance; it is as if there is a deep-seated folkloric feeling that the stones in their normal state have been magically detained and immobilized, and that ideally they should participate in the dance of life that ebbs and flows around them.

TOOTS BARROW   Kings Stanley   ST: 827031

This long barrow lies on the west side of Selsey Common overlooking the Vale of Gloucester and the Severn valley. It is one of the largest in Gloucestershire, 64m long, 27m wide and 3m high. It has been dug into on at least three occasions, although there is no record of any of these excavations. One of the digs cut the barrow in two, creating the illusion that it is two separate barrows. It was probably chambered, but there is no sign of this now.

WEST TUMP   Brimpsfield   SO: 912133

This barrow in the depths of Buckle Wood was both discovered and excavated by G. B. Witts in 1880. He showed that the barrow had been surrounded by a drystone wall and was horned at the east end. Two upright stones marked the false portal between the horns. The mound is 45m long and 20m wide. Witts found a burial chamber 25m in from the horn along the south side. A passage 2m long led into the chamber, made of small upright wallstones; this chamber was 4.5m long and 1.2m wide. It contained the disarticulated and chaotic remains of at at least 20 skeletons; only one burial, perhaps the first, seems to have been that of a complete corpse. It was the body of a young woman, with the remains of a baby, possibly her own, close by. Four more skeletons were found outside the barrow, in front of the false portal. Today, beech trees grow over the barrow and much of its structure has been obscured.

WHITFIELD'S TUMP — Minchinhampton — SO: 854017

This badly damaged long barrow lies amongst other earthworks on Minchinhampton Common. It is 23m long and 11m wide, and its long axis is oriented W–E. It appears to be unexcavated. It was used as a preaching platform in March 1743 by George Whitfield, one of the founders of Methodism.

WINDMILL TUMP — Rodmarton — ST: 932973

A Cotswold–Severn tomb 61m long and 31m wide, with a false entrance at its east end, set between horns built of drystone masonry. The site was dug by Samuel Lysons in 1863 and by Elsie Clifford in 1939. Originally drystone walling ran round the entire barrow. The entrance was marked by two upright slabs 2.4m high with a leaning door-slab between them. In front of this entrance, on the forecourt, animal bones were found and traces of burning. Two burial chambers were discovered, one on each side. The south chamber was entered by descending three steps to a 'porthole' cut into two upright slabs. Beyond this was a chamber 2.4m by 1.2m, which contained pieces of human bone and neolithic pottery. The north chamber also had three steps and a porthole entrance; it measured 2m by 1m and was covered by a large capstone estimated to weigh 8 tonnes. Beneath it were the remains of 13 people, all crouch burials – seven men, three women and three children aged about 2, 3 and 12 years. With them were two leaf-shaped arrow heads. The barrow is overgrown with beech trees and the burial chambers are no longer visible.

GREATER LONDON

EAST BEDFONT — Feltham — SU: 077738

This possible causewayed enclosure is situated on Thames terrace gravels, close to the southern edge of Heathrow Airport. A linear cemetery of at least ten late neolithic or early bronze age ring ditches stretches away from beside the East Bedfont enclosure westwards towards the southern end of the Stanwell Cursus.

HARMONDSWORTH — SU: 055782

A settlement site very close to the River Colne, immediately south of the M4 motorway and north of Heathrow Airport.

HEATHROW

SU: 088767

A settlement site at the north-east corner of the airport. This is one of at least three settlements in the Heathrow Airport area associated with the Stanwell Cursus.

WEST DRAYTON

SU: 075783

A settlement site very close to Junction 4 on the M4 motorway.

———————— HAMPSHIRE ————————

AFTON DOWN BARROW CEMETERY

Freshwater (Isle of Wight)

SZ: 351857

A cemetery of 20 or so round barrows runs along the ridge of the Downs. It includes 17 bowl-barrows, 4 bell-barrows and 2 disc-barrows. Judging from other linear barrow cemeteries, the earliest of the Afton Down barrows is likely to be the long barrow. The Afton Down Long Barrow is 37m long, 1m high and its plan is pear-shaped, with the broader end towards the east. In 1817, the Revd J. Skinner discovered some cremations in the round barrows, but nothing in the long barrow.

BEACON HILL

Kingsclere

SU: 458573

Two slight banks within the iron age contour fort, clearly visible on air photographs, may indicate the presence of a neolithic causewayed camp. Several iron age hilltop enclosures, such as South Cadbury Castle in Somerset and the Trundle in Sussex, have turned out to have neolithic ancestors, which raises some interesting questions. It is not yet clear whether at these sites there was some continuity of purpose, association or tradition from age to age. It may be so, or it may be that the people of the two cultures chose summit sites which were fine vantage points for entirely different reasons, and so made the same choices quite coincidentally.

Inside a railing on the south-west is the tomb of Lord Carnarvon, the patron of Howard Carter's Tutankhamun excavations.

CHILBOLTON DOWN

SU: 393368

A long barrow 60m long, 23m wide, with broad and parallel side ditches. Its long axis is oriented a little south of due W–E, like Willesley Warren South-East, Danebury East and Lamborough barrows.

DANEBURY LONG BARROWS

Nether Wallop   SU: 320383

Three long barrows that were once under the plough are still clearly visible and remain unexcavated. The first, Danebury North-East, at SU: 323387, is at the north-eastern end of the belt of conifers, opposite Down Farm. It is 34m long, 24m wide and 1.2m high; this one is still ploughed over. It is almost a round barrow, but it has clear, parallel side ditches oriented NW–SE, and a long axis which is also aligned NW–SE; these features indicate that it is an unusually fat long barrow. The second, at SU: 320383, is halfway along the south-east side of the belt of conifers. It is 53m long, 18m wide and 1.2m high, with parallel side ditches. It is oriented WNW–ESE. The third is 50m west of the others. It is 64m long, 20m wide and 1.5m high.

Figure 35 Opening a barrow at Snodland, Kent, in August 1844. This contemporary drawing gives a good idea of the unscientific nature of many nineteenth-century digs.

DUCK'S NEST LONG BARROW

Rockbourne   SU: 104203

An overgrown long barrow 40m long, 20m wide and 4.5m high, with side ditches. There is no record of its ever having been opened. It has an unusual, bottle-shaped plan, with a narrow NNW end and a broader SSE end with distinct

117

shoulders between; the flanking ditches are similarly kinked. The peculiar plan suggests that it may have been built in two stages, the later stage resulting in a lengthening of the barrow. This may therefore be a small-scale example of the barrow-lengthening process that apparently occurred at the Pentridge Bank Barrow in Dorset.

FREEFOLK WOOD LONG BARROW · Whitchurch · SU: 498448

A long barrow 50m long near the north-east corner of Freefolk Wood. It stands on a gentle north-facing slope overlooking undulating farmland.

GIANT'S GRAVE · Breamore · SU: 138200

Its western end has been damaged, but this long barrow still stands 3m high at the eastern end. It is 50m long and 24m wide. Probably it was originally longer – up to 70m long. Its long axis is aligned SW–NE. Its contents are still a mystery. The maze cut into the turf in the woods close by may have been created by monks in the twelfth century. The Mizmaze, as it is known, is probably not connected with the Giant's Grave in any way, although even this is not certain.

GRANS BARROW · Rockbourne · SU: 090197

This long barrow is 58m long, 18m wide and 2m high, its long axis running N–S. The ditches that surround the barrow are visible only from the air, as cropmarks, and they flare outwards towards the south, where the barrow is broader. Knap Barrow, which seems to be its pair, lies just 100m away to the north-west.

HOUGHTON DOWN LONG BARROW · Broughton · SU: 329357

This long barrow is 55m long and 12m wide, but only 0.3m high. During the nineteenth century, crouched skeletons and a secondary bronze age cremation were discovered here. The barrow has parallel side ditches and is oriented a little to the north of east.

KNAP LONG BARROW · Martin · SU: 088199

This long barrow lies close to a bridleway across Toyd Down. It is 98m long and about 30m wide. Its side ditches have been destroyed by ploughing, though there are traces of the ditch on the south-west side; the mound still stands to a height of 2m. It has not been excavated. The long axis of the barrow is oriented NW–SE, with the slightly broader end towards the south-east.

LAMBOROUGH LONG BARROW
Bramdean   SU: 593283

This long barrow, aligned W–E, is 67m long and 33m wide. A section cut across the side ditches in 1932 produced a piece of late neolithic pottery. The ditches are 6m wide and 2.5 to 3.5m deep. The mound itself has apparently never been opened.

THE LONGSTONE
Mottistone (Isle of Wight)   SZ: 408843

This pear-shaped mound in a plantation is 21m long and 9m wide, and is thought to be a long barrow. A trial excavation has revealed a kerb on the north side, but no trace of any burials. To the east of the mound stands a large block of sandstone 4m high, with another lying at its base. Both of these stones have probably always stood free of the barrow.

MANOR DOWN LONG BARROW
Longstock   SU: 335381

A long barrow 55m long. It stands on gently sloping land on the north-eastern flank of Danebury Hill, about 1km from the iron age hillfort.

MOODY'S DOWN
Barton Stacey and Chilbolton   SU: 426387

Three long barrows, none of which appears to have been excavated. One, at SU: 426387, is oval, 38m long, 27m wide and 1.5m high. Another, at SU: 417383 in the fields to the south-west, is 46m long and 24m wide; its broader end is towards the south-east, and it has curving side ditches. The last, at SU: 433386, lies to the east of the farm and is 67m long and 23m wide; it is ploughed down but has clear, parallel side ditches 8m wide, and is oriented NW–SE.

NUTBANE LONG BARROW
Penton Grafton   SU: 330495

A long barrow 55m long and 20m wide at its broader east end. It has been radiocarbon dated to 2730 bc (3450 BC). It is roughly trapeze-shaped and, as is usual with barrows of this shape, the flanking quarry ditches are further apart at the broader east end of the barrow. Berms up to 10m wide separate the quarry ditches from the sides of the barrow. The tapering plan, and probably tapering long profile as well, were a common design feature of the long barrows. The intention seems to have been to create an illusion of enormous length when the monument was viewed from the façade or forecourt end; the taper was in effect an architectural device to create a false perspective. Neolithic Britain is full of surprises of this kind.

The remains of a wooden mortuary enclosure and cult house were found underneath the east end of the barrow. The cult house had been rebuilt and enlarged, making it 8m by 6m. The front of the cult house, one of its long sides, was made into a façade for a forecourt, by the addition of two pairs of large posts or totem poles at the corners. From the horns of the forecourt, two lines of posts led away down the sides of the cult house. At the end of the mortuary's enclosure's period of use, it was filled with soil. Then the cult house was set on fire. While it was still aflame, the mound of the long barrow was thrown up over it, stifling the fire and burying the structure completely.

Nutbane is a most important monument, one that has supplied valuable evidence of an elaborate sequence of funerary rituals, and also one that shows us how the physical appearance of a monument can be radically changed during its period of use.

OLD WINCHESTER HILL **Meonstoke** SU: 638196
LONG BARROW

A long barrow 56m long on the south-facing slope of the hill at about 100m OD. It stands near the head of a broad chalk dry valley leading down to the north-west, into the Meon valley; it was probably designed, like many other new stone age burial monuments, to be seen from below, from the gently sloping farmland in the valley, where people were working in the fields.

PRESTON CANDOVER SU: 601409

A rectangular long barrow, originally 70m long and 30m wide, running SW–NE between parallel quarry ditches set 38m apart.

SALT HILL LONG BARROW **East Meon** SU: 672201

A long barrow, 43m long and 18m wide, with parallel flanking ditches, and with its long axis oriented SW–NE. It stands, false-crested, 500m from the summit of Wether Down, at the top of a steep slope down to the WNW into a broad valley. It looks as if, as with so many of the southern English long barrows, the Salt Hill Long Barrow was designed to dominate on the skyline, and be clearly visible from a square kilometre or two of lower cultivable land.

SOUTH WONSTON LONG BARROWS SU: 472362

Two earthen long barrows 120m apart, showing the pairing of barrows that is quite common (though unexplained) in lowland England. Because of the peculiar, diagonal way in which a field boundary crosses one of the barrows, it may be that the field boundaries here are actually older than the barrow; a similar suggestion, based on firmer evidence, has been made in relation to Knap Barrow, which appears to have been built astride a prehistoric lynchet, or cultivation terrace.

South Wonston North Long Barrow is 55m long, 13m wide and oriented towards the south-east. South Wonston East Long Barrow is 94m long and was probably originally about 18m wide, oriented towards the ENE.

UPPER CRANBOURNE FARM   SU: 489424

A long barrow 64m long at about 90m OD on a site which slopes gently down towards the south-west.

WILLESLEY WARREN   Overton   SU: 507527
LONG BARROWS

Willesley Warren South-east Long Barrow is 38m long and 20m wide, with two parallel side ditches. The long axis of the barrow is oriented roughly W–E, and it stands on a gently sloping, southward-pointing spur. Willesley Warren South-West Long Barrow, at SU: 496524, is 60m long, 25m wide and oriented W–E. Both stand at about 130–140m OD on the north side of the Test valley.

WITHERING CORNER   Ashley   SU: 395291
LONG BARROWS

Two long barrows, one 28m long, the other 40m long, stand at the crest of a fairly steep, NNW-facing slope on the flank of Farley Mount.

WOODCOTT LONG   Binley   SU: 428545
BARROW

A long barrow 74m long and 20m wide, rectangular with rounded corners, running SW–NE, apparently between side ditches, although only the north-west ditch has been detected. It stands at 168m OD on the crest of a gentle west-facing slope down into a chalk dry valley.

—————— HEREFORD AND WORCESTER ——————

ARTHUR'S STONE   Dorstone   SO: 318431

A massive six-sided capstone 5.8m by 3m and weighing up to 40 tonnes is supported by nine low uprights, to form a polygonal burial chamber. The entrance passage approaches at an angle from the west side and leads to a small antechamber. This is the most northerly of the Severn–Cotswold group of chambered tombs. It suffered damage recently when a post-and-rail fence was erected within its perimeter. The original mound was oval, 26m by 17m and about 2m high, but only traces of this survive. The western half of the mound appears to have been removed, leaving the chamber, passage and false portal exposed. Three of the nine uprights which supported the capstone have fallen, and the capstone itself has broken in two.

CLIFFORD LONG BARROW   near Llan-y-Coed   SO: 276428

A long barrow 13m long, 10m wide and 2m high. The drystone masonry of a revetment wall can be seen. The lower part of the barrow has been damaged by ploughing at some time.

CROSS LODGE LONG BARROW   Dorstone   SO: 332416

A long barrow that survives as an oval mound 18m by 11m. It is aligned W–E, and is 2m high at the west end, and 2.4m high at the east end. Much of the north side has been damaged by ploughing, and this has made it narrower than it would originally have been. Large stones can be seen in the barrow, some lying loose on the surface.

DORSTONE SETTLEMENT   SO: 326427

A settlement site that was excavated in 1965–70. It looks as if it was originally enclosed by a fence and a low wall on the west side. Finds from the site indicate contact with South Wales and the Cotswolds, as well as evidence of occupation at other times, both before and after the neolithic (mesolithic, iron age and Romano-British).

DUNSEAL LONG BARROW   Abbeydore   SO: 391338

An oval long barrow, 27m by 14m, lying in a natural depression, which makes it inconspicuous. It is in a fair state of preservation, but weathered on the north-west side. The barrow is oriented N–S, and stands about 2m high at the north end.

STANDING STONE   Dorstone   SO: 305422

This pillar of Old Red Sandstone is not in its original position; it seems to have been moved by a farmer at some time unknown to serve as a gatepost. It stands 1.4m high, and is 0.63m by 0.5m in section at the base. There are some interesting cupmarks, apparently of prehistoric origin, concealed underneath the ivy, but these can easily be confused with modern damage to the stone.

──────── HERTFORDSHIRE ────────

BATHEND CLUMP Moor Park TQ: 079926

A 10m length of bank and ditch discovered at Bathend Clump probably belonged originally to a neolithic enclosure. It has been obscured by an iron age chipping floor, and then finally buried with a dump of sand by Capability Brown in 1758–9 as part of his landscaping of Moor Park.

BISHOPS STORTFORD TL: 493213

An occupation site, indicated by a neolithic hearth and associated worked flints found at 6 Limes Crescent, Bishops Stortford. This site is on private land.

BLACKHORSE ROAD Letchworth TL: 233336

A settlement site that has been destroyed and built over. Several funnel-shaped pits were discovered in 1958–67, with the skeleton of a small dog at the bottom of each pit, together with Peterborough and Rinyo–Clacton pottery as well as some flint tools. The evidence of this unusual neolithic dog cemetery strongly implies that ritual dog sacrifices were carried out at Letchworth.

CLAYBUSH HILL LONG BARROW Ashwell TL: 267382

An oval cropmark shows a continuous ditch, though the east end is obliterated by a hedge and a modern road. The cropmark is aligned W–E, along the contour, on a south-facing slope. A ditch belonging to a late iron age field system respects the west end of the enclosure ditch, but cuts through its two long sides. The site is thought to be a ploughed-out neolithic long barrow.

FIVE KNOLLS TL: 007210

A late neolithic ring ditch 9m in diameter is buried under a later round barrow, which is known as Five Knolls 5.

HARPER LANE GRAVEL PIT

Radlett TL: 163018

A flint-working site, indicated by several hundred waste flakes, cores, scrapers, blades, burins, an axe and an adze. There was also possible occupation debris left by the flint-knappers, in the form of burnt flint and grey ash, and this was both mesolithic and neolithic in date.

HITCHIN LONG BARROW

TL: 197322

A rectangular cropmark 50m long and 16m wide, and aligned N–S, probably represents a ploughed-out long barrow. There are cropmarks of ring ditches and two parallel linear ditches close by.

NEWNHAW HILL LONG BARROW

Ashwell TL: 251391

An oval cropmark with its long axis oriented W–E is interpreted as a ploughed-out neolithic long barrow, 65m by 40m. The gap in the ditch at the east end may be an entrance. No internal features have been detected. A double-ditched feature leading towards the supposed barrow may be contemporary and connected with it in some way, perhaps as a processional approach avenue. This suggests parallels with the avenue features that mark the entrances to a significant number of other monuments, such as the Kilham Long Barrow, two of the Stanton Drew stone circles, the Avebury superhenge, and Stonehenge itself,

OFFLEY LONG BARROW

TL: 142241

An oval cropmark 65m by 31m is interpreted as a ploughed-down neolithic long barrow. It is surrounded by other cropmarks that may be contemporary, including six ring ditches, a second oval cropmark and a curvilinear enclosure. Overall, the site may be seen as a neolithic and bronze age cemetery.

PISHOBURY

Sawbridgeworth TL: 473137

A settlement site, indicated by occupation pits with sherds representing the remains of three pots which were similar to Clacton and Grooved ware. There were also petit tranchet derivative arrow-heads, flint scrapers, serrated flakes and bone points. The finds, excavated in 1936, are in Hertford Museum.

RYE MEADS

Hoddesdon TL: 382107

An early flint-working platform or occupation site has been identified in the face of a gravel pit on top of a gravel ridge. Worked flints and burnt flint fragments were recovered. The flints date from the early neolithic.

SANDY LODGE GOLF COURSE TQ: 097937

An occupation site in the north-east corner of the golf course has been identified from finds of scrapers, knives, cores and sherds of neolithic pottery. Arrowheads, pounders, hammers and rubbers were also found at the site. A pit 3m in diameter and 0.6m deep contained many pieces of chipped flint, a fragment of a polished axe, pot-boilers and pieces of pottery.

SAWBRIDGEWORTH TL: 484140

A causewayed enclosure site. A cropmark on a river terrace overlooking the River Stort shows a stretch of three roughly concentric interrupted ditches, but no internal features.

SAWBRIDGEWORTH LONG BARROW TL: 485153

A possible long barrow site, now destroyed. Four inhumation burials were found during levelling work on a building site in 1960. No associated objects were found. There was nevertheless originally a gravel mound here, which was destroyed before the burials were reached; the significance of the mound was not realized until it had been removed and, in retrospect, it looks as if the mound was a long barrow.

THERFIELD HEATH Royston TL: 341401

A relatively small but almost complete long barrow opened by Edmund Nunn in 1855 and excavated by C. W. Phillips in 1935 crowns the golf course. It is 40m long, 22m wide and 3m high. A heap of human bones was found near the lower, western end and it may be that more burials await discovery. A stack of turves had been placed over the bone heap, to make a simple mortuary house. A ditch had been dug all round the turf stack and chalk from the ditch piled up to make the barrow. There is no record of any other primary contents from the barrow, although a Saxon burial was inserted, complete with spear, in the barrow's eastern end.

There are eight round barrows on Therfield Heath immediately to the north of the long barrow. Six of these barrows are known collectively as the Five Hills, and they were opened by Edmund Nunn between 1854 and 1856. One of them, which is probably neolithic, contained the disarticulated remains of nine people, while others held cremations and collared urns. On the summit, above the cricket pavilion, is an unexcavated barrow called Earl's Hill.

WARE PARK NORTH LONG BARROW   TL: 337148

An oval cropmark 65m by 26m is interpreted as a ploughed-out neolithic long barrow. A gap in the ditch may represent the south-east-facing entrance. No internal features are detectable. A second oval enclosure, possibly also a long barrow, lies about 30m to the south.

WARE PARK SOUTH LONG BARROW   TL: 337147

A cropmark 60m by 26m of a roughly oval single-ditch enclosure with slightly squared-off ends. There are no gaps in the ditch and no internal features. It is interpreted as a ploughed-out long barrow.

WESTON HENGE   TL: 256319

A probable henge monument, with a diameter of 85m and two opposed entrances, to east and west. The earthwork comprises a raised central platform, a surrounding ditch 1–2m deep and 7–10m wide, but no sign of an outer bank. It may be that the bank has been destroyed by ploughing. Within the eastern half of the enclosure, there seems to be a ring ditch and there is a large 'macula' (literally, a blot or stain) just to the west of the centre of the monument, which is presumably the dene hole recorded as being filled in some time ago and traditionally the location of 'Jack o' Legs' Cave.

WITCHCRAFT RING DITCH   Ayot St Lawrence   TL: 206165

Circular cropmarks were discovered in 1970 by the landowner, Mr F. Blowey, in a field that was aptly named 'Witchcraft'. Excavation in 1970–1 revealed a circular ditch 1m wide, 20m in diameter and 0.75m deep, with a flat floor. The ditch infill contained flakes of flint waste, a jet pendant ring and pottery sherds belonging to several different pottery traditions – Mildenhall, Mortlake, Fengate and Beaker. There were no traces of a mound or of burials. The enclosure was clearly a neolithic ritual site of some kind; the field name enticingly suggests a survival of ritual use into modern times, but this may be no more than a coincidence.

——————— HUMBERSIDE ———————

BLAKEY TOPPING STONE   Allerston   SE: 873934
CIRCLE

A stone circle 15m in diameter, of which only three stones remain. Each stone stands 2m high, whilst the sockets of the missing stones can still be clearly seen as hollows.

BOYNTON ROUND BARROW   TA: 156704

The site of a round barrow 22m in diameter which has been destroyed. Charcoal from the barrow has been radiocarbon dated to 2890 bc (3600 BC), proving that some round barrows are quite early.

CALLIS WOLD BARROW   **Bishop Wilton**   SE: 830554
CEMETERY

This group of 18 or more barrows was dug between 1860 and 1892 by J. R. Mortimer. His published plans make it difficult to match his discoveries with existing barrow mounds, but this can be achieved to some extent, if allowance is made for the fact that some barrows have been destroyed.

In 1865, Mortimer opened the barrow at SE: 829556. At its centre he found an oval grave containing a crouched burial with a food vessel and a stone battle-axe. Round this burial were two almost concentric circles of posts with diameters of 6.5m and 8.5m. Some of the posts could be seen, still standing 1m high, within the barrow mound. Whether they formed a fence or a free-standing ring of posts round the barrow is open to speculation. Mortimer himself suggested that they marked the walls of a wooden hut, but this would have been very difficult to roof.

A barrow in the wood by Callis Wold Farm produced a number of crouched and cremated burials; at its base, resting on a pavement made of limestone and measuring 3.6m by 0.9m, were the remains of ten people, all adults.

COWLAM ROUND BARROW   SE: 959664

A neolithic round crematorium barrow (Cowlam 277), 17m in diameter and 1.5m high. It was excavated in 1892, when sherds of Grimston pottery were found in it.

CROPTON LONG BARROWS   **Cropton**   site unknown

Two long barrows, one of them 20m long, once existed here, but their sites have been lost.

GARTON SLACK ROUND BARROWS   SE: 978577

A cremation round barrow known as Garton Slack 80. It is 31m in diameter and 1m high. There is a second cremation round barrow, Garton Slack 81, close by, 25m in diameter and 0.5m high.

HUGGATE WOLD ROUND BARROW SE: 871576

A cremation round barrow 18m in diameter and 1m high. It was excavated in 1880.

KILHAM LONG BARROW TA: 056674

Lying to the west of the Thwing–Kilham road, this 50m long barrow was opened by Canon Greenwell in 1868 and again by T. G. Manby between 1965 and 1969. It is now badly ploughed down. The recent excavations located two parallel ditches 40m long and 6.5m apart. They may have marked the outline of an earlier barrow whose mound was destroyed before the later barrow was built. Next, a rectangular bedding trench was dug to hold timber uprights, some of them a massive 70cm square. This substantial mortuary structure was about 55m long and 7.5–9.0m, wide and oriented SW–NE. It had entrances at each end and an avenue of posts about 6m wide led north-east for an uncertain distance, but not less than 15m. Inside the mortuary enclosure a burial chamber was built out of earth and timber; in this, Greenwell seems to have found the remains of two people. Outside the enclosure, quarry ditches were dug, first only at the south-west end, and then, after the burial chamber was destroyed by fire, all the way along both sides. The whole enclosure was then covered with chalk thrown up from the quarry ditches. The finished barrow has been radiocarbon dated to 2880 bc (3470 BC).

In the ensuing bronze age, two bodies with food vessels were buried in the long barrow, and what seems to have been a round barrow was built over the line of the approach avenue at the north-east end.

The neolithic soil layer preserved underneath the long barrow showed signs of lessivation, a type of soil depletion in which the clay fraction is washed down from the topsoil into the subsoil. This was induced by neolithic forest clearance and agriculture. At other sites, this impoverishment led on to the bodily removal of the top layer of the soil: at chalk sites in southern England, buried soils preserved under barrows often appear to have been truncated in this way.

MAIDEN'S GRAVE HENGE TA: 097707

This is the only proven henge in the area, unless we include the newly recognized Duggleby Howe enclosure; even so, this site is unimpressive. It is under cultivation, and only part of the bank is visible. A trial excavation in 1964 by I. McInnes revealed three post-holes and some sherds of Beaker pottery.

MARKET WEIGHTON SE: 906410

An earthen long barrow 33m long. At one end a narrow trench 1m wide had been left open during the mound's construction. The disarticulated, and therefore previously exposed, remains of 26 people were piled up along the trench and set on fire, though it is not clear quite how or why this was done: cremation in an open fire would have disposed of the remains better, but perhaps disposal was not uppermost in the officiants' minds. Scorching or searing by fire was apparently more important. Burning was inevitably more severe at the outer end of the trench, while the bones at the inner end remained untouched by the fire.

RUDSTON CURSUS MONUMENTS TA: 098677

One of the cursus monuments was recognized in 1877, but it was not until air photographs were scutinized in 1961 that it was realized that Rudston had three cursuses. Small-scale excavation of Cursus A, which approaches Rudston from the NNE, revealed some flints and pieces of pottery that suggested a late neolithic or early bronze age date for its origin and period of use. This cursus appears to have crossed the Gypsey Race, a chalk stream which flows intermittently and irregularly, and is associated in folklore with divination; Cursus A resumes on the far side of the valley.

To the west of Rudston is Cursus B, at TA: 085671, which had ditches 82m apart. The west end was associated with circular cropmarks, which may indicate the existence of barrows or ring ditches there in the past. The cursus leads north-eastwards and, where it peters out, it is oriented towards the Rudston Monolith, the pivotal monument in this ancient ritual landscape.

Cursus C passes roughly W–E immediately to the north of the Rudston Monolith, apparently abutting on, but not joining, the west side of Cursus A. It is possible that a fourth cursus may have existed at Rudston. The best preserved cursus segment is to be seen at TA: 099658, where the squared-off end of the cursus still stands as a 1m high bank.

Rudston is proving to be a quite remarkable neolithic cult centre, perhaps originally comparable in scale with Avebury, and it seems likely that more finds await discovery there.

RUDSTON LONG BARROWS in the vicinity of TA: 0967

There were two earthen long barrows in the parish of Rudston, one 77m long and the other 64m, but they have been destroyed and their sites have not been discovered. They were mentioned in nineteenth-century accounts but not accurately recorded or located.

RUDSTON MONOLITH Rudston Church TA: 097677

Reputed to be the tallest standing stone in Britain, this monolith, 7.7m high, 1.8m wide and 0.8m thick, stands in the churchyard, only a few metres from the church itself. Its tip appears to have been broken, perhaps by weathering, perhaps by over-zealous Christians, perhaps by lightning, and its original height is estimated at 8.1m. The top has been protected by a lead cap for at least 200 years; this distinguished monolith is, as far as I know, the only one to sport a hat. The monolith is made of gritstone and must have been brought from Cayton Bay, over 16km away; the effort involved in transporting it implies that it held the highest significance for the Rudston community. Probing by Sir William Strickland in the late eighteenth century is said to have shown that the monolith is deeply buried in the ground, to a depth as great as its height, but this seems very unlikely. The name of the village, 'Rudston', derived from Old English words meaning 'cross-stone', so perhaps Anglo-Saxon missionaries fixed a wooden or even a stone cross-head to the monolith in an attempt to convert it. Similar conversions were performed on several Breton megaliths, such as the standing stone at St Duzec.

There is a smaller stone on the north-east side of the churchyard, also made of gritstone, and close beside it a cist constructed of sandstone slabs. These too seem to be prehistoric structures.

A short section of neolithic ditch preserved underneath a round barrow at Rudston (Rudston 63) is thought to be a chance survival of part of a henge. There was clearly an important cult centre at Rudston, focused on the Rudston Monolith, which must have served as a tribal territorial marker as well as some kind of idol or abode of deities. That the Rudston cult centre was an important centre for quite a large area is proved by the distribution of 'Sunday-best' artefacts in the Yorkshire Wolds. When the findspots of Duggleby axes, Seamer adzes, maceheads, chisels with polished edges, and polished knives are plotted on a map, it becomes apparent that there is a very marked and systematic increase in density as Rudston is approached; it was clearly a focus for high-status goods. Grooved ware, an elaborately decorated type of pottery, is often regarded as a special, elite good, and it must be highly significant that 80 per cent of the Grooved ware in Yorkshire has been found within a 5km radius of the Rudston Monolith. The implication is that either a high-status group lived at Rudston or, more likely, that people from all over the Wolds area and beyond converged on Rudston as their cult centre, bringing their high-status goods with them.

The Rudston Monolith is emerging as one of the finest examples of a prehistoric group identity symbol. Its site, a dominant position on the summit of a knoll in a natural amphitheatre created by a bend in the valley of the Gypsey Race, would originally have underlined this. It is regrettable that the monolith's dominance has been spoilt by the building of the church right next to it – but we may suspect that this was intentional (Plate 4).

SOUTH SIDE MOUNT   Rudston   TA: 107665

Air photographs show that this barrow is surrounded by a square-ditched enclosure, with a round ditch broken by an entrance causeway inside it. The barrow mound has been severely damaged by ploughing. Inside it, the remains of 17 people – men, women and children – were discovered, together with food vessels and beakers. All of these burials must be secondary, which implies that the primary burial has yet to be found.

WESTOW LONG BARROW
SE: 769652

An earthen long barrow 22m long.

WILLIE HOWE
Thwing
TA: 063724

A fine large round barrow covered in trees, this important monument is 40m in diameter and 7m high. It was excavated by Lord Londsborough in 1857 and again by Canon Greenwell in 1886. No dating or burial evidence has survived, but a large pit of shaft-grave proportions was found by Greenwell. The size and location of Willie Howe are comparable with those of Duggleby Howe, which suggests that it too may be late neolithic in origin (Plate 5).

WOLD NEWTON ROUND BARROW
TA: 048726

A well-preserved round barrow 25m in diameter and 3.7m high, located on the valley floor. John Mortimer excavated it in 1894 and found a neolithic inhumation deposit. There was also some kind of internal structure covered by a mound of peat turves. The burials consisted of a closely set group of three adults, an adolescent and a child; one of the skulls had been smashed into small pieces.

———— KENT ————

ADDINGTON PARK
Addington
TQ: 653591

This Medway chambered tomb cut in half by an inconsiderate road is rectangular, its edges marked by a poorly preserved kerb of sarsen stones 1.0–1.5m high. At the north-east end are the remains of a burial chamber which collapsed in the nineteenth century. The barrow is 61m long and 11m wide, with a portal stone 4m long. It stands in urgent need of conservation. Addington Park is one of a remarkable cluster of megalithic tombs in the Medway valley – remarkable for their isolation and wide separation from the other megalithic monuments in Britain. Sir Flinders Petrie found 70 kerbstones, although few of these can now be seen. There has so far been no modern excavation of a Medway chambered tomb site, and this apparently unexcavated and damaged example would seem to be the obvious choice for a scientific dig at some stage.

THE CHESTNUTS   Addington   TQ: 652592

This chambered barrow only 90m away from the Addington Park long barrow has been partly restored in the twentieth century, but without its covering mound. Controversy surrounds this mound, which may have been short and D-shaped, or a long, tapering wedge shape. The entrance, on the straight side of the alleged 'D', led into a roomy chamber 3.7m long, 2.3m wide and 2.1m high. It was divided into two by a septal stone. Two large stones stand on either side of the chamber entrance, to make an imposing façade. When the site was excavated in 1957, traces of nine cremations and one or two infant burials were found, together with Windmill Hill pottery and some late neolithic pottery, three barbed and tanged arrow-heads, and a clay pendant. The site had been occupied in the mesolithic and in the Romano-British period.

The owner has collected an impressive number of flint flakes from the area round the tomb, and just one flake of rose quartz, which implies trade with Guernsey. This in turn implies trade by sea and an orientation to the Medway estuary; it therefore seems all the more significant that the Medway tombs are clustered round this natural harbour.

THE COFFIN STONE   Aylesford   TQ: 739605

A large block of sarsen stone 4.4m by 2.4m, with others lying close to it. In 1836, two human skulls were found under the stone, and this strongly suggests that the stones represent the wreckage of a tomb chamber. The Coffin Stone Long Barrow, if such it was, seems to have been another in the series of Medway megalithic tombs, part of the cluster focusing on the place where the Pilgrims' Way crosses the Medway, which was presumably a fording place or ferry crossing in the neolithic period too. The B2011 leading from the medieval bridge is part of the Pilgrim's Way; it passes within a metre or two of Kit's Coty and Little Kit's Coty.

COLDRUM CHAMBERED   Trottiscliffe   TQ: 654607
TOMB

A short rectangular barrow 21m by 17m, marked out by a kerb of fallen sarsen stones; originally, this kerb would have held in the mound material. At the eastern end, above an artificial slope created by chalk quarrying, stands the burial chamber, which measures 4m by 1.5m and was once separated into two compartments by a stone with a porthole in it. When the site was excavated in 1910, 22 skeletons were discovered, along with neolithic pottery and flint tools. The skeletons showed such strong physical similarities that it must be assumed that the people all belonged to the same family. The tomb itself belongs to the family of Medway megalithic tombs, a group which is strangely isolated from the chambered tombs of the rest of Britain. It has been suggested that they were built as a result of marine contact with the Netherlands and northern Germany: the Medway tombs have some affinities with continental types. They may alternatively be the result of contact, again by sea, between the people of the Medway valley and those living along the west coasts of Britain.

EBBSFLEET   TQ: 617736

A settlement site that has been radiocarbon dated to 2710 bc (3300 BC). The Ebbsfleet settlement has given its name to a distinctive style of neolithic pottery.

GROVEHURST

A settlement site with large, circular, shallow hollows 3–4m in diameter but only 0.5m deep. The hollows contained occupation debris and clay daub from wattle walls, so it seems more than likely that they represent slightly sunken hut floors.

JULLIEBERRIE'S GRAVE   Chilham   TR: 077532

This is one of only three known earthen long barrows in Kent. It is 50m long, 15m wide and 2m high. The northern end has been damaged by a chalk pit. When it was excavated in the 1930s, no burials were found, but it was noted that the barrow was built of turf covered over with chalk rubble. Four Romano-British burials dating from about AD 50 were found in the upper filling of the southern ditch. A neolithic axe from the core of the mound nevertheless proves the

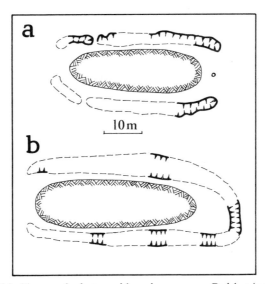

Figure 36   Two partly destroyed long barrows: a – Badshot in Surrey,
b – Jullieberrie's Grave, Kent. Note the single post-hole at the front, i.e. east end,
of the Badshot Long Barrow.

monument's early date. The buried soil beneath the barrow gives us further evidence that the landscape was open scrubland at the time the monument was built.

Jullieberrie's Grave is situated on a chalk hill overlooking the Stour valley; the other two long barrows so far identified in Kent are also in or close to the Stour valley. The north end of the barrow has been destroyed by a chalk quarry, and the south end has been eroded by ploughing, but it looks as if the barrow originally stood in a commanding position on open downland, at the head of a very steep hillslope, designed, like many another long barrow, to be visually impressive when seen from the slopes below (Figure 36).

KIT'S COTY HOUSE   Aylesford   TQ: 745608

The name of Kit's Coty House is surrounded by folklore, and yet it cannot be traced before 1576, when William Lambarde referred to it as 'Citscote House'. It has been connected with Saxon legends as the tomb of Horsa the Sea-king; it has been popularly identified as the Hut of St Christopher, presumably because it stands above what was an important fording-place. Pepys saw it in 1669, and wrote uncomprehendingly, 'Certainly it is a thing of great antiquity and I am mightily glad to see it'. This well-known monument consists of three upright stones set in an H-shaped plan. They rise about 2.4m high and are covered by a large capstone 4m by 2.7m. It has been suggested that the stones may represent a false entrance, but there is no reason to doubt that they are the remains of the tomb chamber itself.

The covering long mound, which has now entirely vanished, ran away to the west from the megalithic structure. It seems likely that a façade of four or six megalithic slabs originally marked the east end of the monument, rather like that at The Chestnuts tomb. In 1723, a correspondent of William Stukeley's wrote to him of stones set in the form of an arc extending from the north-west and south-east of the stone chamber. By the time Stukeley visited the site, though, they had gone, probably removed by the farmer. Stones belonging to a revetment kerb marking the mound's edge are occasionally exposed.

Kit's Coty is the nucleus of a small cluster of wrecked megalithic sites close to the ancient Medway crossing: the Coffin Stone, White Horse Stone, Little Kit's Coty and Smythe's Megalith (destroyed).

LITTLE (or LOWER) KIT'S COTY   Aylesford   TQ: 744604

Demolished in the eighteenth century so that its mound material might be used for road making, this monument now consists of a jumble of 20 sarsen stones that once formed a burial chamber. Only excavation is likely to solve the problem of interpreting and reconstructing the wreckage, by locating the stone sockets. Even so, it is likely that the site originally belonged to the group of Medway megalithic tombs; it should be noted that a reconstruction drawing by Stukeley in 1722, when the monument was relatively undamaged, bears a striking resemblance to Coldrum, a site that Stukeley himself did not know.

UPPER WHITE HORSE STONE

Aylesford   TQ: 753603

A large block of sarsen stone, 2.4m long and 1.5m high, which some people claim once formed part of a burial chamber: bits of other stones scattered round help to give some credence to this view. Local antiquaries felt that the large stone looked like a horse, and some have been quick to latch the god-like White Horse of Kent on to it; there seems no reason to suppose that the similarity is anything but accidental. The site's status as a wrecked Medway tomb is also in doubt.

——— LANCASHIRE ———

CHAPELTOWN (or CHEETHAM CLOSE)

Turton   SD: 716159

Two small stone circles at a height of 320m OD. The northern circle contains six or seven stones all under 1m tall. It has a diameter of 15m. There is an outlying standing stone about 12m away to the south-west.

About 20m to the south-west is a second, smaller, circle which is composed of two concentric rings; the outer circle is 11m in diameter, the inner 9.6m. Between them is a packing of rubble. There are more stones in the centre, which suggests that this is actually a ruined ring cairn, probably raised to cover a burial.

PIKESTONES LONG CAIRN

Anglezarke   SD: 627172

A long cairn 45m long and 18m wide, with a burial chamber made of five stones at the north end. The chamber is long and narrow and it is possible that it was originally divided into two compartments. A drystone-walled circular structure stood to the south of the chamber. At the north end of the cairn are the remains of a double revetment wall, also of drystone masonry.

——— LEICESTERSHIRE ———

BESCABY

SK: 824256

A late neolithic occupation site. Associated finds include an arrow-head, two knives, a piercer and a scraper. Other occupation sites have been discovered at Aston Lane (SP: 477922), Ayston Mill (SK: 861001), Broadnook Spinney

(SK: 586113), Buddon Wood (SK: 567137), Dunbar Acres (SK: 618131), High Close (SP: 445964), Home Barn Farm (SP: 488918), Icehouse (SK: 594104), Johnny Paynes (SP: 798924), Middle Farm (SP: 560840), Rye Close Spinney (SP: 561844), Stonebridge Close (SP: 797955), Warren Farm (SP: 559833) and Woods Farm (SP: 580837). Stone tools of various kinds have been found at all of these places.

LANGHAM LODGE LONG BARROW SK: 850112

A possible long barrow site, which shows up as a cropmark.

REARSBY GRANGE SK: 643141

A cropmark here may be interpreted as a rather small henge. With a diameter of only 20m, it may equally well be a ring ditch.

STATHERN LODGE SK: 747328

The site of an inhumation-burial cemetery. During drainage work here in the 1880s, 'quite a lot of burials were found, some having stone axes with them'. The human remains were reburied, but not the axes. One of the Stathern Lodge stone axes, made of flint, is in Nottingham Castle Museum. Another axe, of petrological type VI, may have come from this cemetery too.

STRAWBERRY HILL　　Charnwood Forest　　SK: 455171

Axe factories where stone of petrological type xx was quarried. These factories have not been definitely located, but it is thought that the outcrop in grid square SK: 4517 is the most likely source. Another axe factory site has been tentatively identified at Warren Hills, SK: 458151.

TIXOVER GRANGE LONG BARROW SK: 981023

A possible long barrow site, which shows up as a cropmark.

TOWER FARM LONG BARROW SP: 575848

A possible long barrow site, showing as a cropmark. Nearby is a rectangular enclosure, which may also be neolithic. The pairing of the sites suggests that the rectangular enclosure may have been the mortuary enclosure, where new stone age people exposed their corpses.

WALK FARM ENCLOSURE
TF: 012116

A rectangular enclosure showing as a cropmark; it may be a neolithic mortuary enclosure.

WARREN HILLS
SK: 458151

This may be the site of a stone axe factory, where Group xx axe-heads were made.

WIGSTON PARVA HENGE
SP: 468893

A possible henge site. Air photographs show a triple ditch circle, about 1km NW of High Cross. Leicestershire is a very poor county in terms of its recorded neolithic sites, there being no certain long barrows, causewayed enclosures or henges, so this site must be regarded as having major (if local) archaeological significance. A second possible henge has been spotted at Enderby, SK: 551002, where a sub-circular enclosure shows as a cropmark.

———— LINCOLNSHIRE ————

ASH HILL LONG BARROW   Binbrook
TF: 209962

This was once considered to be the best preserved long barrow in Lincolnshire. Now, it stands mutilated, having had a wartime dugout excavated into one end. Ash Hill is 38m long and 15m wide at its broader eastern end: it still stands 2m high. The side ditches are no longer visible, although a farm track seems to run along one of them. There is no record that it has ever been opened.

ASH HOLT LONG BARROW   Cuxwold
TA: 190012

This long barrow stands beside a small wood and is overgrown with trees and bushes. Its southern end has had a pit dug into it. It is one of the smallest Lincolnshire barrows, measuring 24m by 12m. Its side ditches are no longer visible.

BARHOLM CAUSEWAYED ENCLOSURE
TF: 0810

A causewayed enclosure standing on a gravel terrace between the River Glen and the River Welland. Three concentric horseshoes of discontinuous ditches enclose an oval precinct about 150m by 120m.

BURGH ON BAIN LONG BARROW TA: 213849

An oval long barrow 27m long, 14m wide and 2m high. It is covered by a clump of beech trees, whose roots must be damaging the interior of the barrow: it has also been damaged by burrowing animals.

CANDLESBY LONG BARROW TF: 459675

An earthen long barrow 30m long.

DEADMEN'S GRAVES   Claxby   TF: 444720

Two long barrows can be seen on the skyline from the road, close to the farm house at TF: 443716. The barrows stand above a narrow, steep-sided valley. The western barrow is 48m long, 17m wide and 2m high; its long axis is aligned W–E and it is apparently unexcavated. The eastern barrow is 52m long, 18m wide and 2m high, standing in a similar location. Neither of the barrows shows any sign of having any side ditches.

GIANT'S HILLS LONG   Skendleby   TF: 428711
BARROW

Although it has been ploughed, the low mound of Giant's Hills is still visible, and it occupies a classic position in neolithic archaeology. Built of chalk, it was 65m long and 23m wide. The mound material came from a ditch that, unusually, completely enclosed the barrow except for a narrow causeway at the north-east. A trench at the south-east end had been dug to provide a foundation for a continuous façade of timbers, which created a shallow, crescent-shaped cyclorama behind the fairly restricted forecourt area. There were also rows of fence-posts extending down the two long sides of the barrow, for some 50m, and these seem to have retained the barrow material. The mound rubble in its turn covered a platform made of chalk blocks, on which the remains of eight people, seven adults and a child, were laid. At the north-west end of the barrow stood a line of eight apparently free-standing tall posts or totem poles, probably symbolizing the eight burials. The body of the barrow had been divided up into irregular segments, possibly representing work-stints, by short lengths of hurdling. Red deer antlers found in the ditch have given radiocarbon dates of 2460 and 2370 bc (3150 and 3050 BC), indicating the period when the quarry ditch was dug and the mound thrown up.

Many of the bones found at Giants' Hills were weathered. Inside one of the skulls was the egg-case of a snail that lays its eggs only in the open air. These pieces of evidence indicate that the corpses were exposed in the open for some time before burial – an important and recurring element in new stone age funerary practice. The barrow also contained the remains of (sacrificed?) oxen, sheep and red deer.

The ritual occupation deposit, which seems to have been laid down as a foundation deposit before the barrow was raised, contained the remains of molluscs, suggesting damper conditions than were evident in other elements in the barrow's construction. This suggests that the builders of the barrow did not live close to it, and that they moreover lived on lower ground, probably near springs in the lightly wooded chalk valley floors. From calculations of the volume of chalk excavated from the quarry ditches, it would appear that the mound when new stood some 6 or 8m high; it would have been a most impressive monument, this huge fake longhouse, when seen from the slopes below.

About 225m to the south there is a second ploughed-down long barrow. It is at TF: 429708, and is some 55m long (Figure 37).

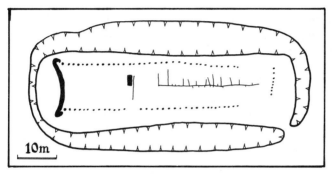

Figure 37 Giant's Hills Long Barrow.

HOE HILL LONG BARROW   Binbrook   TF: 215953

This well-preserved long barrow stands in a small wood which can be seen from the road. It is 54m long and 18m wide, rising to a height of 4m. It has been damaged near its centre. It was built in 2980 bc (3700 BC).

NORMANBY LE WOLD LONG BARROW   TF: 133964

An earthen long barrow 55m long.

SPELLOWS HILL LONG   Partney   TF: 401722
BARROW

This long barrow can easily be mistaken for a row of three round barrows, as it has been cut through in two places. Overall, it is 55m long, 12m wide and 2m high. There is no record of its having been opened, but many human bones are reported to have been found in the neighbourhood, suggesting that its contents were at some time strewn about. This may be the origin of the barrow's alternative name, the Hills of the Slain.

TATHWELL LONG BARROW   TF: 294822

A solitary large tree grows out of this badly overgrown and rabbit-burrowed long barrow. It is 32m long, 16m wide and 2m high at its south-east end.

UFFINGTON CAUSEWAYED   near Stamford   TF: 0607
ENCLOSURE

A causewayed enclosure on a river terrace of the River Welland. Arcs of discontinuous ditches have been detected on the north side. From the curvature of the ditches, the enclosure would seem to have been similar in size to that at Barholm.

WALSMGATE LONG BARROW   TF: 371776

An earthen long barrow almost 80m long.

───────── MERSEYSIDE ─────────

THE CALDERSTONES   Liverpool   SJ: 405875

The wrecked site of an archaeologically important passage grave. Six of its stones survive. They were arranged in a circle in 1845, but they originally formed a chamber within a cairn. The surviving stones are of particular interest because they carry neolithic carvings which are reminiscent of artwork seen in the Boyne passage graves, just across the Irish Sea from Liverpool. One carving shows a stylized foot; another shows a double spiral, a motif which recurs many times in the Boyne tombs. The similarity implies contact by sea between the neolithic people of the Boyne valley and those of Merseyside. The stones have been moved, and are now protected in a conservatory in Calderstones Park, Menlove Gardens, Liverpool.

NORFOLK

ARMINGHALL HENGE   Bixley   TG: 240060

Like Woodhenge, Arminghall was discovered from the air by Wing-Commander Insall in the 1920s. Both of these monuments were important settings of substantial wooden posts surrounded by a bank and ditch. At Arminghall there were two concentric C-shaped ditches, 36m and 66m in diameter, separated by a low bank 15m across and with an entrance that faced south-west, the direction of the midwinter sunset. The outer ditch was 3.7m wide and 1.5m deep; the inner was 8.5m across and 2.5m deep. In the central area there was a horseshoe setting of eight massive oak posts, set into sockets 2m deep and nearly 1m in diameter. Charcoal from the posts has been radiocarbon dated to 2490 bc (3200 BC). Whole tree trunks were raised in the sockets by way of entry ramps sloping in from the SSE; it seems likely that they were raised before the surrounding ditches were dug, since these would have made manœuvring the posts difficult. How high the oak posts reached cannot be gauged; it is possible that they were freestanding, tall, elaborately carved totem poles: alternatively, they may have been connected by lateral timbers and hurdles to form a kind of tower, or even lintels to make a set of four huge trixylons, or wooden trilithons.

Arminghall's site may be significant, as it stands on a promontory above the confluence of the Rivers Yare and Tas. Immediately next to it is a double ring ditch on which many flint scrapers were found early in the twentieth century. A watercolour painted by Samuel Woodward in 1827 shows the promontory occupied by a 'British fortress'. This suggests that either Arminghall or the ring ditch, or both, had significantly upstanding earthworks in the early nineteenth century. Possibly the whole area was developed in the neolithic as an extensive ritual-funerary complex serving the settlement at Eaton Heath, which lay only 1km away to the north-east.

There is virtually nothing to see at Arminghall today.

BROOME HEATH   Ditchingham   TM: 344913

The long barrow at Broome Heath is unusual in several ways. It is one of only three long barrows known in East Anglia in 1960; only the Felthorpe Long Barrow has been added since. The Broome Heath Long Barrow is 35m long and 2m high, its long axis lying roughly NE–SW. At its south-west end is a low tail mound about 40m long, presumably added to give the barrow greater length. The barrow is also unusual in being raised on an earlier settlement site. The neolithic people normally built their barrows on land that they had cleared and farmed, but not actually inhabited. The long barrow has so far not been excavated. East of it is a round barrow 30m in diameter.

Close by are traces of a horseshoe-shaped enclosure, also of neolithic date, which was excavated in 1970–1. Its terminals are 140m apart. The enclosure's bank and outer ditch are visible near the village hall, and further to the south beside Green Lane. The bank was held in place by a timber palisade with a second fence on its summit. The C-shaped structure could have been defensive, but the wide, open part of the circuit presents difficulties if it is interpreted in this way; it seems more likely that the enclosure had a ceremonial function. A wide scatter of post-holes within the enclosure probably represents the remains of a neolithic village, but it has not been possible to unravel any house plans from the post-holes. Pieces of over 400 pots were found during excavation, along with more than 22,000 flint tools. The Broome Heath settlement was inhabited, according to radiocarbon dates, from 4200 BC to 2730 BC (Figure 38).

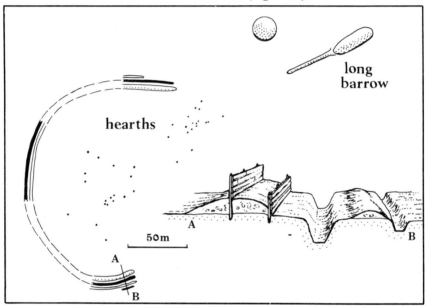

Figure 38 Broome Heath: the C-shaped enclosure, settlement and barrows. The section A–B is reconstructed on the right.

EATON HEATH   TG: 250070

A site of uncertain status on a terrace of the River Yare: it may have been a settlement or a ritual focus. Twenty-one vertical-sided shafts were excavated, some of them 8m deep, as well as the more usual pits and post-holes. The deep shafts have been tentatively identified as wells or even as early forerunners of the ritual shafts that were made in the iron age. It is difficult to visualize how they could have been dug, and it may be that they are entirely natural features – ancient solution pipes, perhaps, into which neolithic occupation debris has collapsed. If this is the case, we can treat Eaton Heath as a normal, if unusually early, neolithic settlement site. It has been radiocarbon dated to 3145 bc (3950 BC). Two hut floors have been identified, one measuring 5m by 3m, the other 3m by 2.5m.

GRIMES GRAVES   **Weeting**   TL: 817898

An area of some 7 hectares of bracken-covered heathland, its surface pockmarked by over 360 craters, represents one of the major industrial centres of the new stone age. The craters mark the tops of buried flint mines, separated from each other by piles of flint and chalk debris, and now grassed over. More shafts lie concealed beneath the flatter ground to the north. In the northern part of the area, exposures of flint were quarried opencast at the surface, or by means of simple bell-shaped pits up to 4m deep. Where the seam of flint was further underground, hour-glass shafts as much as 12m deep were dug, with three or four horizontal galleries opening from their floors. The galleries were up to 9m long, and then usually ran into the galleries of neighbouring, worked-out mines. It has been suggested that about 20 people may have worked each mine, with 10 of them in the galleries prising the flint from the walls and floors with antler-picks, wedges and hammers, and the others carrying the flint to the surface in baskets. Each shaft would have taken about four months, the galleries a further two months. It looks as if, as soon as the work was finished, the mines were immediately backfilled with material from the next shaft.

Three layers of flint were worked at Grimes Graves. The topstone and wall stone layers are of poorer quality, and it appears that it was the lowest layer, the floorstone, that was most keenly prized. The chalk above it was scraped away, and then large slabs were levered up using red deer antlers as wedges, chisels, levers and hooks. The blocks were dragged along the very low galleries and then hauled to the surface with baskets on ropes; the rope marks can be seen on the sides of some of the shafts. The miners themselves probably went down by means of wooden ladders propped against the side or, in the case of the deeper shafts, a wooden scaffolding.

At the time of writing, only one shaft is open to the public. It is 9m deep and there is an iron ladder which provides access to the entrances to the galleries. Among the other mines which have been excavated but not opened to the public is one where the supply of flint seems to have run out. A crude chalk figurine representing the Earth Mother was placed on a ledge. In front of her, a phallus, also made of chalk, was placed on a carefully arranged pile of flint nodules and antler picks. This has been interpreted as an overt appeal to the earth deity to increase the fertility of the mine.

The flint mines at Grimes Graves were in active use for a long time. The shafts and galleries have been radiocarbon dated to between 2340 and 1600 bc (3000–2000 BC). Flint from the mines was traded over a wide area and formed an important element in the neolithic economy.

Occupation seems to have been concentrated in the south-east part of the site. This is the highest part, where the mines are up to 14m deep, and probably approaching their economic limit. In the shallow valley to the south of the occupation site there are pits, which were used for sanitation and refuse. Even so, positive evidence of settlement as such has not yet been found.

HAINFORD CAUSEWAYED ENCLOSURE   TG: 230182

A probable causewayed enclosure site.

HARPLEY LONG BARROW   TF: 809252

A grass-covered long barrow 45m long, which was until recently under the plough and which is, as a result, now very low. The quarry ditches are not visible. A piece of Windmill Hill pottery has been found at the surface. A large, irregular mound to the east (at TF: 871249) may be a second long barrow, but it has been damaged by sand quarrying.

HUNSTANTON   TF: 6740

A Grooved ware settlement dating from 1736 bc (2100 BC) and containing both circular and rectangular houses. It has yielded the earliest 9-post and 6-post buildings in the country, 3.6m and 2.3m across respectively. Buildings like these had previously been known from the iron age, but not from the late neolithic. There was also a palisaded enclosure 47m by 36m with a possible entrance in one corner, facing away from the main part of the settlement: it may have been a livestock pen. Two saddle querns were found, implying cereal cultivation, but most of the food remains were of mussel shells, so seashore gathering was evidently very important to the food supply. The site was only discovered as a result of roadworks in 1970, and probably as much as nine-tenths of this key neolithic settlement site has been left unexcavated.

ROUGHTON CAUSEWAYED ENCLOSURE   TG: 223364

A causewayed enclosure site.

WEST RUDHAM LONG BARROW   TF: 810253

This overgrown long barrow is located in a plantation. It is 66m long, 18m wide and 2m high, and it is one of only four certain long barrows in East Anglia, the others being at Broome Heath, Harpley and Felthorpe. It lies N–S and is surrounded by a ditch, which proved on excavation to be 3.7m wide and 1.2m deep, with an additional forecourt at the southern end. A small pit was discovered in the forecourt, the whole of which was covered by the barrow mound. At the southern end of the main barrow was a platform on which a body had been cremated. The northern end of the mound was not excavated, and further burials and structures may yet be discovered. The West Rudham Long Barrow formed the focus of a now largely destroyed cemetery.

——————— NORTHAMPTONSHIRE ———————

ALDWINCLE ROUND BARROW   SP: 996803

This round barrow, also known as Aldwincle 1, was made of earth and gravel and measured 36m by 31m. The earliest structure on the site was a mortuary enclosure 14m by 11m. This had defining fences on at least two sides. A linear zone was marked out by a pair of post-holes indicating a SW–NE alignment. After the construction of the mortuary enclosure, a D-shaped mound was raised over it; charcoal from its quarry ditch gave a radiocarbon date of 2610 bc (3350 bc). The monument was then covered by a final round mound with an enclosing ditch. Close by was an enclosed cemetery, Aldwincle 4, a pit circle with a 23m diameter; this was later replaced by a ring ditch with a 22m diameter.

BRIAR HILL CAUSEWAYED   Northampton   SP: 736592
ENCLOSURE

A causewayed enclosure constructed in about 4500 BC, and subsequently renovated several times, probably over a long period. Whatever activity went on in the enclosure, it was not a type that has left archaeological traces. After 3200 BC, the earthwork ceased to be maintained, but the enclosure continued in use; there were several structures within it. The period when the enclosure was in use spanned virtually the whole of the new stone age, although it is not clear how or why. It was not a defensive site: the low, north-facing slope below a false crest would have been very vulnerable to attackers approaching unseen from the south. The iron age hillfort of Hunsbury occupies the obvious defensive position, on the hilltop to the south. The Briar Hill site does, however, make sense in terms of a simple mixed economy, as a meeting place for farmers and pastoralists. It has well-drained light soil, just above the spring-line, overlooking clay soils and the gravels and alluvium of the valley floor. It therefore stood at the interface of two ecological zones; possibly, like some later market centres, the causewayed enclosure at Briar Hill integrated the economies and societies of two adjacent zones.

A detailed study of the ditches suggests an unusual departure from the normal 'contiguous pits' or 'beaded ditch' pattern of ditch-digging. At any one time, each 'ditch' at Briar Hill consisted of a series of separate pits; on recutting, different sections of the ditch line were dug out. Therefore, only after a long period would a continuous segment of ditch have been created.

A small, three-sided rectangular structure marked by a bedding trench was discovered on the N–S axis of the central circular enclosure, at the mid-point of the southern half. Its open side faced ENE. It may have been a dwelling, but it seems much more likely to have been an open timber post setting, comparable with the stone coves found within henges. The Briar Hill timber setting should be compared with similar, but megalithic, structures at Stenness, Castlerigg and Avebury (Figure 39).

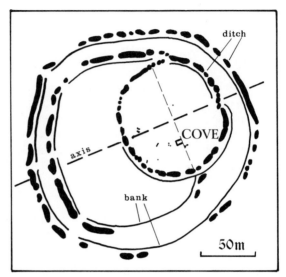

Figure 39 Briar Hill causewayed enclosure. The axes drawn in on this plan show clearly that the design of the enclosure is not as irregular as at first appears. The location and orientation of the timber cove, built in 2600 BC, are related to the main axes.

CLIFFORD HILL   **Little Houghton**   SP: 805606

A large mound standing right beside the River Nene. It has not been excavated, but it is possibly a neolithic 'harvest hill' of the same type as Silbury Hill. It is 26m high and 116m in diameter, which makes it almost exactly two-thirds the size of Silbury Hill. As at Silbury, the lower slopes appear to be composed of solid rock: only the upper half is actually 'built'. The juxtaposition with water, the River Nene, on the north side may have had a ritual significance, just like the shallow moat at Silbury. Local antiquaries have explained the large mound as a Norman motte and its flat summit as, of all things, a bowling green created by the lord of the manor of Little Houghton in the seventeenth century. Yet finds of Roman coins on the summit indicate a much earlier origin. Probably the harvest hill was used as ceremonial focus by the same scattered neolithic communities who built the causewayed enclosure at Briar Hill, 7km up the river to the west.

LODGE FARM   **Northampton**   SP: 724634

A causewayed enclosure that shows as a cropmark on a level plateau. Fieldwalking has failed to reveal a significant associated flint scatter, although there is a high-

146

density 'background' scatter. The enclosure consists of three roughly concentric circuits of interrupted ditches, although the central ditch may be continuous, with a single entrance to the south-east, which makes it rather like a henge.

SOUTHWICK

TL: 041929

A possible causewayed enclosure. Short lengths of discontinuous ditch can be seen on air photographs, marking out a large sub-rectangular enclosure; a similar ditch forms the perimeter of an annexe. An excavation in 1972 showed that the enclosure ditches were 4m wide and 1m deep: the ditch was found to contain iron age pottery and animal bones. Nevertheless, the excavation was of a very small area and the iron age material could have been from the top of the ditch infilling. The cropmarks show up on air photographs as classic neolithic causewayed enclosure ditches.

STANWICK LONG BARROW

SP: 965710

An earthen long barrow.

WEST COTTON ENCLOSURE

West Cotton

SP: 976725

This site consists of an enclosure 120m long, 20m wide, defined by a single ditch about 2m wide and 1.4m deep. No causeways across the ditch have been detected. No internal features have been found either. There is no positive evidence of the enclosure's original function at all, although parallels with mortuary enclosures inevitably present themselves and suggest a possible funerary function. All that can be said on the existing evidence is that it was part of a ritual focus in the Nene valley, comprising several monuments at West Cotton, including a long mound, a ditched enclosure, a turf mound and two round barrows.

WEST COTTON LONG MOUND

West Cotton

SP: 975725

A long mound about 135 metres long and 19m wide, oriented roughly W–E. It was composed of turves and topsoil. There is no sign of any burials. On the old land surface underneath the mound, lines of stake-holes show that a rather desultory construction method, bay by bay, as seen at many long barrows, was followed. There were also signs that the mound had been refurbished during its period of use, and that there were periodic fires. Although its construction was similar in some ways to that of a long barrow, there were no quarry ditches along the sides, and there were apparently no burials. The closest parallel so far seems to be the Crickley Hill long mound, but its function remains a mystery.

NORTHUMBERLAND

BELLSHIEL LAW **Redesdale** NT: 813014

Excavation has proved that this barrow is composed of a stone kerb retaining a mound of boulders. The mound projects into feebly developed horns at the eastern end. Within the barrow at the eastern end an empty grave pit was found, apparently dug for the primary burial. The mound, standing on the south side of Bellshiel Law, is 110m long and 18m wide at its wider eastern end.

BLAWEARIE ROUND CAIRN **Eglingham** NU: 082223

A stone circle 11m in diameter is all that is left of a burial cairn: the circle in effect represents the remains of the retaining wall that surrounded it. The mound material had already gone when the site was excavated by Canon Greenwell. Inside were four grave cists. One cist contained a food vessel, another a jet necklace and a flint knife, but there was no trace of a burial. Two cists are still visible, one with its capstone in place.

COUPLAND HENGE **Ewart** NT: 940330

This is the largest henge in the Milfield group, with a bank some 95m in diameter, sited a few metres above the River Till's floodplain. The ditch is of regular width, and squared off at the two causeway terminals. The Milfield Avenue runs right through the henge, narrowing noticeably in order to pass through the 15m-wide entrance causeways, and proving that the henge was built first. The Milfield ritual complex includes further henges at Akeld Steads (NT: 958307) and Ewart Park (NT: 956316). Although the henges in the Milfield complex are relatively small and unimpressive, the components and the overall design nevertheless recall those of other, and obviously regionally important, monument complexes, such as Stonehenge–Durrington–Coneybury, Knowlton, Thornborough and Priddy.

DEVIL'S LAPFUL **Kielder** NY: 642928

This 60m-long cairn in the forest has been badly damaged by the creation of sheepfolds along its north-west side and three modern cairns built on its summit. There may be horns at the northern end marking the entrance to a burial chamber, but the damage makes it impossible to tell. At NY: 638923 there is a wrecked round cairn 18m in diameter and known as the Deadman. It has been opened for some time in the past, but nothing is known of its contents.

DOD LAW   **Doddington**   NU: 004317

There are some of the finest prehistoric rock carvings in Britain on Doddington
Moor. Some may be seen on the rocks beside the ramparts of the hillfort. There
are others at NU: 009313, and as far to the north-east as the Ringses, at NU:
013328. Their date is unknown, as is their meaning; they may be neolithic or
bronze age.

DUDDO STONE CIRCLE   NT: 931437

This ring, which is almost 10m in diameter, stands on a low knoll. Its site makes
it curiously impressive. Five stones remain, and one of them has irregularities on
it that may be cup marks.

FIVE KINGS   **Holystone**   NT: 955015

There are, in spite of the name, four stones on Dues Hill. They are spread out
along a distance of 18m and vary in height from 1.5m to 2m. One of the stones
has fallen.

HETHPOOL STONE CIRCLE   NT: 892278

This is an untidy arrangement of stones on a level-topped knoll. Eight stones on
average 1.6m high have been put into a horseshoe setting. There are three more
stones to the north-east, one of which carries a ring marking.

MARLEYKNOWE HENGE   NT: 943323

A circular enclosure 25m in diameter, with its main entrance causeway on the
west side. Some 'very large Stones' were reportedly extracted from the interior
of the circle in the nineteenth century. The Milfield Avenue runs past it on the
west side, swerving round it as if to avoid it; this suggests very strongly that the
henge was in existence before the avenue.

MILFIELD AVENUE   NT: 939335–943323

Two roughly parallel ditches 15–30m apart mark this processional route from a
point at least 400m NNW of Milfield South Henge to Marleyknowe Henge. It
has been traced for 1.6km and it may have extended further to the north. The
avenue post-dates both Coupland and Marleyknowe Henges and was certainly
created to link the monuments together. It seems likely that the avenue was
similar in intention to the cursus monuments of Wessex, and indeed the stone
avenues at Avebury.

MILFIELD NORTH HENGE   NT: 934348

This monument consisted of a circle of about 30 posts about 10m in diameter, surrounded by a broad ditch with an outer diameter of 24m. 7 or 8m further out from the ditch was a larger circle of posts, about 37m in diameter, set in the henge bank. These bank posts were substantial, 1m in diameter, and set at least 0.9m into the earth: the implication is that they rose high into the air. The Milfield North Henge forms part of the Milfield ritual complex. A double row of votive pits 2m deep, close to the henge, produced radiocarbon dates of 1820, 1790 and 1650 bc (2250–2100 BC), showing that they, and probably the henge, were in use at the end of the neolithic.

MILFIELD SOUTH HENGE   NT: 939335

This henge is about 35m in diameter, with an irregular, segmented ditch. It has one entrance which faces north-west. A large pit near its centre, 2m across and 2m deep, was surrounded by several smaller pits. The Milfield Avenue, marked by a pair of roughly parallel ditches 15–30m apart, connected Milfield South Henge, running past its western edge, with Coupland and Marleyknowe Henges. The whole complex lies on low gravel terraces of the River Till and River Glen.

OLD YEAVERING HENGE   NT: 929304

An oval henge monument marked by a ditch 3m wide with two entrances. A pit immediately outside one of the entrances contained domestic refuse and yielded a radiocarbon date of 2940 bc (3650 BC). The site evidently attracted a good deal of interest in the Anglo-Saxon period too. The long axis of the henge is aligned with a standing stone 120m away to the ESE. The monument thus belongs to the family of circle-monuments with outliers, like Brodgar, Stenness, Stonehenge and Long Meg and Her Daughters.

ROUGHTING LINN   Doddington   NT: 984368

This is the largest inscribed rock in Northumberland, close to the defences of an iron age fort. The rock measures some 18m long by 3m high, and it is covered with carvings that include cupmarks, concentric circles, and some symbols that look like flowers. The decorated rock is visible for quite a distance and must have been a landmark even at the time when the stone carver's eye first fell on it.

SWINBURN CASTLE   Chollerton   NY: 935753

A standing stone 3.6m high stands in the grounds of the castle, its sides deeply grooved by rainwater running down them. Its faces carry a series of cup markings.

THREE STONE BURN   Ilderton   NT: 972205

An oval setting of 13 stones measuring 36m by 29m has been reduced to five stones. The survivors stand to a height of 1.5m. Excavators in the nineteenth century found a scatter of charcoal on the inside, implying that ritual fires of purification or funeral pyres had been lit there. This would be consistent with what is being discovered at other stone rings.

─────── NOTTINGHAMSHIRE ───────

BARTON IN FABIS   SK: 522329

The site of a ring ditch with a broad outer ditch, visible on air photographs.

BINGHAM HENGE   SK: 703403

This probable henge is known only as a cropmark seen on air photographs. It appears to have a central pit. The monument has been sealed beneath a protective layer of clay in advance of housing development, so, although now completely inaccessible, the Bingham Henge has been safely preserved for some future generation of archaeologists.

EAST STOKE HENGE   SK: 767488

This henge, with possibly two entrances, is marked by two concentric rings of pits. The inner ring is composed of 56 large pits arranged in a circle about 71m in diameter. Interestingly, but probably quite coincidentally, there are also 56 pits (the Aubrey Holes) at Stonehenge; the Stonehenge pits are set in a circle with a diameter of 88m. The outer pit circle at East Stoke is 90–95m in diameter. The henge has been identified from cropmarks on air photographs.

LAMBLEY HENGE   SK: 635642

A cropmark visible on air photographs is interpreted as a possible henge. It is circular, about 100m in diameter, and may have had structures inside it.

MISTERTON CARR   SK: 729951

A neolithic and mesolithic occupation site. Neolithic flints and four polished neolithic axes were found in a peat layer dated to 3000 BC.

NORMANTON ON SOAR SK: 515237

Two parallel lines visible on air photographs have been identified as a likely cursus monument.

NORTH MUSKHAM CURSUS SK: 796601

A cropmark consisting of two parallel lines has been identified as a likely cursus monument.

SHELFORD CURSUS SK: 697415

Two parallel lines visible on air photographs are identified as a possible cursus monument. It seems to have a squared end.

SOUTH MUSKHAM RING DITCH SK: 775578

This monument is known only as a cropmark visible on air photographs. It is interpreted as a double ring ditch.

TUXFORD CAUSEWAYED **Westwood** SK: 714699
ENCLOSURE

This causewayed enclosure was discovered in 1939, since which time it has been destroyed as a landform, although it may survive as cropmarks. The site was evidently in use for a long time, since surface finds ranged in date from the mesolithic to medieval.

——————————— OXFORDSHIRE ———————————

ABINGDON CAUSEWAYED **Abingdon** SU: 511983
ENCLOSURE

A causewayed enclosure built on the southern edge of a level expanse of Summertown–Radley terrace gravels, about 1 km N of the present course of the River Thames. The site was inhabited right at the beginning of the neolithic, and perhaps even earlier. The earliest radiocarbon date for the site, 4070 bc (4900 BC), really represents the closing phase of the mesolithic. The neolithic enclosure which was built on the older settlement site is itself an early structure of its type; its ditches show evidence of silting up and recutting starting as early as 3110 bc (3900 BC), and going on for some 700 years until 2510 bc (3200 BC). Two concentric ditch arcs bounding the enclosure on its north-west side were uncovered in the 1950s (Radley Road area), and these imply a precinct about

100m in diameter; the curvature of the outer, or second, ditch implies a diameter of about 200m. An excavated section across the outer ditch showed a characteristic neolithic form: it was steep-sided, flat-flooted, 2.1m deep and 6m wide at the top.

ASCOTT UNDER WYCHWOOD LONG BARROW   SP: 300175

The site of a long barrow at about 100m OD in the Cotswold Hills. The barrow was an earthen mound 44m long and 1.5m high, revetted by a series of drystone walls. The interior of the mound was divided into a series of bays, probably representing work-stints or annual targets, defined by stone lines and light fences made of hurdles. Irregular quarry pits survived only on the north side, although it seems likely that there was a quarry ditch on the south side originally. At the east end there was a horned façade faced with drystone walling. The primary element in the barrow construction, the burials in two pairs of cists, was about half-way along the mound. There were six separate groups of bones, representing the remains of at least 47 people, and only one cremation deposit. Finds from the barrow include an Abingdon-type bowl, a knife and two leaf-shaped arrow-heads, one of which was embedded in a human vertebra. This last find is often quoted as a rare proof of murderous or war-like behaviour in the neolithic, but the death could as easily have been a hunting accident: at this distance of time we have to be content with an open verdict.

Dense woodland here was cleared for farming at least twice, in 2785 bc (3500 BC) and again in 2650 bc (3390 BC), before the monument was built. Following the initial clearance, the land was probably tilled for cereal cultivation for a while before being turned over to pasture as the soil's fertility deteriorated: then, after quite a short period under grass, the site was abandoned and recolonized by bushes and trees. The Ascott barrow supplies important evidence for what was probably a very common sequence of temporary clearances in the early and middle neolithic. The monument was excavated by D. Benson in 1965–9 prior to road widening.

ASTON CAUSEWAYED ENCLOSURE   SP: 348008

A causewayed enclosure, one of a cluster identified in the upper Thames valley on the Cotswold back slope. It shows from the air as a cropmark. The enclosure is irregular, sub-circular, about 150m across and defined by at least one and possibly as many as three interrupted ditches.

BARROW HILLS OVAL   Radley   SU: 514984
BARROW

An antler from the lowest ditch fill of the barrow has been radiocarbon dated to 4500 bp (3200 BC).

BENSON CURSUS

SU: 624913

A cursus monument.

BROADWELL CAUSEWAYED ENCLOSURE

SP: 265018

A causewayed enclosure in the Leach valley, between two small streams, and not far from the Langford enclosure, which is probably contemporary with it. The Broadwell enclosure consists of three concentric interrupted ditch circles and is visible from the air as a crop-mark.

BUSCOT CURSUS

SU: 218988

A cursus monument identified from cropmarks.

DORCHESTER CEREMONIAL COMPLEX

SU: 570957

Dorchester Big Rings is a large henge monument 150m in diameter. It has two entrances, to north and south. It is the most important ceremonial monument in a major ritual complex including several other circular hengiform enclosures 12–30m in diameter. Some of them seem to have been post circles, such as sites IV, V and VI, whereas others had continuous circular ditches, such as sites I, II and XI. Site II had 20 cremations. Sites I and II yielded many artefacts as well as bones of ox, sheep and pig.

There were two phases of occupation, the first ritual and the second domestic in emphasis; in the second phase, when the ditches and pits were recut, small enclosures or pens for livestock were added. The early date and ritual nature of sites I, II and XI in particular imply that they may have been prototypes for the later full-blown henges. The henges may have evolved partly out of the causewayed enclosure tradition and partly out of small circular ritual structures such as those discovered at Dorchester.

There is also a cursus monument at Dorchester. The extensive and complicated scatter of ritual monuments at this low and level Thames river terrace site has rightly come to be regarded as a major ceremonial centre.

DORCHESTER CURSUS

SU: 575954

The parallel ditches of this cursus ran, 64m apart, for about 1,200m, NW–SE on the north side of the River Thames. It was part of an important complex of ritual monuments, the most notable of which was the double ring feature called Dorchester Big Rings. The south-east end of the cursus was rounded: the north-west end has not been seen. The south-east section produced bones dating from about 3000 BC. Some parallel lines further to the south-east, beyond the River Thames, may have been a continuation of the cursus. The monument passed across the site of an earlier neolithic rectangular mortuary enclosure; the cursus itself was later to be supplanted by a series of circular family cremation cemeteries. The history of the cursus shows how the ritual landscape at Dorchester developed and changed significantly during the neolithic, although funerary practices form a substratum throughout.

The site has unfortunately been destroyed. Part of it has been excavated for gravel and is now flooded gravel pits: part of it is followed by the Dorchester-on-Thames by-pass.

DRAYTON CURSUS   SU: 491947

A substantial cursus monument just south of Abingdon and close to the River Thames. It shows as a cropmark extending SW–NE for 2km; its ditches were 68m apart. The south-west end, close to Mill Brook, was squared off, and the north-east end was not seen. The middle section was obliterated by the development of a Saxon village across the site. The cursus dates from 3750–3550 BC.

EAST ADDERBURY CURSUS   SP: 473372

The cropmarks of this cursus were first identified on photographs in 1972. It lay between East Adderbury and Bodicote, close to the River Cherwell. The north-west terminus was not seen, but the south-east end was visible.

HOARSTONE   Enstone   SP: 378237

The wreckage of a chambered long barrow. Three rough stones, the longest of them 2.7m high, form an unroofed U-shaped chamber with an opening towards the east. Three other stones lie in front of the ruined chamber, and must once have been part of it. The mound of the barrow, which was a metre high in 1824, has now completely gone.

HOAR STONE LONG   Steeple Barton   SP: 458241
BARROW

A long barrow at least 15m long, with the remains of what seems to be a chamber at its east end: this consists of no more than a pile of broken stones. A chambered barrow was described here in 1845, when it had a recognizable false entrance. The monument was probably a Cotswold–Severn chambered tomb.

LANGFORD CAUSEWAYED ENCLOSURE   SP: 245009

A causewayed enclosure in the Leach valley, identified from cropmarks on air photographs. The lines of the ditches are unclear because there are natural fissures criss-crossing the area, and also the cropmarks of later occupation features, which may have been barrows or huts. The neolithic enclosure is 2 or 2.5 hectares in area and has two or three lines of interrupted ditches.

LYNEHAM BARROW SP: 297211

A solitary upright stone nearly 2m high and 1.5m across stands at the north-east end of this long barrow; it may originally have been the blocking stone of the entrance, or have marked the false entrance. In 1894, the remains of two burial chambers were discovered on the south side of the barrow, and skulls and bones of both people and animals were found scattered throughout the mound. Two Saxon graves had also been inserted in the mound. The barrow is still 50m long, but it has been badly damaged by ploughing: odd stones and bones from its damaged edges have been recovered from the field surface.

ROLLRIGHT STONES   Little Rollright   SP: 296308

This is one of the best preserved and most striking stone circles in Britain. The stones look, as William Stukeley wrote in the eighteenth century, as if they had been 'corroded like wormeaten wood by the harsh jaws of time'. The location beside a busy road is the only thing that spoils the drama of this very fine monument.

Rollright was, in the year 1710, the first site of great antiquity that William Stukeley saw. It made a great impression upon him, determined where his future interest would lie, and thus represents a turning point in the development of British archaeology. Stukeley's scientific approach emerged in his treatment of this site; he began with a careful drawing of the remains, and followed it with a considered explanation, as follows. 'There are many different opinions concerning these very venerable pieces of antiquity, many fabulous stories retold of them. I cannot but suppose them to have been a Heathen Temple of our Ancestors, perhaps in the Druids' time.'

The stone circle, which is known as the King's Men, is 31m in diameter and contains about 77 blocks of limestone contorted and gnarled by weathering. There is the usual local legend that the stones cannot be counted, a story that has a peculiar twist at Rollright. There are, in fact, probably far more stones now than there were when the circle was first laid out; Aubrey Burl (1976) estimates that there may originally have been as few as 22 tall stones arranged in a ring. As weathering has fragmented them, one by one, the local people have replanted the broken pieces carefully round the circumference, creating a superficially neat, but archaeologically confusing, monument. There may be an entrance gap on the north side. About 73m NE of the circle is a solitary outlier called the King Stone. This is 2.4m high and 1.5m across. Thom suggested that the King Stone was a marker for the star-rise of Capella in 1790 BC, but that date seems rather too late in relation to the monument's likely date, and alignments on fast-moving star-rises seem unlikely in any case.

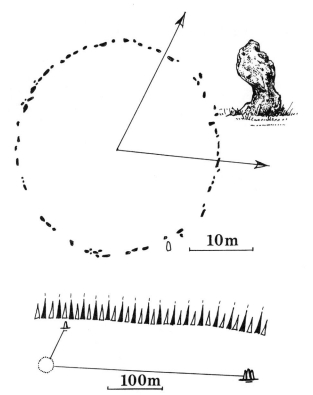

Figure 40 Rollright. Top left – the Rollright Stones or the King's Men. Top right – the King Stone. Bottom – sketchmap showing relationship between the stone circle, its outlier (the King Stone), the tomb chamber (the Whispering Knights) and the steep slope down to the north.

360m ESE of the circle are the ruins of a burial chamber. The stones lean towards one another in a conspiratorial huddle, and they are known as the Whispering Knights. Folklore has it that the Rollright Stones are an ancient king and his frozen army, petrified by a witch. The knights in their turn were changed to stone as they plotted. Rollright is one of those neolithic sites where ancient shamans and enchanters seem still to hold sway, and it is easy to be beguiled by thoughts of witchery.

The high proportion of flints to waste here implies that there was little stone-working and therefore little permanent settlement nearby. This is consistent with a view of Rollright as a taboo place, a cult site that was visited relatively infrequently and for special reasons. Close to the King Stone there seems to be a neolithic round barrow built on top of a neolithic long mound. The cairn stands on a well-structured clay loam, and this may mean that it was built on a virgin, uncultivated site. The later, early bronze age round barrow to the west, at SP:

157

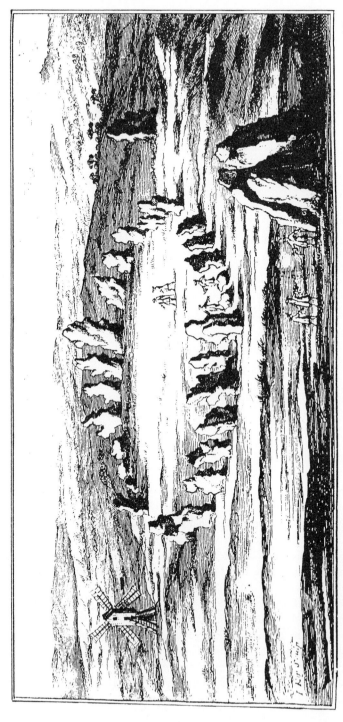

Figure 41 The Rollright Stones as engraved by Kip for Camden's *Britannia* in the seventeenth century. The King Stone is in the right middle distance; the Whispering Knights are in the right foreground.

296309, was built on a leached soil; in other words, the soil had been farmed and suffered soil depletion before the barrow was built. The bronze age barrow has been radiocarbon dated to 3480 bp (1850 BC) and is now ploughed down. Near the stone circle, a neolithic greenstone axe fragment, possibly from Cornwall or Wales, was found in the early 1980s; this implies that the people who used Rollright had trading contacts with people far to the west (Figures 40 and 41; Plates 6 and 14).

SLATEPITS COPSE LONG BARROW   Wychwood   SP: 329165

This chambered long barrow is 30m long, 14m wide and almost 2m high. At the east end there is a wrecked burial chamber, composed of three upright wall stones, but no roofstone. In the 1850s, a gamekeeper found three human skulls in the burial chamber.

WAYLAND'S SMITHY   Ashbury   SU: 281854

This spectacular long barrow, spectacularly located in a beech clump beside the Ridgeway, has a complex history. Excavations in 1962–3 showed that the monument was developed in two separate and distinct periods of construction. In the initial stage, a wooden mortuary house was built with a floor made of sarsen stones: on this the remains of 14 people were laid. In some cases the bones were in piles, showing that the corpses had been exposed and allowed to disintegrate elsewhere, though perhaps not far away, before they were brought into the house of the dead. When the mortuary house was considered to be full, sarsen stones were placed round it and chalk from two flanking ditches was thrown up over the top, burying the whole structure; the loose chalk rubble was held in place by a kerb of stones marking out a rough oval. The end result was a typical, if rather short, earthen long barrow, and there are many other examples of long barrows being raised over timber mortuary houses. What makes Wayland's Smithy unique is the way in which the long barrow went through a second phase of development, engulfing the original mound in much the same way that the original mound had smothered the mortuary building.

The Period 2 barrow was a trapeze-shaped mound of chalk 55m long, 14.5m wide at the south end and tapering systematically and uniformly to 6m at the north end. The taper was an architectural trick, to make the already long and impressive barrow look even longer and even more impressive from the forecourt end. Huge quarry ditches, set apart from the mound by broad berms, supplied the chalk rubble for the large barrow, and also reinforced the tapering effect. The mound material was held in place by a continuous kerb of stones. At the south end this revetment wall was developed on a monumental scale. Six large sarsen monoliths, roughly 3m high, were set up on end, three on each side of the tomb entrance. The gaps between them were carefully filled with drystone masonry, a

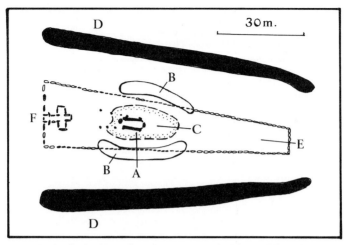

Figure 42 Wayland's Smithy: plan. A – mortuary building of Period 1, B – quarry ditches of Period 1, C – small long barrow mound of Period 1, D – quarry ditches of Period 2, E – large trapeze-shaped mound of Period 2, F – burial chambers, façade and forecourt at south end of Period 2 monument. At first sight, the later barrow seems to override the earlier barrow without regard for it, but some care was taken to make its sides parallel with the converging lines of stones and posts forming the initial mortuary structure.

characteristically neolithic architectural feature. The resulting façade is one of the finest pieces of megalithic architecture in the country (Plate 7).

The tomb entrance, later filled with a blocking stone, just like West Kennet, led – and still leads – into a passage 6.7m long with a single chamber branching off each side. Where the passage roofstones are in place, the ceiling is about 1.8m high: each of the chambers is 1.4m high. When the west chamber was excavated in 1919, the skeletons of eight people were discovered.

The Period 2 barrow was built in cleared, open countryside that had apparently been under cultivation for a long time. The two barrows, one on top of the other, have been radiocarbon dated to 3700 and 3500 BC (Figure 42).

WESTWELL HENGE   SP: 228100

A two-entrance henge monument 150m in diameter, in a field named Barrow Ground, immediately east of Westwell. The henge is visible from the air as a cropmark. In 1951, water pipes were laid from east to west right through the site. Little was found during the pipe-laying operation, other than that the bank was composed of topsoil, not stone, and the ditch sides were cut into stone brash.

Figure 43   The Whispering Knights at Rollright.

THE WHISPERING   **Little Rollright**   SP: 299308
KNIGHTS

These evocative and mysterious stones are the remains of a burial chamber, consisting of four upright stones, two of them forming portals, with a doorstone between them, facing south-east, and a fallen capstone. William Stukeley noted in 1746 that the stones then stood in a round barrow, though the barrow material has now gone (Figure 43 and Plate 8).

———— SCILLY ISLES ————

BANT'S CAIRN   **St Mary's**   SV: 911123

This is probably the largest of the entrance graves in the Scilly Isles. It has two concentric stone walls surrounding it: a retaining wall for the cairn and a lower, outer 'collar'. The cairn is 11.6m across overall, with a circular, kerbed, inner cairn 8.2m in diameter. The passage through the collar is 4.5m long; the chamber to which it leads is 4.5m long and 1.5m wide. When George Bonsor excavated it in 1899, he found four piles of cremated bones at the far end of the chamber, together with pieces of neolithic and late bronze age pottery, the latter dating to a later re-use of the monument.

CRUTHER'S HILL BARROWS   St Martin's   SV: 930152

Each of the three summits of Cruther's Hill carries a barrow. The northern summit bears a barrow with an oval, kerbed mound 12m across and 0.9m high, incorporating natural rock outcrops. The chamber is off-centre near the south-west end of the mound and appears rather cist-like despite its large size (3.8m long and 0.7m wide): its western end is still covered by a capstone.

The tomb on the central summit is unmistakably an entrance grave, 8m in diameter and 1.8m high. It has a massive kerb, broken on the north-east side by the entrance into a roofless chamber 4.7m by 1.2m by 1m high.

The southern summit carries the remains of two barrows side by side. The northern barrow, 6.5m across, incorporates a natural rock outcrop: at its centre are the remains of an entrance grave, but its original plan is hard to reconstruct. The southern barrow, 4.5m in diameter and 0.8m high, still has much of its kerb but there is no trace of its chamber. All these barrows are likely to be late neolithic or early bronze age in date.

INNISDGEN CARN   St Mary's   SV: 921127

A magnificent grass-covered entrance grave at the crest of a hill slope near a rocky outcrop. The mound has a well-preserved stone retaining wall 8.2m in diameter and surviving to a height of three courses. It was probably originally surrounded by a stone collar 3m wide, traces of which survive on the northern side. The entrance passage leads directly into the rectangular burial chamber, which is 4.5m long, 1.5m wide and 1.5m high. Five blocks form the tomb's roof. Paul Ashbee has suggested that the similarities between Innisdgen and Bant's Carn are so strong that the same architect may have been responsible for designing both.

90m N of Innisdgen Carn is Lower Innisdgen, close to the sea and about 7m in diameter. The chamber on the north side is visible. It was dug into illegally in 1950 and the contents were lost. The two tombs have been dated to around 1700 bc (2100 BC).

THE LONG ROCK   St Mary's   SV: 914124

A standing stone 2.5m tall, now secretively enclosed in a clearing in a pine wood. It leans towards the north-east. Before the pine wood existed – and there is no reason to see the wood as a prehistoric feature – the stone would have commanded an extensive view towards the west, north-west and north.

OBADIAH'S BARROW   Gugh   SV: 888085

The island of Gugh can be reached at low water by a sandy tombolo connecting it to the island of St Agnes. The site is 80m NW of the barrow-crowned outcrop of Carn Valla. Obadiah's Barrow is the finest of the ten or so tombs on this small island. It is built into the hill slope and consists of a stone mound 7.3m in diameter. The chamber is 5.2m long, 1.5m wide and 1m high, and entered by way of a short, angled passage. Four large capstones survive, of which two have fallen into the chamber. When it was excavated in 1901, remains of early burials, later cremations and a piece of bronze were found in the tomb chamber.

THE OLD MAN OF GUGH   Gugh   SV: 891085

A fine, leaning standing stone about 2.5m tall and made of granite. The ground round its base has been dug into, but nothing has been found.

PORTH HELLICK DOWN   St Mary's   SV: 928108

This is one of the finest entrance graves in the Scilly Isles, excavated by George Bonsor in 1899 and subsequently restored by the Department of the Environment. It is 12m in diameter and 1.5m high. An entrance on the north-west leads into a roofless passage 4.3m long and 0.9 wide. This curves into the burial chamber, which is 3.7m long and roofed with four covering slabs. Finds of late bronze age pottery tell us that the tomb was re-used at that time, but it was probably built in the late neolithic. A low, degraded stone collar 2.5m wide which once surrounded it was destroyed during the restoration work. To the south, there are several ruinous mounds, four of which show remnants of tomb chambers.

SAMSON HILL   Bryher   SV: 879142

Scilly is incredibly rich in chambered tombs, so rich that it has been alleged that as many as a quarter of all the chambered tombs in southern Britain are in Scilly. They are to be found even on the tiniest islet. Bryher has at least eight cairns. The one on the steep southern slope of Samson Hill is 7m in diameter with a surrounding kerb of largish stones. The chamber, entered from the north-east is 6m long and 0.6m wide at the entrance, widening to 1.4 in the centre. Six capstones, one of which is displaced, still cover much of the partly filled-in chamber. At least two more cairns can be seen close by, although their chambers have been destroyed.

——— SHROPSHIRE ———

HOARSTONE CIRCLE   Chirbury   SO: 324999

This low stone circle, 23m in diameter, lies on a dry 'island' in the middle of boggy wetlands. All 38 stones are less than a metre tall, except for one at the centre which is just a metre high. Two small mounds on the north-west of the circle are probably the remains of barrows.

MITCHELL'S FOLD — Chirbury — SO: 304983

A stone circle 27m in diameter and comprising 16 stones, of which 10 are still upright, the tallest some 1.8m high. The stones are unevenly spaced, and it is certain that there were originally many more. It is possible that, as at Hoarstone, there was once a central stone. The Mitchell's Fold Circle is a conspicuous landmark for some distance. On a cairn 70m to the south-west is an outlying block of stone known locally, and probably misleadingly, as 'the altar'.

——————— SOMERSET ———————

ABBOT'S WAY — ST: 420427

Abbot's Way is one of the later wooden trackways crossing the wetlands of the Somerset Levels. By 2100 bc (2500 BC) the Somerset fens had become a raised bog and thus ecologically less varied and less attractive for human exploitation. The local people built an unusually heavy and substantial timber roadway 2.5km long between the two largest fen islands within the moor. The alder log track may even have been stoutly made so that it could be used for cattle droving. It closely parallels the earlier Bell, Honeycat and Honeygore (3400 BC) trackways, which had by that time foundered in the swamp.

Abbot's Way was probably the first ancient structure to be recognized in the Somerset Levels, in 1835. It was at first assumed to relate to monastic establishments in the area, but its radiocarbon date releases us from that interpretation.

A very large amount of wood and labour was involved in building the Abbot's Way. Over 30,000 alder planks or split logs, each a metre long, and about 15,000 pegs made of alder, hazel and ash were used. A small section of the Abbot's Way, an important example of late neolithic civil engineering, has been reconstructed for posterity, thanks to the generosity of one of the peat companies.

The wooden trackways served people living in the settlements on the higher and drier lands in the Poldens and the fen islands, yet none of the presumed early settlement sites has so far been excavated, so the picture we have of the Somerset Levels in the neolithic is far from complete.

ASHCOTT HEATH — ST: 452405

This site in the Somerset Levels was a fenland pool in which a fine neolithic hunting bow was deposited. Half of the Ashcott Bow was discovered in 1961, and radiocarbon dated to 2665 bc (3235 BC). Close to it was found a Graig Lwyd axe, a Welsh import, in a layer dated to 2580 bc (3130 BC). Whether these artefacts were deliberately deposited in the fen pool as offerings, or simply lost during hunting expeditions, is open to speculation. Several timber trackways, including the Ashcott Track, lead towards this site from the Polden Hills to the SSW, where we may assume the people who owned the artefacts lived.

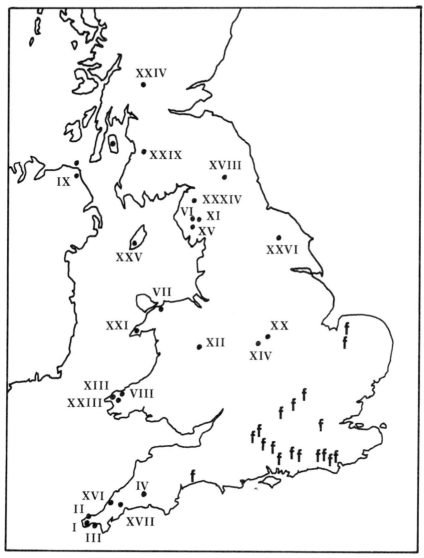

Figure 44   Axe factories and flint mines. f – known flint mine,   I–XXXIV – stone axe factory, e.g. III – Mount's Bay,   VI – Great Langdale,   VII – Graig Lwyd, IX – Tievebulliagh,   XIV – Nuneaton,   XX – Charnwood,   XXI – Mynydd Rhiw.

BELL TRACK ST: 425426

A wooden trackway running west from Westhay in the Somerset Levels. Radio-carbon dates show that it was built, and presumably repaired, between 2800 and 2000 bc (3400–2340 BC). A crudely carved figure of a seated goddess made of ash wood was found buried under the Bell Track, possibly as a foundation offering, and possibly even to enlist the supernatural aid of the earth goddess in stopping the trackway from foundering in the swamp.

CHELM'S COMBE

A Mendip cave used as a burial place. Sherds from several vessels were found along with a group of eight scrapers, which had been laid on a ledge. The remains of a man of 40 and a boy of 13 were also found there.

CHILTON TRACKS ST: 383430

A series of sub-parallel swamp trackways linking the fen 'island' of Burtle with the Polden Hills to the south. Sections of about 13 tracks, all running roughly NNE–SSW, have been discovered. They were probably not all in use at the same time; as one sank into the bog, another was built to replace it. One track has been dated to 2800 bc (3400 BC). The hazel branches used in Chilton 1 Track are long and straight, which conclusively shows that neolithic land management techniques included coppicing. The neolithic community would have found many uses for the long straight wands that coppicing produced, for example in making fencing, hurdles for sheep pens, and in building their wattle-and-daub houses.

THE DEVIL'S BED AND BOLSTER Beckington ST: 815533

This wrecked long barrow is aligned W–E and measures 26m to 20m. Its surface is scattered with loose stones whilst other stones stand at the ends. It is difficult to reconstruct its original form without excavation.

GORSEY BIGBURY Cheddar ST: 484558

This rather inconspicuous henge is overgrown with bracken. It has a bank which is 70m in diameter and up to 1.5m high, with an inner rock-cut ditch, originally in five segments. There is an entrance on the north side, leading to a flat central precinct which is 23m in diameter.

The Gorsey Bigbury Henge was built in the late neolithic, and abandoned for a time before being re-used by Beaker people. The later people deposited pieces of nearly 100 beakers in the ditch. Just to the west of the henge entrance, the ditch was dug deeper and here, in a stone cist, the bodies of a Beaker man, woman and child were buried. They were later disinterred, leaving only the man's skull in the cist, the rest of the bones being scattered along the ditch, except for the skulls of the woman and child, which were reburied to the east of the entrance. Gorsey Bigbury is an interesting example of a ceremonial monument which was re-used by later people of a later period, perhaps because of its association with ancestors and the strength of local tradition. It is also instructive concerning funerary practices; the Beaker people, like the middle neolithic people before them, were using a two-phase funerary rite, relocating human remains after the flesh had gone. They were also treating skulls in a rather different way from other human bones, a distinction which is made in many middle neolithic tombs.

MEARE HEATH TRACKS   ST: 438410

The Meare Heath trackway has been traced for about 1km, and it formed a link between the fen island of Meare and the Polden Hills to the south. In the peat 100m to the west of the trackway was found the Meare Heath Bow, a fine example of a neolithic hunting weapon.

Frank's Hurdle Track, traced near the north end of the Meare Heath Track, at ST: 440410, has been radiocarbon dated to 3500 BC. The hurdles of which it is made are the oldest known in Britain.

PORLOCK COMMON STONE CIRCLE   SS: 846446

A low stone circle composed of 43 stones, of which 10 are still standing. The circle was damaged during the Second World War; originally the circle must have been imposing, with stones about 2m high arranged in a ring 24m in diameter, but today, flattened, Porlock Common Circle is a sorry sight.

PRIDDY CIRCLES   East Harptree   ST: 540530

This important monument consists of four large henges arranged in a line on an undulating plateau. The diameters of the circles are, from south to north, 159m, 150m and 171m; the northernmost, which we may call the Fourth Circle, is similar in scale but seems never to have been completed. The First, Second and Third Circles are 82m apart, but the Fourth Circle – again the odd one out – is 458m beyond. From a trial excavation of the First Circle it is reasonable to assume that each of them consisted of banks of turf, soil and stones dug out of a surrounding ditch which was U-shaped in cross-section. The banks were retained, unusually, by a double line of posts that may have risen high into the air. The external ditch was 1.2m deep and 3.7m wide. Each of the henges seems to have had but one entrance; the First and Second Circles had entrances facing north, the Third Circle's entrance faced south. The position of the Fourth Circle's entrance cannot be ascertained.

Henges are commonly arranged in lines like this, as at Thornborough and

Hutton Moor. They are also often arranged in threes; the first three circles at Priddy, which were clearly built as a set, may be compared with the (less formal) arrangement at Knowlton and the initial design at Avebury.

No internal features have so far been found at Priddy, nor have there been any finds that give any clues as to the date or purpose of the circles. By drawing comparisons with other monuments, though, it seems probable that the Priddy Circles were created in the late neolithic, perhaps between 2700 and 2200 BC, and that they had a ceremonial function. Pollen analysis shows that the area was under pasture at the time the circles were laid out.

The reason for the choice of site is not clear. Possibly the still marshy area between the Second and Third Circles was the source of a stream and this gave the site a cult value. It is probably significant that the centres of the henges form a straight line; continued to the SSW beyond the First Circle this is aligned on the westernmost of the Priddy Nine Barrows, a beautifully preserved close-set row of eight round barrows built on the crest of a low summit. The relationship between the Priddy Circles and the Nine Barrows is obscured by a belt of pine trees, but before the trees were planted the Nine Barrows would have been very conspicuous on the southern skyline when viewed from the circles. It may well be that the barrows should be seen as part of the ritual complex. There can be no doubting that Priddy was a major ceremonial centre serving more than just the people of the immediate area: in scale it rivals Stanton Drew, Mount Pleasant and Knowlton, and, like them, it probably held regional significance as a tribal gathering place.

SOUTH CADBURY CASTLE   South Cadbury   ST: 628252

South Cadbury is an impressive place, its natural, physical qualities drawing human attention to it in one period of prehistory after another – whether for religious cult reasons or for defence. It is a steep-sided, diamond-shaped outlier of the greensand escarpment, offering superb views in all directions. The broad convex shield of the hilltop is surrounded by four sets of impressive ramparts and ditches created in the iron age. Extensive excavations in 1966–70 revealed some elements of the site's complex past.

The earliest occupation on the hill dates to the neolithic, around 3350 bc

Figure 45   South Cadbury, drawn by William Stukeley for his *Itinerarium Curiosum*.

(4200 BC), and pottery, pits and a ditch from this very early period have survived. The pits were found scattered over a wide area. They had been cut into the solid rock and refilled again fairly quickly afterwards with the clayey soil occurring naturally on the hilltop. The pits yielded a wide range of neolithic artefacts including leaf-shaped arrow-heads made of flint, waste flint flakes, potsherds, ox bones, deer antlers, human bones and hazel nuts. The pits were almost certainly domestic in function, either for storage or for refuse, and early neolithic hearths were discovered underneath the iron age rampart; the finds are consistent with the remains of an early neolithic village (Figure 45).

In the later bronze age, the people living on the hill left behind them a gold bracelet, objects of bronze, loom weights and pottery. Then, in about 1180 BC, the site was developed as a hillfort. The hill was to be occupied again, becoming a high-status site between AD 400 and 600, during the Arthurian period, supporting the longstanding local tradition that the dark age fort was Arthur's Camelot.

SWEET TRACK
ST: 422410

An early wooden footpath running 1800m from N to S, linking the fen island of Westhay to the Polden Hills at a time when the Somerset Levels were marshy fens, around 3200 bc (4050 BC). It runs parallel to the modern road and 300m to the east of it. Fire and axes were used to fell 300-year-old oaks on the Poldens, and the tree trunks were then split into planks and notched or perforated ready for incorporation into the track. Ash wood and coppiced limes for the rails were also produced and prepared on the slopes of the Polden Hills. Hundreds of pegs of hazel, holly, alder, ash and elm were driven in obliquely on each side of the rail. Different types of timber were deliberately selected for different components of the track.

Very large amounts of timber were used in making the Sweet Track: an estimated 5km of split oak planks and 10,000 sharpened pegs to hold them in place. This implies a large, permanently settled, well-established, committed and well-organized community. Some of their arrow-heads and other neolithic artefacts were collected by the iron age inhabitants of the area, suggesting that they too may have had a certain antiquarian curiosity about their ancestors.

Blocks of peat were packed along the sides and over the top of the rail to give it extra support and raise the level to about 20cm above the marsh. The heavy planks of oak, ash and lime were laid on top and held in position by the criss-cross pegs, as well as by new, vertical pegs driven through holes or notches cut in the planks. The result was a narrow but firm walkway marked by numerous projecting pegs, which would have been easy to see among the vegetation.

The track builders' settlement was close to the southern end of the track. A good deal of debris was deposited in the swamp along the sides of the track – wooden and stone tools, pottery and flint axes. The system of tracks brought the swamps into a complex mixed economy in which farming, pastoralism, hunting and fowling all played a part. The foot slopes of the Polden Hills next to the fens would have dried out in summer to make excellent summer grazing. In winter, the livestock was probably taken up to higher and drier ground – a kind of inverted transhumance.

TOM TIVEY'S HOLE   ST: 7343

A Mendip cave that was used as a burial place. A round-bottomed cup and some flints, including a leaf-shaped arrow-head, were deposited as grave goods with a woman of about 30 who was about 1.6m tall.

WELLS CATHEDRAL   ST: 551458

Excavations in 1980 revealed remains of a neolithic settlement site, although it was inevitably greatly disturbed by intensive later activity. Quantities of flint, including leaf-shaped arrow-heads, were found. There were also two irregular scoops into the natural gravel, and these contain neolithic flints and a possible potsherd.

—————————— **STAFFORDSHIRE** ——————————

ALREWAS CAUSEWAYED ENCLOSURE   near Lichfield   SK: 154144

A large causewayed enclosure on a gravel terrace of the River Trent, close to the confluence of the River Trent and the River Tame. Three concentric rings of interrupted ditches define an oval precinct 200m by 150m and enclose it on three sides; they have not been preserved, if they ever existed, on the south-east side. It is possible, as at Orsett in Essex, that the monument was C-shaped from the beginning. As at Mavesyn Ridware causewayed enclosure, the Alrewas ditches are set fairly close together, by contrast with, for example, those at Windmill Hill. The monument was detected from the air as a cropmark.

ARBORTON   Alstonefield   SK: 120571

A flint-working site. The finds, which were all discovered in a field known as Aborton, included flint scrapers, arrow-heads, blades, flakes and a large amount of flint-working debris. Several different kinds of flint were used here, implying that the raw material had been imported from various sources; it may eventually prove to be possible to identify precise sources for the flint.

BOWER FARM CAVE   Colwich   SK: 030194

Two skulls, thought to be neolithic, were found in this small sandstone cave. The flints point to mesolithic and neolithic occupation, so it looks as if the cave was a hunting lodge that was in use over a long period.

COURT BANK COVERT   Cannock   SK: 041116

A flint-knapping site belonging to the mesolithic and neolithic periods. Finds here included a leaf-shaped arrow-head, shouldered points, scrapers, flakes and cores.

DARFUR RIDGE CAVE   Ecton Hill   SK: 099557

A solution fissure in a spur of Ecton Hill. The platform in front of the cave has been excavated, revealing mesolithic and neolithic flints. The neolithic occupation was nevertheless represented by no more than a solitary leaf-shaped arrow-head.

DEVIL'S RING AND FINGER   Mucklestone   SJ: 707379

Two stones are built into the wall of Oakley Park. The Ring is a stone that is 1.2m' high and 2m across with a porthole cut through it. The other stone, the Finger, is 1.8m high and 0.9m wide and it leans against the Ring. The two stones were probably part of a burial chamber, but they are not likely to be in their original positions. The site is of interest because it is the only known monument of its type in Staffordshire. It was originally known as 'The Whirl Stones'.

EFFLINCH ENCLOSURES AND CURSUS   SK: 193170

Two small circular earthworks are possibly round barrows. The elongated, elliptically ended structure may be a small cursus of a variant type that is quite common in the Warwickshire Avon valley.

FATHOLME CAUSEWAYED ENCLOSURE   SK: 201173
AND RING DITCH

There is an extensive group of neolithic bronze age ritual monuments located close to the Tame–Trent confluence. The location may be significant for ritual reasons, as an association with water is common in neolithic monuments. It may alternatively be significant for geographical reasons, valley junctions being natural route centres and meeting places.

The ring ditch lay at the western edge of the floodplain, close to an old water course of the River Trent. At least seven circuits of intercutting ditch were found; originally they were continuous rings, but later they were broken by causeways.

There were numerous post-holes and a few pits both inside and outside the ring ditch: where they intersected, the ditch was seen to be later than the post-holes. To the east was a building with a porch projecting on its south side, but it was rebuilt and as a result the original plan is difficult to reconstruct. The building and the structures associated with it were apparently not part of a larger settlement. To the north-west was a group of pits of unknown function which produced Peterborough and Grooved ware pottery and flint, including barbed-and-tanged, leaf-shaped and petit tranchet derivative arrow-heads.

FISHERWICK
SK: 184102

A settlement site. The evidence for occupation includes traces of a probable building, as well as flints and some pottery.

MAVESYN RIDWARE
near Rugely
SK: 084167

A causewayed enclosure on a river terrace of the River Trent. An oval precinct 200m by 170m is surrounded by one, two and on the west side three rings of discontinuous quarry ditches. The enclosure is very similar in size and style to the one a few kilometres downstream at Alrewas. The Mavesyn Ridware enclosure is associated with another enclosure and a ring ditch, and was detected from the air as a cropmark.

SEVEN WAYS CAVE
Manifold Valley
SK: 098549

A neolithic flint arrow-head was found together with other cultural material in a small cave in the rock face overlooking the River Manifold.

ST BERTRAM'S CAVE
Manifold Valley
SK: 106540

This cave above the River Manifold was occupied from the palaeolithic, through the neolithic, and on into the bronze age.

THOR'S CAVE
Manifold Valley
SK: 098549

A neolithic crouched burial and an axe head made of basalt were found here. There is also evidence for occupation later in the prehistoric period, including occupation in the bronze and iron ages.

TUCKLESHOLME FARM BARROW CEMETERY
SK: 208188

Remains of a barrow cemetery have been found 300m to the south-west of Tucklesholme Farm. There are three small circular earthworks, possibly part of

Figure 46   A Stonehenge trilithon drawn by William Stukeley.

a linear barrow cemetery: two are overlapped by the railway margin. A cursus seems to be indicated by parallel lines.

———— SUFFOLK ————

FORNHAM ALL SAINTS CAUSEWAYED ENCLOSURE AND CURSUS   TL: 830680

A causewayed enclosure site. The monument consists of two circuits of inter-rupted ditches, altogether covering an area about 325m by 280m. On the southern side of the main enclosure there was another, also double-circuit, with a possible diameter of 325m.

A cursus of 1.9km long crosses the site from north-west to south-east, appar-ently overriding and therefore post-dating the causewayed enclosure. The cursus is 23m wide at the north-west end, but widens to 40m. It also undergoes two changes in direction. At the south-east end there are gaps, i.e. causeways, in the ditches. There are also four henge-like ring ditches at the south-east end. The north end of the cursus has not been found. Fornham All Saints church is built in the cursus itself, which will appeal to those who like to argue for long-enduring continuity in sacred sites.

FRESTON CAUSEWAYED ENCLOSURE
near Ipswich
TM: 167381

A causewayed enclosure site on low-lying land near the Orwell estuary. The enclosure is roughly circular, 310m by 290m, and encircled by two circuits of interrupted ditches. In terms of scale, it is strikingly similar to the causewayed enclosure at Fornham All Saints.

HONINGTON
TL: 915748

A small settlement site excavated by C. S. Leaf in 1938–9. The surviving remains then consisted of seven storage pits, three outdoor hearths and about eight hut floors. The hut floors were inferred from oval or irregular, discoloured, dark grey patches on the soil, containing concentrations of tools and sherds; some of the hut floors also had 'cooking holes', small holes containing animal bones and showing traces of burning. The huts were about 3m by 2.5m, and may have been lightly built sod houses. One hut floor, set apart from the others, had two post-holes, implying perhaps a ridge-tent structure of some kind.

This type of small farming hamlet, consisting of just five or ten small simple dwellings, was probably very common in neolithic Britain, although there is plenty of evidence from other sites that larger and stouter houses with proper indoor hearths were also built. It is possible that the material standards of living and aspirations of the neolithic population varied significantly from area to area.

HURST FEN
Mildenhall
TL: 725768

A settlement site. Excavations by G. Briscoe in 1951 and J. G. D. Clark in 1954–8 revealed a ditch and a dense scatter of some 200 small storage pits. The pits were probably originally lined or luted and used for storing food. Over 200 square metres of the site were uncovered during the excavation, but not a single identifiable building plan was decipherable from the patternless scatter of pits. The site has become important to archaeologists in that it established a type series of pottery, known as Mildenhall ware, and a seminal classification of worked flint.

KEDINGTON CAUSEWAYED ENCLOSURE
near Haverhill
TL: 701473

A causewayed enclosure site. An arc of causewayed ditches cuts off a small promontory formed by a meander of the River Stour. An area of approximately 1.5 hectares is enclosed by the ditches. A dense flint scatter just to the north-east of the enclosure implies that the settlement was *outside* it, emphasizing the ceremonial nature of the enclosure.

STRATFORD ST MARY TM: 048343

This site is alleged to be a single-entrance henge 27m in diameter, but it may after all be a medieval mill mound. Nevertheless, supporting the henge interpretation is a nearby cursus with a NW–SE axis, roughly 60m wide and 290m long, with several large ring ditches clustered round it. This neolithic ritual complex was largely destroyed by the development of the A12 Stratford by-pass in the early 1970s.

SUTTON HOO **Woodbridge** TM: 288487

This site has become justly famous for the spectacular royal ship burial discovered in 1939. The burial is thought by many to be that of Redwald, king of East Anglia and overking of Southern England, who died in about AD 625.

Yet, long before that, it had been a neolithic settlement site, proved by finds of neolithic pottery, and it was later to be occupied by successive Beaker, bronze age and iron age settlements. This succession of prehistoric settlements culminating in the establishment of a major royal and ancestral cult centre is probably not a chance sequence. Many of the most thoroughly researched cult centres in Britain have proved to be very long-lasting, often surviving one or two major cultural upheavals.

———— SURREY ————

BADSHOT LONG BARROW **Badshot Lea** SU: 861478

Two flat-bottomed parallel ditches were discovered during chalk quarrying in 1936, and correctly interpreted as the side ditches of a ploughed-out long barrow. The sloping site at 85m OD overlooks the Blackwater terrace gravels. The barrow's long axis is oriented just north of east. A single undated post-hole was found in a narrow trench laid out between the ditch terminals at the east end, rather similar to a feature found during the excavation of the long barrow on Thickthorn Down in Dorset. The barrow's original length is estimated to have been 43m, which may link it with a recently recognized group of Hampshire long barrows of roughly oval form and whose lengths lie in the range 30–60m. The long barrow yielded little in the way of finds, although some animal bones from the west end of the north ditch have been radiocarbon dated to 2650 bc (3400 bc) and 2470 bc (3150 bc).

The Badshot Long Barrow is an important monument because of its isolation from others of its type. The nearest proved long barrow that I know of is 25km to the west, at Preston Candover in Hampshire, which is itself on the fringe of the main Wessex group. To the east, Jullieberrie's Grave and its two recently identified companions in the Great Stour valley in Kent are 120km away, and the (chambered) barrows at Addington and Kit's Coty are 78km and 88km away.

The siting of these barrow groups facing gaps in the chalk downs incidentally suggests that a search for others in the Farnham, Guildford and Dorking areas might be fruitful. The Badshot Long Barrow was discovered accidentally, as a chalk quarry intercepted first its southern ditch and then its northern. There was no surface indication of its existence, and the implication is that other long barrows may also have been overlooked or destroyed (see Figure 36).

CHERTSEY   TQ: 042668

A neolithic settlement site close to the south bank of the River Thames. There is a second settlement site to the south-east, at about TQ: 047665.

PENTON HOOK MARINA   Chertsey   TQ: 040690

A settlement site very close to the south bank of the Thames, and now destroyed by gravel working.

RUNNYMEDE   Egham   TQ: 008720
CAUSEWAYED ENCLOSURE

A causewayed enclosure site has been tentatively identified here by Stuart Needham of the British Museum. If correctly identified, this ritual centre on the Thames valley floor probably served the Egham settlements, at SU: 003715 and SU: 018718, dating to 3400 BC (Figure 47).

SHEPPERTON HENGE   TQ: 076686

A henge-like domestic and ritual monument sited on Thames terrace gravels between the River Ash and the north bank of the River Thames. This monument is an important discovery because ringworks of this kind are rare in the lower Thames valley. The monument consisted of a roughly circular ditched enclosure about 23m in diameter, with three entrance causeways that were oriented towards the NE, SE and WSW. The north-east entrance, like that at Stonehenge, seems to have been deliberately aligned on the midsummer sunrise: it was 'guarded' by a human skeleton, a crouched male. It may be that sacrificial rites were performed within the circle to reinforce the solar cycle, at the moment when the sun reached its highest point in the cycle and began its slow descent into autumn. A woman's torso was deposited 10m to the west of this midsummer entrance; a deformed dog's head was buried 10m to the east of it.

Deer antlers were deposited, apparently randomly, in the enclosure ditch. Red ochre lumps were deposited in the ditch at the point on the circumference which marked the most southerly moonrise. This is the position which, at Stonehenge, was marked by offerings of a stone mace-head and several cremated children. The orientations at Shepperton become particularly significant when they are seen to be repeated at other major neolithic monuments. There was a large quantity of rock waste and worked implements, as well as both late and early neolithic pottery. The henge had domestic as well as ritual functions, although not necessarily at the same time.

Next to the Shepperton Henge was an avenue of pits, certainly 200m long and possibly originally as much as 600m long, leading towards the River Ash, a branch of the River Colne. Each pit was rectangular with rounded corners, and there was no evidence that they had ever held posts or stones. Avenues at other neolithic sites are often similarly linked with water, such as the short stone avenues at Stanton Drew and the long Stanwell Cursus not far north of Shepperton.

There was a late neolithic occupation area beside the henge. It included a large pit 9m by 6m and 2m deep, which may have been dug as a water hole for livestock, and a rectangular flat-based pit full of ash and calcined flint; this may have been a boiling pit for cooking. There were two occupation levels, the earlier mid-neolithic, the later probably late neolithic. There were also field ditches to the west of the henge and the pit rows.

There seems to have been a major focus of ritual activity, perhaps water-deity-oriented, at the confluence of the Colne and Thames in a triangle formed by Runnymede, Heathrow and Shepperton (Figure 47).

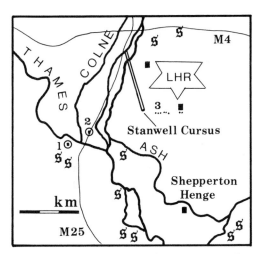

Figure 47 A neolithic landscape in West London. LHR – Heathrow Airport (for orientation), s – neolithic settlement, 1 – Runnymede causewayed enclosure, 2 – Yeoveny (Staines) causewayed enclosure, 3 – linear cemetery of ring ditches, axis apparently oriented towards the southern terminus of the Stanwell Cursus. The black boxes are henge-like monuments. An extensive ceremonial complex developed at what was then, as now, an important route centre.

STAINES

A low-lying settlement site close to the River Thames. It is surrounded on three sides by water, the River Thames to the south-west, the Colne to the west, and the River Ash, a branch of the Colne, to the north-east.

STANWELL CURSUS   Heathrow Airport   TQ: 054745

This cursus monument is a long narrow feature, about 21m wide, at least 4km long, and laid out on Second Terrace gravels at Stanwell, running along the western edge of Heathrow Airport. It was once thought to be a Roman road, but excavation revealed that one of the ditches had been cut by a large late bronze-age pit and a prehistoric trackway. Then, confirming its antiquity, neolithic Peterborough pottery was found in the upper silts of the ditch fill, so the feature has been reinterpreted as a neolithic cursus.

The Stanwell Cursus runs NNW from Stanwell village, apparently to a terminal at Bigley Ditch, close to the M4–M25 intersection, making it the second longest cursus in Britain, the Dorset Cursus being the longest. It runs roughly halfway between the double-ditched enclosures at Yeoveny and East Bedfont, which lie 3.5km to the SW and 2.8km to the ESE respectively. Re-examination of air photographs suggests that the Stanwell Cursus forms part of a large, integrated complex of monuments; at least two other (now inaccessible) narrow linear enclosures, one of them at least a possible cursus, appear to cross under the west end of Runway 5 at Heathrow. The south end of the Stanwell Cursus seems to be aligned approximately on the Shepperton Henge, and it may originally have continued in that direction.

The existence of this important ritual complex on fertile terrace gravels implies that the Stanwell area assumed a particular local importance. It was probably not accidental that it became a focus for late neolithic or early bronze age barrow construction; there is a linear cemetery consisting of at least ten ring ditches running east from the southern terminus of the Cursus, i.e. SU: 078733–060732 (Figure 47).

Here, it may be possible to begin to speak of an organized neolithic landscape, but it is a very difficult area to explore further. The work of archaeologists is impeded by housing, industrial development, road-making and gravel extraction; in addition, many riverine sites must lie buried under a metre or two of alluvium deposited by the Thames and its tributaries over the last 5,000 years. Sites in areas like this are found by chance, or are destroyed unknowingly during development – or simply remain undiscovered.

WALTON-ON-THAMES

A settlement site very close to the south bank of the River Thames. There is another settlement site 1km to the south-west, at TQ: 095658.

YEOVENY (STAINES) CAUSEWAYED ENCLOSURE

TQ: 024726

A causewayed enclosure site with two roughly concentric rings 20m apart. The enclosure had a maximum diameter of about 180m, and an area of 2.2 hectares. It was built on the southern tip of a large spit of First Terrace gravel at the confluence of the River Colne and the River Thames, some 800m north of the present course of the Thames. It may have functioned both as a settlement and as a ritual centre. The evidence suggests that a range of activities took place there, including the manufacture of flint tools and the disposal of human corpses: fragments of two skulls were found on the site. The location, close to the river confluence, and the amount of labour involved in its building suggest that the Yeoveny causewayed enclosure may have been the most important monument in the whole complex. Yeoveny also lies midway between causewayed enclosures at Abingdon in the west and Orsett in the east, and this implies that it and the rest of the 'West London' complex may have functioned as some kind of territorial central place (Figure 47).

This major tribal centre was lost in the development of the M25 motorway, but it has been replaced by the raised reinforced concrete ring of the Junction 13 interchange, which, even if an unconscious back-reference, is as appropriate a modern transformation of the ritual circle as we could wish to find.

——————————— EAST SUSSEX ———————————

BEACON HILL LONG BARROW

Rottingdean

TQ: 364028

A long barrow at 61m OD on open heathland on the eastern flank of Beacon Hill. The barrow is 1.5m high and 33m long; it was once about 3m longer, but has been truncated by small-scale chalk quarrying at its northern end. It was at one time cut in half by a trackway; as a result it has sometimes been identified as two round barrows. The quarry ditches have not been detected.

BELLE TOUT

TV: 557957

A neolithic settlement site very close to the chalk cliffs, although when the site was occupied, during the third millenium BC, the cliffs were probably 1km away to the south. The people who lived here built both circular and rectangular houses and, unusually, enclosed their village at the end of the neolithic with a rectangular bank and ditch.

BISHOPSTONE near Seaford TQ: 467006

An unenclosed settlement on the south-facing slope of Rookery Hill, a chalk hill overlooking the sea to the south and the floodplain and mouth of the Sussex Ouse to the west. In the fourth millenium BC, when the site was first settled, the floodplain would have been an open sea inlet or ria extending inland as far as Lewes, with a shingle spit building across its seaward end from what is now Newhaven harbour. This physical environment would have created a diversity of ecological niches, offering neolithic people many opportunities. The sheltered inlet may also have been used as a harbour for coastwise trade. Concentrations of neolithic artefacts prove that Christchurch Harbour and the now silted Pevensey Bay were used in this way; although there is no positive proof that trade goods were dropped off at Newhaven, it is quite possible that this happened.

The people living at Bishopstone ran a mixed economy based on pastoralism, arable farming, fishing, and probably hunting, fowling and gathering, around 2510 bc (3200 BC). Charcoal from the new stone age hearths shows that hawthorn, hazel, oak, ash, yew and dogwood grew in the vicinity, so the hill was not as bald as it is now.

Farmers were already having problems with weeds invading land cleared for crops: pollen of knotgrass, chickweed, bindweed and burdock was found. Later the fields were given over to pasture and stayed as pasture from then until the iron age. The farmers excavated the hillside a little to make a cultivation terrace or negative lynchet; this is one of the very few downland lynchets of southern England that has been proved to be of neolithic date.

An axe made of quartz-diorite proves that the inhabitants had contacts well outside the region. Many of the flints used there were river-flints, probably from the beaches along the flanks of the Ouse ria.

BULLOCK DOWN Eastbourne TV: 967591

A settlement site at 150m OD on the scarp crest of the South Downs. It was surveyed in 1976–7. The areas of fire-cracked flints suggest hearths, and round these were separate flint-knapping floors marked by concentrations of waste flakes. Between these distinct areas were empty areas and scatters of scrapers and retouched flakes, suggesting that maybe skins were being treated at separate, specific spots. The overall picture is of open, informal, but purposeful and organized activity, with specific areas of the settlement given over to specialized activities.

Finds on Bullock Down include leaf-shaped, barbed-and-tanged, and transverse arrow-heads, scrapers, knives, a polished flint axe, and polished stone axes – one of gabbro from Mount's Bay in Cornwall, others of sandstone and greywacke. Very few flintworking sites have been studied in such depth of detail, or as fruitfully, as Bullock Down.

CLIFFE HILL LONG BARROW

South Malling TQ: 431110

This long barrow, sometimes known as the Warrior's Grave, is 36m long, 15m wide and 2m high. The side ditches are visible, and it is clear that the mound has been disturbed. The centre of the mound has been dug into at some time, so that the mound material has spread laterally. As a result, the monument now has a very distinctive, if un-neolithic, two-humped profile which has led to its nickname, 'the Camel's Humps'. The barrow is false-crested, slightly to the west of the highest point, so that it can be seen, very conspicuous on the skyline, from Lewes in the Ouse valley below.

COMBE HILL CAUSEWAYED ENCLOSURE

Jevington TQ: 574021

Two concentric arcs of interrupted ditches and banks butt onto the South Downs escarpment, which is very steep just here. The enclosure, of about 0.6 ha, offers spectacular views to the north across the Vale of Sussex, and south across rolling downland towards Beachy Head. Interestingly, other Sussex enclosure sites seem to have been selected with a similar aesthetic sense – notably Offham, Bury Hill, Whitehawk and the Trundle.

The inner arc of ditches is broken by at least 16 causeways. Excavation in 1949 revealed that the ditch is U-shaped rather than the usual flat-bottomed trough, 3.7m wide and 1m deep. The ditch contained many pieces of local neolithic Ebbsfleet pottery. No post-holes were discovered, so there was no indication that there had been a palisade or interior buildings. The other arc of ditches remains to be examined.

The enclosure is about 90m across from west to east and 75m from north to south. The banks are degraded to a height of only 0.3m. In 1984, I found a carved chalk object 5cm high and identified as a neolithic talisman in the turf at the centre of the enclosure; it has five parallel lines carved into one of its faces, probably in imitation of the process of arding as part of some fertility ritual, or possibly as a way of imbuing the piece of chalk with fertile magic power.

EXCEAT OVAL BARROW

Westdean TV: 520996

An undated oval barrow 150m NE of Exceat, next to an old flint wall. It stands at 30m OD, in pasture, except for the north-east mound edge and the side ditch, which lie under woodland. The barrow survives to a height of 1.5m, and is 28m long and 18m wide. It is similar in size and shape to the Alfriston oval barrow, which proved on excavation to be neolithic. The Exceat oval barrow is oriented NW–SE.

GIANT'S GRAVE Firle Beacon TQ: 486058

This long barrow, with a long axis aligned W–E, is 33m long, 20m wide and 2.5m high. A hollow area at the eastern end of the mound suggests that there may once have been a wooden burial chamber which subsequently collapsed: only excavation will resolve this. The side ditches turn inwards at the end, and traces of the ditches can still be seen to north, south and east. The barrow is false-crested, and stands at a height of 198m just on the south side of the scarp crest, beside the South Downs Way. The effect of this siting is to make the barrow conspicuous as a skyline feature when viewed from the dip slope valleys to the south; it also has the effect of making the monument appear to be significantly larger than it actually is.

The south side of the mound is badly damaged by rabbit burrowing, but at least the barrow is fenced off now and therefore safe from 'clipping' by the plough; it is unfortunate though that the ditch remnants on the north and east sides have been left unprotected outside the fence.

HIGH ROCKS Frant TQ: 561382

This important site consists of a series of rock shelters in the vertical-sided gulls or gullies formed between projecting rock outcrops of the Tunbridge Wells Sand escarpment. It was in these shallow ravines that mesolithic and neolithic hunters made temporary shelters or hunting lodges, which were probably used seasonally. Several sites in the maze of gullies have been excavated, producing flint tools, hearths and neolithic pottery of Ebbsfleet and Windmill Hill types. Charcoal from the hearths has been radiocarbon dated to 3710 bc (4500 BC) and 3780 bc (4600 BC).

HUNTER'S BURGH Wilmington Hill TQ: 550036

Lying N–S on the steeply sloping scarp face of the South Downs, this long barrow measures 56m long, 22m wide and 2m high. It is quite well preserved, but its height reduces northwards, going down the hillside, so that its north end is very indistinct and indeterminate. Side ditches that were clearly visible to E. C. Curwen in the 1920s are not apparent now, and the most conspicuous feature is a robber pit at the south end. The south end has the appearance of a round barrow 18m in diameter with a concave top, and the 'tail' of the long barrow is relatively inconspicuous; as a result of these peculiarities, it has been incorrectly identified as a round barrow. Its position on the crest of a spur makes it a prominent skyline feature when viewed from the lower slopes of the escarpment near Folkington.

LITLINGTON LONG BARROW   TQ: 535006

There are several oval barrows in Sussex, Hampshire and Wiltshire that have been recognized as a form of long barrow. This example was 20m long and 12m wide. Its greatest height was 1.2m and it is now only 0.8m high. It shows no sign of having side ditches to the west. The mound too is most pronounced in the west. The barrow stands, or rather lies, in a barley field and is a very poorly preserved monument, visible only as a slight, currently unploughed, rise covered in long grass. The barrow is on private land.

LONG BURGH   **Alfriston**   TQ: 510034

This overgrown long barrow is 50m long, 18m wide and reaches a height of 2.4m. On each side are buried ditches, which produced the material from which the barrow mound was made. Part of the barrow was opened in 1767, when a 'skeleton and an urn' were recovered; if accurately reported, these must surely represent a secondary burial, perhaps inserted in the bronze age. A pit was dug, surreptitiously and illegally, in the south end in the 1980s; examples of this kind of vandalism are still depressingly frequent.

Just over 300m to the north of the long barrow was an oval barrow, now totally obliterated by ploughing. This once stood 2m high, and was 28m long and 18m wide. Total excavation prior to deep ploughing in 1974 showed that material from two curving side ditches had been heaped up to form a simple dump mound of chalk rubble, covering a pit that contained a crouched female burial unaccompanied by grave goods. Antler from the oval barrow has been radiocarbon dated to 2360 bc (3050 BC), which makes it a fairly late long barrow.

On each side of the oval barrow, immediately to the west and a little way away to the south-east, areas of struck flint flakes were found, hinting at neolithic occupation of some kind in the area close to the two barrows; perhaps they are traces of the temporary occupation that would have been necessary during the times when the barrows were built. On the whole, it seems likely in Sussex that barrows were built on the boundaries of the small 'band' territories, as far as possible from the permanent settlements. The burial was of a lightly built woman of about 30, 1.5m tall, and apparently in good health at the time of her death. The barrow yielded bones of red deer, roe deer, pig, dog and sheep, and charcoal of hawthorn, crab apple, rose, ivy, hazel, birch and dogwood. Although superficially unimpressive, the oval barrow at Alfriston has acted as a time capsule, supplying us with invaluable detailed information about the animals, vegetation and people of the area in 3050 BC.

MONEY BURGH   **Piddinghoe**   TQ: 425037

A skeleton, probably representing a secondary burial, is the only recorded find

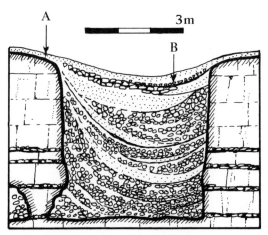

Figure 48   Church Hill, Findon: a section through one of the mine shafts. A – thin modern soil layer,   B – late neolithic flaking floor, showing that the shaft was backfilled while neighbouring shafts were opened and worked.

from this long barrow. The mound is 37m long, 18m wide, 2m high and stands on a low spur projecting from the west side of the Ouse valley, showing up well on the skyline when seen from the north. The barrow has a pronounced eastern end. All traces of lateral ditches have been obliterated by farm trackways and past cultivation. It appears to have had a trench dug along the whole length of the crest in comparatively recent years, but the results of this illicit dig are unknown. The earlier dig, by J. Tompsett in the nineteenth century, is a matter of documentary record, and mound material from that excavation was thrown to the north of the barrow, forming a talus on that side.

Money Burgh stands on private land.

OFFHAM CAUSEWAYED ENCLOSURE   Offham   TQ: 399118

This causewayed enclosure overlooking the Vale of Sussex and the Ouse Gap was excavated in 1976, prior to destruction by ploughing. It consisted of two incomplete circles of discontinuous banks and external ditches. By 1976, the easternmost third of the monument had already been totally destroyed by chalk quarrying. The overall size of the enclosure seems to have been about 100m across; the enclosed central precinct was about 60m in diameter. The enclosure was built in a woodland clearing and it was suggested by the excavator, Peter Drewett, that it was used specifically as a funerary enclosure for the exposure, or excarnation, of human corpses. It therefore seems to have had a different, more limited function than, for instance, Whitehawk. Offham's radiocarbon dates, 2975 bc (3550 BC) and 2790 bc (3390 BC) show that it was built 100–200 years before Whitehawk or Combe Hill. The site was so poor in artefacts that it may conceivably have had only a short lifespan; possibly it was superseded by a neighbouring centre, the much larger enclosure at Whitehawk being an obvious candidate. Alternatively, the Offham enclosure may have been used only for certain ritual, funerary activities, which have left little archaeological trace.

A single chip of Cornish granite found at Offham hints at a trading contact with the outside world.

PLAYDEN   TQ: 921227

A rectilinear ditched enclosure with a palisade immediately inside the ditch. The sub-rectangular space enclosed by the palisade, on at least three sides, was about 12m across. Grooved ware pottery was associated with the site.

Right beside it was a ring ditch about 20m in diameter; at its centre were the post-holes of a round timber building 6m in diameter. The ring ditch contained a lot of charcoal and burnt timber, together with neolithic potsherds. The ditch timbers were up to 0.3m in diameter and 1.5m long, implying that a substantial palisade was set up in the perimeter ditch. The site was destroyed by fire, perhaps deliberately, perhaps as part of a ritual, and the burnt timbers dumped in the ditch. The timbers on the west side were either left unburnt or replaced. The whole of the central area was covered, artificially, with a large quantity of white sand, possibly revetted by planks supported by timbers set in four post-holes. Then a pavement of sandstone blocks was laid over the platform. This unusual site was apparently used, though presumably not primarily used, for flint knapping, with a considerable amount of flint debris building up. The initial inhabitants of the site used the local beach flint for their tool-making. The people of the later phase of occupation used only mined downland flint, which was of a much higher quality, from at least 25km away.

R. M. J. Cleal (1982) has proposed that the central setting in the ring ditch in the first phase was a horseshoe setting of posts, or possibly a timber cove made of timbers set upright in bedding trenches. There seem to be no close parallels for this: the nearest is the very much larger one at Arminghall in Norfolk. The orientation of the cove was to the north-east, a few degrees off an alignment on the midsummer sunrise position in the later neolithic.

WHITEHAWK CAUSEWAYED Brighton Racecourse   TQ: 330048
ENCLOSURE

Where Manor Hill Road crosses the Brighton Racecourse are to be seen the last vandalized remnants of a large causewayed enclosure, which was originally 4.7ha in area, with four concentric circuits of interrupted ditches and banks. The third out from the centre forms a noticeable ridge along the very steep valley side where it drops into Whitehawk Bottom. South of the road, towards the television mast, it is possible to make out segments of the third and fourth ditches. When excavated in 1932–3, the inner ditches proved to be the shallowest, each about 1m deep, whilst the third was the deepest, reaching 2.5m. Large quantities of pottery, flint and animal bones were found, as well as many human bones. Some of the human remains had been carefully and deliberately buried, and others had been thrown into the ditches in an apparently haphazard and casual way: a pattern of behaviour which we see elsewhere.

The radiocarbon dates for Whitehawk are 2750 bc (3450 BC) and 2695 bc (3400 BC). The palisade which evidently topped at least one of the banks may justify our treating Whitehawk as a 'fortified settlement' enclosure, giving it a unique status in East Sussex. Certainly, to judge from the number of ditch circuits and the general elaborateness of its design, it would appear that Whitehawk was the most important enclosure in the county in the middle neolithic. Outside East Sussex, the enclosures at Yeoveny (Staines), the Trundle and Orsett may fall into the same palisaded enclosure category, and the equal spacing of these high-status sites carries an implication of larger-scale territorial organization than hitherto suspected in the middle neolithic. Of the known Sussex causewayed enclosures, Whitehawk and the Trundle are easily the largest in terms of overall size, but the central precincts of these two are not dissimilar in area to those of Combe Hill and Offham. It seems possible that the causewayed enclosures started off much the same in size, with the innermost bank and ditch ring only, and that successive outworks were added later as the enclosures gained in importance – whether for defence or just for show – and some enclosures inevitably became more important than others, in accordance with central place theory. There is firm evidence to support this view from outside this area; at Windmill Hill in Wiltshire the circuits were of significantly different dates.

WINDOVER HILL FLINT MINES   Windover Hill   TQ: 542033

Above and immediately to the south-east of the Long Man of Wilmington there is a well-marked series of about half a dozen hollows which have been identified as flint mines. They were trial-trenched for samples in 1971, and these confirmed Curwen's identification of the cone-shaped pits as flint mine shafts, but as yet they are unexcavated. E. W. Holden's metre-deep trench revealed a filling of chalk blocks, large and small, with very little earth; he found a flint hammerstone, two flakes and numerous flint nodules.

It is probably significant that the only cluster of mines in East Sussex so far identified is at Windover Hill, only 4.5km from the neolithic coastline where the first flint-gatherers probably operated, on the beaches in front of the Seven Sisters and Beachy Head, and where the first attempts at flint quarrying were probably made in the cliff face.

The Windover mines are 200m E of the Long Man and crossed by an ancient terraceway which picks its way among the mines and must therefore post-date them.

WINDOVER LONG MOUND   Windover Hill   TQ: 542033

A very fine long barrow 55m long, 14m wide and 2m high. It stands just to the west of the summit of Windover Hill, false-crested to make it plainly visible from Ewe Dean and from the ridgeway as it ascends from the river crossing. The barrow is aligned, unusually, almost due N–S, like its nearest neighbours, Hunter's Burgh and Long Burgh. The silted quarry ditches are 3m wide and adjoin the mound without intervening berms. The northern tip, a round mound, is separated from the rest of the barrow by a col. This may be part of the original design, or it may have been produced by carts crossing the long barrow to reach the chalk quarry immediately to the east of the mound. The summit of the round mound is a flat circular platform at a lower level than the very even crest line of the main part of the long barrow, and this implies that the separation of the round mound was part of the original design. It nevertheless cannot be treated as an entirely separate barrow, a round barrow in its own right, because the quarry ditch, at least on the west side, runs past the col to flank it. The resulting phallic form of the long barrow may be inadvertent, or it may have been intentional and symbolic.

The Windover Long Mound, as yet unexcavated and still in good condition, is an unusual and important monument, not least because of its proximity to a large mound barrow, clusters of neolithic flint mines, and the Long Man of Wilmington, itself an enigmatic monument which has yet to be dated conclusively (Plate 9).

———————— WEST SUSSEX ————————

BARKHALE CAUSEWAYED   Bignor Hill   SU: 976126
ENCLOSURE

This oval enclosure is one of the largest causewayed enclosures discovered in Britain and encloses about 2.5 hectares in its central precinct. Ploughing has destroyed much of the earthwork, but sections of the interrupted ditches may be seen on the north and north-east sides, together with the internal bank. Excavation has produced late neolithic pottery, confirming the antiquity of the site. Although so far no material suitable for radiocarbon dating has been found at Barkhale, there is no reason to suppose that it is anything but contemporary with the other Sussex causewayed enclosures, in which case it dates from around 3600 BC. The enclosure appears to have been constructed in a temporary and probably quite small clearing in woodland, like Offham and Combe Hill.

Very little has been found at Barkhale. No bone has been found there, and there is very little evidence that it was a settlement. A ceremonial function seems likely. Bronze age barrows cluster round the site, as indeed they do round the Combe Hill, Bury Hill and Offham enclosures. The implication is that enclosures that were evidently foci for funerary ceremonies in the second millennium were also ceremonial foci in the previous millennium, when they were built.

BEVIS'S THUMB North Marden SU: 786155

Lying close to the edge of a ploughed field, this long barrow is 70m long, 21m wide and nearly 2m high. It is the longest of the known long barrows in Sussex. Its north side ditch has been filled by a minor road, and ploughing has obliterated the south side ditch.

A single trench was dug across the ploughed-down ditch for dating and palaeoenvironmental evidence. The ditch was found to be 1.4m deep and contained early neolithic pottery comparable with that found at the Trundle. Some flint flakes and hazelwood and hawthorn charcoal were also found. A radiocarbon date of 2595 bc (3350 BC) was obtained from charcoal in a layer above the lowest layers of silt in the ditch floor, so the monument may have been built a little earlier than 3350 BC. The date is in any case comparable to dates obtained from the enclosures at Whitehawk, Bury Hill and Combe Hill.

BLACKPATCH FLINT MINES Blackpatch Hill TQ: 094089

Low mounds and hollows on the hillside mark the location of about 100 neolithic flint mines. They were discovered by Mr C. H. Goodman as late as 1919, and excavations of seven of the mine shafts were begun in 1922. The new stone age miners were searching for and exploiting a layer of flint about 3.5m below the land surface. When they reached this, they ran radial galleries out from the shaft for about 5m, beyond which daylight did not extend. Once a shaft with its set of galleries was exhausted, a new shaft was dug close by and the excavated material used to backfill the old one, much as in a modern coal mine. Used deer antler picks were cast down in the rubble along with other rubbish; one of these has given a radiocarbon date of 3140 bc (4000 BC). Four flaking floors have also been discovered near the mines. It seems likely that this industrial site was in use for a long time, perhaps intermittently into the bronze age. To the north-east of the mines there are traces of a prehistoric village, which may be where the flint miners lived.

After the mines fell into disuse, Blackpatch became a barrow cemetery; some burials were actually inserted into the rubble filling the old mine shafts, others in barrows built over them. Barrow 3, although a round barrow, is thought to be contemporary with the mines. It may well be that other round barrows in south-east England that have long been thought to be bronze age, or at earliest late neolithic, may also turn out to belong to the pre-3000 BC era.

BURY HILL ENCLOSURE   **Bury Hill**   TQ: 002122

A neolithic enclosure built in a woodland clearing, apparently without 'causeways' and with but a single entrance on the north-west side. Whitehawk's main entrance was also oriented to the north-west. Radiocarbon dates of 2730 and 2620 bc (3450 and 3350 BC) show that Bury Hill was roughly contemporary with the Whitehawk and Combe Hill causewayed enclosures.

The ditch and bank enclose an egg-shaped precinct 124m from SW to NE by 120m from NW to SE. As with many neolithic enclosures, the ditch is seen to resolve into a series of more or less straight segments and it may be that, as at Briar Hill in Northamptonshire, the segments were excavated piecemeal. Pieces of the antler picks used to dig the ditch were found on the ditch floor. The site is noteworthy; at 150m OD and false-crested a little way from the summit of Bury Hill, the gently sloping enclosure commanded one of the most beautiful views in Sussex.

No evidence of domestic occupation was found at Bury Hill. Although there was no evidence for disposal of the dead either, the site's excavator felt that the very dearth of evidence pointed towards a funerary use: a few disarticulated bones were, in fact, found on the site. Certainly a ritual or ceremonial use would seem to be indicated. There is no sign that anything was done to stop the ditch from silting up, and this implies that the ditch was not intended to be defensive.

CHURCH HILL FLINT MINES   **Church Hill, Findon**   TQ: 112083

The chalk here is too soft for flint mines with radiating galleries; instead the pits, approaching 5m deep, flare out into a bell shape at their bases to cover as large a floor area as possible. An antler pick found in one of the bell pits produced a radiocarbon date of 3390 bc (4250 BC), making Church Hill one of the oldest mines in the country. Among the hollows marking the tops of the mines were working places where the raw flint was worked into finished or semi-finished tools. There are not many mines here, but their use seems to have spanned a very long period. In the fill of one shaft, a beaker with 'barbed wire' decoration was found together with a cremation burial and two flint axes: this group of finds was dated to about 2100 BC. This implies that the site was in use, at least intermittently, for over 2,000 years (Figure 48).

CISSBURY FLINT MINES   **Findon**   TQ: 137079

This is one of the most extensive groups of flint mines in Britain, marked by about 200 shallow pits, some lying within and others outside the ramparts of a splendid iron age hillfort. Excavations in the nineteenth century by General Pitt-Rivers and others revealed that the shafts extended down through several layers of flint and chalk, as much as 12m into the rock. At this depth, up to eight radial galleries were dug, enabling the miners to gather large quantities of the prized floorstone. One shaft contained the skeleton of a young woman who may have fallen in accidentally, head first, and died there. Another contained the crouched burial of a youth carefully surrounded by chalk blocks. Neolithic pottery was found in some of the mines, and antler picks from one shaft produced a radio-carbon date of 2700–2780 bc (3400–3500 BC). The Cissbury mines do not seem to have been worked in the bronze age, and the site's history seems to have been forgotten by the time the iron age fort was built on the site; the ramparts neither wholly include nor exclude the mines, but override them randomly.

COURT HILL ENCLOSURE   Singleton   SU: 897137

A hilltop enclosure with an encircling ditch but no surviving bank. The ditch was found to be up to a metre deep on excavation, by Owen Bedwin, and to have a wide flat bottom, characteristic of neolithic ditches. The absence of a bank can be explained by ploughing-down. Very little was found that was datable, but the enclosure has been assumed to belong to the third millennium BC.

HALNAKER HILL   Halnaker Hill   SU: 921097
ENCLOSURE

A small causewayed enclosure with low banks and linked pits. The bank was not revetted. Radiocarbon dated bones place the construction of the enclosure in the third millennium BC.

HARROW HILL FLINT   Harrow Hill   TQ: 081100
MINES

The eastern slope of this conspicuous hilltop is marked by 160 filled-in flint mines. Many of the shafts were as much as 4m deep. One, opened in 1924–5, was 6.8m deep. Roughly oval in cross-section, it cut through three flint seams, the third marking the bottom of the shaft. The lowest level was worked from several radiating galleries; other galleries broke away from the shaft on the way down. The deepest galleries were lit partly by reflected daylight, partly by simple lamps that have left soot on the tunnel roofs. Discarded antler picks, one producing a radiocarbon date of 2980 bc (3700 BC), littered the mine, together with the ox shoulder blades that were used as shovels. The modern excavators estimated that the extraction of the flint from that one mine had involved the removal of 350 tonnes of chalk.

At the entrance to some of the galleries were scratch marks, evidently delib-erately made. It may be that these represent tallies, recording the amounts of flint retrieved, or it may be that they were a magico-religious attempt to induce the earth to yield more flint; the grooves similarly made on portable talisman tablets may have been intended to simulate the ard marks made in the soil in preparation for crop production (Figure 49).

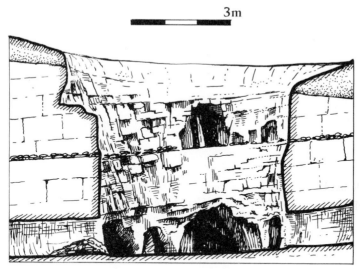

Figure 49   Harrow Hill: a section through one of the mine shafts.

NORTH MARDEN LONG BARROW   SU: 801154

A long barrow that has been extensively plough-damaged, but the ditches have survived to show the original shape and dimensions of the barrow mound. The barrow was oval, 46m long and 30m wide. Although the mound has been badly degraded, its quarry ditches are still over 2m deep in places, and have the steep-sides characteristic of neolithic ditches. In places the ditches are beaded in form, made of rows of irregular pits. No burials were found under or in the mound, but fragments of disarticulated human skeletons were found in the ditches. At the east end the ditch was deliberately filled, an act which was associated with the burial of a series of chalk objects with carved symbols. The radiocarbon date of 2760 bc (3450 BC) makes the North Marden Long Barrow contemporary with Bevis's Thumb and other Sussex long barrows.

RACKHAM COMMON   TQ: 049152

An open flint-knapping site about 3km south of Pulborough. Some 13,000 worked flints have been found, including scrapers, knives, arrow-heads, fabricators, burins and axes. Rough, weathered flint nodules were used, showing that not all the flint used in the neolithic was mined: some at least was gleaned from natural exposures on the land surface. There were two knapping floors here, and the site may have functioned as a seasonal base for hunting wild cattle in the Wealden forest. One of the stones used as an artefact was a piece of mica-schist, which may have come from Brittany, Wales, or the glacial drifts of the English Midlands; any of these possibilities implies long-distance trading contacts. The Arun estuary, then a broader and more open sea inlet before it became silted up, would have had its inland end very close to Rackham Common, so direct contact by sea with Brittany without any intervening transhipment is a real possibility.

SLONK HILL FLINT MINE   Slonk Hill   TQ: 225067

A single flint mine shaft has been discovered here. This may have been a trial pit, the results of which were found to be unsatisfactory, or it may be that the yield of a single shaft was sufficient to meet the needs of a small community.

STOUGHTON LONG BARROWS   Stoughton Down   SU: 822121 and 824120

Two overgrown long barrows on arable land. The north-west barrow is 33m long and 24m wide, and still stands 2m high. The south-east barrow, standing on slightly higher ground, is 25m long and 14m wide. The side ditches of both barrows have been filled by ploughing, and are about 0.7m deep. The barrows are as yet undated.

THE TRUNDLE CAUSEWAYED ENCLOSURE   The Trundle   SU: 877110

This important neolithic centre has been obscured by the superimposition of an iron age hillfort and the addition of an array of ugly radio masts. The choice of site is remarkable: from this conspicuous summit, the neolithic builders of the enclosure had extensive views in all directions. It was the first of the Sussex causewayed enclosures to be constructed, dating from as early as 3290 bc (4150 BC), and it continued in use at least until 2895 bc (3600 BC), by which time the other Sussex causewayed enclosures were also in operation. It was laid out in a landscape that had been recently but extensively cleared of woodland.

    The Trundle was excavated in 1929, when it was shown that the monument consisted of a spiral of banks and ditches with many causeways: it had an inner ring 112m in diameter and an overall diameter of 300m between the gates of the later hillfort. The causewayed ditch sections varied in depth between 1.5m and 2.5m and the material thrown up formed an almost continuous bank on the inner side. One part of the neolithic ditch lies buried underneath the iron age rampart on the north side; there, the skeleton of a woman was found under a pile of chalk blocks. Other finds contemporary with the enclosure included pottery, flint, bone and chalk objects. Among the chalk objects were spindle whorls and line-carved talismans. Cult activity probably went on at the Trundle, but the site seems to have been a thoroughgoing settlement too, like Whitehawk.

A single post-hole found in 1980 adjacent to the ditch on the west side has been interpreted as part of a timber gate structure. The fact that it faces the easiest route up to the enclosure supports this interpretation, but it may be that the post stood quite alone, as an isolated totem pole or flag pole. The single post should not really be advanced as conclusive evidence of a gated palisade. Nevertheless, there are many other parallels between the Trundle and Whitehawk and the latter *was* palisaded and gated. The implication is that by 3600 BC Whitehawk had become a major central place for the eastern South Downs, while the Trundle remained the principal central place for the western South Downs.

WOLSTONBURY HILL HENGE   TQ: 284138

An oval earthwork on a 200-metre high hilltop on the South Downs escarpment. It measures 198m by 183m and encloses some 2.2ha. The bank and internal ditch are now very inconspicuous, the bank crest rising only 0.6m above the top of the silted ditch. The ditch as excavated was 1.8m deep and 2.4m wide at the flat bottom and 4.9m wide at the top. It may have had entrances to the north and south-east, where the perimeter has been destroyed. The internal ditch with a flat bottom, the discovery of a single food vessel sherd at the bottom of the ditch, and the one or two entrances make this monument a very unusual iron age hillfort – if that is what it really is. The suspicion grows that although it may have been used in the iron age it originated as an early bronze age or neolithic ceremonial enclosure. As a henge, Wolstonbury Hill has a unique status in south-east England. Its large area – it is the only known henge of this size in south-east England – suggests a high-status central place. On the whole, Sussex seems to have developed in a rather insular and idiosyncratic way in the middle and late neolithic, remaining untouched by cultural developments to the west and north (Figure 50).

Interpreting Wolstonbury Hill as a neolithic centre fits in rather well with Peter Drewett's view (Drewett *et al.* 1988) that each major enclosure commanded or served a territory with a 4km radius. Since only Offham and Whitehawk are known in the downland block between the Adur and the Sussex Ouse, there is space to the north for a territory centring on Wolstonbury Hill. There is also space to the west for a fourth territory, and, by implication, a fourth neolithic enclosure site; perhaps this awaits discovery on Beeding Hill (TQ: 213095).

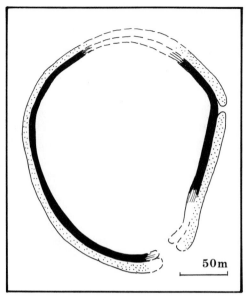

Figure 50 Wolstonbury Hill. This enigmatic monument may be a large late neolithic henge.

TYNE AND WEAR

COPT HILL BARROW   Houghton le Spring   NZ: 353492

A neolithic round cremation cairn 20m in diameter and 2.5m high. The builders of the barrow collected the remains of several disarticulated corpses, stacked wood and limestone blocks over them to make a pile about 10m by 2m, and then set fire to the whole thing. Once the pyre was well burnt a mound of limestone and sandstone chippings was raised over it. Eight more burials were inserted into the barrow in the bronze age.

HASTING HILL

A possible large neolithic ditched enclosure, identified from air photographs.

WARWICKSHIRE

BARFORD CURSUS   SP: 268565

A cursus monument 400m SE of Barford Sheds.

BARFORD HENGE   SP: 2760

A radiocarbon date of 2416 bc (3100 BC) marks the close of this monument's period of use, which would appear to make it one of the earlier henges.

There is a ring ditch 22m in diameter at SP: 289624.

BROOK STREET   SP: 281648

A settlement site that has been excavated. Other settlements, also excavated, have been found at SP: 280648 and 279649.

CHARLECOTE CURSUS   SP: 265563

A possible cursus monument 400m SE of Charlecote. It has a squared-off north end.

FURTHER LODGE BARROW   SP: 283620

A henge-like barrow 200m to the west of Further Lodge.

HOME PASTURES HENGE   SP: 410866

The site of a possible henge 500m to the north-west of Home Pastures.

KING STONE   Rollright   SP: 296309

This gnarled and weathered monolith is part of the Rollright ritual complex, most of which is in Oxfordshire. The King Stone stands 2.5m high and 1.5m wide at its base. It has a semicircular bite out of one side, and this has led some to suggest that the stone once formed part of a porthole entrance to a tomb chamber. On the other hand, many stones in the group have been weathered into odd shapes, so it is an open question. It is probably better to treat the King Stone as an outlier of the stone circle; it may or may not have had some astronomical significance (Plate 10).

NUNEATON AXE FACTORIES   c. SP: 364884

The source of the axe heads belonging to petrological type XIV. I have been unable to trace the exact location of the axe factories, and it seems likely that they have been destroyed by modern quarrying.

OLD BARN COTTAGE CURSUS   SP: 269620

A cursus monument to the south-west of Old Barn Cottage, running to SP: 269617.

ORCHARD FARM HENGE   SP: 468887

A possible henge site, 200m to the north-west of Orchard Farm.

THELSFORD BRIDGE HENGE   SP: 269584

A possible henge 100m to the north-east of Thelsford Bridge.

THELSFORD MORTUARY ENCLOSURE   SP: 269579

A mortuary enclosure 400m to the south-west of Thelsford Farm.

THELSFORD RING DITCH   SP: 268580

A ring ditch 300m to the south-west of Thelsford Farm.

WASPERTON   SP: 261581

An excavated settlement site. A second settlement existed nearby, at SP: 262583.

WASPERTON MORTUARY ENCLOSURE   SP: 263581

A mortuary enclosure some 700m to the south of Wasperton. A long linear feature leading SSW from close to Wasperton to the River Avon may represent a cursus, but it seems to belong to the bronze age rather than the neolithic.

———————————— WILTSHIRE ————————————

ADAM'S GRAVE   Alton Priors   SU: 112634

A very substantial and conspicuous long barrow, 61m long and 6m high. In a hollow at the eastern end are traces of a sarsen stone burial chamber. Excavations by John Thurnam in 1860 revealed fragments of four skeletons and a leaf-shaped arrow-head. He also found a kerb of sarsen stones and some drystone walling. Side ditches are visible, still a metre deep. It is an unusually well-preserved long barrow.

Figure 51 Stonehenge has meant different things to different generations. In 1875, it was the venue for the Wiltshire Champion Coursing Meeting.

AMESBURY BOWL BARROW   Stonehenge   SU: 131420

A bowl barrow enclosed by a ditch, west of the New King Barrows, was excavated by William Cunnington at the beginning of the nineteenth century and re-excavated by Paul Ashbee in 1960. It stands across the valley to the east of Stonehenge near the crest of a gentle west-facing slope, so the monument was built within sight of Stonehenge, and about 900m away from it.

The burnt remains of a pyre or a mortuary structure have been radiocarbon dated to 1670 bc (2100 BC), which means that the site was being developed right at the end of the neolithic. There were indications that a fire had been lit on the old land surface before the mound was raised. Grave goods included amber beads, shale beads and a shale button. A few sherds of a bronze age urn came from the upper fill of the ditch. A lot of occupation debris, including earlier neolithic Peterborough pottery and Grooved ware, worked flints and animal bones, had been incorporated into the loam core of the mound: it is possible that this historic occupation debris was deliberately collected to make a foundation deposit for the barrow.

ASHMORE DOWN LONG   Donhead St Mary   ST: 916196
BARROW

A long barrow 40m long, also known as Donhead St Mary 4.

AVEBURY   SU: 103699

This enormous earthwork, with its damaged stone circles, is one of the most important and impressive archaeological sites in Europe. It lies unobtrusively on low land at the foot of the Marlborough Downs (Figure 52). Large though it is, it cannot be seen from a great distance; we come upon it suddenly and unexpectedly. The main road is, astonishingly, still allowed to slice through the centre of the huge enclosure, which is 427m in diameter, covers 11.5ha, and has an outer circumference of more than a kilometre. Material for the encircling high bank was dug out of an internal ditch, which is about 21m wide and 9m deep, though half full of silt. The ditch was evidently dug in straight or slightly curving sections, and the spoil was carried across a flat berm to be thrown up onto the bank, which still in places has the clear form of a series of dump mounds. Some parts of the bank are as much as 5.5m high, and it seems that the inner face of the bank was originally revetted with a wall of chalk blocks – a technique which was also used to sustain the steep slopes of Silbury Hill at about the same time. The bank and ditch are interrupted by four conspicuous entrances at north, south, east and west, and there seems little doubt that these are original neolithic features. The ditches were dug rather deeper and the banks raised slightly higher beside the entrances, presumably to impress the visitor. These earthwork features constitute one of the largest henge monuments in Britain (Figure 53 and Plate 11).

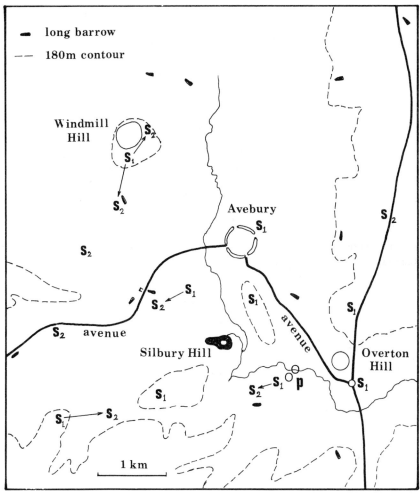

Figure 52 Map of the Avebury area, showing the relationship of the late neolithic henge to the earlier causewayed enclosures of Windmill Hill and Overton Hill. S_1 – early settlement, S_2 – later neolithic settlement. In some cases, sites close to long barrows were settled in the late neolithic; presumably by then the long barrows had ceased to be taboo, 'edgeland' monuments. P – two newly discovered post circles.

Avebury was raised on a site that originally had been a closed woodland landscape, but by the time the monument was built in the late neolithic the land had already been long cleared for agriculture, by people who may have lived at Avebury but used the Windmill Hill and Overton Hill causewayed enclosures, one on each side of Avebury, as their ceremonial centres. A pattern of six late neolithic settlement sites close to Avebury has been identified from flint scatters. Most were on the lower valley slopes, and some of them were quite extensive;

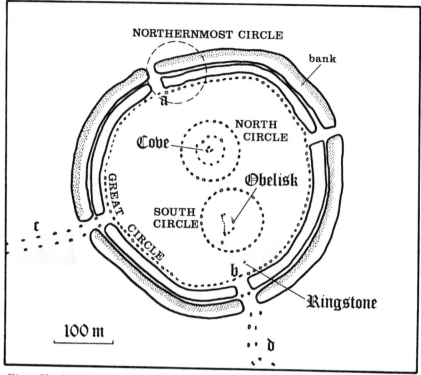

Figure 53 Avebury. a – North Entrance Stones (Swindon Stone survives), b – South Entrance Stones (both survive, including the Devil's Chair), c – Beckhampton Avenue (almost totally destroyed), d – West Kennet Avenue (partly restored). Very few stones of the North, South and Great Circles have survived, so it is all the more remarkable that Avebury is still so impressive.

probably they were permanent farming hamlets. It is hard to believe that these few people supplied all the labour needed to build the superhenge, and we must assume that people came in from further afield to help.

Inside the henge are the remains of three stone circles. The largest and most impressive, still, is the one standing 7m inside the inner lip of the ditch, the Great Circle. It consisted originally of about 98 stones, although only 27 remain standing today (Figure 53). This is Britain's largest stone circle. The sockets of fallen stones that have been destroyed were detected in the 1930s and their positions marked with concrete plinths: these enable us to visualize much more easily what the original monument must have looked like. All the stones are made of a micaceous sandstone called sarsen; this occurs naturally on the downs to the south and east of Avebury. The stones were dragged some 2 or 3km down from the hills, probably on sledges, and probably just one or two stones per year, since the work would have had to be fitted in between agricultural work. Some of them weigh as much as 40 tonnes.

Figure 54   The South Entrance Stones at Avebury.

William Stukeley believed that there was a second large stone circle, concentric with the Great Circle and about 20m inside it, represented by the surviving stump of the Ringstone and another stone on the western circuit. The evidence is too slight to attract much support for a second large circle today, particularly when archaeologists have failed to find any trace of the second alleged survivor. On the other hand, it has emerged that Alexander Keiller, when searching for the western stone, misjudged the scale of Stukeley's plan and was therefore trenching a site 2m to the east of the stone's supposed location! Even so, resistivity surveys in the eastern half of the henge have not produced any indications of a pattern of stone sockets immediately within the Great Circle.

Within the Great Circle there are the ruined remains of two smaller circles. The South Circle seems to have been 104m in diameter and consisted of about 34 to 36 stones. Only five of these survive, but the sockets of at least 12 more can be detected by resistivity survey. A gap in the circle suggests a possible entrance facing towards the SSE; the Ringstone and the huge South Entrance Stones of the Great Circle are in this direction too, which implies some overall design. At the centre of the South Circle a huge monolith, the Obelisk, once stood, but this was broken up and removed in the eighteenth century: its position is now marked by a large concrete pyramid. Close to it there is a line of about a dozen small stones. These mark one edge of a semicircular feature about which little is known, but it seems likely that it represented the semicircular forecourt of an invisible, unbuilt tomb, which in turn was symbolized by the Obelisk itself.

201

The Obelisk was drawn by Stukeley, and it was evidently a very large megalith, probably forming the focal point of the entire monument.

Figure 55   The Avebury Cove. Originally there was a tall, pillar-like flanker on the right hand side as well.

The North Circle was about the same diameter as the South Circle, although only four of its 26 to 30 stones have survived. Resistivity surveys showing the location of many of the empty stone sockets indicate that the North Circle was not smaller than the South Circle: their mean diameters seem to have been identical. The North Circle was laid out to the NNW of the South Circle, diametrically opposite the South Circle's entrance.

Inside the North Circle, three very large stones were arranged round three sides of a square: they have been known for centuries as the Cove. The Cove's open side faces north-east, the direction of the midsummer sunrise. Round this there seems to have been another arrangement of stones, possibly, though not certainly, a circle concentric with the North Circle (see Figures 1 and 55). The seventeenth-century Walter Charleton map that has only just come to light at the Royal Society shows a large fourth stone at the centre of the Cove, apparently lying flat on the ground in front of the large back stone, but Charleton's footnote, to the effect that this large stone was once supported on the other three, need not be believed: 'a Triangular stone, of vast magnitude, lying flat on ye ground; but, (probably) at first imposed on ye heads of ye other stones, in manner of an Architrave.' The two surviving stones of the Cove are so high and set so far apart that this would have presented insuperable engineering problems. Aubrey Burl (1979) estimates that the two flankers were over 10m apart, and the socket of the missing flanker revealed in a resistivity survey (Ucko *et al.* 1991) confirms this, so the fourth stone, if truly a capstone, would have needed to be at least 11m square; the capstone at Tinkinswood, which is believed to be the largest in Britain, is 7m across and weighs 40 tonnes. The substantial difference in height between the back stone and the flankers means that the colossal fourth stone would have sloped unsafely down towards the back of the Cove. It is clear that it would be unwise to suppose that this structure ever existed outside the imagination. Incidentally, the top of the surviving flanker has been inspected and it shows no trace of the sort of wear that we would expect to see if a 100-tonne slab had been dragged into position onto it.

A further point casting doubt on the accuracy of the Charleton map is that the surviving flanker is set at a right angle to the back stone, whereas Charleton shows both flankers twisted through 90°, making them parallel to the back stone. John Aubrey's 1663 plan shows the two surviving stones correctly and, in the plan's top right-hand corner, a reconstruction sketch of the Cove with three upright stones arranged round three sides of a square – and no indication at all of a fourth stone.

It seems that the tall and pointed north-west flanker of the Cove was taken down and destroyed in 1713, before Stukeley had a chance to see it. He noted that there had once been a supine fourth stone, presumably on hearsay evidence, and Stukeley, like Charleton before him, considered that this already-lost stone might once have been a capstone. Professor Peter Ucko (Ucko et al. 1991) feels that the weight of evidence is in favour of the existence of a fourth stone and that this means that Burl's (1988) idea of the Cove as a theatre for display-ing funerary mimes cannot be true. But this is not so, and Burl's sens-ible and considered views should not be so lightly cast aside. The presence of a fourth stone – even a very large stone – lying flat on the ground, which is all that Stukeley and Charleton describe, does not in any way pre-clude the use of the Cove as a theatre; the slab might actually have functioned as a stage.

A third stone circle, the Northernmost Circle, was begun but never finished. This was to have been to the NNW of the North Circle and may have been drawn out to the same dimensions, but the few stones that had been raised were taken down again when it was decided to surround the North and South Circles with a much larger third, the Great Circle. Interestingly, the three circles, the South Circle entrance and the Ringstone all seem to have rested on approximately the same NNW–SSE axis. Ucko et al. (1991) tell us that there is no geophysical evidence for this Northernmost Circle, but the geophysical survey has been confined to the north-east quadrant of the henge and it is in any case suggested only that a Northernmost Circle was begun, not completed. The positive evidence that such a beginning was made exists on the North Entrance causeway, where an arc of three stone sockets survived the major change of design that marked the abandonment of the triple-circle project.

Many of Avebury's stones were deliberately destroyed in the eighteenth century and earlier, partly to clear the land for farming, and partly as an expression of bigoted religious beliefs. Some were smashed up and used for building material, and some were toppled into grave-pits, where they still lie. Between 1936 and 1939 Alexander Keiller re-erected some of the fallen stones, and even mended some that had been smashed. It is worth remembering that many stones still lie unresurrected.

There are faint traces within the soil immediately to the north-east of the North Circle of yet another, previously unsuspected, circular structure (Ucko 1991). This may have been a double post circle with an overall diameter of about 48m i.e. roughly half the diameter of the North Circle. Interpretation is very uncertain, but it begins to look as if there was much more at Avebury than we once thought.

Leading from the southern entrance of the henge, and stretching some 2.5km, is an avenue of paired stones about 15m apart. The West Kennet Avenue, as it is known, winds its way along the valley side and then the valley floor, finally ascending sharply to the Sanctuary on Overton Hill (Plate 12). The West Kennet Avenue was obviously built specifically to connect the two monuments. The stones have been carefully selected so that they are often paired in shape, rectangular (male?) facing diamond (female?) across what is clearly a major processional way. Only the 500m section closest to Avebury has been re-erected, and it is a great pity that Keiller's restoration of the monument has been left unfinished. A settlement site, perhaps a temporary one set up by the people working on the construction of the avenue, has been discovered halfway along the restored section, at SU: 107692.

Soil resistivity surveys have picked up six more pairs of stone holes in the next field to the south of the restored section, which gives us another 60m of the avenue, but beyond that the trail of stone sockets seem to peter out. It may be that the avenue's curving sweep up to the Sanctuary, a feature drawn by Stukeley and for long taken for granted, was not part of the neolithic design. In fact, one of the earliest maps of the monument, in Aubrey's manuscript 'Monumenta Britannica' (Bodleian Library), shows a right-angled bend in the hamlet of West Kennet, so it may be that the missing pairs of stones are buried to the west of the area surveyed.

A second megalithic avenue, the Beckhampton Avenue, once led west from the superhenge's West Entrance, but this has been much more thoroughly obliterated, to the point where many doubt whether it ever existed, except in Stukeley's fertile imagination. Some of its stones have been detected in grave-pits, from which it would be possible to restore them. A second cove, the Beckhampton Cove, was built opening onto the west side of the Beckhampton Avenue; significantly, it faced south-east, the direction of the midwinter sunrise. Adam, the massive, slab-like north-east side stone, is all that remains of this cove. Eve, nearby, is a solitary survivor of the avenue. Professor Ucko's (1991) resistivity survey, undertaken in Longstones Field in the vicinity of Adam and Eve, produced disappointingly inconclusive results, but it does seem to show at least 11 avenue stone sockets, 4 of them clearly arranged in pairs about 10m apart, to the north-east of the Beckhampton Cove. The anticipated linear form does not show up well, but this may be because of a kink in the avenue about 75m NE of the cove.

The recently discovered drawings by John Aubrey and Walter Charleton that were presented at a meeting of the Royal Society in 1663 show the circular henge with its four entrances and a pair of conspicuously large portal stones outside each of the entrances, but there is no reason to believe that the North and East Entrance portals belonged to additional avenues. The discovery of these maps in 1988 led to some premature press speculation that Avebury originally had four stone avenues, which would have made the monument not only cruciform but very large. Cruciform arrangements of megaliths would have been quite possible in the neolithic, and indeed just such an arrangement was built in the Western Isles at Callanish. Nevertheless, there is no archaeological evidence for an east or north avenue at Avebury; a resistivity survey of the area outside the East entrance strongly suggests that there was no east avenue.

The exciting discoveries made in the Avebury ceremonial complex in recent years are a healthy reminder that there is still a great deal that we do not know. Extraordinarily, at the time of writing there are still no definitive radiocarbon dates for Avebury, but the general trend of the archaeological evidence points to the site being in use within the period 2800–2200 BC.

BATTERY HILL LONG BARROW	**Idmiston**	SU: 204348

A long barrow 25m long.

BEACON HILL LONG BARROW	SU: 003652

A long barrow site south-east of Hill Cott. The barrow stood on gently sloping land at 195m OD just south-east of the summit of Beacon Hill. The escarpment drops steeply away about 200m to the south-west.

BECKHAMPTON (or LONGSTONES) LONG BARROW	**Avebury**	SU: 087691

An earthen long barrow 69m long on the crest of a long, low east-pointing spur of West Down. Its long axis is aligned roughly SW–NE. The alternative name of the barrow, Longstones, refers to the two megaliths which stand 200m away to the north-east. One of them, Adam, was part of the Beckhampton Cove. The other, Eve, is a survivor of the Beckhampton Avenue, which passed very close to the long barrow on its downslope side (see Figure 52).

BECKHAMPTON ROAD LONG BARROW	**Avebury**	SU: 066677

A long barrow about 50m long, its long axis oriented SW–NE. The building of the barrow has been dated from an antler to 2517 bc (3250 BC). The mound was trapeze shaped, the broader, north-east end about 12m wide. The quarry ditches, separated from the mound by berms about 5m wide, are parallel to the sides of the mound. The effect, when seen from the broader end of the barrow, would have been to make the monument appear much larger; this false-perspective was used at many of the long barrows. The Beckhampton Road Long Barrow was raised on a site that had originally been closed woodland. The woodland was cleared for agriculture in 3250 bc (4100 BC), some 800 years before the barrow was built.

The measurements of the barrow have suggested to some that it was laid out in body-fathoms. The mound is 27 of these fathoms long, and the south ditch is 30 fathoms long. Like the nearby South Street Long Barrow, Beckhampton Road was laid out using a counting base of 3. The Beckhampton Mound contained three ox skulls, but no human burials at all. The barrow should therefore be considered more of a fertility monument and territorial marker than a burial place (see Figure 52).

BOTLEY COPSE LONG BARROW   Shalbourne   SU: 294599

A long barrow 50m long.

BOWLS (BOLES) BARROW   Heytesbury   ST: 942467

An earthen long barrow 46m long, located unusually on the crest of a W–E ridge at 188m OD. Inside the barrow a large block of bluestone (preselite) was found when William Cunnington excavated it in 1801. This suggests that bluestone was already present in the area well before the building of the bluestone monument at Stonehenge, and is sometimes cited as evidence that bluestones were introduced into Salisbury Plain by an ice sheet and deposited as glacial erratics. The Bowls Barrow bluestone, now on display as a slightly sinister spotlit sentry to the Stonehenge exhibits in Salisbury Museum, is a thick pentagonal slab about 0.9m high and 0.9m across. The two flat faces appear to have been smoothed artificially. The barrow also contained the skulls of seven oxen, lying next to three human skulls.

BRATTON CASTLE LONG BARROW   Bratton   ST: 900516

Although surrounded by arable land, this long barrow lies on grassland inside the iron age hillfort. It is 70m long and 20m wide, and it still stands 4m high at its eastern end. William Cunnington examined the ditches and found 'black vegetable earth for 5 feet (1.5m) deep intermixed with pottery, animal bones, etc.'. Near the surface at the east end of the barrow there were three intrusive skeletons. John Thurnam found 'a heap of imperfectly burnt or rather charred human bones, as many as would be left by the incineration of one or two adult bodies'. These bones seem to have been resting on a mortuary platform at the higher end of the barrow.

BRIXTON DEVERILL LONG BARROWS   ST: 872374

Two long barrows. One, 70m long and 3.7m high at the south-east end, is at ST: 846383. It has clearly defined side ditches and appears to be unexcavated. Its axis is aligned roughly NW–SE, along the contour, and it stands at 250m OD in an impressive situation, false-crested just to the north-east of the summit of Cold Kitchen Hill. The other, 78m long, is at ST: 872374; its long axis is aligned WNW–ESE, along the contour, and it stands at 205m OD, three-quarters of the way up a moderately steep SSW-facing slope.

BROADCHALKE LONG BARROW   Vernditch Chase   SU: 034211

A long barrow 22m long, in woodland on Vernditch Chase. Its long axis is oriented roughly WSW–ENE, along the contour, and it stands at 150m OD. It appears to be the most northerly of the ragged line of long barrows marking the north-east end of the Dorset Cursus.

BULFORD LONG BARROW   SU: 163430

A long barrow 40m long to the south-west of Bulford village. Its long axis lies W–E, following the contour, and it stands on a north-facing slope overlooking the River Avon. It is undated, but presumably it is significantly older than the late neolithic henge of Durrington walls, which is visible 1,200m away across the valley.

CHISELDON STONE CIRCLE   Coate   SU: 181824

A ceremonial circle at Day House Farm, Coate, on the south-western edge of Swindon. It stands perhaps significantly, beside a spring on a gently sloping site at a height of 110m OD.

CLATFORD DOWN LONG BARROW   Preshute   SU: 147713

A long barrow site on an east-facing slope, 1km E of the sarsen stone field on Overton Down.

CONEYBURY HENGE   near Stonehenge   SU: 134416

A henge and early neolithic pit on Coneybury Hill to the south-east of Stonehenge. The site should probably be seen as part of the Stonehenge ritual complex. There was a circle of post-holes concentric with the inner edge of the ditch, and large numbers of stake-holes. The precinct was oval, about 55m by 45m across, with the entrance on the long axis at the north-east end. A small quantity of Grooved ware pottery was recovered. Immediately to the north of the henge was a large pit 2m in diameter and 2m deep: in it was a large quantity of early neolithic pottery, which presumably pre-dated the henge.

Coneybury Henge has been totally flattened by ploughing, and stands on almost level ground above 115m OD within sight of Stonehenge. The site was first noticed from the air in the 1920s, when it was interpreted as a disc barrow. Traces of an external bank were seen on an air photograph of 1934 vintage. The monument has never been described as a standing monument, and was probably levelled during the medieval period or earlier; traces of medieval ridge-and-furrow impinge on it.

CORTON LONG BARROW   ST: 930403

A long barrow 64m long, false-crested on a north-facing spur projecting into the Wylye valley. Its long axis is aligned W–E, along the contour.

CROW'S RUMP LONG   Firs Road   SU: 209329
BARROW

A long barrow in Piccadilly Clump, a hilltop site at 130m OD, just over 2km to the south-east of the Figsbury Rings Henge.

CURSUS BOWL BARROW   Stonehenge   SU: 114427

A bowl barrow to the south of the Stonehenge Greater Cursus. It was excavated by William Cunnington in the nineteenth century and re-excavated by Paul Ashbee in 1960. A large central grave was equipped with a mortuary house made of jointed timbers; it contained a contracted male skeleton together with a trepanned disc of bone from his skull and a Wessex beaker. The barrow was then built, separated from the ditch by a narrow berm. Further, secondary, burials were inserted into the mound and ditch silt. A radiocarbon date of 1788 bc (2200 BC) for a wooden tool buried with one of the later Beaker secondary burials indicates that round barrow building had begun by the end of the neolithic in this area. The barrow is also noteworthy because chips of bluestone (rhyolite) are scattered throughout, showing that the Stonehenge bluestones, which are the only ones known in the locality, were being shaped and dressed at the time the barrow was being built, and also that this must have happened *before* 2200 BC.

DEADHILL WOOD LONG BARROW

Stanton St Quintin   ST: 881804

A long barrow at 110m OD on a gentle south-east facing slope, halfway between Stanton St Quintin and Grittleton.

THE DEVIL'S DEN

Preshute   SU: 152696

A chambered long barrow 70m long. The mound of this long barrow has almost entirely disappeared, but a burial chamber that marks its south-east end can be seen: it consists of four partially collapsed sarsen uprights supporting a capstone that was re-erected in 1921. The chamber was complete when William Stukeley drew it in the eighteenth century.

There is a second chambered long barrow, which is only 20m long, at SU: 151714.

DURRINGTON WALLS

Durrington   SU: 150437

A severely ploughed-down bank can be seen encircling the upper part of a short dry valley running down to the River Avon. This is all that remains of a huge henge monument with a maximum diameter of 520m, enclosing an area of 12ha. Together with Stonehenge, it seems to have supplanted the early hilltop enclosure at Robin Hood's Ball. Although the bank is now only a metre high, excavation proves that it was originally 27m wide and separated from the inner ditch by a berm that varied in width from 6m to 36m. The ditch was 6m deep with a flat bottom and 13m wide at the top. These encircling earthworks are broken by two entrances, to the north-west and south-east; the south-east entrance, at the lower end of the dry valley, opens towards the River Avon, which is only 60m away. The volume of chalk shifted was 50,000 cubic metres, representing an estimated 88,000 man-days of work.

The site of Durrington Walls was originally woodland, and this was cleared in about 3010 BC to make for an open (i.e. unenclosed) settlement consisting of a group of roundhouses. The henge itself was laid out much later, in about 2500 BC, in a short-turfed environment evidently dominated by animal husbandry. As at Marden and Avebury, there was a substantial time-lag between the clearance of the forest and the building of the henge.

It was in 1966–8 that Geoffrey Wainwright carried out his classic excavation along the present route of the A345 road. Just inside the south-east entrance he found a complex structure that originally consisted of five concentric rings of stout wooden posts with a tightly-packed timber façade facing towards the south. The posts increased in size towards the centre, implying that they also increased in height; the structure is usually interpreted as a huge roofed wooden building 38m in diameter. It had been rebuilt two or three times before it finally fell into decay.

209

To the north-east of the Southern Roundhouse was an oval midden 12m long, held in place by arcs of stakes. It contained a large amount of Grooved ware pottery, stone and flint tools, antlers and bones. Some archaeologists have expressed surprise at the amount of domestic refuse represented here, because they have made the assumption that the henge and the roundhouse were ritual in function, but there is no reason why we should see Durrington Walls as anything other than a (ritually protected) settlement. The midden in any case dates from 2320 bc (3000 BC), before the earthworks of the henge were laid out.

A second, smaller circular structure lay 120m to the north of the first. It consisted initially of two concentric rings of posts 27m and 19m in diameter, approached from the SSW by an avenue of posts passing through an arc-shaped screen of totem poles. Later these rings were replaced by two more that were smaller in diameter but composed of larger posts, with an arrangement of four massive posts in the centre suggesting a raised, central, square lantern; there was also a new timber avenue built on a different alignment. The circular structure is interpreted as another large roofed building, the Northern Roundhouse.

Durrington Walls almost certainly has a number of other roundhouses within its precinct, as well as Woodhenge, which lies just outside to the south. Some aerial photographs show tonal variations in the grass which indicate the location of these as unexcavated buildings, as well as a major sub-rectangular structure 10m across, immediately inside the north-west entrance, although this last may well prove to have been a Romano-British farmstead. Each roundhouse would have required vast quantities of timber and taken many man-hours to build. The Grooved ware pottery seems to put the people who built and used the henges in a special class; the implication is that this was prestige or 'Sunday-best' pottery.

Controversy surrounds the site, which may have been a primarily religious, ritual centre or it may have been a thoroughgoing proto-urban settlement. Some have speculated that it might have been a military kraal, a monastery, or even a university. At the end of its period of use, the huge posts were left to decay slowly in their sockets; the thatch and the lighter roof timbers presumably disintegrated first, leaving the uprights and a few lintel-beams. Since this would have left the structure looking very like the sarsen monument at Stonehenge, dating from this period of decay at Durrington, it may well be that Stonehenge III was consciously and deliberately designed as a symbolic roundhouse in decay (Figure 56).

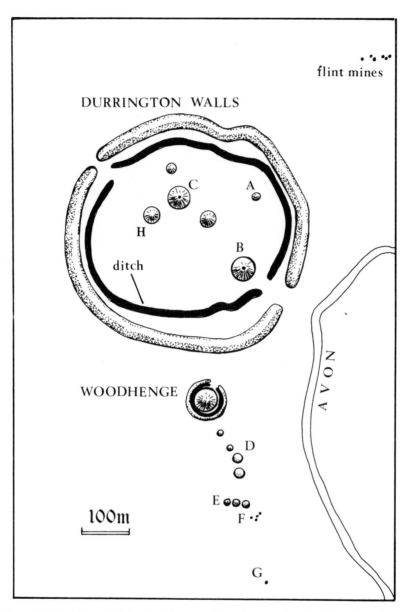

flint mines

DURRINGTON WALLS

C

A

H

B

ditch

WOODHENGE

AVON

D

E

F

100m

G

Figure 56 Durrington Walls. A – Northern Roundhouse,   B – Southern Roundhouse (both proved by total excavation),   C – circular cropmarks seen on air photographs, indicating further roundhouses,   D – later, possibly early bronze age, round barrows,   E – long barrow or three round barrows,   F – Woodlands Pits,   G – Beaker grave,   H – roundhouse indicated by magnetic survey.

EAST KENNET LONG BARROW
SU:116668

An impressive tree-covered mound 105m long and still standing 6m high, probably close to its full neolithic height. At the south-east end there are traces of sarsen stones suggesting a burial chamber, probably along the lines of West Kennet only a kilometre away. Darker growth in the crops in the fields on each side tells us of the presence of side ditches, though these are no longer visible as relief features. The barrow has not been excavated in modern times. A settlement site has been discovered to the north, beside the River Kennet south-east of West Kennet Farm, at SU: 112681 (see Figure 52).

EASTON DOWN FLINT MINES
Winterslow   SU: 237358

A flint-working industrial site on a south-west facing slope at 135m OD. There were at least 90 shafts, each 3–4m deep, and working floors were found among the shafts. The skeleton of a dog was found together with a beaker at the bottom of a pit containing ashes; the dog's skeleton was in an excellent state of preservation. Easton Down was probably the closest major complex of flint mines to Stonehenge.

EASTON DOWN LONG BARROW
Bishop's Cannings   SU: 063661

An earthen long barrow 43m long with sarsens included in its internal structure. Its long axis is aligned roughly W–E, across the contour, and it stands at 200m OD close to the crest of a ridge. The people who built the Easton Down Long Barrow probably lived at Hemp Knoll 1km away to the north-east, where a settlement site has been proved.

ELL BARROW
Wilsford   SU: 073513

A long barrow 52m long, unusually sited on a hilltop at about 180m OD.

FAIRMILE DOWN LONG BARROW
Collingbourne Kingston   SU: 256567

A long barrow 43m long.

FAULKNER'S CIRCLE
Avebury   SU: 109693

A ceremonial circle, probably functioning as part of the great Avebury ceremonial complex. It stood in the shallow dry valley immediately to the east of the West Kennet Avenue, about 750m to the south-east of Avebury itself. A single stone survives in a hedgerow out of a large ring of 12 sarsens, whose filled-up holes were noticed in 1840 by Mr Faulkner, a 'zealous antiquarian' from Devizes. The circle has never been investigated by archaeologists; it may date from the late neolithic or the early bronze age. Its proximity to the West Kennet Avenue implies that the ritual activities there were in some way linked with those of the avenue, but it is not necessarily so.

FIGSBURY RINGS   Firsdown   SU: 188338

A henge monument on a 140m-high hilltop overlooking the valley of the River Bourne, 4km NE of Salisbury and the Bourne's confluence with the River Avon. The hilltop site is exceptional for a henge, though perhaps not unique; the recently re-evaluated site of Wolstonbury in Sussex, probably also a henge, is on a hilltop.

FUSSELL'S LODGE LONG   Clarendon Park   SU: 192324
BARROW

A long barrow 52m long. A wooden mortuary house, radiocarbon dated to 3230 bc (4100 BC), stood on the site before the barrow was built, and it may have housed bodies for excarnation for a long time before it was eventually allowed to collapse. A complete ox hide, skull, hoofs and all, was draped over the mortuary house, with its horned head over the entrance and the skin and legs hanging down the sloping sides. The ox was probably the totem animal of the local community, and its connection with the land's fertility and people's survival is obvious (Figure 57).

FYFIELD AND OVERTON DOWNS   SU: 142710

This is one of the finest prehistoric landscapes in southern Britain, consisting of many examples of 'Celtic' fields, some with banks 3m high, and farm tracks between them. The grassy lynchets or terraces originated when soil moved by rainwash or the plough built up behind rows of boulders, stone walls or fences marking the edges of the fields. Excavation has shown that some fields were cross-ploughed with a simple ard, i.e. using fundamentally neolithic techniques. Farming seems to have gone on here from about 700 BC into the Roman period, and probably intermittently from earlier still. It has for a long time been assumed that the fields date from the iron age, but some may be bronze age or neolithic.

Scattered over the Downs are thousands of sarsen stones, the same stones that were used for the building of Avebury and Stonehenge. The sarsens were freed from the once-continuous layer of silcrete by natural processes of erosion and weathering. The neolithic masons had only to ease them from the soil onto sledges to drag them downhill to the nearby site of Avebury. Taking the consignment of large stones to Stonehenge was, of course, a much larger undertaking. The most accessible groups of 'grey wethers' are at Piggle Dean beside the A4, at

Figure 57 Fussell's Lodge: a reconstruction of the mortuary house, porch and façade palisade to show their relative positions. The mortuary house is shown 'under construction', but it may well have been in a state of collapse by the time the façade palisade and porch were built.

SU: 143688, and Lockeridge Dene, at SU: 145674. A late neolithic settlement has been located on the north-west side of the Downs, close to a large sarsen stone whose surface is deeply scored with grooves resulting from the polishing of stone axes (SU: 128715).

GIANT'S CAVE　　　　　　　**Luckington**　　　　　　　ST: 820829

A trapeze-shaped long barrow 37m long and 15m wide built of limestone. The false entrance at the east end stands between horns that are supported by drystone wall revetments. Passages lead in from the sides of the cairn to four burial chambers, two on the north side, two on the south. The chambers have been opened in the past, so it is difficult to assess how many people were originally buried here. The north-west chamber, which is 2.6m by 1.4m, contained the bones of at least six people: three men, two women and a child. The north-east chamber, 3.4m by 1.2m, held five burials and there were others in the passage leading to it. The south-west chamber was only partially excavated in 1960–2, exposing the remains of at least seven people: a man, three women and three infants. The south-east chamber had been badly disturbed, and the remains of

214

only one woman had survived. A piece of neolithic pottery and a few flint tools were found.

A second long barrow stands 225m to the south-east, at ST: 821828. It too may have had chambers, but it is in a poor state now.

GIANT'S GRAVE   Downton   SU: 161230

A long barrow 60m long, with its long axis aligned N–S along the contours of the Avon valley side. The barrow is false-crested, a little to the east of the highest part of the valley side, presumably to make it clearly visible to the neolithic inhabitants of the valley floor.

GIANT'S GRAVE   Milton Lilbourne   SU: 189583

A long barrow excavated in the nineteenth century by John Thurnam. Built of chalk rubble, it is 96m long, 20m wide and 2m high. At its eastern end it covered a heap of bones representing the remains of three or four people, one of whom had a cleft skull. A leaf-shaped arrow-head lay near the burials. The barrow has quarry ditches running along each side.

It is a matter of controversy whether skull-cleaving like the example discovered here occurred at the time of death, actually causing death, as has long been assumed, or at some time after death. If the cleavage occurred after death, it is not immediately obvious why. Could the purpose have been to release the spirit of the dead person, or possibly even to eat the brains? It is an area that requires further research. Clearly it makes a great deal of difference to our perception of the neolithic people and their culture whether individuals were bludgeoned to death or not. In much the same way, it makes a difference whether we see people dying of arrow wounds as victims of deliberate violence in warfare or as victims of hunting accidents. Much of the accepted evidence for neolithic violence can, in fact, be interpreted in other ways.

GRIMSDITCH LONG   Whitsbury Down   SU: 122220
BARROW

A long barrow sited on a low N–S rise between two shallow chalk valleys.

HORSLIP LONG BARROW   Avebury   SU: 086705

A rectangular long barrow 45m long on the gentle southern slope of Windmill Hill. The site was originally woodland at the beginning of the neolithic, and then it was cleared and used for pasture for a time. Trees had begun to recolonize the site immediately before the barrow was built; in other words, the barrow was built as the area was being abandoned by the farmers.

HORTON DOWN LONG BARROW

Bishop's Cannings   SU: 076658

An earthen long barrow 40m long with sarsens included in its structure.

IDMISTON   SU: 205368

A flint-working site, now in the grounds of the Microbiological Research Establishment.

IMBER CHURCH LONG BARROW

Imber   ST: 962481

A long barrow to the south-west of Imber Church.

KEYSLEY DOWN LONG BARROW

East Knoyle   ST: 879340

A long barrow 40m long, with its long axis aligned WNW–ESE. It stands at 195m OD on a gentle south-east-facing slope.

KING EDWARDS BELT LONG BARROW

Clarendon Park   SU: 179323

A long barrow false-crested on a south-east facing slope. About 1,200m to the east, on the opposite side of the dry valley, is the Fussell's Lodge Long Barrow.

KINGS PLAY HILL LONG BARROW

Heddington   SU: 010659

A long barrow 30m long with its long axis aligned SW–NE, following the contour. It is false-crested 100m to the east of the summit of Kings Play Hill, and was presumably intended to be seen from the gently sloping farmland below it to the south-east, the land which was, in AD 1643, to become the battlefield of Roundway Down.

KITCHEN BARROW

Bishop's Cannings   SU: 066648

An earthen long barrow 30m long with sarsens included in its internal structure. Its long axis, aligned roughly SW–NE, follows the contour, and it is located close to the crest of a steep-sided, south-west-pointing spur, about 1,800m to the north-west of the Rybury causewayed enclosure.

KITTS GRAVE Vernditch Chase SU: 031211

A long barrow on a gentle south-east-facing slope, now concealed in woodland on Vernditch Chase.

KNAP HILL CAUSEWAYED ENCLOSURE Alton Priors SU: 121636

This causewayed enclosure impressively situated on a steep-sided scarp above the Vale of Pewsey was the first such monument to be recognized in Britain. The 1.6ha enclosure is formed by an arc of six or seven ditch sections separated from one another by a series of causeways. The silted-up ditch varies in depth between 1.2 and 2.7m and is about 3.5m wide. The bank inside the ditch is now only very slight. A small amount of Windmill Hill pottery and bone was found in the ditches, providing us with a radiocarbon date of 2760 bc (3450 BC). After the ditches had silted up, a little Beaker pottery, dating to around 2200 BC, was dropped on the site. The Knap Hill enclosure is very clearly visible from the road to the north, especially in a noonday light.

KNIGHTON BARROW Larkhill SU: 127453

A long barrow 55m long. It stands at the north edge of Larkhill, on the summit of a low rise at 147m OD.

KNIGHTON DOWN LONG BARROW Larkhill SU: 124444

A long barrow on a gentle south-facing slope, among buildings at Larkhill.

KNOOK BARROW ST: 956446

A long barrow 30m long. It stands on the shallow crest of a broad, gently sloping ridge, just 200m to the south-west of the 189m summit.

There is a second long barrow 24m long 1km to the east, at ST: 967462, which is also on a south-east-facing slope.

LAKE BARROW CEMETERY Wilsford SU: 107401

This is one of the major barrow cemeteries that aggregated close to Stonehenge during the neolithic and bronze age, confirming the importance of Stonehenge as a sacred site. At least 15 bowl barrows, 4 bell barrows, 2 disc barrows and a long barrow lie in the plantation and on the north side of it, where they have been ploughed down. To the south, outside the wood, are five more barrows. The wedge-shaped long barrow, at SU: 107401, lies apparently unopened in the wood. It is 42m long and 2.4m high with deep side ditches. Although it has not been dated, it is likely to be the oldest of the barrows in the cemetery, and the original focus of the clustering.

'LAKE 22' BOWL BARROW   Wilsford   SU: 114404

A late neolithic bowl barrow 15m in diameter, 0.4m high, and enclosed by an irregularly segmented ditch. The primary grave, lying north to south, was disturbed by William Cunnington; Sir Richard Colt Hoare reported that the grave, opened before 1805, contained unburnt bones and the remains of two 'drinking cups', which were subsequently lost, overlying the skeleton of a child. A secondary cremation burial was tucked into the chalk mound, and the sooty patches of charcoal incorporated in the mound material covering this pit suggest scraped-up pyre material. A large amount of neolithic pottery in fresh condition and some worked flint incorporated in this deposit implies a neolithic date for the burial. Other neolithic sherds were found in the ditch. The pottery includes early neolithic rim-sherds, Peterborough ware (in Ebbsfleet, Mortlake and Fengate styles) and Grooved ware. It was Hoare who named this barrow 'Lake 22'.

'LAKE 24' BOWL BARROW   Wilsford   SU: 114404

The mound of this barrow has been completely destroyed and there is no sign of a surrounding ditch. A large grave, disturbed by William Cunnington's excavation, contained the remains of three successive inhumations above what may have been a primary cremation. Fragments of earlier neolithic pottery and Grooved ware were scattered through the grave fill. Many earlier neolithic sherds and a few of Peterborough ware were found in natural hollows near the grave.

LANHILL LONG CAIRN   Chippenham Without   ST: 877747

A very badly mutilated long barrow about 56m long and 27m wide, aligned W–E with a false entrance at the eastern end removed in 1909. Three side chambers are known to have existed; one still surviving on the south opens out of a passage and measures 2.4m by 1.2m. Originally it had a corbelled roof and contained the remains of 11 or 12 people. On the north side both chambers have been destroyed. One was entered through a roughly shaped porthole entrance and was roofed by a single capstone. When it was excavated in 1936 it contained nine skeletons. In 1938, Dr A. J. E. Cave examined the bones from the northern chamber and identified marked family resemblances among the skulls; from this he deduced that Lanhill had been a family vault. Many of the people buried in the tomb suffered from osteo-arthritis, a complaint that was widespread in the new stone age. The damage done to the Lanhill Long Cairn seems to be mainly modern: most if it has been inflicted since John Aubrey first sketched it in the middle of the seventeenth century.

LIDDINGTON CASTLE   Liddington   SU: 214799

Pits discovered about 800m to the north-east of the hillfort may have been neolithic flint mines.

LIDDINGTON LONG BARROW   SU: 225797

A long barrow 46m long with sarsens, subsequently used as a parish boundary marker.

LUGBURY LONG BARROW   Nettleton   ST: 831786

A fine long barrow 58m long, 27m wide and 2m high. At the east end, as John Aubrey described it, is 'a great Table stone of bastard freestone leaning on two pitched perpendicular stones'. The three big stones form a false entrance. The central stone is 3.7m by 1.8m, with smaller stones on each side. Four sealed burial chambers were found on the south side, containing the remains of 26 people, 10 of them children. None of these chambers can now be seen. In 1821, Sir Richard Colt Hoare found a crouched primary burial near the east end, and in 1854 a further chamber was discovered.

MANTON LONG BARROW   Preshute   SU: 152714

This barrow is 18m long, 12m wide and in a poor state of preservation. At the east end a forecourt leads into a burial chamber with a capstone still in place. A kerb of sarsen stones surrounds the barrow. Excavation has shown that there was a large pit in the forecourt: it contained the skeleton of a pole-axed ox. The style of the pottery found on the site suggests a date of about 3000 BC.

MARDEN HENGE   SU: 091584

The hamlet of Marden stands inside the largest known henge monument in Britain. Oval in shape, 450m by 330m, an area of 14ha is enclosed on the east, north and north-west by a large bank and internal ditch: the meandering River Avon and its floodplain form its west and south sides. Two entrances lie at right angles to each other on the north and east sides.

Excavations at the north entrance in 1969 showed that the ditch was at least

15m wide, but only 1.8m deep. Pieces of Grooved ware pottery, flint tools, antler picks and pieces of animal bone had been dropped into the ditch, or carefully deposited there, by the people who used the site. Just inside the entrance was a timber circle 10.5m in diameter. It had three posts in the centre, presumably to support the highest point of a conical roof. It seems to have been a simpler structure than the wooden rotundas at Woodhenge, Durrington Walls or the Sanctuary. There was a shallow rubbish pit close to it, which contained the bones of cattle, sheep, pigs, horses and red deer. Perhaps there were more roundhouses at Marden.

The great bank surrounding Marden has been badly ploughed down, but it can still be seen for much of its course. The site was cleared of its forest cover and settled as early as 3250 BC, although the henge itself was not laid out until some 750 years later, in 1988 bc (2500 BC).

A huge circular mound, the Hatfield Barrow, once reared to a height of 7m inside the earthwork. It was excavated by William Cunnington in October 1807, using eight men for ten days, but he did not find a primary burial. The barrow, which may have belonged to the 'harvest hill' family of fertility monuments, large round ceremonial mounts with no primary burials, was totally destroyed shortly after the Cunnington excavation (see Figure 28).

MARLBOROUGH MOUND   Marlborough College   SU: 183687

In the school grounds stands one of the largest barrows in England, second only to Silbury Hill. Almost 100m in diameter and 18m high, this huge mound was reshaped in 1650 with a spiral path winding round it and a gazebo at the top. Today Marlborough Mound is in a sad state, overgrown, tree-covered, and with a large water tank on top. Red deer antlers were found buried in the side of the barrow in 1912, finds which are strongly suggestive of a neolithic foundation deposit. The mound has, as far as is known, never been excavated. It seems likely, from its size and its low-lying site next to water, that it belongs to the 'harvest hill' type of large round mound, a ceremonial monument with no primary burial.

MARTIN DOWN LONG   Verndtich Chase   SU: 035204
BARROW

A long barrow 33m long, one of a straggling line of long barrows at the north-east end of the Dorset Cursus and apparently forming its 'destination'. The Broadchalke Long Barrow lies 800m to the north, while 1km to the SSE is a dense linear cluster of barrows actually marking the Cursus terminus.

MILL BARROW

Winterbourne Monkton SU: 094722

A large barrow, once 66m long and with a megalithic tomb chamber at its broader, and probably higher, east end. John Aubrey's sketch shows the mound surrounded by the stones of a revetment wall (see Figure 67). The site was ploughed and wrecked in the eighteenth century. By Sir Richard Colt Hoare's time, it was almost levelled. Eventually the monument was systematically destroyed. In 1849, Dean Merewether met the man who had destroyed it. According to him, the tomb contained 'a sort of room built up wi' big sarsens put together like, as well as a mason could set them; in the room was a sight of black stuff, and it did smill nation bad'. Today there is nothing left except one large stone in the hedge to show where this 'large and flat long barrow set round with stones' once stood.

MILSTON DOWN LONG BARROWS

Milston SU: 217463

Two long barrows lie side by side to the west of the road. Neither of them appears to have been opened. One, at SU: 217462, is 49m long, 21m wide and 2m high; the other, to the north, at SU: 217463, is 27m long, 15m wide and 1m high. Their side ditches are still visible. Further away, there are two more long barrows, at SU: 189459 and SU: 203473.

NETHERAVON LONG BARROW

SU: 114466

A long barrow 33m long on a gentle south-east-facing slope. A second long barrow stands 300m away to the north-west, near the crest of a low ridge.

NORMANTON DOWN BARROW CEMETERY

Stonehenge SU: 118413

Forming one of the most important barrow cemeteries in Britain, these monuments sweep across the horizon south of Stonehenge for more than a kilometre. To the south-west of Bush Barrow, beside a cart track, is a long barrow 36m long and 1.8m high, in which Cunnington found four skeletons 'curiously huddled together' at the east end.

Immediately to the south of the long barrow, at SU: 114410, there was a mortuary enclosure used for storing corpses before burial: it was discovered by air photography and later excavated. The mortuary enclosure was 37m by 20m, with its long axis oriented towards the south-east, where the entrance was situated. The enclosure was marked by a characteristically neolithic beaded ditch broken by 11 causeways; the ditch was up to 1m deep. Inside the entrance were two bedding trenches for posts, apparently to make some sort of ceremonial gateway.

Just above the bedding trench were traces of horizontal timbers that had linked the bases of the posts; perhaps they originally functioned as a revetment to stop bank material from falling into the entrance. Finds include 11 antler picks, the bones of oxen and sheep or goats, and a sherd of a Mortlake-style bowl from a high level in the ditch fill. The mortuary enclosure has been radiocarbon dated to 2560 bc (3250 BC) (Figure 58).

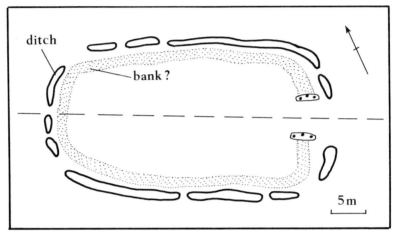

Figure 58 Normanton Down mortuary enclosure.

NORMANTON GORSE LONG BARROW

Stonehenge   SU: 115417

A long barrow standing 800m to the south-west of Stonehenge, and close to the A303.

NORTON DOWN LONG BARROWS

Heytesbury   ST: 925459

The Norton Bavant Long Barrow, at ST: 925459, is 55m long. The other, the Middleton Down Long Barrow at ST: 918459, is 26m long. They stand, false-crested, on neighbouring south-pointing spurs overlooking a broad dry valley, where their builders probably farmed.

OLDBURY LONG BARROW

Calne Without   SU: 046693

A long barrow 55m long with sarsens. A second long barrow lies to the west of Oldbury, at SU: 044693.

OLD CHAPEL LONG BARROW

Rough Hill, Preshute   SU: 129729

A chambered long barrow site high up on Rough Hill. The megalithic long mound had a crescent-shaped forecourt. William Stukeley's reconstruction drawing shows a deep forecourt with no visible means of reaching the chamber behind the façade. Stukeley also saw evidence of a large rectangular ditched and banked mortuary enclosure adjoining the tomb. Both monuments have long since been dismantled by farmers and it is now very difficult to evaluate Stukeley's interpretation of the site.

OLD SHEPHERD'S SHORE LONG BARROW

Bishop's Cannings   SU: 038660

A long barrow to the west of Old Shepherd's Shore.

OVERTON HILL CAUSEWAYED ENCLOSURE

Overton Hill   SU: 117684

A newly recognized causewayed enclosure site, just to the north-west of the Sanctuary and west of the Ridgeway. Overton Hill and Windmill Hill were the two ceremonial centres for the area before the lower site of Avebury was developed. Interestingly, the Avebury henge was built exactly halfway between the two earlier monuments, which suggests that its location was closely linked with the two causewayed enclosures, and also that it may have served or supplanted both of them.

The Overton Hill enclosure has three ditch circuits. Only a part of it has been seen, and it may eventually be found that Overton Hill was as large as Windmill Hill. It is not at all clear how it came about that two major enclosures came to be built so close together – uniquely close, in fact – but their proximity may go some way towards explaining why Avebury later became such an important centre.

PERTWOOD DOWN LONG BARROW

Brixton Deverill   ST: 872374

An unusual long barrow, 76m long and 2m high, with flat berms separating the mound from its clearly marked side ditches. The barrow appears not to have been opened.

ROBIN HOOD'S BALL

Larkhill   SU: 102459

A causewayed enclosure on a gentle south-facing slope, slightly false-crested just to the south of a 140m high summit. Long before neolithic camps or interrupted ditch enclosures were recognized as distinctively neolithic monuments, Sir Richard Colt Hoare described Robin Hood's Ball (1812) as 'one of those ancient circles. This, like the generality of them, is placed on an elevated and commanding situation, but has this peculiarity, of having one circle within the other, with an entrance towards the north. We have to regret the great injury these circles have sustained by the plough, as in their original state they must have been highly curious.'

Robin Hood's Ball, in common with other causewayed enclosures, is irregular in plan. It has two circuits of banks and ditches that enclose 3ha altogether. The inner bank and ditch surround an oval area 1ha in extent, its long axis lying NE–SW. The inner bank has been more completely levelled than the outer and is scarcely visible at all. The second ditch and bank are about 30m outside the first. Both ditches have the characteristic flat floors.

Excavations in 1984 revealed a settlement site just outside the causewayed enclosure. The remains there consisted of small pits dug out of the chalk and containing flint tools, animal bones and round-bottomed pottery. Traces of a hearth were found and, scattered all around the site, discarded flint implements. The implication is that the early farmers living in the settlement built the neighbouring enclosure for ceremonial purposes.

There are two contemporary long barrows to the north-east of Robin Hood's Ball, at SU: 114466 and SU: 112468, and one to the north, at SU: 108467. A fourth, at SU: 108458, is 500m away to the east, its long axis aligned roughly W–E.

ROCKBOURNE DOWN LONG BARROW — SU: 102222

A long barrow 56m long on a south-pointing spur.

ROCKS HILL LONG BARROW — Old Sarum — SU: 141335

A long barrow 600m to the north of Old Sarum.

ROUGHRIDGE HILL LONG BARROW — Bishop's Cannings — SU: 054657

An earthen long barrow 70m long. To the north of Roughridge Hill, at SU: 060660, a settlement site has been located.

ROUND CLUMP LONG BARROW — Whitsbury Down — SU: 112227

A long barrow 60m long on a south-west facing slope.

RYBURY CAMP   All Cannings   SU: 083640

A small iron age fort overlies a small neolithic enclosure. The causewayed
enclosure consists of two concentric oval ditches, of which eight segments of the
outer ring are to be seen on the east side of the hillfort; it measures about 160m
by 140m. About 300m to the south-east is a small knoll called Clifford's Hill,
which bears seven more segments of causewayed ditch. Excavation of the main
part of the enclosure has revealed ditch sections that are 2m deep and flat-
bottomed.

THE SANCTUARY   Overton Hill   SU: 118679

This circular monument marks the end of the West Kennet Avenue, south-east
of Avebury. Systematically destroyed in the eighteenth century, the Sanctuary
was rediscovered and excavated in 1930–1, when digging revealed the sites of
two stone circles and six concentric rings of post-holes. The post-rings represent
a number of successive circular wooden buildings. When the final timber structure
had disintegrated, the site was commemorated by the raising of two stone circles.

At the outset, around 2900 BC, a round thatched-roof house 10m in diameter
was built on the site. Its outer walls consisted of 12 thick oak posts. Inside was
an inner ring of eight huge posts holding up the conical roof. The initial
roundhouse may have stood for as long as 200 years before it disintegrated and
was replaced by another, slightly larger house, which lasted until about 2500 BC.
The stone settings that were probably raised in 2500–2400 BC may have been
intended to commemorate the earlier wooden buildings, and certainly the place
would have gathered ancestral associations.

The positions of both the stones and the posts are today marked by a rather
confusing scatter of concrete plinths.

It is important to see the Sanctuary as a component in the Avebury ritual
complex. Not only was the Sanctuary located at the end of the West Kennet
Avenue, which led to Avebury, but the site lay on the optimal route to Avebury
from Overton Down. It would have been easiest to drag the sarsens south along
the Ridgeway to the Sanctuary, and then west and north-west towards Avebury
along the line later to be followed by the West Kennet Avenue. Some human
remains, such as pieces of jawbone found in a stone hole, suggest a possible
funerary use. The shallow grave of a 14-year-old girl at the east side of the inner
stone ring implies a human sacrifice as a foundation ritual: the body was buried
immediately before one of the stones was hauled upright over the grave.

The number of posts and stones used at the Sanctuary strongly suggests a
counting base of 4, contrasting with the base of 3 noticed among the long barrow
builders (Figure 59).

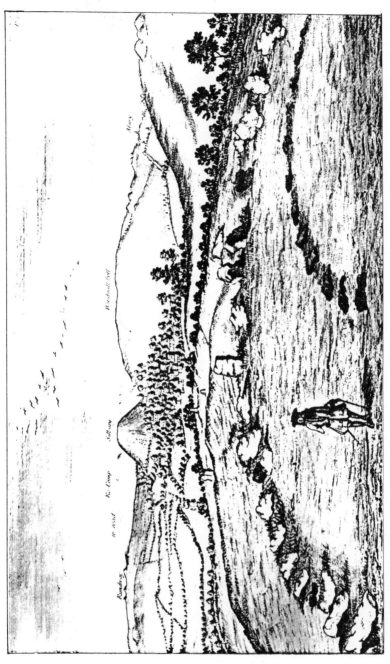

Figure 59   William Stukeley's drawing of himself in the ruins of the Sanctuary. His title for the drawing is 'Prospect of the Temple on Overton Hill 8 July 1723: the Hakpen or head of the Snake in ruins'. On 13 May in the following year, Stukeley had the distressing experience of watching the monument's destruction by farmers Green and Griffiths: 'This day I saw with grief several of the few stones left on Overton Hill carryed downwards towards West Kennet ... The loss of this work, I did not lament alone; but all the neighbours (except the person that gained the little dirty profit) were heartily grieved for it.'

SCOTS POOR LONG BARROW

Chute

SU: 284560

A long barrow to the south-west of Scots Poor.

SHELVING STONES

Winterbourne Monkton

SU: 103715

A destroyed chambered tomb which once had a long mound. Fortunately for us, Shelving Stones was sketched by Aubrey and Stukeley before its destruction. Their sketches show a box-like tomb chamber near one end of a long barrow. The similarity between this megalithic box shape and the form of the cove has been commented on already; coves were probably intended as symbols of the tomb's heart. Stukeley's drawing of Shelving Stones shows a huge gnarled capstone at the tomb's entrance, leaning at 45° against two uprights (Figure 60). Aubrey's earlier sketch shows the same structure.

Figure 60   The Shelving Stones burial chamber, drawn by William Stukeley.

SHERRINGTON LONG BARROWS

ST: 951384

Two long barrows. One to the east of Boyton Field Barn, at ST: 951384, is 46m long. The other, to the east of Sherrington village, at ST: 968391, is 30m long.

SILBURY HILL   **Avebury**   SU: 100685

Silbury's powerful conical profile dominates the chalk landscape today much as it did in the neolithic when it was built. Even the experienced traveller is impressed by Silbury. The neolithic inhabitants of Wessex, who for the most part probably travelled little and were certainly unaccustomed to seeing very large structures like oil rigs, skyscrapers, cathedrals or castles, must have been awe-struck by it. Silbury must have been the Empire State Building or the Severn Bridge of neolithic Britain (see Figure 52).

The huge artificial hill, an 'Unclassified Feature' according to the Wiltshire Sites and Monuments Record, is 40m high and covers an area of more than 2 hectares. Silbury was dug into in 1776, when the Duke of Northumberland employed Cornish miners to tunnel down from the summit. Seventy years later, in 1849, Dean Merewether of Hereford, in an orgy of barrow-plundering, opened 35 barrows in 28 days, including Silbury and the West Kennet Long Barrow. Merewether attacked the big hill by means of a tunnel driven into the centre from the south side, but he found nothing. In 1968–70, Richard Atkinson rediscovered the Merewether tunnel and made a more scientific exploration of the interior of the mound. The Atkinson dig was equally unsuccessful, in that it failed to arrive at a definitive explanation of the monument's purpose, but it did produce a great deal of circumstantial detail about the way it was constructed. It emerged, for example, that there had been four building phases.

First of all a drum-shaped mound 4.9m in diameter and 0.9m high was constructed out of clay and flint, on a stony land surface that may have been cultivated before the work began. This was covered with a heap of soil and turf that spread radially outwards to a low wooden marker fence 20m in diameter. On top of this, the builders laid four layers of chalk, gravel and subsoil, to make a conical mound 34m in diameter and 5m high. Unfortunately, the centre of this structure, probably the key to the whole monument, was completely destroyed.

Shortly after this first phase was completed, the mound was enlarged. A quarry ditch was dug around it and the chalk piled up to create a larger mound 73m in diameter.

There was a change of plan before Phase 2 was completed. The ditch was abandoned and work started on a much larger mound still. This spectacular monument was built of chalk blocks in a series of great steps like a white ziggurat, presumably to give the mound greater stability: the technique is reminiscent of the concentric revetment walls of tombs such as Wideford Hill on Orkney, which were also structural. The uppermost step is still visible, possibly as a result of the later filling weathering out, possibly intentionally. The chalk for this was quarried from a huge new ditch 7–10m deep and 26m wide. Blocks were piled up between concentric and radial retaining walls that were all part of an elaborate and ingenious architectural scheme to counteract the effects of weathering, prevent the sides of the mound from collapsing, and ensure that the monument kept its shape. At around the same time in Egypt, i.e. in about 2670 BC, a similar technique was being employed to stabilize the Step Pyramid of Zoser at Saqqara.

The fourth and last stage at Silbury seems to have been the extension of the ditch towards the west. This was done to procure the extra chalk needed to fill in the steps of the mound and give it its final, smoothed-off appearance.

Radiocarbon dating of the initial phase suggests that the monument was begun in 2750 BC, but its purpose remains one of the great enigmas of British prehistory. Silbury is often regarded as a great neolithic round barrow, raised perhaps to cover the mortal remains and grave goods of some prehistoric king whose paramount rank required an elaborate mausoleum. That may yet prove to be the case, but if so his remains have still to be found. If they existed, they may have been destroyed by Dean Merewether, or it may be that they still lie concealed in a wooden or stone chamber away from the monument's centre, awaiting discovery. It may alternatively be that the 'kingly burial' idea is quite wrong, and that Michael Dames' (1976) interpretation of the monument as a 'harvest hill' is a better explanation. Silbury does seem to be the largest member of a family of later neolithic burial-less barrows, all round, all low-lying near water, all large, all representing major communal work projects. Possibly there is a calendrical function, and almost certainly a magico-religious function.

With Silbury, it is impossible not to speculate. Among the many and varied survivals from the British neolithic, it is unique in scale, grandeur and mystery.

SMAY DOWN LONG BARROW

Shalbourne   SU: 310592

A long barrow 49m long.

SOUTH STREET LONG BARROW

Avebury   SU: 090692

A long barrow 40m long and 16m wide, raised between two parallel quarry ditches; the ditches were separated from the barrow mound by berms that were at least 7m wide. The buried neolithic soil beneath the long barrow has given us invaluable evidence of the forest clearance sequence and early neolithic activity on the site. Dense woodland was totally cleared from the area in around 3500 BC. Then the soil was deeply cross-ploughed for use as arable land. After a time, the land was changed to pasture and there was some flint-knapping on the site; only then was the long barrow built. At some stage before the building of the barrow, a boundary fence seems to have crossed the site, possibly to control the movement of livestock; a line of 34 stake-holes crosses the area covered by the barrow in a straight diagonal. The earth and chalk rubble making up the barrow were contained in a series of bays that were defined by wooden fences, either to support the material or to define work stints. There were no human burials in the barrow, emphasizing the role of the long barrow as a fertility monument and territorial marker (Figure 61).

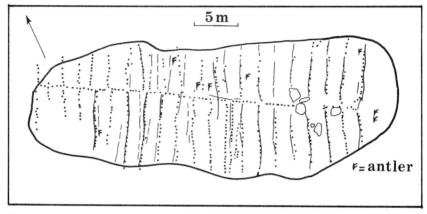

Figure 61   Plan of South Street Long Barrow, showing the pattern of stake-holes (black dots) and hurdles (lines) in the neolithic land surface. The bays between the hurdles may have been seasonal work stints.

STOCKTON LONG BARROW   ST: 965376

A long barrow 33m long, to the south-west of Stockton village.

STONEHENGE   SU: 122422

Stonehenge is the most famous, the most visited and probably the most mis-understood prehistoric site in Europe. It is impossible to do the monument's exceedingly complex history full justice in the limited space we can allow it here, but the main stages in its development at least can be outlined.

One very important fact, and one that is overlooked by many visitors, is that the development of Stonehenge spanned a very long period of prehistory, beginning long before the erection of the sarsen monument at its centre. The three post-holes discovered when the car park was laid out, at SU: 12054237, 12064237 and 12084237, some 253m to the north-west of the monument's centre, represent the earliest known phase in a long evolution. Since they preceded Stonehenge I by many hundreds of years, the three large totem poles – if that is what they were – might be called Stonehenge 0. In fact, as other prehistorians have argued, there is a case for renumbering the phases, but, to avoid confusion, this account sticks to the conventional numbering. Post A has been radiocarbon dated to 7180 bc (about 8000 BC) and post B to 6140 bc (about 7000 BC). Both dates are disconcertingly early, mesolithic rather than neolithic, which is in itself a major problem. Nor is it understood why post A should have been 1,000 years older than post B. The bewildered excavator, who knew that the dated samples were fragments of the original posts, could only speculate that they might have been poor quality samples. An open mind should be kept on the relationship between the three big posts and the later monument, but it is an exciting possibility that there was already a monument of some kind at Stonehenge in the mesolithic.

Stonehenge I, the earliest monument to be generally recognized, dated from around 3000 BC. At that time it consisted of a rather unusual henge monument, a circular bank with an external ditch about 115m in diameter surrounding it. The beaded ditch was dug in a fairly irregular way and it seems to have been regarded by the builders as a quarry for the chalk rubble bank, which was originally about 1.8m high although now scarcely perceptible. The maze of stake-holes on the north-east entrance causeway indicated year-by-year observations of northerly moonrises over a period of a century or more, observations that were summarized by the four or perhaps five large posts, the 'A' posts, to mark the crucial stages in the 19-year lunar cycle. The orientation of the monument's main axis on the midsummer sunrise is well known, so there is clear evidence that Stonehenge was used – either partially or exclusively – to observe, mark and salute both solar and lunar cycles. We can argue from this that the neolithic people, living in the area were intent on fixing religious feast-days in their calendar, and also giving structure to their agricultural programme. Equally, we can argue from the same evidence an awe of nature and an obsession with magico-religious control of the cosmos. Either way, both lunar and solar elements seem to have been present in Stonehenge I (Figure 62).

Inside the ditch and bank were the Aubrey Holes, a ring of 56 pits 0.6–1.2m deep, evenly spaced round the perimeter of the central precinct, and they too belong to this first phase. The original function of the Aubrey Holes, which were named after John Aubrey, who first noticed them, is unknown. They were eventually to hold cremation burials, but they may originally have been excavated as sockets for small circle stones. Although no stones from such a circle survive, except perhaps for the two remaining Station Stones, stones 91 and 93, if they were only 1m high they would have been very easy to remove from the site.

The 4m-high Heel Stone and its now-missing partner were outliers to this circular monument, planted some distance outside the henge's north-east entrance. It was not at all unusual for ceremonial circles to have single outlying marker stones – Brodgar, Stenness, Long Meg and Her Daughters and Stanton Drew all had outliers too – which is why we have been content with the Heel Stone on its own. Nevertheless, it is now clear that the Heel Stone had a partner and that together they formed a ceremonial portal, straddling the main axis of the monument. It is also likely that, at this time, the Slaughter Stone and its missing partner made an inner pair of portal stones at the henge entrance, which would also have made solar observations more accurate. The two pairs of stones defined and emphasized Stonehenge's principal and least controversial alignment, on the

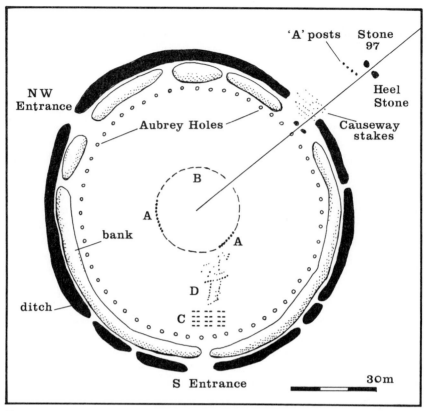

Figure 62 Stonehenge I. A – arcs of post-holes found by Hawley, B – implied circular post setting or roundhouse. The South Entrance was clearly used as an approach to the central structure; there are gaps in both ditch and bank, a trampled area (C) just inside the entrance, and what seems to have been a timber avenue (D) leading towards the post setting. The axis shown is the 3000 BC midsummer sunrise axis. It is apparent that the north-eastern entrance causeway and the scatter of causeway stakes indicate an (earlier) orientation on moonrises. A line passing through the centre of this causeway is aligned on a point midway between the major northern moonrise and the moonrise at midswing.

newly risen sun disc on the summer solstice in 3000 BC. The main axis of Stonehenge does not pass through the Heel Stone's tip, but passes to the north, completely missing the stone. The discovery of the second Heel Stone's socket in 1980 by Michael Pitts was a major event in megalithic archaeology, the significance of which has not been adequately acknowledged.

The final component of the middle neolithic Stonehenge, Stonehenge I, was a central structure of some kind. Unfortunately, the central area has been dug into repeatedly by antiquaries and treasure-hunters, so the archaeological record of the early structure is very hard to read. It appears that there was a ring of posts 29.6m in diameter, roughly coinciding with the later sarsen circle, and this may have been a roofed rotunda of the same type that we saw at Durrington Walls, Marden and Mount Pleasant, and which seems to have preceded the stone circles at Avebury. There may also have been an avenue of posts leading to the rotunda's entrance from a second entrance on the south side of the henge. An area of compacted, trampled earth immediately inside this entrance confirms that it was used as such; in fact it may be that this was the normal, everyday entrance, and that the north-east entrance was a sacred entrance used only by the rays of the sun and moon.

From about 2500 until about 2250 BC there was a significant hiatus in Stonehenge's development. There had been no new building there for some time past, the henge ditch became silted up and the monument became overgrown with grass and bushes. What this hiatus means is not yet clear. It could mean that the small farming communities who collaborated in the building of Stonehenge I were diverting their energies to the development of new sites, and we know that there were new sites just to the east that were built at this time: Coneybury, Durrington Walls and Woodhenge. It may be that, once built, these new monuments attracted ceremonial activity to them, to the detriment of Stonehenge. It may nevertheless be that Stonehenge was still in use throughout this period, but in a lower key and without any interference with the natural processes operating on the site. We know that this sometimes happened at other sites, where trees were permitted to grow in enclosure ditches, where huge roundhouses were allowed to decay, and where ditches were allowed to silt up without any attempt being made at recutting. But, whichever way the evidence is read, in the years around 2500 BC, the Stonehenge people were allowing nature to steal in and take their sanctuary for its own.

In 2250 BC, they changed their minds. They left the partly silted ditch uncleared and made no attempt to rebuild the collapsed and degraded henge bank. They turned their attention instead to the central structure. We can assume that by this time the timber roundhouse that had occupied the centre in Stonehenge I had rotted away and collapsed. It may be that the new development was designed, at least in part, to commemorate the collapsed roundhouse. It may be that diplomacy demanded the acceptance of a gift of a stone circle from Wales. About 85 bluestones, each weighing up to 4 tonnes, were brought from the Preseli Mountains in Dyfed. They may have travelled by raft or composite boat along the South Welsh coast and up the Bristol Avon, then dragged a short distance overland on sledges to reach the River Wylye and the Wiltshire Avon. It seems more likely to me that the journey was made by water all the way: from Milford Haven south across the Bristol Channel via Lundy, round Land's End, along the south coast of England to Christchurch Harbour (a known neolithic importing centre) and then north up the Hampshire–Wiltshire Avon. The idea that the bluestones were delivered to Salisbury Plain by an ice sheet has recently been revived (Keys 1990), on the strength of a geological analysis of the stones. The fact that they represent more than one rock type has been well known for decades, as has the fact that they must have been gathered from more than one site in the

Preseli Mountains. What this implies is not that the bluestones are glacial erratics, an idea which did not convince most geologists and geomorphologists when it was proposed in the 1970s (e.g. by Kellaway 1971), but that the stones had already been gathered together by people in south-west Wales. Possibly the neolithic communities of the Preseli area had gathered them from the hillsides and assembled them into a stone circle, which was then given to, or commandeered by, the Stonehenge people.

At Stonehenge II, the bluestones were arranged in a double circle on the site of the timber structure, with a short avenue emphasizing the entrance and the principal 'midsummer sunrise' axis. Each pair of circle uprights may have been capped by a radial lintel made of wood, an arrangement which was certainly within the architectural vocabulary of the megalithic architects. The intention may have been to develop the stone circle into a symbol of the sun's rayed disc, a common neolithic image. The monument was to consist of 82 uprights and 40 wooden lintels. Inside the double ring, standing upright on the main axis where the dawning midsummer sun would shine squarely onto it, was the most important stone of Stonehenge II. The so-called Altar Stone may have been in place continuously since this first bluestone monument was raised; as such, it should be seen as the most important of the stones of Stonehenge II and III. It is a pity that, even after the repair and reconstruction work of the twentieth century, it should still lie recumbent, obscure and neglected.

Stonehenge II was never finished. Only half the double bluestone circle was in position when, in about 2000 BC, the plan was dramatically changed. The completed bluestone trilithons were uprooted and taken somewhere off-site, and the sockets of the remaining uprights were never dug. In 2200 BC the first of the huge sarsen stones arrived. Possibly the radical change of plan was diplomatically motivated. The sarsens came from the heart of the Avebury territory and may have been offered to the Stonehenge tribe as a gift.

In Stonehenge III, the consignment of sarsens from Avebury was made into a horseshoe of five trilithons arranged symmetrically about the main axis, with the tallest central trilithon facing the midsummer sunrise; the tallest of the uprights is 6.7m high and weighs 45 tonnes (see Figure 46). Surrounding this, the builders raised a massive stone circle of 30 tall blocks surmounted by 30 running lintels, making a unique continuous stone ring. As before, in Stonehenge I and Stonehenge II, the builders were drawing on an existing repertoire of architectural idioms, but using them and combining them in a highly individual way. Planting stones upright in circles had been done before, in a thousand places for nearly a thousand years; large megaliths had been handled, like the very big stones at Avebury; lintels had been built too, every time the entrance passage to a chambered tomb was roofed; even horseshoe-shaped monuments could be seen elsewhere, such as at Arminghall. What was extraordinary was that at Stonehenge the components were put together to create completely new effects. Even though ruined, Stonehenge III still has a magisterial grandeur and power about it that is unrivalled among megalithic monuments. Even more extraordinary is that the builders constructed, in effect, the skeleton – in stone – of a roundhouse in decay, and that, to the late neolithic people of Wessex, would have been a symbol with very powerful resonances. The key to an understanding of Stonehenge is the assimilation and understanding of these layers of allusion and metaphor; we can be sure that to the neolithic people Stonehenge was full of layered symbolism.

At around the same time that the sarsen structure was built, the Avenue was constructed. This consisted of two parallel banks with external ditches, reminiscent of a cursus, and perhaps deliberately so, running north-east from the north-east entrance. Some think the Avenue was laid out as part of Stonehenge II, which may be so. While the ditches and banks were being created, a protecting circular earthwork was built round the one surviving Heel Stone; its partner had, by this early date, already been removed. The Avenue, initially extending dead straight for 0.5km, was perhaps felt to be an adequate alternative salutation to the midsummer sunrise. It is possible that megaliths may have been planted at intervals along this first part of the Avenue, which would have created yet another parallel with the other great sarsen monument at Avebury, with its two stone avenues. Some of the earlier descriptions of the Avenue imply that stones once stood on the Avenue banks. William Stukeley, in his 1722 manuscript, 'The History of the Temples of the Antient Celts', which is now in the Bodleian Library, is very emphatic on the question: 'It may be reckoned bold to assert an Avenue at Stonehenge when there is not one stone left, but I did not invent it, having been able to measure the very intervals of almost every Stone, from the manifest hollows left in their stations'. The first stretch of the ditched and banked Avenue, the section nearest Stonehenge, has been radiocarbon dated to 1770–1728 bc (2200–2100 BC).

Next, the Welsh bluestones, which had been off-site for a century or two, we know not where, were brought back, re-shaped, and arranged in two groups to harmonize with the huge sarsen structure. First an oval, then a horseshoe of 19 bluestone pillars, was set up just inside the sarsen horseshoe, and a circle of about 60 bluestones was raised a couple of metres inside the sarsen ring. The new stone age came to an end amid a flurry of change and experimentation, which is seen at other sites too. The changes at Stonehenge went on into the second millenium, with the Avenue being continued in two additional legs, first turning east to cross the dry valley towards the low ridge where the King Barrows lay, and then, later still, curving towards the south-east to descend to the River Avon. The most likely reason for these final gestures was to commemorate the journey made by the magic bluestones as they were dragged, one by one, towards Stonehenge.

Close to the monument's centre, right in front of the tall central trilithon, the Altar Stone was reinstated – if indeed it had been removed for the building of Stonehenge III: it is possible that it was left in place throughout, from 2200 BC until it was felled in AD 61 when, I believe, it is likely that the Romans slighted Stonehenge as part of their suppression of Druidism. In the popular imagination of the last 200 years, it was the Druids of the iron age who built and worshipped at Stonehenge. Ironically, it looks as if the Romans saw Stonehenge as a Druid temple too, and pulled as much of it as they could down during their campaign against the subversive sect. Time and weather would have toppled some of the stones by the time of the Druids, but it is just possible that they adopted it as their own, in much the same way that a modern coven may adopt a hill figure, chambered tomb or stone circle as a congenial place of worship – or indeed as the modern 'revivalist' Druids and flower-power hippies of the twentieth century have sought to claim Stonehenge.

For its builders, Stonehenge functioned as a temple, a magic circle, an observatory, a shrine and abode of deities, a symbol of home, a symbol of the known universe that they sought to control, and a symbol of the cosmos itself. It was an expression of tribal identity and territoriality, an expression of pride and power. The large number of different pottery styles found in the neighbourhood speaks of the cosmopolitan contacts that the Stonehenge people generated. We may speculate that then, as now, people travelled long distances to see Stonehenge (Plate 13).

| STONEHENGE GREATER | Stonehenge | SU: 109429– |
| CURSUS | | 137431 |

Thought by William Stukeley to have been an ancient chariot-racing track, this long, narrow, rectangular monument may have been constructed for funeral processions or some similar ritual activity. The cursus is certainly aligned on a long barrow, at SU: 137431, which contained the bones of a child. Marked by a bank and an external ditch, the cursus consists of an enclosure 2.8km long and about 90m wide, 700m to the north of Stonehenge. Its closeness to Stonehenge underlines the role of religious ritual in the area at the time of Stonehenge I; it is also a useful reminder that the monument of Stonehenge extends much further than the limits of the sarsen structure at the centre.

The west end of the Stonehenge Greater Cursus lies on fairly level ground; the middle section extends down a shallow coombe, passing out of sight of Stonehenge for a time; in the east it crosses Stonehenge Bottom and rises steadily to an eastern termination about 40m short of one of the largest long barrows in the area. The cursus varies in width from 90m to 150m. Trial sections at the western end have revealed a substantial ditch, nearly 3m wide and 2m deep, some 2.5m away from an internal bank. There was a slighter external bank as well. The western end was damaged when a military installation was built on it in the First World War and it was subsequently used as a piggery.

The cursus' north ditch, as J. F. S. Stone noticed in 1947, is aligned on the site of Woodhenge; the Cuckoo Stone lies on this alignment too, between Woodhenge and the north ditch's east end. This is the sort of evidence that ley-line enthusiasts seize with alacrity, and it does look as if the alignment here was deliberately arranged, but for what reason is unclear.

Excavations at the east end of the Greater Cursus in 1983 showed that the monument was modified during the neolithic. The original ditch was probably dug out to a depth of only 1.5m at first; then it was replaced by a much larger ditch 3m deep. Presumably the completed monument had a correspondingly high bank, which would have been on a similar scale to the long barrows.

The cursus is probably broadly contemporary with Stonehenge I.

STONEHENGE LESSER CURSUS	Stonehenge	SU: 103434–107435

This degraded and almost invisible monument 400m long, 60m wide and aligned WSW–ENE lies along the summit of a broad, flat-topped ridge. Air photographs show that it was still a visible earthwork in 1934, but it had been effectively levelled by ploughing by 1954. It originally comprised a bank with an external ditch, of which only the silted ditch survives. The east end was never closed off, and it may be that this cursus was for some reason left unfinished. The west end tapers slightly and is then squared off like the tip of a screwdriver. A bank and ditch cross the cursus 200m from the west end almost at right angles to its main axis. This feature is accompanied by a narrowing of the sides. It may be that the monument began as a relatively short, coffin-shaped enclosure and was then extended to the east. The Lesser Cursus, like the Greater, was built in two stages. The second stage involved digging out and enlarging the original ditches, which may explain why the cross-ditch, which is in effect the original terminus of the monument, has a bank on each side.

Perhaps the most extraordinary thing about this monument is that as soon as it had been enlarged it was immediately levelled, although not before antlers and antler tools had been carefully placed along the ditch floor. As with many other neolithic monuments, the rituals of making – of digging, depositing and filling – seem to have been more important to neolithic people than the appearance of the resulting structure; it is an approach to architecture that is very different from that of our own time.

STONEHENGE LONG BARROWS	Stonehenge	SU: 137432

Four long barrows. One, at SU: 137432, is 80m long and aligned roughly N–S: it is a very important monument because it marks the east end of the Stonehenge Greater Cursus. The second long barrow, at SU: 115417, is 30m long and forms part of a linear barrow cemetery to the south-west of Stonehenge. The site of a third is at SU: 119421, only 200m to the south-west of Stonehenge. The levelled long barrow at SU: 141419 appears as a pair of parallel crop marks oriented NNW–SSE, 20m long and 12m apart, indicating the location of the flanking ditches. It lay on the north side of a cluster of round barrows or ring ditches and was false-crested so that it would have formed a skyline feature when seen from the Avon valley floor to the south-east; the Stonehenge Avenue, a much later feature, ran past it immediately to the west on its descent to the River Avon. A large ring ditch impinges on the south-east end of this barrow, and the 'cist' referred to in 1864 by Lukis may actually have been the central structure belonging to the ring ditch.

It is likely that all the long barrows in the area were built well before the initial earth circle design of Stonehenge I was laid out; they belong to an even older ceremonial landscape.

SUTTON DOWN LONG BARROW

Swallowcliffe   ST: 983264

A long barrow at 205m OD, just to the north of the hilltop and at the head of a steep north-west slope down towards the village of Swallowcliffe. The barrow was apparently designed to be viewed from the area now occupied by Swallowcliffe. Its long axis is aligned SW–NE.

SUTTON VENY LONG BARROW

ST: 911415

A long barrow 32m long to the east of St Leonard's Church. This barrow is in an unusual location, very low down on a valley side, at the southern edge of the Wylye valley. It is one of a row of three barrows 200m apart along the valley side.

TIDCOMBE DOWN LONG BARROW

Tidcombe   SU: 292576

This substantial long barrow 56m long and 3m high was badly damaged when a trench was dug along it. Four sarsen stones in a hollow at the southern end are the remains of a burial chamber which contained a skeleton when it was raised in 1750 by local treasure hunters. A bank and ditch a few metres to the east may be an iron age farm boundary.

TILSHEAD OLD DITCH

Tilshead   SU: 023468

As it is on Ministry of Defence land this barrow is not accessible, although it is visible from the road to the north. It can lay claim to being the longest true long barrow in England, measuring 120m long, 30m wide and 3.4m high. It was excavated twice in the nineteenth century, by William Cunnington in 1802 and John Thurnam in 1865. On the neolithic land surface at the base of the barrow was a layer of black soil and on this lay the remains of two people. One was the skeleton of a woman that had been partly burnt, whilst the other was a small woman who seems to have died as a result of a blow on the skull. The burnt burial lay on a funeral pyre of flint and ashes, and the remains of both women were covered by a cairn of flints. The three other burials found within the barrow mound were probably added later.

At Tilshead Lodge, at SU: 021475, there is a second long barrow, 50m long, which also contained two burials, one of them with a cleft skull. Beside them were the remains of two slaughtered cattle.

There are other long barrows in the Tilshead area, such as the one at SU: 059494, which is 65m long, and the ominously named Kill Barrow at SU: 000478, 50m long.

TINHEAD HILL LONG BARROW   Edington   ST: 939523

A long barrow 64m long to the west of Tottenham Wood. It stands near the crest of a steep north-west-facing escarpment, a little to the north-west of the highest point. The long axis, oriented SW–NE, is aligned along the contour, presumably so that the full length of the barrow can be seen from the low ground below.

TISBURY HENGE   Tisbury   ST: 951299

A henge monument just to the north of Place Farm, Tisbury. The site is on a south-facing slope at the foot of the valley side, and it is also at the confluence of the River Sem and two tributary streams; the association with water may have a religious significance.

TOW BARROW   Grafton   SU: 274577

A long barrow 28m long.

TOYD CLUMP LONG BARROW   SU: 095224

A long barrow 50m long, 4km SSW of Coombe Bissett and 800m SE of Toyd Clump. Its long axis is aligned W–E, following the contour, and it stands at 120m OD on a moderate southerly slope.

WARMINSTER LONG BARROWS   ST: 897444

Two long barrows, at ST: 897444 (62m long) and ST: 873470 (40m long). A third, on Oxenham Down at ST: 903471, is 32m long.

WEATHER HILL   near Everleigh   SU: 199516

A long barrow 43m long close to a prehistoric field system and a barrow cemetery, centring on SU: 200512. There is also a henge, which may be associated with the long barrow, at SU: 206526.

WELSTONE BRIDGE CAUSEWAYED ENCLOSURE SU: 130965

A causewayed enclosure.

WEST HILL FARM LONG Heytesbury ST: 924441
BARROW

An earthen long barrow 49m long, near the foot of a north-east-pointing spur. The barrow's long axis is aligned roughly N–S.

WEST KENNET AVENUE *see* AVEBURY

WEST KENNET LONG Avebury SU: 104677
BARROW

This fine long barrow can be clearly seen from the A4 as an uneven ridge on the southern skyline. The barrow mound is fully 100m long and 2.5m high. At its east end is a burial chamber 12m long and with a roof high enough to allow most

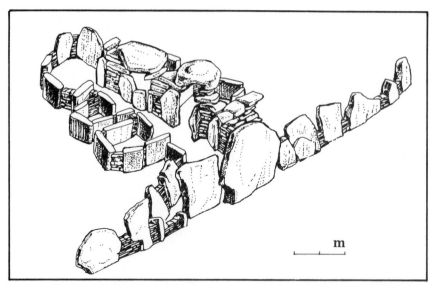

Figure 63 West Kennet Long Barrow: the transepted tomb chambers and façade as reconstructed. The large stone at the centre of the façade was erected to seal the tomb at the end of its period of use. The pile of blocking stones between the large stone and the entrance to the passage has been left out of this reconstruction, as have the upper parts of the western and southern chambers.

people to walk into it without stooping, itself an unusual feature of neolithic monuments. Restoration work following the excavations of 1955–6 revealed that there had been a façade of large sarsen stones at the east end; the huge entrance stone, which was really a blocking stone erected at the close of the barrow's period of use, had fallen over and has now been reinstated. Behind this now-complete façade is a shallow crescent-shaped forecourt. Opening from the centre of this is the central gallery with two pairs of chambers on either side and one at the west end. The barrow has been dug into repeatedly. In 1859 John Thurnam

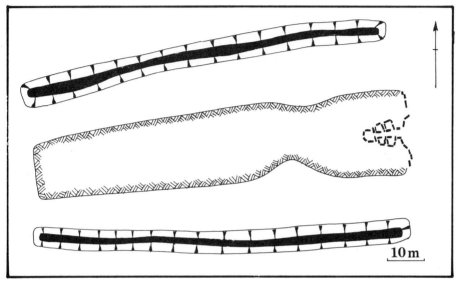

Figure 64 West Kennet Long Barrow: plan. The solid black area represents the floor of the quarry ditch. The chambers occupy a relatively small area of the huge barrow mound.

emptied the end chamber, where he found the remains of five adults and a child. The Stuart Piggott–Richard Atkinson excavations of 1955–6 uncovered the other four side chambers, the existence of which had not previously been suspected; they were found to have corbelled and capstoned roofs about 2.3m high. The north-east chamber contained the remains of a man and two women: the south-east chamber contained a man and a woman together with five young children and four babies. The north-west and south-west chambers are smaller and lower-ceilinged. There was a mass of bones in the north-west chamber which included the remains of at least 12 people. The remains in the south-west chamber included those of nine adults, a youth, a young child and two babies. Mixed up with the bones in all the chambers were fragments of pottery, flints, animal bones and beads. The pottery represents types that were in use for a thousand years, so the tomb may have been reopened many times for the burial of as many as 40 or 50 generations of people. At least 46 people were buried in the tomb, and there is evidence that many more were removed in the seventeenth century. It is also possible that the tomb chambers were periodically cleared in antiquity; there is evidence of this practice at some other neolithic tombs (Figures 63 and 64).

The West Kennet Long Barrow was built in a landscape of open grassland: there is no evidence that the barrow site was ever cultivated. A settlement site, possibly the home of the people who built and used the barrow, has been discovered to the north-west at SU: 102678.

WEST KENNET POST CIRCLES

West Kennet Farm   SU: 110681

A palisade enclosure lying on the Kennet valley floor, halfway between Silbury Hill and the Sanctuary, and only 200m to the south-west of the West Kennet Avenue. Dating probably from the years around 2000 BC, this monument comes at the end of a long sequence of important developments in the Avebury area, and is an expression of this period of experimentation and change. The monument is over 200m in diameter and consists of two concentric palisade ditches 25–30m apart on the south side of the River Kennet: only one ditch has so far been found on the north side. The Kennet seems to have flowed right through the middle of the enclosure. The substantial ditches were rapidly backfilled round large posts set at close intervals and let into sockets cut into the bottom of the trench. Eventually the posts rotted away where they stood.

It seems unlikely, from its valley floor position, that the enclosure was defensive. It may have been a cattle corral or, like the other circular structures in the vicinity, a ritual centre of some kind. The builders may have preferred working in timber to using earth and stone for a variety of reasons. It may have been an economy in labour or time that motivated the choice. It may have been a forest clearance phase, releasing large quantities of timber. Alternatively, the builders may have had some ritual reason for preferring wood at the time. Whatever the reason, this kind of change is typical at the close of the neolithic. The interior of the enclosure has yet to be excavated.

Immediately beside the main circle are the remains of another, about 180m in diameter, and believed to be slightly earlier in date than its neighbour. Grooved ware pottery found on the site suggests that this older circle was built in about 2300 BC; similar pottery was redeposited in the palisade trench of the larger enclosure, implying that it was built rather later. The earlier and slightly smaller enclosure was marked out by posts set in sockets up to 2m deep, but in the rubble of a backfilled trench. Some of the holes were filled with charcoal and ash, showing that the story of the enclosure ended in flames. There are other hints at complex and strange rituals here, with joints of meat deposited round the palisade posts.

Within the smaller circle there are traces of an inner timber circle 40m across and two radial fences linking the enclosure boundary with an as yet unlocated central feature. The late neolithic people of the area must have collected large quantities of timber to build all these structures, which is all the more remarkable in view of the deforested state of the Kennet valley floor at that time; the timber, like the Avebury stones, must have been dragged to the building site from some distance away.

WEST WOODS LONG BARROW — West Overton — SU: 156656

A chambered long barrow 32m long near the head of a dry valley that leads north to join the Kennet valley 3.5km away.

WHITEBARROW — Tilshead — SU: 033468

This fine long barrow is 78m long, 46m wide and 2m high. It has clearly defined berms and side ditches. William Cunnington and Sir Richard Colt Hoare excavated the barrow in the nineteenth century, but the only recorded finds from the site are some pieces of antler. The site has been known as Whitebarrow or Whiteburgh since at least 1348.

WHITE SHEET HILL CAUSEWAYED ENCLOSURE — ST: 802352

This enclosure consists of an oval earthwork covering an area of about 1.6ha. The enclosure's low bank is interrupted at irregular intervals by 21 causeways. An excavation in 1951 proved that the ditch is about 3m wide and 0.3–1.5m deep. On the bottom of the ditch were pieces of Windmill Hill pottery and an ox's skull. A bronze age bowl barrow opened in 1807 by William Cunnington overlies the enclosure ditch on the south-east side.

WHITE SHEET HILL LONG BARROW — ST: 942242

A rectangular long barrow 41m long, 23m wide and 2m high at its east end, with clearly marked side ditches. It seems not to have been excavated.

WICK DOWN LONG BARROW — Collingbourne Ducis — SU: 262528

A long barrow at 180m on a south-facing slope just to the south of the summit of Wick Down.

WILSFORD HENGE — Wilsford — SU: 093573

A henge monument, 500m SSE of the much larger Marden superhenge. The Wilsford henge, on the south side of the River Avon, probably had some functional connection with the Marden henge. It may be that there was originally an extensive ritual complex here, as there was at Avebury and Stonehenge.

WILSFORD LONG BARROWS   SU: 118413

Four long barrows. The first, at SU: 118413, is 20m long. The second, at SU: 114410, is 39m long. The third, at SU: 104411, is 36m long. The fourth, at SU: 108401, is 43m long.

WINDMILL HILL   **Avebury**   SU: 087714
CAUSEWAYED ENCLOSURE

Three not quite concentric circuits of causewayed ditches ring a low hilltop 2km NW of Avebury. Windmill Hill preceded Avebury as a ceremonial centre, and was later superseded by it; it was quite common for early, raised sites to be supplanted by later and lower sites. Windmill Hill is the largest causewayed enclosure so far recognized in Britain. It has an area of 8.5ha and its outermost ditch has a diameter of 360m. The average diameter of the intermediate ditch is 200m: the inner ditch encloses an area about 85m across. Typically, the ditch circuits do not lie round the summit of the hill, but hang lopsidedly over the steeper northern slope, so that the monument is in effect false-crested (see Figures 52 and 65).

The ditch sections are irregular, though they all tend to have flat floors. Both width and depth vary from place to place and the ditches give the appearance of being the work of different groups of people, perhaps digging out the various segments at different times. The 'causeway' gaps between the ditch segments vary from a few centimetres to 7.5m in width. The inner ditch, which was dug first, is shallower than the more substantial outer ring. Each ditch acted as a quarry for a bank thrown up on its inner side, although the banks can be seen only on the east side; elsewhere, the bank material has been pushed back into the ditches, either in the neolithic or as a result of subsequent ploughing. Pieces from more than 1,300 pots of a distinctive 'Windmill Hill' type have been identified from the enclosure, along with flint and stone objects. Much of this material was found deliberately deposited and buried in the ditches, and it is apparent that the ritual practices of the site involved repeated deposition, burial and clearing of objects, possibly as offerings. Radiocarbon dating shows that these ritual acts took place around 3350 BC.

Examination of the pottery found at Windmill Hill has shown that about 30 per cent of it contained fossil shell and oolitic limestone that must have come from rock outcrops in the Bath–Frome area. It may therefore be argued that Windmill Hill, along with several other neolithic settlements in Wiltshire, was importing significant quantities of pottery from the west. Yet stone from the same source was used in the drystone walling of the West Kennet Long Barrow, so it may be that the stone itself was imported into the Avebury area as a raw material, some of it to be used for monument-building and some to be ground up for making local, Windmill-Hill-style pottery.

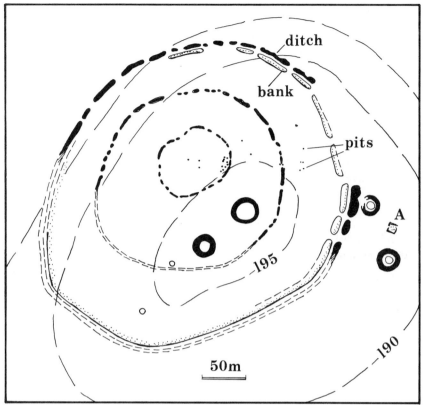

Figure 65   Windmill Hill causewayed enclosure. The round barrows post-date the enclosure, but the little square cult-house (A) belongs, like the enclosure, to the middle neolithic.

WINTERBOURNE BASSET STONE CIRCLE   SU: 094755

A huge but now destroyed stone circle about 71m in diameter. William Stukeley saw its remains, with a 'single, broad, flat, and high stone', evidently an outlying marker stone, outside to the west. By 1881, all the stones had fallen. The Revd A. C. Smith probed the ground and returned the following year with his friend the Revd W. C. Lukis to determine where the pillars had stood. They found only a few remnants of the ring. Today a few collapsed sarsens lie without any distinguishable pattern in a long, hedged field. It seems likely that this circle, in common with Broadstones Circle at Clatford, Langdean Bottom Ring and the Coate Circle, was far enough away from Avebury to form an independent clan centre. There was a long barrow close by, just as at Clatford and Faulkner's Circle. Like so many monuments in the south of England, Winterbourne Bassett has fallen victim to time and the indifference of generations of farmers.

WINTERBOURNE STOKE LONG BARROW

near Stonehenge

SU: 101417

A linear cemetery of ten barrows runs along the edge of a ploughed field beside the plantation. These are under the protection of the National Trust. Further out in the field are two more groups of barrows. The barrow nearest the crossroads roundabout is a fine neolithic long barrow 74m long, 22m wide and 3m high. In 1863 John Thurnam excavated it and found a primary male burial at one end.

A second long barrow, 32m long, stands at SU: 090428. The site of a third, at SU: 101409, lies on a gentle south-eastern slope to the SSE of the crossroads; although now levelled by the plough, it shows as parallel cropmarks 50m long and 18m apart, indicating the positions of the quarry ditches, which were oriented NW–SE.

WINTERSLOW

SU: 225329

A settlement site in the dry valley west of Middle Winterslow, about 300m to the east of Dunstable Farm.

WINTERSLOW FIRS LONG BARROW

Winterslow

SU: 220342

A long barrow on a west-facing slope, just south of the A30.

WOODFORD LONG BARROW

SU: 100377

A long barrow 20m long, north-west of Woodford. The site is at the head of a dry valley leading ESE to the Avon valley.

WOODHENGE

Durrington Walls

SU: 150434

This monument was one of the first major discoveries to be made as a result of aerial photography in Britain, and is for this reason a landmark in British archaeology. It was photographed by Squadron Leader Insall in 1925, and excavated by Mr and Mrs Cunnington in 1926–7. The original monument consisted of six concentric near-circles of posts surrounded by a ditch with an outer bank. There is no agreement yet as to the form of the original building. It may have formed a roofed building or stood open to the sky as a wooden equivalent to Stonehenge, as the excavators' name for the site implies. On the whole it seems more likely that it was a large, roofed rotunda, particularly in view of the similar structures that have been excavated at the adjoining site of Durrington Walls, and at the Sanctuary near Avebury.

The enclosing ditch, dug in about 1850 bc (2300 BC), was irregular in form; on average it was 2m deep and 3.5–4.5m wide. Its internal diameter was 52m.

The ditch was interrupted by an entrance causeway on the north-east side. Rubble quarried from the ditch was thrown up to make an external bank.

Within the enclosure were six concentric, egg-shaped rings of posts, their positions marked now by concrete pillars; they may be, but are not necessarily, all contemporary with one another. Near the centre of the innermost ring of posts

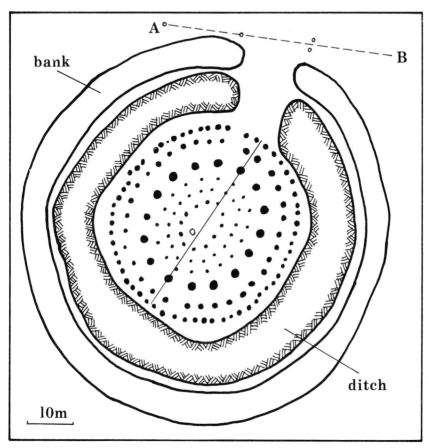

Figure 66 Woodhenge. Note that the long axis of the timber roundhouse does not quite match up with the henge entrance, and that neither of these is oriented towards the midsummer sunrise. A: four widely spaced post-holes at the henge entrance suggest freestanding posts or totem poles; their positions imply a sight-line (A–B), perhaps on a February or November sunrise.

was one of the saddest discoveries that have been made at any neolithic site – the grave of a 3-year-old child whose skull had been split open. It is one of the clearest examples of a child sacrifice forming part of a new stone age foundation ritual. A small cairn of flints marks the spot.

The oldest pottery from Woodhenge belongs to the Grooved ware style, showing that it was broadly contemporary with Durrington Walls. Some Beaker pottery has also been found, suggesting a period of use for the site of some 300 years, from 2300 to 2000 BC.

WOODLANDS PITS near Woodhenge SU: 151431

Four pits on private land, in the garden of 'Woodlands' in Countess Road, about 265m SSE of the centre of Woodhenge. The pits were oval, up to 1.4m across and 0.75m deep. They contained pieces of Grooved ware pottery, part of a Graig Lwyd stone axe, a flaked flint axe, some flint arrow-heads and scrapers, antler picks, bones of ox, sheep, pig, dog, as well as remains of foxes, frogs, scallops, mussels, oysters and carbonized nut shells. Whether these were simple domestic refuse pits or votive offering pits is open to question, although the fact that they form part of an alignment leading south from Durrington Walls makes me feel that they are likely to have been ritual rather than domestic in nature.

─────── NORTH YORKSHIRE ───────

AYTON EAST FIELD East Ayton TA: 000864

This long barrow located at the south-east edge of the North Yorkshire Moors has been radiocarbon-dated to 3080 bc (3800 BC). It is about 26m long and 15m wide, with its long axis aligned N–S. It is only 1m high at the north end and slopes down towards the south. It is built of stones and soil, and has been disturbed by early diggers. The east end is unusual in being convex and built of drystone: possibly it originally had an entrance at the centre. Inside the mound was a wooden structure, probably a mortuary house, measuring 7.5m by 4m; it was slightly trapezoid in shape, with three rows of posts, and may have been built to resemble a neolithic house. The outer rows of posts were supported by rough walling, presumably to help them take the strain when earth and rubble were piled onto the roof. Bodies were placed inside the wooden house, a mound was built over it, and the wood set on fire. Only the outer end was destroyed by the flames before it and its covering mound collapsed, preserving the bodies at the inner end from burning. Two masses of human bones were found together with five leaf-shaped arrow-heads, four partly polished flint axes, two flint knives, some boars' tusks and an axe handle made of antler.

BRANSDALE LONG CAIRN SE: 607967

A ruined long cairn 16m long and 7m wide, situated on the crest of a south-pointing spur of Bilsdale East Moor. It is unusual in being built at such a high altitude (370m OD).

THE DEVIL'S ARROWS   Boroughbridge   SE: 391666

Three massive and weather-fluted blocks of gritstone are spaced out across farmland in an almost straight line on a N–S axis. The stones are, from north to south, 5.5m, 6.4m and 6.9m high. It seems that they were quarried at Knaresborough, 10km away, and the labour involved in dragging them to Boroughbridge must have been considerable. The Devil's Arrows should be seen as part of the extensive Thornborough–Hutton Moor ritual complex that was in use in the late neolithic and early bronze age. The stones almost certainly held some religious significance, but they may also have had a practical function in indicating the river-crossing, possibly originally a ford or even a ferry across the River Ure. The crossing-place has guided communications right up to the present day; heavy traffic on the A1(M) races past the Devil's Arrows as they stalk across the fields (Figure 68).

DUGGLEBY HOWE   Duggleby   SE: 881669

This is one of the great round barrows of northern Britain, dating from the late neolithic period. It is about 36m in diameter and 6m high, consisting of some 5,000 tonnes of chalk. It was trenched by John Mortimer in 1890. At the centre he found a grave pit 2.7m deep and 3m square containing the corpse of a strongly built man in a cramped timber mortuary house. Close to the body of this headman a locally made pot (a Grimston ware bowl), nine flints and some rotted haematite that may have been used, in life as well as in death, for body-painting. Another, shallower grave to the east of this central shaft contained the remains of a 50-year-old man, surrounded by the tools and talismans that had been significant to him in life – flint arrow-heads, a knife, ox bones, 2 beavers' teeth, 12 boars' tusks and a bone pin. A small mound was heaped over this man's body. Each of these 'bigman' burials was followed by the burial of a boy and then of a very young child. This rather sinister pattern – the burial of high-status elders with grave-goods, accompanied by the bodies of pole-axed boys and infants – is highly suggestive of human sacrifice. Yet not all the elders were buried according to this ritual. A very tall 70-year-old man, exceptionally old for these early times, was laid out so that his head hung over the edge of the shaft, looking down into it as if peering into the underworld in search of his ancestors. He held a cushion-shaped piece of translucent flint up to his eyeless sockets as if scrying into a crystal ball.

Perhaps 50 years after the burial of the first headman, a fourth man, aged about 60, was interred in the clay mound that had been raised over the initial graves. Like the earlier chieftains, this man had as his grave-goods weapons that may also have been his symbols of authority: a flint axe, a lozenge-shaped arrow-head and a mace made out of antler. Above him in the mound were, once again, the skeletons of a boy and a child. Offerings of ox, roebuck, red deer, fox, sheep and pig were made to the, so far exclusively male, dead of Duggleby Howe.

In the decades that followed, people raised the barrow by laying more chalk over it. Over 50 cremations were deposited in the chalk layer. Later still, a layer of blue-grey Kimmeridge Clay was added, and then the mound was completed with a further covering of chalk rubble. It had grown into an impressive, multi-generation monument, beginning with the burials of the elders and their sacrificed children, and developing into a communal tomb.

Only about half of the barrow has been excavated, so it is possible that further important discoveries may yet be made here.

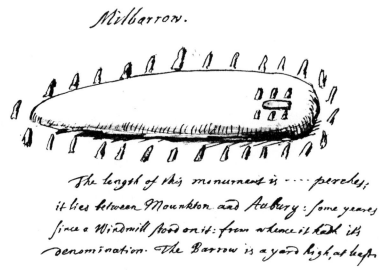

Figure 67 Mill Barrow, Avebury. An invaluable sketch by John Aubrey of a monument that has subsequently been destroyed. Aubrey's note reads, 'The length of the monument is ... perches; it lies between Mounkton and Avbury: some yeares since a Windmill stood on it: from whence it hath its denomination. The Barrow is a yard high, at least'.
Stukeley, who also drew it, described it as 'a most magnificent sepulchre'.

Duggleby Howe lies at the centre of a discontinuous, 300m diameter enclosure ditch, which was only recognized in the 1980s. The area of the ditched enclosure, 10.5ha, puts it among the largest of the third millennium monuments in Britain; it is exceeded in size only by the Wessex superhenges, which lie in the 11–14ha range. The very large precinct may be assumed to be late neolithic, like the barrow, and may be assumed to indicate its territorial importance. A large ring ditch just inside the 'east entrance' to the enclosure is reminiscent of the position of the Hatfield Barrow at Marden. The Duggleby Howe discoveries should alert us to the possibility that there may be other superhenges outside Wessex, as yet unrecognized.

EAST HESLERTON LONG BARROW SE: 938753

An earthen long barrow 125m long. Its long axis is aligned roughly W–E, and it stands at the northern edge of the Yorkshire Wolds, on the crest of the escarpment overlooking the Vale of Pickering. It dates from 3070–2970 bc (3800–3400 BC).

FLOTMANBY LONG BARROW TA: 065787

An earthen long barrow 76m long.

FOLKTON ROUND BARROW TA: 059777

This small, isolated barrow was built to cover the remains of a man and a woman accompanied by a bell beaker. The skeletons seem to have been reburied in prehistoric times, after the skulls had been removed. The beaker that accompanied this burial was a drinking vessel probably made in about 2300 BC, which is so far the only date we have for the barrow. These remains were covered with a layered mound of earth and stones, interspersed with thin layers of chalk. Outside this, but within two concentric surrounding ditches, four adults and a child were buried. Between the concentric ditches was a further child burial accompanied by a bone pin and three chalk 'drums'. The little girl, who was about 5 years old at the time of her death, was buried facing the sunset with her hands covering her face as if in fear. One of the three chalk drums touched her head: the others were placed at her hips. The Folkton Drums are 10–12cm in diameter, and are now on display in the British Museum. Their beautifully restrained and controlled geometric decoration includes what seem to be stylized face patterns reminiscent of megalithic art; their presence here, in this child's grave, suggests that they were endowed with protective magical power. Really, far too much work and artistry went into the creation of these beautiful objects – surely the loveliest things ever made of chalk – for them to have been mere toys, as some have suggested. It may be that the little girl was a sacrifice, buried as a dedicatory offering that would sanctify the funerary precinct and the later burials before the final, larger barrow was raised over them all.

GILLING LONG BARROW   Yearsley   SE: 601741

A long barrow about 40m long, built unusually of sand, close to the northern edge of the Yorkshire Wolds. No interments were found; perhaps there were some originally and they have been destroyed by the acidic conditions within the sand barrow – perhaps there were no burials in the first place. The mound contained parallel lines of sandstone walling 3m inside the barrow's edges, evidently enclosing and revetting a trapeze-shaped mound.

GREAT AYTON   NZ: 593115

This round cairn at the crest of a steep west-facing slope on the northern edge of the Cleveland Hills is 17m in diameter and 1m high, with an added tail some 75m long and 8.5m wide. Inside the cairn is a rectangular, ridged-roofed stone chamber made of four pitched slabs on each side: it was empty when excavated. The mound itself produced collared urns and an incense cup. The tail, a bank of stones 75m long, runs north-west from the cairn, making the structure about 90m long overall. There is an oval enclosure on its north side and two ring cairns to the south-east.

HANGING GRIMSTON LONG BARROW   SE: 810608

An earthen long barrow 24m long which was excavated in 1868 by John Mortimer. No human burials were found, but the site seems instead to have been the focus of a pig cult of some kind. The jaws of 20 young pigs were found in one deposit, arranged in four heaps, and in a ritual pit behind the façade a pig scapula was set on end. Mortimer noted that 'small portions of the points of most of the tusks had been broken off'. This may be explained as a parallel to the ritual breaking which is common in neolithic burials, and in the burials of later cultures too. The breaking of arrow-heads and tools symbolizes the ritual killing of the objects, to enable them too to enter the spirit world already inhabited by the dead.

HEDON HOWE   SE: 784665

A neolithic round cairn 15m in diameter and 2.5m high. It contained five rectangular slab-built stone chambers, of which at least two were paved. They contained disarticulated human bones. The cairn contained fragments of Grimston pottery.

HELPERTHORPE LONG BARROW   SE: 963679

Most of this barrow was removed in the nineteenth century, but it is still about 30m long and 14m wide. When it was opened by John Mortimer in 1868, three circular pits at the higher west end were found to be empty, but a smaller pit near the centre of the mound contained a cremation. The floor of the barrow was covered with wood ash. The side ditches are 1.8m deep, 4m wide at the top and 1m wide at the bottom.

HIGH BRIDESTONES   Sleights Moor   NZ: 850046

These two stone circles stand at a height of 900m on Sleights Moor in the North Yorkshire Moors. The stone rings are both about 10m in diameter, and are now badly damaged; only three stones remain standing in each ring, the tallest of them

2m high. Outside the circle to the north are three outlying stones. A single outlying stone stands away to the south. Close to the stone circles is Flat Howe, a barrow with a kerb of retaining stones.

HUTTON MOOR   Hutton Conyers   SE: 353735

Three ploughed henge monuments stand close together at Hutton Moor and within 3km of the River Ure. All the henges have suffered badly at the hands of farmers. They have circular banks with internal and external ditches, and entrances on the north and south sides. Hutton Moor is part of a larger ceremonial complex that includes the Thornborough Circles and the Devil's Arrows.

NEWTON KYME ENCLOSURE   SE: 459450

This enclosure consists of three circuits of concentric ditches. The innermost ditch, which is fairly wide and has two entrances opposite one another, has been described as a henge. Although it does indeed bear similarities with henge monuments, the two outer rings look much more like the sort of ditch circuits that are found in causewayed enclosures. This unusual monument, which may turn out to have an unusual history, has yet to be excavated.

OVER SILTON LONG   Kepwick   SE: 492904
BARROW

This barrow, at a height of 375m OD is close to the summit of Little Moor in the Hambleton Hills. It is about 34m long, 9m wide at its broadest point and 1m high. Beneath the higher east end Greenwell found a deposit of human bones. The barrow core was of stones, and beneath these lay the disarticulated remains of at least five people.

PEASHOLM LONG BARROW   Scarborough   TA: 031897

The site of an earthen long barrow 20m long.

ROB HOWE   SE: 903860

An earthen long barrow 37m long.

SCAMRIDGE LONG BARROW Ebberston   SE: 892861

This is an almost rectangular long barrow 50m long, its long axis aligned W–E. It is 3m high at the east end, where it is 16m wide. At the east end and along the barrow's centre lay a trench with a floor made of yellow clay, 12m long and 1m wide. In the trench lay the scattered remains of about 14 people, those at the east end completely burnt. At the west end of the trench there was a cairn of stones, whose air passages may have acted as a flue or chimney leading up to the surface of the barrow. The whole mound was constructed of limestone boulders enclosed within a drystone revetment wall.

SCORTON CURSUS   NZ: 243002

A long, straight, regular cursus at least 2.1km long, of which only the south-eastern end has been seen. A post-hole was found which may represent part of the original survey work. Circular cropmarks immediately outside the south-eastern terminus suggest a small cluster of buildings or ring ditches to which the cursus was designed to lead. The north-west end has not been detected, but it may have existed on the summit of a small hill.

SHERBURN ROUND   Sherburn   SE: 960740
BARROWS

A round barrow (Sherburn 8) on the northern rim of the Yorkshire Wolds: it was 15m in diameter and 0.5m high, and contained the remains of five people. Some sherds of Grimston pottery were found resting on the neolithic land surface beneath the barrow. A second round barrow nearby (Sherburn 7) at SE: 960741 had a diameter of 18m and a height of 0.5m. It contained the disarticulated bones of 18 adults.

THORNBOROUGH   East and West Tanfield   SE: 585795

This is an important concentration of religious sites on river terrace gravels between the Ure and the Swale near Ripon. It includes six henge monuments, a cursus and many barrows; Hutton Moor is part of it.

The Thornborough henges lie in a line of three, of which the central one is the most accessible: the northern circle, protected by trees, is the best preserved. This is one of the best examples in Britain of an alignment of prehistoric monuments: it is continued southwards in the Devil's Arrows. All three circles have an approximate diameter of 275m and have the remains of massive banks with ditches both outside and inside. There are entrances on the north-west and south-east of each circle.

When the central circle was excavated in 1952, it emerged that the ditches are 20m wide and 3m deep. The bank was built of large boulders, and it had been coated with crystals of white gypsum, apparently to make the monument look more like the enclosures of the chalklands of southern England.

Under the central circle were found the ditches of a cursus that ran 1.2km from NE to SW, ending in the disused gravel pit to the south-west of the circle where it may still be in cross-section (SE: 289796). The cursus was on average 40m wide. Excavation at its south-west end uncovered a crouched burial in a stone cist. The cursus had already gone out of use at the time the central henge was constructed across it; it seems to be a similar process to that seen at Maxey, where the Great Henge was, apparently deliberately, built astride an earlier cursus in a very similar way.

The south circle has been disturbed by gravel extraction but remains intact. Scattered among the henges are several barrows, including the Centre Hill barrow, at SE: 287791, which is still 1m high; it produced a skeleton with a food vessel and a flint knife lying in a tree-trunk coffin. Three other barrows, the Three Hills, lie to the east of the north circle, at about SE: 286801; W. C. Lukis found cremation burials when he excavated them.

WAYWORTH MOOR STONE CIRCLE   Commondale   NZ: 637108

An oval stone ring sits on a moderately steep, south-west-facing slope overlooking the valley of Steddale Beck. It is 32m across and made of low stones only 0.5m high and set radially. Excavation in 1968 produced little more than a few flints.

WHITEGROUNDS   Burythorpe   SE: 782682

An early neolithic cairn later converted into a round barrow. The site began as an entrance grave under an oval cairn about 15m by 12m. The passage was about 8m long, 0.6m wide and lined with stone slabs: its entrance was sealed with a pile of cobbles. At the inner end of the passage were the remains of three people. They had all been decapitated and their heads buried separately. At the end was a child with an aged fox, probably a pet. In the middle was a woman with an amber pendant round her neck. Beside her was a nest of three skulls, and beyond her the body of a man. Some of the human bone was radiocarbon dated to 3000 bc (3700 BC). In the second phase at Whitegrounds, in about 2500 bc (3200 BC), a large earthen round barrow with a stone kerb and a central grave was raised over the old entrance grave: it was 25m in diameter. The new grave contained a man with a waisted, polished flint axe and a jet slider. A radiocarbon date from this man's bone, 2570 bc (3300 BC), shows that people began building round barrows early in Yorkshire.

WILLERBY WOLD LONG BARROW   Willerby   TA: 029761

This is one of the crematorium long barrows that are peculiar to Yorkshire. The barrow once measured 40m long, 11m wide and 1.2m high, although it is now under the plough and forms only an insignificant rise in a cereal field. The barrow is flanked by ditches to north and south.

Excavations by Canon Greenwell in the nineteenth century and by T. G. Manby in 1958–60 revealed a trapeze-shaped mortuary enclosure, marked by a

Figure 68 The Devil's Arrows, drawn by William Stukeley.

narrow ditch with a concave setting of wooden posts at the east end and a ritual pit at the centre. The wooden posts were burnt down and the bones of several previously exposed corpses were laid out along a crematorium trench following what was to become the central spine of the barrow and covered with chalk rubble and timber. The main part of the barrow mound was then built up and the cremation trench fired; it seems to have acted as a kind of horizontal furnace, producing temperatures reaching an estimated 1,200°C. Timber from the posts has yielded radiocarbon dates of 3010 and 2950 bc (3700 and 3650 BC).

YEARSLEY LONG CAIRN Gilling East SE: 603742

A damaged long cairn 45m long, 12m wide and 2.5m high, built of sand and held in place by a stone kerb. On the old land surface there was a paved area, which is where the burials were very likely laid. A cist burial was added to the mound later.

──────── WEST YORKSHIRE ────────

BRADLEY MOOR CAIRN Bradley Moor SE: 009476

A round cairn 2.4m high with a long tail running away to the west, making a total length of about 70m. The tail feature has been seen at other neolithic burial monuments too, such as the Broome Heath Long Barrow in Norfolk, Bryn yr Hen Bobl in Anglesey and Great Ayton in North Yorkshire: its function is unknown. At a distance of about 18m from the east end is a stone cist 2m long and almost 1m wide with a massive capstone. On the cist floor was a smaller slab covering pieces of unburnt human bone. On top of the slab were traces of a cremation. Both to the south of the cist and in the mound material were some upright stones, three of which may have formed a false entrance to the tomb, whilst others suggest a hidden façade.

BRADUP STONE CIRCLE Keighley SE: 090440

A stone circle 9m in diameter. It originally consisted of about 26 blocks of millstone grit, but only 12 of these have survived. The stones are rather small and form an irregular circle within a bank.

THE BULL STONE Otley SE: 206435

A standing stone 1.8m high with a square cross section at the base, and tapering upwards to a point. The stone seems not to have been artificially shaped at all. It is made of millstone grit, which has probably come from an outcrop to the north.

FERRYBRIDGE HENGE **Knottingley** SE: 474242

A two-entrance henge about 180m across.

GRUBSTONES CIRCLE **Ilkley Moor** SE: 136447

The kerb of a destroyed round cairn, of which 20 stones set on edge survive. It is 10m in diameter and has been destroyed on the south side.

HORNCLIFFE CIRCLE **Ilkley Moor** SE: 134435

An oval setting of 46 stones set edge to edge, with traces of a smaller circle in the centre which may surround a burial. This may represent the remains of a revetted round cairn rather than a true stone circle.

ILKLEY MOOR ROCK CARVINGS **Ilkley Moor** SE: 115472

For a distance of about 8km along the northern and western edge of Ilkley Moor are scattered rock carvings. Most are concentrated on the edge of the escarpment close to the 320m contour. The most easily seen example is the Panorama Stone, which has been brought down from its moorland eyrie to the public garden opposite St Margaret's Church, Ilkley (SE: 115472). The Panorama State is decorated with ringed hollows and ladder patterns. The Swastika Stone, at SE: 094470, is probably the best-known of the carvings, with its double outline of a swastika. In all there are about 40 carved stones; the best preserved are as follows:

Badger Stone	SE: 110460
Barmishaw Stone	SE: 112464
Doubler Stones east	SE: 076466
Doubler Stones west	SE: 072465
Hanging Stones	SE: 128467
Idol Rock	SE: 132458
Pancake Stone	SE: 133462
Panorama Rocks	SE: 104470
Piper Stone	SE: 084471
Silver Well Stone	SE: 104465
Swastika Stone	SE: 094470
Willy Hall's Wood	SE: 115465

The age of the carvings is disputed and opinions vary between neolithic and iron age.

SNOWDON CARR   Askwith   SE: 178513

On the moors above the River Washburn is a small scatter of ancient rock carvings consisting of cup markings, some of them surrounded by circles and lines.

At SE: 179514 there is a D-shaped enclosure marked by a bank, with a cluster of hut footings outside it to the north-west associated with some ancient field walls and some cairns which may cover burials. This early settlement and the rock carvings may prove to be connected in some way.

TWELVE APOSTLES   Ilkley Moor   SE: 126451

The collapsed remains of a large neolithic or early bronze age stone circle, now reduced to 12 stones, set in a bank of earth 15m in diameter.

Plate 1   Arbor Low, Derbyshire

Plate 2   Setta Barrow, Devon

Plate 3   Wor Barrow, Dorset

Plate 4   The Rudston Monolith, Yorkshire Wolds

Plate 5 Willie Howe, Yorkshire Wolds

Plate 6 The Rollright Stones, Oxfordshire

Plate 7 Wayland's Smithy: the façade, entrance passage and chambers

Plate 8 The Whispering Knights tomb chamber, Oxfordshire

Plate 9 Windover Long Mound, East Sussex

Plate 10 The King Stone at Rollright, Warwickshire

Plate 11   Avebury: the East Entrance causeway

Plate 12   The West Kennet Avenue, Avebury

Plate 13 A Stonehenge trilithon (stones 57, 58 and 158)

Plate 14   One of the Rollright circle stones

Plate 15   Deepdale standing stone, Mainland Orkney

Plate 16   The Dwarfie Stane, Hoy

Plate 17 The Hill of Cruaday flagstone quarry

Plate 18 Langstane standing stone, Rousay

Plate 19 Skara Brae: the southern end of House 8

Plate 20 Taversoe Tuick chambered cairn, Rousay

Plate 21   Wideford Hill chambered cairn, Mainland Orkney

Plate 22   Barclodiad y Gawres chambered cairn: the entrance passage

Plate 23 Bodowyr tomb chamber, Anglesey

Plate 24 Bryn-Celli-Ddu Henge and passage grave, Anglesey

Plate 25 Bryn-Celli-Ddu passage grave entrance

Plate 26 Bryn-Celli-Ddu tomb chamber and pillar: entrance passage to the right

Plate 27   Bryn Gwyn stone circle, Anglesey

Plate 28   Bryn yr Hen Bobl, Anglesey: 'the hill of the old people'. The small tomb chamber is protected by the fence visible on the left

Plate 29 Plas Newydd burial chamber

Plate 30 Dyffryn Ardudwy chambered cairn: the smaller, older tomb chamber

SCOTLAND

DRUMELZIER CAIRN   NT: 123326

A cairn on a low knoll at 207m OD on the right bank of the River Tweed. It was excavated in 1929–30. A ring of boulders marks the original cairn boundary, which seems to have been oval and about 10m across. There were seven cists within the cairn, all of typical bronze age style, but a piece of neolithic Peterborough pottery was found in the cairn too, indicating that the cairn may after all have been built in the neolithic.

HARLAW MUIR LONG CAIRN   NT: 179546

The remains of a long cairn on level ground at 284m OD. The cairn consists of a low, ragged, grass-grown mound 58m long, 14m wide and 1m high.

LONG KNOWE   NY: 527862

A long cairn 5km W of Newcastleton, a somewhat enigmatic structure lying east of the 'territories' of the Clyde–Carlingford chambered cairns, and apparently unrelated to these or any other chambered tombs. It is hard to find, because it lies in a clearing in a young forest. The cairn now appears as a stone-pile shaped like a pear 53m long and 14m wide, and the various slabs protruding from the mass may represent remains of cists and burial chambers. Long Knowe has probably been robbed of its stone, but it is known to have been opened in the nineteenth century, with unrecorded results.

MELDON BRIDGE   NT: 207402

A large sub-rectangular enclosure at the confluence of Meldon Burn and Lyne Water. The enclosed area was about 400m by 250m, bounded by the rivers to east and south and a massive L-shaped timber wall 500m long running along the west and north sides. There was a corridor-like entrance passage about 5m wide and 30m long in the west wall. This large enclosure seems to have been a settlement site, although the clusters of domestic pits and post-holes which probably represent the remains of neolithic houses mostly pre-date the great wall and the ritual features. These ritual features consist of standing posts or totem poles and standing stones. It may be that Meldon Bridge is one of the family of major sites which started off as settlements and later became mainly ceremonial centres. The great size of Meldon Bridge suggests a comparison with the Wessex superhenges. Radiocarbon dates show that the main period of use was between 3450 and 2500 BC. It was probably the main ceremonial centre for people living in the Tweed valley.

THE MUTINY STONES   Longformacus   NT: 623590

A long cairn on a ridge at 380m OD. It is 85m long, 8m wide at the west end, 22m wide at the east end, 4m high at the east end, and aligned W–E. It has been damaged by robbing for a sheepfold and by illicit excavation. It is actually cut through at a point about 30m from the west end. An excavation in 1924 found a stretch of internal walling of uncertain purpose. The name of the cairn has varied over the years, from 'the Mittenfull of Stones' in 1794, to 'the Meeting Stones', to its present name.

OVERHOWDEN HENGE   NT: 487524

A degraded henge with a single entrance 6km NW of Lauder. It has been ploughed down, so that the bank rises to a height of only 0.3m and the ditch is entirely filled and levelled. The entrance is recognizable as a 10m-wide gap in the north-western perimeter. In 1950, the henge was proved to exist by excavation. Its diameter was found to measure 100m from bank-crest to bank-crest. The ditch was 3.5m wide and 1m deep. Numerous flint tools have been found in the fields close to the henge, especially round a low knoll 155m away to the north-west, which may represent the henge-builders' settlement.

WORMY HILLOCK HENGE   Clashindarrock Forest   NJ: 449307

A henge 10km S of Huntley, consisting of a low circular bank 16.5m in diameter with a single entrance on the south-east. There is a shallow ditch and a level central area only 6m in diameter. Wormy Hillock's low-lying position close to water is typical for a henge, but it is an unusually confined site, hemmed in by the sides of the glen.

———————— CENTRAL ————————

BANNOCKBURN
NS: 816802

A pit enclosure and alignment, which were revealed as a cropmark by air photography. The pit enclosure produced neolithic pottery. The function of the site remains enigmatic, but there are parallels with a similar ritual site that has been excavated at Balfarg in Fifeshire.

BROADGATE LONG BARROW
NS: 568792

A long barrow 45m long and 2.7m high. A cist was located but not excavated in 1953. This type of site is rare in western Scotland; it may represent an area of mixed culture.

DUNTREATH STANDING STONES
Dumgoyach
NS: 532807

This setting of stones originally consisted of four stones standing in a straight line running SW–NE. Someone has unhelpfully added two field-gathered boulders to the monument in recent years. A radiocarbon date of 2860 bc (3550BC) confirms that the alignment was created in the middle neolithic, and not in the bronze age as is often assumed with this type of monument.

EDINCHIP
Lochearnhead
NN: 575218

A long chambered cairn, 53m long, 16m wide at the wider east end, 10m wide at the west end, and 2m high. The chambers are visible. The monument is important in establishing a communication route between the similar groups of cairns in the lower Clyde estuary and the upper Earn and Tay valleys.

NETHER KINNEIL
NS: 958800

A shell midden excavated in 1978–9 by Derek Sloan. It was regarded as a typical mesolithic site, until it yielded a neolithic date. In coastal areas mesolithic practices and customs may have persisted right through the neolithic and probably, at some sites, on into the bronze age.

STOCKIE MUIR CHAMBERED CAIRN
NS: 479812

8km NW of Milngavie, the remains of a Clyde–Carlingford cairn appear as a long spread-out mound of stones on almost level ground. The cairn is still conspicuous from some distance. It was originally 18m long and 9m wide, but its outline is now lost as the cairn material has spread. Two large earthfast uprights stick up near the east end, the portal stones marking the centre of a shallow façade, and the remains of a chamber about 4m by 1m can be made out a metre or so to the west of them. One lintel remains: the others have fallen in.

WESTER TORRIE STONE CIRCLE   NN: 653048

A stone circle 6.7m in diameter, consisting of five surviving massive stones about 1m high. There may originally have been six.

———————— DUMFRIES AND GALLOWAY ————————

BORELAND   Minnigaff   NX: 405690

A Clyde–Carlingford chambered cairn 2km N of Minnigaff. It is in good condition, standing to a height of 2m and measuring 20m in length by a maximum of 12m in width near the south-east end, where four stones of a crescent-shaped forecourt survive. The cairn edge is marked by more than a dozen boulders, but there are no signs of the passage or chamber.

CAIRN AVEL   NX: 559925

A long cairn 1km S of Carsphairn. It is now only 15m long, having lost about 15m from its west end, by 20m wide at the east end, where it stands to a height of 3m. No upright stones are visible in the cairn, and its general appearance is similar to that of the unchambered long cairns found further to the east and north.

CAIRNDERRY   NX: 315799

A chambered cairn close to the road 18km NW of Newton Stewart. Cairnderry is the only representative in Galloway of a more or less circular type of Clyde–Carlingford cairn, with three chambers set radially within the body of the cairn, showing an affinity with others in Bute and Arran. It measures 28m by 25m. A few boulders of the bounding kerb still show in the south-west. Several slabs of the chambers are visible, still in position, especially those of the south chamber.

CAIRNHOLY CHAMBERED CAIRNS   NX: 517538

These two Clyde–Carlingford chambered cairns are only 140m apart on the hillside overlooking the east shore of Wigtown Bay. They were excavated in 1949.

The south cairn, Cairnholy I, is an impressive and conspicuous monument 50m long and 15m wide, with an imposing crescent-shaped façade and a ruined chamber. A massive forecourt blocking was found to cover hearths, a stone hole, neolithic pottery fragments, a jet bead and a mass of edible mollusc shells. Behind the façade is a two-part chamber. Its outer compartment contained a piece from a jadeite ceremonial axe, fragments of neolithic pottery and a leaf-shaped arrowhead. Late grave-goods included Peterborough and Beaker sherds and a flint knife. The rear compartment had been robbed, but it was found to contain a secondary cist with food vessel sherds and a stone carved with a cup and ring. A hearth near the north portal had beside it pieces of a shallow neolithic bowl and a flake of Arran pitchstone. This hearth had been covered by a clean spread of earth on which four later fires had been lit, probably at different times. A sixth hearth covered a filled-in stone socket on the outer edge of the forecourt on the cairn's main axis: the stone had evidently been removed from the forecourt early on in the site's history.

Cairnholy I, quite apart from being a splendid piece of neolithic architecture, has supplied us with detailed evidence of the complex and changing rituals that went on in the forecourts of chambered tombs.

The north cairn, Cairnholy II, is less spectacular. It is 20m by 12m, with its bipartite chamber exposed, opening between portal stones. The inner compartment was found to have been robbed, and the outer one disturbed.

CAIRNSCARROW — New Luce — NX: 136650

A ruined chambered cairn 3.5km W of New Luce. The megalithic burial chamber is thought to have been part of a Clyde–Carlingford cairn.

CAPENOCH LONG CAIRN — NX: 838926

A long cairn, 36m long, 9.5m wide at the wider north-east end. It now stands 3.5m high, and was probably originally higher.

CAVES OF KILHERN — NX: 198644

A ruined Clyde–Carlingford chambered cairn standing on open moorland 6km N of Glenluce. The cairn is about 30m long, with its long axis oriented WSW–ENE. It is 18m wide at the broader ENE end. The main chamber is well preserved and stands out, still capped, from the robbed cairn material. There are two lateral chambers behind it and another towards the WSW end of the cairn.

CLONFECKLE LONG CAIRN — Dalswinton — NX: 958867

An unchambered long cairn 2.5km NE of Dalswinton. It is 33m long with a maximum width of 25m. Many of the stones of the kerb are visible.

DRANANDOW CHAMBERED Minnigaff CAIRN

NX: 408714

A Clyde–Carlingford chambered cairn 30m long and a maximum of 18m wide, 5km N of Minnigaff. An axial chamber lies centrally towards the east end. There are also four lateral chambers arranged in a regular square formation to the west of the main chamber and a kerb of small boulders.

FLEUCHLARG LONG CAIRN

NX: 854874

A ruined long cairn, apparently without chambers, to the south-west of Fleuchlarg farmhouse. It is 43m long, 9m wide at the northern end and 25m wide at the broader southern end where it reaches a height of 3.5m.

GIRDLE STANES

NY: 254961

A large stone circle about 40m in diameter standing, tree-ringed, in an inconspicuous hollow. The river North Esk has cut away nearly a third of this substantial circle-henge, and several of its stones now lie pathetically in the river. There seems to be an eastern entrance marked by double portal stones. The large diameter of the circle and its situation suggest that it functioned as a central place for several dispersed communities. It was probably built 2500–2100BC. There are two outliers 130m to the north-east, up on a rise, and a sinuous line of standing stones wanders from these outlying stones round a knoll to the megalithic ellipse of the Loupin' Stanes, 500m away.

HIGH GILLESPIE

NX: 255525

A ruinous Clyde–Carlingford chambered cairn 7km SE of Glenluce. It was rather oddly marked as a graveyard on old Ordnance Survey maps. Like Dranandow and the Caves of Kilhern, High Gillespie has lateral chambers, in this case as many as seven, together with the remains of an axial chamber near the broader east end. The cairn is now 23m wide at the east end and 35m long. The cairn material has been severely robbed, so that the remains of the chambers have been exposed.

LOCHHILL LONG CAIRN

NX: 969651

One of a very small elite of earthen long barrows in Scotland; so far only two have been firmly identified: the other is Dalladies. The Lochhill barrow has been radiocarbon dated to 3120 bc (3950 BC). Like some of the southern, i.e. English, long barrows, it was raised over a wooden mortuary chamber which was burnt before the stone cairn was built over it. Associated with the mortuary house was a curved timber façade extending into horns; there were four granite uprights in front of the wooden façade, forming a kind of porch or shrine area. The Lochhill mortuary house was built with walls of granite boulders, a floor of oak planks, and a roof made of birch bark; a thick post stood at each end, presumably to hold up a ridge pole. A single corpse was laid inside it before it was set on fire.

The second phase at Lochhill consisted of a trapeze-shaped long cairn, which covered the mortuary structure and the timber façade. The cairn was fitted with a new, stone façade, which closely copied the plan of the earlier wooden one and was linked to the earlier porch by an additional slab and a panel of drystone walling. It is not known how long elapsed between the building of the mortuary structure and the building of the cairn. The final act at the site in antiquity was the blocking of the forecourt (Figure 69).

The similarities with procedures at English long barrows imply that a common funerary ritual was practised over a very wide area of Britain.

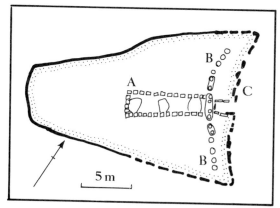

Figure 69 Lochhill Long Cairn. A – timber mortuary house of Phase 1, B – timber façade of Phase 1, C – stone façade of Phase 2.

LOCHMABEN STONE
NY: 311660

The remains of a destroyed stone circle that was originally about 46m in diameter. The Lochmaben Stone is a pear-shaped block on the shores of the Solway Firth, looking across towards the mountains of Cumbria. The name probably derives from 'Locus Maponi' and this implies that the site was used in Romano-British times as a shrine to the hunter-sun-god Maponus; there is thus circumstantial evidence here for a long-continuing tradition. In 1841, the Revd James Roddick wrote that there were 'not many years ago a number of white stones placed upright circling half an acre of ground in an oval form. One of them, the largest, is all that now remains, as some suppose, of a Druidical temple, the rest having been removed for the cultivation of the soil.' The stone is thus the sole survivor of an important ring of stones.

MID GLENIRON NX: 187610

Two Clyde–Carlingford chambered cairns with terminal chambers and crescent-shaped forecourts. The better preserved one is 33m long and 8m wide in the south, 11m wide in the north. Excavation in 1963–6 showed that an original early neolithic chambered cairn 6m in diameter and another of the same period constructed close to it (only 3m away, in fact) were later joined to make a long cairn with a façade at the north end and an additional chamber in the middle. The south chamber was sealed by cairn rubble. Nine cremations in cinerary urns were later inserted in the cairn.

Eventually the forecourt was filled with rubble, and a carefully built wall finally sealed the tomb. Then, much later, the cairn was cut in two again by a cart track. All three chambers had been robbed a century or more before the 1963–6 excavation.

The other Mid Gleniron tomb has been more severely pillaged. It too has a complex history, with multiple phases of construction; its original round cairn was later enlarged to a sub-rectangular shape with a façade facing the south.

This site was a turning-point in our understanding of British megalithic tombs. Its building sequence illustrates the important idea that circular passage graves were early monuments, preceding the fashion for long, horned cairns (Figure 70).

NEWTON NX: 550526

Virtually all that is left of this wrecked Clyde–Carlingford chambered cairn are four fine monoliths over a metre high; traces of slab walling connecting the pillar-bases define an area 2m by 1m.

STIDRIGGS LONG CAIRN NY: 041987

This long cairn stands on the northern toe of Broadshaw Rig. Now, the site is a desolate moorland, but perhaps in the third and second millennia BC the area was more productive. The cairn measures just under 30m long, 9m wide at the north, and 18m at the south where it is 2m high.

TORHOUSEKIE STONE CIRCLE NX: 383565

A superb stone ring 21m across standing beside Wigtown Bay. It stands on the Machars, an area of drumlins and highly calcareous soils that would have been very attractive to early farmers. This is one of the best preserved prehistoric sites in Britain. It is also interesting in being a variant of the recumbent stone circle type, and its south-west location indicates a purely local adoption of a north-east Scottish custom.

Nineteen local granite boulders were laid out on an artificially levelled platform of earth and small stones. The largest stone weighs only about 6 tonnes and

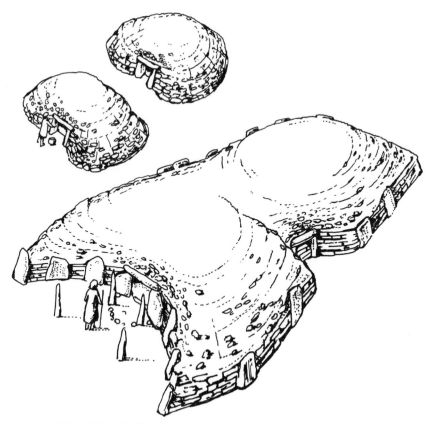

Figure 70   Mid Gleniron II: two stages in the tomb's development.

would not have required many people to move it. Inside the circle, facing ESE, is a small central stone with two large flanking boulders, a setting that recalls the recumbent stone-with-flankers idea from north-east Scotland. There is also a D-shaped ring cairn attached behind it to the WNW.

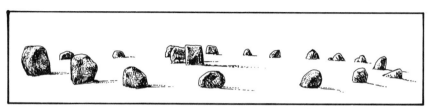

Figure 71   Torhousekie stone circle from the north-east, showing the grading of the stones in height, increasing towards the south-east side.

269

Torhousekie is, as it stands, quite unlike any other stone circle in south-west Scotland. Its date is unknown: it may be late neolithic or early bronze age (Figure 71).

THE TWELVE APOSTLES   Nithsdale   NX: 947794

Eleven out of a probable original 12 boulder stones make up a large 'flattened' circle with a maximum diameter of 88m. Five of the stones are earthfast. The circle sprawls across two low-lying enclosed fields next to a road, so its position does not flatter it; it is actually the largest stone circle on the Scottish mainland, and the fifth largest in Britain. The stone which was the largest in the circle lies, exposed and uprooted, in the south-west sector: it is 3.2m long. The highest standing stone, which is nearly 2m high, is set to the north-east of it. This stone circle is regarded as a northern outlier of the Cumbrian group, among which Long Meg and Her Daughters reign supreme.

WHITCASTLES STONE CIRCLE   NY: 224881

A huge but ruined stone circle 56m by 42m at the foot of Little Hartfell Hill.

WHITE CAIRN   Bargrennan   NX: 353784

A small, ruinous chambered cairn 14km NNW of Newton Stewart. It was excavated in 1949. It is circular, about 14m in diameter and 1m high. The megalithic chamber and passage form a single undifferentiated unit, which had been robbed and gutted earlier, yet the excavators were able to reach an untouched area of paving in the passage where they found cremated bones and fragments of neolithic pottery. These suggested a link with the Ronaldsway culture of the Isle of Man. There was a fire-pit close to the tomb entrance.

WINDY EDGE LONG CAIRN   NY: 429839

This wrecked long cairn stands on the watershed of Liddel and Tarras Waters, 6.5km E of Longholm. It has been badly mutilated by the construction of a large fold and several refuges. The general form of the cairn is a huge stone pile stretching for some 120m. A cist can be made out at the western end.

FIFE

BALBIRNIE STONE CIRCLE

NO: 285029

Balbirnie, together with Balfarg, forms one of the most important ritual complexes in eastern Scotland. There were three phases in the development of the site. The construction of the ellipse of ten stones was clearly the first stage, although the creation of a rectangular kerbed area at the centre probably followed immediately afterwards. Sherds of Grooved ware pottery, in a style similar to that found at Balfarg, were found in the stone socket of one of the uprights. The function of the central area is not known: the crazy paving that can now be seen at the site is entirely modern. After the circle was built, and perhaps long after, the site was used for burials. Two cists were constructed in pits which cut across the corners of the central setting, implying that its function had by then been forgotten. Finally, the interior of the circle was covered with cairn material; the cairn was used to receive deposits of cremated bones.

Following excavation in 1970–1, the main elements of the monument were re-erected by Glenrothes Development Corporation some 125m to the south-east of its original location, to make way for more up-to-date developments.

BALFARG HENGE

NO: 281031

Together with the (possibly later) stone circle at Balbirnie, and the structures occupying the space between them, Balfarg forms one of the most important ceremonial centres in eastern Scotland. Excavations between the two major sites have revealed a ditched enclosure, two timber structures, cairns and burials, and large amounts of pottery.

The 90m-diameter henge was discovered by air photography and excavated in advance of house-building, with the expectation that the site would later be destroyed by building, but the development was imaginatively redesigned to allow it to remain an open area. With its ditch partially cleared out, it now gives a powerful impression of the engineering skills of neolithic people. The ditch encloses a precinct 60m in diameter and originally a large bank surrounded the ditch with a single entrance on the west side. At one stage, a circle of 16 timbers was set up in the precinct, with two unusually large timbers forming a detached gate or portal on the west side. The positions of these uprights are now indicated by short marker posts, but the originals may have been as much as 4m or more high, to judge from the great depth of the sockets.

Then there were stone settings. These have proved difficult to reconstruct because the stones were seated in shallow hollows rather than proper sockets; it has been suggested that there might have been one or two concentric circles of stones in the henge. The two impressive stones 2m and 1.5m high near the entrance are the only traces of this phase; the taller one is a portal stone, the other

271

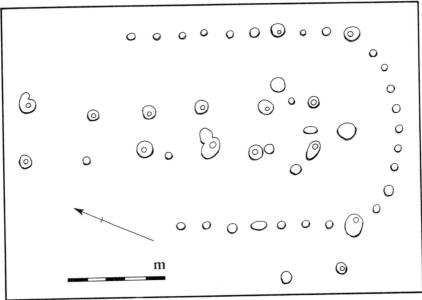

Figure 72 Balfarg: plan of the controversial timber structure. Was it a setting of freestanding posts, or an aisled longhouse?

a ring stone. There was also a timber, 'aisled' structure made of substantial posts and oriented SSE–NNW. This may have been a three-aisled longhouse, comparable with the house at Balbridie, or a setting of free-standing totem poles (Figure 72); how it should be reconstructed is a matter of controversy.

Finally, in the Beaker period, a young person was buried in a pit at the centre of the henge, accompanied by a beaker and a flint knife; the burial was sealed in by a 2-tonne slab, which has been put back in position.

There was a good deal of activity in the middle neolithic period in the area to the west of Balfarg Henge too.

A re-evaluation in the 1980s of the so-called 'natural gully' in the south-west quadrant has led to its reinterpretation as part of the henge ditch. It now looks as though Balfarg was, after all, a henge with two entrances, one to the south and one to the north-west (Figure 73).

GRAMPIAN

BALBRIDIE **Banchory** *c.* NO: 7994

An important house site on a well-drained flat ridge close to the banks of the River Dee near Banchory. The large and stoutly built rectangular hall 26m long and 13m wide had bowed ends and what seem to have been protective timber

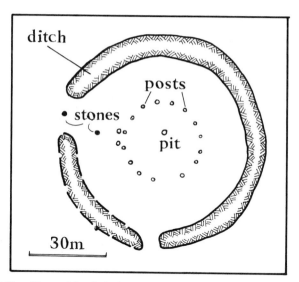

Figure 73   Balfarg Henge. The dashed area is the 'natural gully' that is now thought to be a degraded section of the henge ditch.

screens within the doorways at each end. The architectural style is so similar to that of a dark age hall that the excavators initially assumed that it was a dark age site. The cluster of very early radiocarbon dates, 2790, 2890, 2980 and 3210 bc with a mean of 2967 bc (3650 BC), nevertheless proves that it was a neolithic building. Although it is *just* possible that a dark age hall might have been built of ancient timber such as bog oak, it is not really possible that the fragments of neolithic Unstan ware found on the site can be explained away as coincidental survivals from the same period. The Balbridie house is a rare and highly significant example of a type of dwelling that was common on the European mainland in the neolithic, the timber longhouse (Figure 74).

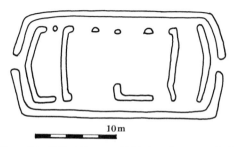

Figure 74   Balbridie: a neolithic longhouse or 'hall'.

273

BALNAGOWAN LONG CAIRN Aboyne   NJ: 500000

The long cairn in Balnagowan Wood, 3km WNW of Aboyne, consists of a series of stone piles stretching over a distance of 70m. Some of the boulders seem to be earthfast. The shape inspired the original recorder to write that 'the plan shows a general resemblance to the outlines of the Milky Way at the section occupied by the constellations Cassiopeia and Cygnus', although it seems to me very unlikely that the neolithic cairn builders had anything of this sort in mind.

BROOMEND OF CRICHIE   Inverurie   NJ: 779196

A third millennium BC ceremonial centre on a gravel terrace of the River Don, 2km to the south of Inverurie. It consists of a subdued circle-henge 33.5m across, which originally formed just one component in an extensive ceremonial complex. The two surviving stones are the remains of a six-stone circle about 13.7m in diameter. The stone now occupying the centre is a fine Pictish symbol stone with beast and crescent, dating from AD 600 and erected here for safety in the nineteenth century. It came from a bank 45m to the north-east. Several standing stones existed in the neighbourhood of the henge, so it is possible that the Pictish symbols were added in the early Christian period to an older stone which was contemporary with the henge and actually part of the original ceremonial landscape. At the base of the neolithic stones were deposits of cremated bones. In 1855 three separate offering deposits were found in front of the north-west stone: a decorated sandstone battle-axe, which was evidently a prestigious status symbol of some kind, a small circular cist and a cordoned urn. In the centre of the circle was a shaft grave about 2m deep with an almost complete human skeleton at the bottom and a deposit of cremated bones.

About 50m to the north of the circle-henge stood a large ring 46m in diameter, consisting of three concentric circles of stones with a small cairn in the centre. A 1757 description mentions 'an altar of one stone, with a cavity in the upper part, wherein some of the blood of sacrifice was put'. This may have been a recumbent stone circle, but, whatever it was, it has since been destroyed by quarrying.

A great avenue of standing stones ran south from this destroyed site to join it to the circle-henge, and on from there to a point close to the banks of the River Don. The avenue was an estimated 18m wide and consisted of 36 stones on each side. Unfortunately, only three stones have survived from this important monument.

CASTLE FRAZER   NJ: 715125

A recumbent stone circle on a site that was first artificially levelled by the circle builders. Aubrey Burl (1976) believes it to be a middle phase recumbent stone circle, i.e. dating from 1700–1850 bc (2100–2300 BC).

CLASHINDARROCK HENGE   NJ: 449307

A single-entrance henge 33m across.

CLOGHILL LONG CAIRN   NJ: 851071

Here are the dilapidated remains of an unchambered long cairn, 8km W of
Aberdeen. Stones are scattered over a distance of 52m; the width of the original
cairn seems to have been about 10m. It has been modified both by robbing for
stone and by the addition of stones thrown onto it by farm workers as they
cleared nearby fields. Significantly, the cairn was described in the 1790s as being
a mere 33m long!

DALLADIES LONG BARROW Fettercairn   NO: 627673

This long barrow was sited on the edge of a fluvioglacial terrace above the River
North Esk at 40m OD. It had side ditches which closely paralleled the curving
revetment walls of the cairn. There were traces of a curved revetment wall at one
end, flanked by horns that had been defaced. The monument has been dated to
3240 bc (4200–4000 BC). Charcoal on the neolithic land surface underneath the
barrow suggests that the site had been cleared of woodland immediately before
the barrow was built. Like the Lochhill Long Cairn, Dalladies had a vertical-
sided, flat-roofed mortuary house inside it, not a stout, ridged-roofed structure
like most of the English earthen barrows; in this, at least, the Scottish long
barrows were different from the English. The Dalladies mortuary house was a
lightly built structure roofed with birch bark. It is possible that it was not intended
to endure for very long, and that its main function was to burn in the ritual fire
that destroyed it.

The remains of the barrow have been totally destroyed by gravel quarrying.

EASTER AQUORTHIES   NJ: 732208

A recumbent stone circle 19.5m across. The recumbent stone itself is 'foreign',
probably because the builders could find no stone large enough for this role
locally: this is true of other recumbent stone circle sites too. Aubrey Burl believes
it to be an early example, i.e. built in about 2000–2100 bc (2500–2700 BC).

FOCHABERS BARROW   near Elgin   NJ: 359592

A barrow site at 60m OD. The tree-covered mound was bulldozed in 1971 during
Forestry Commission road-laying operations, when several skulls and human
long bones tumbled out of the disturbed sand. These bones, it transpired, belonged
to a line of iron age burials right across the crest of the round barrow. The iron

age people had used a place that was already established as a sanctified spot, for there was an extraordinarily long tradition of burial there.

A thousand years before, in about 1500 BC, a mother and child had been buried in the mound. A thousand years before that, a visiting group of Beaker people settled beside the mound, dug a shaft into it and set up a thick, high post, perhaps a totem pole, on it. But the mound is still older than this, having been built by the middle neolithic people who lived in the Spey valley and grew wheat and barley there.

The neolithic soil buried under the barrow was an acidic brown forest soil with traces of oak charcoal, indicating slash-and-burn cultivation on the site in 3100–2800 bc (3850–3500 BC). By comparison, the modern soils in the neighbourhood are strongly leached and podzolic because of their long exposure. The mound was built on a thick layer of charcoal and broken pottery, which was presumably some kind of foundation offering of occupation debris. On top of this black layer, four cairns of heavy cobbles were raised, and then a final capping of tonnes of sand.

The Fochabers Barrow was a monument with a long and rather touching history, showing how some sacred sites are shown respect and reverence from age to age. This makes it all the sadder that twentieth-century man destroyed it; nothing remains of the barrow, but some neolithic pottery from it has been given sanctuary in Elgin Museum.

GOURDON LONG CAIRN   NO: 818707

This long cairn 2.5km SSW of Inverbervie is 47m long, 8m wide at the south end and 13m wide at the north. It is 2.5m high.

KNAPPERTY HILL LONG CAIRN   NJ: 945504

The remains of this long cairn 3.5km NE of Maud are unimpressive, but they yielded some neolithic pottery.

LOANHEAD OF DAVIOT   NJ: 747288

A beautifully preserved recumbent stone circle 6km NW of Old Meldrum. A ring-cairn is surrounded by a circle of standing stones, among which one huge boulder has been placed horizontally. Some of the standing stones are set in a bank, but it is not certain whether the bank is an original feature. Over 100 such monuments are known to exist; Loanhead of Daviot is one of the very few that have been excavated.

The site is a broad shelf near a hill summit, which makes the monument conspicuous from quite a distance. The cairn was used as an occupation site in the early iron age, but its primary use, around 2000 bc (2500 BC), was for burial and funerary ritual.

The central area of the ring-cairn was 3.7m in diameter, the ring of loose stones surrounding this space was about 6m thick, and the outer ring of 10 uprights and one recumbent stone stood 1m outside this. Beaker sherds were found on the site, and also some earlier pottery fragments, including Irish-derived Lyles Hill ware. Although the recumbent stone circle is often regarded as a bronze age phenomenon, the earlier examples, of which Loanhead of Daviot is one, were clearly late neolithic (Figure 75).

Figure 75   Loanhead of Daviot. The ring cairn within the stone circle and the huge recumbent stone can clearly be seen in this view from the north-west.

LONGMAN HILL LONG CAIRN   NJ: 738620

This apparently earthen long cairn 5km ESE of Banff is over 60m long, although in profile it gives the impression of being a round cairn 20m in diameter and 3m high, joined on the south-west by a lower isthmus to a long mound 2m high and tapering from 11m to 8m in width.

OLD KEIG   NJ: 593195

A recumbent stone circle about 26m in diameter. It was built of local stone, although the recumbent stone itself (of sillimanite gneiss) was dragged from somewhere in the Don valley 8km away. This was presumably necessary because no stone large enough was available locally. The recumbent stone is massive – 5m by 2.1m by 2m – and weighs about 53 tonnes. The final leg of its journey was up a 1 in 14 gradient for 0.5km. This must have required the muscle power of 100 people and involved the collaboration of several late neolithic or early bronze age communities – unless teams of oxen were used.

OLD RAYNE   NJ: 679280

A recumbent stone circle about 26m in diameter. A fine greenstone wristguard, of late neolithic date, came from the central pit; it was broken in half, but still plainly visible were the three perforations for binding it to the archer's wrist.

RAEDYKES

NO: 833906

Four small ring cairns 6km NW of Stonehaven.

SUNHONEY

NJ: 716058

A recumbent stone circle 25m in diameter, which was excavated in 1855, producing an urn. Aubrey Burl believes it to be early, i.e. built around 2000–2100 bc (2500–2700 BC).

TOMNAGORN

NJ: 651077

A recumbent stone circle 22m in diameter, which Aubrey Burl believes on architectural grounds to be a middle phase structure, dating from around 1850–1700 bc (2300–2150 BC).

TOMNAVERIE   near Tarland   NJ: 478034

A recumbent stone circle. The outer ring, with its single recumbent stone, is 17m in diameter. The fragmentary inner ring seems to have been 8.5m in diameter.

———————— HIGHLAND ————————

CAITHNESS

ACHANARRAS HILL

ND: 145552

A plain stone circle 18.3m across.

ACHKINLOCH   Latheron   ND: 188417

A round Orkney–Cromarty chambered cairn of Camster type. Robbed and heather-covered, with hardly discernible edges, the 18m diameter cairn stands on a small knoll at 150m OD, only 45m SSE of a large horseshoe setting of standing stones. Three stones of its chamber are visible, projecting up through the debris at the centre.

ACHNAGOUL   Latheron   ND: 156324

The remains of a round Orkney–Cromarty chambered tomb of Camster type placed on a slight knoll, presumably to make it more visible in the neolithic landscape. The cairn has been almost entirely removed, but parts of the edge visible on the south-west side suggest that it was originally 18–20m in diameter.

The entrance passage from the SSE, about 3m long, led to a pair of portal stones set 0.6m apart, opening into the outer chamber 1.5m long: this was divided from the central compartment by another pair of stones. Nothing has survived of the assumed inner compartment.

ALLT NA BUIDHE   **Latheron**   ND: 134268

The remains of a round Orkney–Cromarty chambered tomb of Camster type, 15m by 16m, standing at just over 140m OD beside a stream. The cairn edges are fairly distinct, and its entrance was probably from the south-east side. A few stray stones suggest a chamber about 6m long, which is unusually long.

AULTAN BROUSTER   ND: 045599

A large but badly damaged stone circle 62.8m in diameter, identified by Leslie Myatt as recently as 1973. It seems extraordinary that great megalithic monuments can still be discovered in Britain. The circle stands on low-lying land between Loch Calder and Forss Water. A small cairn, apparently a later addition, stands near its centre.

BACKLASS   ND: 079423

A stone circle 6.7m in diameter.

BEN FREICEADAIN   **Reay**   ND: 059558

A round Orkney–Cromarty chambered cairn of Camster type situated inside the later fort crowning the summit of Ben Freiceadain. The top of the cairn has been lowered to a height of about 2m and the south side severely robbed. The quite distinct edges show that it had a diameter of 16m. There are fragmentary remains of an entrance passage striking in from the ENE side. Stones jutting from the cairn surface suggest the position of the chamber. It is possible to see at least 17 chambered tombs from here, with the aid of field glasses, and it is conceivable that the neolithic tomb builders intended their cairns to be intervisible in this way, though with unaided eyes.

BILBSTER   **Wick**   ND: 269547

An oval Orkney–Cromarty chambered cairn of Camster type stands on a slight ridge in flat, low-lying agricultural land. It has been severely robbed and as a result it is indistinct. The cairn was apparently originally 21m by 17m. There are some stones which seem to be set on end – apparently the remains of two chambers.

BRAWLBIN LONG   Reay   ND: 058570

This horned long chambered cairn of Orkney–Cromarty type lies NE–SW along
a slight ridge. The north-eastern end rises to a 3m-high almost circular mound,
apparently intact. The rest of the cairn has been robbed down. It is 62m long,
12m wide at the south-western end, and 22m wide at the north-eastern. Remnants
of horns project from the south-western end, but not from the north-eastern end.
The cairn was constructed of large flat slabs, but it is in a ruinous condition.

BROUNABAN   Wick   ND: 320437

This long cairn has been almost entirely removed. It seems originally to have
been 50m long with its long axis lying W–E, 15m wide at the eastern end and
10m at the western.

BROUNABAN   Wick   ND: 320437

This long cairn has been almost entirely removed. It seems originally to have
been 50m long with its long axis lying W–E, 15m wide at the eastern end and
10m at the western.

CAIRN OF HEATHERCRO   Bower   ND: 243601

An Orkney–Cromarty chambered long cairn stands on top of an 83m high hill,
in moorland but adjacent to agricultural land. The cairn was originally 48m long
and 15m wide, oriented SW–NE. The north-east end appears to have been
reduced to 2.5m high, but is still a prominent near-circular mound. The excavation
by Sir Francis Tress Barry showed a five-sided undivided chamber formed of
flagstones set on end at the north-eastern end of the mound. An entrance passage
led in from the south-east side. There was probably another chamber in the
robbed area to the south-west of this. At one time the cairn was said to be
surrounded by six or seven concentric circles marked by large stones set on edge,
but there is no sign of these now.

CAMSTER LONG   Wick   ND: 260442

This important and very fine Orkney–Cromarty chambered long cairn of Camster
type stands on a slight ridge in flat moorland at 107m OD. The cairn is 60m long,
with its long axis oriented NE–SW. The width across the horns at the higher
north-east end is 20m, at the south-west end 10m. The maximum height of 4.6m
is reached over the chambers, which are entered by way of passages from the
south-east side (Figure 77).

The east chamber is entered 9m from the north-east end. Most of its passage
is still intact, 0.6m high and 7.5m long, the outer 5m running straight into the

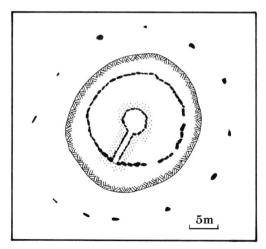

Figure 76   Balnuaran of Clava North-East.

cairn, but at this point two upright slabs were set at a 45° angle, the passage swerving to the right between their faces. The outer 5m of the passage is still lintelled, but the inner end is roofless and broken down. The chamber is an irregular pentagon, 2m in diameter, the lower walls made of five irregular slabs set on edge with drystone masonry above and in between. The masonry oversails above 1m from the floor: at 2m, the roof was closed by a single square stone.

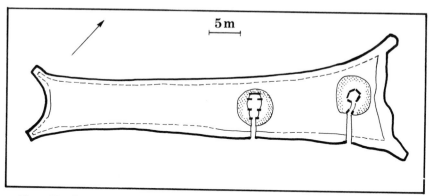

Figure 77   Camster Long: a horned long cairn incorporating two earlier chambered round cairns.

A second chamber, nearly 15m to the south-west, has its own separate entrance passage, with portal stones at the chamber entrance. This chamber has a maximum width of 1m. Another set of portals 2m high marks the entrance to a second compartment 2m by 1.5m. Mingled with the human bones were broken and unburnt bones of horse, ox, pig and deer.

At the south-west end, about 3m in from the cairn edge, a large upright stone is partially exposed; this and a few other slabs lying nearby suggest that there may be a third chamber.

The cairn has been restored, so that the full and almost theatrical effect of the architecture of the north-east façade can be appreciated. The outer drystone revetment wall marked the outer edge of a projecting, stage-like step raised above the forecourt. The restoration is a useful reminder that many monuments which are now fairly shapeless heaps of earth or stones were once as full of detailing and incident as modern buildings – and as full of architectural interest (Figure 78).

Figure 78 Camster Long. The restored cairn, showing one of the horns, the 'platform' running round the cairn edge and the entrance (left) to one of the passage graves.

CAMSTER ROUND   **Wick**   ND: 260440

An Orkney–Cromarty round cairn of Camster type on a slight knoll in flat moorland at 106m OD, only 180m SSE from the long cairn. The high vaulted chamber is almost complete except for a gap beside the capstone, through which the chamber can be entered. The cairn is remarkable because it is virtually intact. The masonry of the chamber is particularly fine. The cairn is 18m is diameter and 3.7m high. A revetment wall seems to surround the cairn, but it is not visible. The entrance was originally from the ESE, along a passage 6m long and only 0.8m high at its outer end. When excavated it was found to have been completely and deliberately blocked with stones to the roof for its entire length; this blocking procedure was quite common at the end of a tomb's period of use. The passage floor was a compacted layer of black earth, ash and burnt bones up to 0.3m thick.

It may be that bodies were placed there in a sitting position and blocking stones packed in round them. Curiously, neither of the skeletons that were propped up in the passage had leg bones. It must be presumed that the bodies had been exposed or buried elsewhere before they were brought here and that somewhere along the way the rotted legs had become detached.

Camster Round has recently been closed for consolidation to make it safe for the public to enter.

Camster Round and Camster Long are sometimes known as the Grey Cairns of Camster. Not included in this grouping is a third cairn, which is round, 8m in diameter, 0.6m high, and located about 120m to the WSW of Camster Round.

CARN LIATH   Latheron   ND: 139320

An Orkney–Cromarty long horned cairn of Camster type on flat moorland at just over 100m OD. The round chambered cairn of Loedebest East is only 30m away to the north-west. Carn Liath is badly damaged and robbed; its length was probably originally 50m and disturbance has lengthened it by 5m. The long axis is aligned W–E. The cairn is 11m wide at the western end, 18m at the eastern, and a maximum of 1.5m high. At the western end, horns project about 3m from the cairn. There were horns at the eastern end too, but the forecourt is so choked with debris that the outline is hard to trace. At the eastern end, five stones on end and parallel to each other stick up through the debris; these are probably the transverse dividing slabs of a chamber aligned along the cairn's main axis.

CARRISIDE   Reay   ND: 072592

This badly degraded Orkney–Cromarty round cairn of Camster type stands on a gentle moorland slope. It is only 2m high, with some stones projecting from it. It is 20–23m in diameter, and has an entrance from the SSE. A lintel stone, 5m in from the cairn edge, probably marks the inner end of the passage. The visible remains suggest a 3m-long passage and a large chamber 8m long divided into three compartments.

CNOC FREICEADAIN   Reay   ND: 013654

This long horned cairn is only 120m N of Na Tri Shean cairn, but has its long axis at right angles to it. Cnoc Freiceadain cairn is 67m long and 16m wide at the south-western end, which has the form of a steep-sided round cairn 2.5m high: the rest is only 1m high. The north-eastern end has two distinct horns, one 5.5 and one 9m long. It is not clear whether there were horns at the south-western end as well; if so, they must have been very low.

Old editions of Ordnance Survey maps indicate 'standing stones' between this site and Na Tri Shean, but there are none visible now.

CNOC NA CISTE   Thurso and Bower   ND: 157619

This round cairn 18m in diameter and 2.5m high crowns the highest point of flat-topped Sordale Hill. There was an irregular kerb of boulders, now visible only to the east, and an entrance from the SSE. The cairn was partially excavated in 1895, revealing a circular chamber and not much else. In 1898, some farm workers moved a lintel and found a cist with a small, well-made cup 10cm in diameter and 10cm high decorated with string impressions.

CNOC NA MARANAICH   Latheron   ND: 131331

This round cairn stands on the summit of a conspicuous hill at 170m OD. It is 18m in diameter and 2m high with a central robber pit. The size of some of the stones suggests that the cairn had a chamber. There is a standing stone 6m to the east, pointed at the top and 2.5m high.

DORRERY   Halkirk   ND: 072553

This round Orkney–Cromarty chambered tomb of Camster type is 14m in diameter and 2m high. It has been eroded, especially on the north and east sides, showing a ring structure composed of slabs laid slanting down from the centre outwards. The chamber slabs can be seen towards the centre. A passage entering from the east led to a chamber 3.3m long, which was divided into three compartments by two pairs of dividing slabs.

EARL'S CAIRN   Dunnet   ND: 263697

A round Orkney–Cromarty chambered tomb of Camster type standing on undulating cultivated land at just over 60m OD. The Earl's Cairn was excavated by Tress Barry some time before 1910. The 12m diameter tomb is badly damaged, but still stands to a height of 2m, and some of the kerb survives. The tripartite chamber is entered from the ESE, but not much of it has survived. The finds from the tomb, including two highly ornamented urns made of blue clay, have also been lost.

FAIRY HILLOCK   Halkirk   ND: 163543

A short horned Orkney–Cromarty tomb stands on a gentle slope at 120m OD. Its oval mound is 18m long, 12m wide and 2m high. The centre has been disturbed.

GALLOW HILL   Thurso   ND: 153615

This long horned cairn lies along the false crest of a hill, making it a conspicuous skyline feature from the west. It is situated in rough pasture which was formerly under the plough; it is, in other words, located in marginal farmland. The cairn is 75m long and 13m wide, widening to 25m at the SSE end, where there are also traces of horns.

GARRYWHIN (CAIRN OF GET)   Wick   ND: 313411

A short horned Orkney–Cromarty chambered tomb in a hollow in undulating moorland at 105m OD, with an open view towards the east and south. The cairn is 2.5m high, with an overall length of 25m and a width across the horns of 17m. The horns project 6m at the front and 4.5m behind the cairn. As at Camster Long, two wall faces define the edges of the cairn. Another revetment wall encircled the chamber. The tomb was entered from the SSW along a passage, which led to a rectangular outer compartment 1.5m long and 2m wide. The inner compartment was entered between two large dividing slabs. The compartment behind was nearly circular and 3.3m in diameter. The walls survived to a height of 2.7m when excavated and are still 1.5m high in places. On the floor of the main compartment was a large accumulation of ashes mixed with pottery and bones; in the centre it formed a mass 0.5m thick. All the finds from the Cairn of Get have been lost.

GUIDEBEST STONE CIRCLE   ND: 181351

A ruined stone circle very close to the Burn of Latheronwheel and surrounded by gorse bushes in an inconspicuous hollow of pasture. It is 57m in diameter and its tallest remaining stone, 1.5m high, stands on the west side of the river bank.

HAM CHAMBERED CAIRN   ND: 235738

A round chambered cairn near the cliffs 5km NW of Mey. For a time this was thought to be a souterrain, but the plan published in 1911 revealed its true identity as a round cairn with a Camster-type chamber. The grass-covered mound is over 2m high and 18m in diameter. There is a passage leading to a 4m-long chamber; the chamber has a corbelled roof capped with flagstones at a ceiling height of 2m. Ham is the northernmost chambered cairn that has been recorded on the British mainland.

HILL OF SHEBSTER LONG CAIRNS   ND: 013653 and 014654

Two long horned cairns stand 80m apart on the northern summit of Shebster Hill. The more southerly, aligned WNW–ESE, is 78m long, 10m wide and 1.5m high. The other cairn, aligned NNE–SSW, is 73m long, 16m wide and 2m high.

HILL OF SHEBSTER   Reay   ND: 011646
ROUND CAIRN

A heavily degraded Orkney–Cromarty stalled round cairn lies on a hilltop close to the two long horned cairns. The round cairn is 25m in diameter. The tops of several upright slabs protrude from it, so that it is possible to detect the internal structure. It looks as if an entrance passage 8m long led in from the south-east to a 7m-long chamber that was divided into four compartments by three pairs of transverse slabs.

HOUSTRY   Latheron   ND: 153331

This round Orkney–Cromarty chambered cairn of Camster type stands on open moorland. It is badly damaged and measures roughly 20m by 17m. The chamber is represented by the tops of five slabs sticking up out of the cairn material. The entrance passage probably ran in from the south edge of the cairn between a pair of portal stones, the tops of which can also be seen. The detail of the interior structure is unclear.

KENNY'S CAIRN   Wick   ND: 310408

A round Orkney–Cromarty chambered cairn in a shallow saddle on rolling moorland. The monument overlooks the Camster–Clyth valley as well as offering views south and east over the coast. It was 12m in diameter and 4m high at the time of excavation in the nineteenth century: now it has been reduced to a jumble of slabs. The entrance was from the south, where the passage corners can still be seen. The passage was 3m long, 0.8m wide, expanding inwards to 1.4m. It was entirely roofed when excavated, but now only three lintels remain. The outer compartment is rectangular, 2.5m wide, 1m long and made of drystone walling. The inner compartment is 3m by 3m, with upright slabs set in the side and back walls: the uprights lean outwards and at their tops the drystone walling begins oversailing to bring the walls in again. At the time of excavation the walls stood to a height of 3m, and the original roof was considerably higher. The entire floor of the main chamber was coated with ashes, burnt bones and fragments of pottery to a depth of 0.3m.

KINBRACE BURN   Kildonan   NC: 875282

This short horned Orkney–Cromarty cairn of Camster type stands on a level moorland site on the east side of the Strath of Kildonan. It is still 3.4m high, but has been severely disturbed. It appears to have had a diameter of 20m. At the north-east and north-west corners there are definite projections, but it is not certain how long these horns originally were. The entrance was from the east, but only a short section of the entrance passage is visible at the inner end, about 0.9m wide. The chamber entrance is marked by miniature portal slabs just 0.3m high.

The outer compartment is 1m long, 1.6m wide, and roofed by two lintels which continue the gradual rise in the level of the passage lintels. The central compartment has curving walls and measures 2m by 2.3m. Today the tomb can be entered through a gap in the north side of the central compartment's roof. The inner compartment is rectangular, 0.8m long and 1.3m wide, with a low roof of lintel stones. The central compartment probably originally had a corbelled dome roof about 2.5m high.

The finds went to Dunrobin Castle Museum at Golspie, but there is unfortunately no trace now of the 'pierced heart-shaped amulet of polished serpentine' that was found in the tomb.

KNOCKGLASS   Halkirk   ND: 056638

This degraded long cairn is now 34m long, but was probably originally longer. The long axis is aligned NW–SE, at right angles to the river, and the higher south-east end is now right on the river bank. The cairn is 1.8m high at the south-east end, 0.6m high at the opposite end. A large stone, possibly belonging to a chamber, was once reported to have projected from the cairn material 9m in from the south-east end, but it is not visible now.

LOWER DOUNREAY   NC: 996677

A short horned Orkney–Cromarty cairn stands on level farmland at 30m OD. At the time of excavation the cairn was a green hillock 2.5m high, and measuring 18m across by 20m long, including the horns. It is surrounded and defined by a wall-face of thin horizontal slabs, visible in places, and the entrance is between the horns on the south-east side. The outer end of the passage is 1.8m inside the apparent edge of the cairn and incredibly narrow – only 0.3m wide. The passage walls expand in width and increase in height up to 1.5m; the walls continue to diverge to form an irregular chamber 5m long and 2m wide. The chamber was carefully built of courses of small thin slabs, strengthened by eight dividing upright slabs set radially into the walls; these uprights are staggered, not paired. The walls rise above the slabs to a height of 2m, and originally higher still. The floor was partly paved. On the paving was a layer of clay in which bones were embedded.

Later in the tomb's history, a long cist was constructed in the debris that filled the chamber: the interior was filled with beach shingle. About 18–20m in front of the cairn is a hollow which seems to be the source of at least some of the cairn material. The chamber has been backfilled, so that none of the interesting internal detail can be seen.

The chamber contained fragments of bones of ox, deer, squirrel, water vole, otter, gannet, grebe, the teeth of ox, sheep and dog, and two bits of oyster shell, as well as the remains of five people. The long cist contained the body of a 25-year-old man.

NA TRI SHEAN   **Reay**   ND: 012653

This long horned cairn stands on the crest of Cnoc Freiceadain, commanding a magnificent view over Caithness and Orkney, and forming a prominent feature on the skyline from all directions. It is one of the largest and most perfect monuments of its type. Even though a field boundary crosses it, the cairn is not seriously damaged. The cairn is 72m long excluding the horns and a maximum of 20m wide at the south-east, but with a predominant width of 10m. At the south-east end, the horns are about 5.5m long and mark out an almost rectangular forecourt 18m across and 4m deep. At the north-west end the horns are 3–4m long, defining a similar but smaller forecourt. Another curious feature is that the cairn rises at both ends to form quite distinct circular mounds. The reference may be to those monuments which began life as one or two round cairns and were then altered to turn them into long cairns.

ORMIEGILL   .   **Wick**   ND: 332429

A short horned Orkney–Cromarty cairn of Camster type standing on a hillock at 60m OD in rough pasture at the foot of the Hill of Ulbster. The cairn is badly damaged: the remains of the interior have been obscured by a modern building inserted inside the chamber. Ormiegill is 20m long overall and 18m wide. The horns at the front were 15m apart, at the back 11m. The edges of the cairn are defined by two revetment walls 0.8m apart, standing 0.6m high at the time the monument was excavated in the 1880s, and battered, i.e. leaning inwards. The chamber is surrounded by further revetments, also battered, and standing to a height of 1m. A short entrance passage starting between the south-east horns led to a tripartite chamber. The roof of the passage and chamber had collapsed some time before the monument was excavated, but large quantities of unburnt bones of people and animals were found on the floor of the chamber. The floor itself consisted of a compacted, trodden-down layer of remains, typical of many of the cairns: this layer was quite thick and extended both above and below the paving.

A mace-head of mottled grey stone and some arrow-heads were found among the debris.

A second cairn once stood nearby. An excavation was begun and abandoned in the middle of the nineteenth century. Now it has completely disappeared.

SHEAN   Stemster   ND: 174626

The mutilated remains of this long cairn stand on a hilltop at 127m OD. They are in moorland, but close to cultivated land. The cairn is aligned NNW–SSE, the SSE end rising into a circular mound 2.5m high, but the rest of the mound is badly damaged and in places only 0.3m high. It is 45m long, but it seems to have been shortened at the SSE end by the construction of a large cistern immediately in front of it. The NNW end may have been truncated by a track passing the site. The width varies between 22m at the SSE end and 10m at the NNW. The monument was excavated in 1904 by Tress Barry, who evidently thought of it as a round cairn. The chamber can no longer be seen, but it was described shortly after excavation as square, central, and containing the unburnt remains of a human skeleton; the area on which the body lay was marked off by an arc of grey boulders. The chamber roof was destroyed when the monument was excavated.

To add to the site's catalogue of woes, all the finds from it have been lost.

SHURRERY CHURCH   Reay   ND: 048587

The remains of a strange and badly damaged large cairn stand on a knoll at a height of 90m OD. The cairn is now only 2m high, 37m long and 35m wide; it was probably originally longer. Its edges are now difficult to detect. Shurrery Church cairn has been severely disturbed and altered; it is crossed by two field walls, a small square building has been built against the east side, and the north end lies partly in a croft garden, partly in a field. The site is mutilated almost out of recognition, but it does seem to have been a cairn with a long stalled chamber, as was suggested at the beginning of the twentieth century. It is a great pity that sites like this cannot be rescued.

SOUTH YARROWS, NORTH   Wick   ND: 305434

A long horned Orkney–Cromarty cairn of Camster type on a moorland rise at 120m OD, with extensive views over the coastline. It is parallel to and 275m to the north of a similar and slightly bigger cairn, South Yarrows South. When the north cairn was excavated it was already reduced and roofless. Since then, it has suffered further damage. The forecourt has been filled with debris and the horns obscured, but some of the walling can be seen at the cairn edge. The cairn is oriented W–E, wider and higher at the east end, 60m long and 14m wide at the east end. Horns at the east end define a forecourt 15m across. A similar forecourt at the west end is 11m across. The entrance to the tomb chamber is at the centre of the east end, leading to a passage 3m long and 0.6m wide, its walls made of horizontally laid drystone. The tripartite chamber is entered between a pair of dwarf portal stones 0.6m high. On the floor was a clay layer containing a large percentage of charcoal and bone-ash: rough paving was laid on top of this.

SOUTH YARROWS, SOUTH   Wick   ND: 304431

This long horned Orkney–Cromarty chambered cairn of Camster type was excavated in 1865. It is more or less bare of vegetation, so its outline is clearly visible: even the exterior wall-faces can be seen in places. The eastern end has been significantly altered by modern walling outside the entrance; the passage and outer compartment of the chamber and original masonry remain in the two inner compartments. It was in this excavation that facing wall-edges, which are now known to be common, were first recognized.

The cairn is 75m long including the horns, 20m wide at the east end, narrowing to 11m at the west end. It was at one time 3.7m high at the east end. The east forecourt is 24m across, the west about 10m. In the horns, the neolithic builders took care to construct alternating courses of large and small stones, to make an interesting visual effect, but along the sides of the cairn just any flat stones were used, indicating that the horns and forecourts in front of them were areas of focal architectural interest.

The entrance passage strikes into the cairn from the centre of the east end, but runs only 3m before opening into the chamber. This drystone structure was in three parts, the largest central compartment being about 2m square, and separated from the other compartments by the usual pairs of dividing slabs. A small subsidiary wedge-shaped chamber opens 20m further along: its passage is only 0.3m wide at the entrance and the chamber roof only 0.4m high, which must have made using the tomb exceptionally difficult. South Yarrows South is a very large monument, and yet a very small area of it was actually used for burials.

WAREHOUSE, SOUTH   **Wick**   ND: 305420

A round Orkney–Cromarty chambered cairn of Camster type, which is one of a group on Warehouse Hill, at just below 180m OD. It is still 3m high, with a diameter of 17m. Remains of two encircling revetment walls have been found. The entrance passage approaching from the north-east is intact, but has been blocked by a recently broken lintel. The passage is 4m long and still fully lintelled. Its entrance is characteristically low (0.8m), rising to 1m at the inner end. The tomb was excavated in 1853, when the passage was found not to have been blocked in antiquity, although the external opening needed clearing. The chamber is entered between portal stones and has a tripartite layout. The finds, which included 'coarse thick pottery', have all been lost.

Of the group of five cairns on the hill, South Warehouse is the largest and East

Warehouse the next in order of size. North and West Warehouse are about half the diameter of South Warehouse. West Warehouse has been completely destroyed. Unfortunately, all the finds from all these cairns have been lost.

INVERNESS

BALNUARAN OF CLAVA   NH: 756443

An important megalithic cemetery immediately south of the Culloden Moor battlefield. Several round cairns are strung out in a line along a low river terrace 3m above the narrow floodplain, in a secluded grove of young beech trees.

The north-east site is a slightly oval, thick ring of stones bounded by an external kerb and a set of upright slabs inside, and measuring 5–7m in thickness. The central circular space is about 6m in diameter, but the external diameter is 21m. This substantial ring cairn lies inside a stone circle consisting of nine standing stones arranged round the circumference of a circle 30m in diameter. These stones vary widely: some are only 0.3m high, others 2.3m. Three of them, on the eastern, SSE and western sides, are connected to the outer kerb of the ring cairn by 'paths' about 2m wide made of small stones. This has not been seen elsewhere in cairns of this type, and their significance at Balnuaran is not known.

Two more, very similar, ring cairns with surrounding stone circles exist, in what was obviously an important clan cemetery. One lies about 55m to the south-west, another about 45m beyond that.

Two of the three cairn passages open towards the south-west and are on the same line; when projected, this line meets the south-western horizon roughly where the midwinter sun sets. The site may thus have affinities with Newgrange and Maes Howe, where the entrance passages of tombs were deliberately oriented to significant sunrise and sunset positions.

The biggest stone on the site weighs about 7 tonnes. Since 15 people could have moved this over level ground, the community that built the monuments may have consisted of no more than 30 or 40 people (Figure 76).

CORRIMONY   NH: 381304

A chambered cairn of Clava type at the head of Glen Urquhart beside the River Ehrick. It is roughly circular, 18m in diameter and 2.5m high, with a kerbed edge. Its entrance passage is 7m long, leading to a circular chamber 3.7m in diameter. Excavation in 1952 revealed the remains of a corbelled roof, which may originally have been 2.5m high, topped by a massive capstone with cupmarkings. A free-standing ring of 11 stones surrounds the cairn 4m away. When the chamber was cleared, its floor was found to be made of sand, with a central area paved with slabs. Under the slabs a crouched burial was secreted in the underlying sand – perhaps the last burial to be placed in the tomb.

CULDOICH   NH: 752438

A ring cairn 17m in diameter within a kerb of boulders. The central space is 6.5m in diameter. Only one stone of the surrounding circle survives, a slab 3.7m high, some 7.5m to the south-west of the kerb, which indicates a likely original diameter of 30m for the stone circle.

Excavation has shown that the central slabs rose 1.5m above the neolithic ground level and contained a deposit of stones and earth up to 0.3m deep. At the centre of this, on the old ground surface, a patch 2m in diameter was heavily impregnated with charcoal and cremated bones, confirming the funerary use of the monument.

NAIRN

EASTER CLUNE   NH: 952516

A Clava ring cairn 22m in diameter. The site of a second ring cairn is 200m away.

ROSS AND CROMARTY

ARDVANNIE   NH: 682874

An Orkney–Cromarty chambered cairn 21m in diameter and 1m high. It has a polygonal chamber to the east of the cairn's centre.

BALNAGUIE   NH: 628547

The remains of an Orkney–Cromarty chambered cairn 620m to the north-west of Balnaguie farmhouse. Much of the cairn material has now gone: probably originally it was 28m in diameter. There is a two-compartment chamber on the east side, flanked by two upright stones which were possibly part of the concave façade.

CASTLE HILL HENGE   Muir of Ord   NH: 527497

A two-entrance henge on a golf course, immediately west of the railway line. The monument measures 25.5m by 19.5m inside a ditch and external bank, with entrances to WNW and ESE.

CONONBRIDGE HENGE   NH: 543551

This is one of three small structures that may be henges. The others are Contin, at NH: 443569, and Culbokie, at NH: 594577.

Cononbridge stands immediately to the west of the Dingwall–Inverness road, the A9. It appears to be a single-entrance henge, 23m in diameter from bank-crest to bank-crest. Contin and Culbokie are 20m and 30m respectively. The problem is that in each case the bank appears to run uninterrupted across the entrance causeway. Possibly there were originally gaps in the banks, but they were filled in subsequently, either in the neolithic or later, or perhaps the banks were always continuous: only excavation will resolve this point. It may emerge that the entrances were deliberately and ritually sealed off at the close of their period of use, in the same way that many of the tombs were ceremonially blocked. The three monuments are hard to classify; they may belong to an obscure transitional phase at the end of the third millennium BC.

DUGARY HENGE   NH: 523526

A possible single-entrance henge 400m to the south-east of Dugary farmhouse. It is 20m in diameter, with a 10m wide ditch and an external bank round it. The entrance lies on the SSW side.

MUIR OF ORD HENGE   NH: 527497

Situated on the golf course 0.4km SW of Muir of Ord, this is the third two-entrance henge of this particular size to have been discovered in Scotland; the others are at Crichie and Ballymeanoch. The diameter from bank-crest to bank-crest in each case lies between 33m and 35m. The monument is used as a green on the Muir of Ord golf course and a part of the north-west arc of the ditch has been filled in to allow golfers in and out. The wasting of the bank may also be accentuated by its present land use. The oval precinct measures 26m by 20m, and the ditch is 5.5m wide and 1m deep.

SUTHERLAND

ACHAIDH   **Creich**   NH: 674910

This short horned Orkney–Cromarty cairn stands at 137m OD, high above Spinningdale; from it, there is a view down the valley and across the Dornoch Firth. The cairn was disturbed to some extent before it was excavated in 1909. In 1909, it was 2.5m high: now it is only 1.5m. The indistinct horns project about 5m at the corners. Part of the rectangular chamber's corbelling remains, so that the mason's technique can be clearly seen: the long stones run back into the cairn, only projecting a short distance into the chamber. The excavators found the apex of the dome intact and examined its structure, 'a large number of flat slabs some 2–3 feet [0.3–0.6m] long radiating from a central block of yellow sandstone: this stone tapered downwards and was firmly inserted in the structure like a keystone'. The chamber ceiling was about 2m high.

ACHANY
NC: 571019

A rectangular Orkney-Cromarty cairn 25m by 20m lies in a level field about 70m above sea level. The cairn is composed of large water-worn pebbles and covered with turf. The boulders round the cairn edge may represent the remains of a kerb. There may be an entrance passage, but its existence has not been proved; presumably it is about 3m long and leads towards the portals which are visible, protruding 0.2m above ground level. The rectangular chamber, 4m long and 1.7m wide, is completely exposed.

ACHU   Spinningdale   NH: 671910

A horned short cairn, measuring only 15m by 15m, 1km NW of Spinningdale. It was excavated in 1910. A 3.5m long passage leads in from the façade at the ESE end to a polygonal chamber 2.5m by 2m. The lower chamber walls are made of seven large slabs, the spaces between them being filled with drystone walling, a standard masonry technique practised the whole length of Britain. The upper walls are corbelled and were originally topped by flat roof slabs about 2.5m above the floor.

ALTNACEALGACH
NC: 262112

There are several chambered cairns in various states of ruination in this significant area, 10km S of Inchnadamph: it was a focal, nodal area, where the route from the north-east coastal area up Strathoykel meets the Inchnadamph–Ullapool section of the north–south route along the west coastal strip.

One of the cairns is a stone heap 14m in diameter and 2m high, with a polygonal chamber 3m long and 2m wide located a bit off-centre. The chamber is constructed of six large slabs, with the spaces between them filled with drystone. Its blocked entrance faces towards the ESE.

AUCHINDUICH STONE CIRCLE
NC: 584002

One of three unusual stone circles in Sutherland – unusual because it has its stones set at right angles to the circumference, which was apparently a local custom. The stone circle is about 9m in diameter.

BADNABAY
NC: 219467

The remains of a round chambered cairn, 12m in diameter. The cairn material has been robbed, leaving the earthfast stones of the chamber standing on their own in the pasture. The entrance passage is 4m long, and the polygonal inner compartment 3m by 3m. The remaining slabs stand about 1m high and, in spite of all the robbing, still make an impressive monument.

CARN LIATH   Torboll   NH: 740995

A ruined chambered cairn stands on a hill 1.2km NW of Torboll, among later clearance cairns. It is a round mound 18m in diameter, with a chamber and passage that have at some stage been cleared of debris. The passage is 4m long and runs in from the south-east to the two-part chamber. The outer compartment is 1.5m square; the inner one is polygonal and 2m by 1.5m. The walls are made of slabs with drystone infilling.

CNOC AN DAIMH   NC: 165428

This round chambered cairn, about 10m in diameter, stands on a rocky knoll. Several slabs protrude from the stony mound, showing that a polygonal chamber exists inside.

CNOC AN LIATH-BHAILD   NC: 728102

The second of three stone circles in Sutherland with its stones set radially. It is elliptical, 9.1m by 6.8m, with a low cairn at its centre. A noticeably taller circle-stone stands on the west side, which may be significant.

COILLE NA BORGIE, NORTH Farr   NC: 715590

A horned long Orkney–Cromarty cairn. Two long bare cairns lie end to end only 10m apart on a moorland terrace above the River Naver, only 15m above sea level. The north cairn is very degraded, and bisected by a cart track, so it was for a long time regarded as two separate cairns. In its original state it was a long horned Orkney–Cromarty cairn oriented N–S, 47m long excluding the horns, 15m wide at the northern end and 13m wide across the centre. The northern end, which was 3.5m high in 1884, has horns defining a forecourt 14m across. There is no sign of an entrance passage, but there are indistinct remains of a polygonal chamber.

COILLE NA BORGIE, SOUTH Farr   NC: 715590

The south cairn has a total length of 72m, with a clear edge marked by an intermittent kerb. It is 19m wide at the higher northern end. Two horns project to form a forecourt 15m across and 4.5m deep, bounded by six monumental, pointed, upright stones set 3–5m apart. The stones were roughly graded, those at the edges being higher than those at the centre. The axis of the passage and chamber is NNE–SSW, which is askew in relation to the long axis of the cairn. Another peculiarity of the tomb is that the entrance is to the east of the centre of the façade. The passage is not visible now, but it is reported to be 0.6m wide,

0.6m high and 5m long, leading to a tripartite chamber. Charred wood and animal bones were found in the inner compartment.

DAILHARRAILD   NC: 678390

The third of three unusual stone circles in Sutherland, with its stones set radially. The significance of the radial setting is not known, although it is possible to see a parallel to it in the circle-setting of radial trilithons of Stonehenge II.

KILLIN   NC: 857077

A chambered cairn in a wood 30m E of the road along the east side of Loch Bora. The cairn is a stony mound 15m in diameter containing a tripartite Camster-type chamber entered from the west. Most of the 6m-long passage has been damaged, but several details of the chamber have been preserved. The first compartment is 2m wide, 1.5m long and made of drystone walling. Large partition stones set vertically 0.6m apart separate it from the second compartment, also made of drystone. There are more portal stones, but the last compartment is choked with debris.

KINBRACE   NC: 875283

Many chambered cairns, both long and round, exist in the Strath of Kildonan immediately south of Kinbrace. This particular one, 3.5km SSE of Kinbrace, has a tripartite chamber reached by way of a 7.5m long passage running in from the east. Its outer compartment, only 0.9m by 1.5m, has side walls of drystone and end walls defined by upright slabs. The central compartment is polygonal, measuring 2m by 2.4m. The inner compartment is 0.9m by 1.5m, with a very low roof only 0.6m above the floor. The central compartment had a corbelled roof that was higher. The cairn now appears as a mass of tumbled boulders; it is not clear whether it was a round cairn or a short horned cairn.

SKAIL   NC: 711465

It is still possible to detect the round mound of this badly damaged chambered cairn. It has a diameter of about 20m and a polygonal chamber with a SW–NE axis. Several slabs indicate the outlines of the chamber's compartments.

SKELPICK   NC: 723566

A long horned cairn about 60m long near the Skelpick Burn. Its long axis is oriented N–S. A 4.5m-long passage enters from the façade between the horns at the north end. The outermost compartment measures 2m by 1m by 1.4m high, and it opens through a portal into a central compartment measuring 3m by 2.5m.

This is separated from the inner compartment by another large lintel resting on portal stones. The inner compartment is 3.7m by 3m and polygonal, formed by six huge slabs with drystone walling in the gaps.

—————————— LOTHIAN ——————————

CAIRNPAPPLE HILL HENGE   NS: 987717

The spectacular view from this ceremonial centre, across to Bass Rock, Goat Fell, the mountains of Arran, the Firth of Clyde, the Border hills, and north-west towards Stirling and the Trossachs, make this an inspiring place. It seems that something about it − and perhaps it was partly the panoramic view − inspired people to treat this as a special centre over an extraordinarily long period.

There were at least five main phases of ceremonial activity at Cairnpapple, the most recent (V) represented by a group of four rectangular full-length graves close to the ditch. These are probably iron age, possibly dating from the first few centuries AD. Before that, some 1,500 years earlier (IV), the site was dominated by a huge, 30m-diameter stone cairn overlooking the western part of the large ditch, and supported by an outer kerb of rounded boulders which are now some 14m away from the cairn edge. In an earlier stage still, around 1800–1700 BC (III), a smaller cairn 15m in diameter existed on the site.

In 2000–1900 BC (II), two small rock-cut graves were made to receive crouched burials. One, possibly originally covered by a small mound, was incorporated into the later cairn and was marked by a standing stone. But the main feature of this 2000–1900 BC phase was a massive oval enclosure containing an egg-shaped setting 35m by 28m, and consisting of 24 standing stones set close to the inner edge of a broad, rock-cut ditch, from which material was thrown up and outwards to create an external bank. This henge had two causewayed entrances.

Well before the building of the henge, and probably not long after 3000 BC, a far less impressive monument existed on Cairnpapple Hill, but it was nevertheless even at that early stage a ritual centre for the area. Seven small pits, probably stone sockets, were arranged in an irregular arc within the area that would later become the enlarged cairn. A second setting of three large stones was also raised, to make a cove. Stone chips originating in the Great Langdale axe factories in Cumbria were found on the site, and they seem to date from around 2800–2700 BC (the dates for Cairnpapple are only approximate).

Cairnpapple was thus a focus of ritual activity, certainly continually and possibly continuously, for 3,000 years that we know of. Cairnpapple stands virtually alone in British archaeology in offering evidence of such long-sustained religious observance at a particular spot; it thus has a virtually unique claim to being a holy place (Figure 79).

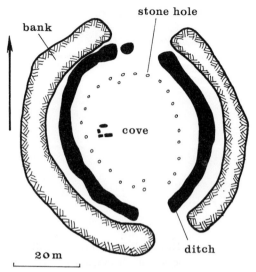

Figure 79 Cairnpapple: a major ceremonial monument.

ORKNEY

BARNHOUSE STONE   **Mainland**   HY: 312121

A standing stone 1km SW of Maes Howe and visible from the tomb chamber. Now looking rather insignificant and out of place in the middle of cultivated land, in the neolithic age it acted as a marker for the midwinter sunset, towards which the main axis and entrance passage of Maes Howe were oriented. The stone should be regarded as an integral part of the Maes Howe ceremonial complex.

BIGLAND LONG   **Rousay**   HY: 435321

A turf-covered cairn with possibly two stalled chambers, sited at the edge of a marine platform close to the valley floor at 15m OD. Its shape is not very clear, but it seems to be rectangular, 28m long, 15m wide and 1m high. Several slabs stick up through the turf, evidently the back and dividing stones of two chambers. The longer chamber, about 11.5m long, follows the NW–SE long axis of the cairn; it seems to have seven pairs of stalls. To the east are three slabs belonging to a second chamber with a different, W–E, alignment.

BIGLAND ROUND   Rousay   HY: 438325

A chambered cairn at 35m OD, on the edge of the lowest marine platform and overlooking the valley in which the present-day farm of Bigland lies. It stands on marginal land just 300m NW of the neolithic settlement of Rinyo, which it probably served. The cairn is 12m in diameter and edged by a wall which now stands to a height of 0.3m but when excavated in 1938 stood to 0.7m. About a metre inside the wall a concentric revetment wall is visible. The passage is only 0.5m wide and 1m long, the thickness of the cairn's outer casing. There is a tripartite chamber 4.8m long by up to 2m wide and divided into compartments by pairs of uprights. There is a substantial back-slab 1m high. The curving side walls are of well-made drystone masonry.

BLACKHAMMER   Rousay   HY: 414276

A rectangular long mound 24m by 10m covering a stalled chamber, one of an archaeologically important series of chambered cairns on the south coast of Rousay. The chamber is 13m long, 1.7m wide and divided into seven compartments or 14 stalls by pairs of upright slabs. The chamber is encased in a stone skin about 2m thick and this in turn is encased by another. The cairn is surrounded by a carefully built wall-face up to 1m high; the foundation course is a single row of flat stones projecting slightly, and above this the courses are laid obliquely, facing left and right alternately in shallow wedges. The original ceiling and upper part of the cairn have been removed and a modern roof now protects the monument; visitors now enter it through the roof. Blackhammer was excavated by Callander and Grant in 1936, when it was found to contain the remains of only two people, both adult males, though it had evidently been much disturbed. Blackhammer's site is similar to that of nearby Taversoe Tuick; it stands on a level shelf at about 60m OD, and overlooks four more level benches which are probably raised shore platforms, and which were almost certainly farmed by the Blackhammer people. Bones from the tomb included those of sheep, ox, red deer, gannet, pink-footed goose and cormorant; whether these animal and bird remains represent 'grave-goods' in any sense, or offerings, or are the remains of ritual meals consumed at or in the tomb, is open to speculation.

BOOKAN   Mainland   HY: 286141

This round chambered cairn is sited on the crest of the isthmus that separates the Lochs of Stenness and Harray, at about 25m OD. The cairn is a slightly irregular oval, 17.5m by 15.5m and up to 1.6m high. At the time of Farrer's excavation in 1861, it was only 0.2m higher than this, but it had apparently been lowered by a still earlier exploration. A wall-face 0.3m high is concealed inside the cairn, about 3m in from the cairn's edge; the function of these internal walls seems to have been structural: they held the cairn material in place. The passage ran in from the wall-face on the SSE side, slightly out of line with the chamber's axis. The entrance passage walls, 1.9m long and 0.5m apart, still stand to a height of 0.8m. The chamber had a rectangular central area 2.1m by 1.3m, with rectangular compartments opening from it, two to the east and two to the west: all four were 1.3m by 0.9m. Human remains were recovered from three of the compartments, but have been lost; this is the common fate of archaeological collections that remain in private hands.

BRAESIDE   Eday   HY: 563375

A rectangular chambered cairn standing in low moorland at 20m OD only 150m away from Huntersquoy. The badly robbed cairn is rectangular and about 30m by 18m. The cairn material has been scooped out to expose a chamber in the cairn's southern half: both cairn and chamber are oriented roughly N–S and the entrance via a short passage was also to the south. The chamber was 6.2m long by 2m wide and divided into three compartments by two pairs of upright slabs.

BURGAR   Mainland   HY: 347278

A round cairn on low-lying land only 10m from the shore. The edge of the cairn is well defined and 17.5 in diameter. The chamber, which has been disturbed, was probably 6m long by 2m wide and tripartite. The entrance passage probably ran in from the north-east, since the chamber's axis is SW–NE and there is an identifiable back-slab at its south-west end. The two large slabs lying askew to the south-east of the chamber are a puzzle: they are probably not in their original positions and were once part of the chamber.

BURRAY   South Ronaldsay   ND: 488988

A wrecked chambered cairn that once stood close to the shore. It was dismantled by farm labourers in 1963, but fortunately George Petrie was able to observe its structure during the demolition. Overall the cairn was 1.6m high, 15.5m across from east to west and 13.5m from north to south. The east and west sides seem to have been straight, while the north and south sides, or ends, were curved; this in effect makes the cairn a short horned type. The stalled chamber seems to have had three or possibly four pairs of stalls and, I think, an entrance passage leading in from the north. The 'cell' detected on the eastern side may have been an additional compartment rather than a section of an entrance passage. The remains of 22 or 23 people were found distributed among the main and side compartments. Seven dog skeletons were also found in the tomb, one in the side cell and one in each of the compartments in the main chamber. This would support the idea that each Orcadian group adopted a distinctive totem animal; if so, the Burray people were 'the Dog People'.

CALF OF EDAY LONG   Calf of Eday   HY: 579387

A rectangular stalled cairn close to the seashore on the hillslope facing Eday. The cairn not only contained a stalled chamber but overlay a small oval house of a type now widely known in Shetland. The house was only 3m long by 2m wide and divided into two unequal parts. It contained peaty soil blackened by fire and a few plain sherds; its entrance was blocked up with stones. It is not clear whether this structure was a house or a tomb, or perhaps even each in turn: it had been severely robbed, and even the walls had been stripped of their facers. Over the remains of this early structure, whatever it was, a stalled chamber was built. An entrance passage 3.5m long from the east entered a chamber with eight stalls arranged in four pairs. The chamber is 8m long and up to 2m wide with walls 1m thick; one corner of the chamber wall overlies and obliterates a corner of the earlier structure. The stalled chamber and the earlier structure were then encased in an oblong mass of masonry 20m by 8m, the sides and ends of which are slightly bowed. The casing and the chamber represent a single construction phase; the little oval building represents an earlier and separate phase, which was nevertheless not completely destroyed when the later building began. The tomb contained the bones of only one person and an otter, in the box below the bench in the end compartment. The neolithic deposits were coated with a layer of blown sand; since this had a level upper surface, it is thought that it accumulated at a time when the roof had been removed. On top of the blown sand was a layer of iron age debris including sherds, suggesting that here, as at several other Orcadian tombs, later people found some new and secular use for the older structure, probably as a windbreak or shelter.

CALF OF EDAY   Calf of Eday   HY: 578386
NORTH-WEST

This chambered cairn can claim to be the smallest in Orkney: 8m in diameter, it covers an area of only 50 square metres. It has a blocking stone at its entrance, and the end compartment was also blocked with masonry almost to the roof. The rectangular chamber, 3m long, has four curvilinear side compartments leading off it. The compartments seem to have had stone benches when the chamber was first opened because Farrer, the excavator, mentioned 'the rude beds of the occupants'.

CALF OF EDAY   Calf of Eday   HY: 580386
SOUTH-EAST

A round chambered cairn 10m in diameter on a gentle hillslope only 40m from the shore. The cairn has a sunken entrance passage to the south-west, facing the shore and the island of Eday; going in from the edge of the cairn, the passage leads after 3m into a roughly rectangular central area with four shallow curved-wall compartments opening from it.

CUBBIE ROO'S (or COBBIE ROW'S) BURDEN

Rousay HY: 437280

A round chambered cairn at 55m OD, the easternmost in the series of well-preserved tombs lining the southern coast of Rousay. The cairn is 16m in diameter and 1.6m high. At the cairn's centre, five upright slabs can be seen, evidently the back-slab and two pairs of dividing slabs of a stalled chamber. The outer part (i.e. the south) of the chamber and the entrance passage, presumably also to the south, have not been traced. Like the other tombs in this Rousay series, Cubbie Roo's Burden is an interesting site in itself; but the whole series taken as an entity is invaluable in implying the social geography of a complete neolithic landscape. Colin Renfrew has made some useful deductions about the organization of band territories from the Rousay tombs, inferring that the territorial boundaries lie half-way between each tomb and the next, each tomb commanding a small patch of low-lying cultivable land.

CUWEEN HILL

Mainland HY: 364127

A chambered cairn of Maes Howe type, one of an almost straight line of Maes Howe cairns marching across the centre of Mainland Orkney. The cairn is 16m in diameter and 2.5m high. An entrance passage 5.5m long and only 0.8m high at the door lintel leads from the south-east, i.e. from the downhill side, to the well-made chamber which measures 3m by 1.5m. The outermost 2.5m of the entrance passage has no roof and takes the form of a trench. The modern replacement roof to the chamber, which is lower than the original roof, is at 2.5m above the floor. Four cells open off the main chamber. Cuween stands high (76m OD) on the hillside, on marginal land but commanding a small area of farmland below. It was well placed to act as a territorial marker for the neolithic population (probably just one family) living on that patch of farmland. The tomb was built on a terrace artificially cut into the hillside, and the rock floor inside the tomb is incredibly smooth and level. In 1901, Charleson found the remains of eight people in the lower layers of the fill in the chamber, along with the skulls of 24 dogs, apparently the Cuween people's totem animal.

DEEPDALE STANDING STONE

Mainland HY: 272117

A standing stone near Stromness. It is a flat slab 1.8m high on a hillside, false-crested, and evidently designed to be seen from the east or north-east, i.e. from the general direction of the Ring of Brodgar. The thin edges of the slab are oriented N–S (Plate 15).

DINGIESHOWE Mainland HY: 548033

A settlement site that has yielded Grooved ware pottery, although no structures have as yet been identified.

DUNCANS GEO Hoy ND: 287878

The remains of a tripartite chambered cairn on the edge of a 5m-high cliffed headland on the south coast of Hoy. The cairn was at least 9m (E–W) by 5m (N–S) and had an outer facing wall. Four upright slabs belonging to its chamber are still visible: one, 1m long and 0.4m high, may have been its back-slab.

THE DWARFIE STANE Hoy HY: 243005

A large block of sandstone, apparently detached by weathering or glacier-ice, rests on the floor of the great glacial through-valley passing right across Hoy. The block is 8.6m long, 4m wide and 2.5m high. A passage and two cells have been laboriously carved out of it. The passage is 2m long, 0.8m high and 0.9m wide. The two cells, each 1.5m by 0.8m by 0.7m high, open out of its sides. Outside, a squared stone measuring 1.5m by 0.7m by 0.6m was obviously used as a blocking stone. It weighs 1.5 tonnes and its measurements correspond closely with those of the tomb entrance; in fact, the stone was in position, blocking the entrance, when seen by 'Jo Ben' in the sixteenth century, although by the eighteenth century the tomb was open. Probably the break in the roof over the entrance occurred when the blocking stone was prised out. Curiously, there is a second stone with very similar dimensions about 30m away; like the blocking stone, it shows signs of having been worn back by chiselling at one end, although it is hard to understand how the tomb can have had two blocking stones, both damaged in the same way by people attempting to break in. As a rock-cut tomb, the Dwarfie Stane is almost unique in the British Isles. The only comparable example that I know of is St Kevin's Bed at Glendalough in Ireland. The technique of carving a tomb out of the living rock is nevertheless exploited in the making of Huntersquoy and Taversoe Tuick, where the lower parts of the tombs are rock-cut (Plate 16).

EARL'S KNOLL Papa Stronsay HY: 665300

A long cairn at least 58m long (and possibly originally 65m), its long axis aligned WNW–ESE and 21m wide at the broader eastern end. At the western end, where the cairn is barely 0.8m high, it has been used as a mill stance: the mill base is still there. This ruined chambered tomb is of great size, comparable to Maes Howe. An estimated 32,000 man-hours went into its building, compared with 39,000 man-hours for Maes Howe. J. W. Hedges speculates that Earl's Knoll formed the tribal focus for the northern part of the Orkney Island group, including the islands of Stronsay, Shapinsay, Rousay, Eday and Westray: whether Sanday and North Ronaldsay were part of this territory is not known. In 1792, the cairn had 'the appearance of old ruins and graves, one of which graves, evidently defined by 2 stones, one at the head, the other at the feet, is 8 feet and a half long [2.6m]; this grave was dug up to the deepness of about 6 feet [1.8m]'. The stones described were apparently still visible in 1878, when the Ordnance Survey showed them at what is now the highest point of the cairn. They may represent the remains of a large tomb chamber: many human bones were found during the 1792 dig. The Earl's Knoll story is a particularly sad example of unscientific tomb-opening – one of the deadliest crazes of the eighteenth and nineteenth centuries.

EDAY CHURCH   Eday   HY: 560335

An irregularly shaped chambered cairn. The main part of the cairn is roughly circular, but it also has two prominent horns. The rectangular chamber, about 5m long and 2m wide, seems to have been divided into three compartments or six stalls.

EDAY MANSE   Eday   HY: 560324

A partially destroyed chambered cairn at 50m OD on a hill slope. It was very badly damaged in about 1821, at the time when the church was built; the church in its turn also stands in ruins next to the ruined cairn. It seems from a description written in the 1860s that 'there was a long passage or room flagged over, and numerous passages branching out and leading to quasi-circular cells. The building [was] externally about 20 yards [18m] in length by about 10 [9m] in breadth'. Hebden found a decorated stone 'lying on its face just at the entrance of one of the passages'. The stone, 1.4m long, is decorated with a grooved design consisting of a pair of spirals joined together, two sets of concentric circles and part of a third set. The ruin as it now stands seems to have been a rectangular cairn 37m from north to south by 16 or 17m from east to west, which is much larger than described in Hebden's account, but it appears from the 1879 OS map that the cairn was then very much its present size.

FARA   Fara   HY: 527379

This round chambered cairn stands about 5m above the rocky shore, and yet on what has apparently always been marginal land; the island has been abandoned since 1947. The cairn is 14m in diameter with the remains of what seem to be four horns projecting from it. The roughly oval chamber, 5m by 2.5m, seems to have been divided into three compartments by pairs of upright slabs.

Figure 80 Knap of Howar. The exterior of a neolithic house doorway, perfectly preserved. Inside, one of the door jambs can be made out.

FARACLETT HEAD WEST   Rousay   HY: 439327

A stalled round cairn 13m in diameter and 1.2m high, only 16m W of the Faraclett Head East round cairn. The central area has been disturbed and there are traces of a rectangular secondary structure, but the broken tops of four upright slabs are visible, and they are probably the remains of a tripartite stalled chamber.

FITTY HILL   Westray   HY: 433445

A chambered round cairn standing in a conspicuous position at 85m OD on a spur of Fitty Hill. Like so many Orcadian tombs, it is on marginal land, in a field of pasture recently converted from rough moorland. The cairn is 17m in diameter and 1m high. The central area has been robbed, but it seems that the broken stumps of five uprights belong to a stalled chamber. The three slabs to the south of this possible chamber are more difficult to explain, but traces of concrete on one of them suggests a modern origin: it is likely that this, like many other Orcadian cairns, has been called into use by a resourceful farmer.

GLIFTER STANDING STONE Rousay   HY: 399289

A standing stone due north of the Knowe of Lairo.

GRICE NESS   Stronsay   HY: 672284

This round chambered cairn, 13m in diameter, stands in a conspicuous position on a low headland of rough pasture about 80m from the seashore. The cairn merges with a surrounding oval platform which is 22m in diameter and has a clearly defined outer edge. The stumps of two pairs of slabs stick up through the turf. They are set 2.7m apart at right angles to the NNW–SSE axis, and possibly represent the remains of a stalled chamber.

HEAD OF WORK   Mainland   HY: 484138

A horned long cairn of the Yarrows type, horned at both ends. It measures 47m by 25m overall, the main body of the cairn being 12–17m wide. There seems to have been some exploratory excavation near the eastern end, where there is a depression and some slabs of what may be a stalled chamber protrude. From the cairn's shape it would appear that it began as a round cairn (the south-east end) with a chamber at its centre, and was then extended to turn it into a long cairn at a later date.

HELLIAR HOLM   Helliar Holm   HY: 484154

This chambered cairn stands on the 28m high summit of the island, which, although uninhabited, is linked to Shapinsay at low tide. The 2m high cairn is an irregular oval, 19m by 17.5m, with well-defined edges. Its chamber is defined by the tops of three pairs of slabs and one stone of a fourth pair; the back-slab is not seen, probably because it is lower than the other stones. The long axis of the chamber is oriented NW–SE and the entrance passage is to the south-east too, a common orientation for neolithic tombs in general.

HESTA HEAD   South Ronaldsay   ND: 462878

This well-defined stalled round cairn stands at a height of 61m OD about 120m back from the cliff edge. The ruined stalled chamber is represented by the stumps of five uprights, with its long axis oriented SW–NE. The big back-slab, 2.2m long, leans outwards slightly from the chamber, a feature seen at some of the other and better-preserved cairns.

HILL OF CRUADAY   Mainland   HY: 246217

This is thought to be the quarry from which the flagstones were taken to build the great monuments of Maes Howe and the Ring of Brodgar in the third millennium BC. It is a 10km haul from Cruaday to Brodgar. Nearby, at Holy Kirk (HY: 249216), a round chambered tomb has been tentatively identified. It is 13m in diameter and only 0.5m high; a group of standing and fallen stones in the centre appears to be a ruined chamber (Plate 17).

HOLM OF PAPA WESTRAY   Holm of Papa Westray   HY: 504522
NORTH

A small stalled cairn at the north end of the island, close to sea level and very close to the neolithic settlement of Knap of Howar. More than a dozen pairs of deer antlers were buried in it, implying an animal totem. The cairn is rectangular, 12m by 6.3m, with its long axis aligned SE–NW and its entrance to the north-west through a straight façade. An inner wall-face seems in this case to represent an earlier exterior, 10m by 5m, with a crescentic façade skewed across the north-west-facing entrance. In its final form, the cairn had an entrance passage 3m long, roughly paved at the outer end, with two courses of sill stones set flush with the outer wall of the monument. The passage is slightly twisted in relation to the cairn's long axis. The chamber is 5m long and 1.7m wide with finely built drystone walls surviving to a height of 1m and divided into four compartments by pairs of uprights. A cell 1m by 1m opens off the southern end of the chamber. Originally it had a corbelled roof. The cell had been assiduously filled with layers of shells, stones, deer antlers and the bones of animals, fish and people. Its entrance had been sealed with carefully built drystone walling early on in the tomb's period of use. The main chamber contained human burials together with deer tines, fish bones, pottery and deposits of periwinkles and limpet shells.

HOLM OF PAPA WESTRAY   Holm of Papa Westray   HY: 509518
SOUTH

A chambered cairn of Maes Howe type or derivation built on the low summit of the island at 15m OD. The outer appearance of the original cairn is not certain, but it seems to have been 38m long and 20m wide, oblong with rounded corners, and 4m high. The chamber is 1.5m wide and subdivided by two cross walls which are open at floor level to allow access between compartments, but solid above. The central compartment is 13.5m long, the west compartment 4m long, and the east compartment 2m long. There are also 12 mural compartments or cubby-holes opening off the main compartments. The passage is 9m long, of which the inner 4m is roofed and original: the outer part was reconstructed to some extent in 1931. Several designs have been sculpted on the chamber's stonework; there are circles, zig-zags and two rectangular symbols carved on as many as 11 stones in the chamber.

THE HOWE   Mainland   HY: 275109

Iron age and Pictish occupation levels overlie, and have largely destroyed, an important neolithic tomb built on low-lying agricultural land. The mound covering the chamber was made of clay, like the mound at Maes Howe; the site and the exceptional quality of the masonry also put it in the same class as Maes Howe, which makes it all the sadder that the Howe has been so badly damaged. The earliest structures on the site were two apparently square and thickly walled buildings separated by a narrow passage. They measured about 4m across internally, but the extent of the damage caused by later occupation makes it impossible to be sure of the detail. Internal divisions by slabs could suggest either an early type of stalled tomb chamber or, considering the presence of the central hearths, the fittings of a domestic dwelling of the same type found at Skara Brae. Whatever they were, the two buildings were demolished and deliberately sealed with clay before the neolithic mound was built. The mound's straight entrance passage, some 11m long, follows fairly closely the long axis of the older 'west' structure, which it partially overlies. It is a great pity that the centre of the mound was almost entirely removed before an early iron age roundhouse was built there, so that many details of the chamber have been utterly destroyed. Its floor level seems to have been higher than that of the iron age souterrain, so the crucial floor deposits of the neolithic chamber have been lost. What is puzzling is the apparently small size of the chamber, given the very large size of the covering mound, 25m in diameter, with two thick concentric revetment walls, and the high quality of the surviving masonry. It seems extraordinary that such a large-scale and apparently important monument should have had a chamber only 1–2m across.

HOXA HILL (THE WART)   South Ronaldsay   ND: 433935

A round chambered cairn 9.7m in diameter on the summit of Hoxa Hill at 60m OD. The cairn was built on a platform 21m in diameter which is edged by a low stony bank. There is no gap in the bank corresponding with the likely position of the entrance passage in the cairn. Five upright slabs were noted by George Petrie in 1869 and his sketch plan suggests a tripartite chamber oriented SW–NE.

HUNTERSQUOY   Eday   HY: 652377

An inconspicuous two-storeyed stalled cairn on the lower slopes of Vinquoy Hill, marked by the stumps of two of the upper chamber stones. The cairn is almost circular, about 10m in diameter, and contains a still-complete lower chamber reached by a passage from the east. Immediately above, and entered from the west, is an upper chamber 4m by 2m and containing six stalls, three on each side of the central space. The upper passage is only 0.4m wide at the outer end, where there was a shallow, flat sill-stone, its outer edge carefully lined up with the footing of the wall marking the cairn's edge. The roof of the upper chamber has been destroyed, but its floor survives – a layer of blue clay 20cm thick spread over the lintels forming the roof of the lower chamber. The floor of the lower chamber is cut into the solid rock. The lower chamber is 4m long, 2.5m wide and 2m high; its ends are divided off by pairs of slabs. Subsidiary compartments and aumbries are built into the walls close to the roof. The entrance to the lower chamber is approached by an open trench lined with drystone masonry; the passage itself is 4m long, 0.75m high and 0.6m wide at the outer end. Huntersquoy and Taversoe Tuick are the only two-storeyed cairns that are known to have been constructed.

ISBISTER　　　　　　　　　South Ronaldsay　　　　ND: 469844

A chambered cairn in an impressive location on the cliffs in the south-east corner of South Ronaldsay. The site is unusual in commanding a view over a natural amphitheatre of bare flagstones at the top of the cliffs, as well as overlooking the sea; from the fields to the west, the cairn makes a conspicuous landmark on the skyline. The cairn was partly opened in 1958, and later excavated more completely. The complete monument was a turf-covered mound 40m long and 15m wide, standing to a height of 3m. The stalled chamber 8m long and 1.5m wide now stands open to the sky. It was encased in two masonry skins, oval in plan, making a cairn 15m long (north to south). Ten metres away from the cairn edge and concentric with it on the west was an arc-shaped retaining wall supporting an outer rubble cairn. Two hornwork walls extended along the cliff top, forming a cycloramic backdrop for the forecourt terrace where, presumably, rituals took place. The human remains – the bones of at least 338 people – are the most complete and best preserved so far found in a neolithic context in Scotland, supplying invaluable evidence of the health and age-structure of the neolithic population. The Isbister bones imply an average life-expectancy at birth of only 20 years. Probably over two-thirds of the population was under the age of 20. The tomb is important also in providing evidence for burial practices. The burials were all very incomplete, proving that corpses were initially deposited or buried elsewhere; only when they had lost their flesh and the skeletons began to dis-articulate were the remains gathered up for burial in the tombs. A wide variety of non-human remains were also found in the Isbister tomb; sheep, cattle, herring gull, kestrel, red grouse, oyster-catcher, woodcock, short-eared owl, goshawk, puffin, snipe, curlew, mallard, pig, otter, and several types of fish; wrasse, lump-sucker, eel, whiting, stickleback and sea bream. The burial of eight white-tailed eagles suggests that the Isbister people adopted eagles as their totem animal. The tomb, naturally enough nicknamed the Tomb of the Eagles, was built in 2480bc

(3150 BC) and its main period of use continued from then until about 1900bc (2350 BC).

KELSBURGH   Stronsay   HY: 617248

A rectangular cairn with a stalled chamber, sited on the shore just above the high water mark; the long axis is aligned NW–SE and the north-west end of the cairn has clearly been eroded away by the sea. As it stands, the cairn is about 23m long and 12m wide; a wall-face seems to run inside the cairn, parallel to the edge and about 1.5m inside it. The broken remnants of a long stalled chamber at least 15m long can be seen projecting from the mound: it probably had seven or more compartments.

KIERFEA HILL   Rousay   HY: 424319

A turf-covered chambered round mound high on the south face of Kierfea Hill. It has a diameter of 9.5m and a tripartite stalled chamber. The cairn has two concentric revetment walls to support it, an entrance passage 2.7m long opening from the ESE, and a chamber 4m long. The monument is badly damaged, and the wall-faces can be traced only on the south-east side.

KNAP OF HOWAR   Papa Westray   HY: 483518

A settlement consisting of two adjoining buildings of the same general type as those at Skara Brae. For a long time the houses were thought to be iron age, but Anna Ritchie's excavation and the resulting radiocarbon dates proved the occupation to be neolithic, making them the earliest known buildings in the Orkneys, dating to 2820–2130 bc (3500–2700 BC). Large fish bones among the remains imply that the neolithic fishermen went some distance from the shore to catch their fish – cod, ling, turbot, flounder, conger eel and halibut. Shellfish were collected, such as oysters, winkles, cockles and razor-shells. Seals were sometimes taken, though only it seems ones that were weak and easily caught. Other finds include flints, pots, bone artefacts, pumice, crude stone objects and polished stone tools. Protected by their own (modern) short sea wall, the two houses have doors opening onto the shore and point out to sea, sitting on the low cliff top like a large pair of clogs. The excavation produced evidence of cereals (carbonized seeds, pollen, rubbing stones), of large cattle (probably more like wild cattle than modern domesticates) and of sheep (similar to those seen today on North Ronaldsay). The inhabitants evidently caught birds in large numbers – especially the great auk, now extinct, which could easily be caught

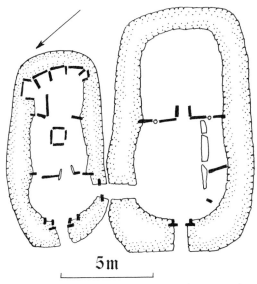

Figure 81   Knap of Howar: a plan of the two neolithic houses, or house and barn, side by side.

when nesting in the cliffs. The site was occupied for some 800 years and the houses excavated and now visible belong to the end of this period: nothing is known of the design of the earlier houses that preceded them. The larger building, the southern, is divided into two rooms by a partition of four upright slabs of flagstone; posts between each outer pair of stones may have held up the roof. The outer room was partially paved and has against one wall a broad low bench which may have served as a bed. The inner room was unpaved, the floor consisting of occupation debris spread on the till: there was a central fireplace, a circular ash-filled hollow, and a large quernstone. The smaller building was originally fitted with an independent door, but it was sealed up and access through a connecting door provided. The smaller building was divided into three rooms: the inner room was intensively equipped with slab-defined recess-cupboards and seems to have served as a storage area (Figures 80 and 81).

KNOWE OF BROCKAN   Mainland   HY: 227181

A large round barrow 36m in diameter, but only 1m high. It would have been visible as a skyline feature from Skara Brae to the NNE, when it was complete. Much of the earthen cairn material has been weathered away, exposing what seem to be the forms of three concentric revetment walls. This may prove to be another tomb of Maes Howe type.

KNOWE OF CRAIE   Rousay   HY: 419315

A chambered round cairn with a tripartite stalled chamber. Standing on level ground at 110m OD, the cairn had been severely disturbed before it was excavated in 1941. The cairn is about 11m in diameter and 0.8m high, with an edging wall-face traceable on the west, north and east sides: on the west it is still 0.5m and six courses high. There is an inner wall-face just 0.7m inside the outer face. The passage, leading in from the east, is 2.8m long. The chamber is 4.6m long and 2.7m wide and there were benches along each side. There seem to have been two floor levels; in the innermost compartment, and possibly throughout the chamber, there was an upper floor of clay and a lower layer of dark ash, which certainly spread through the whole chamber. Outside the cairn, just north of the entrance, there was a small pit cut into the rock, 0.5m across and 0.25m deep, which contained ashes, pieces of burnt bone, flint chips and small bits of pottery. It was evidently connected in some way with a funerary ritual that was carried out at the tomb entrance. This is a small-scale example of a widespread neolithic practice; the crescentic façades, horns and forecourts emphasizing the entrances of other tombs similarly underline the custom of conducting funeral ceremonies in the forecourt area.

KNOWE OF LAIRO   Rousay   HY: 400277

A long horned cairn at 15m OD on the edge of a marine bench; behind it the hillside rises steeply to the terrace where the Knowe of Yarso and Knowe of Ramsay stand. It is conspicuous for its great height and length, and for its architectural style, which is unusual among the stalled and other chambered cairns on Rousay. This may mean that it was erected at a different time from the others, when the Yarrows type was fashionable, or that it was built by a family group contemporary with the others but following different traditions. The long axis follows the contour, from north-west to south-east. The cairn and its chamber appear to be intact: it is still a very impressive long mound, about 60m long, including the horns, at least 25m wide across the horns, and 4m high at the eastern end, above the chamber. The very low-lintelled door (only 45cm high) leads into a passage 4.5m long. This opens into a chamber 5m long, 2.5m wide and 4.1m high. It is thought that the original structure has been altered by the insertion of later stonework, possibly to turn it into an iron age dwelling, but it is not easy to distinguish the work of the two periods. Another problem arises in that the chamber design seems to have been altered while it was being built in the neolithic; a skin of masonry was inserted along each side of the first two compartments, blocking off the third. This end wall was thickened later, probably during the iron age conversion of the monument. The walls oversail towards the capstones forming the chamber's high ceiling. There are also stone beams which rise in height towards the north-west from 2.2m to 3m above the floor. The overall architectural effect is peculiar, awe-inspiring and strikingly original: the ceiling seems much higher than it actually is. What lies beyond the drystone partition wall at the western end of the accessible section of the chamber is not yet known; a 'letterbox' in it gives a glimpse into another chamber which has never been entered: doubtless excavating the sealed section will eventually yield new insights. It may be that the chamber is restricted to the eastern end, as in the English long barrows, or it may extend much further along the cairn; the exterior shape of the cairn suggests an extension 3–4m further to the north-west. Another peculiarity of the site is that there are three large stalled cairns very close together here – Lairo, Ramsay and Yarso. It is a problem area for those who seek to use the otherwise fairly even spacing of the Rousay cairns as an indication of neolithic territories (Figure 82).

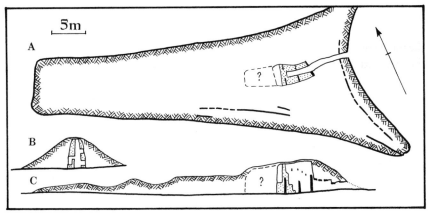

Figure 82   Knowe of Lairo: plan (A), cross section (B) and profile (C). The stippled area represents a neolithic change of plan, narrowing the chamber and sealing off the third compartment. It is possible, as the dashed area with the question mark implies, that the stalled chamber continued further along the mound.

KNOWE OF LINGRO   **Rousay**   HY: 396323

A rectangular stalled cairn on a gentle north slope at 50m OD. It stands in a field that was once cultivated but is now returned to rough pasture, i.e. it is marginal land. The cairn is 21m long, 12.5m wide and 1.5m high. The Knowe of Lingro has not been formally excavated, but a hollow down the centre suggests that someone has opened it. The tops of the dividing slabs of the stalled chamber can be seen. The remains suggest a chamber some 7m long and 2.5m wide, divided into five or more compartments by paired slabs.

KNOWE OF RAMSAY Rousay HY: 400280

A stalled chambered cairn 34m long by 8m wide and 1.5m high, with 14 compartments – the largest number of any of the Orcadian tombs. The cairn is composed of a single skin of masonry, compared with the three at Quanterness. The chamber was covered by a long mound, the long axis following the contour from NW to SE. Radiocarbon dates from the bones show that the tomb was in use from at least 2390 bc to 2060 bc (3050–2600 BC). The bones represented the remains of only three people. Neolithic visitors to the tomb seem to have taken joints of venison there, either to eat or to leave as offerings, just as at Yarso. There were signs of fires in several of the compartments. The chamber is an exceptional 27m long and 1.5m wide; as such, it is the longest of all the Orkney tomb chambers. Unusually, it occupies almost the entire length of the mound. There was, on the north-east corner of the cairn, a wall butting up to it. It was 0.75m wide and 0.8m high, but died away, presumably eroded away, after only 2.5m. This was possibly a vestige of a hornwork comparable with that at Isbister and Midhowe, and may have marked out an area for open-air ceremony.

KNOWE OF ROWIEGAR Rousay HY: 373297

A stalled chambered cairn close to the seashore. It is 27m long, 6m wide, with a wall-face surviving to a height of 0.7m. Inside, there is a chamber 22m long by 2m wide, divided into 12 compartments which originally had benches. Lines in the masonry suggest that the chamber was lengthened in antiquity. Walls extend from each end of the cairn, curving in a way that suggests that they were to continue, and perhaps originally did continue, to form a complete circle enclosing an area between the cairn and the shore. The walls are as yet undated and it may be that they belong to the neolithic, but they may alternatively belong to the iron age: there are signs of iron age occupation immediately beside and indeed on top of the cairn. Radiocarbon dated bones show that the tomb was in use 3000–2600 BC and was probably built in about 3200 BC. Neolithic pilgrims to the tomb brought joints of mutton with them. Curiously, their neighbours, when they visited the nearby tomb of Midhowe, took beef.

KNOWE OF YARSO Rousay HY: 404281

A rectangular stalled cairn 15m long by 8m wide with four compartments. It stands, like several other chambered cairns on Rousay, on the seaward edge of a marine bench. Since it is perched on this site, at 100m OD, it commands an extensive view across the strips of farmland below and the sea beyond. It has all the hallmarks of a territorial marker. It was excavated in 1934, when it was found to contain the remains of 29 people, at least 36 red deer, some sheep, cattle and a dog; possibly the red deer was the totem animal of the Yarso people. Other finds included sherds of food-vessel and Beaker pottery, arrow-heads, flint implements and five bone tools. A radiocarbon date from the bones shows that the tomb was in use in 2275 bc (2950 BC). There is evidence of burning on the walls and finds, which shows that fires were lit in the chamber.

KNUCKER HILL   **Westray**   HY: 428470

A stalled round chambered cairn 15m in diameter, close to the 110m high summit of a hill. The N–S oriented chamber is 9m long and 3m wide, probably opening to the north.

LAMB NESS   **Stronsay**   HY: 689212

A stalled round cairn on low-lying rough pasture 50m from the seashore. The cairn is 12.5m long (W–E) and 9.5m wide (N–S) and its edge was originally revetted with laid stones. Near the centre of the mound the stumps of five upright slabs indicate the position of what was probably a tripartite stalled chamber 5m long, with an entrance passage to the east.

LANGSTANE   **Rousay**   HY: 403275

A standing stone 2.5m high, standing beside a cottage on the roadside. Its flat face has a magnetic bearing of 330°, which is 15° short of the bearing of the Glifter Stone, another standing stone visible on the skyline (Plate 18).

THE LINKS OF NOLTLAND   **Westray**   HY: 4349

The manuscript notebooks of George Petrie tell how he found the neolithic midden among the sand dunes here on 20 September 1866. The significance of his discovery was only realized in the 1970s, and a search was made for the settlement in 1977, when midden and houses covering an area 150m by 150m (i.e. about four times the area of Skara Brae) were found. The site has unfortunately been badly eroded by sea, wind, rabbits, cattle and sand quarrying. The main structure, which is known as Grobust, is a complex, irregular and labyrinthine building: its precise nature and function have yet to be established as excavation funds ran out before the floor had been reached. The settlement was occupied from 2000 bc until 1772 bc (2500–2200 BC). The tens of thousands of shells imply that shellfish were used as food and probably as bait for fishing as well. Other finds included large numbers of beads and a lot of decorated Grooved ware pottery. Parallel lines gouged in the subsoil show that the fields were worked with ards, relatively simple early ploughs fitted with stone shares. Animal manure seems to have been spread on the fields, as was domestic refuse after it had been left to weather for a time; seaweed may have been used as well. This is rare evidence of a serious neolithic attempt at land improvement. A cluster of 13 complete, articulated deer skeletons, mostly of young animals, may indicate a cull of some kind; it nevertheless seems very wasteful, and it is tempting to interpret the deposit as evidence of animal sacrifice, which would be in keeping with the totemic practices seen elsewhere in Orkney.

MAES HOWE   Mainland   HY: 317127

This is without doubt the finest chambered cairn in the British Isles, and one of the most important surviving neolithic monuments of any kind. It was built in about 2800–2700 BC and it represents the culmination of a process of architectural development that began, it is thought, with the Wideford Hill tomb in 3500 BC. It is a monument of outstanding importance: only three other megalithic tombs in north-west Europe approach it in scale and accomplishment – Dowth and Newgrange in Eire, and Gavrinis in Brittany. The tomb was perfectly intact until Farrer broke in through the roof in 1861; the previously conical cairn, reported to have been 11m high, is now pudding basin shaped and only 7.5m high. The cairn is roughly circular, 32–38m across, and stands on an artificially levelled circular platform surrounded by a broad shallow ditch and a bank. The area enclosed by the bank is oval, 103 by 94m, and the longer axes of both the mound and the enclosure are oriented NW–SE. The ditch is 13–18m wide, flat-bottomed and up to 1.4m deep. The bank was retouched in the Viking period. The entrance passage was originally very constricted at the outer end; it has been enlarged partly to allow easier access for tourists. Through the original constricted entrance, it was possible to see the Barnhouse Monolith, obviously a deliberately placed marker for the midwinter sunset. The inner passage, inside the door-checks, is original, but the outer passage has a reconstructed (and higher) roofed section 2m long. Just inside the door-checks is a recess designed to receive the closing stone which originally closed against the door-checks. The inner end of the passage is an extraordinary piece of megalithic masonry composed of very large slabs 5.6m long, 1.2m wide and 0.2m thick. In fact, the architecture of the passage is every bit as remarkable as that of the chamber. The passage opens unusually abruptly into a high square corbelled chamber 4.7m across, with a large square buttress in each corner, each featuring, on the side parallel to the passage, a tall slab 2.4–2.9m high. The walls rise vertically for 1.5m, then begin to oversail. The original ceiling height is unknown, but was probably between 4.5 and 6m. A rectangular cell opens out of each of the south-east, north-east and north-west walls.

Folklore has it that Maes Howe was the lair of the Hogboy, a powerful goblin who was a kind of Norse tomb-ghost. The retouched top of the surrounding bank has been radiocarbon dated to AD 950, showing that the monument was adapted probably for re-use as a Viking royal burial-place: hence the persistent, and probably true, stories about great treasure being found in Maes Howe. The site was nevertheless first developed in 2800–2700 BC, when it was cleared of vegetation, levelled, and the removed soil later piled over the megalithic chambers to make an earthen mound. The ditch, low bank, chambers, passage and mound were all made before 2700 BC. In all, the monument represents a daunting 100,000 man-hours of work, or roughly ten times the amount of labour involved in building the Quanterness tomb. This may imply that Maes Howe functioned as a kind of prehistoric 'cathedral' for a relatively large territory, possibly embracing the whole of Mainland Orkney.

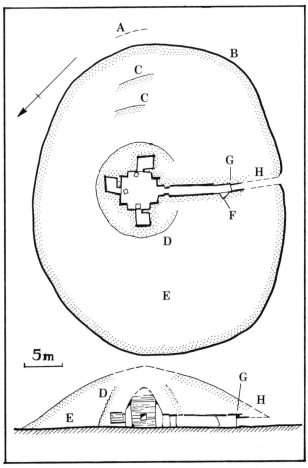

Figure 83   Maes Howe: plan (top) and section (bottom). A – turf bank marking original mound edge,   B – modern mound edge,   C – rough walling representing traces of internal revetment walls,   D – inner core of masonry,   E – clay and stone casing,   F – recess for doorstone,   G – door-checks,   H – outer passage before modern reconstruction.

The tomb is remarkable for the fineness and precision of its masonry. Many of the larger stones are underpinned by small stones to make them level. Some of the slabs are very large too, the largest probably weighing as much as 3 tonnes. But there are other exceptional features; there is not, and seems never to have been, a vertical wall-face revetting the outer edge of the mound, so the mound must always have had a concave lower slope, as now; the blocking stone, the recess designed to accommodate it, and the constriction of the outer passage to create door-checks against which the blocking stone could close; the megalithic masonry of the passage; the square vault of the main chamber with its supporting buttresses. Maes Howe is in every way an extraordinary culmination of a great indigenous architectural tradition.

Its low-lying, central site close to the major ceremonial monuments of the Ring of Brodgar and Stones of Stenness suggests that it served a larger community than the smaller tombs that generally stand higher up in marginal land commanding an identifiable patch of farmland. Its very fine architecture, the very large amount of work involved in building it, and its relatively late date imply to many prehistorians the emergence of a more centralized and stratified society in the third millennium BC. It may be that, in the late neolithic, Maes Howe functioned as a funerary centre and territorial marker for the whole of southern Orkney (Figure 83).

MID HOWE   Rousay   HY: 371306

This is the largest and most impressive of all the stalled cairns, measuring 32m in length by 13m in width. Its long axis lies NW–SE and runs parallel to the shore, which is only 20m away. Before excavation in 1932–4 it was a grassy mound 2.5m high with the vertical slabs of the stalled chamber projecting from it. The cairn consists of an inner drystone construction, which encases the chamber, and an outer skin faced with slabs laid in courses set on a slant. The chamber is 23m long, 2m wide, and divided into 12 compartments, each consisting of two facing cells. Twelve of the cells are fitted with benches made of stone slabs: these were used as shelves where human bones were laid out. Remains of a total of 25 human burials were found. Many of the skeletons were very incomplete, supporting the view that they were buried or exposed in a preliminary funerary rite and only moved into the tomb when the flesh had gone. Many animals (ox, sheep, vole, pig and red deer) and bird (cormorant, guillemot, buzzard, eagle, gannet and falcon) bones were also deposited in the tomb.

The narrowness of the chamber and the repetitive placing of the big uprights give an impression of enormous length. Uniquely, this tomb gives the impression of a great church. It is well preserved under a large, hangar-like building. The original chamber roof and the upper part of the cairn are missing. The walls of the chamber survive to a height of 2.5m and show no sign of oversailing. If they oversailed above that height, in the style of the Knowe of Lairo or Quanterness, the ceiling must have been 4m or more above floor level. It is, in fact, quite likely that many of the large Orkney tombs had ceilings as high as this. It seems more likely, in spite of the chamber width, that the ceiling was spanned by very large stone slabs resting on the tops of vertical walls. These large slabs may have been exposed by weathering early on, or may indeed never have been covered over by cairn material. They would in any case have presented themselves to the iron age inhabitants of Rousay as obvious building material for the construction of the broch that stands close by. Many such stones were used in the broch, and it may be that the broch was located here precisely to exploit the supply of building material (Figure 84).

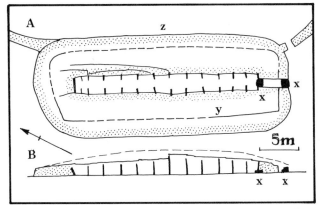

Figure 84   Mid-Howe: plan (A) and section (B). x – blocking stone, y – inner revetment wall,   z – outer revetment wall.

NEV HILL   South Ronaldsay   ND: 428892

A round stalled cairn at about 46m OD and 100m from the cliffs on the west coast of South Ronaldsay. The cairn is 10m in diameter and 1m high. The irregular chamber, about 4m long, is exposed at the centre of the cairn, divided into (probably) three compartments by paved slabs. The entrance was to the south, facing downhill towards the bay.

ONSTAN   Mainland   HY: 282117

This is an almost circular stalled cairn, the lengthening of the chamber slightly affecting the regularity of the cairn's outline. The cairn stands on very low-lying ground almost on the shore of a flat headland jutting into the Loch of Stenness. The chamber is 6m long and 2m wide, divided into five compartments or ten cells by large slabs. The cairn was constructed with great care. The chamber has a well-laid outer face. Two contiguous outer skins encase the chamber, one of which can be detected as a joint in the passage wall, about 3.5m out from the chamber. The chamber was originally floored with white clay, but now this is covered with gravel, apparently for the convenience of visitors. In 1884, Clouston found that the tomb contained large quantities of human bone, but this was not examined in any detail; large quantities of animal bones were also found.

Since excavation, the cairn has been sensitively reconstructed and given a modern roof.

ONZIEBIST   Egilsay   HY: 474278

A round chambered cairn of Maes Howe type on low-lying rough pasture at the southern tip of Egilsay; the site is nevertheless conspicuous because it is on the 15m high summit of a rocky ridge. The cairn is a rough oval, 21m from north to south, which is also the chamber's long axis, 17m from east to west and only 1.5m high, having had its top removed. Part of the walling of the central chamber has been expose at the centre of the mound, together with the 1m-long roofed passage leading to a rectangular cell 1.4m by 0.9m. The cell walls are made of neat oversailing masonry roofed by two slabs 1.1m above the floor.

PIEROWALL   Westray   HY: 438490

A ruined chambered tomb very close to and probably belonging to the Links of Noltland settlement. The tomb was very likely built before 2190 bc (2800 BC), to judge from the radiocarbon dates of secondary occupation in the structures immediately beside it. It was built on a rise at 20m OD, which was sufficient to make it conspicuous in the otherwise flat landscape. There was a low and irregular mound, probably originally 18m in diameter and edged by a revetment wall at least 1m high: the foundation course was of large slabs that project 10cm from the rest of the wall. About 2m behind the facing revetment wall was a second wall concentric with the first. In 1951, remains of a passage were found to the SSW of the cairn centre. Three large stones with pecked decoration were found in the quarry dumps; their original positions are unknown, but the largest stone seems to have been a lintel and probably adorned the entrance to the passage. Pierowall was evidently deliberately destroyed in the late neolithic: perhaps it was considered a threat to new religious practices. The principal find was a large stone, now split in two, which bears an elaborate carving of spirals. The style suggests an affinity with, and possibly contact with, the people of the Boyne valley in Ireland.

POINT OF COTT   Westray   HY: 465474

A damaged chambered cairn situated at the edge of cultivated land, only 4m above the rocky shore. The cairn is oriented N–S, with the entrance and horns to the south. The cairn was originally at least 30m long and about 14m wide at the wider end. The chamber is 12m long by 2m wide and divided into four compartments by pairs of upright slabs. The chamber and inner part of the passage lay within a rectangular cairn core; this was surrounded by several casings of stonework. As at Wideford Hill the exposure of these revetment walls gives the cairn a stepped appearance. One of the two horns, the south-west one, survives. Quite a lot of the northern and eastern part of the cairn has been eroded away by the sea during the twentieth century.

QUANTERNESS   Mainland   HY: 417129

A very well-preserved chambered tomb of Maes Howe type. The tomb was not filled at the end of its period of use, and when the Revd George Barry entered it at the beginning of the nineteenth century he was able to view the last neolithic deposit of human remains still resting on the chamber floor. The tomb was built in 2640 bc (3420 BC); since the last date from the bones was 1920 bc (2430 BC), the tomb's period of use spanned some 900 years, although the period of intensive use seems to have lasted only 200 years. The bones belonged to an estimated 394 people, whose average age at death was only 20–25 years. Probably the tomb received the dead of a relatively small group: a family of 15–20 people would have yielded sufficient corpses. The bones were in very varied condition, suggesting that they were not collected when excarnation was complete, for example two or three years after death, but on a particular feast day, perhaps dictated by the calendar or some event in the community's life. Visitors to the tomb left mutton and sacrifices of song-birds, which suggests that the Quanterness people adopted song-birds as their totem. Bird remains included greylag goose, buzzard, goshawk, grouse, quail, oystercatcher, lapwing, snipe, blacktailed godwit, petrel, great black-backed gull, wryneck, wren, skylark, mistle thrush, fieldfare, song thrush, blackbird, warbler, wheatear, linnet. Charcoal shows that willow, birch, heather, hazel, oak, hawthorn and rowan were growing on Orkney in the neolithic.

The cairn was built on a natural eminence overlooking a territory of arable land to the north, north-west and north-east. The main chamber, oriented N–S, was built on a cleared and levelled platform and then encased in two solidly built revetment walls 7.7m and 10m out from the tomb's centre. The overall diameter of the cairn is 31m. There is no outer kerb (as at Maes Howe). The layering of the fill between the revetment walls was sloping, which shows that the original surface shape was a smooth dome, not a stepped ziggurat as the internal structure might imply, and the revetment walls were in all probability not meant to be seen. The main chamber is 6.4m by 1.8m, and it has six regular side and end chambers. Although Quanterness is not as large as Maes Howe, the masonry is as finely finished. Some of the lintel stones are very heavy (up to a tonne in weight): the stepped revetment walls were very likely used as building platforms.

The first burial at Quanterness seems to have been different from all the subsequent ones. That initial burial was of a 30–40-year-old man, a complete crouch burial lying on its left side at the southern end of the main chamber. It was also different in that the man had been buried immediately after death and not subjected to excarnation. The man was presumably the headman or big man of the Quanterness people, a charismatic figure whose death prompted them to build the tomb.

QUOYNESS   Sanday   HY: 676378

A chambered cairn of Maes Howe type beside the seashore and only just above the modern high-water mark. It was excavated by Gordon Childe in 1951–2. The imposing chamber is roughly rectangular, 4m by 2m by 4m high, with an entrance passage 4m long; originally the passage was 8m long and roofed all the way to the edge of the cairn. There are six irregularly planned cells in the walls. The chamber is encased in an oval cairn which is supported by two revetment walls. The whole structure is covered with cairn material supported by a third retaining wall standing on a raised platform that completely surrounds the cairn and measures 41m by 32m. The edge of the platform was marked by a kerb of stones 0.5m high set on their sides; this only survives on the south and west sides, but it is recorded to have edged the whole circumference. The platform was evidently conceived as a rostrum on which to stand and display the tomb; it probably also served as a precinct for ceremonies. Pottery found on the chamber floor shows kinship with the settlements at Rinyo and Skara Brae. A slate disc, also found in the chamber, is similar to those found in western Scotland, Wales, Portugal and Spain, supporting the idea of a widespread and shared cultural tradition. Quoyness was built around 3200 BC: it was, in other words, roughly contemporary with the tomb at Quanterness. Radiocarbon dates show that it was in use in 2300 bc (3000 BC).

QUOYS   Mainland   HY: 378250

A stalled round cairn about 17m in diameter, standing in low-lying pasture. The cairn has been badly robbed, especially on the south side. The entrance passage, on the south-east side, leads into a tripartite chamber 6m long and 3m wide. The back-slab marking the north-west end of the chamber is an unusually long one, 2.25m long.

RING OF BOOKAN   Mainland   HY: 285147

The cairn material has virtually all gone, but the remnants of the chamber and the scale of the ditch suggest that the monument was of the Maes Howe type. There is a central circular plateau measuring 44.5m by 38m along the axes. Surrounding it is a broad ditch 13m wide and 2m deep. Whilst the central area is smaller than that at Maes Howe, and the tomb itself was therefore probably smaller, the ditch was dug to similar specifications. It is similar in scale to the Stenness henge, but has no entrance causeway, and so cannot be called a henge. Curiously, the Ring of Bookan has been omitted from Davidson and Henshall's list in *The Chambered Cairns of Orkney* (1989), as there is 'no evidence that the mound contained a chamber'. Nevertheless, a few earthfast slabs can still be made out at the centre, and they suggest a rectilinear chamber. The monument was excavated in 1861, and pottery (now lost) which sounds as if it was Grooved ware was found in it.

RING OF BRODGAR   Mainland   HY: 294133

The largest and finest stone circle in Scotland, standing on the low isthmus separating the Lochs of Harray and Stenness. It is a two-entrance henge, with entrances to the north-west and south-east, and with its 10m-wide ditch cut 3.4m down into the rock; this last feature alone involved the cutting and removal of some 4,700 cubic metres of solid rock. The stone circle originally consisted of 60 uprights: 27 remain, on average 2m tall. The stone circle is 104m in diameter, the encircling ditch 3m further out. The former existence of an outer bank is uncertain, though it seems likely: where else did the upcast from the ditch go? It has been argued that the monument was laid out in 'megalithic yards' of 0.829m: the circle would thus have had a diameter of 125 of these units. Radiocarbon dates for the ditch silt are surprisingly late – 255 and 375 bc – which tells us that the ditch remained very clear right through the bronze age. There is as yet no radiocarbon date for the building of the monument, but it was probably the same as Stenness, around 3000 BC. Like Stenness, Brodgar has an outlying standing stone. It is called the Comet Stone and it stands on a specially made low platform 137m SE of the Ring of Brodgar, on a magnetic bearing of 110° from the centre of the circle. The Comet Stone is short and unimpressive. It has two companion stones, of which only the stumps remain, which stand with it on its low mound. There are two more standing stones, leaning and lichen-covered, between the Comet Stone and the Watch Stone. The whole site slopes gently down towards the north-east. This has the effect of raising the stones along the western perimeter so that, when seen from the centre, they could act as skyline markers; the eastern stones are conversely lowered, so that their tips are well below the horizon and they could not conceivably have been used as skyline markers. This must cast some doubt on the use of stone circles in general for astronomical purposes (Figure 85).

RINYO   Rousay   HY: 440321

This settlement of stone houses is similar in type and scale to Skara Brae, but much more ruinous. It was only partially excavated in 1938 and 1946, but with promising results. Numerous potsherds were found, 250 flint implements, including a flint knife, stone axes, stone balls and an oven. The settlement was probably occupied in about 2400 BC; and animal bone from the site has been radiocarbon dated to 1900 bc (2385 BC).

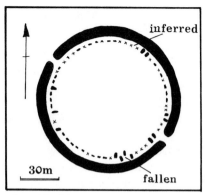

Figure 85   Ring of Brodgar. The black ring represents the deep, rock-cut, henge ditch surrounding the stone circle.

SAEVAR HOWE   **Mainland**   HY: 245269

A Grooved ware settlement site, although no structures have so far been identified.

SALT KNOWE   **Mainland**   HY: 292132

Only 200m WSW of the centre of the Ring of Brodgar stands this impressively large mound, 26m in diameter and 8m high with a flat summit about 4m across. Its scale suggests that it may contain another passage grave of Maes Howe type. If it proves not to contain a primary burial, it could be a 'harvest hill' of Silbury type. Near the summit, vertically set slabs are just visible in the turf, possibly the remains of secondary cist burials. A second large barrow to the south-east of the Ring of Brodgar is almost as big as the Salt Knowe.

SANDS OF EVIE   **Mainland**   HY: 377262

A settlement site that has yielded Grooved ware pottery. No structures have yet been identified.

SANDYHILL SMITHY   **Eday**   HY: 561327

A small round stalled chambered cairn on a moorland knoll at 30m OD. The cairn is 9m in diameter and 0.6m high. The 1937 excavation revealed its distinctive structure – a stone chamber with two masonry casings. The 2m-long passage leads into a rectangular chamber 4m long and about 2m wide. The chamber is divided in three by paired slabs, and at least two of the bays were fitted with slab shelves or benches 0.3m above the floor. The roof and many of the supporting uprights have long gone; layers of peat and blown sand filling the chamber suggest that it was unroofed in antiquity.

SKARA BRAE   Mainland   HY: 230187

This important settlement of stone houses in the southern corner of the Bay of Skaill was buried until 1850 underneath neolithic domestic refuse and later accumulations of beach sand. Its burial and concealment have helped greatly to preserve the site for posterity. A storm in 1850 stripped the grass cover and upper layers of sand from the high sand dune known as Skara Brae, and it was then that the ruined houses were first seen. William Watt, the laird of Skaill, excavated and cleared four of the houses by 1868, and in the process acquired a rich collection of neolithic artefacts.

The settlement consists of the remains of about ten houses huddled together, with a stone-roofed passage winding among them. Each of the houses has a sub-rectangular plan 4–6m across with rounded corners. The walls are thick, well built, and still stand to a height, in places, of 2.4m. The doorways are narrow, low-lintelled and were originally fitted with doors: the jambs, sills and bar-holes survive. The walls corbel in slightly, especially at the corners, but it is unlikely that the houses had beehive vaults. The roofs may have been spanned by whale ribs or North American conifer trunks washed up as driftwood, and then covered with brushwood, skins and turves. The built-in stone furniture, which is a major feature of the site, includes a seat, a large square hearth, box beds, a dresser, wall cupboards and fish or water tanks – for each of the houses. Both the rooms and the furniture are well made and aesthetically pleasing, showing an accomplished handling of material.

Skara Brae was occupied from 2480 bc (3200 BC), the date of the earliest midden, until 1830 bc (2300 BC), which was the date when the phase 2 village was deserted. There were dunes in the area when the village was built, and it may be that a gradual landward advance of the dunes eventually led to the abandonment of the village. The neolithic inhabitants probably abandoned Skara Brae when a series of storms caused the dunes to encroach on their houses. Even after the sand had engulfed their homes, some people returned. The roofs collapsed and the interiors filled with up to a metre of sand, and yet squatters were still prepared to make use of the ruins, presumably because the high wall stumps provided shelter in which fires could be lit; hearth-ashes, shells and deer bones remained from this dismal, late, refugee phase of occupation. The site has yielded a great deal of valuable information about the everyday lives and living conditions of new stone age people. The use made of stone for furniture is particularly illuminating; we can see at Skara Brae the sort of furnishings that were almost certainly created out of wood at a great many other settlements all over Britain, but which have inevitably perished without trace (Figures 86 and 87, Plate 19).

Figure 86 The interior of House 7 at Skara Brae, as seen from the doorway. On the far side of the big square hearth is a block that probably served as a seat, table and working surface. To the left is a fallen stone pillar, which probably held up the roof timbers. To the right is a slab tank, probably for storing water or shellfish. At the back, designed to impress us as we enter the house, is the huge dresser where, no doubt, the family's prized possessions were displayed.

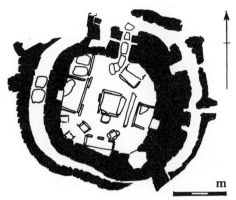

Figure 87   House 7 at Skara Brae. Note the cupboards in the wall, the large square hearth in the middle, the dresser against the south wall, and the two box beds, one on each side of the hearth.

STANEY HILL　　　　　　Mainland　　　　　HY: 318156

A standing stone 2.4m tall and 1m wide at the base, tapering gradually towards its pointed top. This may be one of the missing tribal band centres in the eastern part of West Mainland. It is false-crested, implying that it was designed and intended to be seen from the Brodgar–Maes Howe basin. There are several small earthen barrows on the downslope side.

A long horned chambered cairn has recently been identified at Staney Hill (HY: 316158). It is about 67m long, a maximum of 27m wide, aligned NW–SE, and has horns at its south-east end. Transverse stones stick up near the south-east end, and these may indicate the position of a stalled chamber. Towards the northern end of the low mound there are more uprights, suggesting that there may have been a second stalled chamber.

STONE OF SETTER　　　　　Eday　　　　　　HY: 564372

A standing stone 4.6m high, 2m wide and 0.3m thick. It is irregular in form and has been deeply furrowed by weathering.

STONES OF STENNESS　　　Mainland　　　　　HY: 306125

A 70m diameter henge with a single entrance. The ditch, 7m wide and 2m deep, is cut into solid rock, and follows a circular path with neat squared-off terminals at the entrance causeway; an estimated 1,300 tonnes of rock were dug out to make this ditch, creating some 40,000 man-hours of work. (There is a view, which I share, that one purpose of these huge projects was to create work; this produced not only monuments but social cohesion.) The 61m-diameter bank has been degraded to a 6m broad low swell only 15cm high. Within the ditch and bank is a stone circle 31m in diameter, consisting of 12 standing stones spaced 12 steps apart. Three magnificent 5m-high sandstone slabs still stand complete and intact, and a fourth is broken off to about half its original height. Stumps of four more stones have been discovered, as have the sockets of a further three. Only the position of the twelfth is uncertain. A group of stones within the circle was restored, incorrectly, as a dolmen in 1907; it has subsequently been reconstructed as a type of cove. The slot between the cove's two closely set uprights is oriented towards the east (magnetic bearing 84°); it aligns exactly on the round boss of Maes Howe, whose summit is just visible to an observer squatting in the cove. At the centre of the circle is a rectangular cremation hearth, marked by a frame of large slabs, and strongly reminiscent of the domestic hearths found at Skara Brae.

The ditch was cut in about 2350 bc (3050 BC). The wood charcoal sample taken from the cremation hearth was burnt in 2240 bc (2900 BC). A small timber building, perhaps a cult house, was built next to the hearth in 1730 bc (2200 BC).

Stenness has an outlying standing stone, the Watch Stone. It is 5.6m high and stands to the north of the stone circle, at the narrowest point of the isthmus. Whether Stenness, together with its outliers, was part of the same ritual complex as the Ring of Brodgar, or formed an adjacent but separate complex, is not known: they are remarkably close together if they were foci for two separate clan groups. An additional stone, the Odin Stone, once stood 14m SSW of the Watch Stone. It was broken down to a height of 2.4m in antiquity and the remaining stump was removed in 1930. A custom persisted, right up to 1930, of bearing an offering to the Odin stone – bread, or cheese, or even a piece of rag or a stone; this may represent a folk memory of a neolithic rite.

SWONA   South Ronaldsay   ND: 384837

An oval or round chambered cairn on the seashore, and partly eroded away on the southern and western sides by the sea. Three pairs of tall slabs up to 1.5m high represent the dividers of a stalled chamber.

TAVERSOE TUICK   Rousay   HY: 426276

A rare example of a two-storeyed chambered cairn: Huntersquoy is the other. The cairn is 9m in diameter. The lower chamber, reached by a very constricted entrance passage 5.8m long and only 0.6m high and 0.6m wide at its outer end, includes four cells. The upper chamber has a floor formed by the roof slabs of the lower chamber and is reached by an entrance passage 3m long from the northern side of the cairn. The entrances are both at ground level, on the down hill and uphill sides of the cairn. The upper chamber, 4.7m by 1.9m, is divided into two compartments. A very strange feature exists on the downhill side of the cairn. A drain-like structure, but built like a miniature megalithic passage, continues the line and architecture of the lower chamber's entrance passage for 5m. It ends beside a small, oval, rock-cut chamber 1.6m by 1.1m and only 1.1m high. It is made of very thin drystone masonry, and appears to be a miniature tomb chamber. Two complete Unstan bowls were found in it. No convincing explanation has been offered for these features.

The tomb is built at a height of 61m on a man-made rock-cut platform on a conspicuous knoll overlooking a raised platform and a narrow coastal strip, probably also a raised shore platform. It is a beautiful little circular cairn, covered in grass and flowers: seen from the south, where it appears on the skyline, it is a perfect picture of a fairy mound, with its tiny entrance surrounded by fuchsias (Plate 20).

VERE POINT   **Westray**   HY: 458504

This damaged stalled round cairn stands on low-lying land about 100m from the shore. The cairn is 19m in diameter and contains the remains of a tripartite chamber about 5m long and 3m wide. The entrance was along a passage from the east. The occupier of the nearby house, Mr Thomson, recalled in 1983 that he had seen the tomb chamber opened in 1906, when skeletons were found between the two pairs of transverse slabs. The chamber was subsequently altered to turn it into a byre.

VIA CHAMBERED CAIRN   **Mainland**   HY: 259160

The cairn material has been completely robbed, leaving the monument denuded. The displaced capstone still rests partly on two earth-fast stones belonging to the chamber wall. Five other stones lie around the site, all displaced from their original positions.

VINQUOY HILL   **Eday**   HY: 560382

A round chambered cairn of Maes Howe type which now appears only as a stony and irregular mound 14m in diameter. It stands at the highest point of a long moorland ridge. The chamber has survived, except for the hole smashed through the crown of the corbelled roof to show that Farrer was here. The tomb is built of sandstone, rather than the usual flagstone. The entrance passage is 4m long and 0.6m wide, and at most 90cm high. It leads from the south into a polygonal chamber 2.5m by 2m and 3m high. It has four polygonal cells, two on the east and two on the west. All the entrances to the cells are at floor level, and the cells are on average 1.5m high.

WIDEFORD HILL   **Mainland**   HY: 409121

This round chambered cairn of Maes Howe type stands at 115m OD, halfway up the steep west face of Wideford Hill. The structure contains a main chamber with a cell opening out of each wall except the long west side into which the entrance passage opens. The central structure comprising the chambers and passage was built on a rock-cut terrace specially made for it and it was then encased in a cylindrical mass of laid masonry rising at least 1.5m above the chamber floor. This structure is encased by two concentric, vertically faced annular walls, each a metre thick, in addition to the revetment wall that forms the cairn's edge. When new, the lower part of the cairn would have appeared as a stone drum 11m in diameter. Probably, though not certainly, the walls were carried up progressively higher towards the centre. Whether this 'ziggurat' form was visible is not known: the corners may have been smoothed off into a regular mound with stones, soil and turf; before Petrie's 1849 excavation the cairn was more nearly conical and about 4.5m high when viewed from below. The passage is 5.3m long. The main chamber is 3m long by 1.4m wide at floor level. The chamber walls oversail gradually, like those at Quanterness, not far away, until the gap is reduced to 2m by 0.5m, so that it could easily have been roofed with three slabs at a height of about 2.5m above the floor. The Wideford Hill chambered tomb was built in about 3500 BC, and may represent one of the early stages in the evolution that culminated in the building of Maes Howe (Plate 21).

─────────────────── **SHETLAND** ───────────────────

THE BENIE HOOSE   **Yoxie, Whalsay**   HU: 586652

A stone house 24m by 12m in an area known as Pettigarths Field at about 30m OD on the lower slopes of Gamla Vord. The house has an enclosed forecourt, which has led some to interpret it as the priest's house, although this makes unjustified assumptions about the structure of neolithic society, which seems to have been simple and, until the late neolithic, unstratified. The house walls are 4m thick and the entrance is through a gap between two pincer-like walls that extend forwards from the house façade. The pincers enclose a D-shaped yard or forecourt, which may have served as an animal pen of some kind. In the centre of the façade is a doorway leading into a 4m-long passage, which in turn leads to a roughly rectangular room with two shallow recesses leading off it. There is an elaborate system of drains, ensuring that the floor and interior of the house stayed dry, but no trace of the elaborate stone furniture found in Orkney: presumably the Shetland furniture was wooden.

BURN OF SCUDILLSWICK   HU:474565

Near the east side of the road between Newing and Bretabister are two plantie-crubs, modern walled structures for rearing young vegetables, evidently built out of the ruins of an older structure beside them. This older building is represented by a low, stony, roughly circular mound 12m across. The proportions coupled with the associated field and stone heaps imply that this is a neolithic house site. The prehistoric field measures 130m by 120m and reaches right down to the shore of Nesting Bay. Within the field are lengths of dyke footings, implying field subdivisions.

BUSTA STANDING STONE   HU: 349674

An imposing standing stone, square in cross section and made of granite. It stands on the cliff top, 15m above the waters of Busta Voe. It is 3m high, up to 1.8m wide and weighs about 25 tonnes.

CATPUND BURN   **Dunrossness**   HU: 426273

House 1 lies on a rocky knoll at 100m OD on the slopes of the Clifts of Cunningsburgh. It measures 11m by 10, across walls that are 2m thick: both outer and inner wall-faces are traceable. An entrance passage 2m long and 0.6m wide pierces the wall on the south-west side. House 2 lies on a level plateau near the Thief's Hole, at HU: 424275; it is oval, 14m by 10m, and was robbed of much of its stone when a later rectangular enclosure was built on the same site.

CLUMLIE HOUSE   HU: 397185

This probably neolithic house lies on a grassy slope. It consists of a low bank 0.5m high surrounding an oval hollow 13m by 11m. A gap on the SSE suggests an entrance passage.

CULSETTER   HU: 332677

House 1 lies in a hollow scooped out of the steep slope 200m NE of the loch. The remains consist of a widespread stony bank representing the spread house walls. House 2 lies near the top of the hill on the east side of the loch, 50m from the water's edge. Its remains consist of a hollow oval surrounded by a stony bank 12m by 9m. House 3, at HU: 335674, is 60m S of Culsetter croft. The enclosing oval bank rises to a height of nearly 1m, representing the ruins of walls that were 2m thick. The oval house measures 14m by 9m. House 4, at HU: 334678, is smaller and less stoutly built than the others: it is about 10m across. The surrounding bank is 0.7m high, with straight sides and rounded ends.

THE CUMBLE HOUSE   **Whalsay**   HU: 551654

The ruins of a stone-built house close to the north shore of the South Voe of Brough. Rough stone implements and dish querns were found here.

DALSETTER   HU: 404156

A neolithic farming hamlet, consisting of three houses surrounded by an irregular circular boundary wall; the enclosure was subdivided into smaller allotments. The encircling wall is now badly degraded. There are traces of further field walls beyond it which may represent the remains of a complex field system. There are also mounds of field-gathered stones. The houses are oval and measure roughly 11m by 10m.

DOCK OF LINGNESS   HU: 489545

A cluster of three stone-robbed houses close together on the isthmus at the end of the Dock of Lingness. The houses are oval; two of them measure 14m by 11m and the third 12m by 9m.

EAST HILL OF BELLISTER   HU: 491591

A neolithic house 2km W of Nesting Manse, halfway down the slope of the East Hill of Bellister. The foundations of the oval house, 12m by 10m, are marked by large stones encircling a waterlogged oval hollow.

THE GAIRDIE HOUSE   **Isbister, Whalsay**   HU: 584646

A ruined stone house on sloping ground near a plantie-crub, about 100m SW of the natural arch at Gloupa. The house has three apses at the inner end of the circular principal room, which measures 8m across. The central apsidal recess is 3m across and 3m deep, and contains what seems to have been the base of a stone dresser of the same type found at Skara Brae. The two side recesses are smaller (Figure 88).

GRUNNA WATER   HU: 458549

Near the west shore of Grunna Water several large boulders form a bank enclosing a hollow oval, the remains of a neolithic stone-built house.

GRUTING SCHOOL   HU: 280499

A settlement comprising three neolithic stone houses. The first has its long axis aligned due N–S and its entrance to the south. At the end of the oval main room

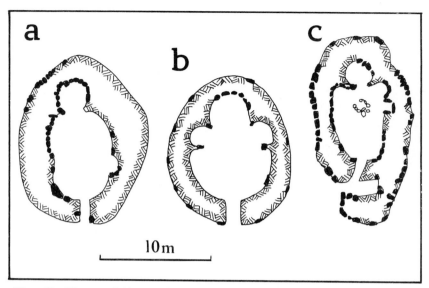

Figure 88   Three neolithic stone houses in the Shetlands. a – Gruting School,   b – the Gairdie House,   c – Stanydale.

opposite the door is a small circular inner chamber. House 2 has been partly built over and destroyed by the schoolmaster's garage, but the curved south-east end is still traceable as a grassy scarp, and some of the outer facing stones project above the surface. The other end was swept away when the garage was built, but the overall size of the original house must have been 15m by 13m. When the schoolmaster was clearing the site, he found a lot of peat-ash and several stone tools. East of the school, at HU: 282498, the road has cut through the middle of a third house site, leaving one curved house-end on each side, defined by stony banks. Near the houses there are several mounds of gathered stones, but no neolithic field boundaries have survived (Figure 88).

HAMAR KNOWE   HU: 479570

There are the very degraded remains of a stone house 200m to the south of the Oxna Burn, and another 200m to the south of that.

ISLEBURGH   **Northmaven**   HU: 334685

The remains of House 1 lie SSW of Isleburgh farmhouse and close to the shore. A plantie-crub has been built into the hollow centre of the house, but the ruined neolithic walls are still visible. House 1 is oval and measures about 16m by 13m. House 2, which is 15m by 13m, lies 20m from the shore near the disused fishing station of Mangaster, at HU: 331700. It now consists of a grass- and heather-covered hollow with a slight bank round it. House 3, which is 15m by 10m and stands at HU: 333698, has a very definite outline, its 0.6m high bank surrounding an oval barrow. A fourth house exists at HU: 334697, some 150m SSE of House 3; it consists of an oval hollow enclosed by a slight stony bank, about 15m by 11m.

JARLSHOF   HU: 399096

A neolithic settlement. The three earliest houses, which form a distinct group and all have courtyards, are oval in plan and have main rooms with subsidiary recesses and an apsidal end chamber. The largest house is 12m by 10m. Their entrances are all oriented towards the south-west; this seems less than prudent, since it is the direction of the prevailing wind.

LOCH OF GIRLSTA   Tingwall   HU: 431529

A farmstead. The site consists of an oval house 12m by 11m and two fields on sloping ground between the Lerwick–Mossbank road and the west shore of the Loch of Girlsta. To the east there is a small pear-shaped field 11m by 8m, leading through a gap on its east side to a much larger field which reaches right down to the water's edge: here a straight line of boulders marks the boundary, whereas elsewhere the walls are curving.

LOCH OF USTANESS   HU: 399428

A house site about 100m from the south end of the loch. It is mantled in heather and peat, but stretches of the curving inner wall faces can be seen. At one end of the connecting passage between the house's two rooms, a jamb stone implies the existence of a door. A field wall runs in a rough circle, starting and ending at the house; a second wall about 30m further out surrounds the entire prehistoric steading.

MAVIS GRIND HOUSES   Mainland   HU: 3368

This group of neolithic houses lies immediately north and south of Mavis Grind, the narrow isthmus connecting the larger part of Mainland with Northmaven. The remains of eight houses have been found, four on each side of the Grind.

NESS OF GRUTING FIELD   Mainland   HU: 280483
SYSTEM

A field system extends in scattered patches down the slope almost to the shore of Seli Voe, covering an area roughly 200m square. The fields are loosely defined by scarps, terraces, stone lines and stony banks. Some of the better defined scarps seem to have been revetted in stone in order to maintain their shape. An oblong structure 26m by 23m may represent a livestock pen or fold, but a stone heap in its centre implies that it had also, perhaps at an earlier time, been cultivated. Remains of five stone houses lie among the clearance cairns and field boundaries. One, excavated in the 1950s, was found to be oval, with a single room featuring a small apse-like recess in the wall facing the entrance. The main room was about 9m by 6m and the apse about 1m deep and 3m across. The entrance, facing south-east, was covered by a porch. Among the finds from the house were some carbonized barley, some stone models of battle-axes and large quantities of domestic pottery, perhaps indicating that a potter lived there. There are other houses at HU: 278484, 277484 and 277485.

NORTH BREMIRE   HU: 388175

An oval house, 14m by 11m, on fairly level ground 200m N of North Bremire. A bank 0.3m high, representing the 2.5m thick house walls, surrounds an oval hollow.

THE PEERIE ROONIE   Whalsay   HU: 554640
HOUSE

The remains of a stone-built house on the west side of the Loch of Houll. Some of the inner face of a drystone wall can be traced, and a stone drain through which water still flows; it may have supplied the house with its fresh water. Peat-ash and stone tools were found here.

PETTIGARTHS FIELD CAIRNS   HU: 585653

These cairns are situated on a slight terrace, about 140m NW of the Benie Hoose. The south cairn is roughly square, about 6m across, with a passage entering from the east side and a small circular chamber 2m across. Four metres away to the north is a round cairn 4.5m in diameter containing a rectangular cist. Both are thought to date from the neolithic or early bronze age; it is likely that at least one of them is contemporary with the Benie Hoose.

RAMNA GEO HOUSE   Lunning   HU: 510671

One of the best preserved house sites is 600m NE of the township of Lunning, halfway up a very steep hillside. The house walls still stand in several courses of drystone masonry to a height of 1m above the original floor level of the one-room house. The exterior and interior wall faces of the 3m-thick wall can be seen. There is a well-built recess in the wall on the northern side, about 2m wide and 1m deep, its walls still standing to a height of 1m. An entrance passage 2.5m long can be made out. The house's exterior is almost circular and 10m in diameter:

the chamber itself is about 4m in diameter. An irregular circular annexe about 9m across was added on the southern side of the house, with a wall 1.5m thick.

SCORD OF BROUSTER   Mainland   HU: 256515

A settlement site on the side of the Scord of Brouster, 300m WSW of Brouster. House 1 is represented by an oval grassy bank 13m by 10m with traces of an entrance passage on the south-east side. There is a series of six recesses round the inner wall of a room 7m by 6m. This house has been radiocarbon dated to 2220

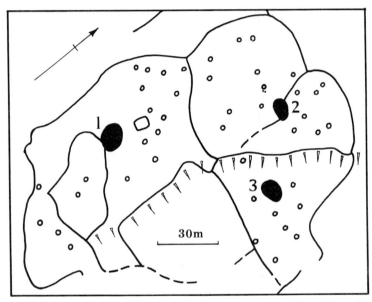

Figure 89   Scord of Brouster, Shetland. 1–3 – houses,   o – stone heap. The solid lines are neolithic field walls. The rectangular structure north of House 1 may have been a livestock pen.

bc (2850 BC). A field system close by comprises five or six irregularly shaped fields. The field walls are badly denuded, but still quite clear in places. Two more oval structures among the fields may also be the remains of neolithic houses. In all the fields there are ancient heaps of stones, gathered out of the fields by the neolithic farmers more than 4,000 years ago to make it easier for them to cultivate the soil (Figure 89).

SOUTH SETTER   Tingwall   HU: 406428

An oval stone-built house 11m by 9m standing on a gently sloping site at 600m OD. Stone banks, evidently once walls, lead from the south end of the house, curving round to enclose a forecourt or livestock compound in front of the house entrance: the forecourt is 10m across.

STANDING STONES OF YOXIE   HU: 587652

A chambered structure, possibly a neolithic house, the north side of which has been weathered away. Originally it had an overall size of 18m by 11m. The building consisted of a large, heel-shaped main block on the west, with a smaller, sub-oval, horned forecourt projecting to the east from a concave façade. There is a passage lined with boulders and paved, with a sill stone placed on edge, but no door-checks were found. The first room is circular and lined with stone slabs. Traces of paving cross the centre of the room, continuing the line of the passage and dividing the chamber into two recesses. Over 120 rough stone tools were found here; some of them were neolithic: others belong to the iron age reoccupation of the site.

STANE FIELD   **Loch of Kirkabister**   HU: 496598

A stone-built house 14m by 12m, indicated by a well-defined 0.7m deep hollow. At the lower south-east end of the house there are traces of an entrance, in front of which a line of nine stones represents the remains of a wall enclosing a forecourt 8m long and 7m wide. At the opposite end of the house a circular enclosure 10m in diameter had been built onto the house in antiquity: this may have been a livestock pen. A second house site lies 100m to the south of the first, at HU: 496597.

STANYDALE   HU:288503

The heel-shaped 'temple' of Stanydale stands amid the remains of five houses that are apparently contemporary with it. Four more house ruins stand a short distance away. One example, House 3 at HU: 288503, is oval in plan and measures 9m by 4m internally, with a wall as much as 3m thick standing up to 1m high. The entrance passage has a protrusion extending beyond the house wall, forming what seems to have been a windbreak: this feature is not found on all the houses. There is a sub-rectangular enclosure built onto the porch wall, but it is not known how much later this feature was added. Peat-ash and quartz scrapers were found inside the house.

The temple and Houses 1 and 3 are all enclosed within the same field, which is a large and irregularly shaped compound measuring 195m E–W and 165m N–S. Its southern boundary rises high on the slopes of the Hamars: to the west its boundary is the edge of the field belonging to House 2 (see Figures 88 and 90).

STANYDALE TEMPLE   HU: 285503

This unique stone building, which combines characteristics of both domestic buildings and sepulchral monuments is a well-made and substantial structure with a wall over 3m thick made of undressed blocks. The wall encloses an oval space 12m by 6m. On the outside, the massive wall is interrupted by a concave façade 10m long, and the entrance to the interior opens from the centre of this. At the far end, the wall is broken up by six beautifully crafted shallow recesses. There are also two post-sockets, each 0.25m across, placed in the chamber floor on its long axis; evidently the posts fitted into these sockets would have supported the roof. Fragments of wood found in the sockets have been identified as spruce. As spruce was not introduced into the Shetlands until AD 1548, this timber must have been imported. It is possible that the timber used in this particular building, and also in others in Orkney and Shetland, arrived as driftwood from the forested coasts of North America. An alternative explanation is that neolithic Shetlanders sailed to Scotland or Scandinavia to collect the timber they needed.

The Stanydale Temple's design seems to be derived from the local heel-shaped cairns – or was it the other way round? – and yet the closest analogue is the Maltese temples. The exact purpose and status of the monument are still matters of controversy, but there is no doubt that it is and was a highly significant monument (Figure 90).

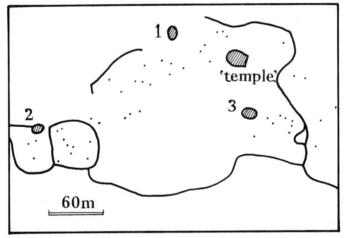

Figure 90   Stanydale. 1–3 – houses. The dots represent stone heaps, the solid lines neolithic field walls.

STROMNESS VOE   **Tingwall**   HU: 388473

A house on the west side of the Voe, on the gentler slopes of the Hill of Oligarth. The house is marked, as is usual, by an oval hollow surrounded by a stony bank. A gap on the ESE side marks the entrance passage. Traces of field wall footings remain in front of the entrance, and to the east there is a large field, quadrangular with rounded corners, extending right down to the shore: it is 66m by 57m.

UYEA BRECK STANDING STONE   Unst   HP: 605606

A leaning standing stone 3m high and made of schist.

VASSO VOE   Railsborough   HU: 464531

Slight remains of an oval house 11m by 8m at the top of the slope, sheltered between two craggy rock outcrops. The oval hollow marking the house interior can be seen, and one course of drystone masonry of the outer wall face survives for part of the perimeter. The wall is up to 2m thick. To the SSE there are traces of a curving field wall enclosing a field about 60m across.

WARD OF BENSTON   HU: 460538

Two probable house sites at HU: 460538 and 460542.

WILTROW   HU: 396143

Originally interpreted as an iron age structure, this is now seen as a neolithic house: probably the odd piece of iron slag found its way in from the later bloomery that was set up beside it. Other finds from the building are consistent with the neolithic date given to similar house sites at Stanydale and Gruting. The house measures 10m by 7.5m, with walls 1.5–3.0m thick.

——————— STRATHCLYDE ———————

ARDMARNOCK   Argyll   NR: 915726

This chambered cairn of Clyde–Carlingford type stands on a ridge 6km SW of Kilfinnan. Its main feature is a cist, 1.4m long, 1m wide and 1.7m deep, formed by side slabs 1.7 and 2m long, an end slab and a septal stone. The broad faces of the septal stone are each marked with a single cup.

ARDNACROSS   Argyll   NR: 768261

The remains of this Clyde–Carlingford chambered cairn are poised precariously above the sea shore. The cairn is now 20m in diameter but the shape has probably been altered by robbing. Several large upright stones stick up through the turf, probably the remains of a megalithic cist.

ARDNADAM   Argyll   NS: 163791

A settlement site at 50m OD, close to a chambered tomb. The site, at the foot of a steep slope, consists of the remains of probably three houses, several hearths and associated pottery, flints, worked slate and hazelnut shells. Charcoal from the hearths has been radiocarbon dated to 2790 bc (3500 BC). A polished Great Langdale axe was also found at the site.

BALLYMEANOCH HENGE   Argyll   NR: 833963

A henge monument 1.6km NW of Lochgilphead, about 100m to the south-west of the Ballymeanoch Standing Stones. There is a low central cairn 20m in diameter, surrounded by the henge ditch and bank. The henge has two entrances and is 35m in diameter. Two cists were found in the cairn; the larger cist had been robbed, but the smaller cist contained parts of a beaker, indicating the late use of the henge site.

BALMALLOCH   Ayrshire   NX: 264845

A circular cairn 15km S of Girvan. Parts of two megalithic cists or chambers arranged radially project from the ruins of the cairn. The south cist appears to be 2m by 0.8m, and formed out of a combination of slabs and drystone masonry leading up through corbelling to a slab roof. The other cist, on the east side, is represented by a 1.8m square capstone, below which sections of the cist wall can be seen.

BEACHARRA   Argyll   NR: 692434

This archaeologically important chambered cairn was opened in 1892, when its famous and distinctive pottery, now housed in Campbeltown Museum 25km away, was found. In 1959 a fresh examination of the cairn ruins revealed a chamber over 6m long and 1.5m wide, with a portal stone and a sill stone remaining in place. The east part of the façade was found to be perfectly straight, its drystone wall still standing 0.6m high. At the far end a right-angled corner joined the façade to the cairn side. It seems likely that the west part of the façade was constructed in the same way.

BICKER'S HOUSES   Bute   NS: 060604

A robbed chambered cairn of Clyde–Carlingford type, 6km SW of Rothesay. The chamber is the cairn's main surviving feature, measuring 4.5m by 1m: it is split into three compartments by dividing slabs.

BLACKSHOUSE BURN ENCLOSURE

Lanark NS: 950405

This strange and enigmatic monument stands in a natural amphitheatre in open moorland, 2.5km N of Thankerton. It has been carefully sited in such a way that its enclosure incorporates the two sources of the Blackshouse Burn. The location has no defensive value and no apparent economic value either, so it can only be assumed that it had a ritual value that was connected with the two springs. The 6.5ha enclosure is ringed by an irregular bank 11m thick, which makes a rough circle. There were eighteenth-century reports that 'urns' had been dug out of rectangular cists at the site, so it is possible that it was a late neolithic or early bronze age ritual enclosure.

Blackshouse is probably a member of a family of later neolithic and early bronze age enclosures that were connected with water cults; other examples that come to mind are the West Kennet Post Circle in Wiltshire and Waulud's Bank in Bedfordshire.

BRACKLEY

Argyll NR: 794418

This chambered cairn 6km NW of Carradale is conspicuous for some distance, even though it is quite low. It has a megalithic chamber with two sets of portal stones, and inhumation burials had been placed within it. Much later, and probably well into the second millennium BC, the chamber floor was paved, and a cremated burial deposited on it together with food vessels and beads from at least two jet necklaces.

BURNGRANGE

Lanark NT: 030495

This chambered cairn within a group of small cairns on gently sloping moorland has been severely robbed and damaged by the building of a sheepfold at its eastern end. It is 12m wide at the broader eastern end, and was originally at least 30m long. A number of earthfast boulders belonging to a kerb can be seen. The chamber, which is under the eastern end, is aligned at right angles to the cairn's long axis, opening towards the south-west. Four side slabs of the chamber are still in place, and the remains of the chamber suggest that it was only 3m by 1m, although it may originally have extended all the way to the kerb, making it 4.5m long.

CAIRN BAN

Arran NR: 991262

A Clyde–Carlingford chambered cairn 10km SSW of Brodick, about 275m up in the heart of the mountains forming the south part of the island. Because it is very inaccessible, it is naturally well preserved. The cairn consists of a mound of stones 30m long and 18m wide, with a deep forecourt and crescentic façade at the east end. The chamber, which is divided into three parts, is 4.5m long and still has its original roof; it is corbelled to a height of 2.5m above the floor and then capped with a slab. Some think that originally there was a complete circular setting of stones at the east end of the cairn, half represented by the semicircular façade, the other half by a free-standing arc, but this is not certain.

CAIRNHOWIT Clydebank NS: 494761

The degraded remains of a chambered cairn on the moors at 275m OD. Two upright stones and one fallen stone are all that are left, probably the remains of the façade and chamber, together with a little of the cairn material.

CAMERON FARM LONG CAIRN Dunbarton NS: 371821

The remains of a Clyde cairn in a forestry plantation, overlooking the sea and Loch Lomond. The cairn is 25m long and 12m wide, and oriented WNW to ESE. Four stones belonging to its façade can be seen at the ESE end, and immediately behind these are the remains of an axial chamber. About 7.5m to the west is another chamber.

CARN BAN Bute NS: 005693

The remains of a chambered cairn lie, mostly in South Wood, near the north end of the island. It is badly damaged and consists of a pile of stones 55m long and 9m wide. The cairn is unusual in having a chamber at each end but no façade or equivalent feature. A side chamber can be distinguished near the eastern end.

CAVE CAIRN Ayrshire NX: 183792

A circular chambered cairn in a clearing in Arecleoch Forest. The cairn is 21m in diameter and 1.5m high. Within it are two chambers placed back to back about 2m apart.

CLACHAIG Arran NR: 950214

An oval chambered cairn of Clyde–Carlingford type, 18m by 15m. It has a simple chamber divided in two. The dividing slab, as is usual in these tombs, rises to only one-third of the height of the chamber. The remains of 12 adults and 2 children were found in the tomb, with Beacharra A pottery, a cord-ornamented bowl, a large stone axe and a flint knife.

CRAGABUS   Islay   NR: 329451

A chambered cairn, which has been robbed to provide building material for the crofts that stand round it. Little remains of the cairn except for parts of the chamber and an isolated stone 3m high.

CRAIGMADDIE MUIR   Lanark   NS: 585764
LONG CAIRN

A severely robbed chambered long cairn of Clyde type on Craigmaddie Muir, about 600m NE of North Blochaim farmhouse. The cairn is 24m long, 14m wide, and aligned S–N. At the north end the remains of the chamber and façade can be seen.

CRARAE   Argyll   NR: 987974

A chambered cairn of Clyde–Carlingford type, situated in the grounds of Crarae Lodge, a well-known Scottish garden 5km SW of Furnace. The cairn was excavated in 1955–7 and found to be 35m long and a maximum of 18m wide. Part of the forecourt area was paved. The drystone walling of a façade, originally 11m long, still stands to a height of 0.6m. Inside, the chamber built of massive slabs measures 5m by 1m. Although the cairn was in a badly damaged condition the excavators were sure that it had once been comparable with the larger Clyde–Carlingford cairns on Arran. Neolithic people deposited two enormous offerings of seafood in the cairn of Crarae; this consisted of at least 5,000 seashells of 15 different varieties. Yet this was no more than a symbolic sacrifice, since it seems that all the shellfish had been eaten first.

DUNAN BEAG   Arran   NS: 027330

A chambered cairn 3km SSE of Brodick. It is roughly rectangular and about 37m by 20m. Dunan Beag is unusual in having a chamber at each end, and yet it lacks a façade or any other focal feature at the entrances. Some fragments of Beaker pottery and the triangular end-piece of a crescent-shaped jet (Beaker?) necklace were found in the south chamber. The finds suggest a late date, at least for the final phase of the cairn's use.

DUNAN MOR   Arran   NS: 028322

A Clyde–Carlingford chambered cairn 3km SSE of Brodick, and located close to Dunan Beag. It consists of the remains of three chambers arranged radially, apparently without any special entrances. Inside, a flint knife representing an early phase in the tomb's use and Beaker sherds representing a late phase were found.

EAST BENNAN   Arran   NR: 994207

A Clyde–Carlingford chambered cairn close to the south coast of the island. It is notable for the large flat slabs which make up the five-compartment, 6m-long gallery. The tomb is fitted with portal stones backed by a septal slab.

EAST CADDER HENGE   Lanark   NS: 642734

A probable single-entrance henge which shows up as a cropmark. It is 6m in diameter, with a broad ditch. In the central precinct there is a concentric setting of large pits, which may well once have held stones or posts.

GIANTS GRAVES   Arran   NS: 043246

A Clyde–Carlingford chambered cairn overlooking Whiting Bay to the north. The cairn is rather degraded. Its chamber is divided into four compartments and fitted with a septal slab immediately within the portal stones. Leaf-shaped arrow-heads and flint knives were found inside the chamber, as well as Beaker sherds. The range of finds once again indicates a long continuity of use; it seems that many of these tombs were in use for centuries.

GLECKNABAE   Bute   NS: 007683

This Clyde–Carlingford chambered cairn was built on top of a mesolithic midden, which had already become covered over with turf before the cairn was raised. Whether the neolithic tomb-builders deliberately chose to commemorate a much earlier settlement site, possibly because it had ancestral associations or reinforced their bond with the territory in some way, is open to speculation. The choice of site may have been coincidental.

Two chambers can be seen in the surviving part of the Glecknabae cairn, and a third probably existed in the robbed part. Pottery of Beacharra A type has been removed from the cairn; some Beaker-type sherds show that the burial sequence was a characteristically long one.

GLENVOIDEAN   Bute   NR: 997705

A chambered long cairn oriented W–E and radiocarbon dated to 2910 bc (3600 BC). The trapeze-shaped cairn is 14m long with a maximum width of 7m at the broader north end, where there are two subdued projecting horns. These shallow horns make a neat, symmetrical façade outlined by four upright slabs on each side of the entrance to a bipartite rectangular chamber 2.5m long. Halfway along the mound there are two further rectangular chambers, opening one on each side of the cairn.

Interestingly, the two side chambers had their own covering cairn, and it is tempting to see here a northern parallel to the sequence seen at Dyffryn Ardudwy in Gwynedd or even Wayland's Smithy in Oxfordshire – in other words, an early round or oval mound with a mortuary chamber incorporated into the centre or back of a later trapeze-shaped long mound with more important new chambers placed at the front. Yet the north chamber at Glenvoidean also has its own round cairn, and it may be, as Marshall and Taylor (the excavators) suggest, that it was this north chamber that came first. The problem of interpretation here has yet to be resolved (Figure 91).

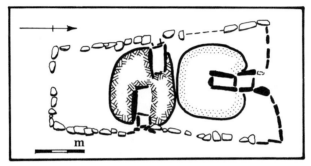

Figure 91 Glenvoidean, a multi-phase tomb. The two round cairns were built first, as at Mid Gleniron, and then the long cairn was built over the top of them: but which of the two round cairns is the earlier is uncertain.

GREENS MOOR **Lanark** NT: 022495

The remains of a long cairn about 82m long, 13m wide and only 1m high made of rounded boulders. Greens Moor is unusual in being oriented exactly N–S. It has been heavily robbed, with a small quarry driven into its east side. At the inner end of the quarry, a single upright slab has been exposed, set at right angles to the long axis, although it does not appear to belong to a chamber.

THE LANG CAIRN **Dunbarton** NS: 457814

This long cairn stands on moorland at 167m OD. It is 56m long, 15m wide and aligned WNW–ESE. At its east end, where it is 1.8m high, there is a façade built of upright stones with panels of drystone walling between them. In the centre of the façade are two pairs of portal stones.

LOCH BUIE   Mull   NM: 618251

A well-preserved small stone circle 13.4m in diameter, standing in a rare patch of flat, cultivable land on the mountainous south coast of Mull. There are two outlying stones, the taller one standing about 36m away to the south-west. This would seem likely to have been a marker for the midwinter sunset, but it has also been suggested that the megalith builders intended an alignment on Antares in 1850 BC or Arcturus in 1740 or 1980 BC instead. The second outlying stone, to the south-east of the circle, is too close to it to have been a marker for any astronomical observation, so it may be that neither of the stones was used in that way. Aubrey Burl (1976) suggests that the taller outlier may have acted as a signpost, since it lies between the circle and the sandy shore: like Long Meg, it may have combined ceremonial and practical signing functions.

MACHRIE MOOR   Arran   NR: 912324

This remarkable series of neolithic or early bronze age stone circles stands near the west coast of the island on a rare expanse of flat land crossed by Machrie Water and joined to east Arran by a mountain pass. Round the edge of this patch of cultivable land is a cluster of late third millennium chambered tombs; they are actually up on the hillsides overlooking the farmland, each one a family grave. Several of the stone circles were excavated in the 1860s. Machrie Moor I, at NR: 912324, is 14.6m by 12.7m. It consisted of ten stones, of which six survive. Machrie Moor II is 13.7m in diameter, and may have consisted originally of ten stones, but only three survive; at its centre there are two rectangular cists aligned NNE–SSW. Circle III, at NT: 910325, is 15.2m in diameter; it consisted of nine stones of which five survive. Circle IV, at NR: 910324, is 6.4m by 5.5m. Circle V, at NR: 909324, is 18.1m diameter and well-preserved. The whole if its interior was covered with small stones, beneath which were two slabs like the sides of a cist. An outer ring consisted of fifteen stones, of which twelve survive; the inner ring consisted of eight stones, of which seven survive.

Aubrey Burl (1976) thinks the concentration of stone circles at Machrie Moor indicates that in the early bronze age the whole of the south-west coastline of Arran was joined in a single chiefdom, centred on the gigantic cairn at Blackwaterfoot to the south of Machrie Moor. At this time Machrie Moor became a cult centre similar to that in the Kilmartin valley. At least three of the circles (II, IV and V) are arranged in a straight line, like the Kilmartin cairns, and oriented towards a conspicuous stone on a ridge 0.5km to the west. This may have directed the prehistoric traveller towards Machrie Bay. The alignment could never have been used astronomically, because the far horizon was, then as now, blotted out by Beinn an Tuire mountain 15km away on Kintyre.

The Machrie Moor stone circles cannot be taken to represent the 'centres' of territorial areas, because they are far too close together. They could nevertheless represent foci for different lineages or clans, and thus be a later, more evolved, more centralized version of the territorial family tomb idea.

MICHAEL'S GRAVE   Bute   NR: 994704

A Clyde–Carlingford chambered cairn. The chamber, which is virtually all that is left, consists of two 1m-long compartments. The portal stones are only 0.3m apart, suggesting that only a symbolic doorway was intended, and this is not fitted with a septal slab. The entrances to neolithic tombs are often constricted like this, either into a narrow vertical slit or into a low-lintelled tunnel. Difficulty of access was evidently a consciously selected design feature. It is open to discussion whether this was a reference to neolithic domestic architecture, which in some cases certainly used small doorways, or had some symbolic and psychological significance; the difficulty of access may for example have symbolized the physical and emotional hurdles that need to be confronted in birth, death and, presumably, if the concept had meaning in the neolithic, rebirth.

MOSS FARM   Arran   NR: 895330

This is Scotland's most remarkable concentration of neolithic and bronze age monuments, with stone circles and cairns clustering round the abandoned steading of Moss Farm, Machrie. The ruins of a chambered cairn are crossed by a track: its location is marked by a single tree. All that is left of the cairn are parts of the chamber and some traces of a mound.

NETHER LARGIE   Argyll   NR: 828979

An important chambered cairn 1km SW of Kilmartin. This is probably the oldest of the long series of burial sites forming the linear cemetery at Kilmartin, and therefore its probable starting-point. There is a well-preserved Clyde-type chamber (the usual neolithic tomb architecture for Argyll) at the centre of a large cairn 40m in diameter, although the final shape of the cairn was probably created when bronze age cists were added. The original cairn was apparently trapezoid in shape. The chamber is rectangular, 6m long and 1.2m wide, separated into four compartments by low dividing slabs. The roof slabs may have been replaced subsequently. Entry now is over the cairn, but there may originally have been a ground-level access through an impressive façade straight into the chamber.

Canon Greenwell's 1864 dig showed that the original chamber floor level was 0.6m lower than the present gravel surface. This means that the transverse slabs would have been much more conspicuous. The innermost pair of compartments were paved with small pebbles, covered with an earthy layer containing cremated bone and quartz chips. Various finds from the cairn, including a round-based neolithic vessel and several beakers, have found their way to the British Museum.

NORMANGILL HENGE   Lanark   NS: 972221

A henge in the Camps Water valley, 2km NE of Crawford. This late neolithic
ceremonial monument was unfortunately only discovered after the railway – now
disused and turned into a road – had been driven right through the middle of the
site. In spite of this vandalism, Normangill is still one of the best examples of a
henge in Scotland.

Its oval enclosure is 40m by 35m within a ditch 4m wide and 0.3m deep,
separated from an external bank by a broad berm. There are two entrances, which
are also unusually wide, to the NNW and SSE. There may originally have been
a circular setting of large timber posts close to the lip of the ditch, leaving an
open central arena for ritual. On the south-west side, a recently built turf sheepfold
has been placed across the bank terminal. The site is an all-too-typical example
of heedless despoliation.

PORT DONAIN   Mull   NM: 738292

A probable Clyde–Carlingford tomb, but interestingly situated on the 'border' of
the Hebridean group of tombs. It stands on the coast of Port Donain. The cairn
is about 30m long and 15m wide, and stands 1.5m high. Portal stones mark the
centre of the façade at the cairn's east end. A chamber just over 4m long opens
inside the portal stones.

SHIELS OF GARTLEA   Dunbarton   NS: 458807

A cairn recently destroyed by quarrying in order to construct a forestry road. It
was 13m long, 8m wide and oriented WSW–ENE. At the time of its destruction,
four façade stones had survived, together with the remains of an axial chamber.

SLIDDERY   Arran   NR: 943238

A cairn with a tripartite chamber, the portal of which has been removed. An
unornamented Beacharra A vessel was found in the chamber, together with a
leaf-shaped arrow-head and a flint knife.

TEMPLE WOOD   Argyll   NR: 826978

This was an important neolithic ceremonial centre, located in the Kilmartin valley.
The recently discovered stone circle in the north-east of the site is about 10.5m
in diameter and belongs to two periods; first there was a timber circle on the site,
the location of its posts now marked by round concrete pillars, and later there
was a stone circle, the uprights of which were subsequently removed. Just one
single upright remains. A radiocarbon date shows that it was one of the earliest
stone circles in Scotland.

The larger and better known stone circle is 13m in diameter, or 16 of Thom's megalithic yards. It was excavated in 1930. This circle was the architectural focus for burials over the course of many centuries, and was reconstructed several times. As it has been restored for us today, the monument is in its final ritual phase, when it was mostly covered by a stone cairn: the circle stones project through it. Near its centre is a cist aligned NNE to SSW, like those on Machrie Moor, Arran, and of a similar size: the cist's capstone had been removed. Re-excavation by J. G. Scott uncovered a small stone ring round the cist, a bit like the central setting of a Clava cairn: the approximate diameter of the inner ring is 3.5m, or 4 of Thom's megalithic yards. An unusual feature is the pecked double spiral carved on one of the circle stones, one half on one side, and the other half on the next face. This elision of carvings from one face of a stone to another is not unique to Temple Wood; we see the same thing on the meander stone at the centre of Bryn-Celli-Ddu on Anglesey.

The Temple Wood complex as a whole shows how neolithic ceremonial centres were very permanent features of the social landscape, continuing in use for many generations. It also shows the close relationship between timber circles, stone circles and burial rites.

TORLIN   Arran   NR: 955211

This chambered cairn contained the remains of six adults and a child, as well as those of otters, birds and fish. Originally the cairn took the shape of a short oval mound enclosing a four-compartment chamber with no façade. Beacharra A pottery was found in the cairn.

TORMORE   Arran   NR: 903310

A Clyde–Carlingford cairn with a tripartite chamber. It was excavated early in the twentieth century, when finds included a fragment of Rinyo I pottery, a plano-convex flint knife, a flint knife with a polished edge and a small perforated stone mace-head. These finds seem to indicate possible colonization from, or contact with, the Orkney–Cromarty region, i.e. the Western Isles, the Northern Highlands, Orkney and Shetland.

WALTON FARM   Dunbarton   NS: 363782

A ruined Clyde–Carlingford chambered cairn at 140m OD on a hillside over-looking the Clyde estuary. When the site was excavated in 1954 it was found that most of the cairn material had been robbed for building. Two portal stones and two side slabs survive to show the design of the former chamber, which must have been about 4m long. About 50 quartz pebbles, thought to be a ritual deposit, were found in the ruined chamber with part of a polished axe. Quartz seems to have had some special magico-religious property within the neolithic belief system; Michael O'Kelly once told me that he believed the sheathing of the Newgrange passage grave in Ireland with quartz cobbles was for magical reasons, perhaps because those stones – and only those – could be made to glow when rubbed.

WESTON HENGE   Lanark   NT: 030457

This oval henge stands in an arable field at a height of 255m OD, commanding a wide view over the South Medwin, which flows past about 850m to the south-east. The main outline of the monument is still visible, but it has been badly damaged by ploughing. It is oval and measures 91m by 66m from bank-crest to bank-crest. The long axis is aligned roughly N–S. The banks are preserved to a height of 1.8m. The ditch, 10.7m wide, is surprisingly shallow, with a maximum depth of only 0.5m.

———————— TAYSIDE ————————

CLACH NA TIOMPAN   NN: 830330

Substantial remains have survived of this 60m-long chambered cairn. There seem originally to have been four chambers, of which one was destroyed quite recently.

CROFT MORAIG   NN: 797472

This stone circle was excavated in 1965, revealing a complex building sequence. In the first phase there was a post setting 8m in diameter, and the sockets for the posts suggest that they may have stood about 2m high. This was later replaced by an oval stone setting. In the third phase a more elaborate stone circle was designed, with the main circular setting built round a horseshoe arrangement, reminiscent of the circle-and-horseshoe idea developed at Stonehenge in contrasting sarsens and bluestones; clearly the combination was part of an island-wide belief system. At the centre of the third phase stone setting there was a flat recumbent stone with a charcoal-filled hollow that may have been a hearth. Many stone circles, when excavated, are turning out to have hearths or hearth-like features: they are thought to have been used for cremation rites or for the ceremonial scorching and purification of bones (Figure 92).

FORTEVIOT   NO: 053169

A large and important palisaded enclosure discovered from air photographs in the 1970s. A river cliff eroded by the Water of May formed its boundary on the south-west side: the rest of the perimeter was marked by a circular palisade some

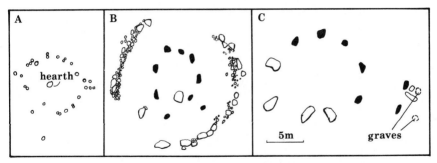

Figure 92 Three phases in the development of Croft Moraig. A – a U-shaped or D-shaped setting of wooden posts and an avenue, B – a stone circle with a surrounding stone bank, C – a second, larger, stone circle.

245m in diameter and 650m long. The posts were spaced 4–5m apart and may have been free-standing or joined together with horizontal planks or poles and hurdles to make a continuous boundary wall.

There is one major circular foundation trench, apparently for a substantial timber building 30m in diameter, within the enclosure and another outside. Three smaller ring ditches 10–20m in diameter lay outside the enclosure; two more, about 6m and 3m across, lay inside the enclosure, close to the large roundhouse. As at Meldon Bridge there was a long, palisaded entrance passage 40m long leading in from the west, its purpose unknown. The size and style of this monument naturally provoke comparison with Meldon Bridge and the Wessex superhenges, such as Durrington Walls, and it seems likely that Forteviot too acted as a ceremonial centre for a large territory (Figure 93).

KINDROCHAT   NN: 723230

This chambered cairn excavated by Gordon Childe in 1929–30 is one of four to be found in the middle reach of Strathearn; the others are Rottenreoch, Clathick and Cultoquhey. The Kindrochat Cairn stands in an unusual position, right down on the floodplain of the River Earn. It looks to be little more than a straggling mass of water-worn boulders. The cairn was originally 40m long and 11m wide, and aligned W–E; it was held in shape by a kerb of boulders embedded in the soil, which had apparently not been cultivated before the barrow was built. The cairn contained three burial cists.

PITNACREE ROUND BARROW   NN: 928533

A round barrow 28m in diameter and 2.7m high. In the first phase at this archaeologically important site dating to 2860 bc (3550 BC), large posts were raised along the monument's principal NW–SE axis. Cremations were deposited

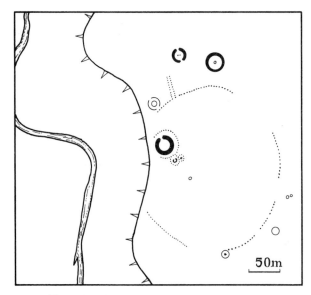

Figure 93   Forteviot: a large timber enclosure.

along what may have been a deliberate astronomical alignment on the midwinter sunrise. In the second phase a rectangular drystone mortuary enclosure was built over the post alignment, and a horseshoe-shaped stone cairn 11m across was raised round the mortuary structure on three sides, leaving its 'entrance' open to the south-east. Then, finally, a round stone-kerbed turf mound was built over the whole structure, about 23m in diameter and perhaps originally 3m high. The site is an important one in illustrating how form is often an expression of ritual gesture in a neolithic monument; form may not be 'architectural' in conception at all, but rather a by-product of ritual action.

ROTTENREOCH   NN: 843206

A chambered cairn 3km SW of Crieff. It is 58m long and 13m wide at the broader north-eastern end. There are stone slabs sticking up through the mound near the north-eastern end, and these may indicate the existence of a chamber on the cairn's long axis. Other slabs near the south-western end may indicate the presence of another chamber.

WESTERN ISLES

AIRIDH NA H'AON OIDHCHE
Benbecula   NF: 816525

A round chambered cairn near the summit of a low hill, 5km NNE of Creagorry, and close to another cairn on Stiaraval. The cairn is 15m in diameter and 3m high. In its top the ruins of the central chamber can be seen. The entrance passage strikes into the cairn from the south-east.

BARPA LANGASS
North Uist   NF: 837657

A chambered cairn on the north-east slope of Ben Langass; it is 24m in diameter and 4m high, with the remnants of a kerb of small flat slabs round the edge. The passage on the east side leads into a polygonal chamber 3m by 2m and 2m high. The spaces between the five chamber slabs are characteristically filled in with drystone walling. The chamber roof is made of three large lintels. Finds include pottery, a scraper, a barbed arrow-head and a pierced disc of talc.

BARPA NAM FEANNAG
North Uist   NF: 856721

A chambered cairn measuring 50m from WNW to ESE and 14m in width near the ESE end, where it stands to a height of 2.5m. A flat slab that probably indicates the position of the tomb chamber can be seen near the centre of the ESE end of the cairn.

BEINN A'CHARRA STANDING STONE
South Uist   NF: 769321

A standing stone on a hillside at 60m OD. At 5m high, it is an exceptionally tall monolith.

BREASCLETE
Lewis   NB: 211355

The remains of a tomb chamber stand on a low hill to the west of Breasclete. The stones are arranged against each other in an arc about 2.5m long and facing the north-east. Most of the cairn material has gone.

CALLANISH
Lewis   NB: 213330

A remarkable composite ceremonial monument consisting of a chambered cairn, a stone circle and stone avenues, all made of slabs of Lewisian gneiss. The focus of the monument is a very tall, wafer-like pillar of stone 5m high, 1m wide, 0.3 thick and weighing about 5 tonnes. It stands, held in its socket by small packing stones, near the centre of a circle that is 11m in diameter and marked by 13 slabs on average 3m high. A stone avenue 8m wide runs north from the circle for a distance of 82m. The avenue, which is really a monument in its own right, may originally have consisted of 20 upright slabs on each side, of which fewer than half have survived. A single row of monoliths runs south from a point outside the southern arc of the stone circle, and it was evidently designed to continue the line of the western side of the north avenue. A single stone represents the sole survivor of what was probably a parallel stone row which would have made a south avenue.

Short lines of standing stones radiate to east and west of the circle, each at the moment consisting of four stones and continuing outwards for 10–15m. The result is to create a stone cross that seems to have been unique in neolithic Britain (but see also Avebury, Wiltshire). In the 1980s, Gerald and Margaret Ponting discovered an additional, fifth, stone at the eastern end of the east row, which inevitably fuels speculation that other fallen and buried stones may yet be recoverable.

The ruined chambered cairn lies between the focal pillar and the stones of the eastern arc of the stone circle in such a way that it implies either that the cairn was carefully and exactly fitted into the space, or that the circle was equally carefully built around it; the latter seems to me more likely, because the 'central' stone, which is likely to have been part of the circle design, is actually 1.2m off-centre, and the only reason for this displacement would be that the space was already occupied by the cairn. A second, and very badly degraded, cairn lies immediately to the north-east of the first and is set against the outside of the circle: its place in the overall design and chronology has yet to be clarified.

Callanish is important in many ways, and not least because it was here, in 1934, when Alexander Thom saw the stones silhouetted against a rising full moon, that a major new phase of research into megalithic archaeoastronomy began. Even before Thom, some had speculated that Callanish had been built as some kind of prehistoric observatory. As early as 1913, Somerville saw the monument as a deliberately despoiled astronomical observatory; he thought the builders had aligned the north avenue on the rising of Capella in 1800 BC, the west row on the equinox sunset and the east row on the rising of the Pleiades in 1750 BC. Thom's calculations of the 1960s were, though precise and accurate in their way, based on the assumption that the raw radiocarbon dates then in use were equivalent to calendar dates; recalibration (see Figure 110) means that his astronomical alignments will have to be reassessed. In fact, no radiocarbon date has yet been obtained for Callanish, so perhaps it is too soon to start searching for star-rise and star-set positions.

A curiosity of the site is that the stones have only relatively recently been revealed to their true height. In 1857 a 1.8m-thick layer of peat which had accumulated and 'drowned' the monument was removed at the orders of the landowner, Sir James Matheson. This had the effect of doubling the height of the stones overnight and exposing the monument in its original impressive state.

Figure 94 Callanish. Colonel Sir Henry James's drawing of 1866 shows how deeply the stones were buried by accumulations of peat. The owner, Sir James Mathes, had 1.8 m of peat removed from the site in 1857. The stones were then, for a time, divided into dark, weathered upper parts and pale, unweathered lower parts.

Colonel Sir Henry James's drawing of Callanish in 1866 (Figure 94) clearly shows
the stones divided into a darker, weathered upper half and a paler lower half
which had been buried in the peat.

This 'Stonehenge of the North' is a great, impressive and mysterious monument; probably it was never finished, and it continues to defy explanation. In
1680, John Morrison observed, bewildered, that 'it is left by traditione that these
were a sort of men converted into stones by ane Inchanter'. Callanish still leaves
both tourists and scholars lost in awe, although we should recognize that, however
extraordinary and original the monument seems, all its components are known
from other neolithic sites in Britain (Figure 95).

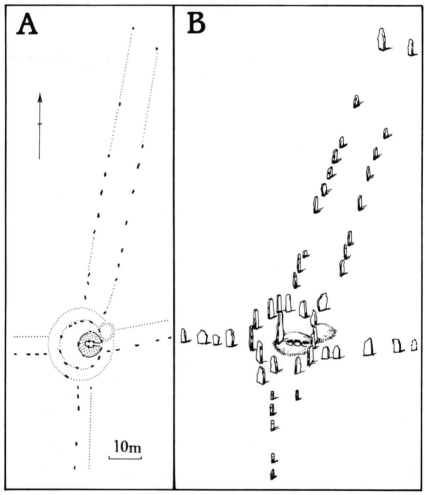

Figure 95 Callanish: plan (A) and oblique view (B). Dotted lines show likely lines of
stones, now missing, to indicate the original design.

CLACH AN TRUSHAL   Lewis   NB: 375537
(THE TRUSHAL STONE)

An impressive standing stone 5.8m high, 1.8m wide and 1m thick.

CLACH MHOR A CHÉ   North Uist   NF: 770662

A standing stone 2.5m high, 1m wide and 0.4m thick, standing like a watcher on the shore, and perhaps once functioning as a neolithic seamark, just 18m from the water's edge.

CLADH MAOLRITHE   Harris   NF: 912805

A robbed chambered cairn: only two upright slabs and two fallen slabs from the chamber are left.

CLETTRAVAL   North Uist   NF: 749714

A chambered cairn that was excavated in 1934. A dun had been built over the western end of the cairn, using material from the old cairn and resulting in its virtual destruction. The cairn was originally wedge-shaped in plan, at least 45m long and 27m wide at its wider eastern end, where there was a straight façade. The chamber is in five sections, the innermost one being the largest. The floor of the now-roofless chamber is made of living rock (gneiss). The cairn was edged at ground level with an elaborate and well-made kerb. Large quantities of neolithic and Beaker pottery were found in 1934. The cairn stands halfway up the southern slope of South Clettraval, with a standing stone below it and a second cairn below that.

CNOC FILLIBHIR   Lewis   NB: 225335

Two concentric stone circles made of tall upright slabs. The outer circle is 16m in diameter, the inner circle 8.5m. The outer circle consists of eight stones, the inner circle four. The highest stone in each circle is nearly 2m high.

COLL   Lewis   NB: 450382

A round chambered cairn 1.5km SW of Coll farmhouse. It is 15m in diameter and 1m high. The remains of a chamber about 2m in diameter are visible on the east side: two large lintel stones seem still to be in position.

CRAONAVAL   North Uist   NF: 842625

A severely robbed circular cairn about 17m in diameter. Remnants of the chamber and passage stick up through the cairn material on the east side.

DUN BHARPA   Barra   NF: 672018

A circular chambered cairn 26m in diameter. It is surrounded by the remnants of a kerb of upright slabs, some of them as much as 2m high. The chamber capstone, which is 3m long, 1.5m wide and 0.3m thick, is exposed near the summit of the cairn, 5m above ground level. The entrance passage is on the east side.

GARRABOST   Lewis   NB: 523330

A badly robbed cairn which now appears as a setting of seven kerb stones lying in a ring 20m across. A setting within the circle represents the remains of the chamber: four large slabs and a fallen capstone. Two earthfast slabs to the south-east of the chamber stones may represent remnants of the entrance passage.

GRESS   Lewis   NB: 472438

This chambered cairn 3km NW of Gress Lodge stands on a site that seems to have been artificially levelled in antiquity. The cairn consists of a mound of stones 28m by 23m and 3m high. The remains of a kerb of earthfast boulders can still be seen on the south-west edge. The large slabs in the south-east quadrant of the cairn may belong to the chamber and entrance passage.

LOCH OLABHAT CRANNOG   North Uist   NF: 7475

A kidney-shaped crannog, a purpose-built artificial island. It was connected to the lake shore by means of a wooden bridge 40m long, and was surrounded by a timber and wattle palisade. Within the enclosure were one main building, which was the dwelling, and several outbuildings presumably used for storage and livestock. The house had internal partitions made of wattle, floors carpeted with heather and straw, and box beds.

The island, which was constructed as early as 3500 BC, was occupied for at least 300 years and was redesigned at least 11 times.

Crannogs are well known from Scottish and Irish lakes, but this is the first crannog that has proved to be of neolithic date.

The Loch Olabhat Crannog very significantly shares design features with tombs, implying that houses for the dead were modelled on houses for the living. The rounded overall shape of the plan, the dimensions (about 25m across), the façade made of large stones, the inturned funnel-like entrance, the narrow entrance – all these characteristics are shared by the crannog and some of the Hebridean cairns.

LOCH ROAG   Lewis   NB: 222335

A stone circle consisting of a setting of tall thin slabs arranged in a ring 20m across, surrounding a small cairn. Five slabs remain standing, the tallest reaching 3m in height. The cairn is set a little to the east of the circle's centre. It is 8.5m in diameter and has a robber pit near its centre.

STEINACLEIT   Lewis   NB: 396540

Remains of a chambered cairn consisting of ten upright slabs arranged in a ring 15m across. The kerb encloses a denuded cairn, through which three earthfast slabs protrude: they belong to the chamber. The cairn stands within an enclosed oval precinct 82m long by 55m wide, which is edged with closely set earthfast boulders.

STIARAVAL   Benbecula   NF: 812526

A denuded chambered cairn about 20m in diameter standing inside the intermittent remains of a kerb of earthfast slabs. The ruin of the chamber can be seen at the centre: it is circular and about 3.5m in diameter.

UNEVAL   North Uist   NF: 800669

A chambered tomb excavated 1935–9; it stands halfway up a steep south-west-facing hillside, commanding the coastal strip. Its remains consist of a polygonal chamber and short passage and several earthfast slabs belonging to the kerb and façade. A two-chambered dwelling dating from the iron age was, much later, built into the north-east corner of the cairn. This sort of iron age 'cannibalism' seems to have been quite common.

WALES

—————————— ANGLESEY ——————————

BARCLODIAD Y GAWRES   Llangwyfan   SH: 328708

This large round barrow was excavated in 1953 and subsequently rebuilt with a modern concrete dome covering the chambers and an inappropriately large new entrance passage, enabling visitors to see the interior of the tomb. The burial chambers themselves are nevertheless sealed off behind iron bars and a locked iron gate. Although the modern building work is well meant, and it conserves the remains well, it is aesthetically disappointing and scarcely a restoration in the true sense of the word (Figure 96, Plate 22).

Even so, it is possible to walk among the ruined remains of the 6m-long entrance passage and look into the main chamber. This central chamber has a single side chamber to the east and a double side chamber to the west. One large capstone survives. The tomb, with its huge covering mound, occupies an unusual coastal location on a headland, but it also commands a view across a shallow basin of agricultural land which lies below it immediately to the north-west; significantly, the entrance passage is oriented in that direction.

Several wallstones in the tomb are decorated with lozenges, chevrons, spirals and zig-zags. The carved, or rather pecked, symbols are similar to those found in tomb art in the Boyne valley. It is certainly the best example of neolithic tomb art so far discovered in the British Isles outside Ireland, with the exception of the beautiful carved spirals found at Pierowall in Orkney.

BEDD BRANWEN   Treffynon   SH: 361850
(BRANWEN'S GRAVE)

According to the Mabinogion the beautiful Queen Branwen, daughter of Llyr and sister of Bran the Blessed, was buried in a square grave on the banks of the Alaw. Local tradition links the site with this ruined cairn, which was excavated in 1813 and 1967–8. Originally the barrow was surrounded by a kerb 19.5m in

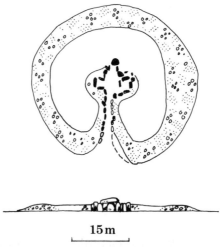

15 m

Figure 96 Barclodiad y Gawres. The shallow barrow consisted of turf in the centre and small stones round the edge. The tomb is now encased in a concrete dome.

diameter. At its centre was a small standing stone and, clustered round it, cinerary urns and cremations. This central area had been surrounded by a ring cairn and then covered with a mound of turves.

BODOWYR   Llanidan   SH: 462683

Bodowyr is a simple passage grave of a type widely distributed round the shores of the Irish Sea, but not found anywhere in large numbers. The three in Anglesey – Bodowyr, Ty-mawr and Ty Newydd – are all situated in the south corner of the island. Bodowyr is the best preserved of the three. This well-tended and well-presented tomb chamber stands on a low summit in open, rolling farmland, almost a picture-book megalithic monument in its grey-railinged enclosure. It dominates the landscape in spite of its small size (Plate 23).

The monument consists of three upright stones 1.5m high holding up a mushroom-shaped capstone 2.4m by 1.8m on the merest trace of a mound. Originally, the small polygonal chamber would have been covered by a small round stone cairn, and access would have been gained by way of a short passage formed of upright stones; indeed, nineteenth-century accounts imply that Bodowyr formerly had a cairn.

Other passage graves in the area are in poorer condition: Ty-mawr near Llanfair Pwllgwyngyll (SH: 539722) and Ty Newydd near Rhosneigr (SH: 344738).

BRYN-CELLI-DDU   Llanddaniel-fab   SH: 508702

Bryn-Celli-Ddu is a beautiful monument, fully excavated in 1925–9, superbly maintained and presented (Plate 24). It stands on a low summit in undulating lowland. There are very few rock outcrops in the area, but there is an eye-catching rocky knoll immediately to the north-west, across a shallow stream valley. It may bear some ritual relationship to the passage grave, since the centre of the passage grave and the summit of the knoll are aligned on a standing stone still further off to the north-west – a very striking alignment.

This is a double monument: a henge and a later passage grave. The circular mound of the passage grave is 26m in diameter and held in position by a very fine revetment wall of large stones planted upright in the ground. Entered on the east side through a well-made stone doorway, the roofed passage, 7.5 m long, leads into a polygonal chamber 2.5m across (Plate 25). Standing rather ominously in the chamber is a single large stone pillar; it had no structural purpose and must therefore have had some ritual function (Plate 26). It is one of the clearest pieces of evidence that neolithic man venerated standing stones. One of the wallstones of the chamber has a spiral pecked into its face. Pieces of human bone, some burnt, some unburnt, were found in both chamber and passage. Along the north side of the passage is a low bench, presumably for offerings or for piles of bones.

The history of Bryn-Celli-Ddu is complex. Underneath the barrow mound, and obviously pre-dating it, was a stone circle consisting of 14 stones; at the centre of this was a pit covered by a recumbent stone. Lying next to this slab was another stone decorated with an incised meandering pattern. A replica of this can be seen at the back of the barrow, which has been left open. The revetment circle of the barrow stands in a buried ditch – the remains of a henge monument that existed on the site before the tomb was built. In front of the entrance, marked by five small stones, were the sockets for five wooden posts; behind them was a pit that contained the carcase of a sacrificed ox. Also beside the entrance were two hearths. The evidence suggests that ritual connected with the site was elaborate, complex and finely detailed. It was not just a tomb but also a temple (Figure 97).

In England, henges evolved and were maintained. Here, on Anglesey, some sort of conflict seems to have arisen. The earlier circle-henge at Bryn-Celli-Ddu was deliberately destroyed by the people who built the tomb, which has left us dramatic evidence of a clash between two traditions. It was a small henge, about 30m in diameter, but elaborately equipped with a free-standing stone circle of 14 large stones inside it and possibly a central feature. There is now no trace of the outer bank, probably because all the material was re-used in building the passage grave mound. The henge ditch is 5m wide, 2m deep and well preserved. The 1929 excavators did not find a causeway across the ditch. This may be because the henge entrance coincided with the later passage grave entrance, which seems very likely. Alternatively, it may be that the henge entrance was overlooked because at that stage the excavators were not expecting such a feature. It is a

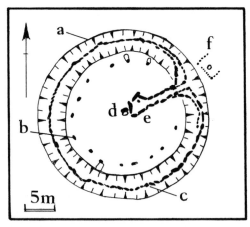

Figure 97 Bryn-Celli-Ddu. a – early henge, b – early stone circle, c – kerb of passage grave mound, d – ritual pit and meander stone, e – burial chamber, f – ox burial in forecourt shrine.

telling fact that three of the fallen circle stones had been broken by having heavy stones dropped on them; they were, in other words, deliberately destroyed by the megalithic tomb builders. Is this archaeological evidence of some prehistoric Reformation?

Other monuments close by include a standing stone 3m high some 450m to the north-west, another standing stone 150m away to the south-west, and a second burial mound containing a small cist 40m away to the SSW.

BRYN GWYN CIRCLE   Llanidan   SH: 462669

About 400m to the south-west of Castell Bryn Gwyn, beside a public footpath across the fields, are two massive stones that once formed part of a circle of about eight stones. One of the stones is over 4m high, 3m wide and wafer-shaped, the other about 3m square and very thick. There are faint traces of a surrounding bank and ditch. These two large and impressive stones are preserved in a hedgerow. Other stones from the circle, exposed in the fields on each side, may possibly have been broken up and cleared by farmers, but there are no recognizable fragments in the stone-studded earthen field wall that runs across the site. The presence of a bank and ditch, however poorly preserved, tells us that the stone circle originally stood within a henge, which is estimated to have had a diameter of 110–130m (Plate 27).

BRYN YR HEN BOBL   Llanedwen   SH: 519690

Bryn yr Hen Bobl, 'the hill of the old people', is a large, tree-grown, kidney-shaped mound 5.5m high and about 13m in diameter (Plate 28). In it, the remains of about 20 people – adults and children – were discovered. On the east side is a hollow which contains the damaged entrance to the burial chamber, a disappointing 2m long, 1m wide and 1.6m high. Its capstone projects to make a porch over the broken notched entrance stone. In 1929 claims were made that a second chamber had been discovered on the south-west side, but this is disputed. In front of the entrance was a large horned forecourt, which was edged by several rather irregular walls and ceremonially blocked by large stones and soil mixed with fragments of neolithic pottery, stone tools and charcoal.

Attached to the southern horn of this large barrow, and now almost imperceptible, was an unusual stone-revetted terrace 100m long, about 5m wide and a little under 1m high. Although built after the barrow, it seems to have been built very soon afterwards. The terrace, which runs straight to the south, has a foundation that was marked out initially with pieces of pottery; then, like the cairn, it was carefully surrounded by a drystone wall. The ground under the terrace was covered with specially laid clay mixed with charcoal, and this flooring was marked with the footprints of the neolithic builders. Professor Grimes suggests (in Lynch *et al.* 1969) that it was a deliberate conversion of the monument into a phallic symbol, but this seems to me unlikely. The attachment of a 'tail' to a tomb is not unique to this site: it happened at Broome Heath too, where there is no suggestion that sexual symbolism of any kind was involved.

The tail at Bryn yr Hen Bobl follows a break-of-slope which, anywhere else, would be taken to mark the course of an ancient field boundary. It may be that the tail is really nothing more than an unusually elaborate and carefully made prehistoric field wall. In support of this interpretation, the same break-of-slope continues to the north of the passage grave, although there without any surviving trace of walling. The tail, which has become part of the mythology of neolithic architecture, may turn out to have little or no ritual significance, although the cinerary urn and cremation secreted at the south end of the tail are hard to explain except in a ritual context.

Bryn yr Hen Bobl is part of a dense concentration of major chambered tombs, many of them along the shores of the Menai Straits: most are on land that was relatively easy to cultivate, which must have been an attraction to early settlers (Figure 98).

CASTELL BRYN GWYN   Llanidan   SH: 464671

A circular precinct 54m in diameter is enclosed by a well-defined bank 3m high and 12m wide. Inside, the ground level is 3m higher than outside, where a surrounding ditch has been discovered by excavation. There was an entrance causeway on the south-west side. Neolithic pottery and flintwork confirm that

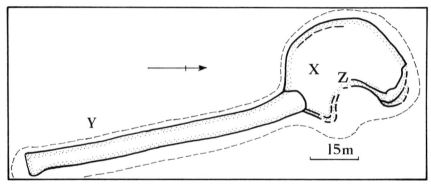

Figure 98 Bryn yr Hen Bobl. Plan showing the kidney-shaped mound with its revetment walls (X), the 'tail' (Y) and location of small tomb chamber (Z). The dashed line represents the outer edge of the cairn spread.

the site was occupied early, perhaps around 2500 BC, as a two-entrance henge with a flat-bottomed ditch 2.5m deep which was subsequently recut several times. Probably the degraded neolithic earthwork was exploited as a defensive site in the iron age, in the first century AD. The site is, significantly, close to the Bryn Gwyn stone circle.

DIN DRYFOL　　　　　　　**Aberfaw**　　　　　　SH: 395725

Originally two large stones marked the entrance to this tomb. Now only one is still standing, 3m high and 2.8m wide. Excavation revealed the socket for the other 2m away to the north. The burial chamber stretches about 9m to the west and now consists of one wallstone with a capstone leaning against it. Ten metres to the east of Din Dryfol's chamber another 3m high stone suggests that the tomb chamber was originally a segmented gallery at least 15m long. This is an unusual site: the tomb nestles under the strange natural hillock called Dinas, on a narrow rock terrace above the valley.

LLANDEGFAN STANDING STONE　　　　　　SH: 554739

A tall thin standing stone plainly visible from the road. It is 3m high and 1m wide at the base, where some packing stones holding it secure in its socket are still visible.

LLANRHWYDRYS　　　　　　SH: 334906 and 334904

Two fine standing stones made of schist, one on each side of Pen-yr-orsedd. The northern one is nearly 4m high and 1.5m wide, the southern 2.5m high and 1m wide.

LLIGWY (ARTHUR'S QUOIT) Penrhos-Lligwy   SH: 501860

This tomb has one of the largest capstones in Britain, weighing an estimated 25 tonnes, and measuring 5.5m long, 4.5m wide and 1m thick. It is supported by only three of its eight wallstones and the burial chamber was created by digging a pit beneath it to make a room almost 2m high. The rock-cut pit accounts for two-thirds of the chamber's height; Lligwy is therefore very close to being a rare example of a British rock-cut tomb. The tomb's entrance was probably at the east end. Excavation in 1908 revealed the fragmentary remains of 30 people, many animal bones, mussel shells and fragments of neolithic and bronze age pottery. There is no trace of the original barrow mound.

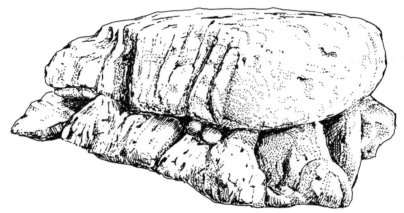

Figure 99   Lligwy chambered tomb.

The filling found in the chamber was layered from the top downwards as follows: 0.6m of topsoil; 0.3m of red clayey soil in and under which were many limpet shells; a deliberate sealing layer with the remains of a feast; 0.4m of black soil or 'occupation earth' with human and animal bones, flint scrapers and bits of pottery; a paved layer made of flat stones; below this 0.2m of black earth with more human bones, teeth and animal bones, with many mussel shells towards the bottom. The human bones had been deliberately broken or trampled to pieces. Unfortunately, no notice was taken of possible differences in the pottery above and below the paved floor, but the tomb seems to have been in continuous use from the neolithic into the bronze age.

The tomb cannot be entered by visitors today because of the railings that surround it, but its exterior is impressive enough (Figure 99).

MAEN ADDWYN   Llanfihangel-Tre'r-   SH: 461834
                          Beirdd

A standing stone 3.2m high, 1m wide and almost 1m thick.

PANT-Y-SAER   Llanfair-Mathanfarn-   SH: 509824
                          Eithaf

A rectangular stone-built burial chamber, open on the south-west side and covered by a capstone 4m square. The chamber stands in a rock-cut pit almost 1m deep, 4m long and 3m wide. An excavation in 1874 showed that a rectangular cist had later been cut into the filling of the pit, and that it contained at least two crouched burials. Further excavations in 1930, in the kidney-shaped cairn, revealed the bones of another 54 people of whom 18 were children, together with pieces of neolithic pottery. Between the drystone horns at the cairn's west end were the remains of a forecourt. Some difference of opinion among the builders as to the correct place for the forecourt seems to have been settled by making two – one where the mound curves inwards, where we would have expected it to be, and another in the western horn of the cairn, cut into the rock and surrounded by walling. Among the human remains, there were not enough skulls for the long bones, implying that the skulls were either deposited elsewhere or kept for magic.

PLAS MEILW   **Holyhead Rural**   SH: 227809

Two tall thin standing stones about 3m high stand 3.3m apart. There is a tradition that a stone cist containing bones, a spearhead and some arrow-heads was found between the stones. The whole site was supposed to have stood within a circle of stones. Excavation might help to determine whether there is any truth in the tradition.

PLAS NEWYDD   **Plas Newydd House**   SH: 519697

On mown grass close to the front of Plas Newydd House, in parkland overlooking the Menai Straits, stands a very large stone burial chamber. There is no trace of its covering mound. The main chamber measures 3m by 2.7m and is topped by a massive capstone 3.5m by 3m and over a metre thick. It was probably entered from the south-west, where there is an antechamber with a broken capstone resting partly on the ground.

This monument stands on a golf course and is not accessible to the public; it can nevertheless be seen clearly, though in the middle distance, from the National Trust car park for Plas Newydd House (Plate 29).

PRESADDFED   Bededern   SH: 348809

Two burial chambers lie 2m apart in a meadow. The south chamber has a capstone
3.2m by 2.4m supported on three upright stones. The north chamber has collapsed
and only two uprights remain. The covering mound has gone, but it may be that
once the two chambers were joined together as a continuous gallery.

TREFIGNATH   Holyhead   SH: 259805

This was once thought to be a continuous gallery grave divided into four
chambers, and it was also thought that it was stone-robbing for gate-posts that
had produced an illusion of separate chambers. Excavations in 1977–9 showed
that the site was developed in more than one period, and that more than one
chamber existed. The oldest structure was a simple box-shaped tomb at the
western end set in a small round cairn. A larger chamber with tall portal stones
was then built to the east of it, with a long cairn and a deeply recessed forecourt.
Finally, a third chamber was built into this forecourt, with its own drystone
forecourt at the eastern end. The cairn was edged with drystone walling. The
junction between the second and third cairns can be clearly seen, now that the
walls have been consolidated and restored. The modern excavations produced
both decorated and plain pottery, but no human burials. No trace of the mound
has survived.

TRE-GWEHELYDD   Llantrisant   SH: 342832

A standing stone that was once called Maen-y-Gored. It is 2.5m high, broken
into three pieces and held together with metal straps.

TY NEWYDD   Llanfaelog   SH: 344738

Only the chamber area of this passage grave survives. It consists of a capstone
4m long and 1.5m wide resting on three uprights. When the chamber was
excavated in 1935 a layer of black earth 5cm thick covered the floor and contained
a lot of charcoal. Mixed into this were 110 pieces of white quartz, a barbed-and-
tanged arrow-head and some Beaker pottery. In 1935, two stone pillars were
added to prevent the crack in the capstone widening. Sections of walling suggested
to the excavator that there had originally been a passage, and these may have
given rise to the stories of a 'second chamber' in some of the early reports. A
fire, mostly of hazel wood, had been lit at the chamber entrance in antiquity.
Only very faint signs of the mound survive; nineteenth-century accounts hint at
the former existence of a circular cairn.

CLWYD

ALLOR MOLOCH
SH: 793747

The rectangular chamber of a megalithic tomb with a large capstone and a pair of uprights forming a portal at the south-east end. No trace of a covering cairn has survived, but the location on a spur of solid rock achieves the visual effect of a long mound, which is what may originally have covered the tomb chamber.

BRYN CASTELL
Llanasa
SJ: 111795

An occupation and burial site. Finds here included pottery – bronze age and Roman as well as neolithic – and flint and chert arrow-heads, of both leaf-shaped and barbed-and-tanged varieties.

BRYN LLWYN
SJ: 071814

The many finds at this settlement site include perforated and unperforated hammer stones, a stone spindle whorl, a quern, a Graig Lwyd stone axe, a leaf-shaped arrow-head, large numbers of flint scrapers, a fragment of a shale bracelet, a bone tool, and fragments of sheep, pig, ox and deer bones. The site has been ploughed up.

BRYN NEWYDD CEMETERIES
SJ: 072827

Two distinct cemeteries, previously thought to be post-Roman, are now thought to be neolithic in date. Most of the human bones are of adults. An ass bone fragment was also found on the site, though it is probably a later intrusion. Other finds include a stone axe, a flint scraper and a flint knife. How the iron bracelet found here is to be interpreted is an open question: for the time being it seems safest to assume that, like the donkey, it is a later intrusion.

CAPEL GARMON
SH: 818543

This well-preserved chambered tomb was thoroughly excavated in 1924, revealing some interesting constructional detail. A false portal in the east end, between the rounded horns of a long cairn, and a double chamber entered by means of a passage from the cairn side show an affinity with the Cotswold–Severn tombs – in spite of the great distance separating the two areas. This affinity is confirmed by other features, such as the use of drystone revetments and the corbelling of the chamber walls. The deposits of Beaker pottery are not inconsistent with a neolithic date for the building of the tomb. There were Beaker people and artefacts about in Britain, in small numbers, from roughly 2600 BC onwards.

CRAIG ARTHUR   SJ: 096788

Finds at this settlement site include a broken stone axe, flint flakes and a stone object with an hour-glass perforation. Close by there was also, in its original position, a deeply scored stone which may have been used for smoothing the shafts or points of arrows.

CRAIG YR ARIAN CAIRN A   SJ: 012358

A chambered round cairn that has been severely damaged by excavation. Originally the cairn was about 20m in diameter and 0.8m high. The stone which was probably the capstone is 2.5m long, 1.5m wide and 0.8m thick.

DYSERTH CASTLE   SJ: 059799

Two pits excavated in 1914 had been used for burning rubbish in the thirteenth century, but the much more ancient finds at their bottom showed that they were neolithic domestic storage pits. Neolithic finds include a fragment of a Group VI stone axe, a hammer stone, a grindstone, a granite pestle, many flint flakes, a bone implement, some bone beads and a piece of pottery.

GOP CAVE   Trelawnyd   SJ: 086800

This rock shelter was used in the neolithic as a burial chamber. Human bones in the cave represented the remains of about 14 people, and sherds of decorated, possibly Peterborough-type, pottery were found with the skeletons. A Graig Lwyd axe was found close to the cave's entrance. Other finds include fragments of broken and burnt animal bone and some jet objects which may have been parts of a necklace.

GOP HILL   Trelawnyd   SJ: 087801

Finds at this occupation site close to the large cairn include leaf-shaped flint arrow-heads, flint scrapers and knives, a flint borer and a large number of worked flint flakes.

GOP-Y-GOLEUNI   Trelawnyd   SJ: 086802
(GOP HILL CAIRN)

Raised up at a height of 250m above the sea, the Gop Cairn is considered to be the largest cairn in Wales, and it is certainly the most imposing. It is some 12m high and 100m in diameter. Excavation from the summit in 1886–7 showed that it is constructed of limestone blocks. No human burial was reached, but the bones of some oxen and horses were uncovered. The enormous size of the cairn suggests that perhaps it contains an important passage grave, comparable to those on Anglesey or in the Boyne valley in Ireland. It is also tempting to draw comparison with 'harvest hills' such as Silbury Hill and Marlborough Mound in Wiltshire, but for its hilltop position, which seems to rule out that possibility. Even the cairn's date is uncertain; the Gop Hill Cairn may be neolithic, or bronze age, or later.

LLANARMON CAVE   SJ: 193562

An occupation site. A finely worked but broken flint arrow-head was discovered here during a partial exploration of the cave in 1905.

MOEL HIRADDUG   SJ: 063784

Finds at this occupation site include fragments of Graig Lwyd (Group VII) polished axes, a flint axe and some neolithic pottery. Some of the material was found in a pit together with animal bone.

MOEL-TY-UCHAF   Llandrillo   SH: 056372

A ring of 41 stones high up on the moors. It is 12m across and there may be an entrance on the south side. A large oval stone stands in the centre, together with the damaged remains of a stone cist.

MOEL Y GAER   SJ: 211690

A neolithic occupation site buried beneath a later rampart. Wood from beneath the rampart has yielded a radiocarbon date of 2100 BC, which may represent the date of the arrow-heads, perforated mace-head and polished axe also found here. The polished axe was a stray (i.e. unstratified) find.

NANT-Y-FUACH ROCK SHELTER   SJ: 067797

This rock shelter was excavated by W. Stead in 1950–7. He found the remains of five people buried in the crouched position close to the entrance, together with animal bones. Neolithic pottery and a barbed-and-tanged arrow-head were also found.

OGOF COLOMENDY CAVE   SJ: 202628

This cave was used as a neolithic burial chamber. In 1975, potholers digging to extend the cave found animal and human bones. Excavations following this discovery, in 1975–6, revealed nothing datable, but in 1977 a neolithic date was confirmed by finds of a leaf-shaped arrow-head and waste flakes.

PENBEDW PARK STONE CIRCLE
Cilcain   SJ: 171679

A stone circle 27m in diameter. Five out of the original 11 stones have survived: the others have their positions marked, rather oddly, by trees. There is an outlying stone 1.5m high which stands 215m to the west and should probably be seen as part of the monument's design. It is difficult to be sure that the circle is a true antiquity; it may be a fake – an eighteenth-century folly. There is nevertheless a genuinely prehistoric barrow in the next field, which has yielded food vessel pottery.

PERTHI CHWARAE FARM CAVE
SJ: 187536

This cave was excavated by Boyd Dawkins in 1869–72; he found human skeletons, some charcoal and a flint flake. It is almost filled in now. The cave entrance is 2m high and 1.8m wide.

RHUDDLAN NURSERY FIELD
SJ: 027778

A flint chipping floor. Excavation in 1969 revealed pits with associated scatters of neolithic worked flints.

RHYL BEACH
Rhyl   SJ: 023824

This may seem an unusual location for an occupation site, but various neolithic artefacts have been found between the high and low water marks, especially in the early twentieth century. Sea level has risen slightly and the intertidal zone, at least in England and Wales, is in effect a submerged neolithic land surface. Three of the Graig Lwyd axes found on Rhyl beach are preserved in the National Museum of Wales: the rest are in private hands. Other finds include a flint scraper and core, and perforated stone fishing net sinkers.

SARN HWLKIN TUMULUS
SJ: 1178

A long barrow site. A long low tumulus was seen here by Pennant in the late eighteenth century, though unfortunately it cannot now be identified.

TAN Y COED CHAMBERED CAIRN
Llandrillo   SJ: 047396

A badly mutilated chambered cairn damaged by farm tracks. The chamber has been exposed and used as a kennel, and is now filled with rubbish. A modern passage leads to it. Though now hard to identify, it may be related to the Cotswold–Severn group.

TYDDYN BLEIDDYN LONG CAIRN   SJ: 007724

A stony oval mound 26m long, 12m wide and 0.8m high, extensively explored and now suffering from neglect. Of the two chambers found during early excavations, only one, the northern, can now be made out. It was 4.5m long, including a short passage, lying crosswise in the end of the cairn. It contained the bones of at least 12 people of all ages. The other chamber was similarly arranged, but further south and with many more burials in it. Quartz pebbles and animal bones, of dog, pig and roebuck, were also found.

TYN Y CEFN CURSUS   Corwen   SJ: 061434

An air photograph shows two slightly converging linear cropmarks, which are interpreted as a possible cursus. This interpretation is supported by the existence of a nearby ring ditch.

WYDHELWERN BURIAL   Llandrillo   SJ: 0335
CHAMBER

A cromlech is mentioned in the records as existing hereabouts, but its location has been lost. It would seem that the monument too has been destroyed.

DYFED

BEDD-YR-AFANC   Brynberian   SN: 113346

This long barrow is 1km SE of the village of Brynberian, set on the northern slope of the Preseli Mountains. The mound, 18m long, 10.5m wide and 0.6m high, is little larger than the chamber within. Along the centre of the mound runs a gallery grave 10.5m long and 2.5m wide; the chamber is simple, rectangular and built of unusually small stones for such a tomb. There are short rows of stones parallel to the gallery on each side. It has been suggested that Bedd-yr-Afanc may be related to similar tombs in Ireland.

CARN LLIDI TOMB CHAMBERS   SM: 735279

Two sub-megalithic chambers, with slabs over rock-cut pits only partly supported by uprights, lie on a north-facing slope. There are no traces of a covering mound, although there presumably was one originally.

CARN MEINI　　　　　Preseli Hills　　　　SN: 144325

This is the ultimate source of the Stonehenge bluestones. The three main varieties of bluestone used at Stonehenge were all taken from outcrops of igneous rocks occurring in the stretch of the Preseli Hills between Carn Meini and the site of the hillfort of Moel Trigarn. The outcrops of Carn Meini are of the blue-grey dolerite with large white spots, confirmed in 1923 by petrological examination as one of the rock types used at Stonehenge in 2250 BC. It weathered naturally into a columnar shape that required little quarrying or shaping beyond prising and levering the blocks out. Suitable shapes were apparently selected from the weathered debris.

Possible routes and methods that may have been used have been widely discussed. Sledging overland seems likely, starting down the slope of the ridge followed by the A478, followed by rafts or composite boats embarking from the head of the tidal eastern branch of the River Cleddau. The alternative glacial explanation proposed in the 1970s and resuscitated in 1990 (Keys 1990) is unconvincing. What has never been satisfactorily explained is the motive behind the massive amount of work and organization involved.

Axes made from stone taken from the Preseli Hills are designated Group XIII, to distinguish them from others.

CARN TURNE　　　　　　　　　　　　SM: 979272

A chambered tomb. The capstone has collapsed, together with its supporters. The V-shaped forecourt in front of the wreckage connects it with the general western family of long cairns. The boulders lying round and behind the chamber are fundamentally the remnants of a weathered outcrop which the neolithic tomb builders could have exploited relatively easily as a foundation for their cairn.

CARN WEN　　　　　　　　　　　　　SM: 948390

At this site there are three round cairns, each containing a tomb chamber of a distinctive sub-megalithic type, partly built, partly cut into the living rock. The southernmost chamber is the best preserved of the three.

CARN WNDA　　　　　　　　　　　　SM: 932392

A sub-megalithic type of burial chamber, in which the capstone is not entirely supported by its two uprights but rests partly on the edges of a rock-cut pit. It seems to represent, stylistically, though not necessarily chronologically, a halfway house between the rock-cut tomb and the megalithic built tomb. Early excavation here yielded a cremation burial in an urn of some kind.

CARREG COETAN ARTHUR (ARTHUR'S QUOIT)   SN: 061393

The massively thick, sloping capstone and the two tallest stones of the four remaining uprights give an impression of an Irish portal dolmen, to which this monument may be related. There are some vestiges of a covering mound and a few outlying stones (Figure 100).

Figure 100   Carreg Coetan Arthur.

CARREG SAMSON   **Longhouse**   SM: 847335

Three of the seven uprights of Carreg Samson's well-formed polygonal burial chamber support a large capstone 4.5m by 2.7m. There is no surviving cairn or covering mound, or any other distinctive feature. Excavation has proved that there was an entrance at the north-west corner and a passage leading in from it. It also showed that the uprights were planted round the edges of a single large pit. The gaps between the wallstones have been filled with smaller stones in modern times, to convert the tomb into a shelter for sheep.

CERRIG LLWYDION   SN: 374326

A large flat slab rests on three uprights; further slabs standing at right angles to the modern wall show that this was once a megalithic tomb of the segmented cist type also seen at Trefignath. No forecourt has survived, so it is not clear to what extent this tomb may have been related to the Irish court cairns.

CERRIG-Y-GOF

SN: 039389

A megalithic tomb 2km to the west of Newport. It consists of a roughly circular mound, now badly damaged, with five rectangular cists or chambers placed round its edge. Tombs of this type occur in Ireland and south-west Scotland as well, and it may be that architectural ideas were communicated by way of Irish Sea trading routes. Only one of the tomb chambers has retained its capstone. The radial arrangement of the chambers seems to have been a local development at the very end of the neolithic or even early bronze age, apparently without any parallel in the Irish Sea area. Excavation in about 1800 yielded charcoal, pottery, bones and 'a quantity of black sea pebbles'.

CLEGYR BOIA   St David's   SM: 737252

The ramparts of a small iron age fort about 100m long and 25m wide occupy this rocky hilltop: in some places the natural rock outcrops are rugged enough to provide the defensive barrier. The site has been excavated and, although no precise date for the fort was procured, the remains of two neolithic houses were exposed. One of the houses was oval, the other rectangular. Two sides of the larger, rectangular house were cut into the hillside: two rows of posts supported its roof. It was 7.5m long and 3.7m wide. The many cattle bones associated with the houses imply that the occupants were livestock farmers. They also used polished stone axes and pottery which shows affinities with Irish ware.

COETAN ARTHUR

SM: 725280

A round barrow containing a megalithic tomb chamber, 1km west of the Carn Llidi megalithic chambers. The chamber seems to have collapsed, but a passage leading into it has been tentatively identified.

COYGAN CAMP

SN: 284092

An early settlement site dating to 3050 bc (3750 BC). The hilltop attracted settlement in most periods of prehistory; both mesolithic and neolithic material were found during an excavation of the iron age hillfort.

DOLWILYM BURIAL CHAMBER

SN: 170256

Dolwilym burial chamber is sometimes known as Bwrdd Arthur or Gwalyfiliast. In 1872, this cromlech was said to have been covered by a barrow with a surrounding circle of 32 stones, but there is now no trace of either of these; only four uprights remain to support the capstone. The site seems to have suffered robbing on an astonishing scale during the past 100 years, unless the original report was incorrect.

FFYST SAMSON
SM: 906349

A wrecked megalithic tomb, consisting of a capstone supported on two broad uprights.

GORS FAWR STONE CIRCLE Mynaclog-ddu
SN: 134294

A stone circle 22m in diameter, consisting of 16 surviving stones graded in size towards the SSW. It is one of a group of monuments of neolithic or early bronze age date set on the south-east edge of moorland at the foot of the Preseli Hills. The largest stone in the circle is just 1m high. Two tall standing stones – outliers – stand 134m away to the NNE of the circles. Alexander Thom speculated that they may have been intended to mark the midsummer sunrise in the direction of Foel-Drych: whether that is so or not, the outliers should probably be seen as part of the stone circle design.

THE HANGING STONE   Burton
SM: 972082

This is one of the best preserved examples of a cromlech to be found in Dyfed, but it is even so marred by field walls. It consists of a small megalithic burial chamber. A second capstone and two uprights in the hedge may have been part of a passage leading to the main chamber. The covering mound has gone, which makes the monument difficult to classify.

HIRFAEN GWYDDOG   near Fflad-y-brenin
SN: 625464

A 4.6m-high standing stone shaped like a knife blade. It was used as a boundary marker for the border between the old counties of Carmarthenshire and Cardiganshire, and is the tallest standing stone in Dyfed.

MEINI-GWYR
SN: 142267

A single-entrance henge monument 36m in diameter, with an 18.3m-diameter circle of 17 stones set inside it. William Stukeley's drawing of the site shows a large three-stone setting that looks exactly like a cove '200 paces' away to the NNE. His drawing also shows a short avenue consisting of three pairs of stones leading into the circle on the west side. With its bank, stone circle, cove and stone avenue, Meini-Gwyr had all the components of the Avebury superhenge except the ditch; the neolithic ritual language varies in dialect and accent from place to place, but the vocabulary invariably remains recognizable.

PARC Y MEIRW   Llan Llawer   SM: 999359

A neolithic and early bronze age chambered tomb and a short stone row, about 1.5km east of the village of Llan Llawer.

PENDINE HEAD BURIAL CHAMBERS   SN: 222075

These four small chambered cairns stand in a straight line on a terrace 60m above the sea. The southernmost cairn consists of a closed rectangular chamber within an oval mound. The second, an irregular pentagonal chamber within a round cairn, is 40m away to the north. A collection of stones 75m further to the north is interpreted by some as the site of the third, but it should be noted that the so-called 'Druid's Altar' near it is a natural rock, probably not an altar, and certainly nothing to do with Druids. The fourth cairn, 75m further north, is the best preserved, with its capstone in place. A natural slab has been underpinned to make a rectangular chamber 2m by 1.5m partly cut into the ground; it is approached by a short passage leading in from the edge of the round cairn. It therefore belongs, together with its slighted and less recognizable neighbours, to the passage grave tradition, but it seems to be at a final stage of degeneration from the primary idea as seen at Barclodiad y Gawres.

PENTRE IFAN   Nevern   SN: 099370

This is one of the best-known tombs in South Wales, 2km N of Brynberian. The exposed and impressive chamber is 3m high – lofty by neolithic standards – with its capstone supported delicately on three uprights. Two of these on the south side form portal stones for a lower doorstone. There is a semicircular forecourt, which originally consisted of two stones standing on each side of the portal stones. The destroyed mound was originally about 40m long and 17m wide.

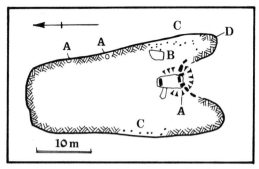

Figure 101   Pentre Ifan. A – pits,   B – fallen stone,   C – pre-barrow stone settings,   D – probable cairn edge. Note the curved stone setting creating a façade in front of the tomb chamber.

379

The crescentic façade, high portals and slightly tapering cairn all suggest links with the court cairns of Northern Ireland and south-west Scotland, and it may be that contacts by sea in the neolithic explain these affinities. A floor level was made by cutting into the hillside; then the sides of the chamber were completed with drystone walling, with a false blocking stone built into the entrance. The N–S orientation of the cairn is unusual. It also, unusually, contains within its length some alignments of stones and ritual pits, the purpose of which is unknown, but they suggest a phase of ritual activity on the site before the cairn was built, which is something that occurred at many other tomb sites (Figure 101).

PONT-DDU   Llangynog   SN: 314139

Within a relatively short distance of only 1.5km, and close to the Afon Cywyn, there are several standing stones. Examples occur at SN: 308148, SN: 312141 and SN: 314139. Such stones are common in Dyfed and, whilst many of them may be prehistoric, and some of them neolithic, not all of them are. Some have been set up by well-meaning farmers in modern times for cattle to scratch their backs against.

RHOS Y CLEGRYN   SM: 913354

A fine monolith 2.75m high stands beside a degraded round cairn. Modern excavation has revealed that there was a neolithic settlement on the site before the monolith and cairn were built; whether there was any connection between the earlier settlement and the later monuments is uncertain.

SAMSON'S QUOIT   near Trevine   SM: 848336

This splendid tomb chamber stands at a farm called Ty Hir. The massively thick capstone is 5m long and 3m across (Figure 102).

TRELYFFANT   near Nevern   SN: 082425

An ill-defined megalithic tomb chamber with two compartments. The upper surface of its capstone carries 22 cupmarks. It is not clear whether the builders intended these to be seen or not; there is disagreement among archaeologists as to whether the large capstones were covered over by barrow material or left standing proud as a summit feature. Giraldus Cambrensis said that Trelyffant (Toads' Town) was so called because the chieftain buried inside it was eaten by toads, which seems very improbable.

Figure 102   Samson's Quoit.

WAUN PWTLYN CAIRN   SN: 709260

A mound 40m long, about 20m wide and 2m high, clearly visible from the road
to the west. It is sited on the valley bottom and is therefore comparable in site,
as well as in size, to several other Cotswold–Severn tombs of Glamorgan and
Brecknockshire. There is no trace of a chamber.

YSBYTY CYNFYN CHURCH STONE CIRCLE   SN: 752791

Ysbyty churchyard is surrounded by a circular bank. The church is built into the
west side of it, and the rest has been damaged by a wall. Five stones of a prehistoric
stone circle survive, but only the block on the north side, 3.3m high, is clearly
in its original position. Two of the others are in use as gateposts to the churchyard,
and they must have been moved from their original positions. The remaining
two have been built into the churchyard wall, although it is possible that they
are in their original places. This is a site that will appeal to those who like to see
continuity of worship at sacred sites.

———————— GLAMORGAN ————————

MAEN CATWG   ST: 127974

This isolated block of stone bears an apparently random series of 50 cupmarks
up to 11.5cm in diameter and 6cm deep. Some are nearly weathered away. Rare
in Wales, cupmarks are often treated as bronze age phenomena, but some at least

are known to have been cut in the neolithic, such as those on the capstones of the Trelyffant and Bachwen cromlechs.

MAEN CETI   Reynoldston   SS: 491905

Often known as Arthur's Stone and once described as one of 'the 3 wonderful works of Britain', Maen Ceti is a circular ring cairn about 23m in diameter with a burial chamber at the centre. The rectangular chamber may originally have been divided into two irregularly shaped compartments. The capstone, a huge, unshaped glacial boulder, is massive: when complete it must have weighed 30 tonnes, but the western quarter has broken off. Even after this loss it is 4m long, 2m wide and 2.2m thick, and held up by four of the ten uprights which make up the chamber's walls. It may be that the tomb chamber has always been freestanding, never covered by a mound: it is often argued that the builders must have wanted to show off spectacularly large capstones like Maen Ceti's. It is also possible that the monument was never finished. The larger boulder lying on the west side may have broken off at the time the monument was being erected and that led to the project being abandoned. Excavation might resolve some of these uncertainties.

NICHOLASTON LONG CAIRN   SS: 507888

A Cotswold–Severn long cairn with a small closed chamber in the centre equipped with a small porthole opening. The presence of the porthole has led some to see this tomb as the latest in the series of Cotswold–Severn tombs in Glamorgan.

PARC-LE-BREOS CWM   Pen-maen   SS: 537898

A Cotswold–Severn long cairn 22m long and 12m wide. It was only recognized as a long barrow when the north end was quarried for road metal in 1869. The site was then excavated by Sir John Lubbock, who uncovered the plan of the forecourt and burial chambers and the bones of about 20 people 'much broken and in no regular arrangement'. Parc-le-Breos was excavated again in 1960–1, by Richard Atkinson, when the monument was taken into Department of Environment guardianship. The tomb is a transepted arrangement consisting of a straight central passage 6m long with two side chambers on each side, built of thin limestone wallstones set on end; gaps between the wallstones are infilled with drystone walling. The entrance to the passage and three of the side chambers are marked by low sill stones. The chambers and passage would originally have been roofed by a series of capstones, but these have long since gone. The cairn and the rounded horns projecting from the southern end were kept in shape by two parallel drystone walls (Figure 103).

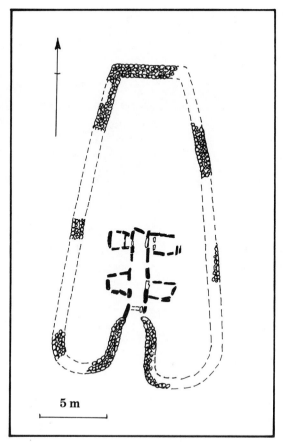

Figure 103   Parc-le-Breos, a Cotswold–Severn chambered tomb.

PENMAEN BURROWS   SS: 531881

The remains of the chambers of what was probably a Cotswold–Severn tomb similar to Parc-le-Breos. Sand driven across the site by a rising sea level and onshore winds has obscured whatever may have survived of the surrounding cairn.

ST LYTHANS CROMLECH   ST: 101723

A chambered long barrow 1km W of St Lythans village. The subdued long mound is 27m long, 11m wide and 1m high, with its long axis aligned W–E. At its east end a group of four large slabs of mudstone, gnarled by weathering, forms an impressive rectangular chamber 2.5m long, 1.5m wide and about 2m high, which makes a classic megalithic monument in itself. Its open side faces south.

383

Figure 104   St Lythans tomb chamber, a beautiful example in a beautiful setting, standing in 'the Accursed Field' near Dyffryn.

The heavy capstone is 4m long, 3m wide and 0.6m thick. The field in which the cromlech stands is known as the Accursed Field and it has been said that nothing will grow there. The monument has never been excavated, but material that was removed from the chamber in 1875 included coarse pottery and human bones (Figure 104).

SANT-Y-NYLL   ST: 101783

A neolithic settlement site found by chance in 1958 on the old land surface when a bronze age cairn was excavated. An oval ring of post-holes 4.6m by 3.7m represented a hut: it replaced two smaller huts, and was associated with domestic refuse that indicates a sheep-farming economy. The pottery was of a late neolithic type distinct from that of the long cairns; as such, it may represent a phase of peasant farming life that was transitional to the bronze age.

SWEYNE'S HOWES
SS: 421898

This site, sometimes incorrectly called Swine Houses, consists of two ruined megalithic tombs about 100m apart at the foot of Rhosili Down. The shape of the chambers can no longer be made out properly, but the principal point of interest is the near-circular shape of their cairns, which puts them outside the main Cotswold–Severn tradition of south-east Wales.

TINKINSWOOD   St Nicholas   ST: 092733

This chambered long barrow was excavated and very carefully restored by John Ward in 1914. The mound is almost rectangular, 40m long and 17m wide, and held in shape by a drystone revetment wall round the edge. Halfway along the north side and 2m in from the cairn edge is a stone-lined cist about 2.9m square, lined with thin upright slabs. It may be later or earlier than the main barrow and it contained no human burials when excavated. Between the rounded horns at the north-east end of the cairn is a trapezoid chamber 5m long and 3.5m wide. The straight façade at the back of the forecourt was walled to the chamber roof; the chamber was all but sealed off, except for a narrow and low entrance gap at the north-west corner leading into a short slab-lined passage 0.8 wide.

The enormous capstone at Tinkinswood is believed to be the largest in Britain, weighing some 40 tonnes. The south wallstone of the chamber was destroyed by early stone robbers. The bones of at least 50 people were found in the chamber: 21 women, 16 men and at least 8 children. The style of the pottery suggests that the tomb was in use in the late neolithic (Figure 105).

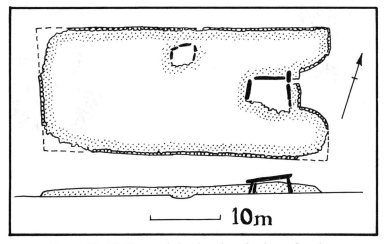

Figure 105   Tinkinswood chambered tomb: plan and section.

GWENT

GAERLLWYD BURIAL CHAMBER   ST: 447968

A badly damaged burial chamber, with its covering mound, if it ever had one, completely robbed. Nevertheless, the chamber stones show – in the two transverse portal stones, for instance – that the tomb was probably linked with a western, 'Irish Sea' tradition rather than with the Severn–Cotswold tradition. Five of the conglomerate supporting stones remain, although the one at the north end has fallen in, but they are only 1m high. Several of the other stones from the cromlech have been taken to be used in local buildings. Remnants of the covering mound are visible on the north-west side, but it has been totally destroyed on the other side by road construction (Figure 106).

Figure 106   Gaerllwyd Cromlech.

GWERN-Y-CLEPPA   ST: 276851

About 40m from the M4 are the remains of a substantial cromlech. Three of the stone uprights are still in position, but a fourth lies under the fallen capstone, part of which lies buried in the soil.

HAROLD'S STONES   **Trellech**   SO: 499052

Three tall pointed stones by the roadside form an alignment 12m long. Only the central stone seems to have been given any artificial shaping, and it is this one that has two large cupmarks on its south side. The date when the stones were shaped and raised is unknown, although it is rightly assumed that they must be antiquities since the name of the village means 'the village of stones'; there is also a carving of the stones dated 1689 on the sundial in Trellech Church. The stones all lean in different directions, but were presumably once vertical. They are difficult to date, but probably belong to the neolithic or bronze age. They are also difficult to interpret; they may be a remnant of a longer and more impressive alignment, but it seems certain that they were not, as has sometimes been said, part of a stone circle.

HESTON BRAKE   Portskewett   ST: 506887

This much-disturbed cairn, at least 21m long and aligned W–E, has an unroofed chamber set in its eastern end. Two tall portal stones mark the entrance to a passage 4m long leading into a chamber 3m long. Both passage and chamber are 1.5m wide and would form a simple gallery but for a crook or offset separating the two. This feature suggests that possibly the passage was added to a pre-existing chamber. Human bones were found when the tomb was excavated in 1888. In spite of its location by the River Severn, almost within sight of the Cotswolds, Heston Brake seems to belong to a more westerly tradition, distinct from that of the Black Mountains chambered tombs.

Y GARN LLWYD   Newchurch West   ST: 447968

The ruined remains of a chambered tomb, with two upright stones flanking the entrance to make either a narrow square entrance or the dividing wall between two parts of the chamber. Either possibility would link the tomb with others in the Cotswold–Severn tradition. The site has been damaged by road making and it has not been excavated.

—————— GWYNEDD ——————

(see 'Anglesey' for sites on Anglesey)

ALLOR MOLACH (MOLACH'S ALTAR)   SH: 793747

A collapsed megalithic tomb chamber lying in a field above the River Conway. It has a capstone estimated to weigh 20 tonnes, one of the largest in Wales.

BACHWEN   Clynog   SH: 407495

A megalithic burial chamber consisting of four upright stones about 1m high supporting a large triangular capstone. This is a particularly interesting monument, as the upper surface of the capstone is decorated with about 110 cupmarks, each roughly 5cm in diameter and 2cm deep. There are two shallow grooves, each of which links three of the cupmarks together. Eight more cups can be seen on the east ridge of the capstone. Some have inferred that this means that the capstone was exposed in antiquity, but this should not be assumed. It may be that the cups were not necessarily meant to be seen by mortal eyes, but were part of a making or validating ritual.

BARCLODIAD-Y-GAWRES   Caerhun   SH: 716716

This cairn, whose name means 'the giantess's apronful', stands at a height of 396m OD in a natural hollow. It is a dramatic site close to the summit of a major col (a glacial watershed breach), later to be utilized by a Roman road, and overlooking the valley head of the Afon Tafalog. The cairn is an oval mass of boulders, with a cist on the north side about 2.5m long and 1.2m wide.

BRON-Y-FOEL ISAF CAIRN   SH: 608246

A chambered tomb at about 200m OD on a west-facing slope. The tomb's stone portal has a doorstone or blocking stone still in position. The capstone leans on one side of the side stones, and the cairn has been reduced to 18m by 9m by robbing.

BRYN CADER FADER   Llandecwyn   SH: 648353

This is a very dramatic cairn circle made of small stones, out of which 15 long, pointed stones jut like teeth or the spires of a ragged crown. Inside is a low cairn with a central burial cist. Outside is a ring of boulders.

CAPEL GARMON   Llanrwst   SH: 818542

Lying west-to-east in a hollow behind Tyn-y-Coed farm, Capel Garmon is a wedge-shaped long barrow 28m long and 13m wide at the wider east end. Excavation has shown that it was supported by a revetment wall that was deliberately buried beneath the barrow mound. At the eastern end well-developed horns jutted out on either side of the false entrance, which was made of two slabs of slate. The true entrance is on the south side, where a passage 5m long leads into a rectangular antechamber, from which roughly circular chambers 3m across open to east and west. The west chamber has a large capstone still in position. When it was excavated the entrance passage was still blocked, just as it had been after the last burials were deposited in the tomb in antiquity. Finds included neolithic pottery, flints and fragments of human bone. In 1853, one chamber was rescued from use as a stable and the other two chambers were discovered and cleared. By 1924, the site was in such a poor state, with trees growing out of it, that the then Ministry of Works decided to excavate. The restored cairn has been kept low enough to reveal the chambers, only one of which is still roofed with its original capstone. We should assume that originally the whole lot was covered.

The skilful neolithic building technique can be clearly seen in the dumb-bell-shaped arrangement of chambers, with the gaps between the megaliths packed with drystone walling.

CARNEDDAU HENGWM   Llanaber   SH: 614205

Two long cairns lie side by side on open moorland, the northern one 33m long and about 18m wide, with at least two burial chambers set back to back. At the west is a large capstone, which seems to have been displaced. The south cairn is larger, 57m long and 21m wide. It has two chambers, one a portal dolmen at the eastern end: this is now wrecked, but it was still standing in the late eighteenth century. The other chamber, in the centre, is approached by a passage from the north. The south cairn seems to have been a multi-period construction, but they have both been badly robbed to build field walls, one of which crosses the south cairn.

CIST CERRIG   Treflys   SH: 543384

Three stones of this fine portal dolmen survive: the two uprights of the portal and the doorstone. The burial chamber lay to the west. There is no trace of the covering mound.

An outcrop of rock 23m to the south-east has a sloping face on which 15 cupmarks can be seen.

COETAN ARTHUR   Llanystumdwy   SH: 499413

This passage grave, sometimes called Ystum Cegid Isaf, is half-engulfed by a field wall. Five uprights, the largest 2m high, support a rather lightweight capstone. The chamber has been restored, possibly in its original position. The entrance was on the north side, and a drawing of 1769 shows that there was originally a passage nearly 5m long. Although the passage capstones that existed in 1769 have gone, traces of the passage wallstones can still be seen on both sides of the field wall. Probably, originally, this was a passage grave under a 20m diameter circular covering mound.

DRUID'S CIRCLE   Dwygyfylchi   SH: 722746
(MEINI HIRION)

The Druid's Circle is the finest of the ruined cairns and circles situated on a low saddle 700m to the east of the Graig Lwyd axe factory. On a bank of boulders 26m in diameter were 30 stones, of which 10 still remain standing, some of them 1.8m high. At the south-west is a gap in the bank with two large doorstones. At the circle's centre there was a cist containing the cremated remains of a 10-year-old child and an inverted food vessel. To the north-west of the cist there was a pit with a second food vessel and a second child cremation; it may be that these remains represent further examples of child sacrifice.

The shape of the circle is slightly flattened where an old trackway crosses the site just north of the circle. This can be taken as evidence that the track was there first: a rare example of a datable prehistoric track. It is, significantly, only when the site is approached along this track that the circle is at all conspicuous, and it was presumably built here in order to be visible from the track.

The stones vary a lot in size and spacing, but they are set on the inner side of a bank of small stones. None are of local rock: they are probably glacial erratics from Snowdonia. The surface of the bank was deliberately coated with white quartz fragments. This procedure, which is reminiscent of the painting of Thornborough's banks with gypsum crystals, was evidently to make the monument white, like the (higher status?) monuments of the English chalk country; mimicry and symbolic references are the hallmarks of neolithic architecture. The entrance, which was badly damaged by nineteenth-century blasting to remove the stone, is to the west.

A small circle 250m to the north-east of the Druid's Circle was excavated at the same time as the Druid's Circle, but all that was found there was a thick scatter of quartz fragments and, close to the centre, a small pit crammed full of quartz fragments. The area is dense with ceremonial circles, cairns and hut circles.

DYFFRYN ARDUDWY   SH: 589229

This chambered cairn on the hillside overlooking the sea is of two periods of construction. First of all a small rectangular stone chamber 2.7m long and 2m high was built with two portal stones set on either side of a high closing slab or doorstone, and roofed with a single capstone (Plate 30). This was then covered over with a cairn – probably circular or kidney-shaped – made of water-rolled cobbles. The early cairn was at least 3m in diameter and its outline can still be clearly seen at the site. Although the chamber was found to be empty when it was excavated in 1961, the pit in the forecourt contained fragments of plain neolithic pottery.

A second, more spacious burial chamber was later built, to the east of the first and further up the hillside, but still on roughly the same axis. The new chamber was 3.6m long, 2.4m wide and 1.5m high, with two wallstones on each side, an end stone and a low sill stone that did not prevent people from entering the chamber. The cairn covering the east chamber was roughly rectangular in plan and built large enough to cover not only the new chamber but the old one as well. Neolithic and bronze age pottery was found in the east chamber, and in the forecourt on its east side. The forecourt had been carefully and systematically blocked in prehistory, presumably in the early bronze age, and much of the blocking remained in position until the 1961 excavation.

Dyffryn Ardudwy is a key site in the development of archaeological thought. In the 1950s and 1960s it was believed that portal dolmens were late monuments because their entrances were usually blocked, or blind: in Irish examples, the true 'entrance' or access is usually over one of the side stones. But Dyffryn Ardudwy has a portal dolmen, complete with impenetrably high doorstone, as its starting-point. The fact that it and its small round cairn were incorporated into a long cairn proves its early date; it is also associated with the earliest pottery yet found in Wales. The portal dolmens may generally, therefore, be early. They may even have supplied the idea for the blind entrances found in many Cotswold–Severn tombs (Figure 107).

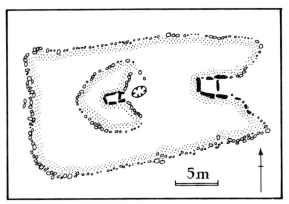

Figure 107   Dyffryn Ardudwy. The early round cairn with its small chamber can be seen just to the west of the centre of the long cairn.

FOUR CROSSES   Aberech   SH: 399385

A small closed rectangular burial chamber with no traces of a covering mound. The chamber measures 1.3m by 0.8m and is 1.5m high. The east stone probably formed the entrance: it is only 1m high and does not support the capstone. The pentagonal capstone is 2.5m by 2m and 0.6m thick. The stones were straightened up in 1936: at that time nothing was found in the chamber.

   To the north-east of the burial chamber are two 1.7m-high standing stones, at SH: 400389 and SH: 400388.

GRAIG LWYD AXE   Penmaenmawr   SH: 717750
FACTORY   Mountain

The outcrops and screes at the eastern end of Penmaenmawr Mountain are the source of material used by neolithic stone axe makers. Excavations in 1920 revealed much about the technology. Rough-outs made here were traded all over Britain, as far afield as Cairnpapple, Woodhenge and Upware. A fragment of a

Graig Lwyd mace-head was found at the Windmill Hill causewayed enclosure. The neolithic quarry sites are now largely destroyed by modern quarrying, or buried beneath modern quarry waste. The rock gathered by the neolithic axe factors is an augite granophyre, worked from the scree slope.

A stone plaque 13cm across and decorated with hatched chevron symbols was found on the site. It may have been a talisman: ritual finds at other sites, such as Grime's Graves in Norfolk and Harrow Hill in Sussex, imply that supernatural help was regularly sought by miners and axe factors. There is no sign of any continuing interest in the Graig Lwyd site after the neolithic came to an end.

GWERN EINION Llanfair SH: 587286

A rectangular burial chamber forming a portal dolmen, with five wallstones holding up a sloping capstone 2.7m long. All of this has been built into a drystone wall and is used as a cattle shelter. There is no trace of a mound. Somehow the portal dolmen has survived incorporation into the field wall, although the cairn has certainly been lost. The capstone typically slopes sharply back from the portal, which retains its blocking stone or doorstone.

HENDRE WAELOD Llansantffraid-glan- SH: 793748
Conway

A very fine portal dolmen above the River Conway. Two portal stones 1.7m high stand at the south-eastern end of a low chamber. The entrance is closed by a thin slab that rises right up to the capstone, a massive block 3m long and 1.5m thick, resting on the ground on the north side. Some remains of the covering long cairn survive in the hedgerow.

LLANBEDR SH: 585269

Inside the church, skulking behind the font, is a stone slab with a megalithic spiral 0.3m across carved on its face. It is an elaborately designed, pecked spiral with seven turns. It is not known where this intriguing piece of megalithic art came from, but it is believed to have been taken from a tomb on the hillside above the village.

Two stones stand 90m to the north-west of the church, one 3m and the other 2m high. They are known as Meini Hirion and they may once have been part of a stone circle.

LLANDEGAI CURSUS near Bangor SH: 593712

Air photography in 1961 revealed this cursus as a cropmark. There were straight ditches 15m apart, running side by side for at least 275m. The eastern end disappeared under a modern road and a plantation, but the rounded western end was seen, close to two henges. Other cropmarks that were possibly associated with the Llandegai Cursus were also seen on the air photographs. The site of this once-important ceremonial complex 1km from the Menai Strait, a busy thoroughfare for axe traders in the neolithic, is now covered by modern factories.

LLANDEGAI HENGES near Bangor SH: 593711

Two henges, each about 70m across, and discovered by air photography; there were also a cursus and some small circular ditched structures, the whole forming an important ceremonial complex near the northern end of the Menai Strait.

One of the henges, Llandegai North, had a single entrance with internal bank and a miniature cremation circle just outside the entrance causeway. The circle of pits containing cremation deposits is reminiscent of the henges at Dorchester in Oxfordshire, another site where henges developed early. It had no internal features except for a series of refilled holes near the centre. An unusual axe had been placed in a pit at the bank-foot, probably as an offering, and also suggesting a connection with the axe traders who must regularly have used the Menai Strait as a sheltered-water short cut. Pottery suggests that the henge-builders were local people, not incomers.

The second henge at Llandegai had two entrances, with a multiple cremation burial in a large pit outside the more important south entrance. The centre was marked by another cremation, and three beakers were found in small pits in the south-west quadrant. There were no other internal features: no pits, posts or stones.

The henges yielded radiocarbon dates of 2470 bc (3150 BC) and 2790 bc (3500 BC). These relatively early dates show that henges were already evolved during the middle neolithic, when the causewayed enclosures were being constructed. The Llandegai henges are nevertheless among the earliest known in Britain.

LLETY'R FILIAST Llandudno SH: 772829

An oval barrow about 25m long has been partly quarried away at the southern end, revealing a ruined burial chamber, which may originally have been rectangular. A broken capstone is partly in position on the west side. The mound is badly damaged, so that it is difficult to be sure of its original shape. Like Capel Garmon, which also belongs to the Conway Valley series of tombs, Llety'r Filiast may have been related to the Cotswold–Severn group. Contact with the main Cotswold–Severn group of tomb builders may have been established by way of inland routes, along the major valleys.

MAEN Y BARDD   Roewen   SH: 741718

A fine cromlech consisting of a large capstone 4m by 2m by 0.7m thick, resting on four upright stones. The local name for the structure is Cwrt y Filiast, the Greyhound's Kennel. There are traces of a long cairn on each side of a modern wall. To the west, along the lane, there are two fine standing stones: the Giant's Stick at SH: 738717 and another at S: 736716. It may or may not be a coincidence that the two standing stones are aligned on the cromlech.

MYNYDD AMWLCH   Penllech   SH: 230345

A wedge-shaped capstone supported by three upright stones, forming a roughly rectangular chamber. This may have been closed originally by a fourth stone which now lies beside the chamber. Another flat stone to the north-west may have been the capstone of another chamber. Possibly the chamber or chambers were once covered by a circular mound 8.5m in diameter.

MYNYDD RHIW   SH: 234299

A drift mine and stone axe factory. A 1.5m-thick layer of glacial drift rests on a shale layer, which in turn rests on dolerite. The shale in contact with the igneous dolerite has been metamorphosed: it was this 1m-thick contact seam of metamorphosed shale, or hornfels, that the neolithic miners were interested in quarrying. The stone axes from here are known by their petrological type number, xxi, but they seem not to have been widely distributed.

RHOSLAN   Llanystumdwy   SH: 483409

These are the merest bones of a megalithic tomb: a single large capstone 3.5m long and 2.7m wide supported on four wallstones. The chamber is open to the south and there is no trace of a covering mound.

TAN-Y-MURIAU   SH: 238288

An interesting tomb on the Lleyn peninsula, with a portal dolmen at its north-west end. Above the H-shaped closed doorway is a large capstone 4m long, 3m wide and 1.5m thick. The chamber has lost its sidestones, and the cairn has gone to make field walls. To the south-east, 7.5m down the slope, is a side chamber entered from the west: from here the cairn is quite well preserved for nearly 30m to the south. It has been suggested that the portal dolmen formed part of an early cairn on the site and that the rest of the mound is a later addition.

YSTUM-CEGID-ISAF   SH: 498413

A passage grave 3km N of Criccieth. It has a large slab 4m long for a capstone, and this rests on four low uprights.

──────────── POWYS ────────────

CERRIG DUON   Glyntawe   SN: 852206

This egg-shaped ring of 22 stones near the source of the River Tawe is dominated by a great block of sandstone almost 2m high, called 'Maen Mawr', which stands about 10m away from the circle. The 20m-diameter stone circle is formed out of rather small stones, none of them over 0.6m tall.

There are two more small stones behind Maen Mawr to the north, which seem to mark the circle's axis. Aubrey Burl believes these to be directional indicators, as at Long Meg, while Alexander Thom believes they marked the rising of Arcturus in 1950 BC. 14m NE of the circle is an irregular avenue 46m long and 5m wide near the circle, and also made of small stones. The avenue does not reach the ring; even if projected, it would pass by on the south-east side. None of these monuments has been dated.

CRICKHOWELL   SO: 210192

A chambered long barrow 1km W of Crickhowell. It was badly damaged by eighteenth- and early nineteenth-century excavators, to the extent that the capstone of the chamber, the monument's principal stone, is now missing. The eight upright slabs of the polygonal chamber can still be seen.

CWM FFOREST LONG CAIRN   SO: 183294

A long cairn, lying in the same valley as Ty Isaf, with which it has similarities. Its drystone walling survives, together with a capstone, but there are no signs of the upright slabs.

CWM-MAWR   near Corndon Hill   not known

There was a stone axe factory in this area, but the location has not been identified. Picrite was used for making the axes, which are known by their petrological type number, XII. A few axes of this type have been found in Wales and Wessex, and one in East Anglia, but most have been found in the English Midlands. It was quite common for neolithic axe factories to have particular 'market areas', to judge from the distribution of finds.

CWRT Y GOLLEN SO: 236167

A fine example of a standing stone 3km S of Crickhowell.

FFOSTILL LONG CAIRNS SO: 179349

An interesting pair of chambered tombs. The south cairn is better preserved and has a single chamber in the form of a gallery just over 3m long at its north-east end; it is lined by ten uprights which supported the two displaced capstones. The second cairn, to the north, is larger and lies more exactly west to east. Its main chamber, which is wrecked, was at the east end; it also had a small chamber in the middle of the north side and possibly a third at the south-west corner. Both cairns were excavated, though not very thoroughly, in 1921–3.

FFRIDD FALDWYN SO: 216970

A neolithic occupation site on a hilltop that was later, in the third century BC, to be developed as a palisaded hillfort.

THE FISH STONE near Crickhowell SO: 183198

A standing stone near the River Usk. At 5.5m high, it is probably the tallest standing stone in Wales; the Rudston Monolith easily overtops it, at 7.7m. The slab somewhat resembles a fish standing on its tail. It is said that on Midsummer Eve it leaps into the river for a swim.

GWERNVALE SO: 211192

Close to the north side of the A40 are the remains of a long cairn in the Cotswold–Severn tradition, which was built, very unusually, on the site of an earlier neolithic settlement. The cairn was wedge-shaped, nearly 45m long, horned, with a forecourt and false portal at the eastern end. Along the south side were two lateral chambers, with traces of a third at the damaged western end. Another single chamber was situated on the north side. The only traces of burials were found in the south-east chamber. Six post-holes in the forecourt suggest that some sort of mortuary structure or shrine stood in front of the tomb. The cairn had double revetment walls. The monument had been badly damaged by the changing routes of the A40, which was most recently altered in 1978. No human remains were found in the 1978 excavation by the Clwyd–Powys Archaeological Trust, but they may have been removed during an earlier excavation, such as the one in 1804.

LLANGYNDIR Coed-yr-ynys SO: 156204

Close to the track along the valley bottom, on the north bank of the River Usk, this is the largest standing stone in the area. As with many other such stones its date or origin is unknown, but assumed to be prehistoric.

MAEN LLWYD Pen-y-Gader Fawr SO: 226276

A large standing stone high in the Black Mountains to the north of Crickhowell. At 570m OD, it is higher above the sea than any other standing stone in Wales.

MAEN SERTH Llansanffraidd SN: 944698

A standing stone just over 2m tall. It has a cross incised on it, which may support the tradition that it marks the site of the murder of Einion Clud in the twelfth century AD. It may be that it was erected in the neolithic or bronze age and the cross added in the twelfth century.

PENYWYRLOD LONG CAIRN SO: 225398

A fairly small cairn 18m long with a rectangular chamber in its north-eastern end, consisting of four uprights but with no surviving capstone. Another chamber lies to one side at the south-western end. The cairn was partially excavated in 1920, but this added little in the way of constructional detail. It seems to be a degenerate form of the Cotswold–Severn type of long cairn found nearer the Bristol Channel. Houlder (1978) suggests that it is 'somewhere near the end of a natural devolution' from the type.

PIPTON CAIRN SO: 160373

At the end of a spur above the River Wye is a trapeze-shaped cairn 32m long with a drystone revetment wall. It is squared off at the narrow south-western end, and divided by a dummy entrance between two rounded horns at the broader north-eastern end. The dummy entrance consists of two upright stones side by side. There are two burial chambers, both on the west side. One has a long articulated passage and antechamber before the burial chambers proper are reached. The burial chambers lie roughly north to south along the spine of the barrow. The arrangement resembles that of Arthur's Stone in Hereford and Worcester. The second chamber, further to the south, is a simple rectangular structure without a passage. This tomb evidently represents and incorporates more than one cultural tradition.

The pretence of the dummy entrance may indicate that it is late in the Cotswold–Severn series, as may also the concealment of the true entrance, the complicated gallery at the side, and the decided irregularity of the chambers. The tomb as a whole has many points in common with Ty-Isaf, even to the 'incorporated' oval mound implied by the second chamber and its curving drystone revetment walls.

RHOS-Y-BEDDAU   Llangynog   SJ: 058303

This site is difficult to find as it is overgrown with rushes. It consists of a stone circle 12m in diameter, of which nine stones survive, none higher than 0.8m. To the east of the circle is a double avenue of stones 48m long and about 3m wide. The stones are only 0.1–0.4m high. 42m away from the east end of the avenue and to the north-east is a wrecked cairn, which is recognizable by the surviving fragments of its retaining kerb. The site is particularly interesting because stone rows and avenues are fairly uncommon in Wales.

TALGARTH   SO: 151316

This large trapeze-shaped Cotswold–Severn chambered tomb with rounded horns was discovered as recently as 1972, when Mr Griffiths discovered human remains in a stony mound on his farm. The cairn is 60m long, 25m wide and 3m high, and it has been damaged by the small quarry that led to its recognition as a burial monument. Its long axis is oriented NW–SE. Traces of at least three chambers opening from the cairn sides have been found and what may be the main chamber behind the 'entrance' between the horns.

TRECASTLE MOUNTAIN   Trecastle   SN: 833311

Two stone circles stand 45m apart. The larger of the two is 22m in diameter and is made up of 18 small stones, all less than 0.6m high, surrounding a low central mound. Sockets or hollows for other stones can still be detected. The second circle, also composed of small stones, is only 8m in diameter. Four stones once stood in a line to the west – another of the rare Welsh stone rows – but now only two remain.

TRELYSTAN   near Welshpool   SJ: 277070

Traces of a late neolithic Grooved ware settlement have been discovered beneath two round barrows, including the remains of two stake-walled buildings 40m apart, one of which is much better preserved than the other. The four radiocarbon dates for the site range from 2185 (bc) (2800 BC) to 2005 bc (2500 BC). The better preserved house was lightly built, even flimsy, by neolithic standards, with stakes set vertically in the ground 0.5m apart round the four sides of a square with rounded corners, 4.5m by 4m, and a 1.5m gap for the doorway. The square hearth was originally edged with upright slabs, reminiscent of the hearths at Skara Brae. There were pits in the floor, probably for food storage. If the site had been eroded instead of protected, only the pits would have survived; this might give us a useful guide to the interpretation and reconstruction of many other occupation sites in Britain where only the pits have survived (Figure 108).

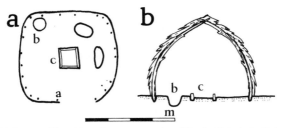

Figure 108   Trelystan. Plan (a) and reconstruction (b) of a lightly built hut. a – stake-hole,   b – storage pit,   c – hearth.

TY ILLTUD   Llanhamlach   SO: 098263

Near the centre of an unusually well-preserved oval cairn is a rectangular burial chamber with three wallstones and a low capstone sloping forwards. There seems to be part of a rectangular forecourt to the north. Most of the wallstones are decorated with faint incised patterns, but these are not neolithic; they are mostly crosses, some in lozenges, some with circles at the ends of their arms, and amongst them are traces of writing including the date 1312. These decorations are almost certainly medieval, possibly the work of shepherd boys. It is possible, although not probable, that St Illtud used this burial chamber as his hermit's cell. The chamber has been called 'the House of Illtud' for a long time, and the saint is reputed to be buried at Maen Illtud, a few kilometres away from this site.

TY ISAF   Talgarth   SO: 182291

Ty Isaf is one of the best known neolithic tombs in South Wales, largely because of the careful excavation and restoration of 1938. It is often used as a type site for the whole series of long cairns found in the Black Mountains, which are related to the classic Cotswold–Severn tombs. Ty Isaf is a trapeze-shaped mound 30m long and 16m at the broader northern end. It is held in shape by drystone revetment walls, which form rounded horns and curve inwards to focus attention on the false doorway at the northern end. Halfway along the barrow were two side chambers opening from the east and west. The west chamber contained the crushed remains of 17 people, neolithic pottery, leaf-shaped arrow-heads and a polished axe. The east chamber contained only one skeleton, but pieces of at least six neolithic bowls; there were the remains of two people in the passage. At the southern end of the barrow were the remains of another rectangular chamber. Between the two side chambers and the end chamber was a very curious feature – an oval cairn surrounded by two curving revetment walls that had been incorporated into the long barrow. The oval cairn had its own entrance passage 4.5m long, leading diagonally into the mound from the long cairn's south-east corner; it led diagonally into the cairn to a transepted burial chamber divided into three parts. The central section was about 2m long, with a small chamber opening out of it to the north-east and a larger chamber, about 3m long, opening out of it to the south-west. The bones of several people were found in this chamber together with neolithic pottery; once again, the bones of two people were deposited in the entrance passage (Figure 109).

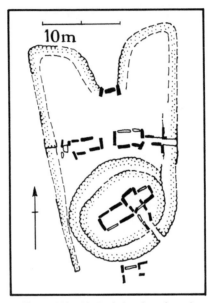

Figure 109 Ty Isaf chambered tomb.

The oval cairn is a matter of controversy. It may be that it was added to the long cairn as a later intrusion or, more likely, it was an early monument that was incorporated into a later long cairn. This second interpretation would be more in harmony with what we see at other sites, such as Dyffryn Ardudwy in Gwynedd.

WELSHPOOL CURSUS   SJ: 216048

A cursus monument. It was the Greater Cursus at Stonehenge that was the first such monument to be discovered, by William Stukeley on 6 August 1723, and he immediately identified it (probably wrongly) as a running track for the 'games, feasts, exercises and sports' of Druidical feast days, 'the finest piece of ground that can be imagin'd for the purpose of a horse race' (Stukeley 1740). As time has passed, so too has the unique status of the Stonehenge Greater Cursus; it turned out that there was a Lesser Cursus not far away, and there were others further afield. The Dorset Cursus has proved to be much longer, though with no great stone circle anywhere within sight of it, and many another cursus monument, albeit much smaller in scale than the Stonehenge 'original', has been revealed by modern air photography. It is now clear that the cursus was a regular part of the ritual landscape of the British neolithic; funerary in implication, often by association with nearby ring ditches or long barrows, they were possibly used as processional ways. It is perhaps appropriate to end with a type of monument that was discovered for us by Stukeley, one that remains an archaeological enigma, but which is also becoming increasingly well known to archaeologists in terms of numbers, construction and distribution. The cursus is emblematic of the span of the study of prehistory as it has evolved over the last 300 years, since the pioneering days of William Stukeley and John Aubrey before him. For all the great strides that prehistory has made since then, we can still stand in awe of the mysteries of the new stone age in Britain, just as John Aubrey did over 300 years ago (Dick 1972):

> This Inquiry, I must confess, is a gropeing in the Dark; but although I have not brought it into a clear light, yet I can affirm that I have brought it from an utter darkness to a thin mist ... These Antiquities are so exceeding old that no Bookes doe reach them, so that there is no Way to retrive them but by comparative antiquitie, which I have writt upon the spott, from the Monuments themselves.
>
> Historia quoquo modo scripta, bona est.

APPENDIX: RADIOCARBON DATES

The radiocarbon dating method, which has now been in use for some 40 years, depends on the inclusion in the remains of all living things of the isotope carbon-14. When an organism dies, the carbon-14 it contains decays at a constant and known rate. The dating method uses precise laboratory measurements of the amount of carbon-14 remaining to calculate the date of death; the result is the 'raw' radiocarbon date which is normally expressed, as in this book, in years bc. Occasionally the text uses years bp, which means raw radiocarbon date before present.

A complication arises because other dating methods, notably the one that uses the rings of the long-lived bristlecone pine tree, indicate that the levels of carbon-14 in the atmosphere have fluctuated with time. Raw dates thus need correcting to allow for this. The conversion graph, the dashed line on Figure 110 (see p. 404), shows the best available conversion of radiocarbon dates, resulting mainly from the evidence of the bristlecone pines. The fluctuations mean that some raw dates can be corrected to three possible calendar dates, which is unsatisfactorily clumsy: 3200 bc can be corrected to 4000, 4130 and 4220 BC. To get round this problem, the line has been smoothed mathematically (the heavy black line) so that each radiocarbon year bc has only one conversion date in calendar years BC.

The corrected dates are significantly older than the raw dates, and they lengthen the neolithic by several centuries: the gap also widens with age, as Figure 110 shows. It should nevertheless be remembered that even the corrected dates are only approximate and may prove to be in error by a century or so.

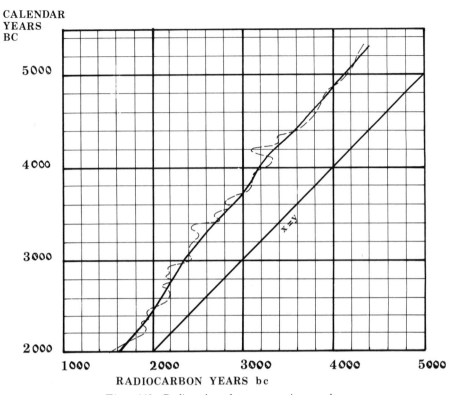

Figure 110 Radiocarbon dates conversion graph.

BIBLIOGRAPHY

The following abbreviations are used in the Bibliography:

CA – *Current Archaeology*
PDNHAS – *Proceedings of the Dorset Natural History and Archaeological Society*
PPS – *Proceedings of the Prehistoric Society*
PSAS – *Proceedings of the Society of Antiquaries of Scotland*
RCAHM – *Royal Commission for Ancient and Historical Monuments*

Ashbee, P. (1966) The Fussell's Lodge Long Barrow Excavations, 1957, *Archaeologia*, 100: 1–80.
——(1974) *Ancient Scilly*, Newton Abbot: David and Charles.
——(1978) *The Ancient British*, Norwich: Geo Abstracts.
——(1984) *The Earthen Long Barrow in Britain*, Norwich: Geo Abstracts.
Ashbee, P., Smith, I. F. and Evans, J. G. (1979) Excavation of three long barrows near Avebury, Wiltshire, *PPS*, 45: 207–300.
Aston, M. A. and Burrow, I. C. (1982) *The Archaeology of Somerset*, Taunton: Somerset County Council.
Atkinson, R. J. C. (1951) *Excavations at Dorchester, Oxon.*, Oxford: Ashmolean Museum.
——(1965) Wayland's Smithy, *Antiquity*, 39: 126–33.
——(1979) *Stonehenge: Archaeology and Interpretation*, Harmondsworth: Penguin Books.
Balfour, M. (1983) *Stonehenge and its Mysteries*, London: Hutchinson.
Bamford, H. M. (1985) *Briar Hill Excavations 1974–8*, Northampton: Northampton Development Corporation.
Barker, G. and Webley, D. (1978) Causewayed camps and early neolithic communities in central southern England, *PPS*, 44: 161–86.
Barnatt, J. (1982) *Prehistoric Cornwall: the Ceremonial Monuments*, Wellingborough: Turnstone Press.
Bell, M. (1977) Excavation at Bishopstone, *Sussex Archaeological Collection*, 115: 1–291.
Bird, J. and Bird, D. G. (1987) *The Archaeology of Surrey to 1540*, Guildford: Surrey Archaeological Society.
Bowden, M., Bradley, R., Gaffney, V. and Mepham, L. (1983) The date of the Dorset Cursus, *PPS*, 49: 376–9.
Bradley, R. (1983) The bank barrows and related monuments of Dorset in the light of recent fieldwork, *PDNHAS*, 105: 15–20.
Bradley, R. and Thomas, J. (1984) Some new information on the henge monument at Maumbury Rings, Dorchester, *PDNHAS*, 106: 132–4.
Britnell, W. (1979) The Gwernvale Long Cairn, Powys, *Antiquity*, 53: 132–4.
Buckley, D. G. (1980) Archaeology in Essex to AD 1500, *Council for British Archaeology Research Report*, No. 34.

Bunch, B. and Fell, C. I. (1949) A stone axe factory at Pike of Stickle, Great Langdale, Westmorland, *PPS*, 15: 1–20.

Burgess, C. (1980) *The Age of Stonehenge,* London: Dent.

Burl, A. (1976) *The Stone Circles of the British Isles,* New Haven and London: Yale University Press.

——(1979) *Prehistoric Avebury,* New Haven and London: Yale University Press.

——(1987) *The Stonehenge People: Life and Death at the World's Greatest Stone Circle,* London: Dent.

——(1988) Coves: structural enigmas of the neolithic, *Wiltshire Archaeological and Natural History Magazine,* 82: 1–18.

Bushell, W. D. (1911) Amongst the Prescelly Circles, *Archaeologia Cambrensis,* 11: 287–333.

Calder, C. S. T. (1950) Report on the excavation of a Neolithic Temple at Stanydale, Shetland, *PSAS.*

——(1958) Report on the discovery of numerous stone age house-sites in Shetland, *PSAS,* 89: 340–97.

——(1963) Excavations in Whalsay, Shetland, 1954–5, *PSAS,* 94: 28–45.

Case, H. J. (1956) The neolithic causewayed camp at Abingdon, Berkshire, *Antiquaries Journal,* 36: 1–30.

——(1962) Long barrows and causewayed camps, *Antiquity,* 36: 212–16.

Castleden, R. (1987) *The Stonehenge People: an Exploration of Life in Neolithic Britain,* London and New York: Routledge.

Childe, V. G. (1931) *Skara Brae,* London: Kegan Paul.

Clayton, P. (1985) *Guide to the Archaeological Sites of Britain,* London: Batsford.

Cleal, R. M. J. (1982) A re-analysis of the ring-ditch site at Playden, East Sussex, *Sussex Archaeological Collection,* 120: 1–17.

Close-Brooks, J. (1986) *Exploring Scotland's Heritage: The Highlands,* London: HMSO.

Coles, B. and Coles, J. (1986) *Sweet Track to Glastonbury,* London: Thames and Hudson.

Coles, J. M. and Hibbert, F. A. (1968) Prehistoric roads and tracks in Somerset, England, *PPS,* 34: 238–58.

Coles, J. M. and Simpson, D. D. A. (1965) The excavation of a Neolithic round barrow at Pitnacree, Scotland, *PPS,* 31: 34–57.

Corcoran, J. X. W. P. (1969) Excavation of two chambered cairns at Mid Gleniron Farm, Glenluce, Wigtownshire, *Trans. Dumfriesshire Galloway Nat. Hist. Antiq. Soc.,* 46: 29–90.

Cunnington, M. E. (1929) *Woodhenge,* Devizes: G. Simpson.

——(1931) The 'Sanctuary' on Overton Hill, near Avebury, *Wiltshire Archaeological Magazine,* 45: 300–35.

Dames, M. (1976) *The Silbury Treasure,* London: Thames and Hudson.

Daniel, G. E. (1950) *The Prehistoric Chambered Tombs of England and Wales,* Cambridge: Cambridge University Press.

Darvill, T. (1981) Excavations at the Peak Camp, Cowley: an interim note, *Glevensis,* 15: 52–6.

Davidson, J. L. and Henshall, A. S. (1989) *The Chambered Cairns of Orkney,* Edinburgh: Edinburgh University Press.

Dick, O, L. (1972) *Aubrey's Brief Lives,* Harmondsworth: Penguin Books.

Drewett, P. (1982) *The Archaeology of Bullock Down, Eastbourne, East Sussex,* Lewes: Sussex Archaeological Society.

Drewett, P., Rudling, D. and Gardiner, M. (1988) *The South East to AD 1000,* London: Longman.

Dyer, J. (1981) *The Penguin Guide to Prehistoric England and Wales,* Harmondsworth: Penguin Books.

Dymond, C. W. (1877) The megalithic antiquities at Stanton Drew, *Journal of the British Archaeological Association,* 33: 297–307.

——(1879) The Hurlers: three stone circles near St Cleer, Cornwall, *Journal of the British Archaeological Association,* 35: 297–307.

Dymond, D. P. (1966) Ritual monuments at Rudston, East Yorkshire, England, *PPS,* 32: 86–95.

Evans, J. G. (1971) Notes on the environment of early farming communities in Britain, in *Economy and Settlement in Neolithic and Early Bronze Age Britain and Europe,* edited by D. D. A. Simpson, Leicester: Leicester University Press.

Feachem, R. (1977) *Guide to Prehistoric Scotland,* London: Batsford.

Field, N. H., Matthews, C. L. and Smith, I. F. (1964) New neolithic sites in Dorset and Bedfordshire, with a note on the distribution of neolithic storage pits in Britain, *PPS,* 30: 352–81.

Forde-Johnston, J. (1976) *Prehistoric Britain and Ireland,* London: Dent.

Fox, A. (1973) *South-West England, 3500 BC–AD 600,* Newton Abbot: David and Charles.

Gray, St G. H. (1903) On the excavations at Arbor Low, 1901–2, *Archaeologia,* 58: 461–98.

——(1935) The Avebury excavations, 1908–22, *Archaeologia,* 84: 99–162.

Green, C. P. (1973) Pleistocene river gravels and the Stonehenge problem, *Nature,* 243: 214.

Grimes, W. F. (1938) Excavations at Meini Gwyr, Carmarthen, *PPS,* 4: 324–5.

Grinsell, L. V. (1978) Dartmoor barrows, *Proceedings of the Devon Archaeological Society,* 36: 85–180.

——(1983) The barrows of south and east Devon, *Proceedings of the Devon Archaeological Society,* 41: 5–46.

Hawkins, G. S. (1965) Callanish: a Scottish Stonehenge, *Science,* 147: 127–30.

——(1966) *Stonehenge Decoded,* London: Souvenir Press.

Heathcote, J. P. (1980) The Nine Ladies Stone Circle, *Derbyshire Archaeological Journal,* 100: 15–16.

Hedges, J. and Buckley, D. (1978) Excavations at a neolithic causewayed enclosure, Orsett, Essex, *PPS,* 44: 219–308.

Hemp, W. J. (1930) The chambered cairn of Bryn-Celli-Dbu, *Archaeologia,* 80: 179–214.

Henshall, A. S. (1963) *The Chambered Tombs of Scotland,* Vol. 1, Edinburgh: Edinburgh University Press.

——(1972) *The Chambered Tombs of Scotland,* Vol. 2, Edinburgh: Edinburgh University Press.

Higham, N. (1986) *The northern Counties to AD 1000,* London: Longmans.

Hillam, J., Groves, C. M., Brown, D. M., Baillie, M., Coles, J. and Coles, B. (1990) Dendrochronology of the English neolithic, *Antiquity,* 64: 210–20.

Hoare, Sir Richard Colt (1812) *The Ancient History of Wiltshire,* London.

Houlder, C. H. (1961) The excavation of a neolithic stone implement factory on Mynydd Rhiw in Carnarvonshire, *PPS,* 27: 108–43.

——(1978) *Wales: An Archaeological Guide. The Prehistoric, Roman and Early Medieval Field Monuments,* London: Faber.

Houlder, C. H. and Manning, W. H. (1966) *Regional Archaeologies: South Wales,* London: Cory, Adams and Mackay.

Jessup, R. (1970) *South-East England,* London: Thames and Hudson.

Keen, L. (1979) Dorset Archaeology in 1979, *PDNHAS,* 101: 133–43.

Keiller, A. and Piggott, S. (1936) The West Kennet Avenue, Avebury. Excavations 1934–5, *Antiquity,* 10: 417–27.

Kellaway, G. A. (1971) Glaciation and the stones of Stonehenge, *Nature,* 233: 30–5.

Keys, D. (1990) The green answer to the riddle of Stonehenge, *The Independent,* 24 April, 1990.

Lewis, B. and Green, M. (1980) Excavation of a ring ditch at Down Farm, Gussage St Michael: interim report, *PDNHAS,* 102: 85.

Lynch, F. (1970) *Prehistoric Anglesey,* Llangefni: Anglesey Antiquarian Society.

Lynch, F., Scott, J. G., Corcoran, J. and Powell, T. (1969) *Megalithic Enquiries,* Liverpool: Liverpool University Press.

Manby, T. G. (1976) Excavation of the Kilham Long Barrow, East Riding of Yorkshire, *PPS,* 42: 111–59.

Marshall, D. N. and Taylor, I. D. (1978) The excavation of the chambered cairn at Glenvoidean, Isle of Bute, *PSAS,* 108: 1–39.

Masters, L. J. (1973) The Lochhill Long Cairn, *Antiquity,* 47: 96–100.

——(1978) Camster Long Chambered Cairn, *PPS,* 44: 453–4.

Mercer, R. J., Barclay, G. J., Jordan, D. and Russell-White, C. J. (1988) The neolithic henge-type enclosure at Balfarg – a re-assessment of the evidence for an incomplete ditch circuit, *PSAS,* 118: 61–7.

Morgan, F. (1959) The excavation of a long barrow at Nutbane, Hampshire, *PPS,* 25: 15–51.

Newham, C. A. (1966) Stonehenge – a neolithic 'observatory', *Nature,* 211: 456–68.

O'Kelly, C. (1969) Bryn-Celli-Ddu, Anglesey. A reinterpretation, *Archaeologia Cambrensis,* 118: 17–48.

Peek, R. A. and Parsons, D. (1972) *Provisional List of Sites in Leicestershire Recognised from Air Photographs,* Leicester: University of Leicester Department of Adult Education.

Penny, A. and Wood, J. E. (1973) The Dorset Cursus complex: a neolithic astronomical observatory, *Archaeological Journal,* 130: 44–76.

Phillips, C. W. (1936) The excavation of the Giant's Hills Long Barrow, Skendleby, Lincs., *Archaeologia,* 85: 37–106.

Piggott, S. (1948) The excavations at Cairnpapple Hill, West Lothian, *PSAS,* 82: 68–123.

——(1954) *The Neolithic Cultures of the British Isles,* Cambridge: Cambridge University Press.

——(1962) *The West Kennet Long Barrow: excavations 1955–6,* London: HMSO.

——(1974) Excavation of the Dalladies Long Barrow, Fettercairn, Kincardineshire, *PSAS,* 104: 23–47.

Piggott, S. and Powell, T. G. E. (1951) The excavation of three neolithic chambered tombs in Galloway, 1949, *PSAS,* 83: 103–61.

Powell, T. G. E. (1973) Excavation of the megalithic chambered cairn at Dyffryn Ardudwy, Merioneth, Wales, *Archaeologia,* 104: 1–49.

Powell, T. G. E. and Daniel, G. E. (1956) *Barclodiad y Gawres,* Liverpool: Liverpool University Press.

Pryor, F. (1978) Excavation at Fengate, Peterborough, England: second report, *Royal Ontario Museum Archaeological Monograph,* No. 5.

——(1985) Maxey, *CA,* 96: 11–13.

Radley, J. (1969) The origins of the Arbor Low monument, *Derbyshire Archaeological Journal,* 88: 100–3.

RCAHM (1979) *Long Barrows in Hampshire and the Isle of Wight,* London: HMSO.

——(1979) *Stonehenge and its Environs: Monuments and Land Use,* Edinburgh: Edinburgh University Press.

Reed, R. C. (1974) Earthen long barrows: a new perspective, *Archaeological Journal,* 131: 33–57.

Renfrew, C. (1979) *Investigations in Orkney,* London: Society of Antiquaries and Thames and Hudson.

——(ed.) (1985) *The Prehistory of Orkney,* Edinburgh: Edinburgh University Press.

——(1986) participating in the BBC television 'Horizon' programme 'Who built Stonehenge?' written and produced by Dominic Flessati.

Richards, J. (1978) The archaeology of the Berkshire Downs, *Berkshire Archaeological Committee Publication,* No. 3.

Ritchie, G. (1974) Excavation of the stone circle and cairn at Balbirnie, Fife, *Archaeological Journal*, 131: 1–32.

Ritchie, G. and Harman, M. (1986) *Exploring Scotland's Heritage: Argyll and the Western Isles*, London: HMSO.

Savory, H. N. (1973) Pen-y-wyrlod: a new Welsh long cairn, *Antiquity*, 47: 187–92.

Scott, J. G. (1974) Temple Wood, Kilmartin. Stone circle, *Discovery and Excavation, Scotland*, 76.

Selkirk, A. (1972) Waulud's Bank, *CA*, 30: 173–7.

Shepherd, I. A. G. (1980) *Exploring Scotland's Heritage: Grampian*, London: HMSO.

Shore, W. (1911) *Prehistoric Man in Cheshire*, London: Simpkin, Marshall, Hamilton, Kent.

Simpson, D. D. A. (1968) Timber mortuary houses and earthen long barrows, *Antiquity*, 42: 142–4.

Smith, C. (1979) Trefignath burial chambers, Holyhead, Anglesey, *PPS*, 45: 340.

Stell, G. (1986) *Exploring Scotland's Heritage: Dumfries and Galloway*, London: HMSO.

Stevenson, J. B. (1986) *Exploring Scotland's Heritage: Clyde Estuary and Central Region*, London: HMSO.

Stukeley, W. (1740) *Stonehenge. A Temple Restored to the British Druids,* London.

——(1743) *Abury, a Temple of the Druids, with Some Others, Described*, London.

——(1766) *Itinerarium Curiosum*, London.

Thom, A. (1967) *Megalithic Sites in Britain*, Oxford: Oxford University Press.

Thomas, N. (1964) The neolithic causewayed camp at Robin Hood's Ball, Shrewton, *Wiltshire Archaeological and Natural History Magazine*, 59: 1–27.

Tratman, E. K. (1966) Investigations at Stanton Drew Stone Circles, Somerset, *Proceedings of the University of Bristol Speleological Society*, 11: 40–2.

——(1967) The Priddy Circles, Mendip, Somerset, henge monuments, *Proceedings of the University of Bristol Speleological Society*, 11: 97–125.

Trow, S. (1985) An interrupted ditch enclosure at Southmore Grove, Rendcomb, Gloucestershire, *Transactions of the Bristol and Gloucester Archaeological Society*, 103: 17–22.

Ucko, P. J., Hunter, M., Clark, A. J. and David, A. (1991) *Avebury Reconsidered*, London: Unwin Hyman.

Varley, W. J. (1964) *Cheshire Before the Romans*, Chester: Cheshire Community Council.

Vatcher, F. (1961) The excavation of the long mortuary enclosure on Normanton Down, Wiltshire, *PPS*, 27: 160–73.

Vatcher, L. and Vatcher, F. (1975) Excavation of three postholes in Stonehenge car-park, *Wiltshire Archaeological Magazine*, 68: 57–63.

Wainwright, G. J. (1969) A review of henge monuments in the light of recent research, *PPS*, 35: 112–33.

——(1971) The excavation of a late neolithic enclosure at Marden, Wiltshire, *Antiquaries Journal*, 51: 177–239.

——(1970) Excavations at Marden, Wiltshire, *Antiquity*, 44: 56–7.

——(1972) The excavation of a neolithic settlement on Broome Heath, Ditchingham, Norfolk, *PPS*, 38: 1–97.

Wainwright, G. J. and Longworth, I. H. (1971) *Durrington Walls: Excavations 1966–1968*, London: Society of Antiquaries.

Watson, K. (1965) *Regional Archaeologies: North Wales*, London: Cory, Adams and Mackay.

Weatherhill, C. (1985) *Cornovia: Ancient Sites of Cornwall and Scilly*, Penzance: Alison Hodge.

INDEX

Abbot's Way, Som. 164
Abingdon Causewayed Enclosure, Oxon. 152
Abingdon-style pottery 112, 153
Achaidh Horned Cairn, Sutherland 293
Achanarras Hill Stone Circle, Caithness 278
Achany Chambered Cairn, Sutherland 294
Achkinloch Chambered Cairn, Caithness 278
Achnagoul Chambered Cairn, Caithness 278
Achu Chambered Cairn, Sutherland 294
Adam's Grave Long Barrow, Wilts. 196
Addington Park Chambered Tomb, Kent 131
Afton Down Barrow Cemetery, Hants 116
Airidh na H'Aon Oidhche Chambered Cairn, Western Isles 353
Aldwincle Round Barrow, Northants 145
Alington Avenue Long Barrow, Dorset 81, 86
Allor Molach Tomb Chamber, Gwynedd 387
Allor Moloch Chambered Tomb, Clywd 370
Allt na Buidhe Chambered Cairn, Caithness 279
Alrewas Causewayed Enclosure, Staffs. 170
Altnacealgach Chambered Cairns, Sutherland 294
amber 84, 198
Amesbury Bowl Barrow, Wilts. 198
animal sacrifice 53, 76, 123, 139, 154, 176, 212, 220, 239, 249, 315–16, 321, 363
antler 14, 20, 22, 23, 26, 54, 101, 153, 169, 176, 183, 188, 220, 230, 237, 249, 307
antler pick 76, 94, 143, 189, 190, 220, 222, 237, 248

Arbor Low Henge, Derby. 62–3, 64, 66
Arborton Flintworking Site, Staffs. 170
architecture, concept of 24–6, 59, 86, 90, 120, 198, 201, 210, 233, 236, 237, 264–5, 282, 312–13, 316–18, 325–6, 338, 352, 358, 363–4
ard 21, 190–1, 315
ard-marks 181, 229
Ardmarnock Chambered Cairn, Strathclyde 339
Ardnacross Chambered Cairn, Strathclyde 339
Ardnadam Settlement, Strathclyde 340
Ardvannie Chambered Cairn, Ross and Cromarty 292
Arminghall Henge, Norfolk 141, 185, 234
arrow-heads 15, 16, 19, 21, 22, 27, 32, 65, 66, 67, 68, 70, 72, 73, 74, 76, 88, 105, 107, 112, 114, 124, 132, 153, 169, 170, 180, 191, 215, 248, 249, 314, 370, 372, 399
arthritis 21, 218
Arthur's Stone, Hereford and Worcs. 121–2, 397
artwork 26, 86, 140, 149, 150, 181, 190, 191, 192–3, 251, 258, 259, 304, 307–8, 320, 349, 361, 392
Ascott under Wychwood Long Barrow, Oxon. 153
ash 166, 169
Ash Hill Long Barrow, Lincs. 137
Ash Holt Long Barrow, Lincs. 137
Ash Tree Cave, Derby. 63
Ashbee, Paul 16, 162, 198, 208
Ashcott Bow 164
Ashcott Heath, Som. 164–5
Ashmore Down Long Barrow, Wilts. 198
Ashover Occupation Site, Derby. 63

Aston Barrow, Derby. 64
Aston Causewayed Enclosure, Oxon. 153
Aston Cursus, Derby. 64
Aston Lane Occupation Site, Leics. 135
Astonhill Settlement, Derby. 65
astronomy 22, 29, 48, 55, 57, 59, 85, 88,
    141, 156, 176, 185, 195, 231–2, 274, 291,
    298, 316, 323, 346, 351–2, 354, 378, 395
Atkins, Martin 16
Atkinson, Richard 228, 241, 382
Aubrey, John 1, 7, 111, 203, 204, 219, 221,
    227, 231, 250, 401
Auchinduich Stone Circle, Sutherland 294
auk, great 310–11
Ault Hucknall Occupation Site, Derby. 65
Aultan Brouster Stone Circle, Caithness
    279
Avebury 1, 2, 7, 8, 59, 60, 91, 95, 96, 124,
    146, 149, 198–205, 223, 242, 243
Avening Burial Chambers, Glos. 105
avenue 10–11, 58, 59, 61, 79, 81, 124, 128,
    148, 149, 150, 200, 204–5, 213, 225, 235,
    274, 351, 352, 353–6, 378, 395, 398
axe manufacture 35, 40, 44, 51, 60, 77, 136,
    164, 195, 391–2, 394, 395
Ayston Mill Occupation Site, Leics. 135
Ayton East Field Long Barrow, N. Yorks
    248

Bachwen Tomb Chamber, Gwynedd 387–
    8
Backlass Stone Circle, Caithness 279
Badnaby Round Cairn, Sutherland 294
Badshot Long Barrow, Surrey 133, 175–6
Balbirnie Stone Circle, Fife 271
Balbridie Longhouse, Grampian 272–3
Balfarg Henge, Fife 271–2, 273
ball 94, 323
Ballowall Barrow, Corn. 29, 30
Ballymeanoch Henge and Standing Stones,
    Strathclyde 293, 340
Balmalloch Chambered Cairn, Strathclyde
    340
Balnagowan Long Cairn, Grampian 274
Balnaguie Chambered Cairn, Ross and
    Cromarty 292
Balnuaran of Clava, Inverness 291
bank barrow 82, 83, 90, 92, 93, 98
Bannockburn Enclosure, Central 263
Bant's Carn, Scilly 161, 162
Barbook Circles, Derby. 65
Barclodiad-y-Gawres, Gwynedd 388

Barclodiad-y-Gawres Chambered Tomb,
    Anglesey 361, 362, 379
Barford Henge and Cursus, War. 194–5
Barholm Causewayed Enclosure, Lincs.
    137, 140
bark 21, 22, 267, 275
Barkhale Causewayed Enclosure, W.
    Sussex 187–8
Barnack Cursus, Cambs. 19
Barnatt, John 38, 47
Barnhouse Stone, Orkney 298, 316
Barpa Langass Chambered Cairn, Western
    Isles 353
Barpa nam Feannag Chambered Cairn,
    Western Isles 353
Barrow Hills Oval Barrow, Oxon. 153
Barry, Revd George 321
Barton Hill Farm Henge, Beds. 12
Barton in Fabis Ring Ditch, Notts. 151
Bateman, Thomas 68, 69, 71, 73, 74
Bathend Clump Enclosure, Herts. 123
Battery Hill Long Barrow, Wilts. 205
battle axe 127, 274, 335
Beacharra Chambered Cairn, Strathclyde
    340
Beacharra pottery 342, 344, 348, 349
Beacon Hill Causewayed Enclosure, Hants
    116
Beacon Hill Long Barrow, E. Sussex 179
Beacon Hill Long Barrow, Wilts. 205
Beaker culture 4, 27, 64, 71, 126, 128, 166,
    167, 208, 248, 251, 276, 340, 343, 344,
    357, 370
Beckhampton Avenue, Wilts. 199–200, 204
Beckhampton (Longstones) Long Barrow,
    Wilts. 205
Beckhampton Road Long Barrow, Wilts.
    205–6
bed 24, 311, 325, 327
Bedd Branwen, Anglesey 361–2
Bedd-yr-Afanc Long Barrow, Dyfed 374
Bedwin, Owen 190
Beenham Ring Ditch, Berks. 16
Beer Head Axe Factory, Devon. 77
Beinn a'Charra Standing Stone, Western
    Isles 353
Beisgawen yn Dumnonia 30
Belas Knap Chambered Tomb, Glos.
    105–6
Bell Track, Som. 166
Belle Tout Settlement, E. Sussex 179
Belleville, Guy 78

Bellshiel Law Long Barrow, Northd. 148
Ben Freiceadain Chambered Cairn, Caithness 279
Benie Hoose, Shetland 330
Benson Cursus, Oxon. 154
Bere Down Long Barrows, Dorset 81
Bescaby Occupation Site, Leics. 135
Bevis's Thumb Long Barrow, W. Sussex 188
Bicker's Houses Chambered Cairn, Strathclyde 340
Big Wood Long Barrow, Dorset 82
Bigland Round and Long Chambered Cairns, Orkney 298–9
bigman burial 112, 249, 321
Bilbster Chambered Cairn, Caithness 279
Bincombe Hill Long Barrow, Dorset 82
Bingham Henge, Notts. 151
birch 21, 62, 267, 275, 321
Biscot Mill Long Barrow, Beds. 12
Bishops Stortford Occupation Site, Herts. 123
Bishopstone Settlement, E. Sussex 180
Black Hill Ring Cairn, Devon. 78
blackbird 321
Blackhammer Chambered Cairn, Orkney 299
Blackhorse Road Settlement, Herts. 123
Blackpatch Flint Mines, W. Sussex 188
Blackshouse Burn Enclosure, Strathclyde 341
Blakeley Raise Stone Circle, Cumbria 54
Blakey Topping Stone Circle, Humberside 126
Blawearie Round Cairn, Northd. 148
Blight, J. T. 31, 42, 45, 47
Blind Fiddler, Corn. 29
bluestone 206, 208, 233–5, 375
blocking (of tomb) 105, 160, 240, 241, 264, 267, 268, 282, 301, 318, 319, 380, 388, 390, 392
Bodowyr Passage Grave, Anglesey 362
Bokerley Long Barrows, Dorset 82
Boleigh Stone Circle, Corn. 43, 44
Bonsall Lane Rock Shelters, Derby. 65
Bonsor, George 161, 163
Bookan Chambered Cairn, Orkney 299–300
Boreland Chambered Cairn, Dumfries and Galloway 264
Borlase, W. C. 18, 33, 35, 39, 42, 43, 44, 50, 51, 53

Boscawen-Un Stone Circle, Corn. 29–30, 31
Botley Copse Long Barrow, Wilts. 206
bow 164, 167
Bower Farm Cave, Staffs. 171
Bowls (Boles) Barrow, Wilts. 206
Boyne Valley culture 26, 140, 320, 361
Boynton Round Barrow, Humberside 127
Brackley Chambered Cairn, Strathclyde 341
Bradford Peverell, Dorset 82
Bradley Moor Cairn, W. Yorks. 257
Bradley, Richard 98
Bradup Stone Circle, W. Yorks. 257
Braeside Chambered Cairn, Orkney 300
Brane Entrance Grave, Corn. 30–1, 32, 51
Brane Long Barrow, Corn. 31
Bransdale Long Cairn, Wilts. 248
Brats Hill Stone Circles, Cumbria 54
Bratton Castle Long Barrow, Wilts. 206–7
Brawlbin Long and Round Cairns, Caithness 280
bream 309
Breasclete Chambered Tomb, Western Isles 353
Bretton Racecourse Occupation Site, Derby. 65
Briar Hill Causewayed Enclosure, Northants 145, 146, 189
Bridestones Burial Chamber, Ches. 28
Brierlow Grange Flintworking Site, Derby. 65
Brittany 78, 130, 192, 316
Brixton Deverill Long Barrows, Wilts. 207
Broadchalke Long Barrow, Wilts. 207
Broadgate Long Barrow, Central 263
Broadmayne Long Barrow, Dorset 82–3
Broadsands Passage Grave, Devon. 78
Broadstones Stone Circle, Wilts. 245
Broadwell Causewayed Enclosure, Oxon. 154
Bron-y-Foel Isaf Cairn, Gwynedd 388
bronze age 13, 14, 22, 24, 27, 36, 40, 41, 45, 47, 55, 59, 64, 70, 74, 76, 78, 82, 85, 100, 128, 173, 187, 190, 194, 263, 297, 347, 381, 384
Brook Street Settlement, War. 195
Broome Heath, Norfolk 72, 103, 141–2, 144, 257, 365
Broomend of Crichie Henge, Grampian 274, 293
Brounaban Long Cairn, Caithness 280

Brown, Capability 123
Brown Edge Occupation Site, Derby. 65
Brushfield Hough Barrow, Derby. 66
Bryn Cader Fader Cairn Circle, Gwynedd 388
Bryn Castell Occupation Site, Clwyd 370
Bryn-Celli-Ddu Henge and Passage Grave, Anglesey 349, 363–4
Bryn-Gwyn Circle, Anglesey 364
Bryn Llwyn Settlement, Clwyd 370
Bryn Newydd Cemeteries, Clwyd 370
Bryn yr Hen Bobl Passage Grave, Anglesey 72, 257, 365, 366
Buckden Gravel Pit Occupation Site, Cambs. 19
Buckworth Long Barrow, Cambs. 19
Buddon Wood Occupation Site, Leics. 136
Bulford Long Barrow, Wilts. 207
Bull Ring Henge and Stone Circle, Derby. 66
Bull Stone, W. Yorks. 257
Bullock Down Settlement, E. Sussex 180
Burgar Round Cairn, Orkney 300
Burgh on Bain Long Barrow, Lincs. 138
Burl, Aubrey 5, 22, 156, 202, 203, 274, 275, 278, 346, 395
Burn of Scudillswick Stone House, Shetland 331
Burngrange Chambered Cairn, Strathclyde 341
Burray Chambered Cairn, Orkney 300
Burwell Settlement, Cambs. 19
Bury Hill Enclosure, W. Sussex 181, 189
Buscot Cursus, Oxon. 154
Busta Standing Stone, Shetland 331
buzzard 318, 321

Cairn Avel, Dumfries and Galloway 264
Cairn Ban Chambered Cairn, Strathclyde 341–2
Cairn of Get, Caithness 285
Cairn of Heathercro, Caithness 280
Cairnderry Chambered Cairn, Dumfries and Galloway 264
Cairnholy Chambered Cairns, Dumfries and Galloway 264–5
Cairnhowit Chambered Cairn, Strathclyde 342
Cairnpapple Hill Henge, Lothian 297–8, 391
Cairnscarrow Chambered Cairn, Dumfries and Galloway 265

Calderstones, Merseyside 140
Calf of Eday Chambered Cairns, Orkney 301
Callanish, Western Isles 59, 205, 353–6
Calling Low Dale Rock Helter, Derby. 66
Callis Wold Barrow Cemetery, Humberside 127
Calton Hill Settlement, Derby. 66
Cambridge Settlement, Cambs. 19
Came Down Settlement, Dorset 83
Came Wood Barrow Cemetery, Dorset 83, 84
Camelot 169
Cameron Farm Long Cairn, Strathclyde 342
Camster Long and Round Cairns, Caithness 280–3
Candlesby Long Barrow, Lincs. 138
Cannons Hill, Berks. 16
Capel Garmon Chambered Tomb, Clwyd–Gwynedd border 370, 388
Capenoch Long Cairn, Dumfries and Galloway 265
capstone 29, 30, 32, 33, 34, 36, 37, 40, 41, 44, 45, 46, 50, 51, 52, 53, 78, 81, 87, 90, 105, 115, 121, 148, 161, 163, 209, 219, 227, 240, 241, 257, 291, 340, 358, 362, 370, 375, 376, 377, 378, 379, 380, 382, 385, 387, 389, 391, 392, 393, 394, 395, 399
Cardington Causewayed Enclosure, Beds. 12
Carn Ban Chambered Cairn, Strathclyde 342
Carn Brea Enclosure, Corn. 32–3, 37, 77
Carn Gluze Barrow, Corn. 33–4
Carn Liath Chambered Cairn, Sutherland 295
Carn Liath Long Cairn, Caithness 283
Carn Llidi Chambered Tomb, Dyfed 374
Carn Meini, Dyfed 375
Carn Turne Chambered Tomb, Dyfed 375
Carn Wen Round Cairns, Dyfed 375
Carn Wnda, Dyfed 375
Carneddau Hengwm Long Cairns, Gwynedd 389
carpentry 23–4, 71, 96, 138, 145, 164, 169, 209–11, 214, 234, 246, 266–7, 272, 273, 325, 330, 350–1
Carreg Coetan Arthur Chambered Tomb, Dyfed 376

Carreg Samson Chambered Tomb, Dyfed 376

Carriside Round Cairn, Caithness 283

carving 26, 86, 140, 143, 149, 150, 166, 181, 190, 191, 251, 258, 259, 304, 307–8, 320, 349, 361

Carwynnen Quoit, Corn. 34, 41

Castell Bryn-Gwyn Henge, Anglesey 365–6

Casterton Stone Circle, Cumbria 54

Castilly Henge, Corn. 34–5

Castle Frazer, Grampian 274

Castle Hill Henge, Ross and Cromarty 292

Castlehowe Scar Stone Circle, Cumbria 54

Castlerigg Stone Circle, Cumbria 54–5, 146

Castlewitch Henge, Corn. 35

Catpund Burn Stone Houses, Shetland 331

cattle 21, 105, 112, 220, 309, 377

causewayed enclosure 12, 14, 17, 20, 23, 80, 83, 89, 97, 103, 106, 108, 114, 115, 123, 125, 137, 140, 144, 145, 146–7, 152, 153, 154, 155, 170, 171, 172, 173, 174, 176, 177, 178, 179, 181, 184, 185–6, 187, 190, 192, 217, 223–4, 240, 243, 244–5, 253, 393

Cave Cairn, Strathclyde 342

Caves of Kilhern Chambered Cairn, Dumfries and Galloway 265

cereals 17, 144, 276, 335

ceremonial centre 16, 22–3, 30, 39, 61, 91, 92, 93, 130, 154, 168, 171, 177, 178, 187–8, 192–3, 198–205, 250, 261–2, 271–3, 318, 348–9, 350–1, 352, 392–3

Cerrig Duon Stone Circle, Powys 395

Cerrig Llwydion Segmented-Cist Tomb, Dyfed 376

Cerrig-y-Gof, Dyfed 377

chambered tomb 9, 11–12, 28, 29, 30, 32, 34, 36, 37, 40, 41, 42, 44, 45, 46, 48, 49, 50, 51–2, 53, 68, 69, 70, 72, 75, 78, 81, 87, 89, 105, 109, 110, 111, 112, 114, 121, 122, 131, 132, 134, 140, 148, 155, 156, 159–60, 161, 162, 163, 171, 182, 209, 212, 214, 219, 221, 223, 227, 240–2, 243, 250, 261, 263, 264, 265, 266, 267, 268, 269, 270, 291, 292, 293, 294, 295, 296, 298, 299, 300, 301, 302, 303, 304, 305, 306, 307, 308, 309, 310, 311, 312, 313, 314, 315, 316–19, 320, 321, 322, 327, 328, 329, 330, 339, 340, 341, 342, 343, 344, 345, 347, 348, 349, 350, 351, 352, 353, 354, 357, 358, 359, 361, 362, 363,

364, 365, 366, 367, 368, 369, 370, 371, 373, 374, 375, 376, 377, 378, 379, 380, 381, 382, 383, 384, 385, 386, 387, 388, 389, 390, 391, 392, 393, 394, 395, 396, 397, 398, 399, 400

changing land use 20, 92, 141, 153, 154, 188, 199, 209, 215, 229, 233, 262, 301, 308, 344, 363–4, 380, 396

Chanter, J. F. 78

Chapel Carn Brea, Corn. 35–6

Chapeltown Stone Circles, Lancs. 135

Chapman Barrows, Devon. 78

Charlecote Cursus, War. 195

Charleton, Walter 1, 202, 203, 204

Chatsworth Park Farm Shop, Derby. 67

Cheesewring, Corn. 48

Chelm's Combe, Som. 166

Chelmsford Cursus, Essex 103

Cherry Hinton Settlement, Cambs. 19

Chertsey Settlement, Surrey 176

Chestnuts Chambered Tomb, Kent 132

Chettle Long Barrow, Dorset 84

chevron symbol 26, 361, 392

Chew Park, Avon 9

Chilbolton Down Long Barrow, Hants 116

child sacrifice 13–14, 93, 247, 249, 251, 389–90

Childe, Gordon 322, 351

Chilton Tracks, Som. 166

Chiseldon Stone Circle, Wilts. 207

Chun Quoit, Corn. 36, 44

church, related to neolithic site 10, 91, 129–30, 173

Church Hill Flint Mines, W. Sussex 184, 189

Cissbury Flint Mines, W. Sussex 189–90

cist 16, 29, 33, 34, 35, 40, 44, 49, 58, 63, 71, 72, 75, 76, 130, 148, 166, 238, 257, 270, 271, 324, 335, 339, 340, 346, 349, 377, 385, 388, 389

Cist Cerrig Portal Dolmen, Gwynedd 389

Clach an Trushal, Western Isles 357

Clach Mhor a Che Standing Stone, Western Isles 357

Clach na Tiompan Chambered Cairn, Tayside 350

Clachaig Chambered Cairn, Strathclyde 342

Cladh Maolrithe Chambered Cairn, Western Isles 357

Clandon Long Barrows, Dorset 84

Clashindarrock Henge, Grampian 275

Clatford Down Long Barrow, Wilts. 207

Claybush Hill Long Barrow, Herts. 123
Cleal, R. M. J. 185
Clegyr Boia Wooden Houses, Dyfed 377
Clettraval Chambered Cairn, Western Isles 357
Cliffe Hill Long Barrow, E. Sussex 181
Clifford Hill, Northants 146
Clifford Long Barrow, Hereford and Worcs. 122
Cloghill Long Cairn, Grampian 275
Clonfeckle Long Cairn, Dumfries and Galloway 265
Clumlie House, Shetland 331
Clyde-Carlingford chambered cairns 28, 261, 263–4, 265, 266, 268, 269, 339, 340, 341, 342, 343, 344, 347, 348, 349
Cnoc an Daimh Chambered Cairns, Sutherland 295
Cnoc an Liath-Bhaild Stone Circle, Sutherland 295
Cnoc Fillibhir Stone Circles, Western Isles 357
Cnoc Freiceadain Long Cairn, Caithness 283
Cnoc na Ciste Round Cairn, Caithness 284
Cnoc na Maranaic Round Cairn, Caithness 284
Cockpit, Cumbria 55
cod 310
Coetan Arthur Chambered Tomb, Dyfed 377
Coetan Arthur Passage Grave, Gwynedd 389
Coffin Stone, Kent 132
Coille na Borgie, North and South Long Cairns, Sutherland 295
Cold Fell Cairn, Cumbria 55
Coldrum Chambered Cairn, Kent 132–3
Coll Chambered Cairn, Western Isles 357
Colt Hoare, Sir Richard 218, 219, 221, 224, 243
Combe Hill Causewayed Enclosure, E. Sussex 114, 181
Comet Stone, Orkney 323
Condicote Henge, Glos. 106
Coneybury Henge, Wilts. 208, 233
Cononbridge Henge, Ross and Cromarty 292–3
Conquer Barrow, Dorset 84, 86
constricted tomb entrance 45, 312, 347
continuity of sanctity 23, 91, 174, 276, 297, 344, 348–9, 367, 381

coppicing 20, 166, 169
Copt Hill Barrow, Tyne and Wear 194
corbelling 111, 218, 241, 285, 291, 293, 294, 296, 307, 325, 329, 330, 340, 342, 370
cormorant 299, 318
Corrimony Chambered Cairn, Inverness 291
Corringdon Ball Gate Long Barrow, Devon. 78
Corton Long Barrow, Wilts. 208
Cotswold-Severn tomb 9, 11–12, 105, 109, 110, 115, 122, 155, 373, 382, 383, 384, 385, 387, 391, 396, 397, 398, 399, 400
counting 71, 95, 151, 156, 206, 228
Coupland Henge, Northd. 148, 149
Court Bank Covert Flintworking Site, Staffs. 171
Court Hill Enclosure, W. Sussex 190
cove 2, 10, 11, 55, 62, 94, 96, 145, 185, 200, 202–3, 204, 205, 227, 297, 298, 328, 378
Cow Common Long Barrow, Glos. 106
Cowlam Round Barrow, Humberside 127
Cowleaze Long Barrow, Dorset 84
Coygan Camp Settlement, Dyfed 377
Cragabus Chambered Cairn, Strathclyde 343
Craig Arthur Settlement, Clwyd 371
Craig yr Arian Round Cairn, Clwyd 371
Craigmaddie Muir Long Cairn, Strathclyde 343
Craonaval Round Cairn, Western Isles 358
Crarae Chambered Cairn, Strathclyde 343
cremation 13, 50, 51, 54, 55, 57, 58, 61, 63, 65, 72, 75, 79, 84, 86, 92, 111, 116, 118, 127, 128, 144, 154, 161, 163, 177, 189, 194, 206–7, 218, 231, 238, 248, 250, 252, 253–4, 257, 268, 274, 292, 328, 341, 347, 350, 351, 362, 365, 375, 389, 393
Cresswell Crags Occupation Site, Derby. 67
Crickhowell Chambered Tomb, Powys 395
Crickley Hill Enclosure, Glos. 106–7, 112, 147
Croft Moraig Stone Circle, Tayside 350, 351
Cropton Long Barrows, Humberside 127
Cross Lodge Long Barrow, Hants 122
crouched burial 12, 14, 16, 21, 26, 67, 70, 74, 112, 113, 118, 127, 172, 219, 291, 321, 368
Crow's Rump Long Barrow, Wilts. 208
Cruther's Hill Barrows, Scilly 162

c-shaped monument 24, 103, 141–2, 170, 234, 235, 352
Cubbie Roo's Burden Chambered Cairn, Orkney 302
Cuckoo Stone, Wilts. 236
Culdoich Ring Cairn, Inverness 292
Culliford Tree Long Barrow, Dorset 84
Culsetter Stone Houses, Shetland 331
cult-house 92, 108, 120, 172, 328, 338
cultivation terrace 180
Cumble House, Shetland 331
Cunnington, William 198, 206, 218, 220, 221, 238, 243
cupmarks 49, 51, 59, 123, 149, 150, 258, 259, 265, 291, 339, 381, 386, 387–8, 389
cursus 12, 13, 19, 20, 24–5, 27, 64, 68, 76, 77, 84–5, 94, 102, 103, 110, 129, 149, 152, 154, 155, 171, 173, 177, 178, 194, 195, 196, 254, 255, 374, 392–3, 400–1
Cursus Bowl Barrow, Wilts. 208
Cursus Long Barrow, Dorset 84
Curzon Lodge Occupation Site, Derby. 67
Cuween Hill Chambered Cairn, Orkney 302
Cwm Fforest Long Cairn, Powys 395
Cwm-Mawr Axe Factory, Powys 395
Cwrt y Filiast Cromlech, Gwynedd 394
Cwrt y Gollen Standing Stone, Powys 396

Dailharraild Stone Circle, Sutherland 296
Dalladies Long Barrow, Grampian 275
Dalsetter Settlement, Shetland 332
Dames, Michael 229
Danebury Long Barrows, Hants 117
Darfur Ridge Cave, Staffs. 171
Darvill, Timothy 112
Deadhill Wood Long Barrow, Wilts. 209
Deadmen's Graves Long Barrows, Lincs. 138
decapitation 255
Deepdale Standing Stone, Orkney 302
deer 26, 74, 76, 183, 220, 249, 281, 299, 314, 315–16, 318, 325, 370
Derwent Reservoir Occupation Site, Derby. 67
destruction by road-building 7–8, 20, 28, 50, 51, 86, 131, 134, 175, 179, 276, 386, 396
destruction of neolithic sites 7–8, 9, 14, 15, 18, 20, 22, 25, 26, 31, 36, 43, 97, 98, 110, 125, 134, 137, 155, 203, 220, 221, 224, 225, 250, 276, 333, 348, 377, 392

Devil's Arrows, N. Yorks 249, 254, 256
Devil's Bed and Bolster, Som. 166
Devil's Coyt, Corn. 36
Devil's Den Long Barrow, Wilts. 209
Devil's Lapful Long Cairn, Northd. 148
Devil's Ring and Finger, Staffs. 171
Din Dryfol Chambered Tomb, Anglesey 366
Dingieshowe Settlement, Orkney 303
ditch shape 4, 17, 19, 53, 80, 91, 92, 99, 103, 104, 108, 138, 145, 148, 152, 167, 189, 190, 191, 222, 316, 327, 366
ditch-recutting 13, 20, 88, 106, 145, 152, 237
Dock of Lingness Stone Houses, Shetland 332
Dod Law, Northd. 149
dog 67, 74, 123, 183, 212, 248, 288, 300, 302, 314, 374
Doghouse Hill Settlement, Dorset 85
Dolwilym Burial Chamber, Dyfed 377
donkey 370
Dorchester, Dorset 86, 87
Dorchester Ceremonial Complex, Oxon. 154
Dorrery Round Cairn, Caithness 284
Dorset Cursus, Dorset 88, 98, 100, 102, 220, 400
Dorstone Settlement, Hereford and Worcs. 122
Dorstone Standing Stone, Hereford and Worcs. 122–3
Dowel Cave, Derby. 67
Down Farm Occupation Site, Dorset 85
Dranandow Chambered Cairn, Dumfries and Galloway 266
Drayton Cursus, Oxon. 155
Drewett, Peter 184, 193
Drive Plantation Long Barrow, Dorset 86
Drizzlecombe Barrow Cemetery and Stone Rows, Devon. 78–9
Druid Stoke, Avon 9
druids 53, 156, 235–6, 267, 379
Druid's Altar, Dyfed 379
Druid's Circle, Gwynedd 389–90
Druids' Temple Stone Circle, Cumbria 55
Drumelzier Cairn, Borders 261
Dry Tree Menhir, Corn. 36
drystone walling 33, 35, 66, 72, 109, 112, 114, 122, 135, 153, 196, 214, 240, 248, 267, 281, 282, 294, 295, 297, 299, 313, 318, 335, 339, 340, 343, 345, 369, 382, 385, 389, 395, 397, 398, 399

D-shaped structure 9, 15, 20, 24, 87, 91, 132, 145, 200, 259, 269, 330, 338, 350, 351
Duck's Nest Long Barrow, Hants 117
Duddo Stone Circle, Northd. 149
Dugary Henge, Ross and Cromarty 293
Duggleby Howe, N. Yorks. 128, 130, 249–50
Dun Bharpa Chambered Cairn, Western Isles 358
Dunan Beag Chambered Cairn, Strathclyde 343
Dunan Mor Chambered Cairn, Strathclyde 343
Dunbar Acres Occupation Site, Leics. 136
Duncans Geo Chambered Cairn, Orkney 303
Dunseal Long Barrow, Hereford and Worcs. 122
Dunstable Down Long Barrow, Beds. 13
Duntreath Standing Stones, Central 263
Durrington Walls Henge, Wilts. 87, 209–11, 233, 246
Dwarfie Stan Rock-Cut Tomb, Orkney 303
Dyer, James, Beds. 14
Dyffryn Ardudwy Chambered Cairn, Gwynedd 105, 345, 390–1, 400
Dyserth Castle Settlement, Clwyd 371

eagle 309, 318
Earl's Cairn, Caithness 284
Earl's Knoll Long Cairn, Orkney 303–4
earth mother 143, 166
East Adderbury, Oxon. 155
East Bedfont Causewayed Enclosure, Greater London 115
East Bennan Chambered Cairn, Strathclyde 344
East Cadder Henge, Strathclyde 344
East Heslerton Long Barrow, N. Yorks. 251
East Hill of Bellister Stone House, Shetland 332
East Kennet Long Barrow, Wilts. 212
East Stoke Henge, Notts. 151
Easter Aquorthies Stone Circle, Grampian 275
Easter Clune Ring Cairn, Nairn 292
Eastleach Causewayed Enclosure, Glos. 108
Easton Down Long Barrow and Flint Mines, Wilts. 212

Eathorne Menhir, Corn. 36
Eaton Heath, Norfolk 141, 142
Ebbsfleet Settlement, Kent 133
Eday Church Chambered Cairn, Orkney 304
Eday Manse Chambered Cairn, Orkney 304
Edensor Occupation Site, Derby. 67
Edinchip Chambered Long Cairn, Central 263
eel 309, 310
Efflinch Enclosures and Cursus, Staffs. 171
Eggardon Barrow, Dorset 86
Ehenside Tarn Settlement, Cumbria 56
Ell Barrow, Wilts. 212
'elm decline' 27
Elton Common Settlement, Derby. 68
Elton Enclosure, Cambs. 19
Elton henge, Cambs. 20
Elva Plain Stone Circle, Cumbria 56
Englefield Ring Ditches, Berks. 16
entrance grave 30–1, 32, 33, 34, 35–6, 46, 50–1, 161, 162, 163, 255
erosion by the sea 179, 321, 325, 328
Etton Causewayed Enclosure, Cambs. 20, 24–5
Etton Woodgate Settlement, Cambs. 21
excarnation 39, 129, 136, 138, 159, 184, 213, 257, 283, 309, 318, 321
Exceat Oval Barrow, E. Sussex 181

façade 24, 69, 119, 132, 134, 138, 153, 160, 214, 240, 241, 257, 264, 266–7, 281, 282, 292, 295, 312, 338, 340, 341, 342, 343, 344, 345, 347, 348, 357, 358, 379–80, 385
Fairmile Down Long Barrow, Wilts. 212
Fairy Hillock, Caithness 284
Fairy Toote, Avon 9
falcon 318
false-cresting 17, 78, 101, 120, 181, 182, 187, 189, 207, 208, 215, 216, 238, 239, 244, 252, 327, 353
false entrance 105, 109, 111, 115, 122, 134, 155, 219, 257, 390–1, 397, 399
false perspective 59, 120, 206
Fara Chambered Cairn, Orkney 304
Faraclett Head Round Cairns, Orkney 305
farmers, destruction by 225, 245, 289, 300, 350, 389
farming 4, 50, 120, 128, 159–60, 169, 180, 229, 268, 276, 302, 315, 377, 384
Fatholme Causewayed Enclosure and Ring Ditch, Staffs. 171–2

Faulkner's Circle, Wilts. 212–13
Felthorpe Long Barrow, Norfolk 141, 144
fence 138, 228, 229, 230
Fengate Settlement and Field System, Cambs. 21
Fengate-style pottery 16, 22, 65, 126, 218
Fernacre Stone Circle, Corn. 37
Fernworthy Stone Circle, Devon. 79
ferry 132, 134
Ferrybridge Henge, W. Yorks. 258
fertility ritual 50, 181, 213
Ffostill Long Cairns, Powys 396
Ffridd Faldwyn Occupation Site, Powys 396
Ffyst Samson Chambered Tomb, Dyfed 378
field system 20, 21–2, 61, 120–1, 213, 331, 334, 335, 336
fieldfare 321
Figsbury Ring, Wilts. 213
Findern Cursus, Derby. 68
Fish Stone, Powys 396
Fisherwick Settlement, Staffs. 172
fishing 180, 309, 310, 325
fishing net sinker 373
Fissure Cave, Derby. 68
Fitty Hill Round Cairn, Orkney 305–6
Five Kings Standing Stones, Northd. 149
Five Knolls Ring Ditch, Herts. 123
Fivewells Round Cairn, Derby. 28, 68, 69
Flagstones Ritual Enclosure, Dorset 86, 93
Fleucharg Long Cairn, Dumfries and Galloway 266
flint mine 17, 143, 165, 184, 185, 186, 188, 189–90, 191, 192, 211, 219
flint tool making 67, 77, 89, 99, 123, 170, 171, 180, 184, 191–2, 216, 229, 373
Flotmanby Long Barrow, N. Yorks 251
flounder 310
Fochabers Barrow, Grampian 275–6
Folkton drums 251
Folkton Round Barrow, N. Yorks. 251
forecourt 17, 28, 75, 87, 108, 109, 112, 113, 119, 138, 144, 201, 219, 223, 264, 282, 288, 289–90, 295, 312, 330, 337, 341, 365, 366, 368, 369, 375, 379, 385, 390–1, 399
forest clearance 21, 29, 56, 62, 110, 128, 153, 187, 199, 206, 215, 220, 229, 242, 275
Fornham All Saints Causewayed Enclosure and Cursus, Suffok 173–4
Forteviot Enclosure, Tayside 350–1, 352

Forty Acre Plantation Long Barrow, Dorset 87
Foulmire Fen Settlement, Cambs. 22
Four Crosses Burial Chamber and Standing Stones, Gwynedd 391
fowling 170, 180
fox 248, 249, 255
Fox, Lady 35
Fox Hole Cave, Derby. 68
Frank's Hurdle Track, Som. 167
Freefolk Wood Long Barrow, Hants 118
Freston Causewayed Enclosure, Suffolk 174
funerary practices 24, 25–6, 39, 40, 49, 58, 61, 67, 71, 76, 84–5, 104, 111–12, 120, 128, 138–9, 147, 151, 159, 167, 184, 187–8, 194, 213, 236, 241, 249–50, 251, 265, 267, 283, 289, 292, 299, 312, 314, 318, 321, 341, 350, 368, 393, 401
furniture 325–7, 330, 332
Further Lodge Barrow, War. 195
Furzenhill Farm Cursus, Beds. 13
Fussell's Lodge Long Barrow, Wilts. 101, 213, 214
Fyfield and Overton Downs, Wilts. 213–14

Gaerllwyd Burial Chamber, Gwent 386
Gairdie House, Shetland 332–3
Galley Hill Long Barrow, Beds. 13
Gallow Hill Long Cairn, Caithness 285
Gamelands Circle, Cumbria 56
gannet 299, 318
Garrabost Chambered Cairn, Western Isles 358
Garrywhin Chambered Tomb, Caithness 285
Garton Slack Round Barrows, Humberside 127
Gatcombe Lodge Barrow, Glos. 109
Giant's Cave Long Barrow, Wilts. 214
Giant's Grave Long Barrow, E. Sussex 182
Giant's Grave Long Barrow, Hants 118
Giant's Grave Long Barrow, Wilts. 215
Giants Graves Chambered Cairn, Strathclyde 344
Giant's Hills Long Barrow, Lincs. 24, 138–9
Giant's Quoit, Corn. 37
Gib Hill, Derby. 63, 66, 72
Gilling Long Barrow, N. Yorks. 251
Giraldus Cambrensis 380

Girdle Stanes, Dumfries and Galloway 266
glacial erratics 28, 206, 233–4, 375, 390
Glecknabae Chambered Cairn, Strathclyde 344
Glenvoidean Long Cairn, Strathclyde 344–5
Glifter Standing Stone, Orkney 306
Godmanchester Enclosure, Cambs. 22–3
Godwin, Sir Harry 27
godwit 321
Goldington Henges, Beds. 13–14
Goodman, C. H. 188
goose 299–300
Gop Cave, Clwyd 371
Gop Hill Occupation Site and Cairn, Clwyd 371
Gors Fawr Stone Circle, Grampian 378
Gorsey Bigbury Henge, Som. 166–7
goshawk 321
Gourdon Long Cairn, Grampian 276
Graig Lwyd axe 65, 67, 164, 370, 371, 372, 373, 391–2
Graig Lwyd Axe Factory, Gwynedd 165, 248, 389, 391–2
Grange Farm Long Barrow, Essex 103
Grange Farm Settlement, Derby. 68–9
Grans Barrow, Hants 118
Great Ayton Round Cairn, N. Yorks. 252, 257
Great Langdale axe 16, 57, 60, 66–7, 68, 73, 76, 340, 371
Great Langdale Axe Factory, Cumbria 60, 62, 164, 297
Great Wilbraham Causewayed Enclosure, Cambs. 23
Green Low Round Cairn, Derby. 69
Green Sitches Occupation Site, Derby. 70
Greens Moore Long Cairn, Strathclyde 345
Greenwell, Canon 61, 106, 128, 131, 148, 253, 255
Gress Chambered Cairn, Western Isles 358
Gretigate Stone Circles, Cumbria 56
Grey Croft Stone Circle, Cumbria 56–7
Grey Mare and Her Colts, Dorset 87
Grey Wethers Stone Circles, Devon. 79
Greyhound Yard, Dorset 87, 93, 94
Grice Ness Round Cairn, Orkney 306
Grimes Graves Flint Mines, Norfolk 143
Grimsditch Long Barrow, Wilts. 215, 252
Grimston/Lyles Hill pottery 21, 65, 74, 249, 254, 277
Grobust Stone Building, Orkney 315

Grooved Ware pottery 15, 16, 19, 26, 27, 68, 85, 94, 102, 105, 107, 124, 130, 144, 172, 208, 210, 218, 220, 247, 248, 271, 303, 315, 323, 324, 398
grouse 321
Grovehurst Settlement, Kent 133
Grubstones Circle, W. Yorks. 258
Grunna Water Stone House, Shetland 332
Gruting School Settlement, Shetland 332–3
Guidebest Stone Circle, Caithness 285
guillemot 318
gull 309, 321
Gunnerkeld Stone Circle, Cumbria 58
Gussage Down Long Barrows, Dorset 88
Gwern Einion Portal Dolmen, Gwynedd 392
Gwernvale Chambered Tomb, Powys 396
Gwern-y-Cleppa Tomb Chamber, Gwent 386

Haddenham Causewayed Enclosure, Cambs. 23
Haddenham Long Barrow, Cambs. 22, 23–4
Haddon Grove Occupation Site, Derby. 70
Hainford Causewayed Enclosure, Norfolk 144
Haldon House, Devon. 77, 79
halibut 310
Halnaker Hill Enclosure, W. Sussex 190–1
Ham Round Cairn, Caithness 285
Hamar Knowe Stone Houses, Shetland 333
Hambledon Hill Enclosures, Dorset 88–9
Hambledon Hill Long Barrows, Dorset 89
Hampton Barn Long Barrow, Dorset 89
Hampton Stone Circle, Dorset 89
Hand-in-Hand Flint Cairn, Dorset 89
Hanging Grimston Long Barrow, N. Yorks. 252
Hanging Stone Chambered Tomb, Dyfed 378
Harborough Cave, Derby. 70
Harborough Rocks Round Cairn, Derby. 70
Harlaw Muir Long Cairn, Borders 261
Harold's Stones, Gwent 386–7
Harper Lane Gravel Pit Flintworking Site, Herts. 124
Harpley Long Barrow, Norfolk, 144
Harrod Low Long Barrow, Derby. 70
Harrow Hill Flint Mines, W. Sussex 191

harvest hill 146, 220, 229, 324, 372
Hasting Hill Enclosure, Tyne and Wear 194
Hatfield Barrow, Wilts. 220, 250
Hawkslow Farm Occupation Site, Derby. 70
hawthorn 180, 183, 188
Hazard Hill Settlement, Devon. 77, 79
hazel 21, 58, 59, 63, 166, 169, 180, 188, 321, 340, 369
Hazleton North Long Barrow, Glos. 109–10
Head of Work Long Cairn, Orkney 306
hearth 56, 71, 79, 80, 174, 264, 326, 328, 340, 350, 351, 398
heather 321
Heathrow, Greater London 116
Hedges, J. W. 303
Hedon Howe Round Cairn, N. Yorks. 252
Hell Stone Barrow, Dorset 89–90
Helliar Holm Chambered Cairn, Orkney 306
Helman Tor, Corn. 37, 41
Helperthorpe Long Barrow, N. Yorks. 252
Hembury Causewayed Enclosure, Devon. 77, 80, 86
Henbury Henge, Cambs. 28
Hendre Waelod Portal Dolman, Gwynedd 392
henge 4, 13, 14, 19–20, 25–6, 28, 34–5, 58, 59, 62–3, 66, 75, 90–1, 102, 106, 126, 128, 130, 136, 137, 141, 148, 149, 150, 151, 154, 160, 166, 175, 176, 193, 194, 195, 196, 198–205, 208, 209–11, 213, 220, 230–6, 243, 246–8, 250, 253, 254–5, 258, 262, 271–2, 273, 274, 275, 323, 327, 340, 341, 344, 348, 350, 363–4, 365–6, 378, 393
Hesta Head Round Cairn, Orkney 306
Heston Brake Chambered Tomb, Gwent 387
Hethpool Stone Circle, Northd. 149
Hetty Pegler's Tump Chambered Tomb, Glos. 110
Hicken's Bridge, Derby. 71
High Bridestones Stone Circles, N. Yorks. 252–3
High Close Occupation Site, Leics. 136
High Gillespie Chambered Cairn, Dumfries and Galloway 266
High Peak Causewayed Enclosure, Devon. 77, 80

High Rocks Hunting Lodges, E. Sussex 182
Higher Drift Standing Stones, Corn. 37
Hill of Cruaday, Orkney 307
Hill of Shebster Round and Long Cairns, Caithness 286
Hirfaen Gwyddog Standing Stone, Dyfed 378
Hitchin Long Barrow, Herts. 124
Hoarstone, Oxon. 155
Hoarstone Circle, Shropshire 163–4
Hodder, Ian 23
Hoe Hill Long Barrow, Lincs. 139
Holden, E. W. 186
Holdenhurst Long Barrow, Hants 90
Holm of Papa Westray Chambered Cairns, Orkney 307
Home Barn Farm Occupation Site, Leics. 136
Home Pastures Henge, War. 195
Honington Settlement, Suffolk 174
Horncliffe Circle, W. Yorks. 258
horns 12, 66, 75, 105, 109, 110, 112, 113, 114, 148, 153, 266–7, 280, 281, 282, 283, 284, 285, 286, 287, 288, 289, 290, 293, 294, 295, 296, 309, 312, 313, 314, 320–1, 327, 344, 365, 368, 370, 379, 382, 385, 391, 397, 398, 399
horse 74, 220, 281, 371
Horslip Long Barrow, Wilts. 215
Horton Down Long Barrow, Wilts. 216
Houghton Conquest Long Barrow, Beds. 14
Houlder, Christopher 397
house 9, 20, 21, 24, 46, 47, 71, 77, 79, 92, 102, 104, 133, 139, 142, 144, 174, 179, 248, 262, 272–3, 301, 308, 310–11, 325–7, 330, 331, 332, 333, 334, 335, 336, 337, 338, 339, 347, 358, 377, 384, 398
Houstry Round Cairn, Caithness 286
Howe Chambered Tomb, Orkney 308
Hoxa Hill Chambered Cairn, Orkney 308
Huggate Wold Round Barrow, Humberside 128
human remains 9, 12, 13, 14, 16, 17, 20, 21, 23, 26, 29, 40, 50, 51, 54, 61, 66, 68, 69, 70, 71, 72, 74, 75, 76, 84, 86, 87, 88, 93, 102, 105, 106, 109, 110, 111, 112, 113, 114, 115, 118, 125, 127, 128, 129, 130, 131, 132, 136, 138, 139–40, 153, 159, 163, 166, 169, 170, 183, 186, 190, 192, 194, 196, 206–7, 208, 214, 215, 218, 219,

225, 229, 238, 241, 246, 247, 248, 249, 250, 251, 252, 253, 254, 255, 257, 274, 275, 281, 282–3, 288, 289, 292, 299, 300, 301, 307, 309, 314, 318, 319, 321, 329, 342, 347, 349, 368, 370, 371, 372, 373, 374, 385, 387, 398, 399
human sacrifice 53, 176, 225, 247, 249, 251, 389–90
Hunstanton Settlement, Norfolk 144
Hunter's Burgh Long Barrow, E. Sussex 182
Huntersquoy Stalled Cairn, Orkney 303, 308–9
hunting 15, 68, 74, 153, 165, 167, 169, 171, 180, 182, 191–2
Huntley, Matthew 111
hurdle 153, 166, 167
Hurlers, Corn. 37–9
Hurst Fen Settlement, Suffolk 174
Hutton Moor Henges, N. Yorks. 253

Icehouse Occupation Site, Leics. 136
Idmiston Flintworking Site, Wilts. 216
Ilkley Moor Carvings, W. Yorks. 258
Imber Church Long Barrow, Wilts. 216
imported timber 338
Innisdgen Carn, Scilly 162
Insall, Wing-Commander 246
intervisibility 279
iron age 'overlay' 14, 23, 32, 51, 80, 83, 92, 106, 116, 123, 147, 150, 168–9, 190, 192, 193, 206, 225, 235–6, 238, 267, 275, 276, 297, 301, 308, 312, 319, 320, 339, 359, 366, 377, 396
Isbister Chambered Cairn, Orkney 309–10
Islesburgh Stone Houses, Shetland 333–4

James, Col. Sir Henry 354, 355
Jarlshof Settlement, Shetland 334
jet 57, 126, 148, 255, 265, 341, 343, 371
Johnny Paynes Occupation Site, Leics. 136
Jullieberrie's Grave Long Barrow, Kent 133, 176

Kedington Causewayed Enclosure, Suffolk 174
Keiller, Alexander 201, 203
Kelsburgh Chambered Cairn, Orkney 310
Kenny's Cairn, Caithness 286
kestrel 309
Keysley Down Long Barrow, Wilts. 216

kidney-shaped structure 17, 358, 365, 366, 368, 390
Kierfea Hill Chambered Cairn, Orkney 310
Kilham Long Barrow, Humberside 124, 128
Killin Chambered Cairn, Sutherland 296
Kinbrace Burn Horned Cairn, Caithness 287
Kinbrace Chambered Cairn, Sutherland 296
Kindrochat Chambered Cairn, Tayside 351
King Arthur's Hall, Corn. 39, 40
King Arthur's Round Table, Cumbria 58, 59
King Arthur's Stone Circles, Corn. 40
King Edwards Belt Long Barrow, Wilts. 216
King Stone, War. 195
Kings Play Hill Long Barrow, Wilts. 216
Kingston Russell Long Barrows, Dorset 90
Kingston Russell Stone Circle, Dorset 90
Kirkby Moor Ring Cairn, Cumbria 58
Kitchen Barrow, Wilts. 216
Kit's Coty House Chambered Tomb, Kent 132, 134, 176
Kitts Grave Long Barrow, Wilts. 217
Knap Hill Causewayed Enclosure, Wilts. 217
Knap Long Barrow, Hants 118, 121
Knap of Howar Settlement, Orkney 305, 310–11
Knapperty Hill Long Cairn, Grampian 276
Knighton Barrow, Wilts. 217
Knighton Down Long Barrow, Wilts. 217
Knighton Settlement, Dorset 90
Knockglass Long Cairn, Caithness 287
Knocking Knoll Long Barrow, Beds. 14
Knook Barrow, Wilts. 217
Knowe of Brockan Round Barrow, Orkney 311
Knowe of Craie Round Cairn, Orkney 312
Knowe of Lairo Long Cairn, Orkney 312–13
Knowe of Lingro Stalled Cairn, Orkney 313
Knowe of Ramsay Chambered Cairn, Orkney 312, 314
Knowe of Rowiegar Chambered Cairn, Orkney 314
Knowe of Yarso Stalled Cairn, Orkney 312, 314–15

Knowlton Circles, Dorset 90–1, 96, 101, 148
Knucker Hill Chambered Cairn, Orkney 315

Lacra Circles, Cumbria 58–9
'Lake 22' Bowl Barrow, Wilts. 218
'Lake 24' Bowl Barrow, Wilts. 218
Lake Barrow Cemetery, Wilts. 217
Lamb Ness Round Cairn, Orkney 315
Lambley Henge, Notts. 151
Lamborough Banks Long Barrow, Glos. 110
Lamborough Long Barrow, Hants 119
Lambourn Long Barrow, Berks. 16
Land's End Axe Factory, Corn. 40
landscape awareness 33, 46–7, 54–5, 59, 102, 106, 130, 167–8, 169, 181, 182, 187, 189, 192, 276, 297, 302, 309, 323, 361, 363, 388, 397
Lang Cairn, Strathclyde 345
Langdean Bottom Ring, Wilts. 245
Langford Causewayed Enclosure, Oxon. 155–6
Langham Lodge Long Barrow, Leics. 136
Langstane Standing Stone, Orkney 315
Lanhill Long Cairn, Wilts. 219
Lanivet Quoit, Corn. 40
Lanyon Quoit, Corn. 31, 40–1
lapwing 321
Lathkill Dale Burial Site, Derby. 71
Leagrave Long Barrow, Beds. 14
Leaze Stone Circle, Corn. 40, 41
Lechlade Cursus, Glos. 110–11
Leighterton Barrow, Glos. 111
Lesquite Quoit, Corn. 41
Liddington Long Barrow, Wilts. 219
life expectancy 309, 321
Liffs Low Round Cairn, Derby. 71
Lindow Moss, Ches. 29
linear barrow cemetery 81, 82, 83, 84, 97, 98, 100, 116, 173, 221, 246
ling 310
Links of Noltland Settlement, Orkney 315–16
linnet 321
Lismore Fields House, Derby. 71
Litlington Long Barrow, E. Sussex 183
Little Bromley Henge, Essex 103
Little (Lower) Kit's Coty Chambered Tomb, Kent 132, 134–5
Little Paxton House, Cambs. 24

Litton Cheney Settlement, Dorset 91–2
Llanarmon Cave Occupation Site, Clwyd 372
Llanbedr Standing Stones and Carving, Gwynedd 392
Llandegai Cursus and Henges, Gwynedd 392–3
Llandegfan Standing Stones, Anglesey 366
Llangyndir Standing Stone, Powys 397
Llanrhwydrys Standing Stones, Anglesey 366
Llety'r Filiast Chambered Tomb, Gwynedd 393
Lligwy Chambered Tomb, Anglesey 367
Loanhead of Daviot Stone Circle, Grampian 276–7
Loch Buie Stone Circle, Strathclyde 346
Loch of Girlsta Stone House, Shetland 334
Loch of Ustaness Stone House, Shetland 334
Loch Olabhat Crannog, Western Isles 358
Loch Roog Stone Circle, Western Isles 359
Lochhill Long Cairn, Dumfries and Galloway 266–7
Lochmaben Stone, Dumfries and Galloway 267
Lodge Farm Causewayed Enclosure, Northants. 146–7
Lodge Park Long Barrow, Glos. 111
long barrow or cairn 9, 12, 13, 14, 15, 19, 23–4, 31, 53, 59, 61, 63, 66, 70, 72, 74, 75, 78, 81, 82, 83, 84, 85, 86, 87, 88, 89, 90, 91, 92, 93, 97, 98, 99, 100, 101–2, 103, 105, 106, 107, 108, 109, 110, 111, 112, 113, 114, 115, 116, 117, 118, 119, 120, 121, 122, 123, 124, 125, 126, 127, 128, 129, 131, 132, 133, 135, 136, 137, 138, 139, 140, 141, 142, 144, 147, 148, 153, 155, 156, 157, 159–60, 175–6, 179, 181, 182, 183, 184, 187, 188, 191, 192, 196, 198, 199, 205, 206, 207, 208, 209, 212, 213, 214, 215, 216, 217, 218, 219, 220, 221, 222, 223, 224, 225, 227, 228, 229, 230, 237, 238, 239, 240–2, 243, 244, 245, 246, 248, 250, 251, 252, 253, 255, 257, 261, 262, 263, 264, 265, 266–7, 268, 269, 270, 274, 275, 276, 277, 280, 281, 282, 283, 285, 286, 287, 288, 289, 290, 295, 296, 298, 299, 300, 301, 303, 306, 312, 313, 314, 318–19, 320, 327, 341, 342, 343, 344, 345, 348, 350, 351, 352, 353, 357, 370, 382, 383, 385, 387, 388, 389,

390, 393, 394, 395, 396, 397, 398, 399–400
Long Burgh, E. Sussex 183
Long Knowe Long Cairn, Borders 261
Long Low Cairn, Derby. 72
Long Man of Wilmington, E. Sussex 186, 187
Long Meg and Her Daughters, Cumbria 57, 59, 270, 346, 395
Long Rock Standing Stone, Scilly 162
Long Stone, Devon. 78
Longlands Long Barrow, Dorset 92
Longman Hill Long Cairn, Grampian 277
Longstone, Corn. 41
Longstone, Glos. 111
Longstone, Hants (IOW) 119
Longstone Moor Long Barrow, Derby. 72
Louden Hill Stone Circle, Corn. 37
Loupin' Stanes Stone Circle, Dumfries and Galloway 266
Lower Dounreay Horned Cairn, Caithness 287–8
Lower Swell Barrow, Glos. 111
lozenge 361
Lugbury Long Barrow, Wilts. 219
Lukis, Revd W. C, 52, 238, 245, 255
lump-sucker 309
lunar orientation 22–3, 231
Luton Down Long Barrow, Dorset 92
Lyneham Barrow, Oxon. 156
Lysons, Samuel 109, 115

McInnes, I. 128
mace 71, 177, 249, 289, 349, 372, 392
Machrie Moor Stone Circles, Strathclyde 346–7
Maen Addwyn Standing Stone, Anglesey 368
Maen Catwg Tomb Chamber, Glamorgan 381–2
Maen Ceti Tomb Chamber, Glamorgan 382
Maen Llwyd Standing Stone, Powys 397
Maen Mawr Standing Stone, Powys 395
Maen Serth Standing Stone, Powys 397
Maen y Bardd Chambered Cairn, Gwynedd 394
Maes Howe Chambered Cairn, Orkney 291, 298, 303, 307, 316–18
Maes Howe-type tombs 302, 311, 316–18, 321, 322, 329

Maiden Bower Causewayed Enclosure, Beds. 14, 15
Maiden Castle Causewayed Enclosure, Dorset 77, 83, 84, 92, 93
Maiden's Grave Henge, Humberside 128
Manby, T. G. 128, 255
Manor Down Long Barrow, Hants 119
Manton Long Barrow, Wilts. 219
Marden Henge, Wilts. 15, 91, 96, 219–20, 243, 250
marginal land 45, 50, 304, 305, 313, 318, 321
Market Weighton Long Barrow, Humberside 128–9
Marlborough Mound, Wilts. 220
Marleyknowe Henge, Northd. 149
Martin Down Long Barrow, Wilts. 220
Martin's Down Bank Barrow, Dorset 82, 93–4
Martin's Down Cursus, Dorset 94
Matheson, Sir James 354
Maulden Henge, Beds. 14
Maumbury Rings Henge, Dorset 81, 86, 93, 94, 102
Mavesyn Ridware Causewayed Enclosure, Staffs. 170, 172
Mavis Grind Houses, Shetland 334
Maxey Cursus and Great Henge, Cambs. 20, 24–6
Mayburgh Henge, Cumbria 59–60
Meare Heath Tracks, Som. 167
Medway chambered tombs 131, 132, 134–5
Melbourne Occupation Site, Derby. 72
Meldon Bridge Enclosure, Borders 261–2
Meini Hirion Standing Stones, Gwynedd 392
Meini-Gwyr Henge, Dyfed 378
Men Gurta Standing Stone, Corn. 43
Men-an-Tol, Corn. 42
Merewether, Dean 221, 228, 229
Merrivale Stone Circle, Devon. 80
Merry Maidens Stone Circle, Corn. 43, 44, 51
mesolithic 4, 27, 62, 76, 109, 122, 124, 132, 151, 152, 171, 230–1, 263, 344, 377
Michael's Grave Chambered Cairn, Strathclyde 347
Mid Gleniron Chambered Cairns, Dumfries and Galloway 268, 269
Mid Howe Stalled Cairn, Orkney 314, 318–19

Middle Farm Occupation Site, Leics. 136
Middle Hill Occupation Site, Derby. 72
Mildenhall pottery 20, 27, 126, 174
Milfield Avenue and Henges, Northd. 149–50
Mill Barrow, Wilts. 221, 250
Mill Farm Occupation Site, Derby. 72
Mill Hill Long Barrow, Beds. 15
Milston Down Long Barrow, Wilts. 221
Minning Low Chambered Barrow, Derby. 72
Misterton Carr Occupation Site, Notts. 151
Mitchell's Fold Stone Circle, Shropshire 164
Mizmaze, Hants 118
Moel Hiraddug Occupation Site, Clwyd 372
Moel y Gaer Occupation Site, Clwyd 372
Moel-ty-Uchaf Stone Circle, Clwyd 372
Money Burgh Long Barrow, E. Sussex 183–4
Moody's Down Long Barrows, Hants 119
Moorgate Standing Stone, Corn. 43
Morrison, John 356
Mortimer, John 127, 131, 249, 252
Mortlake pottery 16, 65, 74, 126, 218, 222
mortuary enclosure 12, 26, 39, 40, 100, 102, 120, 128, 136, 138–9, 145, 147, 196, 222, 255–7, 352
mortuary house 17, 23, 61, 100, 102, 120, 125, 159, 160, 198, 213, 214, 248, 266–8, 275, 345
Moss Farm Stone Circles and Cairns, Strathclyde 347
Mount Pleasant Superhenge, Dorset 81, 86, 91, 93, 95–6, 97
Mounts Bay Axe Factory, Corn. 44, 165, 180
Muir of Ord Henge, Ross and Cromarty 293
Mulfra Quoit, Corn. 44
multi-phase development 13–14, 19, 21–2, 24–6, 29, 30, 33–4, 62–3, 91, 92–3, 94–6, 106–7, 119, 228, 230–6, 237, 249–50, 271, 276, 297, 345, 347, 348, 350, 351, 352, 377, 389
Mutiny Stones Long Cairn, Borders 262
Myatt, Leslie 279
Mynydd Amwlch Tomb Chamber, Gwynedd 394
Mynydd Rhiw Mine and Axe Factory, Gwynedd 165, 394

Na Tri Shean Long Cairn, Caithness 288
Nant-y-Fuach Roch Shelter, Clwyd 372
National Trust 6, 246, 368
necklace 16, 148, 341, 343, 371
Needham, Stuart 176
Ness of Gruting Field System, Shetland 334–5
Nether Kinneil Shell Midden, Central 263
Nether Largie Chambered Cairn, Strathclyde 347
Netheravon Long Barrow, Wilts. 221
Nev Hill Stalled Cairn, Orkney 319
New Littlewood Farm Long Barrow, Dorset 96
Newbridge Farm Settlement, Derby. 73
Newgrange Passage Grave, Ireland 12, 291, 316, 350
Newhaven House Occupation Site, Derby. 73
Newnhaw Hill Long Barrow, Herts. 124
Newton Chambered Cairn, Dumfries and Galloway 268
Newton Kyme Enclosure, N. Yorks. 253
Nicholaston Long Cairn, Glam. 382
Nine Barrow Down Long Barrow, Dorset 97
Nine Ladies Stone Circle, Derby. 73
Nine Maidens Stone Row, Corn. 44–5
Nine Stones, Dorset 97
Nine Stones Close, Derby. 74
nine-post building 144
Norden, John 51
Normanby le Wold Long Barrow, Lincs. 139
Normangill Henge, Strathclyde 348
Normanton Down Barrow Cemetery, Wilts. 221–2
Normanton Gorse Long Barrow, Wilts. 222
Normanton Long Barrows, Wilts. 222
Normanton on Soar Cursus, Notts. 152
North Bremire Stone House, Shetland 335
North Marden Long Barrow, W. Sussex 191
North Muskham Cursus, Notts. 152
Norton Down Long Barrows, Wilts. 222
Notgrove Long Barrow, Glos. 112
Nuneaton Axe Factories, War. 165, 195
Nunn, Edmund 125
Nutbane Long Barrow, Hants 24, 119–20
Nympsfield Long Barrow, Glos. 112

oak 23, 26, 56, 59, 141, 169, 180, 267, 276, 321
Obadiah's Barrow, Scilly 162–3
Odin Stone, Orkney 328
Offham Causewayed Enclosure, E. Sussex 181, 184–5
Offley Long Barrow, Herts. 124
Ogof Colomendy Cave, Clwyd 372
O'Kelly, Michael 350
Old Barn Cottage Cursus, War. 196
Old Chapel Long Barrow, Wilts. 223
Old Keig Stone Circle, Grampian 277
Old Man of Gugh Standing Stone, Scilly 163
Old Rayne Stone Circle, Grampian 277
Old Shepherd's Shore Long Barrow, Wilts. 223
Old Winchester Hill Long Barrow, Hants 120
Old Yeavering Henge, Northd. 150
Oldbury Long Barrow, Wilts. 222
One Ashe Cave, Derby. 74
Onstan Chambered Cairn, Orkney 319–20
Onziebist Chambered Cairn, Orkney 320
Orchard Farm Henge, War. 196
Orkney-Cromarty chambered tombs 278, 279, 280, 282, 283, 284, 285, 286, 287, 288, 289, 290, 292, 293, 294, 295
Ormiegill Horned Cairn, Caithness 288–9
Orsett Causewayed Enclosure, Essex 103–4, 170, 186
Orton Longueville Settlement, Cambs. 26
otter 301
outlying stones 38, 43, 45, 57, 59, 80, 135, 150, 156, 164, 195, 231–2, 253, 298, 323, 328, 346, 373, 378, 395
oval barrow 12, 25–6, 97, 122, 138, 181, 183, 191, 393, 399, 400
Over Silton Long Barrow, N. Yorks. 253
Overhowden Henge, Borders 262
Overton Hill Causewayed Enclosure, Wilts. 199, 223
ox 23, 63, 74, 76, 154, 169, 206, 213, 219, 222, 243, 248, 249, 277, 281, 288, 299, 318, 363, 370, 371
oyster 248, 310
oyster-catcher 321

paint 26, 249
pairing of long barrows 117, 120, 121, 132, 136, 183, 192, 389
palisade 20, 23, 26, 80, 87, 94, 96, 102, 103,
107, 138–9, 142, 185, 186, 193, 242–3, 262–3, 350–1, 352, 358
palisaded entrance passage 103, 262, 351, 352
Panorama Stone, W. Yorks. 258
Pant-y-Saer Chambered Tomb, Anglesey 368
Parc y Meirw Chambered Tomb, Dyfed 379
Parc-le-Breos Cwm Long Cairn, Glam. 382–3
Parsonage Hill Barrow, Dorset 97
pasture 16
Pawton Quoit, Corn. 45
Peak Camp Causewayed Enclosure, Glos. 112
Peasholm Long Barrow, N. Yorks. 253
Peerie Roonie House, Shetland 335
Penbedw Park Stone Circle, Clwyd 373
Pendine Head Burial Chambers, Dyfed 379
Penmaen Burrows Chambered Tomb, Glam. 383
Pennance Entrance Grave, Corn. 45, 46
Penton Hook Marina Settlement, Surrey 176
Pentre Ifan Chambered Tomb, Dyfed 379–80
Pentridge Bank Barrow, Dorset 98, 118
Pentridge Hill Settlement, Dorset 98
Penywyrlod Long Cairn, Powys 397
Perryfoot Long Barrow, Derby. 74
Perthi Chwarae Farm Cave, Clwyd 373
Pertwood Down Long Barrow, Wilts. 223
petrel 321
Petrie, George 300, 308, 315, 330
Petrie, Sir Flinders 131
Pettigarths Field Cairns, Shetland 335
phallus 94, 101, 143, 187, 365, 366
Pierowall Chambered Tomb, Orkney 12, 320
pig 74, 75, 76, 105, 154, 183, 220, 248, 249, 252, 281, 318, 370, 374
Pigeon House Long Barrow, Dorset 99
Piggott, Stuart 241
Pike of Stickle Stone Axe Factory, Cumbria 60
Pikestones Long Cairn, Lancs. 135
Pimperne Long Barrow, Dorset 99
pine 62
Pipers, Corn. 44, 45, 47
Pipton Cairn, Powys 397
Pishobury Settlement, Herts. 124

Pistle Down Long Barrow, Dorset 99
Pitnacree Round Barrow, Tayside 351–2
Pitstone Hill Flint Mines, Bucks. 17
Pitt-Rivers, General 102, 189
Pitts, Michael 232
Plas Meilw Standing Stones, Anglesey 368
Plas Newydd Chambered Tomb, Anglesey 368
platform, levelled 302, 316, 321, 322
Playden Enclosure and Ring Ditch, E. Susses 185
ploughing 87, 190–1, 229
Point of Cott Chambered Cairn, Orkney 320–1
Poles Wood Long Barrows, Glos. 113
Pont-Ddu Standing Stones, Dyfed 380
Ponting, Gerald and Margaret 354
Porlock Common Stone Circle, Som. 167
Port Donain Chambered Tomb, Strathclyde 348
portal dolmen 376, 389, 390–1, 392, 394
portal stones 51, 58, 59, 61, 68, 69, 131, 161, 201, 205, 231–2, 254, 265, 266, 271–2, 279, 281, 287, 290, 296, 340, 341, 344, 345, 347, 348, 349, 370, 386, 387, 388, 389, 390, 391, 392
Portesham Hill Long Barrow, Dorset 99
Porth Hellick Down Entrance Grave, Scilly 163
porthole 42, 49, 105, 132, 195, 218, 382
post circle 7, 13, 26, 87, 127, 150, 154, 204, 208, 220, 225, 232–3, 242–3, 246–7, 271, 344, 348, 384
Presaddfed Chambered Tomb, Anglesey 369
Preseli Hills 233
Preston Candover Long Barrow, Hants 120, 176
Priddy Circles, Som. 148, 167–8
Priddy Nine Barrows, Som. 168

quail 321
Quanterness Chambered Tomb, Orkney 112, 321
quartz 43, 347, 349–50, 369
quern 144, 311, 332, 370
Quoyness Chambered Cairn, Orkney 322
Quoys Stalled Cairn, Orkney 322

Race Down Long Barrow, Dorset 99
Rackham Common Flintworking Site, W. Sussex 191–2

Radford, Raleigh 39
radial stone circle 234, 294, 295, 396
radiocarbon dates 5, 16, 20, 21, 22, 27, 29, 32, 51, 56, 62, 64, 65, 79, 80, 81, 84, 85, 86, 87, 89, 93, 94, 101, 102, 109, 127, 133, 138, 141, 142, 143, 145, 150, 152, 153, 159, 160, 164, 166, 167, 175, 180, 182, 183, 184, 186, 188, 189, 190, 191, 192, 195, 198, 208, 210, 213, 217, 222, 229, 230, 231, 235, 244, 246, 248, 255, 257, 262, 263, 266, 273, 309, 310, 314, 315, 321, 322, 323, 325, 328, 336, 340, 351, 354, 372, 393, 398, 403–4
Raedykes Ring Cairns, Grampian 278
Rains's Cave, Derby. 74
Raiset Pike Long Cairn, Cumbria 61
Ramna Geo House, Shetland 335–6
Randwick Barrow, Glos. 113
Ransom, William 14
Ravencliffe Cave, Derby. 74
rayed sun symbol 294, 296
Rearsby Grange Henge, Leics. 136
reconstruction 30, 34, 36, 38–9, 40, 42, 43, 46, 52, 79, 81, 89, 102, 105, 110, 140, 163, 164, 209, 240, 271, 320, 328, 349, 361, 385, 399
recumbent stone circle 5, 268, 274, 275, 276, 277, 278
Red Barn Long Barrow, Dorset 99
red paint 71
regional ritual centre 141, 147, 148, 154, 177, 250, 261–2, 271–3, 318, 348–9, 350–1, 392–3
Rendcomb Causewayed Enclosure, Glos. 114
Renfrew, Colin 4, 302
revetment wall 33, 89, 109, 110, 112, 113, 114, 122, 134, 148, 153, 159–60, 161, 162, 163, 198, 214, 219, 221, 228, 251, 255, 275, 282, 294, 309, 318, 319, 320, 330, 365, 366, 370, 382, 385, 388, 397, 398, 399
Reynard's Cave, Derby. 74
Rhos y Clegryn Monolith and Round Cairn, Dyfed 380
Rhoslan Tomb Chamber, Gwynedd 394
Rhos-y-Beddau Stone Circle, Powys 398
Rhuddlan Nursery Field Flintworking Site, Clwyd 373
Rhyl Beach Occupation Site, Clwyd 373
ring ditch 16, 17, 19, 21, 25, 27, 64, 68, 71, 86, 115, 123, 124, 126, 129, 136, 145,

151, 152, 173, 178, 185, 237–8, 250, 254, 351, 352, 374
Ring of Bookan Chambered Cairn, Orkney 322–3
Ring of Brodgar Stone Circle and Henge, Orkney 307, 318, 323, 324
Ringham Low, Derby. 75
Rinyo Settlement, Orkney 299, 322, 323
Ritchie, Anna 310
ritual breaking 252, 367, 399
ritual dance 55, 108
ritual fire 24, 26, 28, 33, 55, 58, 120, 128, 147, 151, 242, 248, 257, 265, 270, 275, 314, 350, 369
river erosion 31, 266
Rob Howe Long Barrow, N. Yorks. 253
Robin Hood's Ball Causewayed Enclosure, Wilts. 223–4
Rockbourne Down Long Barrow, Wilts. 224
rock-cut tomb 303, 367, 374
Rocks Hill Long Barrow, Wilts. 224
roebuck 374
Rollright Stones, Oxon. 156–9, 195
Romano-British period 9, 66, 69, 73, 113, 122, 132, 133, 146, 210, 235–6, 267
Rookery Farm Flintworking Site, Dorset 99
Roseland Wood Occupation Site, Derby. 75
Rottenreoch Chambered Cairn, Tayside 352
Rough Tor Enclosure, Corn. 46–7, 48
Roughridge Hill Long Barrow, Wilts. 224
Roughting Linn Rock Carving, Northd. 150
Roughton Causewayed Enclosure, Norfolk 144
round barrow or cairn 12, 14, 27, 40, 44, 53, 54, 64, 70, 72, 75, 76, 78, 80, 83, 84, 86, 91, 97, 98, 106, 116, 127, 128, 130, 131, 139, 141, 145, 147, 148, 157, 161, 171, 188, 194, 198, 211, 218, 220, 228–9, 243, 245, 249–50, 251, 252, 254, 255, 257, 258, 261, 268, 269, 270, 275, 278, 279, 281, 282, 283, 284, 285, 286, 290, 292, 294, 295, 296, 299, 300, 301, 302, 304, 305, 306, 308, 311, 312, 315, 316–18, 319, 320, 321, 322, 324, 328, 329, 330, 335, 339, 340, 342, 351, 353, 354, 356, 357, 358, 361, 362, 363, 364, 365, 369, 371, 377

Round Clump Long Barrow, Wilts. 224
Round Hill Henge, Derby. 75
roundhouse, timber 95, 96, 127, 210–11, 220, 225, 233, 246–7, 351, 352
rowan 321
Rudston Monolith and Cursus Monuments, Humberside 91, 129–30, 396
Runnymede Causewayed Enclosure, Surrey 176
Rybury Camp Causewayed Enclosure, Wilts. 225
Rye Close Spinney Occupation Site, Leics. 136
Rye Meads Occupation Site, Herts. 124–5

Saevar Howe Settlement, Orkney 324
St Bertram's Cave, Staffs. 172
St Kevin's Bed Rock-cut Tomb, Ireland 303
St Lythans Cromlech, Glam. 383–4
Salt Hill Long Barrow, Hants 120
Salt Knowe, Orkney 324
salt production 22
Samson Hill Chambered Tomb, Scilly 163
Samson's Bratful Long Cairn, Cumbria 61
Samson's Quoit Chambered Tomb, Dyfed 380, 381
Sanctuary, Wilts. 96, 225–6
Sands of Evie Settlement, Orkney 324
Sandy Lodge Golf Course Occupation Site, Herts. 125
Sandyhill Smithy Chambered Cairn, Orkney 324
Sant-y-Nyll Settlement, Glam. 384
Sarn Hwlkin Tumulus, Clwyd 373
sarsen stones 10, 16, 81, 86, 89, 131, 132, 134, 159, 196, 200, 209, 212, 213–14, 219, 221, 225, 231–6, 245
Sawbridgeworth Causewayed Enclosure, Herts. 125
Sawbridgeworth Long Barrow, Herts. 125
Scamridge Long Barrow, N. Yorks. 253–4
Scord of Brouster Settlement, Shetland 336
Scorhill Stone Circle, Devon. 80
Scorton Cursus, N. Yorks. 254
Scots Poor Long Barrow, Wilts. 227
Setta Barrow, Devon. 80
settlement 9, 20, 21–2, 26, 27, 32–3, 37, 56, 63, 64, 65, 66, 67, 68–9, 70, 71, 72, 73, 74, 75, 76, 77, 79, 83, 84, 85, 87, 90, 91,

settlement – *contd*
98, 102, 104, 106–7, 115, 116, 123, 124,
133, 135, 139, 141, 142, 143, 144, 151,
165, 168–9, 170, 172, 174, 175, 176, 177,
178, 179, 180, 192–3, 195, 196, 199, 210–
11, 242, 259, 261–2, 301, 315–16, 323,
324, 325–7, 330–9, 340, 370, 371, 372,
373, 377, 384, 396, 398–9
Seven Barrow Plantation Long Barrow,
Dorset 100
Seven Ways Cave, Staffs. 172
shaft, ritual 94, 142
Shap Ceremonial Centre, Cumbria 61
Shean Long Cairn, Caithness 289
sheep 76, 154, 183, 220, 222, 248, 249, 288,
299, 309, 318, 370
Shelford Cursus, Notts. 152
shellfish and shells 16, 144, 248, 263, 265,
288, 307, 310, 315, 325, 326, 367
Shelving Stones Chambered Tomb, Wilts.
227
Shepperton Henge, Surrey 176–7
Sherburn Round Barrows, N. Yorks. 254
Sherrington Long Barrows, Wilts. 227
Shiels of Gartlea Chambered Cairn,
Strathclyde 348
Shippea Hill Settlement, Cambs. 27
Showery Tor, Corn. 47
Shurrery Church Stalled Cairn, Caithness
289
Silbury Hill, Wilts. 1, 7, 63, 146, 199, 228–
9
siting of burial monuments 17, 30, 31, 33,
41, 45, 50, 51, 53, 74, 82, 83, 84, 85, 86,
87, 88, 89, 90–1, 92, 93, 97–8, 99, 100,
101, 113, 116, 119, 120, 121, 122, 130,
131, 134, 138–9, 161, 162, 163, 176, 181,
182, 187, 205, 206, 207, 208, 212, 215,
216, 217, 218, 221, 238, 239, 243, 246,
251, 252, 280, 282, 283, 284, 285, 286,
287, 288, 289, 291, 293, 295, 302, 304,
312, 313, 319, 329, 330, 346, 351, 353,
357, 361, 362, 363, 388
Skail Chambered Cairn, Sutherland 296
Skara Brae Settlement, Orkney 322, 325–
7, 398
Skelpick Long Cairn, Sutherland 296–7
Skinner, John 12, 116
skylark 321
Slatepits Copse Long Barrow, Oxon. 159
Slaughter Barrow, Dorset 100
sledge 200, 233

Sliddery Chambered Cairn, Strathclyde 348
Slonk Hill Flint Mine, W. Sussex 192
Smacam Down Long Barrow, Dorset 100
Smay Down Long Barrow, Wilts. 229
Smerrill Moor Round Cairn, Derby. 75
Smith, Revd A. C. 245
snipe 321
Snowdon Carr Carvings, W. Yorks. 259
social stratification 71, 210, 318, 321
sod house 24, 174
soil 128, 157, 228, 229, 276
soil depletion 128, 153
solar orientation 11, 22–3, 29, 48, 55, 59,
88, 108, 141, 176, 185, 231–2, 234, 235,
291, 298, 316, 346, 351–2, 378
Sonning Settlement, Berks. 17
South Cadbury Castle, Som. 116, 168–9
South Muskham Ring Ditch, Notts. 152
South Setter Stone House, Shetland 336–7
South Side Mount Enclosure, Humberside
130
South Street Long Barrow, Wilts. 229–30
South Warehouse Round Cairn, Caithness
290–1
South Wonston Long Barrows, Hants 120–
1
South Yarrows North and South Long
Cairns, Caithness 289
Southwick Causewayed Enclosure,
Northants 147
Spellows Hill Long Barrow, Lincs. 139–40
Sperris Quoit, Corn. 48
Spinsters' Rock Tomb Chamber, Devon.
81
spiral 12, 57, 140, 192, 304, 320, 349, 361,
392
Springfield Cursus, Essex 104
Staden Low Henge, Derby. 75
Staines Settlement, Surrey 178
stalled chamber 289, 298, 299, 300, 301,
304, 305, 306, 307, 308, 309, 310, 312,
313, 314, 315, 318, 319, 320, 322, 324,
327, 328, 329
standing stone 10, 11, 29, 30, 36, 37, 38–9,
41, 42, 43, 45, 47, 51, 59, 78, 111, 119,
122–3, 129–30, 135, 150, 156–9, 162, 164,
195, 231–2, 249, 257, 262, 266, 298, 302,
306, 315, 323, 327, 328, 331, 339, 340,
353, 357, 362, 363, 364, 368, 369, 378,
380, 391, 394, 396, 397
Standing Stones of Yoxie, Shetland 337
Stane Field Stone House, Shetland 337

Staney Hill Chambered Cairn and Standing Stone, Orkney 327

Stannon Stone Circle, Corn. 48

Stanton Drew Stone Circles, Avon 10–11, 60, 91, 124

Stanwell Cursus, Surrey 115, 178

Stanwick Long Barrow, Northants 147

Stanydale Settlement and 'Temple', Shetland 337–8

Stathern Lodge Cemetery, Leics. 136

Steinacleit Chambered Cairn, Western Isles 359

Stepleton Enclosure, Dorset 88

Stiaraval Chambered Cairn, Western Isles 359

stickleback 309

Stidriggs Long Cairn, Dumfries and Galloway 268

Stockie Muir Chambered Cairn, Central 263

Stockton Long Barrow, Wilts. 230

Stone, J. F. S. 236

stone axe 12, 19, 23, 35, 51, 57, 60, 65, 66–7, 68, 70, 71, 73, 75, 76, 77, 124, 130, 133, 136, 151, 159, 172, 180, 214, 342, 371, 372, 373, 375, 391–2, 394, 395

stone circle 4, 5, 10–11, 28, 29–30, 37–9, 41, 43, 48, 49, 52, 54, 55, 56, 57, 58, 59, 61, 62, 64, 65, 66, 73, 74, 79, 80, 90, 97, 108, 126, 135, 148, 149, 150, 156–9, 163–4, 167, 198–205, 207, 212–13, 225–6, 233–6, 245, 252–3, 255, 257, 259, 264, 266, 267, 268–9, 270, 271, 274, 275, 276, 277, 278, 279, 281, 285, 291, 294, 295, 296, 297–8, 323, 327, 342, 346, 347, 348–9, 350, 351, 353–6, 356, 359, 363, 364, 372, 373, 377, 378, 381, 388, 389, 392, 395, 398

stone heap 333, 336

Stone of Setter Standing Stone, Orkney 327

Stone Point Settlement, Essex 104

stone row 44–5, 48, 59, 78, 79, 80, 149, 249, 263, 266, 379, 386

stone tools 19, 22, 27, 29, 44, 65, 68, 69, 70, 71, 72, 73, 76, 80, 98, 124, 132, 141, 170, 174, 180, 191–2, 224, 248, 323, 335, 349, 370, 371

Stonea Grange Cursus and Occupation Site, Cambs. 27

Stonebridge Close Occupation Site, Leics. 136

Stonehenge, Wilts. 1, 23, 41, 91, 96, 124, 148, 151, 173, 176, 197, 210, 217, 230–6, 350, 375

Stonehenge Cursus Monuments, Wilts. 85, 236–8, 400

Stonehenge Long Barrows, Wilts. 237–8

Stones of Stenness Stone Circle and Henge, Orkney 146, 318, 327–8

Stoney Littleton Chambered Tomb, Avon 9, 11–12

Stoney Low Round Cairn, Derby. 75–6

Stoughton Long Barrows, W. Sussex 192

Stowe's Pound Tor Enclosures, Corn. 39, 48–9

Stratford St Mary Henge, Suffolk 175

Strawberry Hill Axe Factory, Leics. 136

Stripple Stones Henge, Corn. 37, 49

Stromness Voe Stone House, Shetland 338–9

Stukeley, William 2, 7, 8, 14, 15, 59, 75, 85, 134, 156, 161, 201, 202, 203, 209, 223, 227, 235, 236, 378, 400–1

Sunhoney Stone Circle, Grampian 278

superhenge 4, 94–6, 198–205, 209–11, 219–20, 250, 262, 350–1, 352

Sutton Down Long Barrow, Wilts. 238

Sutton Hoo Settlement, Suffolk 175

Sutton Poyntz Settlement, Dorset 83, 100

Sutton Veny Long Barrow, Wilts. 238

Swaffham Prior Settlement, Cambs. 27

Swastika Stone, W. Yorks. 258

Sweet Track, Som. 169–70

Sweyne's Howes Chambered Tombs, Glam. 385

Swinburn Castle Standing Stone, Northd. 150

Swinside Stone Circle, Cumbria 61–2

Swona Chambered Cairn, Orkney 328

'tail' 72, 98, 141, 142, 252, 257, 365, 366

talc 353

Targarth Chambered Tomb, Powys 398

talisman 181, 190, 191, 192–3, 392

Tan y Coed Chambered Cairn, Clwyd 373

Tan-y-Muriau Chambered Tomb, Gwynedd 394

Tathwell Long Barrow, Lincs. 140

Taversoe Tuick Chambered Cairn, Orkney 303, 328

Telegraph Clump Long Barrow, Dorset 100

Temple Wood Ceremonial Centre, Strathclyde 348–9
territorial organization 53, 63, 130, 183, 186, 193, 230, 250, 302, 303–4, 313, 317–18, 321, 327, 344, 346–7, 351
Thelsford Bridge Henge, Mortuary Enclosure and Ring Ditch, War. 196
Therfield Heath Long Barrow, Herts. 125
Thickthorn Long Barrows, Dorset 100–1
Thom, Alexander 57, 349, 354, 378, 395
Thornborough Circles, N. Yorks. 59, 148, 253, 254–5
Thornbury, Nathaniel 105
Thor's Cave, Staffs. 172
Three Brothers of Grugwith Burial Chamber, Corn. 49
Three Stone Burn Stone Setting, Northd. 151
thrush 321
Thunacar Knott Axe Factory, Cumbria 62
Thurnam, John 110, 196, 206, 215, 238, 241, 246
Tidcombe Down Long Barrow, Wilts. 238
Tideslow Round Barrow, Derby. 76
Tilshead Old Ditch Long Barrow, Wilts. 238–9
Tinglestone Barrow, Glos. 114
Tinhead Hill Long Barrow, Wilts. 239
Tinkinswood Chambered Tomb, Glam. 385
Tisbury Henge, Wilts. 239
Tixover Grange Long Barrow, Leics. 136
Tollard Farnham Long Barrow, Dorset 101
Tolvan Stone, Corn. 49
Tom Tivey's Hole, Som. 170
Tomnagorn Stone Circle, Grampian 278
Tomnaverie Stone Circle, Grampian 278
Toots Barrow, Glos. 114
Torhousekie Stone Circle, Dumfries and Galloway 268–9
Torlin Chambered Cairn, Strathclyde 349
Tormore Chambered Cairn, Strathclyde 349
Torside Reservoir Occupation Site, Derby. 76
totem animal 76, 213, 252, 300, 302, 314, 315–16
totem pole 13, 22, 100, 108, 120, 133, 138–9, 141, 193, 230–1, 262, 272, 276, 309
Tow Barrow, Wilts. 239
Tower Farm Long Barrow, Leics. 136
Toyd Clump Long Barrow, Wilts. 239

trackway 89, 132, 134, 182, 186, 187, 249, 289–90
trackway, timber 165, 166, 167, 169
trade route 35, 44, 55, 67, 132, 133, 140, 141, 159, 171, 180, 185, 192, 294, 380, 391–2, 393, 395
transhumance 92, 170
transport of megaliths 206, 213–14, 233–4, 249, 277, 375
Treak Cliff Cavern, Derby. 76
Trecastle Mountain Stone Circles, Powys 398
Treen Entrance Graves, Corn. 45, 50
Trefignath Chambered Tomb, Anglesey 369
Tregeseal Entrance Grave, Corn. 50
Tregiffian Entrance Grave, Corn. 44, 50–1
Tre-Gwehelydd Standing Stone, Anglesey 369
Trelyffant Chambered Tomb, Dyfed 380
Trelystan Settlement, Powys 398–9
Tremenheere Farm Menhir, Corn. 51
Trencrom Castle Enclosure, Corn. 51
Trenow Axe Factory, Corn. 51
Trenuggo Stone, Corn. 29
Tress Barry, Sir Francis 280, 284, 289
Trethevy Quoit, Corn. 51–2
triad of rings 10–11, 37–9, 59–60, 167, 203, 254–5
Triganeeris Stones, Corn. 37
trilithon 141, 234
tripartite chamber 281, 283, 284, 287, 290, 296, 297, 300, 303, 304, 308, 312, 313, 341
Trippet Stones, Corn. 49, 52
Trundle Causewayed Enclosure, W. Sussex 108, 116, 181, 186, 192–3
Trushal Stone, Western Isles 357
Tucklesholme Farm Barrow Cemetery, Staffs. 172–3
turves 13, 16, 24, 26, 58, 102, 125, 228, 352, 362
Tuxford Causewayed Enclosure, Notts. 152
Twelve Apostles Stone Circle, Dumfries and Galloway 270
Twelve Apostles Stone Circle, W. Yorks. 259
two-phase burial monument 13–14, 23–4, 29, 50, 62–3, 72–3, 76, 91–2, 98, 101, 116, 119–20, 141, 142, 145, 154, 159–60, 161, 213, 252, 255, 257, 267, 268, 269,

281, 341, 345, 347, 354–6, 363–4, 390–1, 394, 398, 399
two-storey tomb 308–9, 328
Twyford Cursus, Derby. 76
Ty Illtud Chambered Tomb, Powys 399
Ty Isaf Chambered Tomb, Powys 398, 399–400
Ty Newydd Passage Grave, Anglesey 369
Tyddyn Bleiddyn Long Cairn, Clwyd 374
Tye Field Settlement, Essex 104–5
Tyn y Cefn Cursus, Clwyd 374

Ucko, Peter 7, 203, 204
Uffington Causewayed Enclosure, Lincs. 140
Uneval Chambered Tomb, Western Isles 359
Unstan ware 273
Upper Cranbourne Farm Long Barrow, Hants 121
Upper White Horse Stone, Kent 135
Uyea Breck Standing Stone, Shetland 339

Valley of Stones, Dorset 89, 101
Vasso Voe Stone House, Shetland 339
Vere Point Round Cairn, Orkney 329
Via Chambered Cairn, Orkney 329
Viking period 316
Vinquoy Hill Chambered Cairn, Orkney 329
vole 318
votive pit 123, 150, 151, 177, 231, 248

Wainwright, Geoffrey 209
Walk Farm Enclosure, Leics. 137
Walmsgate Long Barrow, Lincs. 140
Walton Farm Chambered Cairn, Strathclyde 349–50
Walton-on-Thames Settlement, Surrey 178
warbler 321
Ward, John 385
Ward of Benston Stone Houses, Shetland 339
Ware Park Long Barrows, Herts. 126
warfare 15, 32, 88, 106, 107, 153, 215
Warminster Long Barrows, Wilts. 239
Warren Farm Occupation Site, Leics. 136
Warren Hills Axe Factory, Leics. 137
Wasperton Settlement and Mortuary Enclosure, War. 196
Watch Stone, Orkney 328

water cult 11, 15, 20, 24–5, 41, 61, 129, 146, 171, 177, 207, 220, 229, 239, 262, 341
Watt, William 325
wattle-and-daub 21, 24, 79, 133, 166
Waulud's Bank, Beds. 15, 341
Waun Pwtlyn Cairn, Dyfed 381
Wayland's Smithy Long Barrow, Oxon. 16, 159–60, 345
Wayworth Moor Stone Circle, N. Yorks. 255
Weather Hill Long Barrow, Wilts. 239
Wells Cathedral Settlement, Som. 170
Welshpool Cursus, Powys 400–1
Welstone Bridge Causewayed Enclosure, Wilts. 240
West Cotton Enclosure and Long Mound, Northants 147
West Drayton Settlement, Greater London 116
West Hill Farm Long Barrow, Wilts. 240
West Kennet Avenue, Wilts., see Avebury
West Kennet Long Barrow, Wilts. 228, 240–2
West Kennet Post Circles, Wilts. 7, 199, 242–3, 341
West Rudham Long Barrow, Norfolk 144
West Tump Long Barrow, Glos. 114–15
West Woods Long Barrow, Wilts. 243
Wester Torrie Stone Circle, Central 264
Weston Henge, Herts. 126
Weston Henge, Strathclyde 350
Westow Long Barrow, Humberside 131
Westwell Henge, Oxon. 160–1
Whaley Rock Shelter, Derby. 76
wheat 17, 276
wheatear 321
Whispering Knights Tomb Chamber, Oxon. 156–9, 161
Whitcastles Stone Circle, Dumfries and Galloway 270
White Cairn, Dumfries and Galloway 270
White Sheet Hill Causewayed Enclosure and Long Barrow, Wilts. 243
Whitebarrow, Wilts. 243
Whitegrounds Round Barrow, N. Yorks. 255
Whitehawk Causewayed Enclosure, E. Sussex 108, 181, 185–6
Whiteleaf Barrow, Bucks. 17
Whitfield's Tump Long Barrow, Glos. 115
whiting 309
Whittle, Alasdair 7

Wick Down Long Barrow, Wilts. 243

Wideford Hill Chambered Cairn, Orkney 330

Wigber Low Occupation Site, Derby. 76

Wigston Parva Henge, Leics. 137

Willerby Wold Long Barrow, N. Yorks 255

Willesley Warren Long Barrows, Hants 116, 121

Willie Howe Round Barrow, Humberside 131

Willington Settlement, Derby. 77

willow 321

Wilsford Henge, Wilts. 243

Wilsford Long Barrows, Wilts. 244

Wilson Scar Stone Circle, Cumbria 62

Wiltrow Stone House, Shetland 339

Wimblington Occupation Site, Cambs. 27

Windmill Hill Causewayed Enclosure, Wilts. 170, 199, 223, 244–5, 392

Windmill Hill pottery 13, 14, 16, 65, 101, 144, 182, 217, 243, 244

Windmill Tump Long Barrow, Glos. 115

Windover Hill Flint Mines, E. Sussex 186

Windover Long Mound, E. Sussex 187

Windy Edge Long Cairn, Dumfries and Galloway 270

winkle 310

Winterbourne Bassett Stone Circle, Wilts. 245

Winterbourne Stoke Long Barrow, Wilts. 246

Winterslow Firs Long Barrow, Wilts. 246

Winterslow Settlement, Wilts. 246

witchcraft ceremonies 73

Witchcraft Ring Ditch, Herts. 126

Withering Corner Long Barrows, Hants 121

Witts, G. B. 113, 114

Wold Newton Round Barrow, Humberside 131

wolf 76

Wolstonbury Hill Henge, W. Sussex 193, 194, 213

Woodcott Long Barrow, Hants 121

wooden artefacts 20, 21, 23

Woodford Long Barrow, Wilts. 246

Woodhenge, Wilts. 14, 211, 246–8, 233, 236, 391

Woodlands Pits, Wilts. 248

Woods Farm Occupation Site, Leics. 136

Wooley Long Barrow, Corn. 53

Wor Barrow, Dorset 101–2, 111

Wormy Hillock Henge, Borders 262

wrasse 309

wren 321

wryneck 321

Wydhelwern Burial Chamber, Clwyd 374

Wyke Down Henge, Dorset 102

Wymer, John 16

Y Garn Llwyd Chambered Tomb, Gwent 387

yard, megalithic 349

Yearsley Long Cairn, N. Yorks. 257

Yellowmead Down Round Cairn, Devon. 81

Yeoveny Causewayed Enclosure, Surrey 179, 186

Ysbyty Cynfyn Church Stone Circle, Dyfed 381

Ystum-Cegid-Isaf Passage Grave, Gwynedd 395

Zennor Quoit, Corn. 48, 53

ziggurat 228, 321, 330

zig-zag 308, 361